THE SABBATH IN SCRIPTURE AND HISTORY

THE SABBATH IN SCRIPTURE AND HISTORY

Editor
KENNETH A. STRAND

CONTRIBUTORS

Including those to the appendixes:

Daniel Augsburger, Samuele Bacchiocchi, Roy Branson, Raymond F. Cottrell, Raoul Dederen, Walter B. Douglas, Lawrence T. Geraty, Roy Graham, Gerhard F. Hasel, Robert Johnston, Sakae Kubo, Hans K. LaRondelle, C. Mervyn Maxwell, W. G. C. Murdoch, Walter F. Specht, Kenneth A. Strand, Werner Vyhmeister, S. Douglas Waterhouse, Kenneth H. Wood.

REVIEW AND HERALD PUBLISHING ASSOCIATION
WASHINGTON, D.C. 20012

Copyright © 1982 by the
Review and Herald Publishing Association

Printed in U.S.A.

    Bible texts credited to A.S.V. are from the American Standard Version, copyright 1901 by Thomas Nelson & Sons.
    Bible texts credited to Goodspeed are from Smith and Goodspeed, *The Complete Bible: An American Translation.* Copyright 1939 by the University of Chicago.
    Scripture quotes credited to N.A.B. are from *The New American Bible* and are used by permission of the Confraternity of Christian Doctrine, copyright owner.
    Scripture quotations marked N.A.S.B. are from the *New American Standard Bible,* © The Lockman Foundation, 1960, 1962, 1963, 1968, 1971, 1972, 1973, 1975, and are used by permission.
    Bible texts credited to N.E.B. are from *The New English Bible.* © The Delegates of the Oxford University Press and the Syndics of the Cambridge University Press 1961, 1970. Reprinted by permission.
    Texts credited to N.I.V. are from *The Holy Bible: New International Version.* Copyright © 1978 by the New York International Bible Society. Used by permission of Zondervan Bible Publishers.
    Bible texts credited to N.J.V. are from the New Jewish Version. © 1962 by the Jewish Publication Society of America.
    Bible texts credited to R.S.V. are from the Revised Standard Version of the Bible, copyrighted 1946, 1952 © 1971, 1973.
    Bible texts credited to R.V. are from the Revised Version, copyright 1911 by the Oxford University Press.
    Bible texts credited to T.E.V. are from the *Good News Bible*—Old Testament: Copyright © American Bible Society 1976; New Testament: Copyright © American Bible Society 1966, 1971, 1976.

Library of Congress Cataloging in Publication Data
Main entry under title:

The Sabbath in Scripture and history.

    Bibliography: p.
    Includes index.
    1. Sabbath—Addresses, essays, lectures. 2. Seventh-day Adventists—Doctrinal and controversial works—Addresses, essays, lectures. I. Strand, Kenneth Albert, 1927-   . II. Augsburger, Daniel André, 1920-
BV125.S2   263'.1   82-3724
ISBN 0-8280-0037-9   AACR2

Table of Contents

LIST OF ABBREVIATIONS 7
ABOUT THE AUTHORS 9
PREFACE 15
INTRODUCTION 17

PART I: SABBATH AND SUNDAY IN THE BIBLICAL PERIOD

Chapter 1. The Sabbath in the Pentateuch (Gerhard F. Hasel) 21
Chapter 2. The Sabbath in the Prophetic and Historical Literature of the Old Testament (Gerhard F. Hasel and W. G. C. Murdoch) 44
Chapter 3. The Sabbath in the Intertestamental Period (Sakae Kubo) 57
Chapter 4. The Rabbinic Sabbath (Robert Johnston) 70
Chapter 5. The Sabbath in the New Testament (Walter F. Specht) 92
Chapter 6. Sunday in the New Testament (Walter F. Specht) 114

PART II: SABBATH AND SUNDAY IN CHRISTIAN CHURCH HISTORY

Chapter 7. The Rise of Sunday Observance in Early Christianity (Samuele Bacchiocchi) 132
Chapter 8. The Sabbath in Asia (Werner Vyhmeister) 151
Chapter 9. The Sabbath in Egypt and Ethiopia (Werner Vyhmeister) 169
Chapter 10. The Sabbath and Lord's Day During the Middle Ages (Daniel Augsburger) 190
Chapter 11. Sabbath and Sunday in the Reformation Era (Kenneth A. Strand) 215
Chapter 12. The Sabbath in Puritanism (Walter B. Douglas) 229
Chapter 13. The Sabbath in the New World (Raymond F. Cottrell) 244

PART III: SABBATH THEOLOGY

Chapter 14. The Sabbath in Modern Jewish Theology (Roy Branson) 266
Chapter 15. Contemporary Theologies of the Sabbath (Hans K. LaRondelle) 278
Chapter 16. Reflections on a Theology of the Sabbath (Raoul Dederen) 295

APPENDIXES

Appendix A. The Planetary Week in the Roman West (S. Douglas Waterhouse) 308

Appendix B.	The Sabbath and Sunday From the Second Through Fifth Centuries (Kenneth A. Strand)	323
Appendix C.	On Esteeming One Day as Better Than Another—Romans 14:5, 6 (Raoul Dederen)	333
Appendix D.	The "Sabbath Days" of Colossians 2:16, 17 (Kenneth H. Wood)	338
Appendix E.	A Note on Hebrews 4:4-9 (Roy Graham)	343
Appendix F.	The "Lord's Day" in the Second Century (Kenneth A. Strand)	346
Appendix G.	Joseph Bates and Seventh-day Adventist Sabbath Theology (C. Mervyn Maxwell)	352
Appendix H.	The Sabbath on a Round World (Raymond F. Cottrell and Lawrence T. Geraty)	364
GLOSSARY		371
SCRIPTURE INDEX		375
GENERAL INDEX		379

List of Abbreviations

ANET—J. B. Pritchard, ed., *Ancient Near Eastern Texts*
ANF—*The Ante-Nicene Fathers*
APOT—*Apocrypha and Pseudopigrapha of the Old Testament*, R. H. Charles, ed.
AUSS—*Andrews University Seminary Studies*
BDB—F. Brown, S. R. Driver, and C. A. Briggs, *Hebrew and English Lexicon of the Old Testament*
BHK—R. Kittel, *Biblia hebraica*
BHS—*Biblia hebraica stuttgartensia*
CD—Cairo (Genizah text of the) Damascus (Document)
CHAL—*Concise Hebrew and Aramaic Lexicon*
CJ—*Codex Justinianus*
CSEL—*Corpus scriptorum ecclesiasticorum latinorum*
CT—*Codex Theodosiamus*
DACL—*Dictionnaire d'archéologie chrétienne et de liturgie*
GCS—*Griechische christlicke Schriftsteller*
HAD—*Hebrew-Aramaic Dictionary*
HALAT—W. Baumgartner et al., *Hebraisches und aramaisches Lexikon zum Alten Testament*
IB—*Interpreter's Bible*
ICC—*International Critical Commentary*
IDB—G. Buttrick, ed., *Interpreter's Dictionary of the Bible*
IDBSup—Supplementary volume to *IDB*
JBL—*Journal of Biblical Literature*
KB—L. Koehler and W. Baumgartner, *Lexicon in Veteris Testamenti libros*
LCC—Library of Christian Classics
LCL—Loeb Classical Library
LW—*Luther's Works* (American edition)
MB—*Mäṣḥafä Birhan* ("Book of Light")
MGH—*Monumenta Germaniae historica*
   Cap—*Capitularia regnum Francorum*
   Conc—*Concilia*
   Ep—*Epistolae*
   Ep sel—*Epistolae selectae*
   L—*Leges*
   LL—*Libelli de lite*
   SS—*Scriptores*
MT—Masoretic Text
NCE—*New Catholic Encyclopedia*
NIC—*New International Commentary*
NPNF—*Nicene and Post-Nicene Fathers*

PG—J. Migne, ed., *Patrologia graeca*
PL—J. Migne, ed., *Patrologia latina*
PO—*Patrologia orientalis*
PS—*Patrologia Syriaca*
SBL Diss Ser—Society of Biblical Literature Dissertation Series
SC—Sources chretiénnes
SDABC—*Seventh-day Adventist Bible Commentary*
SDABSSB—*Seventh-day Adventist Bible Students' Source Book*
SDB—*Seventh Day Baptists in Europe and America*
TDNT—Gerhard Kittel, ed., *Theological Dictionary of the New Testament*
TDOT—G. J. Botterweck and Hehmer Ringgren, eds., *Theological Dictionary of the Old Testament*
THAT—Ernst Jenni and Claus Westermann, eds., *Theologisches Handwörterbuch zum Alten Testament*
TWAT—G. J. Botterweck and Hehmer Ringgren, eds., *Theologisches Wörterbuch zum Alten Testament*
VT—*Vetus Testamentum*
ZAW—*Zeitschrift für die alttestamentlicke Wissenschaft*
ZDMG—*Zeitschrift der deutschen*

About the Authors

Daniel Augsburger is professor of historical theology at the Seventh-day Adventist Theological Seminary, Berrien Springs, Michigan. He joined the faculty of Andrews University in 1942 (at that time Emmanuel Missionary College) and subsequently served as chairman of the Modern Languages Department for nineteen years. In 1976 he joined the Seminary faculty after having served for a number of years as a member of the college's religion department. In 1950 he earned a Doctor of Philosophy degree from the University of Michigan in French language and literature, and in 1976 the Doctor of Theology degree from the University of Strasbourg, France. For his theology doctorate he wrote a dissertation on John Calvin in relationship to the Mosaic code. He also serves as secretary for the American Society for Reformation Research, and for several years has coordinated its spring meetings held in Kalamazoo, Michigan.

Samuele Bacchiocchi, a professor in the Religion Department of Andrews University since 1974, was the first non-Catholic to obtain a doctorate from Rome's Pontifical Gregorian University in its more-than-four-century history. He earned the doctorate at the Gregoriana in 1974, and was awarded two medals for his academic achievements there. Born in Rome, Bacchiocchi studied at Newbold College in England and at Andrews University, followed by five years of service for the Seventh-day Adventist Church in Ethiopia, where he was chairman of the theology department of Ethiopian Adventist College; he also taught religion and history in that school. His subsequent doctoral work at the Pontifical Gregorian University dealt with Sabbath and Sunday in the early church, and eventuated in the publication in 1977 of his *From Sabbath to Sunday*. He has also published other works in the same field.

Roy Branson is senior research scholar at the Kennedy Institute for Ethics, Georgetown University, Washington, D.C., where he has worked since 1973. Prior to that, for six years he was a professor of Christian ethics at the Seventh-day Adventist Theological Seminary at Andrews University. He earned a Doctor of Philosophy degree at Harvard University in 1968 with a dissertation on "Theories of Religious Pluralism and the American Founding Fathers." He is the editor of *Spectrum*, "A Quarterly Journal of the Association of Adventist Forums." He is author of numerous articles in a wide variety of journals, and also of an article on Judaism in the *Encyclopedia of Bioethics*. In 1976 he coedited, with Robert Veatch, *Ethics and Health Policy* (Ballenger Press).

THE SABBATH IN SCRIPTURE AND HISTORY

Raymond F. Cottrell, retired, was book editor for the Review and Herald Publishing Association, Washington, D.C., from 1970 to 1976. Prior to that, he had been an associate book editor and associate editor of the *Review and Herald,* general church paper for the Seventh-day Adventist Church. He served eighteen years as a Bible teacher in China and at Pacific Union College, Angwin, California. He has done special research in Biblical studies, and was awarded the Doctor of Divinity degree by Andrews University in 1972. He is author of *Beyond Tomorrow* and *Reason and Faith,* as well as numerous journal articles; he was also a contributor to *The Seventh-day Adventist Bible Commentary.*

Raoul Dederen, professor of theology and chairman of the Theology Department of the Seventh-day Adventist Theological Seminary, served as a pastor and educator for seventeen years in Belgium and France prior to joining the Seminary faculty in 1964. His service in France included chairmanship of the Theology Department of the French Adventist Seminary in Collonges-sous-Salève near Geneva, Switzerland. In 1963 he completed a doctoral program at the University of Geneva. Dr. Dederen is active as a writer and is an internationally recognized lecturer on ecumenical studies. He is also an associate editor of *Ministry,* a well-known magazine for clergy.

Walter B. Douglas, from Grenada in the West Indies, is a professor in the Church History and World Mission departments of the Seventh-day Adventist Theological Seminary; he joined the Seminary faculty in 1969. His doctoral studies were completed in 1972 at McMaster University in Hamilton, Ontario, and centered on seventeenth-century Puritanism. The research for his dissertation involved a new approach to the interpretation of the history of the English Church from 1660 onward. Prior to joining the Seminary faculty, Dr. Douglas was active in church work for the Seventh-day Adventist denomination in the West Indies and in Canada.

Lawrence T. Geraty is professor of archeology and history of antiquity for the Seventh-day Adventist Theological Seminary and is also the curator of the Siegfried H. Horn Archaeological Museum at Andrews University. He joined the Seminary faculty in 1966; in addition to teaching in the Old Testament Department, he has led several of the university's archeological expeditions to Heshbon, Jordan. Geraty earned his Doctor of Philosophy degree at Harvard University in 1972, with a concentration in Syro-Palestinian archeology. He has received numerous honors, awards, grants, and fellowships from universities, archeological organizations, and government offices, and is in wide demand as a lecturer in the field of Biblical archeology.

Roy E. Graham, provost of Andrews University, Berrien Springs, Michigan, since March, 1979, is also a professor in the Theology Department of the Seventh-day Adventist Theological Seminary, whose faculty he joined in 1976. His earlier service includes pastoral work and educational superintendency for the Seventh-day Adventist Church in Great Britain, as well as the presidency of the South England Conference of Seventh-day Adventists, with offices in Watford (near London). From 1971 to 1976 he was the president of Newbold College in

ABOUT THE AUTHORS

Bracknell, Berkshire, England. His Doctor of Philosophy degree in theology was earned at the University of Birmingham, England, in 1978, his dissertation being "The Role and Influence of Ellen G. White in the Seventh-day Adventist Church, With Particular Reference to Ecumenism and Race Relations."

Gerhard F. Hasel, from Germany, is dean of the Seventh-day Adventist Theological Seminary and professor of Old Testament and Biblical theology. Prior to joining the Seminary faculty in 1967, he had served as a pastor in New England and as a teacher in the religion department of Southern Missionary College, Collegedale, Tennessee. His Ph.D. degree was earned in 1970 at Vanderbilt University in Nashville, Tennessee. He is author of numerous scholarly articles and books, including the popular *Old Testament Theology: Basic Issues in the Current Debate* (1972, 1975). His doctoral dissertation has been published by the Andrews University Press under the title *The Remnant: The History and Theology of the Remnant Idea From Genesis to Isaiah*.

Robert M. Johnston is a professor in the Theology Department of the Seventh-day Adventist Theological Seminary, whose faculty he joined in 1972. He earned the Ph.D. degree from the Hartford Seminary Foundation in 1977, his dissertation being entitled "Parabolic Interpretations Attributed to Tannaim"; he is a specialist in ancient Judaism and early Christianity. Prior to his appointment to the Seminary faculty, Dr. Johnston served as a missionary in the Far East for twelve years. He was chairman of the theology department of Korean Union College in Seoul, Korea, and acting dean of the Graduate School of Religion at Philippine Union College in Manila, the Philippines.

Sakae Kubo is president of Newbold College in Bracknell, Berkshire, England, taking up service there in 1980, after having been the dean of the school of theology at Walla Walla College, College Place, Washington, during the two previous years. Early in his career, Kubo spent a number of years in pastoral service in Hawaii and California. From 1955 to 1978 he was connected with Andrews University, Berrien Springs, Michigan, in its Religion Department, and in the Seventh-day Adventist Theological Seminary as a professor in the New Testament Department and as Seminary librarian. His doctorate was earned at the University of Chicago in 1964. He is author of numerous articles and books: his *Reader's Greek-English Lexicon of the New Testament* is a widely used reference tool, and he coauthored with Walter F. Specht the popular and widely acclaimed *So Many Versions?* (1975).

Hans K. LaRondelle is a professor in the Theology Department of the Seventh-day Adventist Theological Seminary, whose faculty he joined in 1967. He had earlier been engaged in ministerial service for the Seventh-day Adventist Church in the Netherlands, his homeland, for some fourteen years. He earned the Doctor of Theology degree in systematic theology at the Free University of Amsterdam in 1971, and his dissertation on *Perfection and Perfectionism* has been published by the Andrews University Press. His recent *Christ Our Salvation* (1980) is a more popular book on the same general topic. Currently he is actively engaged in writing in the field of eschatology.

C. Mervyn Maxwell is professor of church history and chairman of the Church History Department of the Seventh-day Adventist Theological Seminary, whose faculty he joined in 1968. His doctorate was earned at the University of Chicago in 1966, his dissertation being entitled "Chrysostom's Homilies Against the Jews: An English Translation With Introduction and Notes." Prior to joining the Seminary faculty, Dr. Maxwell served as a pastor and then as a religion teacher and as departmental chairman at Union College, Lincoln, Nebraska. He has written numerous articles and five books, including a Seventh-day Adventist history textbook, *Tell It to the World* (1976). Presently he is writing commentaries on the Bible books of Daniel and Revelation.

W. G. C. Murdoch is dean emeritus of the Seventh-day Adventist Theological Seminary, and has served in various educational posts, including the presidency of Newbold College in England and the presidency of Avondale College in Australia. He has also served as a theology professor at the Seminary since 1953. Doing graduate study in both the U.S.A. and Great Britain, he earned the Ph.D. degree in 1946 from the University of Birmingham, England, his dissertation being entitled "Tertullian as a Montanist." The Medallion of Merit Award, highest educational award in the Seventh-day Adventist Church, was presented to Dr. Murdoch in 1972 for his contribution to the education of the Adventist ministry.

Walter F. Specht is dean emeritus of the School of Theology at Loma Linda University. His earlier service included pastoral work for the Seventh-day Adventist Church in Montana, Oregon, and Oklahoma. He also was chairman of the religion department at La Sierra College in Riverside, California, for a number of years, followed by chairmanship of the New Testament Department of the Seventh-day Adventist Theological Seminary from 1966 to 1976. His doctorate was earned at the University of Chicago in 1955 in the field of New Testament and early Christian literature; his writings include contributions to *The Seventh-day Adventist Bible Commentary* and coauthorship with Sakae Kubo of the widely acclaimed *So Many Versions?* (1975).

Kenneth A. Strand is a professor in the Church History and New Testament departments of the Seventh-day Adventist Theological Seminary, Andrews University. Receiving his early education in his home State of Washington, and with a number of years of ministerial service in the Michigan Conference of Seventh-day Adventists, he joined the faculty of the Seminary in 1959. He is also editor of the scholarly journal *Andrews University Seminary Studies*. His doctorate was completed at the University of Michigan in 1958. He is author or editor of some twenty-five books in the fields of Biblical studies and church history, as well as author of numerous articles in scholarly journals and religious periodicals. Two of his publications are standard reference works on early German Bibles, and he has written several books and articles treating the New Testament book of Revelation.

Werner K. Vyhmeister is a professor in the Department of World Mission of the Seventh-day Adventist Theological Seminary. Born in Chile, he received his early education in his homeland, after which he did graduate study in the United

ABOUT THE AUTHORS

States. He then returned to Chile, earning a doctorate in history from the University of Chile in Santiago in 1968, with a dissertation treating church-state relationships in Elizabethan England. Prior to joining the Seminary faculty in 1975, Dr. Vyhmeister had served as academic vice-president for Chile College, Chillán, Chile, and subsequently as academic vice-president for River Plate College in Argentina. He also taught church history and Biblical studies in both schools.

S. Douglas Waterhouse is a professor in the Religion Department at Andrews University, having joined its faculty in 1963. After spending his early years in Hawaii and doing college study in California, he did graduate work at Andrews University, the University of Chicago, and the University of Michigan. His Doctor of Philosophy degree was earned at the University of Michigan in 1965, his dissertation being entitled "Syria in the Amarna Age: A Borderland Between Conflicting Empires." He has also done extensive research into the historical backgrounds for Bible symbolism, especially symbols in the apocalyptic books of Daniel and Revelation.

Kenneth H. Wood is editor of *Adventist Review,* general organ of the Seventh-day Adventist Church. He joined the staff of that paper as an associate editor in 1955, when it was known as the *Review and Herald,* and became editor in 1966. Prior to that, he served as a pastor, evangelist, and church departmental leader for seventeen years. In 1979 he was awarded the Doctor of Letters degree by Andrews University. In addition to innumerable journal articles, he is author of *Meditations for Moderns* and *Relevant Religion,* and coauthor with Miriam Wood of *His Initials Were F.D.N.* He is also chairman of the board of the Ellen G. White Estate.

Preface

MANY years have elapsed since publication of the monumental fourth edition of *History of the Sabbath and First Day of the Week* by J. N. Andrews and L. R. Conradi (published in 1912 by the Review and Herald Publishing Association). This important work has long been out of print, and used copies appear for sale only rarely.

A need has been felt, therefore, to produce a new book dealing comprehensively with the two main days of Christian worship. This need has been augmented by the fact that since 1912 a considerable amount of new information has come to light and deserves attention.

The present work differs from that of Andrews and Conradi in at least two significant respects. First, it represents a community effort of nearly twenty specialists, each dealing with a limited portion of the total subject. This fact alone carries obvious implications with regard to the authoritativeness and reliability of this new publication.

Second, the present book treats certain important areas not dealt with, or covered only very cursorily, by Andrews and Conradi. For instance, in the present volume an entire chapter (chapter 4) is devoted to the kind of Jewish Sabbath observance that was contemporary with the rise of the Christian church, and three chapters (chapters 14-16) present theological perspectives. In addition, various appendixes both broaden and deepen the coverage, as does also the considerable amount of newly researched data treated within a number of the chapters.

In a very real sense this publication is a pioneer work, for the authors have endeavored to probe the frontiers of knowledge. As is inevitably the case when unexplored territories are entered, the uncharted terrain leaves some gaps in knowledge. These have to be filled in by the historian with as plausible a reconstruction as the data will allow. It is in such instances that *slight* differences of opinion may at times appear, but such differences are not central or crucial to the significance of the broad picture that is presented.

It should be further noted that a multiauthored work of this nature inevitably results in some duplication or overlap of material. The editor and publishers have endeavored to minimize such duplication, inserting cross-references at appropriate places in the text. Where duplicated material has been essential to the particular author's line of argument, it has been retained, albeit at times in substantially reduced form.

It may appear to the reader that this volume is exceptionally large—which admittedly it is! Nevertheless, the wealth of material on the subject is even greater, and the authors have been constricted by the page limitations given them.

Nevertheless, their effort has been to touch all essential points. Also, they have written in such a way as to secure a balance between breadth and depth of coverage. For the reader who is interested in further information, the rather extensive notes at the end of each chapter provide reference to a wealth of sources to explore.

For convenience, the main text has been divided into three sections (see Introduction, page 17). Also, for the general reader who may not be familiar with some of the technical terms, a glossary is included in the appendix section.

I wish to express my deep appreciation to each of the authors and to the many others who, as readers, participants in the production process, or in other ways, have had a vital part in making this volume possible.

Among these "many others," several deserve special mention. The genius and inspiration for this multiauthored volume came from Raymond F. Cottrell when he was book editor of the Review and Herald Publishing Association. He launched the project and saw it through its initial stages. Although Dr. Cottrell retired long before the project's completion, he has in his retirement continued to contribute to it by helpful counsel and by preparing, on short notice, one of the chapters and one of the appendixes.

The long and tedious process of verification has been in the capable hands of Shirley Welch, who has also given assistance in various other aspects of the editorial process. Miss Welch is responsible, too, for simplifying the method of source citation and for the list of abbreviations that appears at the beginning of the volume.

The helpful glossary has been provided by my secretary, Jeanne Jarnes, who also gave the entire manuscript a critical reading and especially checked the need for cross-referencing. In addition, Mrs. Jarnes has spent many hours typing and retyping manuscript copy.

Last, but not least, mention must be made of Raymond H. Woolsey, who succeeded Dr. Cottrell as book editor of the Review and Herald; he has enthusiastically taken on the responsibility of this project and supported it generously with his time and expertise. Indeed, during the past several years Woolsey has given his capable, careful, and constant attention to a multitude of details, both great and small, necessary to the satisfactory completion of this volume, and his continuous helpfulness and encouragement to the volume's editor and authors are most deeply appreciated.

To all the foregoing and to all others who have in any way had part in making this volume possible, I express herewith my deep gratitude and thanks.

Kenneth A. Strand
Editor

Introduction

A WEEKLY day for special worship services has been a significant part of the Hebrew-Christian religious tradition since antiquity. In Old Testament times this day, designated as the "Sabbath," was the seventh day of the week, now called Saturday. It was a day of rest from normal secular pursuits—a day for giving attention more exclusively to spiritual concerns, including attendance in religious assembly. It also served as a memorial of Creation, as it commemorated God's rest on the seventh day of Creation week (Gen. 2:1-3).

In earliest Christianity a similar Sabbath attitude was in evidence, as early Christians, too, observed this seventh-day Sabbath as a memorial of Creation. As one Christian source of the fourth century A.D. has put it, "Oh Lord Almighty, Thou hast created the world by Christ, and hast appointed the Sabbath in memory thereof, because on that day Thou hast made us rest from our works, for the meditation upon Thy laws."[1]

It has been aptly stated by some modern researchers, J. N. Andrews and L. R. Conradi, that had this weekly day of rest and worship been faithfully observed by all human beings "as God ordained it, there never would have been, there never could have been an atheist, an infidel, an agnostic, or an idolater in the world."[2]

Historical records reveal that during the early Christian centuries another day, Sunday, the first day of the week, also came to have importance in Christian worship. It was looked upon as a memorial of Christ's resurrection. Though at first it was considered by Christians as a workday with a joyous memorial service, this new Christian Sunday eventually took on the aspect of rest, similar to the rest accorded the seventh-day Sabbath. Although sources from the fifth Christian century reveal that there were at that time special religious services on *both* Saturday and Sunday, the new "Sabbath" type of emphasis on Sunday finally led to Sunday's substitution for Saturday quite widely throughout Europe. This substitution was mainly a development of the sixth century and onward. In Ethiopia, interestingly enough, both Saturday and Sunday were observed as "Sabbaths."

With the Protestant Reformation of the sixteenth century there arose in Europe a diversity of views toward this Sunday Sabbath. The more prominent Reformers "desabbatized" Sunday and even concluded that any day of the week would be satisfactory for worship services. Nevertheless, they retained Sunday for such religious services on purely practical grounds—as being the day traditionally and commonly observed.

However, certain of the early Continental Reformers, and especially the English Puritans in the seventeenth century, reinforced the concept of a Sunday

"Sabbath." In addition, there was increased observance of the Saturday Sabbath, both on the continent of Europe and in England. And at the present time—and widely throughout the world—there are, of course, varying types of Sundaykeeping, as well as a significant number of observers of the Saturday Sabbath.

The account of the historical developments, from the earliest Biblical records to the present day, is given in fair detail in the present volume. Also, several chapters are devoted to current theological perspectives on the Sabbath and Sunday.

For convenience, the main text is divided into three parts: Part I, "Sabbath and Sunday in the Biblical Period"; Part II, "Sabbath and Sunday in Christian Church History"; and Part III, "Sabbath Theology." In a sense, each part is a major unit in itself, though the sequence of chapters has been arranged so that the volume can with profit be read from beginning to end. (Further information on the purpose, scope, and contents of this publication is given in the Preface.)

It should be mentioned that although this volume is one that deals with the day of worship mainly from the Christian perspective and in Christian history, two chapters have been devoted to Jewish Sabbath attitudes: chapter 4, which treats Jewish Sabbath observance at the time of the rise of the Christian church, and chapter 14, which gives theological perspectives of major present-day Jewish authorities. With regard to the latter, it should be noted that some of these Jewish authorities, especially Abraham Joshua Heschel, have influenced considerably the thinking of various Christian writers who treat the theology of the Sabbath.

It is hoped that this publication will serve not only as a general reference tool but also as a source of pleasurable and informative reading for all who are concerned with the vital topic of the weekly Christian day of worship.

Kenneth A. Strand
Editor

NOTES

[1] *Apostolic Constitutions*, 7.36 *(ANF* 7:474). See the further treatment and quotations in appendix B.
[2] J. N. Andrews and L. R. Conradi, *History of the Sabbath and First Day of the Week*, 4th ed. (Washington, D.C., 1912), p. 11.

Sabbath and Sunday in the Biblical Period

PART I

CHAPTER 1

The Sabbath in the Pentateuch

Gerhard F. Hasel

NO other part of the Bible has the breadth, depth, and height of ideas, themes, and motifs pertaining to the Sabbath as does the Pentateuch. It remains the major source for information on the origin, institution, purpose, and meaning of the seventh-day Sabbath. The Sabbath is grounded in Creation and linked with redemption. It is an agent of rest from work and confronts man's religious and social relationship. It is a perpetual sign and everlasting covenant. It relates to the meaning of time. Its nature is universal and it serves all mankind. It is concerned with worship as well as with joy and satisfaction. The themes of Creation, Sabbath, redemption, and sanctification are inseparably linked together, and with the Sabbath's covenant aspect they reach into the eschatological future.

It will be the purpose of this chapter first to survey the quest for Sabbath origins and then to investigate the Creation Sabbath and the Sabbath before Sinai, at Sinai, and after Sinai. Finally, the topics of the Sabbath as sign and covenant will conclude this study of the Sabbath in the Pentateuch.

The Quest for Sabbath Origins

A century ago the quest for the origin of the Sabbath[1] was stimulated by the discovery of alleged Babylonian parallels and became part of the Bible-Babel controversy.[2] Since 1883 there have been many attempts to find the origin of the Sabbath outside of Israel.[3]

The oldest astrological hypothesis suggested that the Sabbath originated in Babylon in connection with astrological observations. Some Babylonian menologies revealed regularly recurring evil (taboo) days *(ûmê lemnûti)* that were associated with lunar phases and fell on days 7, 14, 19, 21, and 28 of the month. It was hypothesized that the Sabbath derived from these evil days.[4] Other scholars, following Babylonian texts that identify the Akkadian term *šab/pattu*[5] with the monthly full moon day, suggested that the Sabbath was originally a monthly full moon day. Only at a later period did it develop into a weekly day of rest.[6] These hypotheses are beset with such grave difficulties that many scholars have rejected them.

Another astrological hypothesis claims that the Sabbath is of Kenite origin and governed by the planet Saturn and therefore unsuited for work.⁷ The Israelites are said to have adopted the Sabbath from Kenite smiths at the time of Moses. The evidence for a Kenite Saturn day is too slender to recommend this hypothesis.⁸ "The theory of Kenite origin is merely an attempt to explain one unknown by means of another."⁹

An agricultural hypothesis for the origin of the Sabbath was developed on the basis of the *ḫamuštum* unit in Babylon, i.e., a supposed fifty-day period made up of seven weeks plus one day from which a pentecontad calendar was reconstructed.¹⁰ But there is no generally accepted evidence for a supposed early Semitic pentecontad calendar, and there is not even any clear evidence in support of the position that *ḫamuštum* was a fifty-day period.¹¹

The most prominent of the sociological hypotheses holds that the Sabbath originated through an adaptation of market days, which recurred at intervals of three, four, five, six, eight, or ten days.¹² There is, however, no evidence that such market-day cycles existed in Israel or among its ancient Near Eastern neighbors. It is also curious that in the later societies where such market-day cycles are known, there is no evidence for a recurring seven-day cycle of market days.¹³

Some recent studies have attempted to explain the origin of the Sabbath in connection with the number seven in Mesopotamia and/or Ugaritic texts.¹⁴ There is, however, no evidence that the periodic sequence of seven years or seven days leads to the origin of the recurring week and/or Sabbath.¹⁵ There is likewise no indication that there is a link between a seven structure and the Biblical Sabbath.¹⁶

The quest for the origin of the Sabbath that began about a century ago has been unsuccessful. No single hypothesis or attempted combination of hypotheses has succeeded in providing a conclusive solution to the quest of Sabbath origins.¹⁷ It may be concluded that from the point of view of religiohistorical investigation the Sabbath is unique to Biblical religion.

Recent research reveals a twofold shift. A number of scholars have turned their attention to the Biblical texts for the origin and development of the Sabbath,¹⁸ and many others have turned to look for the theological, sociological, and anthropological significance of the Sabbath and its relevance for modern man.¹⁹ It will be our attempt to investigate the pentateuchal passages²⁰ regarding their own witness to the origin, meaning, and relevance of the Sabbath.

Sabbath and Creation

The Creation Sabbath appears in Genesis 2:1-3, Exodus 20:8-11, and Exodus 31:12-17.²¹ These texts provide the basic Biblical motivation for observing the Sabbath and point to the Biblical view of the origin of the Sabbath. In Exodus 31:12-17, the command to observe the Sabbath finds its ultimate reason in the statement "For in six days the LORD made heaven and earth, but on the seventh day he rested, and was refreshed" (verse 17b).* In Exodus 20:8-11 the commandment to refrain from work on the seventh-day Sabbath is also motivated by an explicit reference to Creation and the divine example: "For in six days the LORD made the heavens, and the earth, the sea, and all that is in them, and rested on the seventh day; therefore the LORD blessed the sabbath day and made it holy" (verse 11). These texts point to the origin of the Sabbath at Creation, and the

---

* All Bible quotations in this chapter are translations by the author, unless otherwise indicated.

language for the motivation reminds us of the Creation account,[22] especially Genesis 2:1-3.

Creation Sabbath and Genesis 2:1-3.—Genesis 2:1-3 forms the conclusion of the Biblical Creation account. These verses are not an "etiological myth"[23] but a carefully structured literary unit.[24] Verse 1 affirms what was finished: "the heavens and the earth" (cf. Gen. 1:1; 2:4; Ex. 20:11; 31:17),[25] i.e., the totality of the world in its bipartite division, together with "all the host of them," namely the fullness of the host of creatures contained in the bipartite world.[26] Verse 2 is linked to verse 1 through the common verb "finished" *(klh).*[27] God had finished "his work which he had done" on "the seventh day."[28] The expression "the seventh day" appears two more times in this unit (verses 2b and 3a), so that four ideas are associated with "the seventh day": (1) God "had finished" His creative work on that day; (2) God "rested" from all His creative work on that day; (3) God "blessed" that day; and (4) God "made it holy."

Creation Sabbath and Weekly Sabbath.—The unique threefold emphasis on the seventh day with its four different aspects at the conclusion of the Genesis creation story indicates that just as man is the crown of Creation so the seventh day, the Sabbath,[29] is the final goal of Creation.[30] If this is the case, then the Creation Sabbath is not merely directed toward Creation and Creator,[31] but has equally significant aspects for the future of man, his life and worship.[32] This twofold purpose for the past and the future makes the Creation Sabbath the archetype of the weekly Sabbath. G. H. Waterman provides the following summary: "It seems clear, therefore, that the divine origin and institution of the sabbath took place at the beginning of human history. At that time God not only provided a divine example for keeping the seventh day as a day of rest, but also blessed and set apart the seventh day for the use and benefit of man."[33]

What does it mean that God "had finished" His creation on the Sabbath? The exact idea of the Hebrew verb *(klh)* is difficult to ascertain. Basically *klh* means "to stop, come to an end."[34] The Piel form as used in Genesis 2:2 means neither "declared finished"[35] nor necessarily "brought to a (gratifying) close,"[36] but expresses the positive idea of an achievement of a desired goal. The task of creating is "completed" and thus finished: on the seventh day God had His task completed and was finished with His creative work.[37] God looked back to His completed creation and finished work with joy, pleasure, and satisfaction and pronounced it "very good" (chap. 1:31). God set here the pattern for His creation. As He created the world in six days, so that it was completed and finished on the seventh day, so man is to accomplish his work and purpose in this creation during the six working days of the week and is to follow his Creator's example of rest on the seventh day, the Sabbath. Following the pattern of the Creator, he too may look back upon his finished work with joy, pleasure, and satisfaction. In this way man may rejoice[38] not only in God's creation but also in his responsible rulership, not exploitation, over creation (chap. 1:28).

Creation Sabbath and Sabbath Rest.—The idea that God "rested" on the seventh day appears in Genesis 2:2, 3, Exodus 31:17, and Exodus 20:11. The latter text uses the Hebrew verb *nwḥ,* "to rest, take a rest,"[39] while the former passages employ the verb *šbt,* "to cease (working), stop (work), rest."[40] The relationship between these terms has been frequently discussed,[41] but one should be cautious lest one presses the differences so much that one denies any relationship between

Genesis 2:1-3 and Exodus 20:8-11.[42] Not only is the motif of divine rest common to the three texts referring to the Creation Sabbath but the expressions "the seventh day" (Gen. 2:1-3; Ex. 20:10), "bless" (Gen. 2:3; Ex. 20:11), "make holy" (Gen. 2:3; Ex. 20:11; cf. Ex. 31:14), "make" (Gen. 2:2, 3; Ex. 20:9, 10; 31:14, 15; cf. Ex. 35:2; Deut. 5:13, 14), and "work" (Gen. 2:2-4; Ex. 20:9, 10; 31:14, 15) connect these texts most closely. Genesis 2:2, 3 is filled with language that belongs to pentateuchal Sabbath texts,[43] so that it has been concluded that the seventh day of the Creation Sabbath is "at the same time instituted as man's day of rest."[44] The fact that the noun "Sabbath" is not present in Genesis 2:1-3 and that no explicit commandment to keep the Sabbath is provided may find its reason in one of the purposes of Genesis 2:1-3, namely to present the divine Exemplar whose example man is to follow (cf. Ex. 20:11; 31:17).

The question of the origin of the verb šābat, "to cease (working), stop (work), rest," and the noun šabbāt, "Sabbath," is widely debated.[45] It has been suggested that these words derived from the Arabic sabata, "to cut off, interrupt; rest,"[46] or the Arabic root šbb, "to grow, increase, be great,"[47] or the Akkadian šab/pattu,[48] the exact meaning of which is itself disputed,[49] or the word šb, "seven," via the Akkadian.[50] These attempts proved fruitless and remain unconvincing because they are not supported by philological considerations of comparative Semitics and lack the support of the usage of forms of the Hebrew root šbt in the Old Testament.

At the present there is no evidence for the root šbt outside of Hebrew except for Punic.[51] The verb šbt, "to cease (working), stop (work), rest," and the noun šabbāt, "Sabbath," seem to share a common Hebrew root. Some scholars derive the noun from the verb,[52] while others derive the verb from the noun.[53] There seems to be no conclusive proof for either suggestion. The issue of the exact relationship of the noun to the verb and vice versa is not settled. Nevertheless, it is linguistically possible that both words derive from a common root.[54] On the basis of Old Testament contexts it may be suggested that the verb šābat and the noun šabbāt are related to each other from the beginning (Ex. 16:29, 30).[55]

The idea of the verb šābat, "to cease (working), stop (work), rest," as applied to God when He had finished His creation (Gen. 2:3; cf. Ex. 31:17) expresses the notion that He ceased from His creative activity and thus rested. This cessation and resting on the part of God can hardly be explained as an etiology[56] or a divine retirement (otiositas) from heavy activity, as is the case in pagan mythologies,[57] but as something that is related to man. Creation takes place with reference to time, to which belongs the duality of days of work and day of rest. The latter is the "seventh day," the Sabbath. God's cessation from work, His resting, on the seventh day is not necessitated because He grew tired or weary (cf. Isa. 40:28) but because of His function as Exemplar for man. Man is the "image of God" (Gen. 1:26-28) and is taught by his Model's example how to function in the usage of the sequence of time (cf. Ex. 31:17; 16:23-26; 20:8-11).

The Sabbath commandment in Exodus 20 also affirms God's "rest" on the seventh day, but chooses the Hebrew nuaḥ (verse 11; cf. Deut. 5:14), while Exodus 31:17 and Genesis 2:3 employ the verb šābat. In the Sabbath texts the Hebrew verb nuaḥ means "to rest, take a rest"[58] and, along with the thought that God "was refreshed" (npš)[59] in Exodus 31:17, is part of the Sabbath vocabulary that expresses God's most intimate self-identification with man. God rests on the seventh day of Creation week in order to provide a day of meeting in rest with the crown of Creation, man, made in His image. The three texts (Gen. 2:1-3; Ex. 20:11; 31:17) dealing with the Creation Sabbath assert that the world is no longer being created, because God rests from the work of Creation on the seventh day; a day of rest as contrasted with the days of Creation. These texts connect God's rest with the institution of the Sabbath. The weekly Sabbath has "its legitimation in the primal Sabbath (Ursabbat) of creation."[60] In resting on the Sabbath, man participates in God's rest, meeting with his Creator.

Creation Sabbath and Sabbath Blessing.—Genesis 2:3 affirms that the Creator "blessed" *(brk)*[61] the seventh day just as He had blessed animals and man on the day before (Gen. 1:22, 28). The blessing of the Sabbath referred to in Exodus 20:11 links the Creation Sabbath with the weekly Sabbath.

What does it mean that the seventh-day Sabbath is blessed? When God is the subject, "blessing" means generally that "man and things are imbued with the power of fruitfulness and prosperity, he gives life, happiness and success."[62] In terms of the seventh day, it means that this day is "a gift of the Creator for man,"[63] imbued with a blessing that no other day possesses. The "blessing" provides this day of rest with a gift that makes it full of power. This power makes this day fruitful and vital for man's life.[64] The seventh day receives through its blessing a beneficial and vitalizing power through which human existence is enriched and comes to fulfillment. As such, the Sabbath is man's source of unequaled benefit in the weekly cycle.

Creation Sabbath and Sabbath Holiness.—Genesis 2:3 also affirms that the Creator "hallowed" (R.V., R.S.V.) the seventh day, "made it holy" (N.E.B., N.A.B.), "declared it holy" (N.J.V.), or "sanctified it" (N.A.S.B.). Both here and in the Sabbath commandment (Ex. 20:11) the Hebrew text uses the verb *qidāš* (piel)[65] from the root *qdš*, "holy."[66] Most basically, the idea is that God made the seventh day "holy" by putting it into a state of holiness. Since the more elemental meaning of the Hebrew idea of "holy" and "holiness" is "separation,"[67] the meaning of the holiness of the seventh day as affirmed in Genesis 2:3 and Exodus 20:11 expresses that the seventh-day Sabbath is that very day that God has separated from the rest of the days. The separation of the seventh day from the six working days is a gift of the Creator for all mankind. It should be emphasized that God, not man, has separated this seventh day. The seventh day is God's day for mankind as a whole and not merely His day for Israel.

It is because of God's separation of the seventh day from the six days and His assigning holiness to it[68] that the Sabbath is designated a "holy Sabbath" (Ex. 16:23; 31:14, 15; 35:2; cf. Isa. 58:13). The holiness of the Sabbath does not stem from man's keeping it, but from an act of God.

Man is commanded to keep the Sabbath "holy" (Ex. 20:8; Deut. 5:12)[69] by refraining from work (Ex. 20:10; Deut. 5:14).[70] The injunction not to "profane" *(hl, hll)*[71] the Sabbath (Ex. 31:14, et cetera)[72] is the counterpart to the commandment to keep it holy.

The Pentateuch has a number of specific instructions regarding activities prohibited on the Sabbath. Exodus 16:23 prohibits baking and cooking on the Sabbath, indicating rest also from the daily chores of women. Exodus 34:21 enjoins the Sabbath rest also in the seasons of plowing and harvesting, indicating that the Sabbath is not kept holy only during times of normal activity. Exodus 35:3

directs that no fire is to be kindled, and Numbers 15:32 that no wood is to be gathered. These specific prohibitions illustrate the broad aspects of keeping the Sabbath holy. Yet, priests do not profane the Sabbath when they put the shewbread in order (Lev. 24:8) and bring additional sacrifices (Num. 28:9).

In short, the Creator has made the seventh day holy by separating it from the six workdays and has thus provided a gift for the whole of mankind for all time. The person who keeps the seventh-day Sabbath holy follows the Exemplar's archetypal pattern (Gen. 2:3) and meets with Him on that day of rest. He acknowledges his God as Creator, accepts His gift, and has a part in God's rest. The Sabbath "is a steady reminder of the Creator, [and] of the origin and goal of creation.... Every Sabbath grants anew to those who stand under [God's] royal dominion the freedom [from the struggle for existence] that belongs to God's children; although at first in a limited measure, it is given with the renewed promise of complete fulfillment." [73]

Sabbath and Manna

The gift of the manna is the occasion for renewing the greater gift, the Sabbath. The noun "Sabbath" *(šabbāt)* appears unannounced in the Bible for the first time in Exodus 16:25 within the narrative of the manna miracle.[74] It has been pointed out correctly that the Sabbath appears already before Israel's arrival at Mount Sinai,[75] i.e., the Sabbath was kept before it was formally commanded to be kept holy in the Decalogue.[76]

The setting of the appearance of the Sabbath during Israel's wilderness sojourn is the murmuring of the whole Israelite congregation (Ex. 16:1-3).[77] God revealed to Moses that bread would rain from heaven; on each of the first five days a portion had to be gathered in, but on the sixth day "it shall be twice as much as they gather daily" (verse 5).

Following this instruction, "on the sixth day they gathered twice as much bread" (verse 22—this and the following discussion quote from the R.S.V.), Moses explained to the people, "This is what the Lord has commanded: 'Tomorrow is a day of solemn rest [*šabbātôn*],[78] a holy sabbath [*šabbāt-qōdeš*] to the LORD; bake what you will bake and boil what you will boil, and all that is left over lay by to be kept till the morning'" (verse 23). On the following morning, the Sabbath, "Moses said, 'Eat it today, for today is a sabbath [*šabbāt*] to the LORD; today you will not find it in the field. Six days you shall gather it; but on the seventh day, which is a sabbath [*šabbāt*], there will be none'" (verses 25, 26).

Some doubters went out in disbelief to gather the manna on the Sabbath (verse 27). They found nothing. God rebuked them, saying to Moses, "How long do you refuse to keep my commandments and my laws?" (verse 28). Then comes the revelation that they have received the Sabbath from Yahweh (verse 29a), and the injunction follows: "Remain every person in his home, let no one go out of his place on the seventh day" (verse 29b). The narrative concludes, "So the people rested [*šabāt*] on the seventh day" (verse 30).

The didactic character of this narrative is obvious throughout. The wilderness generation was to learn to rest on the seventh day (verse 30). They were taught to be obedient to their Lord, to keep His "commandments" (*miṣwôt*) and His "laws" (*tôrōt*). Does this imply that Israel had known "laws and commandments" even before Sinai? Was there a Sabbath commandment known before Sinai? The present form of Exodus 16 appears to hint in that direction.[79] If this be the case, nothing is revealed about the origin of such a divine law or instruction. It is assumed to exist.[80] It may be concluded that the Sabbath "is not introduced for the first time even in the wilderness of Sin, where the manna is found. Here, too, it is proclaimed as something which is already in existence."[81]

The manna narrative is filled with Sabbath terminology and Sabbath theology. It has already been noted that for the first time the nouns *šabbāt*, "Sabbath," and *šabbātôn*, "Sabbath feast" (Ex. 16:23) appear.[82] The word "Sabbath" is qualified by the adjective *qōdeš*, "holy" (verse 23). In verse 26 there is the first identification of the "seventh day" as the Sabbath. All of this is part of the Sabbath teaching.[83] The three usages of "sixth day" (verses 5, 22, 29) and the four usages each of "seventh day" (verses 26, 27, 29, 30) and "sabbath" (verses 23, 25, 26, 29) reveal an additional aspect of the preoccupation with Sabbath ideology.

The major ideas regarding the Sabbath in Exodus 16 may be summarized as follows: 1. The "sixth day" prepares for the Sabbath (verses 5, 22, 29). On it a double portion of food is collected (verses 5, 22) so that no one needs to go out of his house on the seventh day (verse 29). 2. The Sabbath is the day following the sixth day. "On the sixth day they gathered twice as much." "'Tomorrow is a sabbath feast, a holy sabbath to the LORD'" (verses 22, 23, R.S.V.). The "seventh day" is the Sabbath (verse 26). 3. A divine commandment enjoined the keeping of the Sabbath (verse 28). 4. The Sabbath is "holy" (verse 23; cf. Gen. 2:2, 3; Ex. 20:11). 5. The Sabbath is a day of "rest" (verses 23, 29, 30). Rest means refraining from work. In this instance it means refraining from gathering food, from engaging in the pursuit of a livelihood. God had made ample provisions for sustenance. The prohibition to stay in one's house on the Sabbath in verse 29 has contextually nothing to do with lunar phases[84] but is designed to keep the wilderness generation from gathering manna (verses 27-29). Both a religious ("holy") and humanitarian ("rest") interest come to expression. 6. The Sabbath is a "sabbath feast" *(šabbātôn)*[85] and not a day of taboos, fasting, and mourning. It has a "festive ring,"[86] a day on which one is not to go hungry. Israel is to eat, "for today is a sabbath to the LORD" (verse 25). The Sabbath is God's special day and is designed to bring joy, happiness, and satisfaction upon the keeper. 7. The Sabbath is a testing ground of man's relationship with God. Some Israelites went out "either through unbelief or through curiosity"[87] to collect manna (verses 25-27). In this connection God's rebuke is heard, "How long do you refuse my commandments and my laws?" (verse 28). A refusal to keep the seventh-day Sabbath means a refusal to obey God's will as expressed in His commandments and laws. The Sabbath has the character of a test of obedience and faith.[88] God demands of His faithful a particular life style.[89]

Exodus 16 contains key notions regarding the origin, purpose, function, and meaning of the Sabbath. It reveals that the Sabbath institution was known before the giving of the law on Mount Sinai and before its appearance in the wilderness of Sin, as indicated by both the incidental matter in which it is introduced in Exodus 16 and the divine remonstrance of the people's disobedience.

Sabbath and Decalogue

We now turn to the Sabbath commandment of the Decalogue in Exodus 20 and Deuteronomy 5. A discussion of the Sabbath commandment in the Decalogue involves first a brief look at major trends in the recent study of the Decalogue itself,[90] inasmuch as these trends have influenced the debate on the interpretation and meaning of the Sabbath commandment.

A Survey of Trends.—Recent critical studies on the Decalogue have been dominated by form-critical approaches pioneered for Old Testament laws by A. Alt,[91] who argued that casuistic law grew out of secular justice and apodictic law from a cultic setting. His views dominated the field for two decades until they were supplemented, broadened, and modified by G. Mendenhall's thesis that there is a similarity between the form of the Decalogue and Hittite state treaties.[92] This was refined by a flood of studies.[93] Opposition to these alleged parallels continues to be strong, with incisive arguments.[94] The last decade of critical study has attempted to modify the sharp distinction between apodictic and casuistic law and suggested that clan wisdom is the source of prohibitive law.[95]

A unifying element of form-critical and religiohistorical studies is the traditiohistorical claim that the present form of the Decalogue is the product of a long evolutionary development. Its present shape is rooted in the institutional life of Israel. A recent observation by a thoroughgoing form-critic is noteworthy: "The danger of exegesis being built on ill-founded hypothetical projections has increased dramatically during the last half-century. As a result, few passages have suffered such divergent interpretations as has the Decalogue."[96] Great caution is demanded because it is evident that modern Decalogue research has led to irreconcilable conclusions. This is true for the Decalogue as a whole and the Sabbath commandment in particular.[97] It must be admitted that present methods of research are inadequate and that their conclusions do not allow even a fair degree of certainty.

Some scholars have suggested that an alleged form of the Sabbath commandment was originally formulated negatively,[98] while other scholars have maintained that it was positive.[99] There is no agreement regarding the wording of the hypothetical form, although it is often believed to go back to Mosaic times along with the remainder of the so-called "primitive decalogue" (Urdekalog).[100] For example, H. H. Rowley suggests that the original Sabbath commandment was: "Six days shalt thou labor and do all thy work; but the seventh day is a sabbath unto the Lord thy God."[101] G. Fohrer's proposal is "Remember the day of the Sabbath."[102] H. Gese argues for "Remember the Sabbath day, to keep it holy";[103] but K. Rabast believes it was negatively formulated: "You shall not do any work on the sabbath."[104] In view of such insurmountable methodological problems and subjective judgments, it is safe to proceed on the basis of the context of the Decalogue (and the Sabbath commandment) in the book of Exodus itself. This context views the Decalogue in its present form to be God's revelation in Mosaic times.[105]

The Sabbath in Exodus 20.—The Sabbath commandment (Ex. 20:8-11) consists of fifty-five Hebrew words and is the longest of the Ten Commandments. This length has given rise to the assumption that it was originally short, but ancient Near Eastern law codes disprove that laws developed from short to long and from simple to complex ones.[106] Long and short laws can stand side by side from the beginning, as pre-Mosaic law codes from the ancient Near East demonstrate.[107] Hittite laws, which are more or less contemporary with Moses, reveal that a later version of the same law can be shorter[108] or longer[109] (cf. Deut. 5:12-15), and that both short and long laws are found next to each other.[110] Accordingly, ancient Near Eastern laws do not support the assumption of a short original law. Comparative evidence of ancient Near Eastern law codes militates against the view that the Sabbath commandment in Exodus 20 is necessarily the result of slow growth over a long period of time.

The Sabbath commandment is a carefully structured unit. The following structure seems to be present:

A	Introduction	Remember the sabbath day to keep it holy. (Verse 8, R.S.V.)
	B¹ Command	Six days you shall labor and do all your work; (verse 9)
	C¹ Motivation	but the seventh day is a sabbath to the LORD your God; (verse 10a)
	B² Command	in it you shall not do any work, you, or your son, or . . . (verse 10b)
	C² Motivation	for in six days the LORD made heaven and earth, the sea, . . . and rested . . . (verse 11a)
D	Conclusion	therefore the LORD blessed the sabbath day and made it holy. (Verse 11b)

This structure[111] reveals the following: A contains, in the form of an introductory opening statement, the key principle of the Sabbath commandment as a whole. B¹ expresses the positive command to engage in work on six days, whereas B² gives the other side in the prohibitive command of refraining from any work on the Sabbath day. B² makes clear that this prohibition has broad application for the entire family and domestic animals, as well as for the stranger or resident alien (*gēr*).[112] C¹ and C² provide the motivation for the commands. C¹ motivates the sequence of time in the six-days-seventh-day duality by emphasizing that "the seventh day is a sabbath to the Lord your God." The identification of the seventh day with the Sabbath has already taken place in the earlier manna experience in the wilderness of Sin (Ex. 16:23, 25, 26). It should be noted that the seventh-day Sabbath is "for [to] the LORD" (see verses 23, 25; chap. 31:15; 35:2; Lev. 23:3),[113] indicating that God is the owner of this day that comes as a gift to His people (cf. Ex. 16:29) and is filled with His special blessing. C² contains the formal motivation clause with the introductory "for" *(kî)*. It provides the detailed motivation in terms of the LORD's six days of work and His resting on the seventh day. This motivation has its roots in the Creation Sabbath. The links between Exodus 20:11 and Genesis 2:2, 3 have already been discussed. D is an independent clause, joined by a connective-result particle "therefore" *('al-kēn)*. It forms the conclusion. The last words of the commandment, "and made it holy," have a correspondence to the exhortation of the introductory principle A, "to keep it holy."

The key words that frame the Sabbath commandment are (1) "the sabbath day" *('et-yôm haššabbāt)* in verses 8 and 11, and (2) the expressions "to keep it holy" *(l⁽qadd⁽šô)* in verse 8 and "he made it holy" *(y⁽qadd⁽šēhû)* in verse 11. This outer frame of the introduction A and conclusion D brackets the entire commandment, while both A and D keep their own identity. The reason for man's keeping the Sabbath is that God had made it holy at Creation. Accordingly, a major thrust of the Sabbath commandment falls on its holiness, which has already been the subject of discussion in connection with the Creation Sabbath. Sabbath holiness and

Sabbath blessing stem from acts of God. The commandment to keep the Sabbath holy means (1) to accept God's gift for man, (2) to follow the divine Exemplar's pattern, (3) to acknowledge Him as Creator, and (4) to participate in God's rest. It also means a cessation from activity of the work that man is engaged in during the six days appointed for such work. The tie between the Sabbath commandment and Creation[114] is so close that God's six-day creation, followed by His rest on the seventh day, serves as the theological motivation for the seventh-day Sabbath of the fourth commandment.

The introductory word "remember" (zākôr)[115] carries great weight for the total meaning of the Sabbath commandment. The Hebrew root zkr has retrospective and prospective aspects.[116] Both retrospection and prospection are part of the meaning of the first word of the Sabbath commandment in Exodus 20.

The retrospective aspect of remembering focuses on the past. It wishes to bring something to remembrance. Thus it indicates that the Sabbath "is not introduced for the first time on Sinai, it is already there. . . . However, it is not introduced for the first time even in the wilderness of Sin, where the manna is found. Here, too, it is proclaimed as something which is already in existence."[117] A pre-Mosaic Sabbath[118] or early pre-Israelite Sabbath[119] is pointed to by several scholars. W. W. Cannon suggested a number of decades ago that the ancestors of the Hebrews who migrated to Canaan brought with them some memory of the Sabbath institution, its name, weekly recurrence, and cessation from work.[120] More recently a similar view has been put forth by M. H. Segal, who believes "that Abraham bequeathed to his descendants the conception of the seventh day as a divine rest day and that this conception was known among the Israelites in Egypt and had received among them the name of Sabbath. . . ."[121] On account of the sudden appearance of the Sabbath in fairly full-fledged form in Exodus 16, its broad grounding in the fourth commandment (Exodus 20), and the unique choice of the word "remember" (verse 8), one is led to assume a knowledge of the Sabbath before the time of Moses. Unfortunately, our present extra-Biblical sources do not allow us to trace the Sabbath. The Old Testament answer to the origin of the Sabbath is indicated in the link of the seventh day with Creation. Exodus 20:11 and 31:17 connect God's rest on the Creation Sabbath with the institution of the weekly Sabbath, which appears to be legitimized in the Creation Sabbath (Gen. 2:2, 3).[122]

The word "remember" in Exodus 20:8 also contains a prospective aspect,[123] aside from the psychological one that looks to the past.[124] The prospective aspect of "remember" relates to the future. The immediate purpose of remembering is directed toward definite action in the present.[125] This comes to expression in the wording "Remember [zākôr] . . . to keep holy [l^eqadd^ešô]."[126] This is also the case in the searching question of Exodus 16:28: "How long do you refuse to keep the divine commandments and laws?" To refrain from refusing to keep the laws of God is the same as to "remember," or to observe, or to keep them (chap. 31:13-17). To "remember" means to keep or to observe (cf. Deut. 5:12). The memory of the past (retrospective aspect) is to lead to right action in the present and to faithful obedience in the future (prospective aspect). Past, present, and future are united in the pregnant opening word of Exodus 20:8. The imperative "remember" calls for an awareness that makes the seventh day special through separation from the ordinary working days of the week. The remembrance motif points man back to the past, even back to Creation, and provides a meaningful purpose for the observance of the Sabbath in the present and points forward to a promising future.

The Sabbath in Deuteronomy 5.—The Sabbath commandment of Deuteronomy 5:12-15 has sixty-four Hebrew words. This difference in length, and new aspects of content as compared with Exodus 20:8-11, have exercised scholars for generations.[127] No consensus is emerging, because the issues are extremely complex and overshadowed by conflicting methodological problems.[128] It should, however, be reemphasized that short and long laws are found next to each other in Hittite legal tradition, and short later versions of the same laws may be expanded or contracted. Thus great caution is demanded in drawing radical conclusions from the differences between the Sabbath commandment in Exodus 20 and the oral reaffirmation of the same commandment in Deuteronomy 5.

The version of the Decalogue in Deuteronomy 5 has its own contextual life setting in an oral sermon to Israel on the eve of their entrance into the Promised Land. The book of Deuteronomy attributes it to be orally delivered by Moses to the Israelites (Deut. 5:1). Accordingly, the present text of the Decalogue in Deuteronomy 5 presents it to be a later oral version than the one written in Exodus 20.

The structure, based on content, of Deuteronomy 5:12-15 seems to be as follows:

A	Introduction	Observe the sabbath day, to keep it holy, as the LORD your God commanded you. (Verse 12)
B¹	Command	Six days you shall labor, and do all your work; (verse 13) but the seventh day is a sabbath to the LORD your God; (verse 14a)
C¹	Motivation	
B²	Command	in it you shall not do any work, you, or your son, or your daughter, or your manservant, or your maidservant, or your ox, or your ass, or any of your cattle, or the sojourner who is within your gates, (verse 14b)
C²	Motivation	that your manservant and your maidservant may rest as well as you and you shall remember that you were a servant in the land of Egypt, and the LORD your God brought you out thence with a mighty hand and an outstretched arm; (verses 14c-15a)
D	Conclusion	therefore the Lord your God commanded you to keep the sabbath day. (Verse 15b)

This structure[129] has many similarities and few significant differences compared with that of the fourth commandment in Exodus 20. The opening section (A) contains (again in the form of an introductory statement) the key principle of the commandment as a whole. It should be noted that its concluding clause, "as the LORD your God has commanded you" (verse 12c), contains the reason or motivation for the commandment as a whole. The question of the "why" of the Sabbath commandment is answered with the statement that God had commanded it to be thus.[130] The conclusion comes back to this motivation as being rooted in God's commandment. This theological motivation[131] in parts A and D bracket the commandment as a whole. Deuteronomy 5 does not reject the motivation of the Sabbath in Exodus 20 but affirms that it is rooted in a commandment and elaborates one aspect of the Sabbath. The recognition of the theological motivation of the grounding of the Sabbath in a commandment of God cannot be emphasized enough, because it introduces an element that seems implicitly affirmed in Exodus 20:10a (C¹) and repeated in Deuteronomy 5:14a (again C¹). But in Deuteronomy 5 something is made explicit in the commandment itself for the first time: the Sabbath is to be kept because God has ordained it—nay, commanded it—to be so.

Deuteronomy 5:13 (B¹) and verse 14b (B²) contain once more the positive command to do all work in six days and the prohibitive command to refrain from any work on the Sabbath day, just as in Exodus 20 (B¹ and B²). The short expansion "or your ox, or your ass" is new. This elaborates what is already implicit in "or your cattle" in Exodus 20:10.

Deuteronomy 5:14c (C²), which opens with the preposition *l'ma'an*, "that," provides the motivation for the prohibitive command "in it you shall not do any work," but not for the entire Sabbath commandment,[132] as has been maintained too often.[133]

The purpose of the cessation from work on the seventh day is "rest" (verse 14). It is significant that here the same verb—*nwh*, "to rest, take a rest,"[134]—is employed as in Exodus 20:11 and 31:17, where God is the subject of the "rest." Now the entire household, including manservant and maidservant, those of an inferior status in society, are to rest together. This brings liberation and freedom; it is a pointer to do away with all inequalities in the social structure. Before God all men are equal. Man's original status before God is to be reenacted in society. The Sabbath is an institution that is designed to bring this about. This amplification of the purpose of the Sabbath with its social or humanitarian aspect, its emphasis on liberation from work and freedom in society, is captured in Jesus' own words: "The sabbath was made for man, and not man for the sabbath" (Mark 2:27).

A further aspect comes into view with the "remembrance" clause: "and you shall remember that you were a servant in the land of Egypt, and the LORD your God brought you out thence with a mighty hand and an outstretched arm" (Deut. 5:15).[135] This introduces a soteriological aspect and elaborates the sphere of the rest aspect of the Sabbath commandment. It brings to remembrance the deliverance from Egyptian slavery through God's saving activity in the Exodus experience. It is definitely not aimed to provide a motivation for the Sabbath commandment as a whole,[136] which is provided in God's command (verses 12, 15b) itself. Contextually, the soteriological aspect relates to the Sabbath rest of the slaves.[137] The social or humanitarian emphasis[138] in Deuteronomy 5:12-15, which is likewise present in Exodus 20:8-11 (and Exodus 16:27-29), where Sabbath rest is extended to the whole household, is linked with the soteriological aspect, the divine deliverance from servitude in Egypt. On every Sabbath God's people are to remember that their God is a Saviour who has put an end to all bondage and who is the superior of all who wield power in the world. The fundamental significance of the Sabbath is both to remind us of God's creation (Ex. 20:8-11) and to bring to remembrance the freedom from servitude of any form, achieved by God and extended to all human beings (cf. Ex. 23:13).

There is also a variation between the opening term of the Sabbath commandment in Exodus 20:8 and the one in Deuteronomy 5:12. The former is "remember" *(zākôr)* and the latter "observe" *(šāmôr)*. It has been suggested that

THE SABBATH IN THE PENTATEUCH

there is little difference between these words.[139] Nevertheless, they are not synonyms, and their variations are important. Few hold that "observe" is original.[140] The present canonical context makes it later[141] than "remember." It is a favorite word in Deuteronomy[142] and sharpens one of the semantic aspects of "remember."

The term šāmar has the meaning of "to observe, keep" when followed by an accusative in the form of an order, commandment, agreement, or obligation.[143] Just as the Lord "observes, keeps" (šāmar) the covenant (Deut. 7:8, 9, 12; Ex. 34:7)—i.e., He is faithful in observing His part of the obligation—so His people, who are the other party in the covenant, are to "observe, keep" their part of the covenant. The Ten Commandments are known as "the words of the covenant" (Ex. 34:28; cf. Deut. 29:1, 9) or "the tables of the covenant" (Deut. 9:9, 11, 15), and the oral recitation of the Decalogue in Deuteronomy 5 is part of a covenant renewal. Accordingly, the choice of "observe" as the first word stresses the keeping of the Sabbath. This we have seen to be a part of the meaning of the word "remember." The term "observe" appears to include special covenantal overtones,[144] which will be discussed in a later section.

The goal of observing the Sabbath is "to keep it holy" (Deut. 5:12; cf. Ex. 20:8). This means that it is directed toward definite action. One aspect regarding the meaning of the phrase "to keep it holy" (l'qadd'šô) should now be added. The idea expressed by the words "to keep holy" (qiddaš) contains also the idea "to consecrate for usage in behalf of God."[145] Just as priests[146] or Nazarites (Num. 6:2, 6-8; Judges 13:5, 7; 16:17) are placed in a state of holiness and consecration in order that they may perform their service before God, so the Sabbath is placed in a state of holiness and separation for service in behalf of God (Lev. 23:1-3).

This separation of the Sabbath with its own holiness for service in behalf of God includes activity in communal worship. Worship (cultic activity) is part of the Sabbath institution, as Leviticus 23:1-3 indicates. This passage contains many themes that have already surfaced, such as "a sabbath to the LORD" (see Ex. 16:23, 25; 20:10; 31:15; 35:2); "six days shall work be done; but on the seventh day is a sabbath of solemn rest" (Ex. 23:12; 31:15; 34:21; 35:2); and "you shall do no work" (Ex. 20:10; Deut. 5:14).[147] Its significance rests in the fact that the Sabbath is listed as belonging to the sacred festivals, "the appointed feasts of the LORD" (Lev. 23:2). The Sabbath, like the other "holy convocations" of the annual festal calendar,[148] is proclaimed to be "a holy convocation" (verse 2)[149] that belongs to God's "appointed feasts" (verse 2). The Sabbath belonged to the festal days on which the congregation gathered for worship as a festal assembly. Leviticus 23:1-3 claims that in the early history of Israel, the Sabbath was a day of joyous rest from weekly labor and a time of solemn, festal worship of God.

Sabbath and Sign

An exceptionally rich Sabbath text appears in Exodus 31:12-17.[150] Before we discuss some of the new ideas expressed for the first time in this passage, we need to recognize its contextual setting. The instructions for keeping the Sabbath as related in Exodus 31:12-17 follow the directions of Yahweh (Ex. 27:20; 31:11) for the sanctuary and its service (chaps. 25:1-31:11). Both are part of the same oral communication of Yahweh to Moses (chaps. 25:1; 30:11, 17, 22, 34; 31:1, 12) on Mount Sinai. The divine communication had outlined in detail the work to be done regarding the building of the sanctuary. The instructions concerning the Sabbath, coming at the conclusion, (1) connect the Sabbath and the sanctuary (cf. Lev. 19:30),[151] (2) specify details about the Sabbath revealed for the first time, and (3) remind the people of the limits of work: "Six days shall work be done, but the seventh day is a sabbath of solemn rest, holy to the LORD; whoever does any work on the sabbath day shall be put to death" (Ex. 31:15).[152] The present context indicates that the Sabbath, which had been included as one of the Ten Commandments (Ex. 20:8-11), is formally explained to Moses in its manifold aspects on Mount Sinai.

Many of the aspects associated with the Sabbath in Exodus 31:12-17 are already known. God's six-day creation and rest on the seventh day in verse 17 is known from Genesis 2:2, 3 and Exodus 20:11. The command to "keep" (*šāmar*) the Sabbath of verses 13, 14, and 16 is encountered in Deuteronomy 5:12, 15, as is also the injunction to "observe" (verse 16; Deut. 5:12) it. The holiness of the Sabbath of verses 14 and 15 takes us to Genesis 2:3; Exodus 16:23; 20:8 (cf. Ex. 35:2; Deut. 5:12). The identity of the seventh day as the Sabbath comes in both Exodus 16:26 and 29 and 20:10, and the idea of the Sabbath as a "sabbath feast" (*šabbātôn*)[153] is already known in Exodus 16:23.

The statement that the Sabbath "is a sign between me and you throughout your generations, that you may know that I, the LORD, sanctify you" (Ex. 31:13) is entirely new. These words appear in similar form[154] again in Ezekiel 20:12, 20. Exodus 31:13 specifies that the "sign" (*'ôth*)[155] is "between me and you," i.e., between God and His people.[156] The fact that the Sabbath functions as an external, visible, and perpetual sign between God and His people is an essential part of the total meaning of the Sabbath as a sign. But the sign functions of the Sabbath go far beyond this.

The very nature of a "sign" is that it points to something beyond itself. The "sign" serves to mediate an understanding and/or to motivate a kind of behavior.[157] A sign can impart knowledge about God's activity in shaping history.[158] It may motivate people to believe in God, to worship Him, and thus produce and confirm faith.[159] A sign may serve as a memorial that brings remembrance.[160] It can function as a mark or sign of separation.[161] It can put attention on, confirm, or corroborate something beyond itself and thus be a sign of confirmation.[162] Finally, there can be signs of the covenant between God and His elected people.[163]

Several of these functions of signs are part of the sign nature of the Sabbath.[164] It has been frequently emphasized that the Sabbath is a "sign of observation,"[165] which exhorts to fulfill a duty,[166] and brings to mind an obligation.[167] In Exodus 31:13 the Sabbath is a "sign between me and you" and quite naturally emphasizes the obligation and duty of God's covenant community to keep the Sabbath "holy to the LORD" (verse 15).

The Sabbath is also a "sign of separation."[168] It has been pointed out that one of the functions of a "sign" (*'ôth*) is to mediate knowledge and understanding.[169] The Sabbath as a "mark of separation" mediates to men of different religions or faiths the knowledge that a peculiar or unique relationship exists between God and the people that keep the Sabbath holy "by which the whole world is to recognize the existence of this relationship."[170] The Sabbath is a "sign of recognition" that marks God's people off from those around them.[171] Just as the sign placed by God on Cain did not disgrace him (Gen. 4:15),[172] but separated him from the rest of men and assured his future existence,[173] so the Sabbath is a sign given to the believer that separates him from the rest of men and assures his future existence. As such the Sabbath is a distinguishing mark.

Aside from being a "sign of observation" and a "sign of separation," the Sabbath is a "sign of remembrance."[174] The retrospective aspect of "remembrance" has already been recognized to be part of the Sabbath commandment in Exodus 20. The Sabbath functions as a "sign of remembrance" in that it takes man's memory back to the origin of the Sabbath as the seventh day of Creation week on which God "rested, and was refreshed" (Ex. 31:17; cf. Gen. 2:3; Ex. 20:11). It is thus a sign that memorializes Creator and Creation. Remembrance not only includes the past but actualizes[175] this knowledge in present and future action: "to keep the sabbath, observing the sabbath throughout their generations" (verse 16). God's people remember the gracious acts of deliverance[176] and God's plan of redemption.

The Sabbath is also a "sign of knowledge."[177] This is made explicit in Exodus 31:13: "this is a sign . . . that you may know *(lāda'ath)*." The sign serves the purpose of knowledge.[178] The Sabbath is a sign that imparts to Israel the knowledge (1) that Yahweh is her God[179] and (2) that her God "sanctifies" His people[180] by making them a holy people,[181] i.e., a people separated for a special covenant with Him.[182] The holiness of God's people, therefore, is derived from their being related to the holy God, and not from any intrinsic quality of the people. The redemptive character of the Sabbath comes into view.

The discussion of the Sabbath as a sign of observation, separation, remembrance, and knowledge, which stressed the Sabbath as a sign for man, needs to be supplemented by the Sabbath as a sign for God. The meaning of the Sabbath as a sign for God has come into focus by designating the Sabbath as a "sign of guarantee."[183] Just as the rainbow is the perpetual sign of guarantee between God and the earth (Gen. 9:13) that "the waters shall never again become a flood to destroy all flesh" (verse 15), so the Sabbath is a "sign of guarantee" whereby God assures His sanctifying purposes for His people.[184] It is a sign of efficacious grace, a powerful sign of salvation. The Giver of the sign guarantees His pledge of making His people holy.

Another phase of the Sabbath as a sign of God's pledge and guarantee for the covenant community has been offered recently by M. G. Kline on the basis that the Sabbath is part of God's covenant and thus carries its seal.[185] He states emphatically, "The Creator has stamped on world history the sign of the Sabbath as His seal of ownership and authority."[186] This interpretation is based on the parallelism of external appearance between international treaty documents, in some of which the suzerain's dynastic seal comes in the midst of the treaty document. Whether or not this parallelism can be sustained is beside the point. The Sabbath regulation appears as a sign or seal of ownership and authority. God is identified as the Creator (Ex. 20:11; 31:17), distinguishing Him from the other gods;[187] and the sphere of ownership and authority is identified as "heaven and earth" (chaps. 31:17; 20:11; Gen. 2:1-3).[188] These are ancient constituents of the seal, namely the identity of the owner and the sphere of ownership and authority. They are present in the written[189] and oral[190] Sabbath commandments revealed on Mount Sinai and thus make the Sabbath a unique sign or seal with momentous meaning for the believer. Any person who imitates the Creator's example by keeping the Sabbath holy as did his Lord acknowledges Him both as Creator and Re-creator (Redeemer). He accepts the Sabbath as God's gracious and life-renewing gift and acknowledges God's ownership and authority over himself and all creation. This sets the believer off from the rest of mankind and makes him part of the covenant community of true worshipers of God. The celebration and keeping of the Sabbath is the "outward sign" and "external seal." God's election, covenant, and sanctifying activity are the "inward grace" and "internal sanctification" that give it present reality.

Sabbath and Covenant

The Sabbath is directly connected with the "covenant" *(bᵉrîth)* in Exodus 31:12-17: "Therefore the people of Israel shall keep the sabbath, observing the sabbath throughout their generations as a perpetual covenant [*bᵉrîth 'ôlām*]" (verse 16). It is true that the Sabbath, in contrast to the rainbow as a "sign of the covenant" (Gen. 9:13, 17) in the Noachic covenant and to circumcision as "a sign of the covenant" (chap. 17:11) in the Abrahamic covenant, is not explicitly called a "sign of the covenant." [191] Nevertheless, the Sabbath doubtlessly functions as a covenant sign of the Sinai (Horeb) covenant, because it is called a "sign between me and you" (Ex. 31:13; cf. Eze. 20:20) or a "sign between me and the people of Israel" (Ex. 31:17).[192] The expression "a sign between me and you" brings to mind the phrases "a sign of the covenant between me and the earth" (Gen. 9:13)[193] and "a sign of the covenant between me and you" (chap. 17:11) in the covenants of Noah and Abraham, respectively.[194] The language of the entire passage of Exodus 31:12-17 is filled with covenant terminology. The verbs "keep" *(šāmar)*[195] in verses 13, 14, and 16 and "know" *(yāda')*[196] in verse 13 are filled with covenant overtones. The term "profane" *(hll)*,[197] which is used not infrequently with the Sabbath,[198] is a term for the breaking of or doing away with the covenant.[199] In short, just as the Noachic covenant has an eternal sign in the rainbow (Gen. 9:13, 17) and the Abrahamic covenant has an eternal sign in circumcision (chap. 17:11), so the Sinai (Horeb) covenant has an eternal sign in the Sabbath.

The Sabbath is a "sign of confession"[200] on the basis of which the validity of God's "eternal covenant" is maintained throughout the generations of the covenant community (Ex. 31:16). The perpetual celebration of the Sabbath reminds God's covenant people that the intimate covenant relationship established by her God between Him and them was rooted in His gracious election and eternal covenant that was formally established on Mount Sinai. The ongoing celebration (keeping, observing) of the Sabbath does not so much secure God's relationship with His people[201] as it serves as an indicator that the "eternal covenant" relationship is still in existence.

Retrospectively, the Sabbath looks back. As a sign of remembrance the Sabbath memorializes God as Creator and His creation as undisturbed by sin (Gen. 2:2, 3; Ex. 20:8, 11; 31:17).[202] Prospectively, the Sabbath, as a sign of an "everlasting covenant" (Ex. 31:16) in which God bound Himself[203] to His covenant people and they accepted the obligation of celebrating the Sabbath, contains an "emphatic promise"[204] for all generations. As covenant sign and rooted in Creation, the Sabbath makes possible redemptive history, i.e., covenant history[205] that moves forward to its ultimate goal.

The Sabbath has a key part in reaching into the future toward the ultimate goal of redemptive, covenant history. First, the Sabbath is a sign of man's basic posture in the presence of God. It is a day that provides freedom and liberation from the work and anxiety in present existence. It brings communion with God and thus physical, mental, and spiritual regeneration and renewal. As such, it is a proleptic token of an eschatological reality in the future.[206] It is a covenant sign in the here and now about an ultimate future[207] with its hoped-for redemption. Second, the Sabbath stands as a sign of an "everlasting covenant" between Creation (Gen. 2:2, 3; Ex. 20:11; 31:17) and redemption (Deut. 5:15; Isa. 56:1-4), pointing to the great consummation.[208] In this sense the Sabbath's commemorative retrospection to Creator and Creation shows itself as a powerful token of divine obligation[209] that makes man look forward to complete redemption and total freedom, awaited by the entire sin-ridden creation.

The extraordinary redeeming qualities inherent in the Sabbath are a sign of guarantee on the basis of which the hope in ultimate redemption with its new heaven and new earth has a secure anchor. Thus the Sabbath directs us to the past from which this day receives its deepest meaning for the present and points constantly anew to a most glorious future of total freedom and everlasting joy. Finally the interruption of unhindered communion between God and His people comes to an end. The Sabbath is a promise and guarantee that this will take place. The Sabbath is a covenant sign through which God has pledged that the present proleptic experience of freedom, liberation, joy, and communion on the weekly Sabbath is but a foretaste of the ultimate reality in the glorious future.

NOTES

[1] See the informative surveys by T. J. Meek, "The Sabbath in the Old Testament," *JBL* 33 (1914):201-212; E. G. Kraeling, "The Present Status of the Sabbath Question," *American Journal of Semitic Languages and Literature* 49 (1932-33):218-228; R. North, "The Derivation of Sabbath," *Biblica* 36 (1955):182-201; R. de Vaux, *Ancient Israel: Its Life and Institutions* (London, 1961), pp. 476-479; J. H. Meesters, *Op zoek naar de oorsprong van de sabbat* (Assen, 1966), pp. 4-83; C. W. Kiker, *The Sabbath in the Old Testament Cult* (Th.D. dissertation, Southern Baptist Theological Seminary, 1968), pp. 5-39; W. Rordorf, *Sunday* (Philadelphia, 1968), pp. 19-24; N.-E. A. Andreasen, *The Old Testament Sabbath*, SBL Diss. Ser. 7 (Missoula, Mont., 1972), pp. 1-16; N. Negretti, *Il Settimo giorno* (Rome, 1973), pp. 31-108; G. Robinson, *The Origin and Development of the Old Testament Sabbath* (Hamburg, 1975), pp. 6-24.

[2] F. Delitzsch, *Babel and Bible* (Chicago, 1903), pp. 37, 38.

[3] G. Lotz, *Questiones de historia Sabbati libri duo* (Leipzig, 1883), pp. 57, 58, 106, is at times credited to be the first to seek the origin of the Sabbath from Babylonian sources.

[4] G. Smith, *Assyrian Discoveries* (London, 1876), p. 12; C. H. W. Johns, *Assyrian Deeds and Documents II* (London, 1901), pp. 40, 41; idem, "The Babylonian Sabbath," *Expository Times* 17 (1905-06):566, 567; cf. W. Kornfeld, "Der Sabbath im Alten Testament," *Der Tag des Herrn*, ed. by H. Peichl (Wien, 1958), pp. 11-21, esp. 18, 21; M. Noth, *The History of Israel* (New York, 1958), p. 296; G. von Rad, *Old Testament Theology* (New York, 1962), 1:16, n. 3; P. R. Ackroyd, *Israel Under Babylon and Persia* (London, 1970), p. 155.

[5] Cf. appendix A, pp. 308-322.

[6] H. Zimmern, "Sabbath," *ZDMG* 58 (1904):199-202; idem, "Nochmals Sabbat," *ZDMG* 58 (1904):458-460; T. G. Pinches, "Sapattu, the Babylonian Sabbath," *Proceedings of the Society of Biblical Archaeologists* 26 (1904):51-53, 162, 163; J. Meinhold, *Sabbat und Woche im Alten Testament* (Göttingen, 1905), p. 5; idem, "Die Entstehung des Sabbats," *ZAW* 29 (1909):81-112; idem, "Zur Sabbatfrage," *ZAW* 36 (1916):108-110; idem, "Zur Sabbathfrage," *ZAW* 48 (1930):121-138; K. Marti, *Geschichte der israelitischen Religion*, 4th ed. (Strassburg, 1903), pp. 43, 44; G. Beer, *Schabbath: Der Mischnatractat "Sabbat"* (Tübingen, 1908), pp. 11-21; idem, "Sabbat," *Pauly-Wissowa Realencyclopädie*/2 (Stuttgart, 1920), cols. 1551-1557; E. Mahler, "Der Sabbat: Seine etymologische und chronologisch-historische Bedeutung," *ZDMG* 62 (1908):33-79, esp. 47-56; Meek, *loc. cit.*; G. Hölscher, *Geschichte der israelischen und jüdischen Religion* (Giessen, 1922), p. 80; S. Mowinckel, *Le Décalogue* (Paris, 1927), p. 90; A. Lods, *Israel* (New York, 1932), pp. 437-440; S. H. Hooke, *The Origins of Early Semitic Ritual* (London, 1938), pp. 58, 59; O. Procksch, *Theologie des Alten Testaments* (Gütersloh, 1950), p. 544; N. H. Tur-Sinai, "Sabbat und Woche," *Biblica et orientalia* 8 (1951):14-24, esp. 21 (note the critique of the latter by M. Gruber, "The Source of the Biblical Sabbath," *Journal of the Ancient Near Eastern Society of Columbia University* 1 [1969]:14-20); J. Morgenstern, "Sabbath," *IDB* (New York, 1962), 4:135, 136; idem, "The Festival of Jerobeam I," *JBL* 83 (1964):111; J. M. Baumgarten, "The Counting of the Sabbath in Ancient Sources," *VT* 16 (1966):277-286; A. Lemaire, "Le Sabbat à l'époque royale Israélite," *Revue biblique* 80 (1973):161-185; Robinson, *op. cit.*, pp. 145, 146, 171-185.

[7] In modern scholarship it was first proposed by A. Kuenen, *The Religion of Israel* (London, 1874), 1:276; while the Kenite aspect was added by B. D. Eerdmans, "Der Sabbath," *Vom Alten Testament* (Festschrift für K. Marti) (Giessen, 1925), pp. 79-83, and supported by K. Budde, "The Sabbath and the Week," *Journal of Theological Studies* 30 (1928-29):1-15; idem, "Antwort auf Johannes Meinhold's 'Zur Sabbathfrage,'" *ZAW* 48 (1930):138-145; L. Köhler,

"Der Dekalog," *Theologische Rundschau* Neue Folge 1 (1929):163-165; W. W. Cannon, "The Weekly Sabbath," *ZAW* 49 (1931):325-327; H. H. Rowley, "Moses and the Decalogue," *Bulletin, John Rylands Library* 34 (1951-52):81-118; idem, *Worship in Ancient Israel* (Philadelphia, 1967), pp. 45, 46, 90, 91; W. H. Schmidt, *Alttestamentlicher Glaube und seine Umwelt* (Neukirchen-Vluyn, 1968), p. 84.
    [8] See the critiques by Meesters, *op. cit.*, pp. 53-57; Kiker, *op. cit.*, pp. 5-14; De Vaux, *loc. cit.* On the lunar-phase hypothesis, see D. Nielsen, *Die altarabische Mondreligion und die mosaische Überlieferung* (Strassburg, 1904), pp. 52-58; J. Hehn, *Siebenzahl und Sabbat bei den Babyloniern und im Alten Testament* (Leipzig, 1907), pp. 58-62, 112-114; cf. Negretti, *op. cit.*, pp. 71-81.
    [9] H. Ringgren, *Israelite Religion* (Philadelphia, 1966), p. 202.
    [10] Developed by H. Lewy and J. Lewy, "The Origin of the Week and the Oldest West Asiatic Calendar," *Hebrew Union College Annual* 17 (1942-1943):1-152, and supported by J. Morgenstern, *op. cit.*, pp. 135-141. Note the critical reaction by Tur-Sinai, *op. cit.*, p. 16; K. Balkan, "The Old Assyrian Week," *Studies in Honor of Benno Landsberger*, ed. by H. G. Güterbock and Th. Jacobsen (Chicago, 1965), pp. 159-174.
    [11] Among the negative reactions to the astrological and agricultural hypotheses are the following: Meesters, *op. cit.*, pp. 16-57; De Vaux, *loc. cit.*; Kiker, *op. cit.*, pp. 31-35; Rordorf, *op. cit.*, pp. 23, 24; Robinson, *op. cit.*, pp. 16, 17; B. E. Shafer, "Sabbath," *IDBSup.* (Nashville, 1976), p. 760; J. B. Segal, "Intercalation and the Hebrew Calendar," *VT* 7 (1957):250-307; J. A. Brinkman, "Note on Old Assyrian *ḫamuštum*," *Journal of Near Eastern Studies* 24 (1965):118-120; B. Z. Wacholder, "Sabbatical Year," *IDBSup.* (Nashville, 1976), p. 762.
    [12] With some variation, H. Webster, *Rest Days* (New York, 1916), pp. 101-123; M. P. Nilsson, *Primitive Time Reckoning* (Lund, 1920), pp. 323-334; M. Weber, *Ancient Judaism* (Glencoe, Ill., 1952), p. 151; E. Jenni, *Die theologische Begründung des Sabbatgebotes im Alten Testament* (Zurich, 1956), pp. 12, 13.
    [13] Rordorf, *op. cit.*, p. 22; F. Mathys, "Sabbatruhe und Sabbatfest," *Theologische Zeitschrift* 28 (1972):257; H.-J. Kraus, *Worship in Israel* (Richmond, Va., 1966), p. 82; Robinson, *op. cit.*, p. 12; F. Stolz, "שבת *sbt* aufhören, ruhen," *THAT*, 2:869.
    [14] First proposed by W. A. Heidel, *The Day of Yahweh: A Study of Sacred Days and Ritual Forms in the Ancient Near East* (New York, 1929), pp. 438, 439, and expanded by Kraus, *op. cit.*, pp. 81-87; Kornfeld, *loc. cit.*; Kiker, *op. cit.*, pp. 50, 51, 67-131; J. Guillén, "Nuevas aportaciones al estudio del sábado," *Estudios biblicos* 26 (1967):77-89; idem, "Motivación deuteronómica del precepto del Sabat," *Estudios biblicos* 29 (1970):73-99; idem, *Motivación deuteronómica del descanso sabatico* (Madrid, 1971), pp. 121-144; F. Stolz, "Sabbath, Schöpfungswoche und Herbstfest," *Wort und Dienst* 11 (1971):159-175; Negretti, *op. cit.*, pp. 31-91; Lemaire, *loc. cit.*, esp. pp. 167-170.
    [15] Schmidt, *loc. cit.*
    [16] With Ringgren, *loc. cit.*, and Robinson, *op. cit.*, p. 10, against Negretti, *op. cit.*, pp. 33, 41-43, and Kraus, *op. cit.*, pp. 85-87. Important critiques are also provided by De Vaux, *op. cit.*, p. 478; Meesters, pp. 66-80; Andreasen, *op. cit.*, pp. 113-121, and G. J. Botterweck, "Der Sabbat in Alten Testamente (II)," *Theologische Quartalschrift* 134 (1954):454.
    [17] See Meesters, *op. cit.*, pp. 1-83; Kiker, *op. cit.*, pp. 1-66; Andreasen, *op. cit.*, pp. 1-16; Robinson, *op. cit.*, pp. 6-24; Shafer, *op. cit.*, pp. 760, 761.
    [18] Meesters, *op. cit.*, p. 201; Kiker, *op. cit.*, pp. 67-187; Robinson, *op. cit.*, pp. 29-313.
    [19] R. D. Congdon, "Sabbatic Theology" (Th.D. dissertation, Dallas Theological Seminary, 1949); A. J. Heschel, *The Sabbath* (New York, 1951); Jenni, *op. cit.*, pp. 3-40; A. Rosenfeld, "The Sabbath in the Space Age," *Tradition* 7 (1964-65):27-33; J. W. Leitch, "Lord Also of the Sabbath," *Scottish Journal of Theology* 19 (1966):426-433; W. Dignath, "Der biblische Ruhetag—Urmodell humaner Daseinsstruktur," *Stimne* 23 (1971):357-360; Mathys, *op. cit.*, pp. 241-255; H. W. Wolff, *Anthropology of the Old Testament* (London, 1974), pp. 134-142; N.-E. A. Andreasen, "Festival and Freedom: A Study of an Old Testament Theme," *Interpretation* 28 (1974):281-297; C. R. Biggs, "Exposition and Adaptation of the Sabbath Commandment in the OT," *Australian Biblical Review* 23 (1975):13-23.
    [20] In view of the confusion and contradiction in more recent pentateuchal criticism, which throws into total disarray the traditional division and dating of the strata assigned to JEDP (see, for example, R. Rendtorff, "Traditio-Historical Method and the Documentary Hypothesis," *Proceedings of the Fifth World Congress of Jewish Studies* [Jerusalem, 1969], pp. 5-11; idem, "The 'Yahwist' as Theologian? The Dilemma of Pentateuchal Criticism," *Journal for the Study of OT* 3 [1977]:2-10; idem, *Das überlieferungsgeschichtliche Problem des Pentateuch* [Berlin, 1977]; J. Van Seters, *Abraham in History and Tradition* [New Haven and London, 1975]; idem, "The 'Yahwist' as Theologian? A Response," *Journal for the Study of OT* 3 [1977]:15-19; H. H. Schmid, *Der sogenannte Jahwist* [Zurich, 1976]; idem, "In Search of New Approaches in Pentateuchal Research," *Journal for the Study of OT* 3 [1977]:33-42), it appears methodologically sound to attempt to treat the pentateuchal Sabbath passages in the sequence in which they are textually provided and to bring together those passages that emphasize certain topics, settings, or motifs.
    [21] Literary critical questions or modernistic scholarship need not detain us. See previous note.
    [22] H. W. Wolff, "The Day of Rest in the Old Testament," *Concordia Theological Monthly* 43 (1972):501; Meesters, *op. cit.*, pp. 91-99.
    [23] Against H. Gunkel, *Genesis*, 8th ed. (Göttingen, 1969), p. 115, and M. Greenberg, "Sabbath," *Encyclopaedia Judaica* (Jerusalem and New York, 1971-72), 14:558, with Andreasen, *OT Sabbath*, p. 65, n. 1., and Jenni, *op. cit.*, p. 21.
    [24] C. Westermann, *Genesis* (Neukirchen-Vluyn, 1974), pp. 231-233; Andreasen, "Recent Studies of the Old Testament Sabbath: Some Observations," *ZAW* 86 (1974):465; and now especially Negretti, *op. cit.*, pp. 150, 151.
    [25] B. Hartmann, "Himmel und Erde im AT," *Schweizer Theologische Umschau* 30 (1960):221-224; M. Ottosson, "'erets," *TDOT* (1974), 1:394-397.
    [26] Cf. Gunkel, *op. cit.*, p. 114; E. A. Speiser, *Genesis*, Anchor Bible (Garden City, N.Y., 1964), p. 7.
    [27] *HALAT*, p. 454; G. Gerleman, "*klh* zu Ende sein," *THAT*, 1:831-833.
    [28] *The New English Bible* reads "sixth day" and follows the Septuagint, Syriac, and Samaritan. Nevertheless, the Hebrew text is well preserved.
    [29] Although the noun "Sabbath" does not appear in Genesis, it is the *communis opinio* that this is what is meant.
    [30] Jenni, *op. cit.*, p. 25; W. Zimmerli, *1. Mose 1-11: Die Urgeschichte*, 3d ed. (Zürich, 1967), p. 103; N. Füglister, *Gottesdienst am Menschen: Zum Kultverständnis des Alten Testaments* (Salzburg, 1973), p. 9; O. Loretz, *Schöpfung und Mythos* (Stuttgart, 1968), p. 70, formulates sharply: "The goal of the whole creation and of man is God's Sabbath. The creation of the world reached its completion only through the Sabbath, the seventh day."
    [31] Andreasen, *OT Sabbath*, p. 194, affirms with others (G. von Rad, M. Noth, W. H. Schmidt) that Genesis 2:1-3 is "not concerned with the Sabbath institution at all, but only with God's rest.... It [the Creation Sabbath] explains the divine *otiositas* as the seventh day of Creation." This judgment is not sustained in the text itself. It is noteworthy that this one-sided emphasis is somewhat corrected in his more recent essay "Recent Studies of the Old Testament

Sabbath: Some Observations," *ZAW* 86 (1974):466, 467.

[32] K. Elliger, "Sinn und Ursprung der priesterlichen Geschichtserzählung," *Zeitschrift für Theologie und Kirche* 49 (1952):122; Westermann, *op. cit.*, p. 236; H. Riesenfeld, *The Gospel Tradition* (Philadelphia, 1970), pp. 112, 113; Füglister, *op. cit.*, pp. 9-11; M. F. Unger, "The Significance of the Sabbath," *Bibliotheca Sacra* 123 (1966):53-55; et al.

[33] G. H. Waterman, "Sabbath," *The Zondervan Pictorial Encyclopedia of the Bible* (Grand Rapids, Mich., 1975), 5:183.

[34] *HALAT*, p. 454; *CHAL*, p. 158; *KB*, p. 437.

[35] See E. König, *Die Genesis*, 3d ed. (Gütersloh, 1925), p. 163; A. Heidel, *The Babylonian Genesis*, 2d ed. (Chicago, 1963), p. 127, n. 118.

[36] Speiser, *op. cit.*, p. 8.

[37] Gerleman, *op. cit.*, col. 832.

[38] Riesenfeld, *loc. cit.*; Andreasen, "Recent Studies," p. 466.

[39] *CHAL*, p. 231, *KB*, p. 601, *HAD*, p. 172.

[40] *CHAL*, p. 360, *KB*, p. 946, *HAD*, p. 277.

[41] Budde, *Die biblische Urgeschichte* (Giessen, 1883), pp. 494, 495; Jenni, *op. cit.*, pp. 19-21; W. H. Schmidt, *Die Schöpfungsgeschichte der Priesterschrift* (Neukirchen-Vluyn, 1964), p. 72.

[42] G..von Rad, *Die Priesterschrift im Hexateuch literarisch untersucht und theologisch gewertet* (Stuttgart, 1934), pp. 168, 169; M. Noth, *Überlieferungsgeschichte des Pentateuch* (Stuttgart, 1948), pp. 261, 262; Schmidt, *Schöpfungsgeschichte*, p. 157; E. Nielsen, *Die zehn Gebote* (Kopenhagen, 1965), pp. 37, 38; Negretti, *op. cit.*, pp. 155-162.

[43] This is especially emphasized by Schmidt, *Schöpfungsgeschichte*, p. 157.

[44] W. Bienert, *Die Arbeit nach der Lehre der Bibel*, 2d ed. (Stuttgart, 1956), p. 25; cf. Waterman, *loc. cit.*; W. Zimmerli, *Grundriss der alttestamentlichen Theologie* (Stuttgart, 1972), p. 26: ". . . but in this resting of God the Sabbath is obviously established."

[45] Among leading studies are: H. Hirschfeld, "Remarks on the Etymology of Šabbāth," *Journal of the Royal Asiatic Society* 28 (1896):353-359; P. Jensen, "Assyrio-hebraica," *Zeitschrift für Assyriologie* 4 (1889):274-278; Meinhold, *Sabbat und Woche*, pp. 12, 13; D. Nielsen, *op. cit.*, pp. 51-69; Hehn, *op. cit.*, pp. 91-106; Beer, *Schabbath*, pp. 11-21; Mahler, *loc. cit.*; S. Langdon, "The Derivation of *šabattu* and other notes," *ZDMG* 62 (1908):29-32; Meek, *op. cit.*, p. 204; B. Landsberger, *Der kultische Kalender der Babylonier und Assyrer* (Leipzig, 1915), pp. 132-134; North, *op. cit.*, pp. 184-193; G. Yamashiro, "A Study of the Hebrew Word Sabbath in Biblical and Talmudic Literatures" (Ph.D. dissertation, Harvard University, 1955); De Vaux, *op. cit.*, pp. 475, 476; Meesters, *op. cit.*, pp. 6-16; Kiker, *op. cit.*, pp. 40-53; Andreasen, *OT Sabbath*, pp. 100-106; Negretti, *op. cit.*, pp. 94-97; Lemaire, *op. cit.*, pp. 172-174.

[46] See D. Nielsen, *op. cit.*, pp. 51, 67, 69; cf. H. Wehr, *Arabisches Wörterbuch* 4th ed. (Wiesbaden, 1968), p. 365. For critical reactions, see Meesters, *op. cit.*, pp. 6-8; Andreasen, *OT Sabbath*, pp. 100, 101; Negretti, *op. cit.*, pp. 94, 95; Robinson, *op. cit.*, p. 184.

[47] H. Cazelles, *Études sur le Code de L'Alliance* (Paris, 1946), p. 93; Lemaire, *op. cit.*, pp. 173, 174.

[48] Jensen, *loc. cit.*; Langdon, *op. cit.*, p. 30; cf. Landsberger, *op. cit.*, pp. 132, 133; and many others.

[49] See Zimmern, "Sabbath," p. 202; North, *op. cit.*, pp. 189-193; *The Assyrian Dictionary of the Oriental Institute of the University of Chicago*, 5:25.

[50] See Hirschfeld, *op. cit.*, pp. 355-359; Hehn, "Zur Sabbatfrage," *Biblische Zeitschrift* 14 (1917):210-213; idem, *Siebenzahl*, p. 30; Landsberger, *op. cit.*, p. 134.

[51] See J. Friedrich and W. Röllig, *Phönizisch-Punische Grammatik*, 2d ed. (Rome, 1970), p. 68, sec. 146.

[52] Hirschfeld, *op. cit.*, pp. 355-359; J. Barth, *Die Nominalbildung in den semitischen Sprachen* (Leipzig, 1894), pp. 24, 145; F. Bohn, *Der Sabbat im AT und im altjüdischen religiösen Aberglauben* (Gütersloh, 1903), pp. 2, 3; A. Bentzen, *Den israelitske Sabbats Oprindelse og Historie indtil Jerusalems Erobring aar 70 E. Kr.* (Kopenhagen, 1923), pp. 10, 11; North. *op. cit.*, pp. 185-187; E. Kutsch, "Sabbat," *Die Religion in Geschichte und Gegenwart*, 3d ed. (Stuttgart: Kohlhammer, 1956), Vol. V., col. 1259; De Vaux, *op. cit.*, pp. 475, 476, B. S. Childs, *The Book of Exodus* (Philadelphia, 1974), p. 413.

[53] Recently most vigorously by North, *op. cit.*, pp. 182-201, and at some length by Kiker, *op. cit.*, pp. 42, 43.

[54] Kiker, *op. cit.*, pp. 44-53, put forth the hypothesis of a common Hebrew biliteral root *šb* from which the noun and verb derived and also the word *šbʿ*, "seven," so that cessation from work, rest on the seventh day, and Sabbath are closely related. Whether the hypothesis of a biliteral root is superior to the suggestion of a triliteral root *šbt* with the word *šbʿ*, "seven," deriving from a separate root is an open issue. The hypothesis of a common triliteral root has seemingly more in its favor.

[55] Noth, *Exodus* (Philadelphia, 1962), p. 136.

[56] See note 23.

[57] Schmidt, *Schöpfungsgeschichte*, pp. 158, 159, explains that this "mythical notion" is taken over in Genesis 2:2 but applied to the Sabbath. See also Westermann, *op. cit.*, p. 125, and W. G. Lambert, "A New Look at the Babylonian Background of Genesis," *Journal of Theological Studies* 16 (1965):297. Andreasen, *OT Sabbath*, p. 186, follows these suggestions, claiming that Genesis 2:1-3 "understood the *otiositas* simply as a Sabbath, the first Sabbath."

[58] F. Stolz, "נוח *nuᵃh* ruhen," *THAT*, 2:43, 44. See Jenni, *op. cit.*, p. 20, and A. R. Hulst, "Bemerkungen zum Sabbatgebot," *Studia Biblica et Semitica: Theodoro Christiano Vriezen* (Wageningen, 1966), pp. 162, 163, who respectively seek to determine whether Genesis 2:2-3 is prior to Exodus 20:11, or Exodus 20:11 is prior to Deuteronomy 5:11. On the theme of rest, see G. von Rad, "There Remains Still a Rest for the People of God: An Investigation of a Biblical Conception," *The Problem of the Hexateuch and Other Essays* (New York, 1966), pp. 94-102, esp. 100-102.

[59] The verb *npš*, "exhale," or "catch one's breath, refresh oneself" (*CHAL*, p. 242), is used only in the Old Testament in Exodus 23:12; 31:17; 2 Samuel 16:14. On *npš*, see Jenni, *op. cit.*, pp. 20, 21. Wolff, "Day of Rest," p. 501; *idem, Anthropology of the OT*, p. 138, has suggested that God *must* rest because He had become exhausted from His work of creation. This runs counter to the context of Exodus 31:17 and the theme of God's rest in the Old Testament.

[60] Jenni, *op. cit.*, p. 23.

[61] See G. Wehmeier, *Der Segen im Alten Testament* (Basel, 1970); C. A. Keller and G. Wehmeier, "*brk* segnen," *THAT*, 1:353-376; J. Scharbert, "*brk*," *TWAT* (Stuttgart, 1972), 1:827-841.

[62] Keller and Wehmeier, *op. cit.*, col. 362.

[63] Westermann, *op. cit.*, p. 237.

[64] F. Horst, *Gottes Recht* (Munich, 1961), pp. 198, 199; Scharbert, *loc. cit.*; Wehmeier, *op. cit.*, p. 134; Keller and Wehmeier, *op. cit.*, col. 369; and the following commentaries on Genesis: Gunkel, *op. cit.*, p. 115; S. R. Driver, *The Book of Genesis*, 14th ed. (London, 1943), p. 18; J. Skinner, *Genesis*, 2d ed. (Edinburgh, 1930), p. 38; König, *op. cit.*, p. 168; C. A. Simpson, "The Book of Genesis," *The Interpreter's Bible*, vol. 1, p. 490; O. Procksch, *Die Genesis* (Leipzig, 1913), p.

451; Westermann, *op. cit.*, p. 237.

[65] *KB*, p. 825; *CHAL*, p. 313.

[66] Cf. N. H. Snaith, *The Distinctive Ideas of the Old Testament* (Philadelphia, 1946), pp. 24-55; H.-P. Müller, "קדש *qdš* heilig," *THAT*, 2:589-609.

[67] W. W. Graf von Baudissin, *Studien zur semitischen Religionsgeschichte* (Giessen, 1878), 2:20; Snaith, *op. cit.*, pp. 35-37; J. Muilenburg, "Holiness," *IDB*, 2:617.

[68] Westermann, *op. cit.*, p. 236.

[69] Cf. Jer. 17:22, 24, 27; Eze. 20:20; 44:24; Neh. 13:22.

[70] Cf. Ex. 16:23; Isa. 58:13; Jer. 17:22, 24; Neh. 13:15-22.

[71] F. Maass, "*hll* pi. entweihen," *THAT*, 1:571-575, esp. 573.

[72] Isa. 56:2, 6; Eze. 20:13, 16, 21, 24; 22:8; 23:38; Neh. 13:17-18.

[73] W. Vischer, "Nehemia, der Sonderbeauftragte und Statthalter des Königs," *Probleme biblischer Theologie: Gerhard von Rad zum 70. Geburtstag* (Munich, 1971), p. 609.

[74] Discussions of Exodus 16:23-30 are provided from a variety of perspectives by Meesters, *op. cit.*, pp. 115-118; Andreasen, *OT Sabbath*, pp. 67-69, 129, 130; Negretti, *op. cit.*, pp. 173-224.

[75] Jenni, *op. cit.*, p. 20.

[76] Critical scholars working with the theory of source division (see the long list by Negretti, *op. cit.*, p. 174, n. 47) have never accomplished an exact division of the chapter into sources (Childs, *op. cit.*, p. 274). There are recent attempts to explain the present form of Exodus 16 without recourse to literary criticism (see B. Jacob, *Das Zweite Buch der Tora* [Jerusalem, n.d.], pp. 647ff.; U. Cassuto, *A Commentary on the Book of Exodus* [Jerusalem, 1967]; E. Galbiati, *La Struttura letteraria dell' Esodo* [Milan, 1956]) that may be more fruitful. Even literary critics now point out that early elements are contained in Exodus 16 (B. J. Malina, *The Palestinian Manna Tradition* [Leiden, 1968], pp. 3-41), but there is no agreement on what is early.

[77] The murmuring motif is investigated by G. W. Coats, *Rebellion in the Wilderness* (Nashville, 1968).

[78] The noun *šabbātôn* means "sabbath feast" (P. Joüon, *Grammaire de l'Hébreu biblique*, 2d ed. [Rome, 1947], p. 808; *CHAL*, p. 360; *KB*, p. 948) here and in Exodus 31:15 and Leviticus 23:24 and 39, but with *š^enat* it means "sabbatical year" (Lev. 25:5) and in the expression *šabbāt šabbātôn* it means "most solemn sabbath" (Ex. 35:2; Lev. 23:3; 25:4), which can be the Day of Atonement (Lev. 16:31; 23:32). As used in Exodus 16:23 in connection with *šabbāt-qōdeš*, "holy sabbath," it seems to intensify or qualify "sabbath" in some way (Meesters, *op. cit.*, p. 116; K. Elliger, *Leviticus* [Tübingen, 1966], pp. 305, 306; Negretti, *op. cit.*, pp. 270-272).

[79] Childs, *op. cit.*, p. 290: "The existence of the sabbath is assumed by the writer."

[80] This is the case from the point of view of the author. Modern critical theories seek vastly different explanations, see most recently Negretti, *op. cit.*, pp. 173-224, and Robinson, *op. cit.*, pp. 270-275.

[81] M. Buber, *Moses: The Revelation and the Covenant* (New York, 1958), p. 80.

[82] See note 78.

[83] Negretti, *op. cit.*, pp. 196, 197, speaks of the announcement of the Sabbath.

[84] Against those who attempt to link prohibitions to astrological hypotheses, see notes 4, 6-9.

[85] See note 78.

[86] Childs, *op. cit.*, p. 290.

[87] Noth, *Exodus*, p. 136.

[88] C. F. Keil and F. Delitzsch, *The Pentateuch* (Grand Rapids, Mich., 1952), 2:69.

[89] Whether this is to be viewed as "the restrictive side of the day set aside for God" (Childs, *op. cit.*, p. 290) is debatable.

[90] There are numerous critical discussions; the following studies give an overview of these critical endeavors: Köhler, *op. cit.*, pp. 161-184; Rowley, "Moses and the Decalogue," pp. 81-118; J. J. Stamm, "Dreissig Jahre Dekalogforschung," *Theologische Rundschau* Neue Folge 27 (1961):189-239, 281-305; A. S. Kapelrud, "Some Recent Points of View on the Time and Origin of the Decalogue," *Studia Theologica* 18 (1964):81-90; J. P. Hyatt, "Moses and the Ethical Decalogue," *Encounter* 26 (1965):199-206; A. Jepsen, "Beiträge zur Auslegung und Geschichte des Dekalogs," *ZAW* 79 (1967):277-304; J. J. Stamm and M. E. Andrew, *The Ten Commandments in Recent Research* Naperville, Ill., 1967); E. Nielsen, *The Ten Commandments in New Perspective* (Naperville, Ill., 1968); E. Zenger, "Eine Wende in der Dekalogforschung?" *Theologische Revue* 3 (1968):189-198; H. Cazelles, "Les Origines du Décalogue," *Eretz Israel* 9 (1969):14-19; A. J. Phillips, *Ancient Israel's Criminal Law* (Oxford, 1970).

[91] Alt's essay of 1934 is translated as "The Origins of Israelite Law" in *Essays on Old Testament History and Religion* (Oxford, 1966), pp. 79-132.

[92] G. Mendenhall, "Ancient Oriental and Biblical Law," *Biblical Archaeology* 17 (1954):26-46; idem, "Covenant Forms in Israelite Tradition," *Biblical Archaeology* 17 (1954):50-76.

[93] K. Baltzer, *The Covenant Formulary* (Philadelphia, 1971); W. Beyerlin, *Origins and History of the Oldest Sinaitic Traditions* (Oxford, 1965), pp. 12-14, 49-67; D. R. Hillers, *Covenant: The History of a Biblical Idea* (Baltimore, 1969), pp. 48-56, 61, 62, 70; W. L. Moran, "Moses und der Bundesschluss am Sinai," *Stimmen der Zeit* 70 (1961-62):120-133; H. B. Huffmon, "The Exodus, Sinai and the Credo," *Catholic Biblical Quarterly* 27 (1965):101-113; M. G. Kline, *The Structure of Biblical Authority* (Grand Rapids, Mich., 1972), pp. 113-130; and others.

[94] D. J. McCarthy, *Treaty and Covenant: A Study in Form in the Ancient Oriental Documents and in the Old Testament* (Rome, 1963); Kraus, *op. cit.*, pp. 136-141; E. Gerstenberger, *Wesen und Herkunft des "apodiktischen" Rechts* (Neukirchen, 1965); idem, "Covenant and Commandment," *JBL* 84 (1965):38-51; F. Nötscher, "Bundesformular und 'Amtsschimmel,'" *Biblische Zeitschrift* 9 (1965):181-214; D. J. McCarthy, *Old Testament Covenant: A Survey of Current Opinions* (Oxford, 1972), pp. 10-30, with a good survey of the whole problem; W. M. Clark, "Law," *Old Testament Form Criticism*, ed. by J. H. Hayes (San Antonio, Tex., 1974), pp. 122-124.

[95] Gerstenberger, *Wesen und Herkunft*, ushered in this new phase of the debate in 1965. Among those following his line of thought are: W. Richter, *Recht und Ethos* (Munich, 1966); H. Schulz, *Das Todesrecht im Alten Testament* (Berlin, 1969); cf. R. Kilian, "Apodiktisches und kasuistisches Recht im Licht ägyptischer Analogien," *Biblische Zeitschrift* 7 (1963):185-202.

[96] Childs, *op. cit.*, p. 392.

[97] The length of this commandment is assumed to show many signs of growth and expansion as argued by many scholars using critical methods. See recently Hulst, *op. cit.*, pp. 152-164; N. Lohfink, "Zur Dekalogfassung von Deuteronomium 5," *Biblische Zeitschrift* 9 (1965):17-32; Meesters, *op. cit.*, pp. 90-111; Robinson, *op. cit.*, pp. 186-200.

[98] E. Sellin, *Geschichte des israelitisch-jüdischen Volkes* (Leipzig, 1924), 1:83, 84; Alt, *op. cit.*, p. 118; K. H. Rabast, *Das*

apodiktische Recht im Deuteronomium und im Heiligkeitsgesetz (Berlin, 1949), p. 35; Von Rad, *Old Testament Theology*, 1:191; Stamm, *op. cit.*, p. 201; E. Nielsen, *Ten Commandments*, pp. 88, 89; Meesters, *op. cit.*, p. 101; Negretti, *op. cit.*, pp. 142, 143.

[99] R. H. Charles, *The Decalogue* (Edinburgh, 1923), p. XLVIII; O. Procksch, *Theologie*, p. 85; Rowley, "Moses and the Decalogue," p. 114; H. Graf Reventlow, *Gebot und Predigt im Dekalog* (Gütersloh, 1962), pp. 12, 54-59, 63; Andreasen, *OT Sabbath*, pp. 84-89; G. Fohrer, *Geschichte der israelitischen Religion* (Berlin, 1969), p. 187.

[100] Among critical scholars who affirm or allow that the Decalogue may be Mosaic are H. Ewald, *Geschichte des Volkes Israel bis Christus*, 2d ed. (Göttingen, 1853), 2:22, 23; T. K. Cheyne, "Dr. Driver's Introduction to the Old Testament Literature," *Expositor* 5 (1892):109; W. P. Paterson, "Decalogue," *A Dictionary of the Bible*, ed. by J. Hastings (Edinburgh, 1908-1909), 1:581; E. Kautzsch, "Religion of Israel," *Hastings*, extra vol., p. 634; S. R. Driver, *The Book of Exodus* (Cambridge, 1911), p. 415; G. A. Smith, *The Book of Deuteronomy* (Cambridge, 1918), p. 85; Köhler, *op. cit.*, p. 184; P. Volz, *Mose und sein Werk*, 2d ed. (Tübingen, 1932), pp. 20-27; Procksch, *Theologie*, pp. 89, 90; A. Weiser, *Introduction to the Old Testament* (London, 1961), pp. 120, 121; Botterweck, *op. cit.*, pp. 140, 141; Rowley, "Moses and the Decalogue," p. 83; Kapelrud, *loc. cit.*; Hyatt, *loc. cit.*; Beyerlin, *op. cit.*, pp. 49-67, 145-157; Stamm and Andrew, *op. cit.*, pp. 25-27; T. C. Vriezen, *The Religion of Ancient Israel* (London, 1967), pp. 142, 143; W. Eichrodt, *Religionsgeschichte Israels* (Bern, 1969), pp. 21-23; J. Bright, *A History of Israel*, 2d ed. (Philadelphia, 1972), p. 142. J. K. Kuntz, *The People of Ancient Israel* (New York, 1974), p. 113; and, among many others, those listed by Andreasen, "Recent Studies," p. 455, n. 10.

[101] Rowley, "Moses and the Decalogue," pp. 113, 114.

[102] Fohrer, *loc. cit.*

[103] H. Gese, *Vom Sinai zum Zion* (Munich, 1974), p. 67; see also R. Kittel, *A History of the Hebrews* (London, 1895), 1:244, 245; Mowinckel, *op. cit.*, pp. 4, 5; Stamm, *op. cit.*, p. 200; Hyatt, *op. cit.*, p. 202; cf. Andreasen, *OT Sabbath*, p. 85: "Remember [observe] the sabbath day [to keep it holy]" is not certain whether or not to include "to keep it holy."

[104] Rabast, quoted by Stamm and Andrew, *op. cit.*, p. 20.

[105] With A. Dillmann, *Exodus und Leviticus*, 2d ed. (Leipzig, 1880), pp. 219, 220; E. König, "Neueste Verhandlungen über den Dekalog," *Neue Kirchliche Zeitschrift* 17 (1906):565-584; R. Kittel, *op. cit.*, pp. 235, 236; W. Möller, *Grundriss für alttestamentliche Einleitung* (Berlin, 1958), pp. 52-54, 107-110; G. C. Aalders, *A Short Introduction to the Pentateuch* (London, 1949); Buber, *op. cit.*, pp. 80-82, 119-144; A. Neher, *Moses and the Vocation of the Jewish People* (New York, 1959); A. Eberharter, *Der Dekalog* (Münster, 1930); K. A. Kitchen, *Ancient Orient and Old Testament* (Chicago, 1966), pp. 98, 99; M. H. Segal, *The Pentateuch* (Jerusalem, 1967), pp. 39, 40; R. K. Harrison, *Introduction to the Old Testament* (Grand Rapids, Mich., 1969), pp. 569, 570; and others.

[106] Note the incisive observations of Kitchen, *op. cit.*, pp. 130-135.

[107] See the short laws (Nos. 9, 10, 15, 16, 33-37) next to the long ones in the Lipit-Ishtar Law Code, nineteenth century B.C. *(ANET*, pp. 160, 161); cf. long laws (No. 9), short ones (Nos. 10, 11), long ones (Nos. 12-14), et cetera, in the Law Code of Eshnunna, *c.* 1925 B.C. *(ANET*, pp. 162, 163). The same can be observed in the famous Code of Hammurabi, late eighteenth century B.C. *(ANET*, pp. 166-177).

[108] Nos. 3, 4, 9, 14, 15, 16, 17, 18, 46. See *ANET*, pp. 189-191.

[109] Nos. 5, 6, 13, 45, 47.

[110] For example, Nos. 43 (short), 44 (long), 45 (short), 46 (long), 47 (long). Careful studies of Hittite laws are by E. Neufeld, *The Hittite Laws* (London, 1951); J. Friedrich, *Die hethitischen Gesetze* (Leiden, 1959).

[111] This differs from the structure of Andreasen, *OT Sabbath*, p. 170, with an (a), (b), (c), (d) sequence that seems to be in tension with the (a), (b), (b¹), (a¹) pattern (p. 198 and his "Festival and Freedom," pp. 283, 284).

[112] R. Martin-Achard, "*gūr* als Fremdling weilen," *THAT*, 1:409-412.

[113] The related expression "my/your Sabbath(s)" appears in Exodus 31:13; Leviticus 19:3, 30; Isaiah 56:4; 58:13; Ezekiel 20:12; 22:26; 23:38; 44:24; Nehemiah 9:14.

[114] Rightly affirmed among others recently again by Childs, *op. cit.*, p. 416, but questioned by some because of the dating problems brought about by literary criticism. See Reventlow, *op. cit.*, pp. 38, 60; Hulst, *op. cit.*, pp. 159-161.

[115] This Qal infinitive absolute functions as a strong imperative. Cf. R. J. Williams, *Hebrew Syntax: An Outline*, 2d ed. (Toronto, 1976), p. 39, sec. 211; J. D. Watts, "Infinitive Absolute as Imperative and the Interpretation of Exodus 20:8," *ZAW* 74 (1962):141-145.

[116] There are important recent studies: P. A. H. de Boer, *Gedenken und Gedächtnis in der Welt des AT* (Leiden, 1962); B. S. Childs, *Memory and Tradition in Israel* (Naperville, Ill., 1962); W. Schottroff, *"Gedenken" im Alten Orient und im Alten Testament* (Neukirchen-Vluyn, 1964); *idem*, "*zkr* gedenken," *THAT*, 1:507-518.

[117] Buber, *op. cit.*, p. 80.

[118] For example, Jenni, *op. cit.*, pp. 8, 9.

[119] Rowley, "Moses and the Decalogue," pp. 109-113, points to a Kenite usage. But see above on the Kenite hypothesis.

[120] Cannon, *op. cit.*, p. 325.

[121] M. H. Segal, *op. cit.*, p. 152.

[122] Greenberg, *loc. cit.*: ". . . here for the first time is given a rationale, drawn directly from the formulation of Genesis 2:1-3 and expressly identifying the Sabbath with the seventh day of Creation (Ex. 20:8-11)."

[123] Childs, *Memory and Tradition*, pp. 49-56; Schottroff, "*Gedenken*," pp. 153-156.

[124] J. Pedersen, *Israel: Its Life and Culture I, II* (London, 1926), pp. 106, 107, 256, 257; Childs, *Memory and Tradition*, pp. 17-30.

[125] Schottroff, "*zkr* gedenken," col. 510.

[126] The significance of this also comes to expression in other instances with *zkr* followed by l^e with infinitive construct: Ps. 103:18; cf. Ps. 109:16; 119:55.

[127] E. Auerbach, *Moses* (Amsterdam, 1953), pp. 196-197; Stamm and Andrew, *op. cit.*, pp. 13, 14; G. Schrenk, "Sabbat oder Sonntag?" *Judaica* 2 (1946):176; Lohfink, *loc. cit.*; Hulst, *op. cit.*, pp. 152-164; Andreasen, "Festival and Freedom," pp. 281-297.

[128] For recent reviews of the issues in critical scholarship, see the standard introductions by O. Eissfeldt, G. Fohrer, O. Kaiser, and E. W. Nicholson, *Deuteronomy and Tradition* (Philadelphia, 1967); S. Loersch, *Das Deuteronomium und seine Deutungen* (Stuttgart, 1967). For other approaches, that date Deuteronomy to the second millennium, see the introductions by E. J. Young, G. L. Archer, R. K. Harrison, and G. T. Manley, *The Book of the Law* (Grand Rapids, Mich., 1957); M. G. Kline, *Treaty of the Great King: The Covenant Structure of Deuteronomy* (Grand Rapids, Mich., 1963); *idem*, *The Structure of Biblical Authority*; Kitchen, *op. cit.*, p. 128, and his "Ancient Orient,

'Deuteronomism,' and the OT," *New Perspectives on the OT,* ed. by J. B. Payne (Waco, Tex., 1970), pp. 1-24; G. J. Wenham, "The Structure and Date of Deuteronomy" (Ph.D. dissertation, 1971); M. H. Segal, "The Book of Deuteronomy," *Jewish Quarterly Review* 48 (1957-58):315-351; idem, *The Pentateuch,* pp. 75-102; P. C. Craigie, *The Book of Deuteronomy* (Grand Rapids, Mich., 1976), pp. 24-29.

[129] Lohfink, "Dekalogfassung," p. 22, put forth a symmetrical-chiastic structure built upon catchwords. Recently Andreasen, "Festival and Freedom," p. 283, suggested a thematic structure. Our proposal differs from both, but the latter has pointed in the right direction.

[130] So correctly Hulst, *op. cit.,* p. 156.

[131] This is not to affirm the kind of "theological" motivation argued for by Childs, *Memory and Tradition,* pp. 52, 53; idem, *Exodus,* p. 417; Jenni, *op. cit.,* pp. 15-19; Reventlow, *op. cit.,* pp. 57, 58; E. Nielsen, *Ten Commandments,* p. 40; Füglister, *op. cit.,* p. 17; Loretz, *op. cit.,* p. 71; and others, because they base it on verse 14 and not on verses 12 and 15.

[132] See for this correct emphasis Hulst, *op. cit.,* pp. 155, 156, and the amplification by Andreasen, "Festival and Freedom," pp. 284-294.

[133] Recently again G. von Rad, *Deuteronomy* (Philadelphia, 1966), p. 58; Schrenk, *op. cit.,* p. 178; Rordorf, *op. cit.,* p. 15; and others.

[134] See note 39, and on its meaning Hulst, *op. cit.,* pp. 155-156; Mathys, *op. cit.,* pp. 245-247.

[135] It should be noted that 4QDeut^m contains in Deut. 5:15 the same motivation as in Ex. 20:11. For the text, see F. M. Cross, *Scrolls from the Wilderness of the Dead Sea* (San Francisco, 1969), pp. 18 (plate 19), 30.

[136] We cannot agree with J. L'Hour, *Die Ethik der Bundestradition im Alten Testament* (Stuttgart, 1967), p. 52: "Yahweh gives Israel the Sabbath commandment because of the slavery and the liberation from the land of Egypt. Slavery and liberation are the objective reason for the commandment." Similarly G. A. Smith, *op. cit.,* p. 89, n. 15; Von Rad, *Deuteronomy,* p. 58; Childs, *Memory and Tradition,* pp. 52, 53; M. Weinfeld, *Deuteronomy and the Deuteronomic School* (Oxford, 1972), p. 222.

[137] Andreasen, "Festival and Freedom," p. 287: "The real purpose of the 'remembrance clause' recalling the exodus deliverance here again is to provide a reason or a motive for extending the sabbath to those who are not free to observe it."

[138] It has been emphasized time and again that the social or humanitarian motive fits into the total emphasis of Deuteronomy. See S. R. Driver, *A Critical and Exegetical Commentary on Deuteronomy* (New York, 1902), p. 85; Weinfeld, *op. cit.,* pp. 282-297; M. H. Segal, *Pentateuch,* p. 93; Andreasen, "Festival and Freedom," pp. 285-287; and others.

[139] Noth, *Exodus,* p. 164; Reventlow, *op. cit.,* p. 45; Schottroff, "Gedenken," p. 155, call them "interchangeable terms." Meesters, *op. cit.,* p. 101; Andreasen, *OT Sabbath,* p. 83; idem, "Recent Studies," p. 457, n. 18; cf. Negretti, *op. cit.,* p. 131.

[140] Köhler, *op. cit.,* p. 180, because it does not presuppose a lengthy existence for the Sabbath institution; Hulst, *op. cit.,* pp. 158, 159, who believes that *šāmôr* was original because *zākôr* puts special emphasis on the Sabbath. Is this not equally applicable with *šāmôr?* See Lohfink, *op. cit.,* pp. 21-23.

[141] See also E. König, *Das Deuteronomium* (Leipzig, 1917), p. 92; Childs, *Memory and Tradition,* p. 55; Lohfink, *op. cit.,* pp. 22, 23; Meesters, *op. cit.,* p. 101; and others.

[142] Forms of *šāmar* appear a total of sixty-six times in Deuteronomy, but *zākar* in comparison only fourteen times.

[143] *CHAL,* p. 377.

[144] They are explicit in Exodus 31:12-17.

[145] Jepsen, *op. cit.,* p. 292; Mathys, *op. cit.,* p. 244.

[146] Ex. 28:3, 41; 29:1, 33, 44; 30:30; 40:13; Lev. 8:30; 21:15; 1 Sam. 7:1.

[147] The passages in the Decalogue are identical in form but with reversed word order.

[148] See the discussion in Kiker, *op. cit.,* pp. 101-112.

[149] This phrase appears eight times in Leviticus 23 and is traditionally understood to mean "festal assembly." Some scholars have proposed the meaning "festal time"; see J. Morgenstern, "Two Compound Technical Terms in Biblical Hebrew," *JBL* 43 (1924):314-320; E. Kutsch, "מקרא," *ZAW* 65 (1953):247-253; P. Katz, "'מקרא' in der griechischen und lateinischen Bibel," *ZAW* 65 (1953):253-255.

[150] On the whole pericope, see Meesters, *op. cit.,* pp. 124-125; Negretti, *op. cit.,* pp. 291-295. The widely discussed question of critical scholarship whether the idea of the Sabbath as a "sign" is earlier (see C. A. Keller, *Das Wort OTH als "Offenbarungszeichen Gottes"* [Basel, 1946], pp. 140, 158, n. 69) or later (see W. Eichrodt, "Der Sabbat bei Hesekiel: Ein Beitrag zur Nachgeschichte des Prophetentextes," *Lex tua Veritas: Festschrift für Hubert Junker,* ed. by H. Gross and F. Mussner [Trier, 1961], pp. 65-74) than Ezekiel 20 is answered more recently on the basis of traditiohistorical analysis: Ezekiel 20 reflects ancient traditions (see Jenni, *op. cit.,* pp. 30, 31; G. Fohrer, *Die Hauptprobleme des Buches Ezechiel* [Berlin, 1952], pp. 151, 152; W. Zimmerli, *Ezechiel* [Neukirchen-Vluyn, 1969], part 1, p. 447; Andreasen, *OT Sabbath,* pp. 42, 43; Mathys, *op. cit.,* pp. 253, 254).

[151] Childs, *Exodus,* p. 541.

[152] The subject of Sabbath and death penalty for violators cannot be treated in detail (Ex. 31:14, 15; 35:2, 3; Num. 15:32-36). See Andreasen, *OT Sabbath,* pp. 150-157; Meesters, *op. cit.,* p. 125; Negretti, *op. cit.,* pp. 283-285; Schulz, *op. cit.,* pp. 42-46, 55-63.

[153] See note 78.

[154] Andreasen, *OT Sabbath,* p. 42, n. 1 (p. 210) argues against direct literary dependency of Ezekiel on Ex. 31:13, because the material is used differently in the two places.

[155] Recent key studies on the Old Testament usage of the word *'ôth,* "sign," see F. Stolz, "'*ōt* Zeichen," *THAT,* 1:91-95; F. J. Helfmeyer, "אות *'ôth,*" *TDOT,* 1:167-188.

[156] So correctly Jenni, *op. cit.,* p. 31; Andreasen, *OT Sabbath,* p. 210; Wolff, *Anthropology,* p. 142; idem, "Day of Rest," pp. 504, 505; Mathys, *op. cit.,* pp. 252, 255.

[157] Helfmeyer, *op. cit.,* p. 171.

[158] Ex. 7:3, 5; 8:18, 19, 22, 23; 10:2; 13:8, 14; Deut. 6:20; Jer. 44:29; Eze. 14:8.

[159] Num. 14:11, 22, 23; Deut. 1:22-46; 4:34; 11:3; 13:1-3; 26:8; 29:2, 3; Joshua 24:17; Ps. 65:8 (9); 78:43; 86:17; Isa. 7:11.

[160] Ex. 13:9, 16; Num. 17:25; Deut. 6:8; 28:46; Joshua 4:6; Isa. 55:13; Eze. 14:8.

[161] Gen. 4:15; Ex. 8:19; 12:13; Num. 2:2; Joshua 2:12; Job 21:29.

[162] Ex. 3:12; Judges 6:17; 1 Sam. 2:34; 10:7, 9; 2 Kings 19:29; 20:8; Isa. 7:11, 14.

[163] Gen. 9:12, 13, 17; 17:11.

164 Ex. 31:13, 17; Eze. 20:12, 20.
165 See L. Köhler in *KB*, p. 23. This is taken over in *HALAT*, p. 25. Jenni, *op. cit.*, p. 31; Eichrodt, "Der Sabbat bei Hesekiel," p. 65; Negretti, *op. cit.*, p. 93; Füglister, *op. cit.*, p. 11.
166 *KB*, p. 23.
167 *CHAL*, p. 7.
168 Jenni, *op. cit.*, p. 31.
169 Helfmeyer, *op. cit.*, p. 171.
170 Noth, *Exodus*, p. 241.
171 *Ibid.*
172 G. von Rad, *Genesis* (Philadelphia, 1961), p. 103.
173 This comparison does not wish to overlook the distinctions between the subjects involved, nor to underestimate other differences. Cf. Westermann, *op. cit.*, pp. 423-427.
174 This is evident from the present context and falls into line with the pentateuchal theology of remembrance. Cf. G. J. Botterweck, *"Gott erkennen" im Sprachgebrauch des Alten Testaments* (Bonn, 1951), pp. 87, 88.
175 Helfmeyer, *op. cit.*, pp. 186-188.
176 Stolz, "'ōt Zeichen," col. 92.
177 On the function of "sign of knowledge," see Helfmeyer, *op. cit.*, pp. 171-175.
178 Jenni, *op. cit.*, p. 31.
179 The story of the plagues with the climax in the death of the Egyptian firstborn sons are "signs" (Ex. 7:3, 5; 8:18-23; 10:2; 18:22) by which Israel can know the power and help of her God.
180 Cf. Lev. 20:8; 21:8; 22:32; Eze. 37:28.
181 Ex. 19:6; Lev. 19:2, 3; Deut. 7:6.
182 Lev. 18:1-5; 19:2, 3; 20:26; 22:31-33.
183 See Keller, *op. cit.*, p. 145; Jenni, *op. cit.*, pp. 31, 32; Eichrodt, "Der Sabbat bei Hesekiel," p. 65; Mathys, *op. cit.*, p. 254; Füglister, *op. cit.*, p. 12.
184 Keller, *op. cit.*, p. 145.
185 Kline, *Treaty of the Great King*.
186 *Idem*, *The Structure of Biblical Authority*, p. 120.
187 Job 31:15; Isa. 44:24; Mal. 2:10. On the idea of "one Creator," see N. Lohfink, "אֶחָד, 'echādh," *TDOT*, 1:197.
188 The seal of the famous treaty between the Hittite Hattusilis and the Egyptian Ramses II in 1280 B.C. identifies the maker(s) of the treaty by name and the sphere of ownership and authority. See *ANET*, p. 202. For Mitannian practice, see D. J. Wiseman, *The Alalakk Tablets* (London, 1953), Plates VII and VIII, Texts 13, 14.
189 Ex. 20:8-11.
190 Chap. 31:12-17.
191 Keller, *op. cit.*, pp. 140, 141.
192 Helfmeyer, *op. cit.*, pp. 182, 183.
193 The phrase "between me and you" appears in verse 12.
194 This correspondence is pointed to by Keller, *op. cit.*, p. 140; W. Zimmerli, "Sinaibund und Abrahambund: Ein Beitrag zum Verständnis der Priesterschrift," in *Gottes Offenbarung: Gesammelte Aufsätze zum Alten Testament* (Munich, 1963), pp. 210, 211; Andreasen, *OT Sabbath*, p. 211; Helfmeyer, *op. cit.*, pp. 182, 183.
195 See the covenant context in Genesis 17:9, 10; Exodus 19:5; Deuteronomy 5:12; 7:9; 1 Kings 11:11; Psalm 78:10; 103:18; Ezekiel 17:14.
196 The peculiarly flexible Hebrew verb "to know" (*yāda'*) is connected with the covenant in so-called "covenant lawsuit" passages of Amos 3:1, 2; Hosea 4:1, 2; 13:4, 5; Isa. 1:2, 3; Jer. 24:7, in which it carries the meaning "to recognize." It is also used in a similar way in international treaties of the ancient Near East. See H. B. Huffmon, "The Treaty Background of Hebrew *Yāda'*," *Bulletin of the American Schools of Oriental Research* 181 (1966):31-37; H. B. Huffmon and S. B. Parker, "A Further Note on the Treaty Background of Hebrew *Yāda'*," *Bulletin of the American Schools of Oriental Research* 184 (1966):36-38; Hillers, *op. cit.*, pp. 120-125.
197 Maass, *op. cit.*, cols. 570-575.
198 See Ex. 31:14; Isa. 56:2, 6; Eze. 20:13, 16, 21, 24; cf. chap. 22:8; 23:38; Neh. 13:17, 18.
199 See Ps. 55:21; Mal. 2:10; cf. E. Kutsch, "*b^erît* Verpflichtung," *THAT*, 1:345.
200 Zimmerli, *Ezechiel*, part 1, p. 447; Helfmeyer, *op. cit.*, p. 183.
201 Eichrodt, "Der Sabbat bei Hesekiel," p. 65.
202 Unger, *op. cit.*, p. 58.
203 E. Kutsch, "Sehen und Bestimmen: Die Etymologie von בְּרִית," *Archäologie und Altes Testament: Festschrift für Kurt Galling* (Tübingen, 1970), p. 170; *idem*, *Verheissung und Gesetz* (Berlin, 1973), p. 76.
204 Wolff, "Day of Rest," p. 505.
205 Jenni, *op. cit.*, p. 27.
206 Wolff, "Day of Rest," p. 505: "The sabbath becomes an eschatological event in the midst of man's provisional existence."
207 K. Barth, *Church Dogmatics* (Edinburgh, 1958), III/1, 98; *idem*, III/4, 51-59; J. Brown, "Karl Barth's Doctrine of the Sabbath," *Scottish Journal of Theology* 19 (1966):409-425.
208 Unger, *op. cit.*, p. 59.
209 Kutsch, *Verheissung und Gesetz*, p. 76.

CHAPTER 2

The Sabbath in the Prophetic and Historical Literature of the Old Testament

Gerhard F. Hasel
and
W. G. C. Murdoch

THE emphasis on the Sabbath voiced by the writing prophets and the inspired writers of the historical literature is rooted in a deep-seated covenant conception in which Yahweh is the covenant Lord and Israel His covenant people. Their teaching on the Sabbath is also rooted in their knowledge of God as Creator of the heavens and the earth and His resting on the Creation Sabbath to commemorate a finished work.[1] The themes of Creation, covenant, sign, sanctification, acknowledgment of God as Lord, deliverance from bondage, and re-creation, which are well known from the Pentateuch,[2] reappear with application to the Israelite community in its checkered history. Israel's future is dependent upon obedience or disobedience to the divine law and particularly to the Sabbath. Thus the keeping of the Sabbath relates ultimately to the matter of life and death for the community and the individual; it addresses itself with force to the very essence of man's existence, whether it is relational, liberated, joyful, and redemptive, or the opposite.

The Sabbath in Prophetic Literature

Our purpose is to investigate the Sabbath first in the prophetic writings. Aside from the appearance of this subject in the three major prophets, it is present also in the minor prophets Amos and Hosea.

The Sabbath in the Eighth-Century Prophets.—*Amos*. A saying of the prophet Amos against the wicked merchants and the sins of the marketplace contains one explicit reference to the Sabbath. He quotes those who trample upon

THE SABBATH IN THE LITERATURE OF THE OLD TESTAMENT

the needy and bring the poor of the land to an end:
"When will the new moon be over,
   that we may sell grain?
And the sabbath,
   that we may offer wheat for sale,
that we may make the ephah small
   and the shekel great,
      and deal deceitfully with false balances" (chap. 8:5).*

It is evident from this reference that at the time of Amos (and Hosea), legislation was known in the northern kingdom that prohibited business dealings on the Sabbath.[3] This application assumes that the Sabbath was conceived of as a day of rest from work.[4] Rest from work was part of the Sabbath law of the Decalogue (Ex. 20:8-11; Deut. 5:12-15) and other legal passages (Ex. 23:12; 34:21).

Amos is known as a champion of the underprivileged, the poor, and the oppressed. In the passage under discussion the prophet champions the Sabbath because it was a day of liberation from work and thus safeguarded the rights of working persons: complete rest from everyday activity on the Sabbath. This right included rest from business enterprises of any form and kind, even those that included the trading of food items ("wheat"), a task of women and slaves (cf. Ex. 23:12; Deut. 5:14, 15). While there is here an emphasis on the social-humanitarian aspect of the Sabbath as a day of rest for all men, women, and children,[5] there is also an emphasis on the moral aspect of the Sabbath as a day on which avarice, greed, and selfishness need to be overcome by refraining from engaging in business enterprises of any kind.[6]

A detailed investigation of the ideas put forth on the relationship of Sabbath and new moon would take us too far afield.[7] There are but six passages in the Old Testament in which Sabbath and new moon are joined together in virtually the same way (Amos 8:5; Hosea 2:11; Isa. 1:13; Eze. 45:17; 46:3; 2 Kings 4:23). There is no support for the claim that Sabbath and new moon "occurred at equal intervals."[8] Amos 8:5 makes no such claim. There is no evidence in the entire Old Testament that the new moon day was a weekly day or that the Sabbath was a monthly recurrence. Furthermore, Hosea 2:11, which mentions new moon and Sabbath, as well as "feasts" and "appointed feasts," militates against equating these terms as indicating equal intervals. But in sequences that indicate increasing frequency the Sabbath is given as the most frequently (namely, weekly) celebrated festival.

In the prophetic writings the nature of observances on both Sabbath, the weekly day of rest, and new moon, the monthly festival (Ps. 81:3; 1 Sam. 20:24, 29), remains vague, except that Amos suggests complete rest from normal business enterprises, which appears to be part of the proscription of rest from work in general (Isa. 58:13, 14). Ezekiel 46:3 prescribes "worship" before Yahweh at the gate of the future temple (cf. Isa. 66:23).

Hosea. The prophet Hosea refers to the Sabbath (chap. 2:11 [Heb. 2:13]) within a unit of an indictment of the faithless wife Israel.[9] In this speech the Lord announced, "I will put an end to all her mirth, her feasts, her new moons, her sabbaths, and all her appointed feasts.... And I will punish her for the feast days

---

* All Bible quotations in this chapter are translations by the authors, unless otherwise indicated.

of the Baals" (verses 11, 13).[10] The "feasts" *(ḥag)* possibly designate the great autumn harvest festivals,[11] or more likely the three major annual festivals of unleavened bread, of weeks, and of booths (cf. Deut. 16:16; 2 Chron. 8:13).[12] The "new moons" *(ḥōdeš)* are presumably monthly days of festivity.[13] The "sabbaths" *(šabbāt)* are the weekly days of worship and rest.[14] The sequence of "feasts, new moons, and sabbaths" is not a descending order[15] nor an ascending order[16] of festivals, but a sequence of festivals of increasing frequency of celebration: yearly (feasts), monthly (new moons), weekly (sabbaths). The concluding phrase "and all her appointed feasts" *(wᵉkol mōᶜᵃdāh)* may refer collectively to the days and seasons of festivity included or not included in the former sequence.[17] There is here indisputable evidence along with Amos 8:5 for the celebration of the Sabbath in northern Israel in the eighth century B.C. There is, however, no evidence that the Sabbath at that time was a "new moon" day celebrated only once a month,[18] or a kind of "tabu-day."[19]

In Hosea, as also in Amos, the mentioning of the Sabbath is not within the context of a positive exhortation. Both prophets condemn the misuse or neglect of the Sabbath, respectively. In the message of Hosea the Sabbaths had apparently deteriorated into days of "her pleasures" (verse 11a), which were with the other feasts but "feast days of Baal" (verse 13). Yahweh, the lover of Israel, designed the various occasions of religious festivals, including the Sabbath, to be reflective of the covenant relation between Him and His people. If this relation is broken, then He must divorce His people (verse 2) and He "will bring to an end"[20] these festal days, including the Sabbath, which is the covenant sign.

Isaiah. The gospel prophet Isaiah has an exceptionally rich Sabbath teaching. The Sabbath is encountered for the first time in Isaiah 1:13: "'Bring your worthless offerings no longer, their incense is an abomination to Me. New moon and sabbath, the calling of assemblies—I cannot endure iniquity and the solemn assembly'" (N.A.S.B.). The usage of the expressions "new moon" and "sabbath" has been discussed already. The third expression "the calling of assemblies"[21] is unusual,[22] but is probably best understood as an expression similar to "all her appointed feasts" in Hosea 2:11, i.e., as a reference to festal assemblies inclusive of but far beyond "new moon and sabbath" as is evident from Leviticus 23. This implies that "new moon and sabbath" are not identical with the "assembly." The latter term stands in opposition to the former expressions. If this is recognized, then one cannot speak of an "ascending order—new moon (monthly), sabbath (?), calling of assemblies (annual)."[23] Instead one must take the "new moon and sabbath" together as a sequence of festivals within the year of increasing frequency of celebration: new moon (monthly) and sabbath (weekly). The expression "the calling of assemblies," which is inclusive of the weekly Sabbath (Lev. 23:1-3), the passover (verses 4-15), the feast of weeks (verses 15-22; Num. 28:26; Deut. 16:10), the first day of the seventh month (Lev. 23:23-25), the Day of Atonement (verses 26-32) and the feast of booths (verses 33-43), includes weekly, monthly, and yearly feast days, the yearly extending from one to a number of days.

The appearance of the Sabbath in Isaiah 1:13 is evidence for the fact that the weekly Sabbath was celebrated in the kingdom of Judah in the eighth century B.C. as a seventh-day institution of rest and worship. "We have no reason to suppose that the Sabbath was in Isaiah's time a day different from the seventh day of the week and that it was connected with lunar phases."[24] In favor of the weekly Sabbath stands the fact that the Sabbath is indisputably a weekly celebration in the familiar Decalogue of Exodus 20 and Deuteronomy 5 and in the law of Exodus 34, which go back to the time of Moses, and in all other legislation.

The polemic against "new moon and sabbath" is part of Isaiah's message against sacrifices, religious assemblies, and prayers (chap. 1:10-20). This can hardly be construed as an outright rejection of Israel's cult and worship. It is rather a repudiation of the emptiness of formal ritual without true heart religion. Even a keeping of the regular weekly Sabbath cannot be pleasing to God when the covenant relationship is broken and when empty ritual takes the place of genuine heart religion. Isaiah's message indicates that the keeping of the Sabbath by itself or together with other feast days, or any other ritual act, does not assure man's good standing with God aside from a true relationship with Him based on His covenant.

Several chapters in the latter part of the book of Isaiah (chaps. 56:1-8; 58:13, 14; 66:23)[25] contain very important references to the Sabbath. The Sabbath is mentioned repeatedly in Isaiah 56:1-8. We find here an identification of the Sabbath as Yahweh's Sabbath ("my sabbaths," verse 4),[26] a theme that is known elsewhere in the Old Testament.[27] Blessedness is pronounced over the person "who keeps from profaning the sabbath" (verse 2). The opposite of this beatitude is the profanation of the Sabbath. To "keep my sabbaths" (verse 4) means to hold fast "my covenant" (verse 6). Sabbathkeeping is identified with covenant keeping. "Whoever keeps the covenant keeps the sabbath, and whoever profanes the sabbath breaks the covenant" (Lev. 26:42, 45).[28] The reason for singling out the Sabbath as the particular occasion for maintaining the covenant between God and His community is the fact that the Sabbath is understood as the covenant sign (Ex. 31:13, 17; Eze. 20:12, 20). The universalistic tendency of Isaiah 56:1-8 that grants admission into the messianic kingdom even to eunuchs (cf. Deut. 23:1) reaches back to the universal quality of the Sabbath as encountered in the Creation Sabbath of Genesis 2:1-3.[29]

The high point of the Sabbath in Isaiah 58:13, 14, must be seen as part of the chapter as a whole and not as an isolated fragment.[30] If it is taken as a part of a larger whole, then a harmonious association between social interests and religious action, the keeping of the Sabbath, may be recognized. The combination of both of these concerns is also attested in the Sabbath commandment (Ex. 20:8-11; Deut. 5:12-15). Nevertheless, it has been claimed—and in many ways quite correctly—that "the ideal of Sabbath observance proposed here is found in no other passage in the Old Testament."[31] Isaiah 58:13, 14, has certainly played an important role in Pharisaic Judaism, the Talmud, and in modern Jewish society.[32]

A somewhat detailed look at translations of Isaiah 58:13, 14, reveals their divergencies. We will therefore attempt a literal translation based on the Hebrew text:

"If[33] you turn[34] your foot away[35]
    from the sabbath, from[36] doing your business on my holy day,
and[37] call the sabbath a delight,
    the holy (day)[38] of the LORD honorable,
and you honor it by not doing[39] your ways,
    by not[40] seeking after[41] your business or[42] speaking words,

then you shall delight in the LORD,
 and I[43] will cause you to ride on the heights[44] of the earth,
 and I will feed you with the heritage of Jacob, your father,
  for the mouth of the LORD has spoken."

The keeping of the foot on the Sabbath means to profane and dishonor it (chap. 56:1-8). To turn the foot away from the Sabbath means to turn away from doing one's business on the Sabbath, God's holy day. The Sabbath is, as it were, holy ground[45] or actually holy time. The faithful one is to keep himself on such ground, or in such time, not by trampling it with his foot but by heeding the following injunctions:

1. Refusing to engage in one's own business (affairs) on the Sabbath. The Hebrew term *ḥēpeṣ* is traditionally translated "pleasure" (K.J.V., R.S.V., N.A.S.B., et cetera), a term that means in English "gratification," "diversion," "enjoyment of the senses or the mind," in short, something that gives delight and satisfaction and to which one devotes time to gain it.[46] Recent lexicographers have suggested that the best rendering of the term *ḥēpeṣ* in our text is "business, affair,"[47] which has found support in word studies.[48] Man is not to engage in his own pleasure in the sense that he seeks his own business or affairs on the Sabbath (chap. 58:13b, 14b).

2. Not doing one's own ways. The term for "ways" is *derek*, a word that has rich connotations and that can mean "understanding" or "enterprise." Without doubt emphasis is placed on the pronoun "your" in connection with "ways." These are the "ways" of human endeavor, undertaking, and enterprise. The keeping of the Sabbath involves a period of rest from such ways of human activity, so that one can reflect on the ways of God.

3. Refraining from "speaking words" on the Sabbath. This counsel, in verse 13d, is not aimed at maintaining total silence on the Sabbath.[49] The vexing phrase *dabbēr dābār*, which is variously rendered with "talking idly" (R.S.V., T.E.V.), "speaking idle words" (N.I.V.), or in closer affinity to the original text with "'speaking your own word'" (N.A.S.B.),[50] if kept in the spirit of the immediate context, appears to refer to any oral communication involved in the pursuit of man's secular affairs, enterprises, and undertakings.

These three prohibitive injunctions are counterbalanced by several affirmative precepts. If the Sabbath is emptied of man's own affairs, his own enterprises, his own ways, and all the talk related thereto, then it is not only a day of freedom and liberation[51] from all everyday pursuits, but also a day "providing time"[52] for the deepening of the relationship between God and man. The Sabbath turns out to be a day of highly positive import: Sabbath observance is not a burden; it liberates man for meeting God.[53]

Among the most significant precepts related to the Sabbath in the Bible is the one that enjoins the calling of the Sabbath a delight. The noun *ʿoneg* appears in connection with the Sabbath only here and means "delight, enjoyment,"[54] as it does in its only other appearance in the Old Testament (chap. 13:22). The Sabbath is no day of gloom or sadness, but a day of joy and delight. The person who calls the Sabbath a delight is also the one who is to delight in the Lord (chap. 58:14). The same verbal form[55] for delighting in the Lord appears in other passages parallel to the lifting up of the face to the Lord (Job 22:26) and the calling upon God (chap. 27:10), i.e., acts of worship by the godly person who stands in humility before God (Ps. 37:4, 11). It appears also in connection with the joy found in being satisfied with food (Isa. 55:2; 66:11).[56] Thus the idea of delight with regard to the Sabbath combines both worship of the Lord and finding enjoyment through and in Him and what He provides both spiritual and physical.

The Sabbathkeeper is promised (1) to delight in Yahweh, (2) to ride on the heights of the earth, and (3) to be fed with the heritage of Jacob. The Sabbathkeeper will delight in God, because true Sabbathkeeping cannot be separated from a genuine faith relationship with the Lord of the Sabbath. The Sabbath is not a burdensome, ritualistic, and legalistic institution.[57] It is the sign of God's lordship over the Sabbathkeeper. The Lord of the Sabbath will make him ride on the heights of the earth. This picture communicates in metaphoric language associated with theophanic descriptions[58] that God grants triumph and victory to the Sabbathkeeper. The Sabbathkeeper is also promised to be fed with the "heritage of Jacob," i.e., the gifts of produce of the land (Deut. 32:13), promised to the forefather Jacob (Gen. 28:12-17). The Sabbath is God's "holy day." In honoring His day the loyal worshiper acknowledges God to be his covenant Lord who fulfills His covenant promises. The Sabbathkeeper also enters each Sabbath on his Lord's "holy day" (cf. Gen. 2:3).

Finally we must turn to the last chapter in the book of Isaiah for a consideration of the Sabbath in the new heavens and the new earth. Just as we find new moon and Sabbath in the first chapter of the book, so we find new moon and Sabbath in the last one. Isaiah 66 carries the reader into the realm of the future judgment and salvation of apocalyptic eschatology.[59] It is within the setting of the creation of the new heavens and the new earth that the following saying appears:

"'And it shall be, from new moon to new moon,
and from sabbath to sabbath,[60]
all flesh will come to worship before me,'
says the LORD" (verse 23).[61]

In the realm of the new creation beyond history there will be total restoration of the break brought about by sin. "All flesh" in the sense of all mankind, the redeemed remnant of all times, will worship before the Lord Sabbath after Sabbath. As the Sabbath was the climax of the first creation and destined for all mankind (Gen. 2:1-3), so the Sabbath will again be the climax of the new creation and destined again for all mankind in the new heaven and the new earth. The Sabbath will thus be the only institution designed by the Creator that will link the first heaven and earth with the new heaven and earth. As such, the Sabbath is a powerful catalyst of apocalyptic eschatology and its future hope.

The Sabbath in the Seventh- to Sixth-Century Prophets.—*Jeremiah.* The book of Jeremiah contains a key prose sermon on the observance of the Sabbath (chap. 17:19-27).[62] Jeremiah reveals that he was to preach publicly a sermon that demonstrates the conditional nature of the prophecies of doom. Destruction could be avoided if sinful Israel would evidence true repentance. The reference to the Sabbath commandment comes in connection with the phrase "as I commanded your fathers" (verse 27; cf. chap. 7:1-8, 30), and it is explicit in the expression "sabbath day" *(yôm haššabbāt,* chap. 27:21, 22, 24; cf. Ex. 20:8, 10, 11; Deut. 5:12, 14, 15) and in the precepts "keep holy the sabbath" (Jer. 17:22, 24; cf. Ex. 20:8; Deut. 5:12) and "do no work" (Jer. 17:22, 24; Ex. 20:9, 10; Deut. 5:14). If Israel would be obedient to God's law (Jer. 7:8-10; cf. chaps. 5:30, 31; 6:13-15; 14:14) by turning from its apostasy (chaps. 6:20; 7:21, 22, 30, 31; 19:5) and from desecrating the Sabbath through refraining from the carrying of burdens (chap. 17:21, 22, 24, 27) and from working (verses 22, 24), and would keep the Sabbath holy (verses 22-24) and obey the Lord wholeheartedly (verses 24, 27), then the Lord could maintain His covenant relationship with them and save them from fiery destruction (verse 27). Sabbathkeeping is a condition of salvation, but not the only one,[63] because wholehearted obedience, though inclusive of the Sabbath, goes beyond the keeping of the covenant sign. It includes right living in all areas of life—moral, social, and religious (chap. 22:1-9).

Lamentations. The book of Lamentations, which is often ascribed to Jeremiah and dated in the sixth century after the fall of Jerusalem in 586 B.C., contains one clear reference to the Sabbath (chap. 2:6) and one disputed one (chap. 1:7).

The King James Version translation of Lamentations 1:7 renders the last line "The adversaries saw her, and did mock at her sabbaths." The expression "at her sabbaths" is a translation of the Hebrew word ʿal-mišbatehā in dependence upon the Latin Vulgate's reading, "her sabbaths."[64] Different ancient versions had difficulties with the Hebrew text.[65] This fact led to emendations[66] and reconstructions. There are some scholars who follow the Vulgate and the consonantal Greek readings, suggesting that the original Hebrew was šabbᵉtoteha, "her sabbaths."[67] The majority of scholars believe that the original word is mišbat, "cessation, ruin."[68] If the former position is correct, then this text laments the mocking and laughter of the victorious adversary about the celebration of the Sabbath, i.e., the end of public worship.

Without dispute the Sabbath is mentioned in Lamentations 2:6:
"He has broken down his booth like a garden,
    he has destroyed his feast,[69]
the LORD has caused to be forgotten in Zion
    feast and sabbath,
and he has despised king and priest
    in the indignation of his anger."

The context is the destruction of Israel and Zion through the blazing wrath of God on the day of Yahweh (verses 1, 21, 22). Yahweh has caused "feast and sabbath" to be forgotten. The holy city and its holy temple is destroyed. Therefore the celebrations of the appointed feasts and the weekly Sabbath have been terminated. This passage is part of the description of the fulfillment of the conditional threats of the prophet Jeremiah (Jer. 17:19-27; 22:1-9). The fall of Judah and the destruction of Zion are due not to a lack of political wisdom but to the sin of leaders and people.

Ezekiel. Several chapters in the book of Ezekiel speak of the Sabbath (chaps. 20:12-24; 22:8-26; 23:38; 44:24; 45:17; 46:1-4, 12).[70] We note the frequent identification "my sabbaths,"[71] i.e., Yahweh's Sabbaths, a designation that is not new[72] and one that indicates that the Sabbath is the Lord's possession, a gift of God to man. The injunction "sanctify [hallow] my sabbaths" (chaps. 20:20; 44:24) is reminiscent of the fact that the Creator had sanctified (hallowed) the Sabbath Himself at Creation (Gen. 2:3)[73] and that it is so commanded in the Sabbath commandment (Ex. 20:8; Deut. 5:12). It aims toward definite action for usage in behalf of God.[74] The idea of festal worship (Eze. 46:3), including the bringing of sacrifices (verse 4) as envisioned for the future temple (verses 1-12), is included in the notion of Sabbath sanctity (cf. Lev. 23:1-3).

The prophet Ezekiel emphasizes the "sign" *('ôth)*[75] nature of the Sabbath (Eze. 20:12, 20), which is closely related to that in Exodus 31:13.[76] The identification of the Sabbath as a sign "between me and you" proves it to be a covenant sign between Yahweh, the covenant God, and His chosen people Israel (cf. Gen. 17:11; Ex. 31:13). Intimately related to the Sabbath as the unique covenant sign between God and His people is the stated purpose "that they/you may know that I am Yahweh" (Eze. 20:12, 20).[77] The Sabbath is not only a covenant sign of identifying God's people,[78] it is also a sign of knowledge[79] that communicates that Yahweh is Israel's God, keeping His covenant and sanctifying His people.

There is a strong condemnation of the profaning of the Sabbath in the past (verses 13, 16, 21, 24) and present (chaps. 22:8; 23:38). It is to be noted that in the "history of sin" in Ezekiel 20, there is in addition to the profanation of the Sabbath a condemnation of idolatry and other infractions of God's law (verses 13, 16, 21, 24, 26).[80] The same is true in Ezekiel 22 and 23, so that it is missing the point to conclude "that the exile was the result of the profanation of the sabbath" and that this is the intention of Ezekiel 20.[81] The profanation of the Sabbath is pointed out by Ezekiel to be a major sign of the refusal of Israel to acknowledge her God as Lord, Saviour, and protector. It is an external manifestation, in addition to others, that she has broken the covenant.

We find, in the regulations for the future service at the new Temple, instructions for the bringing of sacrifices "on the feasts, and on the new moons, and on the sabbaths, on all the appointed feasts" (chap. 45:17). This sequence is identical to that of Hosea 2:11 (Heb. 2:13), and it again is best understood as referring to an order of increasing frequency of celebration. "Feasts" are the *yearly* celebration of the major annual festivals (unleavened bread, weeks, and booths); "new moons" are the *monthly* celebrations; "sabbaths" are the *weekly* celebrations; "all the appointed feasts" stands in apposition to the former, including them all and any other feasts not included in them.[82]

The Sabbath in Historical Literature

In the historical literature of the Old Testament, references to the Sabbath are relatively sparse. The Sabbath appears only in 2 Kings and in the work of the chronicler.

The Sabbath in 1 and 2 Kings.—The narrative of the Shunammite woman (2 Kings 4:8-37) contains a reference to the Sabbath from the ninth century B.C.[83] When her son had suddenly died, the Shunammite woman decided to ride to the prophet Elisha for help. Her husband said to her, "Why will you go to him today? It is neither new moon nor sabbath" (verse 23). The obvious implication is that a prophet was normally visited on "new moon and sabbath." No travel restrictions existed for visiting a man of God on the Sabbath.[84] There is no suggestion here that the day of the accident, which was a regular working day, was a Sabbath.[85] Thus there is no tension with the Sabbath legislation of the Pentateuch (Ex. 20:8-11; Deut. 5:12-15; Ex. 23:12; 34:21). It is held correctly that this Sabbath text gives evidence for the keeping of the Sabbath as a day of rest in preexilic times.[86] It was a weekly day of rest.[87]

The account of the *coup d'état* arranged by the high priest Jehoiada in 2 Kings 11:4-12 (2 Chron. 23:4-11) suggests "that the Sabbath in the end of the ninth century was regularly observed."[88] The changing of the guard of the Temple was undoubtedly a weekly occurrence (1 Chron. 9:24, 25) that took place on each Sabbath (verse 32).[89] The ruling monarch visited the Temple on the Sabbath, presumably for worship purposes, and the Temple court was filled with people (2 Chron. 23:1-15).

The Sabbath is also mentioned in connection with King Ahaz (735 [732]-715 B.C.)[90] and the removal of a structure[91] used on the Sabbath (2 Kings 16:17, 18).

The Sabbath in the Work of the Chronicler.—The chronicler[92] refers to the Sabbath in a variety of connections.[93] It is stated that the Kehathites had charge of preparing bread for each Sabbath (1 Chron. 9:32) and that burnt offerings were to be sacrificed in the Temple on the Sabbaths, new moons, and appointed feasts (chap. 23:31; 2 Chron. 2:4; 8:13; 31:3)[94] from the time of Solomon onward. The gatekeepers at the Temple who change each Sabbath are priests and Levites (2 Chron. 23:4, 8).

The concluding chapter of 2 Chronicles contains a unique reference to the Sabbath: "To fulfill the word of the Lord by the mouth of Jeremiah, until the land had enjoyed its sabbaths. All the days that it lay desolate it kept sabbath, to fulfill seventy years" (chap. 36:21). It would take us too far afield to discuss the various opinions on the "seventy years," and related subjects,[95] but it is clear that the author conceived of the Exile as the time of paying off or compensation for the neglect of keeping the Sabbaths.[96] There is here a close association of the themes of land and Sabbath, rest and Sabbath, redemption and Sabbath, restitution and Sabbath, and covenant and Sabbath.

The Sabbath in Nehemiah.—The penitential prayer in Nehemiah 9:6-37 mentions the "holy sabbath" (verse 14) as a gift from God through Moses. The so-called code of Nehemiah (chap. 10:31-40), which put obligations on the community that were sealed by a covenant, forbids any trade on the Sabbath (verse 31). It is likely that this regulation resulted from the practices noted in Nehemiah 13:15-22,[97] but undoubtedly it is rooted in the pentateuchal laws that command the keeping of the Sabbath. Evidently when Nehemiah came to Jerusalem, he found a lax attitude toward Sabbathkeeping.[98] The precept against buying or selling on the Sabbath is also extended to "a holy day" (*yôm qodeš*),[99] which means either the other holy days in the sense of the yearly festivals (Numbers 23, 28, 29)[100] or more likely any holy days, including the monthly new moons and all other festivals.[101] This reform was necessitated because of the widespread disregard for the Sabbath in Judah and Jerusalem. The Sabbath was "profaned" (Neh. 13:17, 18)[102] by working and trading (verses 15-22). Nehemiah also reminded the returnees that it was "this very thing for which our God brought upon us and upon this city all this misfortune."[103] Here the reformer Nehemiah reflects the announcements of the prophets (Jer. 17:19-27; Eze. 20:12-24), who referred among other things to the violation of the Sabbath as the cause of future misfortune. He stopped the foreign traders from peddling their wares on the Sabbath by closing the gates of Jerusalem from sunset on Friday to sunset on Sabbath and made the winepress operators, farmers, fruit growers, and transportation workers to sanctify the Sabbath.

Conclusion

Our investigation of the Sabbath in the prophetic and historical literature of the Old Testament has indicated that the Sabbath was known and honored or

THE SABBATH IN THE LITERATURE OF THE OLD TESTAMENT

dishonored from the time of the united monarchy through the divided monarchy to the time of Nehemiah in the post-Exilic period. The Sabbath has had its ups and downs. Among the most significant aspects of prophetic proclamation regarding the Sabbath are its inseparable links with covenant, sign, and faithfulness, land and liberty, delight and human fulfillment, and last but not least, eschatology and new creation. The inevitable impression is that the Sabbath will remain as God's gift to man from the first creation even to the new heavens and the new earth (Isa. 66:22, 23).

NOTES

[1] T. C. Vriezen, *An Outline of Old Testament Theology*, 2d ed. (Oxford, 1970), p. 64, where it is pointed out also that "the fact that God sanctified the seventh day at the Creation is to be explained in the same way: God, who appoints the days, months, and years, has instituted the Sabbath from the beginning."

[2] See the chapter "The Sabbath in the Pentateuch," pp. 21-43.

[3] So particularly F. Stolz, "שבת" *šbt* aufhören, ruhen," *THAT*, 2:865, 866.

[4] This is correctly emphasized by many scholars; see, for example, R. S. Cripps, *A Critical & Exegetical Commentary on the Book of Amos* (London, 1960), p. 243; W. Rudolph, *Joel-Amos-Obadja-Jona* (Gütersloh, 1971), p. 262, no. 2; H. W. Wolff, *Dodekapropheton 2: Joel und Amos* (Neukirchen-Vluyn, 1969), p. 375; F. Mathys, "Sabbatruhe und Sabbatfest: Überlegungen zur Entwicklung und Bedeutung des Sabbat im Alten Testament," *Theologische Zeitschrift* 28 (1972):249.

[5] G. A. Smith wrote on Amos 8:5: "The interests of the Sabbath are the interests of the poor: the enemies of the Sabbath are the enemies of the poor.... The Sabbath was made for man."—*The Book of the Twelve Prophets Commonly Called the Minor* (New York, 1908), p. 183.

[6] A. Weiser, *Das Buch der zwölf Kleinen Propheten*, 5th ed. (Göttingen, 1967), 1:194, 195.

[7] For the hypothesis that the Sabbath derived from lunar or new moon days and its problems, see the chapter "The Sabbath in the Pentateuch," pp. 21-43.

[8] This claim is made again by G. Robinson, *The Origin and Development of the Old Testament Sabbath* (Hamburg, 1975), p. 39. Before him it appeared by E. Mahler, "Der Sabbat: Seine etymologische und chronologisch-historische Bedeutung," *ZDMG* 62 (1908):249, and A. Lemaire, "Le Sabbat a l'époque royale Israélite," *Revue biblique* 80 (1973):163. See note 82.

[9] It has recently been dated to about 750 B.C. See H. W. Wolff, *Hosea: A Commentary on the Book of the Prophet Hosea* (Philadelphia, 1974), p. 33, followed by Robinson, *op. cit.*, p. 46.

[10] The terms "feasts" (*ḥaq*), "new moons" (*ḥōdeš*), "sabbaths" (*šabbāt*), and "appointed feasts" (*mōʿēd*) are in Hebrew collective nouns in singular form. The Septuagint rendered them as plurals.

[11] Wolff, *Hosea*, pp. 38, 156.

[12] W. Rudolph, *Hosea* (Gütersloh, 1966), p. 71, followed by N.-E. A. Andreasen, *The Old Testament Sabbath: A Traditio-Historical Investigation*, SBL Diss. Ser. 7 (Missoula, Mont., 1972), p. 61.

[13] The Old Testament reveals little detail about the new moon day and its celebration (cf. 1 Sam. 20:5-11, 18-23; Ps. 104:19; Isa. 1:13). See H.-J. Kraus, *Worship in Israel* (Richmond, Va., 1966), pp. 76-78.

[14] The fact that there is a *waw* before the term *šabbāt* seems to indicate that the sequence of three separate recurring festivals, namely "feasts, new moons, and sabbaths," has come to an end. This would stand against the view that "feasts" is a collective noun referring to both "new moons and sabbaths" (see Robinson, *op. cit.*, pp. 53-55). See also Eze. 45:17, where there is also a *waw* connecting the three festival celebrations of "feasts, and new moons, and sabbaths" but no *waw* before "all appointed feasts."

[15] Wolff, *Hosea*, p. 38; Rudolph, *Hosea*, p. 71.

[16] Robinson, *op. cit.*, pp. 53, 62.

[17] Andreasen, *loc. cit.*, understands *mōʿēd* as an all-inclusive reference that encompasses also "feasts, new moons, and sabbaths." Although this is possible, it is less likely in view of our extensive listing of yearly, monthly, and weekly feast days.

[18] Despite repeated efforts in that direction (cf. Lemaire, *op. cit.*, Robinson, *op. cit.*), the observation of R. de Vaux regarding these attempts still stands: "One thing, however, is certain: it is useless to try to find the origin of the sabbath by connecting it in some way with the phases of the moon."—*Ancient Israel: Its Life and Institutions* (London, 1961), p. 480.

[19] Against Wolff, *Hosea*, p. 38. Sabbath rest has nothing to do with a tabu.

[20] There is in Hebrew a striking wordplay both in Hosea 2:11 and Amos 8:5 between the verb *šbt* (in Hiphil as used here "to bring to an end") and the noun *šabbāt*, "Sabbath." The close association between both has been seen time and again as indicating a relationship between the verb *šbt* and the noun *šabbāt* (cf. Gen. 2:1-3; Ex. 16:30; 31:17; Lev. 23:32; 25:2; 26:34, 35; 2 Chron. 36:21). See also R. North, "The Derivation of Sabbath," *Biblica* 36 (1955):186; Stolz, *op. cit.*, cols. 864, 865.

[21] This expression follows the first two without a conjunction in the MT. Thus the translation "and the calling of assemblies" (R.S.V.; Robinson, *op. cit.*, p. 57) or merely "and assemblies" (N.E.B.) is inexact and not supported by the MT.

[22] It has been claimed that the term *miqra'*, "assembly," is an abbreviation of *miqra' qodeš*, "holy assembly," in the sense of a "feast day," on which no work was to be done (see E. Kutsch, "מקרא," *ZAW* 65 [1953]:247-253). But this does make as little sense (see H. Wildberger, *Jesaja 1-12* [KAT X/1; Neukirshen-Vluyn, 1972], p. 34) as the claim that the entire third phrase is a later interpolation (against F. Schwally, "Miscellen," *ZAW* 11 [1891]:257; K. Marti, *Das Buch Jesaja* [Tübingen, 1900], p. 12; J. Morgenstern, "Two Compound Technical Terms in Biblical Hebrew," *JBL* 43 [1924]:316; with Wildberger, *loc. cit.*; Andreasen, *op. cit.*, p. 58).

[23] See Robinson, *op. cit.*, p. 62.

24 Wildberger, *op. cit.*, p. 42, against K. Marti, J. Meinhold, and followers (T. J. Meek, G. Hölscher, S. Mowinckel, A. Lods, N. H. Snaith, O. Procksch, A. Lemaire, and G. Robinson), who have thought that the linking together of new moon and Sabbath means that the Sabbath was at one time a monthly observance.

25 Whereas it is widely customary in modernistic scholarship to assign Isaiah 56-66 to one or several authors, J. H. Meesters, *Op zoek naar de oorsprong van de Sabbat* (Assen, 1966), pp. 148-151, argues that Isaiah 66:23 is a genuine saying from Isaiah and that Isaiah 56:1-8 and 58:13 contain genuine kernels of material from Isaiah. Among scholars who have argued since the 1950s for the unity of authorship of the entire book of Isaiah are E. J. Young, W. Möller, R. K. Harrison, G. L. Archer, O. T. Allis, and R. Margalioth, not to mention such great commentators of the past century as J. A. Alexander, R. Stier, and Franz Delitzsch.

26 Some have seen in the plural a reference to all festivals (cf. Lemaire, *op. cit.*, pp. 180, 181; E. J. Young, *The Book of Isaiah* [Grand Rapids, Mich., 1972], 3:391), but this can hardly be correct, because in Ezekiel 45:17 the plural "sabbaths" appears and the other festivals are mentioned separately.

27 So also in Ex. 31:13; Lev. 19:3; 26:2, aside from Eze. 20:12, 13, 16, 20, 21, 24; 22:8, 26; 23:38; 44:24.

28 Robinson, *op. cit.*, p. 302.

29 See the previous chapter, "The Sabbath in the Pentateuch," pp. 21-43, and N.-E. A. Andreasen, "Recent Studies of the Old Testament Sabbath: Some Observations," *ZAW* 86 (1974):467.

30 Note the persuasive arguments of J. Muilenburg, "The Book of Isaiah: Chapters 40-66," *The Interpreter's Bible* (New York, 1956), 5:677.

31 J. L. McKenzie, *Second Isaiah, Anchor Bible* (Garden City, 1968), p. 165.

32 Among the Pharisees, see J. Z. Lauterbach, "The Pharisees and Their Teachings," *Rabbinic Essays* (Cincinnati, 1951), pp. 87-159, esp. p. 123; in the Talmud, see BT Sabbath 117b; in modern times, see I. Eisenstein, "Oneg Shabbat," *The Universal Jewish Encyclopedia* (New York, 1942), 8:300.

33 The conditional particle *'im* ("if") is employed here with the imperfect to indicate a real condition capable of fulfillment (R. J. Williams, *Hebrew Syntax: An Outline*, 2d ed. [Toronto, 1976], p. 74, sec. 453).

34 The verb *šûb* followed by the preposition *min* means "to turn away from." This is supported by such passages as Numbers 14:43, "turn away from following the Lord," and 1 Kings 8:35, "turn away from their sin," where we find also *šûb min*. Cf. J. A. Soggin, "שוב *šûb* zurückkehren," *THAT*, 2:888.

35 The proposed emendation of the *min* to a *b^e* *(BHK, BHS)* is unnecessary. See previous note. Thus the MT does not support such translations as "If you cease to tread the sabbath underfoot" (N.E.B.), "'If because of the sabbath, you turn your foot'" (N.A.S.B.), and "If you hold back your foot on the sabbath" (N.A.B.).

36 Although the MT lacks the preposition while 1QIsa^a provides it, it is known that it is understood, because in poetic parallelism *min* serves to govern coordinate clauses (cf. E. Kautzsch and A. E. Cowley, *Gesenius' Hebrew Grammar*, 2d ed. [Oxford, 1910], p. 384, sec. 119hh).

37 The *waw* may here be considered to have an adversative force, i.e., "but."

38 The difficult expression *liqdôš YHWH* (also attested in 1QIsa^a and 1QIsa^b) means literally "the holy of Yahweh" where the prophet employs the adjective "holy" in parallelism to "sabbath," so that the intention is "holy day."

39 The infinitive *^casôt* construed with the privative meaning of *min* (Williams, *op. cit.*, p. 56, sec. 321) literally means "without doing . . ."

40 Here we find again a privative *min*. See note 39.

41 Although the verb *ms'* means normally "to find, meet, reach," it also carries the meaning of "to seek, to seek out, seek after" (*HALAT*, p. 586; G. Gerleman, "מצא *ms'* finden." *THAT*, 1:924).

42 The *waw* may be taken with the alternative force.

43 1QIsa^a has the third person masculine singular form *whrkybkh (w^ehirkîbkāh)*, "and he will cause you to ride." *BHS* states incorrectly that the form in 1QIsa^{a, b} is *kîbkā*.

44 1QIsa^a has for MT *bom^otê* the reading *bwmty*, which may be vocalized as *bômetê*. The translation "heights" is to be preferred over "high places," because there is no explicit association with the cultic high places of idolatrous worship (Micah 1:5; Hosea 10:8; Amos 7:9, et cetera).

45 Young, *op. cit.*, p. 426.

46 *Webster's New Twentieth-Century Dictionary of the English Language Unabridged*, 2d ed. (Cleveland, 1976), 2:1378.

47 *HALAT*, p. 327; *CHAL*, p. 112; *HAD*, p. 89.

48 G. Gerleman, "חפץ *ḥpṣ* Gefallen haben," *THAT*, 1:625, and literature cited.

49 So correctly D. N. Freedman in McKenzie, *loc. cit.*

50 The translations "attending to your own affairs" (N.E.B.) or "speaking with malice" (N.A.B.) are off the mark.

51 Among many, see A. J. Heschel, *The Sabbath* (New York, 1951), pp. 13-32; S. H. Dresner, *The Sabbath* (New York, 1970), pp. 36-64; H. W. Wolff, "The Day of Rest in the Old Testament," *Lexington Theological Quarterly* 7 (1972):72; Muilenburg, *op. cit.*, p. 414.

52 Andreasen, "Recent Studies," p. 467.

53 McKenzie, *loc. cit.*

54 *KB*, p. cf. *CHAL*, p. 277.

55 Hithpael is attested in the Old Testament in Deuteronomy 28:56; Job 22:26; 27:10; Psalm 37:4, 11; Isaiah 55:2; 57:4; 58:14; 66:11.

56 The emphasis on worship on the Sabbath as the exclusive meaning of delight in Isaiah 58:14 by Robinson, *op. cit.*, pp. 307-309, misses the other aspects of usage of the same Hithpael forms.

57 J. D. Smart, *History and Theology in Second Isaiah* (Philadelphia, 1965), p. 252, misses the point by assigning this passage to a late orthodox community.

58 See Micah 1:3; Amos 4:13; Deut. 32:13.

59 So correctly Muilenburg, *op. cit.*, p. 772.

60 A literal translation is "from the abundance of new moon in its new moon and from the abundance of sabbath in its sabbath." Gesenius explains the whole to mean "as often as the new moon comes in its new moon, i.e., its appointed time" (as cited by J. A. Alexander, *Commentary on the Prophecies of Isaiah* [reprint ed., Grand Rapids, Mich., 1953], 2:480). Accordingly the phrases indicate the meaning "whenever new moon and Sabbath appear in the new creation" (cf. C. von Orelli, *The Prophecies of Isaiah* [Edinburgh, 1895], p. 346; Young, *op. cit.*, p. 536).

61 The claim that Isaiah 66:23 is secondary (see B. Duhm, *Das Buch Jesaia*, 5th ed. [Göttingen, 1968], p. 489, who

THE SABBATH IN THE LITERATURE OF THE OLD TESTAMENT

is followed by a great number of exegetes) is countered by Meesters, *op. cit.*, p. 150, because of the link between new moon and Sabbath. Cf. E. A. Leslie, *Isaiah* (New York, 1963), pp. 244, 245.

[62] The authenticity of this sermon has been questioned since A. Kuenen (see the commentaries and studies by B. Duhm [1903], C. H. Cornill [1905], S. Mowinckel [1914], P. Volz [1920], A. C. Welch [1928], J. Steinmann [1952], J. W. Miller [1955], J. P. Hyatt [1958], W. Rudolph [1958], E. W. Nicholson [1970], and W. Thiel [1973]), but the authenticity is upheld by W. E. Barnes, "Prophecy and the Sabbath: A Note on the Teaching of Jeremiah," *Journal of Theological Studies* 29 (1928):386-390; E. Kalt, "Sabbat," *Biblisches Reallexikon*, 2d ed. (Paderborn, 1939), 2:553; A. Condamin, *Le livre de Jérémie* (Paris, 1936), p. 150; J. Bright, "The Date of the Prose Sermons of Jeremiah," *JBL* 70 (1951):23, 24; H. Freedman, *Jeremiah* (London, 1949), p. 122; R. K. Harrison, *Jeremiah and Lamentations: An Introduction and Commentary* (Downers Grove, Ill., 1973), pp. 107, 108. The comprehensive study on the prose speeches in Jeremiah (except chap. 17:19-27) by H. Weippert, *Die Prosareden des Jeremiabuches* (Berlin, 1973), has led to the conclusion that "the prose speeches *do not derive* from the hand of a redactor."—Page 234. Italics hers.

[63] Robinson, *op. cit.*, p. 226, misses the point by claiming this.

[64] Without the initial *m*, i.e., *šabtotehā* (cf. *BHK*).

[65] Several manuscripts (MSS^{Ken} and ₁₃MSS^G) read *mišbatêhā*, i.e., the plural (see H. Bauer and P. Leander, *Historische Grammatik der hebräischen Sprache des Alten Testaments* [Halle, 1922], sec. 252r).

[66] *BHK* suggests $m^e \check{s}ûbôt\hat{e}h\bar{a}$, "her apostasies," from $m^e \check{s}ûb\bar{a}h$.

[67] See H.-J. Kraus, *Klagelieder (Threni)*, 3d ed. (Neukirchen-Vluyn, 1968), pp. 21, 22, in brackets with question mark; Robinson, *op. cit.*, p. 229.

[68] *BDB*, p. 982; *KB*, p. 572; *HALAT*, p. 607; *CHAL*, p. 218; *HAD*, p. 163. It is a hapax legomenon derived from *šbt* (Bauer and Leander, *op. cit.*, sec. 490z, 558c; Stolz, *op. cit.*, col. 864).

[69] The Hebrew $m\hat{o}^ced$ can mean "[appointed] place" (N.A.B. "dwelling," N.A.S.B. "appointed meeting place") or "[appointed] feasts" (see R.S.V., K.J.V., et cetera). See *HALAT*, pp. 528, 529; *CHAL*, p. 186; G. Sauer, "יעד y^cd bestimmen," *THAT*, 1:742.

[70] Many modernist exegetes assign all (or most) of these passages to later hands. See also W. Eichrodt, "Der Sabbat bei Hesekiel: Ein Beitrag zur Nachgeschichte des Prophetentextes," *Lex Tua Veritas: Festschrift für Hubert Junker*, ed. by H. Gross and F. Mussner (Trier, 1961), pp. 65-74. For a penetrating critique of these hypotheses, see Andreasen, *OT Sabbath*, pp. 40-48.

[71] Eze. 20:12, 13, 20, 21, 24; 22:26; 23:38; 44:24.

[72] Ex. 31:13; Lev. 19:3, 30; 26:2; Isa. 56:4; 58:13, "my holy day."

[73] See the chapter "The Sabbath in the Pentateuch," pp. 21-43.

[74] A. Jepsen, "Beiträge zur Auslegung und Geschichte des Dekalogs," *ZAW* 79 (1967):293; Mathys, *op. cit.*, p. 244.

[75] Key studies are F. Stolz, "אות *'ôt* Zeichen," *THAT*, 1:91-95; F. J. Helfmeyer, "אות *'ôth*," *TDOT*, 1:167-188.

[76] The evident relationship between Exodus 31:13 and Ezekiel 20:12, 20, "a sign between me and you" and "that you may know," et cetera, should not be explained as a direct literary dependence of one on the other (with A. Bertholet and K. Galling, *Hesekiel* [Tübingen, 1936], p. 70; W. Zimmerli, *Ezechiel* 2d ed. [Neukirchen-Vluyn, 1977] p. 447; Andreasen, *OT Sabbath*, p. 42 n. 1, against N. Negretti, *Il Settimo Giorno* [Rome, 1973], p. 256, and Robinson, *op. cit.*, p. 238, who claims that Exodus 31:17 is dependent on Ezekiel 20:12 or another early post-Exilic source).

[77] The infinitive form of yd^c is identical in Ezekiel 20:12, 20, and Exodus 31:13, but unusual in other formulae of recognition. Cf. Zimmerli, *op. cit.*, p. 60.

[78] W. Zimmerli, *Old Testament Theology in Outline* (Atlanta, 1978), pp. 125, 126.

[79] E. Jenni, *Die theologische Begründung des Sabbatgebotes im Alten Testament* (Zurich, 1956), p. 31.

[80] Correctly emphasized by F. Maass, "חלל *hll* pi. entweihen," *THAT*, 1:573.

[81] Robinson, *op. cit.*, p. 239.

[82] The argument that "sabbath could not have taken place at an interval shorter than that of new moon" (with reference to the sequence in Hosea 2:11 as maintained by Robinson, *op. cit.*, p. 62, and equally applicable to Ezekiel 45:17) stands without support from the Old Testament. Once the order of increasing frequency of celebration is recognized, i.e., yearly (feasts), monthly (new moons), weekly (sabbaths), as in Hosea 2:11 and Ezekiel 45:17, or monthly (new moons), weekly (sabbaths), as in Isaiah 1:13; 66:23; Amos 8:5; and 2 Kings 4:23, either with or without the appositional phrase "all the appointed feasts" (Hosea 2:11; Eze. 45:17), then a consistent and harmonious understanding emerges for all texts in which Sabbath appears in relationship to new moon and other festivals. See note 94.

[83] See Robinson, *op. cit.*, p. 30. Andreasen, *OT Sabbath*, p. 48, suggests the first part of the eighth century B.C., or perhaps earlier.

[84] Contrary to the Rabbinic restriction of 1,000 steps (Sotah 5. 3; CD X. 20, 21). Shunem and Carmel were separated by 25 km. (16 mi.). Cf. A. Sanda, *Die Bücher der Könige* (Münster, 1912), 2:31.

[85] Some scholars suggest on the basis of 2 Kings 4:22, 23, that servants and cattle were employed on the Sabbath and that it was not a rest day (A. Phillips, *Ancient Israel's Criminal Law: A New Approach to the Decatogue* [Oxford, 1970], p. 68; Robinson, *op. cit.*, p. 33). The husband's question would make no sense if it had been a Sabbath. The contrast is between "today" *(hayyôm)* and the new moon or Sabbath. Cf. S. J. DeVries, *Yesterday, Today, and Tomorrow* (Grand Rapids, Mich., 1975), p. 235.

[86] F. Bohn, *Der Sabbat im Alten Testament und im Altjüdischen religiosen Aberglauben* (Gütersloh, 1903), p. 11; K. Budde, "Antwort auf Johannes Meinholds 'Zur Sabbathfrage,'" *ZAW* 48 (1930):140; W. W. Cannon, "The Weekly Sabbath," *ZAW* 49 (1931):326; G. J. Botterweck, "Der Sabbat in Alten Testamente," *Theologische Quartalschrift* 134 (1954):137, 138; Lemaire, *op. cit.*, pp. 163, 164; Stolz, "שבת *šbt* aufhören, ruhen," col. 866.

[87] It is going far beyond the evidence to suggest that the Sabbath was at this stage a full-moon day (Robinson, *op. cit.*, p. 33). The sequence "new moon"—"sabbath" gives no support to this, because it follows the natural order of increasing frequency of celebration (see note 82).

[88] J. Gray, *I & II Kings: A Commentary* (Philadelphia, 1963), p. 516.

[89] The monthly change of the commanders of the army (1 Chron. 27:1) as instituted at the beginning of kingship is not related to the Sabbath (see Robinson, *op. cit.*, p. 90), because the gatekeepers of the sanctuary/Temple were not identical with the former and changed each week on Sabbath (chap. 9:17-32). Only Levites and priests were to enter the Temple (2 Chron. 23:4, 6).

[90] For dates, see E. R. Thiele, *A Chronology of the Hebrew Kings* (Grand Rapids, Mich., 1977), p. 75.

⁹¹ For a detailed discussion of the obscure words, see Meesters, *op. cit.*, p. 146; Andreasen, *OT Sabbath*, p. 52 nn. 2, 3; Robinson, *op. cit.*, pp. 99-108.
⁹² We conceive of him as the author of 1 and 2 Chronicles, Ezra, and Nehemiah.
⁹³ 1 Chron. 9:32; 23:31; 2 Chron. 2:4; 8:13; 23:4, 8; 31:3; 36:21; Neh. 9:13, 14; 10:32-34; 13:15-22.
⁹⁴ The order is one of decreasing frequency in 1 Chronicles 23:31, i.e., weekly (sabbaths), monthly (new moons), and possibly yearly (appointed feasts) (cf. 2 Chron. 8:13). 2 Chronicles 2:4 proves this order of decreasing frequency of sacrifices in its sequence of daily (morning and evening), weekly (sabbaths), monthly (new moons), and yearly (appointed feasts). The chronicler always has the sequence from most to least, whereas other Old Testament writings prefer the order from least to most. See note 82.
⁹⁵ Representative views are A. Orr, "The Seventy Years of Babylon," *VT* 6 (1956):304-306; C. F. Whitley, "The Term Seventy Years Captivity," *VT* 4 (1954):60-72; idem, "The Seventy Years Desolation—A Rejoinder," *VT* 7 (1957):416-418; O. Plöger, "Siebzig Jahre," *Festschrift F. Baumgärtel zum 70. Geburtstag*, ed. by L. Rost (Erlangen, 1959), pp. 124-130; B. Z. Wacholder, "Sabbatical Year," *IDBSup.* (Nashville, 1976), pp. 762, 763.
⁹⁶ J. M. Myers, *II Chronicles* (Garden City, 1965), pp. 222, 223; P. R. Ackroyd, *Exile and Restoration* (Philadelphia, 1968), pp. 240-243.
⁹⁷ J. M. Myers, *Ezra-Nehemiah* (Garden City, 1965), p. 178.
⁹⁸ B. E. Shafer, "Sabbath," *IDBSup.* (Nashville, 1976), p. 761.
⁹⁹ The Expression *yôm qodeš* appears only here in the Old Testament. Although the Sabbath is several times called "holy" (Ex. 16:23; 31:14, 15; Lev. 27:23; Isa. 58:13), here it does not refer to the Sabbath.
¹⁰⁰ C. F. Keil, *The Books of Ezra, Nehemiah, and Esther* (reprint ed., Grand Rapids, Mich., 1952), p. 252.
¹⁰¹ Myers, *Ezra-Nehemiah*, p. 178.
¹⁰² The phrase "profaning the sabbath" is familiar from Ezekiel 20:16, 21, 24; 22:8; 23:38. Its idea is present in Exodus 31:14; Isaiah 56:2, 6.
¹⁰³ Translation of Myers, *Ezra-Nehemiah*, p. 210.

CHAPTER 3

The Sabbath in the Intertestamental Period

Sakae Kubo

THE intertestamental period brings to view several new facets regarding the history of the Sabbath. First, aside from the Sabbath commandment itself (Ex. 20:8-11; Deut. 5:12-14; Lev. 23:3), the Old Testament provides surprisingly few specific statements regarding the manner of observing the day.* The intertestamental sources carry us beyond these and serve as a transition between the Old Testament and the Rabbinic period. Furthermore, these sources give information on Sabbath observance in wartime and in situations where the Jews were subjects of foreign powers. While such situations were present in the Old Testament, we have no similar information there regarding Sabbath observance in conjunction with them. A still further aspect of the Sabbath that first appears during this period is the setting forth, especially by Philo, of a kind of theology of the Sabbath necessitated by Jewish contacts with Hellenistic society. Other facets include the contents of the Sabbath service and the Jewish sectarian views on the Sabbath.

The Observance of the Sabbath

Ostraca found at Elephantine in Egypt (fifth century B.C.) mention the Sabbath four times.[1] One of these merely mentions the Sabbath, and nothing can be inferred from this except that there was an awareness of the Sabbath. A second ostracon is addressed to the woman Islah, who, according to Rosenthal,[2] is told to "meet the boat tomorrow on Sabbath lest they [the vegetables] get lost/spoiled *('rqy 'lp' mḥr bšbh lmh hn y'bd)*. By the life of YHH, if not, I shall take your lif[e] *(npšk[y] 'lkh)!*" The third ostracon refers to something, perhaps the dispatching of fish, being done before the Sabbath. The fourth has the sentence, "I am going and will not come until the eve (of the Sabbath) *('rwbh)*."

Porten also discusses the name Shabbethai, which is found four times in the Aramaic papyri of Elephantine-Syene and once on a sarcophagus. According to

---

* Texts such as Exodus 16:29, Jeremiah 17:22, Isaiah 58:13, and Nehemiah 13:15-22 are noted in chapters 1 and 2. See pp. 25-27, 47-49.

Tcherikover, this name was given especially in Egypt only to Jewish children born on the Sabbath during the Hellenistic period, but later on to others without this connotation. Still later, during the Roman period, the name was changed to Sambathion and was given to Egyptians, as well. His explanation for this is that the Sabbath made a deep impression on non-Jews, so that many of them adopted its observance without becoming Jews.[3] Porten feels that three occurrences of this name belong to non-Jews who were attracted by Sabbath observance.[4] If this is so, it would be highly significant, since Tcherikover finds this phenomenon only in the Roman period. If Porten is right, then we have non-Jews already keeping the Sabbath in the fifth century B.C., and this practice probably continued on through the Hellenistic period.

Regarding the mention of Sabbath in the ostraca, he concludes: "At first glance, the person who wrote to Islaḥ to meet the boat on the Sabbath lest the vegetables which he was sending that day get lost/spoiled is reminiscent of the contemporary men of Judah who brought grain, wine, and figs into Jerusalem on the Sabbath (Neh. 13:15). On the other hand, concern for the preservation of the vegetables and the threat to take Islaḥ's life unless she met the boat on the Sabbath may imply some extraordinary situation and indirectly attest the regular observance of the Sabbath. The possible dispatch of fish and the individual's arrival before the day of the Sabbath may indicate a deliberate unwillingness to profane the Sabbath by traveling or dispatching an object on that day."[5]

In this same article, Porten seeks to show that the Jews were not as syncretistic in their worship as has been held formerly. The only clear case of this he finds in the worship of AnathYHW, which he attributes to the worship of heavenly bodies introduced during the days of Manasseh (2 Kings 21:5; 2 Chron. 33:3, 5). The cult of Bethel, he feels, belongs to the Aramaeans who had a garrison at Syene in close proximity to the Jews.[6]

A practice that is clearly in evidence in the Rabbinic period but not mentioned in the Old Testament comes into view for the first time in the book of Judith, which is dated by most scholars between 150 and 125 B.C. The heroine "fasted all the days of her widowhood, except the day before the sabbath and the sabbath itself, the day before the new moon and the new moon itself, and the feasts and days of rejoicing of the house of Israel" (chap. 8:6). Even in her mourning, since the Sabbath and the feasts were considered days of rejoicing, she refrained from fasting on those days. She also set up a tent on the roof of her house where she wore garments of her widowhood, but the Sabbath and feast days she spent in her home wearing different garments (verse 5). While the story is considered fictional and takes place in the days of Assyria, nevertheless it reflects customs and practices of the period in which it was written.

The Book of Jubilees, written in the form of a revelation given to Moses on Sinai, is dated about the same time as Judith. Here for the first time we have a series of prohibitions regarding the Sabbath, and a forerunner of the later Rabbinic laws regarding the Sabbath. Fragments of this book have also been found at Qumrân and are believed to be a part of the literature of the sect that lived there. According to Frank Cross, "The concrete contacts in theology, terminology, calendrical peculiarities, and priestly interests, between the editions of Enoch, Jubilees, and the Testaments of Levi and Naphtali found at Qumrân on the one hand, and the demonstrably sectarian works of Qumrân on the other, are so systematic and detailed that we must place the composition of these works within a single line of tradition."[7]

This being so, when God on Sinai revealed to Moses on the Sabbath that Israel would forsake His law, commandments, and judgments and would "go astray as to new moons, and sabbaths, and festivals, and jubilees, and ordinances" (Jub. 1:14, 15), Bietenhardt[8] considers this as a polemic against the calendar and feasts of Israel that were different from those of Qumrân.

Bietenhardt also sees the Sabbath in Jubilees obtaining cosmic and metaphysical meaning.[9] The Sabbath is not simply observed on earth by men; it is observed in heaven, as well, and by God Himself with the angels of presence and the angels of sanctification (chap 2:17, 18). In fact, it was kept by the angels "in the heavens before it was made known to any flesh to keep Sabbath thereon on the earth" (verse 30). This heavenly celebration of the Sabbath with men not only took place after Creation (Gen. 2:2) but takes place every Sabbath. And it is for Israel alone that the Sabbath was made (Jub. 2:31).

The death penalty for breaking the Sabbath is mentioned emphatically (verses 25, 27; chap. 50:8). As in the Old Testament, work and one's own pleasure are prohibited, as well as the preparation of food and drink, drawing of water, and the carrying of burdens in or out of the city gates (chaps. 2:25-29; 50:7). Other things prohibited are cohabiting with one's wife; the mere mention that one will do something or set out on a journey on the Sabbath in regard to any buying or selling (chap. 50:8); going on a journey; tilling one's farm; lighting a fire; riding on a beast; traveling by ship; striking or killing anything; slaughtering a beast or a bird; catching an animal, bird, or fish; fasting; and making war (verse 12). The only work allowed is "burning frankincense and bringing oblations and sacrifices before the Lord for days and for Sabbaths" (verse 10).

The Zadokite Document, which scholars believe also comes from the Qumrân community, has similarities as well as differences from the Sabbath prohibitions of the Book of Jubilees. It is similar not only in forbidding work on the Sabbath but further in allowing only that to be eaten that has been prepared on the previous day (10:22),[10] not allowing a man to strike a stubborn beast (11:6), not fasting (11:5),[11] and not allowing anything to be carried from or to the house (11:7-9a). There are other passages that look similar but are not. These include: 10:19, "Let him not speak of matters of labour and work to be done on the morrow," which sounds similar to the prohibition against one's saying that he will do something on the Sabbath or that he will set out on a journey on the Sabbath in regard to buying or selling; 10:23, "And let him not drink *water* unless it is in the camp," which is similar to the command in Jubilee 50:8 prohibiting one from drawing water without having prepared it for himself on the sixth day (but in fact, the latter appears more strict). According to Rabin, the Zadokite Document is more liberal in allowing the drawing of water anywhere inside the camp. The rabbis forbid drawing from a watercourse even inside a courtyard but allow this from a well inside the house.[12]

There are some additional items that go beyond those found in Jubilees. Among these is the fact that work should cease on Friday "from the time when the orb of the sun is distant from the gate by its own fulness" (10:15, 16). According to Charles, this means "just before the sun touches the horizon."[13] A man may not draw water on the Sabbath, but if a man is "on a way and 'goes down to bathe,'" let him drink where he stands, but let him not draw *water* into any [vessel]" (11:2). He must not strike a beast; if it is stubborn, he must not take it out of his house (11:6, 7).

Additional prohibitions not found in Jubilees are:

1. "Let no man speak a lewd or villainous word" (10:18).
2. "Let him not lend anything to his neighbour (or: press his neighbour for repayment of anything)" (10:18).
3. "Let them not shed *blood* for (or: dispute about) property and gain" (10:18).
4. "Let no man walk about in the field *on Sabbath* in order to do the work he requires ‹after› the Sabbath *ends*" (11:20, 21).
5. "Let him not walk about 'outside his town above' one thousand cubits" (10:21).
6. "And of that which is lying about (lit.:lost) in the field [let him not] eat" (10:23).
7. "Let him not send a proselyte (or: gentile) 'to do what he requires' on the Sabbath day" (11:2).
8. "Let no man put upon himself (on the Sabbath) dirty clothes or such as have been put into store, unless they have [been washed] in water or are rubbed with frankincense" (11:4).
9. "Let no man go after a beast (on the Sabbath) to pasture it 'outside his town' for more than 'two thousand cubits'" (11:5, 6).
10. "[Let him not open] a pitch-sealed vessel on the Sabbath" (11:9).
11. "Let no man carry upon himself medicaments to go out and [to go in] on the Sabbath" (11:10).
12. "Let no man pick up in his dwelling-house a stone or dust" (11:11).
13. "Let 'the pedagogue[14] not carry the young child' to go out and to go in on the Sabbath" (11:11).
14. "Let no man urge on his (Jewish) slave or maidservant or [hired laborer] on the Sabbath" (11:12).
15. "Let no man assist a beast in birth on the Sabbath day. Even if she drops *her new-born young* into a cistern or a pit, let him not keep it (the young) alive on the Sabbath" (11:13, 14).
16. "Let no man [spend the Sabbath] in a place near gentiles on the Sabbath" (11:15).
17. "Let no man profane the Sabbath for the sake of property and gain on the Sabbath. But every living (lit.:soul of) man who falls into a place *full* of water or into a place [from which one cannot come up], let *any* man [bring him up] with a ladder or a rope or *any* instrument" (11:15-17).[15]
18. "Let no man offer on the altar on the Sabbath except the burnt-offering of the Sabbath; for thus it is written: 'apart from your Sabbath-offerings'" (11:17, 18).

There is agreement that the Qumrân sect generally had a stricter view of Sabbath observance than the rest of the Jews. Josephus bears this out when he writes: "They . . . are stricter than all Jews in abstaining from work on the seventh day; for not only do they prepare their food on the day before, to avoid kindling a fire on that one, but they do not venture to remove any vessel or even to go to stool."[16] Kimbrough disagrees with this judgment and puts forth his own thesis that what the Zadokite Document gives us is "precise evidence as to the nature of 'normative' Jewish tradition at a very early stage." He accepts G. F. Moore's evaluation that the strictness of the laws "was not particularly sectarian" but "was the character of the older Halakah in general."[17]

One of the most striking differences between the Zadokite Document and Jubilees is the fact that the death penalty for Sabbath desecration is not mentioned at all. Instead, the former reads: "But everyone who goes astray so as to profane the Sabbath and the appointed times shall not be put to death, for it falls to men to guard him; and if he is healed from it, they shall guard him for a period of seven years, and afterwards he shall come into the assembly" (12:4-6). In this it seems to be more liberal even than Rabbinic Judaism, which kept the death penalty but emphasized that the transgression must be a complete act of work or done presumptuously in spite of the warning of witnesses.*

Other differences between the two documents are: (1) The Zadokite Document does not mention lighting a fire on the Sabbath, although this is probably assumed on the basis of Exodus 35:3 and Numbers 15:32-35 and the command to eat only that which has been prepared on the previous day; (2) Jubilees prohibits traveling on sea, which is not mentioned in the Zadokite Document, as well as riding on an animal, slaughtering a beast or bird, catching an animal, bird, or fish, and making war.

According to Bietenhardt, the Zadokite Document is stricter than the Rabbinic praxis in the following: the time of beginning the Sabbath; speaking a foolish or idle word; the length of a Sabbath day's journey; the opening of a pitch-sealed vessel; the carrying of medicaments; the picking up of stone or dust in the house; the carrying of a young child in and out of the house; the helping of a man who has fallen in water.[18]

Philo, after mentioning that the Sabbath rest is to include one's family, neighbors, freemen, and slaves, as well as his beasts, goes further than anything mentioned thus far. The Zadokite Document forbids a man to eat what is lying about in the field (10:23), but Philo says that the Sabbath "extends also to every kind of trees and plants; for it is not permitted to cut any shoot or branch, or even a leaf, or to pluck any fruit whatsoever."[19]

Sabbath Observance in Situations of Conflict

Although it really falls under the previous section, we are treating this aspect of Sabbath observance separately because of its prominence during this period. There are surprisingly no such cases mentioned in the Old Testament, even though there were situations of conflict during which the people of God had to live under foreign rulers, as in Egypt, Assyria, and Babylon. The Israelites also engaged in wars during this period, but nothing is said about this aspect, although the rabbis discussed Joshua's march around Jericho, and Alger F. Johns seems to think that Nebuchadrezzar attacked Jerusalem specifically on the Sabbaths because presumably he knew that they would not resist him then.[20]

We hear nothing about Sabbath problems during the Egyptian oppression before the Exodus. Presumably most of the Israelites forgot the laws of their fathers. However, the Sabbath seems to have great importance for the Diaspora

---
* See pp. 82, 83.

Jews in Egypt during the Ptolemaic period. The three most popular Hebrew names during this period were Sabbathai, Simon, and Joseph.[21] The first was given to a child born on the Sabbath. Mention has also been made of the fact that many non-Jews also took this name and that Gentiles bearing the name Sambathion (a corruption of the name) were keeping the Sabbath without becoming Jews. Nevertheless, in a total pagan environment it was not easy for a Jew to remain faithful. There is one instance of a man on the estate of Apollonios in Philadelphia, probably a manager of building works, who did not work on the Sabbath. "We should recall the vast amount of work carried out by the new settlers in Philadelphia, the tempo of the work, and the severity of such taskmasters as Apollonios or Zenon, to appreciate the steadfastness of a Jew observing the Sabbath under such conditions."[22]

Life for a Jew could be very difficult working under foreign taskmasters but well-nigh impossible in a foreign army. Josephus lists a letter of Dolabella, governor of Syria, who wrote to Ephesus about 44 B.C., giving instruction concerning the Jews' insistence that they "cannot undertake military service because they may not bear arms or march on the days of the Sabbath." In this case he granted them exemption from military service and allowed them to follow their native customs.[23] The papyri have shown clearly that Jews served as soldiers in Egypt in the Ptolemaic period and even before that in the Persian period, as the Jewish garrison at Elephantine indicates. This continued to the Roman period, when the Ptolemaic army was abolished.[24] But there are no indications of Sabbath problems. Perhaps in a peacetime situation, accommodation could be made or the Jews acquiesced. There is one account where they were forced into the army and compelled to fight on the Sabbath against their own countrymen. Nicanor wanted to attack Judas and felt he could do so "with complete safety on the day of rest." The Jews who were forced into his army tried to dissuade him, beseeching him to "'show respect for the day which he who sees all things has honored and hallowed above other days.'" When Nicanor asked who commanded this, they replied, "'It is the living Lord himself, the Sovereign in heaven.'" Nicanor then replied, "'And I am a sovereign also, on earth, and I command you to take up arms and finish the king's business.'"[25] Apparently they were forced to attack but did not succeed.

But how did they relate to the Sabbath when they were fighting for themselves, when they could control what they did on the Sabbath (at least on their part)? The first such situation we have recorded took place when Ptolemy Soter entered Jerusalem on a Sabbath unopposed and "became master of the city without difficulty and ruled it harshly."[26]

Later, about 168 B.C., Antiochus sent Apollonios to Jerusalem, where he remained peaceably until the Sabbath, when he ordered his men to parade in arms since the Jews were idle. When the people came to see them, they were slain. He also destroyed the city walls and built the Acra, a fortified citadel occupied by troops.[27]

In the next such occasion under Antiochus Epiphanes, when a determined plan of Hellenization was added to conquest, there was a different reaction. Many Jews submitted by sacrificing to idols and profaning the Sabbath.[28] But some refused and fled into the wilderness. The enemy pursued them and intentionally attacked them on the Sabbath. Mattathias and his followers refused to defend themselves, saying, "'Let us all die in our innocence.'" The result was disaster.

THE SABBATH IN THE INTERTESTAMENTAL PERIOD

Faced with the dilemma of fighting on the Sabbath or suffering annihilation, the survivors chose the former. "'Let us,'" they determined, "'fight against every man who comes to attack us on the sabbath day; let us not die as our brethren died in their hiding places.'"[29] Josephus adds, "We continue the practice of fighting even on the Sabbath whenever it becomes necessary."[30] The Book of Jubilees, written a little later than this event, prohibits war on the Sabbath. Perhaps it represents a group that rigidly maintained the strict observance of the Sabbath even if it meant annihilation. At any rate, it must have been made with conscious awareness of the problem of the observance of Sabbath in wartime.

During the Maccabean period, this practice of defending themselves when attacked but not fighting offensively on the Sabbath seems to have been followed. Judas fought against Nicanor when the latter attacked him on the Sabbath,[31] and Jonathan did likewise when Bacchides attacked him on the Jews' sacred day.[32] Josephus, also, during the Great War, followed this practice when he was in command of a troop at Tarichaeae.[33] Apparently, the enemy generals were not fully aware of the Jews' decision to defend themselves on the Sabbath. However, even when the Jews could take advantage, they did not attack the enemy on the Sabbath. Even though Judas and his forces had routed Nicanor and had pursued him for some distance, "they were obliged to return because the hour was late. For it was the day before the sabbath, and for that reason they did not continue their pursuit." They kept the Sabbath, and on the next day they distributed the spoils.[34] On another occasion Judas had Gorgias in flight, but since the Sabbath was coming on, he stopped so his forces could observe the day.[35]

Even though they fought to defend themselves on the Sabbath, the Sabbath remained very important for the Jews, and their enemies were well aware of this. Thus when Demetrius sought the alliance of Jonathan, one of his proposals was that "on the Sabbaths and all festivals and the three days preceding a festival the Jews shall be exempt from labour."[36] and John Hyrcanus, who was forced to accompany Antiochus VII Sidetes to fight against the Parthians, even in this type of relationship persuaded the king to remain in one place not only for the Sabbath but also for Pentecost, which happened to precede the Sabbath that year, since on those days the Jews were not permitted to march.[37]

Different strategies could be used against the Jews, assuming that the enemies knew how they would behave on the Sabbath. Knowing that they would defend themselves only if attacked and that therefore if there were no imminent sign of attack the Jews would relax, their enemies could attack them by surprise. This is exactly what Ptolemy Lathyrus did (c. 100 B.C.) when he attacked "Asochis, a city of Galilee, on the Sabbath, and taking it by storm, captured about ten thousand persons and a great deal of booty besides."[38] Another type of strategy would be for the enemy to make other types of military preparations short of an attack. This is the tack that Pompey followed in capturing Jerusalem. Concerning this, Josephus says:

"But if it were not our national custom to rest on the Sabbath day, the earthworks would not have been finished, because the Jews would have prevented this; for the Law permits us to defend ourselves against those who begin battle and strike us, but it does not allow us to fight against an enemy that does anything else.

"Of this fact the Romans were well aware, and on those days which we call the Sabbath, they did not shoot at the Jews or meet them in hand to hand combat, but instead they raised earthworks and towers, and brought up their siege-engines in order that these might be put to work the following day."[39]

Under Roman rule, the Jews were quite free to practice their religion, including the observance of the Sabbath. We have already mentioned Dolabella's letter to Ephesus exempting the Jews from military service so that they would not have conflicts over the Sabbath and problems concerning their food. Josephus lists several other decrees and letters granting the Jews permission to observe their Sabbaths.[40] Their conflicts centered upon the question of images rather than the Sabbath.

Nevertheless, there were incidents that related to the Sabbath. Philo mentions one such case, although his interest is more to point out an example of vainglory. He mentions "one of the ruling class" who wanted to do away with the Sabbath. He commanded the Jews to do things forbidden on the Sabbath, "thinking that if he could destroy the ancestral rule of the Sabbath it would lead the way to irregularity in all other matters, and a general backsliding." But the Jews refused, so he tried to persuade them through reason:

"'Suppose,' he said, 'there was a sudden inroad of the enemy or an inundation caused by the river rising and breaking through the dam, or a blazing conflagration or a thunderbolt or famine, or plague or earthquake, or any other trouble either of human or divine agency, will you stay at home perfectly quiet? Or will you appear in public in your usual guise, with your right hand tucked inside and the left held close to the flank under the cloak lest you should even unconsciously do anything that might help to save you? And will you sit in your conventicles and assemble your regular company and read in security your holy books, expounding any obscure point and in leisurely comfort discussing at length your ancestral philosophy? No, you will throw all these off and gird yourselves up for the assistance of yourselves, your parents and your children, and the other persons who are nearest and dearest to you, and indeed also your chattels and wealth to save them too from annihilation.

"'See then,' he went on, 'I who stand before you am all the things I have named. I am the whirlwind, the war, the deluge, the lightning, the plague of famine or disease, the earthquake which shakes and confounds what was firm and stable; I am constraining destiny, not its name but its power, visible to your eyes and standing at your side.'"[41]

Philo does not tell us whether the ruler succeeded or failed; but since he could not force them through pressure, it is likely that he failed through persuasion. Nevertheless, Philo provides us here with a good example of the type of reasoning that must have been presented to persuade the Jews in some instances to go further than they were accustomed in their observance of the Sabbath.

At the beginning of the Jewish revolt after Vespasian landed in Syria, Antiochus, whose father was chief magistrate of the Jews in Antioch, not only denounced his father and other Jews but did not allow them "to repose on the seventh day," instead compelling them "to do everything exactly as on other days; and so strictly did he enforce obedience that not only at Antioch was the weekly day of rest abolished, but the example having been started there spread for a short time to the other cities as well."[42]

In the desperate war that broke out between the Romans and the Jews, the Romans could not rely on what the Jews would do on the Sabbath. In the past their enemies surprised them because they knew what they would do. But in this war we find the opposite taking place. Since the Romans expected the Jews to act in a certain way, and they did not, the Romans were surprised. The first instance of this was the massacre of the Roman garrison on the Sabbath, "a day on which from religious scruples Jews abstain even from the most innocent acts."[43] Josephus expresses his disapproval of this Sabbath massacre when he adds further, "The same day and at the same hour, as it were by the hand of Providence, the inhabitants of Caesarea massacred the Jews who resided in their city."[44] Another instance of this was when John tricked Titus into postponing the surrender of the people of Gischala from the Sabbath to the next day so that he could escape during the night.[45]

And as the war came to its climax and reached Jerusalem, Josephus writes: "The Jews, seeing the war now approaching the capital, abandoned the feast and rushed to arms; and, with great confidence in their numbers, sprang in disorder and with loud cries into the fray, with no thought for the seventh-day of rest, for it was the very sabbath which they regarded with special reverence."[46]

The Jewish dilemma of keeping the Sabbath holy and dying or fighting on the Sabbath and surviving is well expressed in Agrippa II's speech just before the Jewish rebellion.

"'If you observe your sabbath customs and refuse to take any action on that day, you will undoubtedly be easily defeated, as were your forefathers by Pompey, who pressed the siege most vigorously on the days when the besieged remained inactive; if, on the contrary, you transgress the law of your ancestors, I fail to see what further object you will have for hostilities, since your one aim is to preserve inviolate all the institutions of your fathers. How could you invoke the aid of the Deity, after deliberately omitting to pay Him the service which you owe Him?'"[47]

The answer to this is given aptly by Asinaeus, who with his brother Anilaeus had set up an independent enclave in Mesopotamia about the time of Gaius' death (A.D. 41) and when the Jews were being massacred there. When Asinaeus heard of the satrap of Babylonia's plan to attack him on the Sabbath, he sent scouts out to investigate. They came back with the report that it was true and that they were caught in a trap and "our hands are tied because the commandment of our ancestral law orders us to do no work." Apparently they thought it improper even to defend themselves on the Sabbath. However, Asinaeus' response was that it was "better observance of the law, instead of gladdening the foe by a death without anything accomplished, to take his courage in his hands, let the straits into which he had fallen excuse violation of the law, and die, if he must, exacting a just vengeance."[48] His resolve strengthened his forces, and they defeated the enemy.

Later on, after Asinaeus had been poisoned, Anilaeus learned that the Parthian leader Mithridates had set up camp with the idea of attacking him the next day, which was the Sabbath. He made a night march (Friday night) and attacked the Parthians at 3:00 A.M. Sabbath morning, slew a host of soldiers, captured Mithridates, and put the rest to flight.[49] Thus the Jews chose not only self-defense on the Sabbath but even attack to defeat their enemies and preserve their way of life. For them it was "better observance of the law" to fight and die if need be to protect their religious rights, even if it meant at the moment that they had to transgress the very laws they sought to uphold.

Religious Activities on the Sabbath

Very little is mentioned of the religious activities that were carried on on the Sabbath. Josephus mentions that one of the priests stood near the tower of the southwest corner of the Temple "to give notice, by sound of trumpet, in the afternoon of the approach, and on the following evening of the close, of every seventh day, announcing to the people the respective hours for ceasing work and for resuming their labours."[50]

At the Temple the priests served daily; but on the Sabbath, new moons, and feast days the high priest accompanied them. Philo discusses the Sabbath sacrifices, the placing of the shewbread on the table and the frankincense and salt on the loaves,[51] but does so on the basis of the Old Testament rather than current practice.

Every Sabbath the Jews gathered in the synagogues "to listen to the Law and to obtain a thorough and accurate knowledge of it."[52] Philo describes in some detail what goes on in the synagogue: "And indeed they do always assemble and sit together, most of them in silence except when it is the practice to add something to signify approval of what is read. But some priest who is present or one of the elders reads the holy laws to them and expounds them point by point till about the late afternoon, when they depart having gained both expert knowledge of the holy laws and considerable advance in piety."[53]

Philo more frequently describes these activities as "studying philosophy" and occupying themselves "with the philosophy of their fathers, dedicating that time to the acquiring of knowledge and the study of the truths of nature." He summarizes the truths and principles studied under two heads: "one of duty to God as shewn by piety and holiness, one of duty to men as shewn by humanity and justice." Moreover, he calls the synagogues "schools of good sense, temperance, courage, justice, and the other virtues," as well as prudence, piety, and holiness.[54]

The Sabbath was to be devoted to the "one sole object of philosophy with a view to the improvement of character and submission to the scrutiny of conscience."[55] Every Sabbath they should examine "whether any offence against purity had been committed in the preceding days, and exact from themselves in the council-chamber of the soul, with the laws as their fellow-assessors and fellow-examiners, a strict account of what they had said or done in order to correct what had been neglected and to take precaution against repetition of any sin."[56]

According to Philo, the Therapeutae isolated themselves for six days but came together on the Sabbath. His description of the service itself is quite similar to the regular synagogue worship that he described above.

"But every seventh day they meet together as for a general assembly and sit in order according to their age in the proper attitude, with their hands inside the robe, the right hand between the breast and the chin and the left withdrawn along the flank. Then the senior among them who also has the fullest knowledge of the doctrines which they profess comes forward and with visage and voice alike quiet and composed gives a well-reasoned and wise discourse. He does not make an exhibition of clever rhetoric like the orators or sophists of to-day but follows careful examination by careful expression of the exact meaning of the thoughts, and this does not lodge just outside the ears of the audience but passes through the hearing into the soul and there stays securely. All the others sit still and listen showing their approval merely by their looks or nods."[57]

THE SABBATH IN THE INTERTESTAMENTAL PERIOD

He further describes the synagogue as having a double enclosure, with the women segregated from the men with a low wall between.

However, the synagogue seems to have been used on the Sabbath for other purposes than instruction in the law. Josephus describes a meeting held in the synagogue of Tiberias on Sabbath where a political discussion was carried on that could easily have led to a riot "had not the arrival of the sixth hour, at which it is our custom on the Sabbath to take our midday meal, broken off the meeting."[58]

The Theology of the Sabbath

Here we deal with the Sabbath not from the standpoint of what can and cannot be done or what religious activities are performed on it, but from the standpoint of its deeper meanings as derived from its various components, such as its being the seventh day, a day of rest, or a day of spiritual emphasis. The one who developed this aspect of the Sabbath more than anyone else, in fact almost exclusively, was Philo. Naturally, some of his reasoning will seem fanciful to us today, but in the context of his time, especially for those who understood the philosophical currents that influence Philo, it would have been cogent.

Philo develops his theology on the Sabbath with reference to the meaning of the number seven,[59] to the universal significance of the Sabbath as the birthday of the world,[60] to the philosophical meaning of resting,[61] and to the equality and freedom to which it points.[62]

Miscellaneous Elements

The Numbering of the Sabbaths.—According to the Qumran calendar, every year and every quarter began on a Wednesday. Since there were 364 days in a year, 30 days in a month, and with an extra day added every three months, each quarter had exactly 13 weeks. Thus the feast days always fell on the same day of the week every year, and none of these fell on the Sabbath.[63] There is also evidence that the Sabbaths were numbered throughout the year. Baumgarten thinks that this practice of numbering the Sabbaths was not confined to the Qumran sect but was common practice among the Jews and Samaritans of the time.[64]

Sabbath Observed Before Creation.—Philo, in the context of the falling of manna, says that the Sabbath "has held the place of honour in nature, not merely from the time when the world was framed, but even before the heaven and all that sense perceives came into being."[65]

Samaritans Kept Sabbath, but for Different Reason.—Josephus relates that at the time of Antiochus Epiphanes the Samaritans sought to dissociate themselves as much as possible from the Jews and their practices. They thus gave different reasons for their observance of the Sabbath: "Our forefathers because of certain droughts in their country, and following a certain ancient superstition, made it a custom to observe the day which is called the Sabbath by the Jews."[66]

Etymology of Sabbath.—Apion's explanation for the Sabbath is that on the sixth day after the Jews left Egypt they developed tumors in the groin and so when they reached Judea they rested on that seventh day and called it sabbaton, preserving the Egyptian terminology of the disease of the groin that is called "sabbo." Josephus attributes this to "either gross impudence or shocking ignorance; there is a wide difference between *sabbo* and *sabbaton*. *Sabbaton* in the Jews' language denotes cessation from all work, while *sabbo* among the Egyptians signifies, as he states, disease of the groin."[67]

The Eighth Day.—Although 2 Enoch 33:1, 2 connected the days of Creation with the history of the world as consisting of a world-week of 7,000 years and did not refer to a day of worship, it did mention the term "eighth day," and this was most probably the basis for Barnabas' use of this term for Sunday.[68] Barnabas had earlier used the Creation scheme in the same way as 2 Enoch.[69] The author of 2 Enoch considers the eighth day as the commencement of "a time of not-counting, endless, with neither years nor months nor weeks nor days nor hours."[70] He does not explicitly mention the seventh thousand-year period as a millennium, but Barnabas does this. In a sense, then, according to the scheme of the world-week, the Sabbath serves not only as a type of this millennium of the seventh thousand-year day but also for the age to come, which begins with the eighth thousand-year period. It is interesting to find that at the death of Eve, the archangel tells Seth: "'Man of God, mourn not for the dead more than six days, for on the seventh day is the sign of the resurrection and the rest of the age to come; on the seventh day the Lord rested from all His works.'"[71]

NOTES

[1] Bezalel Porten, "The Religion of the Jews of Elephantine in Light of the Hermopolis Papyri," *Journal of Near Eastern Studies* 28 (1969):116-121.

[2] Franz Rosenthal, ed., *An Aramaic Handbook*, Porta Linguarum Orientalium n.s., X (Wiesbaden, 1967), I/1, pp. 12, 13, as translated by Porten, *op. cit.*, p. 116. This is quite a different translation from that given by A. Dupont-Sommer in "L'ostracon araméen du Sabbat," *Semitica* 2 (1949):31.

[3] *Corpus Papyrorum Judaicarum*, ed. by Victor A. Tcherikover in collab. Alexander Fuks, 3 vols. (Cambridge, 1957-1964), 1:95. See also his full discussion of the Sambathions (3:43-56).

[4] Porten, *op. cit.*, pp. 117, 120.

[5] *Ibid.*, pp. 117, 118.

[6] *Ibid.*, pp. 120, 121.

[7] Frank Moore Cross, Jr., *The Ancient Library of Qumran and Modern Biblical Studies*, rev. ed. (Garden City, N.Y., 1961), p. 199.

[8] Hans Bietenhardt, "Sabbatvorschriften von Qumrân im Lichte des rabbinischen Rechts und der Evangelien," in *Qumran-Probleme: Vorträge des Leipziger Symposions über Qumran-Probleme vom 9. bis 14. Oktober 1961* (Berlin, 1963), p. 54.

[9] *Ibid.*

[10] The numeration and translation followed is that of Chaim Rabin, ed. and trans., *The Zadokite Documents*, 2d rev. ed. (Oxford, 1958).

[11] Some dispute the meaning of this passage. The original reads: אל יתערב אישמרצובו ביום השבת. R. H. Charles translated this, "No man shall fast of his own will on the Sabbath" *(APOT*, 2:827), by proposing the reading יתעבה for יתערב. Some have emended the reading to יתרעב with the same meaning, others have accepted the original with reference to the *erub* implying opposition by the sectaries of this Pharisaic enactment, and still others understand the passage as prohibiting competition or making a wager, or "pooling property" on the Sabbath. S. Hoenig translates the passage, "Let no man socialize, of his own free will, on the Sabbath" (see Hoenig's article "An Interdict Against Socializing on the Sabbath," *Jewish Quarterly Review* 62 [1971-1972]:77-83).

[12] Rabin, *op. cit.*, p. 53.

[13] *APOT*, 2:826.

[14] The Hebrew is enigmatic. Charles translates it as "nursing father" *(APOT*, 2:827), while S. T. Kimbrough, Jr. ("The Concept of Sabbath at Qumran," *Revue de Qumran* 5 [1964-1966]:495) translates it "foster-father." Samuel Belkin *(Philo and the Oral Law* [Cambridge, Mass., 1940], p. 203) suggests that the sect permitted carrying, but only by the parent.

[15] Charles translates this, "And if any person falls into a place of water or into a place of . . . he shall not bring him up by a ladder or a cord or instrument."—*APOT*, 2:828. Kimbrough *(op. cit.)* follows Rabin with this explanation: "The text is extremely corrupt. Lit. it is: 'But every human being who falls into a place full of water, or into a place . . ., let him not be made to climb out.' I have accepted the proposal of RABIN, GINZBERG, and DUPONT-SOMMER in order to get around the inhumanity of the rule as it stands. This is, of course, only surmise."—Page 497. How one accepts this will, of course, affect one's judgment of the strictness of the sect.

[16] Josephus *Jewish War* 2. 8. 9. (All citations from Josephus are from LCL.)

[17] Kimbrough, *op. cit.*, pp. 484, 486.

[18] Bietenhardt, *op. cit.*, pp. 56-60.

[19] Philo *Moses* 2. 4. (All citations from Philo are from LCL.)

[20] Regarding Joshua's attack on Jericho, Moshe David Herr ("The Problem of War on the Sabbath in the Second Temple and the Talmudic Periods," *Tarbiz* 30 [1960-61]: ix [the original Hebrew article is on pp. 242-256 and 341-356]) says: "The answer that God explicitly permitted it presents an even greater difficulty. There are others who add that Joshua destroyed Jericho so as not to benefit from Sabbath desecration. Admittedly the legend itself of the conquest of Jericho on the Sabbath is found in a Tannaitic Midrash, but we have no record of any Tanna or Amora

asking why Joshua desecrated the Sabbath. On the other hand, Pirqoi ben Baboi who lived in Babylon circa 800 c.e. explicitly states that the waging of war is obligatory on the Sabbath just as Joshua and the kings of Israel did in the time of the Bible. These sentiments were voiced, as is known, to combat Karaitic views that all war was forbidden on the Sabbath.... This strange retreat in the opinions of the rabbinic sages is no cause for wonder since we find a more extreme example in the controversy with the Karaites and their followers in Se'adya's *Emunot Wede'ot* (tenth century), where he stated, contrary to the Midrash, that Joshua never fought at all on the Sabbath in order to brush away his opponents 'with a straw'—a typical attitude adopted in polemic."

For Nebuchadrezzar's Sabbath attacks on Jerusalem, see Alger F. Johns, "The Military Strategy of Sabbath Attacks on the Jews," *VT* 13 (1963):482-486.

21 Tcherikover, *op. cit.*, 1:29.
22 *Ibid.*, p. 44; see also Papyrus 10 on pp. 136, 137.
23 Josephus *Jewish Antiquities* 14. 10. 12.
24 Tcherikover, *op. cit.*, pp. 11, 12, 52.
25 2 Macc 15:1-4. (All references to the Apocrypha will be from the Revised Standard Version.)
26 *Jewish Antiquities* 12. 1. 1.
27 2 Macc 5:24-26; 1 Macc 1:30-33.
28 1 Macc 1:43.
29 Chap. 2:32-41.
30 *Jewish Antiquities* 12. 6. 2.
31 2 Macc 15:1-4.
32 1 Macc 9:24-49; *Jewish Antiquities* 13. 1. 3.
33 *Life* 32.
34 2 Macc 8:25, 26.
35 Chap. 12:38.
36 *Jewish Antiquities* 13. 2. 3.
37 *Ibid.*, 13. 8. 4.
38 *Ibid.*, 13. 12. 4.
39 *Ibid.*, 14. 4. 2, 3; see also *Jewish War* 1. 7. 3.
40 *Jewish Antiquities* 14. 10. 20, 21, 23, 25; 16. 6. 2, 4.
41 *On Dreams* 2. 18.
42 *Jewish War* 7. 3. 3.
43 *Ibid.*, 2. 17. 10.
44 *Ibid.*, 2. 18. 1.
45 *Ibid.*, 4. 2. 3; also 7. 8. 7.
46 *Ibid.*, 2. 19. 2. It was a special Sabbath since it fell within the week of the Feast of Tabernacles.
47 *Ibid.*, 2. 16. 4.
48 *Jewish Antiquities* 18. 9. 2.
49 *Ibid.*, 18. 9. 6.
50 *Jewish War* 4. 9. 12.
51 *The Special Laws* 1. 35.
52 Josephus *Against Apion* 2. 17.
53 *Hypothetica* 7. 13.
54 *The Special Laws* 2. 15; *Moses* 2. 39.
55 Philo *On the Creation* 43.
56 Philo *The Decalogue* 20.
57 *The Contemplative Life* 3.
58 *Life* 54.
59 *Moses* 2. 39; *The Special Laws* 2. 15; *Allegorical Interpretation* 1. 4-6; *On the Creation* 30, 31, 33-42.
60 *Moses* 1. 37; 2. 39; *On the Creation* 30; *The Special Laws* 2. 15, 16.
61 *On the Cherubim* 26; *On the Creation* 33; *Allegorical Interpretation* 1. 2, 3, 6; *The Special Laws* 2. 15, 48; *On Flight and Finding* 31; *On Abraham* 5.
62 *The Special Laws* 2. 16.
63 Karl Georg Kuhn, "Der gegenwärtige Stand der Erforschung der in Palästina neu gefundenen hebräischen Handschriften: 43. Zum heutigen Stand der Qumranforschung," *Theologische Literaturzeitung* 85 (1960):654.
64 Joseph M. Baumgarten, "The Counting of the Sabbath in Ancient Sources," *VT* 16 (1966):277-286. He proposes to explain Luke 6:1 and Horace's use of the term *tricesima sabbata* in *Sat.* 1. 9, 69 on the bases of this ancient practice.
65 *Moses* 2. 48.
66 *Jewish Antiquities* 12. 5. 5.
67 *Against Apion* 2. 2.
68 Barnabas 15:9.
69 Barnabas 15:4, 5.
70 2 Enoch 33:1. See J. Daniélou, "La typologie millenariste de la semaine dans le Christianisme primitif," *Vigiliae Christianae* 2 (1948):1-16.
71 *Vita Adae et Evae* 51. 2; see also *Apocalypsis Mosis* 43. 3.

CHAPTER 4

The Rabbinic Sabbath

Robert M. Johnston

OF the numerous Jewish denominations in existence before A.D. 70, only two survived the destruction of Jerusalem and the Temple.[1] One of these was Christianity and the other was Pharisaism.[2] Deprived of the Temple and finding it necessary to adjust to the devastating results of a tragic war and a dramatically altered outlook, Pharisaism necessarily changed. This post-A.D. 70 continuation of Pharisaism is referred to as Rabbinic Judaism, and from it virtually all modern forms of Judaism are descended. The present chapter provides a brief sketch of the Sabbath as it is regarded and observed in classical Rabbinic Judaism.[3]

One of the distinguishing features of Pharisaism had been its high regard for oral tradition. The Pharisees claimed to be heirs of Ezra the scribe and his court known as the Great Assembly, the beginning of the Sanhedrin. Indeed, Ezra and the Great Assembly were regarded as transmitters of oral laws that could be traced all the way back to Moses.[4] The oral laws usually took the form of an interpretation or application of some proof text from the Old Testament Scriptures, given as the considered opinion of a noted rabbi and supported by the majority vote of the other rabbis in the court or academy.[5] But legal decisions by the Sanhedrin or even individual rabbis could be authoritative even when they could not be proved from the Bible. The charter for such nonscriptural laws, known as *geziroth* (rabbinical prohibitions; singular, *gezerah*) and *takkanoth* (positive enactments by court or rabbi; singular, *takkanah*), was seen in Deuteronomy 17:11. Rabbinic Judaism is thus the Old Testament interpreted by the tradition.[6]

For a long time the oral law was indeed oral; there was an inhibition against writing it down for fear that it might be treated as Scripture. Instead, it was stored up in the heads of the rabbis and their disciples. However, as scholars continually added to the body of tradition, it grew so massive that memories were too severely taxed. Even more seriously, the deaths of large numbers of leading scholars in the great Jewish wars of the first and second centuries (A.D. 66-70 and 132-135) and the persecution that followed the latter war made it apparent that the memories of men were too fragile a record. A teacher's head severed from his body is a book that can no more be read! And hence, the oral tradition came to be written down.

Sometime after A.D. 135 Rabbi Meir made a compilation of laws known to him. To this collection more was added, and at the beginning of the third-century Rabbi Judah the Prince made the basic codification of Rabbinic law known as the Mishnah, which remains the fundamental guide for orthodox Jewish life to this day. The Mishnah consists of sixty-three books, or "tractates," each dealing with a different subject. The tractates dealing the most with the Sabbath laws are entitled *Shabbath* and *Erubin*.[7] One can as little understand the Jewish religion without a knowlege of the Mishnah as one can understand Christianity while ignorant of the New Testament.[8]

But Rabbinic interpretation and lawmaking did not terminate, and the process of amplification continued. This produced a massive elaboration of the Mishnaic tractates known as the Gemara. The basic Mishnah texts together with their Gemara expansions are known as the Talmud.[9] There are actually two Talmuds: the Palestinian (or "Jerusalem") Talmud, compiled about A.D. 400, and the more authoritative Babylonian Talmud, compiled about a hundred years later. These are the most important sources for our study of the Rabbinic Sabbath.

Roughly speaking, the works so far mentioned are topically arranged. Besides these Rabbinic works that are topically arranged, there are other works in the form of running commentary on the Biblical texts; these are called *midrashim* (singular, *midrash*). *Midrashim* are of various types: *halakic* (legal; these are the oldest type), expositional and homiletic. Reference will be made in this chapter to *Mekilta* of Rabbi Ishmael, the *Midrash Rabbah, The Midrash on Psalms,* and *Pesikta Rabbati*.[10]

Even after the Talmud was completed, the rabbis continued to deliver legal decisions about the Sabbath, as they did about all other important questions in Jewish life. The opinions are known as *responsa*. Attempts have been made to digest all of these vast materials for easy reference. Perhaps the most readable such digest was made by Maimonides (Moses ben Maimon) in the twelfth century, but the most authoritative digest of Jewish law today is the *Shulchan Aruch*, prepared by Joseph Karo in the sixteenth century.[11]

We shall now see what these sources have to tell us about the Sabbath.

Importance of the Sabbath

No other institution is more important to Judaism than the Sabbath, and only circumcision comes near equaling it. The rabbis regarded the Sabbath as equaling in importance all the other precepts of the Torah combined.[12] It was said, "He who observes the Sabbath is kept far from sin."[13] One sermon has the Lord declaring, "O My people, behold, you have annulled all Ten Commandments. Nevertheless, if you had kept one Commandment . . . I would have forgiven you. And which Commandment is this? It is the Commandment concerning the Sabbath day."[14] Shabbath is the longest tractate in the Mishnah, and the subject is dealt with repeatedly in the other tractates.[15]

Not only was the Sabbath an essential feature of Jewish identity, but it was regarded as a way of witnessing to men about the Creator[16] The matter was graphically put this way: "The Sabbath adds holiness to Israel. Why is the shop of so-and-so closed? Because he keeps the Sabbath. Why does so-and-so abstain from work? Because he keeps the Sabbath. He thus bears witness to Him by whose word the world came into being that He created His world in six days and rested on the seventh. And thus it says: 'Therefore ye are my witnesses, saith the LORD, and I am God' (Isa. 43:12)."[17]

Cardinal gifts of privileges, blessings, and deliverances were promised to Israel as a reward for success in Sabbathkeeping.[18] Above all, the final redemption was said to hinge upon correct observance of the Sabbath. Rabbi Johanan said in the name of Simeon ben Yohai: "If Israel were to keep two Sabbaths according to the laws thereof, they would be redeemed immediately."[19] Rabbi Levi said: "If Israel kept the Sabbath properly even for one day, the son of David would come. Why? Because it is equivalent to all the commandments."[20] Isaiah 30:15 was cited to show that true repentance ("returning") and Sabbathkeeping ("rest") were the conditions of salvation, the way to hasten the coming of the Messiah.

The Sabbath in Haggadah

As to content, all Jewish teaching is divided into two categories: Halakah (law) and Haggadah (lore). The latter, which includes strictly theological questions and speculations as contrasted with standards of conduct, draws our attention first. Simeon ben Lakish made this comparison: "It is the way of the world that even a king who considers himself enlightened might say to his servants: 'Work one day for yourselves and six days for me.' Not so the Holy One, blessed be He. This is what the Holy One, blessed be He, says to Israel: 'My children, keep six days for yourselves, and keep only one day for Me.'"[21]

It is characteristic of Haggadah that it is filled with parables, legends, and lively imaginary dialogues such as this one, which hinges on the fact that the seventh day, unlike the other days of the week, is not followed by an even-numbered day, and the fact that in late Hebrew the same word, *kiddash*, meant both to hallow and to betroth:[22] "The Sabbath spoke right up to the Holy One, blessed be He: Each of the days has a mate, but I have no mate. The Holy One, blessed be He, replied: The congregation of Israel will be thy mate. And when Israel stood on Mount Sinai, God said: Remember the special thing I told the Sabbath, namely that the congregation of Israel is to be thy mate, as it is said: 'Remember the Sabbath day to hallow it' (Ex. 20:8)."[23]

It became the custom of many Jews to follow the example attributed to the first-century Rabbi Hanina, who donned his best robe and stood at sunset on the beginning of Sabbath, exclaiming, "Come and let us go forth to welcome the queen Sabbath," and the example of Rabbi Jannai, who similarly attired himself and met the Sabbath with the words, "Come, O bride, Come, O bride!"[24] Friday night was a time of connubial consummation.

Altering the metaphor, Israel is the bride, God her husband, and the Sabbath the time of their union.[25] These figures imply that the Sabbath is Israel's exclusive privilege, for it is like the wife of another to the heathen. Rabbi Johanan put it thus: "In mundane affairs, when a king and his consort are sitting and conversing together, should one come and interrupt them, does he not thereby make himself liable to punishment of death? So, too, the Sabbath is a reunion between Israel and God, as it is said, It is a sign between Me and the children of Israel (Ex. 31:17); therefore any non-Jew who, being uncircumcized, thrusts himself between them incurs the penalty of death."[26]

The foregoing parable was told to explain a point made by both Jose ben Hanina and Simeon ben Lakish: "A Gentile who keeps the Sabbath deserves death."[27] It was considered that the Lord gave the Sabbath only to Israel, not to the heathen.[28]

A corollary to this exclusivistic idea of the Sabbath was the common Rabbinic view that the Sabbath command was given first at Sinai, though there were many deviations from that opinion.[29] According to one variation, the Sabbath was known to Adam, who composed Psalm 92.[30] Indeed it was said that Adam sinned on the day he was created, but because the Sabbath interceded for him, he was not driven out of the Garden until the end of the Sabbath.[31] Thereafter, according to this view, the Sabbath was forgotten until the time of Moses.[32]

Many of these ideas can be traced back to intertestamental times, as can be the view that many of the patriarchs observed the Sabbath, particularly Jacob and Joseph; the case of Abraham was more debated.[33] There was also a belief that Moses obtained for the Israelites in Egypt the privilege of Sabbathkeeping before his flight.[34] Sanhedrin 56b reasons that the fourth and fifth commandments were part of a special revelation to the Israelites at Marah (Ex. 15:25) prior to the giving of the law at Sinai, or even before the giving of manna (Exodus 16); the rabbis recognized that "your God commanded you" (Deut. 5:15, 16, R.S.V.) must refer to pre-Sinaitic commandments. But it is nowhere suggested that anyone before Abraham kept the Sabbath except Adam and God, and possibly other celestial beings.[35]

If these were the Rabbinic views of the Sabbath's past, what of its future? The Sabbath is seen as an island of eternity within time, a foretaste of the world to come. Tamid 7:4 declares that Psalm 92, the psalm sung by the Levites in the Temple on the Sabbath, is "a song for the time that is to come, for the day that shall be all Sabbath and rest in the life everlasting."[36]

Closely related to this conception was the ancient teaching about the cosmic week, deduced from Psalm 90:4, according to which six thousand years of earth's history would be followed by a thousand years of desolation, which corresponds also to the sabbatical year of release, when slaves were freed and the land lay fallow (Ex. 21:2; 23:11; et cetera). This conception, which can be traced back at least to the intertestamental pseudepigrapha,[37] is also connected with Psalm 92 and the idea of the eschatological Sabbath in Sanhedrin 97a, b. Pirke de Rabbi Eliezer, chapter 19, states the doctrine concisely: "The Holy One, blessed be He, created seven millennia (*olamin*), and of them all He chose the seventh millennium only; the six millennia are for the going in and coming out for war and peace. The seventh millennium is entirely Sabbath and rest in the life everlasting."[38]

Somehow parallel to the doctrine of the eschatological Sabbath is the notion that lost souls are given respite from punishment in the nether world on the Sabbath. As soon as the Sabbath begins, an angel named Dumah, who is in charge of the souls, cries out, "Come out of Gehenna!" And the souls are released and not judged on the Sabbath. When the Jews finish the service that closes the Sabbath, Dumah again cries aloud and says, "Come out and come to the house of the shadow of death and of chaos."[39]

The rabbis were called upon to explain God's own activity on the Sabbath. Tinneus Rufus, the Roman governor who martyred Rabbi Akiba, stated to Akiba, "'If it is as you say that the Holy One, blessed be He, honours the Sabbath, then He should not stir up winds or cause the rain to fall on that day.' 'You fool!' Akiba exclaimed; 'it is like one who carries objects four cubits.'"[40] Here Akiba appeals to the rule of *erub,* according to which a man is permitted to carry most objects within his private domain, or four cubits in the public domain. But the whole universe is God's private domain.

In another illustration, three other rabbis are depicted as silencing objections when, while visiting Rome, they taught that God keeps His own commandments: "There happened to be a sectarian there, who accosted them as they were going out with the taunt: 'Your words are only falsehood. Did you not say that God says a thing and fulfils it? Then why does He not observe the Sabbath?' They replied: 'Wretch! Is not a man permitted to carry on the Sabbath in his own courtyard?' He replied: 'Yes.' Whereupon they said to him: 'Both the higher and the lower regions are the courtyard of God, as it says, "The whole earth is full of his glory" [Isa. 6:3], and even if a man carries a distance of his own height, does he transgress?' The other agreed. 'Then,' said they, 'it is written, "Do not I fill heaven and earth?"' (Jer. 23:24)."[41]

An alternative explanation for God's activity on the Sabbath was that work was permitted to be done on the Sabbath within the sanctuary, but the whole universe is God's Temple: "To you it shall be a holy day. To God however it is like a profane day."[42] In any case, against such a background, the statement of Jesus in John 5:17, "'My Father is working still, and I am working'" (R.S.V.), is a claim to divinity in more than one way.

The Sabbath in Halakah

When we turn from Jewish beliefs (Haggadah) about the Sabbath to the rules (Halakah) about keeping it, we are prone to think that we are on familiar ground, for who has not heard about the burdensome legalism, so well known from the Gospels? It may come as a surprise, therefore, to learn that the Rabbinic laws were in certain significant aspects a relaxation from far stricter Halakah held by earlier Jewish sects.[43] Stricter rules about many Sabbath practices are found not only in earlier non-Rabbinic documents, such as the Book of Jubilees (especially chapter 50), the Zadokite Document (13:1-27; 14:6),[44] and the Dead Sea scrolls, but also in the recorded practices of the Essenes, the Samaritans, and the Falashas.[45]

Rabbinic practices represent an alleviation of the stricter rules, accomplished either by flatly contradicting them, or—more characteristically—by elaborating more rules that permit exceptional or general circumvention of prior rules. There are several striking illustrations of this tendency. The so-called "older" Halakah interpreted Jeremiah 17:22 very literally as a prohibition against carrying anything out of or into a house; but Shabbath 1:1 circumvents this by allowing two persons, by a carefully prescribed procedure, to pass an object between them from outside to inside or the reverse. The Samaritans, Falashas, and Karaites interpreted Exodus 16:29 very strictly, never leaving their dwellings on the Sabbath; but the Pharisees set up limits within which a person could lawfully move on the Sabbath—the "Sabbath day's journey" of 2,000 cubits mentioned in Acts 1:12. Indeed, the Mishnah contains an entire tractate, Erubin, describing a legal fiction whereby these limits could be joined together to extend freedom of movement even further.

In some cases the Rabbinic rules seem deliberately to have contravened the rules of earlier sects, and the contraventions are generally in the direction of greater convenience or humanitarianism. This relaxation had already begun in the time of Jesus. The Zadokite Document lays down among its Sabbath rules: "No man shall help an animal in its delivery on the Sabbath day. And if it falls into a pit or ditch, he shall not raise it on the Sabbath.... And if any person falls into a place of water or into a place of darkness he shall not bring him up by a ladder or a cord or instrument."[46] That such rules were already reversed or repudiated by the Pharisees in Jesus' time can be seen from Luke 14:5, which is in harmony with Rabbinic principles, as will appear below.

Still more striking are two further examples. The Book of Jubilees 50:8 declared that "whoever lies with his wife" desecrates the Sabbath and "shall die," which agrees with the principles of the Samaritans, Falashas, and Karaites; but marital cohabitation on Friday night was encouraged by the rabbis, as will be seen below.[47] Finally, Exodus 35:3 was understood by Samaritans, Essenes, Falashas, and Karaites to forbid all fire on the Sabbath. Hence, these groups passed Friday night in darkness. But the rabbis understood the prohibition to apply only to *kindling* a fire (or extinguishing one) on the Sabbath; if a lamp was lit before the commencement of the Sabbath, it could be left burning. In fact, the lighting of the Sabbath lamps was, as we shall see, a positive duty in every home.[48]

The Rabbinic multiplication of rules was largely intended to make the law easier to obey, to spell out exceptions, to explain contraventions.[49]

Activities Taking Precedence Over Sabbath Rest

The essence of the Rabbinic understanding of the Sabbath prohibitions was the avoidance of purposive, productive labor, as will be illustrated below. But certain circumstances were recognized in which the Sabbath law could be suspended so that activities that otherwise would have been regarded as breaking the Sabbath were permitted. For the most part these activities that took precedence over the Sabbath rest were connected with ceremonial duties, military action, and the saving of life.

The most notable ritual that superseded the Sabbath was circumcision, which normally had to take place the eighth day after birth. "R. Jose the Galilean says: Great is circumcision, for it sets aside the Sabbath, which is very important and the profanation of which is punishable by extinction."[50] If the eighth day fell on the Sabbath, even the necessary preparations for the operation were lawful, though Rabbi Akiba laid down the rule, "Any act of work that can be done on the eve of the Sabbath does not override the Sabbath, but what cannot be done on the eve of the Sabbath [for ceremonial purposes] overrides the Sabbath."[51] But this was done only if the birth had clearly taken place the previous Sabbath, making the eighth day also a Sabbath. If the case was doubtful, as when the boy was born at twilight Friday, the circumcision was put off until what might be considered the tenth day, Sunday.[52]

As Jesus pointed out on one occasion (Matt. 12:5), work done in connection with the Temple ritual was lawful on Sabbath. Even after the Temple was destroyed, the rabbis carefully preserved and even elaborated the laws about its services, for they still retained a wistful hope that these services would some day be restored. Thus we find: "The offerings of the congregation override the Sabbath and the laws of uncleanness, but the offerings of the individual override neither the Sabbath nor the laws of uncleanness," exceptions being "the baken cakes of the high priest and the bullock offered on the Day of Atonement," because "they must be offered at a fixed time."[53] While the baken cakes of the high priest (Lev. 6:21) could be made on the Sabbath, the two loaves of Leviticus 23:17 and the shewbread could not be made then, following Akiba's rule.[54] In general, if the Mosaic law fixed a calendrical day for any ceremonial act, that date was observed even if it fell on a Sabbath. Such acts included removing and burning all leavened bread before Passover; slaughtering the Passover lamb, but not roasting it; and reaping the omer of barley that was offered on the second day of Passover according to Leviticus 23:10, 11.[55]

The matter was carried back one step further, for how were the calendrical dates determined? It should be recalled that the Jewish calendar was lunar, and during the Tannaitic period, at least, the beginning of the lunar month was determined by observation, not calculation: the day after the new crescent was sighted was declared by the Sanhedrin to be the first day of the month. But for this, the court was dependent on witnesses. So important was their testimony considered, since the set feasts were determined accordingly, that such a witness was permitted to profane the Sabbath in order to go and give testimony to the court of the appearance of the new moon, particularly of Nisan and Tishri. Such a witness could transgress the Sabbath limits, take anything necessary for his journey, and even be carried on a litter if he could not walk.[56]

Ever since Maccabean times defensive warfare had also been permitted on the Sabbath.[57] Indeed, the rabbis noted that the wars waged by Joshua and David must have overridden the Sabbath.[58] They taught: "Gentile cities must not be besieged less than three days before the Sabbath, yet once they commence they need not leave off. And thus did Shammai say: 'until it fall' [Deut. 20:20], even on the Sabbath."[59] If an Israelite city was besieged by Gentiles, self-defense was permitted on the Sabbath, but only just so long as necessary, according to Judah ben Bathyra.[60] Individuals also were permitted to take necessary measures for self-protection: "If a man is pursued by gentiles or by robbers, what is the law as regards his breaking the Sabbath? Our Rabbis taught as follows: If a man is pursued by gentiles or by robbers, he may desecrate the Sabbath in order to save his life."[61] However, a man not under military orders may not go out on the Sabbath carrying arms.[62]

Self-protection comes under the third type of circumstance that overrides the Sabbath: mortal danger *(pikkuach nephesh)*. As a matter of principle, any life-or-death emergency superseded the Sabbath.[63] That the duty of saving life supersedes the Sabbath laws was deduced by Rabbi Ishmael from Exodus 22:2, by Rabbi Eleazar ben Azariah from circumcision, and by Rabbi Akiba from the fact that capital punishment for murder supersedes the Temple service (which in turn supersedes the Sabbath, and saving life is surely better than taking it!).[64] Rabbi Nathan argued that Exodus 31:16 implies "that we should disregard one Sabbath for the sake of saving the life of a person so that that person may be able to observe many Sabbaths."[65]

More problematic was a decision reached by majority vote of the sages at a secret meeting in the upper room of a house at Lydda after the war of A.D. 135, when the practice of Judaism was outlawed and many were suffering martyrdom for keeping the Sabbath. It was decided: "In every law of the Torah, if a man is commanded: 'Transgress and suffer not death' he may transgress and not suffer death, excepting idolatry, incest [including adultery], and murder."[66] Rabbi

Ishmael justified this ruling on the basis of Leviticus 18:4—"Ye shall therefore keep my statutes and my judgments, which if a man do, he shall *live* by them," but not *die* by them.[67] These rationalizations were not universally accepted, however, and Rabbi Dimi hedged and said: "This was taught only if there is no royal decree, but if there is a royal decree, one must incur martyrdom rather than transgress even a minor precept." Rabbi Johanan hedged further: "Even without a royal decree, it was only permitted in private; but in public one must be martyred even for a minor precept rather than violate it."[68]

The rabbis considered that the motive of the persecutor must be considered: if he was commanding the Jew to break the Sabbath only for his personal pleasure, the Jew might transgress; but if the command were religiously motivated, martyrdom must be chosen: "For Raba said: If a Gentile said to a Jew, 'Cut grass on the Sabbath for the cattle, and if not I will slay thee,' he must rather be killed than cut it; 'Cut it and throw it into the river,' he should rather be slain than cut it. Why so?—Because his intention is to force him to violate his religion."[69]

The danger to life need not be absolutely certain. "Whenever there is doubt whether life is in danger, this overrides the Sabbath." In certain cases medication could be taken on Sabbath. One may even warm water for a sick person: "Nor do we say: Let us wait, because perchance he will get well, but we warm the water for him immediately."[70] Midwifery was legitimate on Sabbath, and the midwife could transgress the Sabbath limits if necessary to go where she was needed. But a chronic illness for which treatment could be postponed could not be treated on Sabbath, for it did not involve the principle of *pikkuach nephesh*.[71]

The *shofar* of alarm could be sounded on Sabbath for a city surrounded by Gentiles or a flood, and for a ship in danger.[72] One could rescue a child fallen into the sea or locked into a room by accident, and "one must remove debris to save a life on the Sabbath, and the more eager one is, the more praiseworthy is one; and one need not obtain permission from the Court."[73] One could also extinguish and isolate a fire in the case of conflagration, and certain things could be rescued from it.[74]

These activities would not be permitted on Sabbath except to save life. It was only the dire emergency that made them legitimate.

Sabbath Prohibitions

It is perhaps arbitrary to distinguish sharply between circumstances that allowed suspension of the Sabbath laws in toto and those things that were regularly permitted. Was warfare a permitted activity or a suspension of the Sabbath? Nevertheless, the distinction is convenient. We turn now to the most characteristic feature of the Rabbinic Sabbath: the multitudinous laws stipulating what was prohibited and what was permitted.

In the Old Testament, only a few prohibited Sabbath activities are specifically mentioned: doing work, kindling a fire, trading. In addition, the rabbis understood Exodus 16:29 to forbid travel beyond certain limits, and Jeremiah 17:21, 22 to forbid carrying burdens from one's domicile to the public domain, or vice versa.

But what counts as work? In the scientific sense, raising an arm is work, and obviously the rabbis needed a different definition from that used by modern physicists. The Biblical word used in the fourth commandment and elsewhere was *melakah*—task, project, employment, and the essential thing about it was not the amount of effort involved, but the purpose.[75] *Melakah* was something done intentionally to gain or produce a temporal benefit, conceived in the broadest sense of the word.

But that is an abstraction, and the rabbis preferred to think in very concrete terms, making not definitions, but lists. They obtained their basic list from an exegesis of Exodus 35, where Moses solemnly forbids Sabbath work and kindling of fire on pain of death, and then proceeds to set the tasks for constructing the tabernacle. Here, then, was the key: all the different activities that must have contributed to the building of the tabernacle must come under the rubric of "work." By a process of deduction that need not concern us, they also decided on the basis of Deuteronomy 25:3 that the number of prohibited basic works was thirty-nine: "The main classes of work are forty save one: sowing, plowing, reaping, binding sheaves, threshing, winnowing, cleansing crops, grinding, sifting, kneading, baking, shearing wool, washing or beating or dyeing it, spinning, weaving, making two loops, weaving two threads, separating two threads, tying, loosening, sewing two stitches, tearing in order to sew two stitches, hunting a gazelle, slaughtering or flaying or salting it or curing its skin, scraping it or cutting it up, writing two letters, erasing in order to write two letters, building, pulling down, putting out a fire, lighting a fire, striking with a hammer and taking out anything from one domain into another. These are the main classes of work: forty save one."[76]

This list was taken to constitute the basic categories of work, which could be infinitely subdivided and extrapolated. The Mishnah itself contains a considerably detailed discussion of many of them. Out of hundreds of examples, we may here cite only a few. "They may not squeeze fruits to press out the juice, and even if the juice comes out of itself it is forbidden."[77] Squeezing came under the category of threshing. The rule also illustrates the principle that one must not receive personal benefit from inadvertent or unavoidable production that takes place on the Sabbath.[78] One could not eat on the Sabbath, for example, fruit that lay fallen under the tree, because it may have fallen on the Sabbath itself.[79] There was lengthy debate about whether and when an egg laid on the Sabbath might be eaten, some maintaining that it had been formed the day before. It was finally concluded that such an egg might not be removed from the nest, but could be protected until after the Sabbath, when it might at last be eaten.[80]

The category of "striking with the hammer" was extended to include any act needed to finish a work or complete an article. By this token, "he who removes threads from garments on the Sabbath is liable on the score of striking with the hammer; but that is only when he objects to them."[81] Under the same rubric instrumental music was forbidden on the Sabbath. Nor could food be prepared."[82]

Prohibition of kindling fire on the Sabbath was explicit in Exodus 35:2, 3, and the Mishnaic list added the extinguishing of fire. What to do in case of a house fire was a thorny issue. It was felt that this might be done to save life, as noted above, but not to save property.[83] The severity of this rule was alleviated by certain circumventions. Thus, "If a gentile came to put out the fire they may not say to him, 'Put it out', or 'Do not put it out', since they are not answerable for his keeping the Sabbath. But if it was a Jewish minor that came to put it out they may not permit him, since they are answerable for his keeping Sabbath." "All sacred books may be saved from burning," as well as enough food and drink for the remaining Sabbath meals and other absolute essentials.[84]

The rabbis saw it as their duty to place a hedge around the sanctity of the Sabbath (in accordance with the principle found in Aboth 1:1) by forbidding not only things that clearly profaned the Sabbath but also things that might increase the danger of profaning the Sabbath. To tilt a lamp in order to make more oil run to the wick and thus cause it to burn brighter was like kindling a fire, a cardinal transgression. Therefore the rabbis forbade anything that might tempt one on this score. One was not allowed to search his garments for vermin or read by the light of a lamp on the Sabbath.[85] There was scholarly debate on other grounds as to whether it was proper to kill vermin on the Sabbath, and one rabbi declared, "If one kills vermin on the Sabbath, it is as though he killed a camel."[86] But a clear distinction was made between a cardinal transgression and the breach of merely a Rabbinic enactment.

The Sabbath laws were of various kinds. The thirty-nine prohibited forms of labor were primary. There were also *muktzeh* laws about things that had to be set apart and not handled on Sabbath, even though no labor was involved—dirty things, and things such as fruit that fell or eggs that were laid during Sabbath. Under these laws a man, for the sake of appearances, might not touch money or any of the tools of his craft, even though he did not intend to work with them.

Then there were the *shebuth* laws of Sabbath rest, forbidding things that were not considered labor in themselves, but that were felt to detract from the restfulness and sanctity of the Sabbath. A list of such acts is found in Betzah 5:2—climbing a tree, swimming, clapping the hands, slapping the thighs, and stamping the feet. Forbidden also were "acts of choice" such as sitting in judgment, concluding a betrothal, performing *halitza* (Deut. 25:9), or contracting levirate marriage. Capital punishment, burial, and weddings could not take place on the Sabbath.[87] Many of these acts led to writing out some document, and writing was forbidden on the Sabbath.

Culpability of Sabbath activities depended on intention, purpose, and whether benefit was received,[88] as well as appearances.[89] A distinction was made between intentional and unintentional Sabbathbreaking.[90] It was even said, "He who mistakenly did a forbidden act on the Sabbath whilst intending to do another is free from penalty, because the Torah prohibited only a calculated action."[91] Thus one was not to blame if by dragging a chair across an earthen floor he made a "furrow," unless he intended to do so! The question was asked, "What if one forgot a pot on the stove and cooked it on the Sabbath?" Rabbi Hiyya bar Abba replied: "If one cooks on the Sabbath unwittingly, he may eat it; if deliberately, he may not eat it; and there is no difference." But the rabbis soon discovered that many began to leave the pot on the stove intentionally and then pleaded, "We forgot"; so the sages "retraced their steps and penalized him who forgot."[92] Such are the perils of leniency!

The professional, skilled task was forbidden, while the casual, amateurish deed was sometimes permitted.[93]

It cannot be denied that the rabbis often, and with considerable zest, plunged deep into casuistic reasoning; and some of their rulings seem arbitrary. Against some opposition, they decided that it was permissible to scrape honey from a beehive on the Sabbath; it was also permitted to set a vessel to catch dripping rain.[94] From a conflagration one may rescue Scriptures, phylacteries, and their cases, but not prayer books.[95] Objects could not be lifted off a cushion or the mouth of a jar, but they could be shaken off or wiped off.[96] While a man might not directly carry a stone, he was permitted to lift up his child even if the child had a stone in his hand.[97]

The rabbis were somewhat more relaxed about what children did on the Sabbath. While children could not be commanded to do some task, spontaneous acts, such as plucking and throwing, might be allowed.[98]

While food might not be heated, it could be kept warm, and there were various devices for this purpose. For example, a vessel containing cold water could be put into hot water to warm it.[99] Acts were permitted if a whole act of work was not completed at one time.[100] Work that completes itself (soaking, dyeing, baking, et cetera) could not be begun unless there was time to complete itself before Sabbath; but "water may be conducted into a garden on the eve of the Sabbath just before dark, and it may go on being filled the whole day."[101]

Treatment of nonmortal ailments and handicaps was not permitted; but "an eye salve may be placed on the eye [before sundown Friday] and a plaster on a wound and the process of healing continues all day."[102] One should not go out to war, go out with a caravan, or set out in a ship less than three days before the Sabbath.[103] On the Sabbath a corpse could be anointed and washed as long as the limbs were not moved,[104] but it could be moved if a loaf of bread or a child were placed on it: these could be moved within the domicile, and the body moved therewith.[105] Within certain limitations, cattle and other animals could be fed on the Sabbath.[106]

Restrictions on Sabbath bathing were concerned only with heating of the water, which was not allowed; but swimming was prohibited.[107] Indeed, ritual immersion of the body because of any pollution was required.[108] The use of public bathhouses operated by Gentiles posed a problem, since the water was heated on the Sabbath. This meant that one had to wait an interval after the Sabbath before bathing, so as not to benefit from heat generated on the Sabbath.[109] Bathing presented other problems: "If one bathes in water, he should first dry himself and then ascend, lest he come to carry [the water upon him] four cubits in a *karmelith* [semipublic domain]"; so after bathing on Sabbath, one may dry himself with a towel but not wring it out—the towel may be placed on the windowsill.[110]

If a deer wandered into a house on the Sabbath, trapping it would be wrong if done by one man, but permissible if done by two.[111] Women were forbidden to play with nuts or apples on Sabbath only because it might level the ground; but R. Huna said certain places were visited with destruction because "they used to play a game with ball on the Sabbath."[112] It was forbidden to read secular documents on the Sabbath.[113] Eating utensils needed for subsequent meals on Sabbath could be washed, but not if the next meal was after the Sabbath.[114]

A Gentile was not held accountable for the Sabbath, but could he work for a Jew on the Sabbath? The rule was: A Gentile must not do a Jew's work on the Sabbath, but he may do his own work.[115] There was no objection, however, if work inadvertently done by a Gentile for a Gentile also benefited a Jew; but no Sabbath work was to be done purposely for a Jew.[116]

The School of Menasseh, interpreting Isaiah 58:13, said: *"Thy* business is forbidden, but the affairs of Heaven are permitted;" hence one may make arrangements on Sabbath for betrothals and for religious instruction of a child.[117] Some religious duties were considered appropriate on Sabbath, but others were inappropriate. The rabbis took turns waiting on the scholars each Sabbath.[118] In fact, certain officials of the synagogue were paid for duties they performed on the Sabbath.[119] We have already seen that while on the Sabbath day itself one was not permitted to kindle a fire, one could on Friday kindle a fire for the Sabbath, the example par excellence being the Sabbath lights; but in the sanctuary one might even kindle a fire on Sabbath.[120]

On the other hand, certain other duties could not be performed on Sabbath. It was forbidden on that day to tithe, and tithing was usually done on the eve of the Sabbath.[121] Untithed produce could not be eaten, carried around, or even touched in the home on Sabbath. Hence every Friday evening before Sabbath a man asked his family three questions: "Have you tithed? Have you prepared the *erub?* Have you kindled the lamp?" Phylacteries were not worn on the Sabbath, and Rabbi Isaac explained it thus: "Since the Sabbath is called a sign and the phylacteries are called a sign, one should not add one sign to another." [122]

Perhaps the most ingenious casuistry was expended upon defining and circumventing the Sabbath limits *(techum)*. In Rabbinic times there were two limits with which to be concerned: 2,000 cubits, and four cubits. These were based on an interpretation of Exodus 16:29—"It was taught: 'Abide ye every man in his place' refers to the four cubits; 'let no man go out of his place' refers to the two thousand cubits." [123] The figure 2,000 was obtained from Numbers 35:5. On the Sabbath no Jew was to move more than 2,000 cubits beyond the city limits where he abode.[124] The place of abode was rather crucial. According to Rabbi Hanina, if Sabbath comes to a man on a journey, his abode is an imaginary circle with the man at its center and a radius of four cubits. If it is in an inhabited place the whole town plus 2,000 cubits outside it is the abode. If the man is in a cave, the cave is his abode.[125]

The four-cubit limit also applied to a person on shipboard.[126] But the main application of the four-cubit figure was to the basic work of "carrying," derived from Jeremiah 17:21, 22. Most objects were not to be carried from a private domain to a public one or vice versa, and no more than four cubits in the public domain.[127] Within one's private domain one could move most objects necessary, but there were even limitations in that area.[128] There were also special rules concerning a *karmelith,* an area that was neither a public nor a private domain, such as a community bath.

Obviously there would be times when the limits would be most inconvenient. There would be times, for example, when a four-cubit limit would be embarrassing to one experiencing a call of nature. The rabbis carefully discussed all the possibilities and attempted to make exact provision for them. They even went further and devised some clever circumventions: For instance, "If a man was on a journey and darkness overtook him, and he recognized a tree or a fence and said, 'Let my Sabbath resting-place be under it,' he has said nothing; but if he said, 'Let my Sabbath resting-place be at its root,' he may walk from where he stands to its root two thousand cubits, and from its root to his house two thousand cubits. Thus he can travel four thousand cubits after it has become dark." [129]

Is throwing an object different from carrying it? Yes and No. The rabbis debated the question: What if one intended to throw an object two cubits, but threw it four? They could come to no better answer than what amounts to saying, It depends. The rabbis also said: "If a man threw anything from a private domain to the public domain, . . . he is culpable; but if from a private domain to another private domain with the public domain between . . . [he is] not culpable."[130] It behooved one to have a good aim!

But the most important circumvention of the Sabbath limits was the *erub,* an institution that probably arose in the first century of our era, but which Shabbath 14b attributes to Solomon, doubtless because of its ingenuity. There were many types of *erub,*[131] but the basic idea in all of them was the fusion or pooling of Sabbath limits. To mitigate the 2,000-cubit limit, one need only deposit enough food for two meals at 2,000 cubits' distance and declare the spot his temporary abode; this device gave him twice the range he would otherwise have had.

To alleviate the limits on carrying, the residents of dwellings fronting on a common courtyard all contributed their share to a dish that could be placed in the courtyard or in one of the dwellings; by this device all the dwellings were considered common to all, and unrestricted access was had by all to all, so that anything that might be carried within one's private domicile could now be carried anywhere within the common one. This second type of *erub* was also called a *shittuf* (partnership). Needless to say, the rabbis laid down careful rules about the matter. For example, the entry into the courtyard could not be higher than twenty cubits nor wider than ten cubits,[132] but this qualification could be met, if necessary, by the installation of some temporary beams. Also, needless to say, the *erub* must be prepared before the Sabbath began,[133] hence the presundown question, "Have you prepared the *erub?*"

Punishable Sabbathbreaking

We have seen that a number of the Sabbath prohibitions are listed as resting solely on rabbinical authority.[134] About such prohibitions it was said: "The rules about the Sabbath, Festal-offerings, and Sacrilege are as mountains hanging by a hair, for Scripture thereon is scanty and the rules many."[135] But the rabbis felt that where the Scriptures were silent they had power to bind or loose, as it were, in order to safeguard the sanctity of the Sabbath. "R. Simeon says: Wheresoever the Sages have permitted aught to thee they have but given thee what is already thine, for what they have permitted thee is only that which they had withheld by virtue of the Sabbath rest."[136] If they had power to lay down a limit, they had power to modify it with exceptions and circumventions. So the rabbis commanded Jews not only to refrain from activities regarded as labor *(melakah),* but prohibited also even such activities as only detract from the restfulness *(shebuth)* of the Sabbath day.[137]

But while a clear distinction was made between a scriptural command, such as the prohibition against kindling a fire (which was punishable by death), and a purely Rabbinic precept, such as taking off the phylacteries on Sabbath,[138] this does not mean that the Rabbinic teachings were taken lightly by the pious. "R. Aibu said: Rest even from the thought of labor. A story is told, said R. Berechiah, of a pious man who took a walk in his vineyard to find out what it required. When he saw a breach in it, he resolved to repair it at the departure of the Sabbath. But then he said: Since the thought of repairing it came to me on the Sabbath, I will leave it forever unrepaired. How did the Holy One, blessed be He, reward him? A caper bush which grew up in the vineyard fenced the breach, and on the fruit of the bush he sustained himself the rest of his life." [139]

The principle of Sabbath restfulness *(shebuth)* was not always articulated into rules, but it was respected: "When the mother of R. Simeon ben Yohai used to talk too much on the Sabbath, he would say to her: 'It is Sabbath,' and she would keep silent." [140] While women were exempted, by virtue of their domestic responsibilities, from many of the Rabbinic rules, no distinction was made between man and woman in regard to the Sabbath.[141]

Perhaps the most crucial difference between the scriptural and Rabbinic Sabbath precepts was in the matter of punishments. There were three levels of punishment for Sabbathbreaking: (a) death by stoning, (b) *kareth,* and (c) liability for a sin offering.

Sabbath profanation is listed among the offenses punishable by stoning, which was the second-gravest form of capital punishment, after burning, and followed by beheading and strangling—all penalties that the Sanhedrin had power to inflict.[142] Stoning was inflicted only for cardinal offenses against the Sabbath, such as kindling a fire, prescribed in Scripture (Ex. 35:3). But such a penalty was indicated only if there were two witnesses to the act, and if the offender were warned.[143] In other words, there had to be deliberate and stubborn intent.

Kareth (cutting off), often translated "extirpation," is a punishment often referred to in the Old Testament ("that soul shall be cut off from among his people"). Kerithoth 1:1 lists thirty-six transgressions for which the Bible prescribes *kareth*. Whatever it may have meant originally, the rabbis understood it to mean divine punishment, apparently premature death; and by the time of Maimonides, at least, it was believed that a person incurring *kareth* would have no life in the world to come. Flogging or repentance could annul *kareth*.[144] Deliberate Sabbathbreaking for which there were no witnesses incurred *kareth*.[145]

If the profanation of the Sabbath was unintentional, and the offender realized his mistake, he was liable to a sin offering. "'He that profanes the Sabbath' [Num. 15:32-36] is liable, after warning, to death by stoning if he committed an act which renders him liable to Extirpation if he acted wantonly, or to a Sin-offering if he acted in error." [146] He is, however, not liable "unless the beginning and the end" of the act "were done in error." [147] Rabbi Akiba maintained that "if a man did many acts of work of the like kind on many Sabbaths during one spell of forgetfulness, he is liable to one sin-offering for all of them" [148] But if the many acts were of different kinds, or if the one act involved many differing species of Sabbathbreaking (according to the thirty-nine categories), a sin offering was required for each kind.[149] If a man "did an act of work on either a Sabbath or a weekday but it is not known on which he did the act, he must bring a Suspensive Guilt-offering [Lev. 5:17-19]." [150]

The Positive Side of Rabbinic Sabbath Observance

A recital of Rabbinic Sabbath rules such as the foregoing might give the impression that the Sabbath was considered negative and burdensome, and for many it may have been so. But such an impression in general would be one-sided and distorted. The rabbis were concerned to make the Sabbath a delight (Isa. 58:13), and it would seem that they largely succeeded. "The Holy One, blessed be He, said to Moses, I have a precious gift in My treasure house, called the Sabbath, and desire to give it to Israel; go and inform them."[151] We now view the positive side of Rabbinic Sabbath observance.

The rabbis applied their considerable exegetical ingenuity to the fact, perplexing to them, that the fourth commandment in Exodus begins "Remember" *(zekor)*, but in Deuteronomy it begins "Keep" *(shemor)*. Several theories were put forth to explain the discrepancy.[152] One often-repeated explanation was that the two different words "were pronounced in a single utterance—an utterance which the mouth cannot utter, nor the ear hear."[153] The following exposition was less metaphysical but more practical: *"Remember* and *observe.* Remember it before it comes and observe it after it has gone.—Hence they said: We should always increase what is holy by adding to it some of the non-holy.[154]—Thus it can be compared to a wolf moving backward and forward. Eleazar b. Hananiah b. Hezekiah b. Garon says: 'Remember the day of the Sabbath to keep it holy,' keep it in mind from the first day of the week on, so that if something good happens to come your way fix it up for the Sabbath. R. Isaac says: You shall not count them in the manner in which others count them. But you should count them with reference to the Sabbath."[155]

The Sabbath was thus the climax of the week; it was approached with increasing expectation and left behind reluctantly. Even in times of proclaimed fasting, it was permitted to open the shops all day on Thursday "because of the honour due to the Sabbath"; the Sabbath was to be honored with food, drink, and fresh clothing, in fulfillment of Isaiah 58:13.[156] In the spirit of Nehemiah 8:9-12, the Sabbath was to be honored by indulgence in some unusual luxury, especially food and drink; and in order to have a better appetite for the first Sabbath meal, one ate sparingly on Friday.[157] "Even a trifle, if it is prepared in honour of the Sabbath," is called Sabbath delight, and it was said that the less money a person spends for Sabbaths, the less money will he earn.[158]

On Friday the Jewish housewife baked the special bread called *challah,* from the dough of which she had separated a portion for the priests, according to Numbers 15:17-21. (After the disappearance of the Temple system, it became the custom simply to throw this portion into the fire.) Though a man might eat two meals on weekdays, it was considered meritorious to eat three meals on Sabbath—on Friday night, after the Sabbath morning services, and a light meal following the afternoon services. Rabbi Zerikah based the custom of three meals on Sabbath on Exodus 16:25, and it was said: "He who observes the practice of three meals on the Sabbath is saved from three evils: the time of trouble before the Messiah comes, the retribution of Gehinnom, and the wars of Gog and Magog."[159] Of course, all food preparation had to be done before the Sabbath, and the third and fourth chapters of the Mishnah tractate Shabbath describe devices for keeping food warm—they could not be heated on the Sabbath, but the heat they already had might be conserved.

The Sabbath was a favorite time for inviting guests to dinner, and if it was known that anyone in the community or a transient visitor was too poor to eat well that day, it was a virtuous deed to provide for him. Also, it was strictly forbidden to fast on Friday or Sabbath, or to mourn on Sabbath, the only exception being when the Day of Atonement fell on Sabbath. Not only was mourning forbidden, but it was only with difficulty that the rabbis agreed to allow mourners to be comforted and the sick to be visited on the Sabbath. When a sick person is visited, the Sabbath visitor should say, "It is Sabbath, when one must not cry out, and recovery will soon come." [160] On the Sabbath one was not even to give voice to distress in his prayers.

On Sabbaths one should not only consume a special treat but he should wear a special garment.[161] From Ruth 3:3 Rabbi Hanina inferred that "a man should have two sets of garments, one for weekdays and one for Sabbath," but when Rabbi Simlai expounded the same precept his hearers "wept and said: As our raiment on weekdays, so is our raiment on the Sabbath. He said to them: It is nevertheless necessary to change," meaning that the same garment may be worn differently.[162] Because so many Jews did make the practice of having a special Sabbath garment, the Gentiles mockingly said to one another: "How long do you wish to live?" To which the jocular reply was: "As long as the shirt of a Jew which is worn on the Sabbath!" [163]

One further indulgence encouraged on the Sabbath by the rabbis was marital relations; Psalm 1:3 was said to refer to the man who performs his marital duty every Friday night.[164] Even a wife living separately from her husband had the right to have relations with him on Friday nights.[165]

As the Sabbath drew on, the home was supposed to be especially cheery and bright.[166] There was much bustle on Friday to complete the preparations for this weekly festive occasion. In ancient Jewish communities, the approach of the Sabbath was signaled by the synagogue sexton *(chazzan)* with blasts on the *shofar* (ram's horn). According to one account, "six blasts were blown on the eve of the Sabbath. The first, for people to cease work in the fields; the second, for the city and shops to cease work; the third, for the lights to be kindled: that is R. Nathan's view. R. Judah the Nasi said: The third is for the phylacteries to be removed. Then there was an interval for as long as it takes to bake a small fish, or to put a loaf in the oven, and then a long blast, a series of short blasts, and a long blast were blown, and one commenced the Sabbath." [167] Work must be completed or stopped at least half an hour before sunset. A question on the interpretation of Exodus 20:9 arose: "But is it possible for a human being to do all his work in six days? It simply means: Rest on the Sabbath as if all your work were done. Another interpretation: Rest even from the thought of labor." [168]

The Sabbath began at sunset on Friday, and this time was anciently determined by observation: "When one star is visible, it is day; when two, it is twilight; three, it is night." [169] Although in later custom the Sabbath was ushered in by a service in the synagogue, more anciently the greeting of the Sabbath was a home affair.

Lighting of the Sabbath lamps just before sundown is one of the oldest customs for welcoming the Sabbath, apparently already an established custom in the time of Jesus.[170] With the performance of this ceremony—assigned to the woman of the household, if there was one—the Sabbath was felt to have palpably arrived.

Then came the *Kiddush* (sanctification) ceremony, which was believed to be a Biblical requirement: "'To keep it holy' [Ex. 20:8]—To consecrate it with a benediction. On the basis of this passage the sages said: At the entrance of the Sabbath we consecrate it by reciting the sanctification of the day over wine." [171] Commenting on the different ways by which God hallowed the Sabbath (Ex. 20:11), Rabbi Judah said: "God hallowed it by prescribing a blessing for it. From this teaching it follows that at the arrival of the Sabbath one declares it holy by reciting a blessing over a cup of wine." [172] Though ordinarily women were excused from observing positive precepts that depended on set times, they were required to recite or hear the recital of the Kiddush at the beginning of Sabbath.[173]

Following this the first Sabbath meal proceeded, which from early times was accompanied with singing: "When the Sabbath comes, we welcome it with psalmody and song, as it is said, 'A Psalm, a song for the Sabbath.'" [174] Later, when it became customary to gather in the synagogue for services before the Friday-evening meal, the father, upon returning home, would lay his hands on each child in turn and bless him, greet the Sabbath angels, and then recite to his wife the thirty-first chapter of Proverbs; and after this came the Kiddush and meal. Rabbi Jose reports that it was taught: "Two ministering angels accompany man on the eve of the Sabbath from the synagogue to his home, one a good angel and one an evil angel. And when he arrives home and finds the lamp burning, the table laid and the bed covered with a spread, the good angel exclaims, 'May it be even thus on another Sabbath also,' and the evil angel unwillingly responds, 'amen.' But if not, the evil angel exclaims, 'May it be even thus on another Sabbath also,' and the good angel unwillingly responds, 'amen.'" [175]

On Sabbath morning the family would arise somewhat later than usual and go to the synagogue, if it were within the Sabbath limits for them. There the ritual differed from that of other days, most notably in that the Eighteen Benedictions were reduced in number to seven, for all prayers with reference to sickness or other trials were omitted.[176]

About noon came the second Sabbath meal. Sabbath dishes were declared to be more tasty than on other days, even though cold.[177] The following story was often told: "God blessed the Sabbath with tasty dishes. Our Teacher [Judah the Prince] made a meal for Antoninus on the Sabbath. Cold dishes were set before him; he ate them and found them delicious. [On another occasion] he made a meal for him during the week, when hot dishes were set before him. Said he to him: 'Those others I enjoyed more.' 'These lack a certain condiment,' he replied. 'Does then the royal pantry lack anything?' he exclaimed. 'They lack the Sabbath,' he replied; 'do you indeed possess the Sabbath?'" [178]

After the noon meal there was a period of relaxation. Later in the afternoon one went to the Beth ha-Midrash, or synagogue school. It was thought better to attend the Sabbath-afternoon lectures than to read the Scriptures privately at that hour. This time of study, discussion, and lecture was followed by the afternoon Minha services. "It is not permitted to read the Hagiographa [on Sabbath] except from Minha time onwards, but one may recite them by heart and deliver expositions on them, and if it is required for some purpose to examine, one may take up [a copy] and examine it." [179]

Anciently, after the Minha service the family would gather before sundown for the third Sabbath meal, which was lighter than the others. As it grew dark, the sexton once again blew a blast on the shofar, and the family conducted the ceremony of *Habdalah* (separation), marking the boundary between the Sabbath and the secular time ensuing. Lights were kindled, spices on burning coals were brought in and smelled, and grace after the meal was recited over a cup of wine. The Habdalah was not concluded until an interval after sundown, for the people were loath to see the Sabbath pass; indeed, the custom of smelling spices was regarded as a consolation for its passing.

THE RABBINIC SABBATH

Most Jews looked forward to the Sabbath with anticipation of pleasure, whether rabbi or day laborer: "R. Berechiah taught in the name of R. Hiyya bar Abba: The Sabbath was given solely for enjoyment. R. Haggai said in the name of R. Samuel bar Nachman: The Sabbath was given solely for the study of Torah. And the two do not differ. What R. Berechiah said in the name of R. Hiyya bar Abba about the Sabbath's being given for enjoyment applies to the disciples of the wise who weary themselves in the study of Torah throughout the weekdays, but on the Sabbath come and enjoy themselves. What R. Haggai said in the name of R. Samuel bar Nachman about the Sabbath's being given for study of Torah applies to workingmen who are busy with their work throughout the weekdays, but on the Sabbath come and occupy themselves with the Torah." [180]

For the Jews the Sabbath was a temple in time, an irremovable place of meeting with God, the inalienable rallying point of all Jews. They read Exodus 31:17, "It is a sign... for ever," and declared, "This tells that the Sabbath will never be abolished in Israel. And so you find that anything to which the Israelites were devoted with their whole souls has been preserved among them." [181] It is worthy of note that insofar as they have preserved the Sabbath, the Sabbath has also preserved them.

NOTES

[1] This statement leaves out of account the Samaritans, who had for many generations been considered as not quite Jews. Less than a thousand of them remain today. Many groups of Diaspora (overseas) Jews remained isolated from the main stream of Jewish history, such as the Falashas, the black Jews of Ethiopia, of whom only some thirty thousand are left today. In later Jewish history other groups arose that may be regarded as throwbacks to pre-Rabbinic forms of Judaism, most notably the Karaite movement, which arose in the eighth century A.D., and Reform Judaism of contemporary America.

[2] The Nazoreans (Jewish Christians) survived by fleeing at an opportune moment to Pella beyond the Jordan. Pharisaism survived because of the dramatic escape from Jerusalem by Rabbi Johanan ben Zakkai, who received permission from the Romans to set up a school at Jabneh (Jamnia), a short distance from the Palestinian coast. The Sadducees could not survive without the Temple and its sacrifices, but the Pharisees had ready at hand the local synagogues as alternative religious centers. Though the Essenes had little to do with the Temple, as a group they seem to have been wiped out in other Roman military actions during the disastrous war. Many of them may have become Christians or Gnostics.

[3] By "classical Rabbinic Judaism" is meant primarily the religion of the Talmud; but this was further elaborated and finally codified by later rabbis, as explained below.

[4] The classic statement of this theory of the chain of tradition is in the Mishnah, Aboth 1:1. The rest of this tractate illustrates how the chain was carried on from Ezra's day to the time when the Mishnah was compiled.

[5] It may be wondered how a legal decision presented as the opinion of a rabbi could be somehow attributed to Moses. The answer is probably that the accepted Rabbinic opinions were regarded as the natural and necessary unfolding of what was contained in principle or implied by the Mosaic legislation.

[6] Judaism regards the Five Books of Moses as the primary revelation from God, and the fact that subsequently in the Old Testament further details and applications of the Mosaic laws are given is cited as proof for the necessity of a continually developing tradition. For example, the prophetic strictures against trading and bearing of burdens on the Sabbath (Amos 8:5; Jer. 17:21-24) make more explicit what is intended by the general prohibitions of labor in the Decalogue and the laws of Moses, and it is felt that this Biblical precedent for explicating and elaborating the laws legitimizes the process that was carried on by the rabbis. The opinions of the rabbis were based on their interpretations of Scripture, upon established custom, and upon clever casuistic deductions. The point was reached where the Rabbinic rulings carried more weight than the Bible, from which they were supposed to have been ultimately derived: "The words of the Scribes are more beloved than those of the Torah" (*Midrash Rabbah, The Song of Songs*, 1:2:2; cf. Ellen G. White, *Christ's Object Lessons* [Washington, D.C., 1941], p. 304). This may not have been the case in theory, but it was so in practice; if the teaching of the rabbis is a magnifying glass for reading the instruction of Moses, who would dare to read the latter without the former?

[7] References to the Mishnah are customarily made by citing the particular tractate in a manner analogous to Biblical references, thus: Shabbath 8:2. References to the Palestinian Talmud are made by prefixing "J." to the Mishnah which is being elaborated upon, thus: J. Shabbath 8:2. References to the Babylonian Talmud are customarily made according to folio enumeration, thus: Shabbath 73a (each folio in Hebrew had two sides, designated "a" and "b"). Thus the reader can tell which work is being cited by the form of the reference, even though the tractate has the same title in all. In footnotes hereafter, Shabbath will be abbreviated Shab., and Erubin will be Erub. The names of other tractates will not be abbreviated. As far as possible, only those Rabbinic works will be cited that are available in English. The most convenient translation of the Mishnah is by Herbert Danby; the standard translation of the Babylonian Talmud is the edition edited by Isidore Epstein (the Soncino edition), which we have usually but not always followed.

[8] The rabbis who are quoted in the Mishnah are called *tannaim;* they were contemporary with the New Testament writers and earliest Church Fathers.

THE SABBATH IN SCRIPTURE AND HISTORY

⁹ The rabbis who are quoted in the Gemara of the Talmuds are called *Amoraim*. The Amoraitic period ended about A.D. 550. Finishing touches were put on the Babylonian Talmud by scholars called *Saboraim*, whose period ended about A.D. 600.

¹⁰ *Mekilta* is a commentary on the legal portions of Exodus; references to it are by tractate and chapter, thus: Mek. Bachodesh 2. *Midrash Rabbah* is a series of commentaries on the Five Books of Moses and the Five Megilloth (Ruth, Lamentations, Ecclesiastes, Esther, and Song of Solomon), the scrolls that were read on the Jewish festivals. References to the *Midrash Rabbah* are hereafter made in this fashion: Gen. R. 97:2. References to the other *midrashim* will not employ abbreviations but will use the standard chapter and verse systems of those works. In addition to the works mentioned, reference will be had to the so-called Minor Tractates, which are sometimes thought of as appendexes to the Talmud; in this article their titles will be prefixed by "M.T."

¹¹ The Code of Maimonides *(Mishneh Torah)* deals with the Sabbath in Book Three, "The Book of Seasons." The translation (Yale University Press ed., New York, 1961) will be referred to as Maimonides, Code. An abridgment of the *Shulchan Aruch* has been translated (Goldin, New York, 1963); this will be referred to hereafter as Ganzfried, Code.

¹² Hullin 5a; J. Berakoth 1:5; J. Nedarim 3:14; Ex. R. 25:12; Deut. R. 4:4.
¹³ Mek. Vayassaʻ 6.
¹⁴ Pesikta Rabbati 27:4.
¹⁵ Cf. Eugene J. Lipman, *The Mishnah: Oral Teachings of Judaism* (New York, 1970), p. 79.
¹⁶ Mek. Bachodesh 8.
¹⁷ Mek. Shabbata 1.
¹⁸ Mek. Vayassaʻ 5.
¹⁹ Shab. 118b.
²⁰ Ex. R. 25:12; J. Taanith 1:1.
²¹ Pesikta Rabbati 23:2.
²² The basic meaning, "to set apart or consecrate," is behind both usages. The noun form *kiddush* is used both for the prayer of sanctification of the Sabbath and for the wedding ceremony.
²³ Pesikta Rabbati 23:6.
²⁴ Shab. 119a. For other customs and legends connected with the idea of the Sabbath as Israel's bride, see Abraham Joshua Heschel, *The Sabbath* (New York, 1966), pp. 45-62, 124-128.
²⁵ Deut. R. 1:21; cf. Ex. R. 33:7.
²⁶ Deut. R. 1:21.
²⁷ Sanhedrin 58b (my translation); Deut. R. 1:21.
²⁸ Mek. Shabbata 1; Ex. R. 25:11. Other Jews, particularly in the Diaspora, had a more universal view of the Sabbath obligation. See Robert M. Johnston, "Patriarchs, Rabbis, and Sabbath," *AUSS* 12 (1974):94-102. But while most rabbis were saying, "The Sabbath was given to *you*" (meaning Israel), Jesus was saying, "The sabbath was made for *man*" (Mark 2:27).
²⁹ Besides Johnston, see Kurt Hruby, "Le sabbat et sa célébration d'après les sources juives anciennes" (suite), *L'Orient Syrien* 8 (1963):72-79; and Jacob Z. Lauterbach, "The Sabbath in Jewish Ritual and Folklore," in *Rabbinic Essays* (Cincinnati, 1951), pp. 439, 440.
³⁰ M. T. Aboth de Rabbi Nathan 1:8 [17b]; Eccl. R. 1:2:1.
³¹ Pesikta Rabbati 23:6; 46:1. An eighth-century work that draws not only from earlier Rabbinic traditions but also from early apocalyptic pseudepigrapha *Pirke de Rabbi Eliezer*, 18 [19] (Friedlander trans., pp. 125, 126) says: "The Sabbath day arrived and became an advocate for the first man, and it spake before Him: Sovereign of all worlds! No murderer has been slain in the world during the six days of creation, and wilt Thou commence (to do this) with me [on the Sabbath]? Is this its sanctity, and is this its blessing? ... By the merit of the Sabbath day Adam was saved from the judgment of Gehinnom." It was also said that, out of consideration for Adam's fears, on the first Sabbath light continued for thirty-six hours (Midrash on Psalm 92:4).
³² *Pirke de Rabbi Eliezer*, 18 (Friedländer, p. 126).
³³ For references, see the three articles referred to in notes 28 and 29. Cf. Pesikta Rabbati 23:9.
³⁴ Ex. R. 1:28; 5:18.
³⁵ There was a Rabbinic doctrine concerning what was known as the Noachide Law, according to which the antediluvian saints were given six laws to obey: prohibitions against the worship of other gods, blaspheming the name of God, cursing judges, murder, incest, and robbery; to Noah was given the additional prohibition of eating flesh with the blood of life in it (Sanhedrin 56a, b; Gen. R. 16:6). The moral demand upon Gentiles did not go beyond these seven laws, which did not include the Sabbath.
³⁶ Cf. M.T. Soferim 42a.
³⁷ See The Book of the Secrets of Enoch 33:1-2, which may reflect Christian redaction of the same mentality that produced Barnabas 15:4-9; but see the note in *APOT*, 2:451. Cf. also *Vita Adae et Evae* 51:2, where the seventh day is "the sign of the resurrection and the rest of the age to come," which could hardly have been said by a Christian for whom the Resurrection is associated with Sunday.
³⁸ On this whole subject see Theodore Friedman, "The Sabbath: Anticipation of Redemption," *Judaism* 16 (1967):443-452; George Wesley Buchanan, "Sabbatical Eschatology," *Christian News From Israel* 18 (December, 1967):49-55. It is of interest that the New Testament book of Revelation endorses the last part of the cosmic week schema but is loudly silent about the first part (the six thousand years). It is difficult to harmonize the concept of an endless Sabbath with such a passage as this one in Midrash on Psalm 73:4—"R. Simeon said in the name of R. Simeon the Pious: In this world, if a man goes about gathering figs on a Sabbath, the fig tree says nothing at all; but in the World to Come, if a man should go to glean a fig tree on a Sabbath, the tree will call aloud to him and say: 'It is the Sabbath!'"
³⁹ Midrash on the Ten Commandments, Fourth Word; Pesikta Rabbati 23:8. The former is in German translation in August Wünsche, *Aus Israels Lehrhallen* (Leipzig, 1909; reprinted Hildesheim, 1967), 4:91.
⁴⁰ Gen. R. 11:5; Pesikta Rabbati 23:8.
⁴¹ Ex. R. 30:9.
⁴² Mek. Shabbata 2. Or perhaps the meaning is that to God, who is unlimited by sun, moon, or revolving earth, all time is alike. But such a concept would clash with other Rabbinic statements, such as the comment in Midrash on Psalm 92:2, "In all the forty years that the children of Israel were in the wilderness, God would give manna to them on

the six days of labor, but on the Sabbath the manna did not fall: not because God had no strength to send it down, but because it was Sabbath in His presence."

[43] On this general question see especially George Foot Moore, *Judaism in the First Centuries of the Christian Era: The Age of the Tannaim* (Cambridge, Mass., 1927), 2:27-32. Moore speaks of an "older Halakah" that was more stringent than that of the Pharisees and later tannaim, who sought to make the laws more practicable. It is unclear, however, whether the differences between the rules of the Mishnah and those of earlier sources (Jubilees, Zadokite Document, Dead Sea scrolls, et cetera) represent the difference between newer and older or sectarian differences. It is possible that a group such as the Essenes represents not only conservatism but also a tendency toward greater rigor. See Barbara Thiering, "The Biblical Source of Qumran Asceticism," *JBL* 93 (1974):432, 433. However that may be, there is every probability that the Pharisaic rules of Sabbathkeeping in Jesus' time were stricter and more onerous than they were later when the Mishnah was completed.

[44] These first two works are found in *APOT*, 2:1-82, 785-834. The Zadokite Document is now often called the Covenant of Damascus; it is usually included in published translations of the Dead Sea scrolls, such as that by Theodor H. Gaster, *The Dead Sea Scriptures* (Garden City, N.Y., 1956).

[45] On this general question, see especially S. T. Kimbrough, Jr., "The Concept of Sabbath at Qumran," *Revue de Qumran* 5 (1964-1966):486-501; and Judah Rosenthal, "The Sabbath Laws of the Qumranites or the Damascus Covenanters," *Biblical Research* 6 (1961):10-17. These two articles unfortunately tend to minimize the differences between the Rabbinic rules and those of the others; this comes from overlooking some of the illustrations given below. Cf. also two articles by Louis Finkelstein: "The Book of Jubilees and the Rabbinic Halaka," *Harvard Theological Review* 16 (1923):39-61; and "Some Examples of the Maccabean Halaka," *JBL* 49 (1930):20-42. On the differences in respect to Sabbath lights, see Lauterbach, *op. cit.*, pp. 458-461.

[46] 13:22, 23, 26. Gaster, *op. cit.*, p. 78, emends the latter rule to change it from a prohibition to a positive command because "this would be against the universal Jewish rule that sabbath laws may be broken in cases of life and death."—Page 104. But such an emendation fails to take into account the whole tenor of the Sabbath rules in this and cognate documents, in contrast to the Rabbinic rules. It is illegitimate to transfer Rabbinic principles to the group that produced this work. The emendation is even more unlikely on formal grounds, for the command stands in the midst of some twenty-five other commands, every one of which is a prohibition.

[47] See note in *APOT*, 2:81, 82.
[48] See Lauterbach, *op. cit.*, pp. 454-458.
[49] Cf. White, *op. cit.*, pp. 38, 39, 278, 279.
[50] Mek. Amalek 3.
[51] Shab. 19:1.
[52] Shab. 19:5.
[53] Temurah 2:1.
[54] Menahoth 11:2-3; cf. Shab. 19:1; Pesahim 6:2.
[55] Pesahim 3:6; 6:1-6; Menahoth 10:1-3, 9.
[56] Rosh ha-Shanah 1:4, 5, 9.
[57] After a thousand pious Jews allowed themselves to be massacred rather than defend themselves on the Sabbath, Mattathias and the other Jewish leaders in the struggle against Antiochus Epiphanes decided that in the future they would fight in such a situation (1 Macc 2:29-41). According to 2 Maccabees 8:25-28, after Jews defeated the army of Nicanor they ceased pursuit because the Sabbath was drawing on. There seems to have been less compunction about even routine military service on Sabbath in Old Testament times; 2 Kings 11:4-11 tells of soldiers doing guard duty and even participating in the *coup d'état* against Queen Athaliah.

[58] Gen. R. 70:15.
[59] Shab. 19a.
[60] Mek. Shabbata 1.
[61] Num. R. 23:1.
[62] Shab. 6:4.
[63] Such cases are systematically discussed by Maimonides (Code, Sabbath 2:1-25).
[64] Mek. Shabbata 1.
[65] *Ibid.* It will be seen immediately that two of these arguments are almost identical with those used by Jesus. Rabbi Eleazar's argument as it appears in *Mekilta* is virtually identical with that found in John 7:23. In Yoma 85b it is somewhat expanded: "R. Eleazar answered and said: If circumcision, which attaches to only one of the two hundred and forty-eight members of the human body, suspends the Sabbath, how much more shall the saving of the whole body suspend the Sabbath!" The saying of Simon ben Menasiah is quite similar to Mark 2:27. Because of these similarities, some Jewish scholars have insisted that Jesus was saying nothing new but merely echoing the standard humanitarianism of the Pharisees. This view runs aground on a chronological difficulty, for both Rabbi Eleazar and Rabbi Simon ben Menasiah taught two or more generations later than Jesus. I. Abrahams, *Studies in Pharisaism and the Gospels*, First Series (London, 1917), p. 130, tries to meet this difficulty by noting that in Yoma 85b Simon's saying is attributed to Jonathan ben Joseph, and "the variation in assigned authorship suggests that the saying originated with neither, but was an older tradition"; he traces the teaching ultimately to the decision of Mattathias in 1 Maccabees 2:39. To this I would reply, Abrahams is quite right in saying that the saying originated with neither rabbi, but is older—the unknown originator of the teaching was Jesus, whose striking sayings must have passed into common coinage even among nonfollowers, who would have had no reason to remember the source, and indeed every reason not to recall it. There is no verbal parallel in 1 Maccabees, nor any statement of a general principle.

[66] Sanhedrin 74a; Yoma 85a; and elsewhere.
[67] Sanhedrin 74a. Rabbi Ishmael's dictum is attributed to Rabbi Samuel in Yoma 85b, where it occurs in the same context as the saying of Rabbi Eleazar and the saying attributed there to Jonathan ben Joseph but in *Mekilta* to Simon ben Menasiah. The saying that *Mekilta* attributes to Rabbi Nathan is assigned by Yoma 85b to Simon ben Menasiah.

[68] *Ibid.*
[69] Sanhedrin 74b.
[70] Yoma 8:6; 84a, b.
[71] Shab. 18:3; 22:6.
[72] Taanith 3:7.

[73] Yoma 84b.
[74] *Ibid.*; but see also Shab. 16:1-6.
[75] I. Grunfeld, *The Sabbath: A Guide to Its Understanding and Observance* (Jerusalem, 1972), p. 19, concludes to define a *melakah* as "an act that shows man's mastery over the world by the constructive exercise of his intelligence and skill."
[76] Shab. 7:2. Cf. Mek. Shabbata 2; Shab. 97b.
[77] Shab. 22:1.
[78] For this reason Orthodox Jews who find it necessary to milk cows on Sabbath pour out the milk obtained rather than receive any benefit from it.
[79] Peshahim 4:8.
[80] Betzah 1:1; Betzah 2a-4b; Shab. 43a.
[81] Shab. 75b.
[82] Erub. 104a; Mek. Pischa, 6.
[83] Maimonides, Code, Sabbath 12:3.
[84] Shab. 16:6, 1; 117b.
[85] Shab. 1:3.
[86] Shab. 12a.
[87] Betzah 5:2; Mek. Shabbata 2; Shab. 23:4, 5.
[88] Shab. 12:1-6; Shab. 73b; Sukkah 3:14; cf. Maimonides, Code, Sabbath 1:6.
[89] Shab. 22:3-5.
[90] Cf. Terumoth 2:3.
[91] Sanhedrin 62b.
[92] Shab. 38a.
[93] Cf. Shab. 46b.
[94] Shebiith 10:7; Betzah 5:1.
[95] Shab. 16:1, 2; Ruth R. 6:4.
[96] Shab. 21:2, 3.
[97] Shab. 21:1.
[98] Yebamoth 113b-114a.
[99] Shab. 3:1-5; 4:1, 2; 22:4.
[100] Shab. 10:2, 5; 20:5; Mek. Shabbata 1.
[101] Shab. 1:5, 10, 11; 18a.
[102] Shab. 22:6; 18a.
[103] M.T. Semahoth 46a.
[104] Shab. 23:5; cf. Ruth R. 3:2.
[105] Eccl. R. 5:10:2.
[106] Shab. 24:2-4; Ruth R. 3:2.
[107] Shab. 39b-40b.
[108] Betzah 2:2.
[109] Lev. R. 34:16.
[110] Shab. 141a, 147b.
[111] Shab. 13:5-7.
[112] Erub. 104a; Lam. R. 2:2:4.
[113] M.T. Soferim 41a.
[114] Shab. 118a.
[115] Mek. Pischa 9.
[116] Shab. 23:4.
[117] Shab. 150a.
[118] Shab. 74a.
[119] M.T. Kallah Rabbathi 55a.
[120] Mek. Shab. 2.
[121] Shab. 2:7; Demai 4:1.
[122] Mek. Pischa 17.
[123] Erub. 51a; Mek. Vayassaᶜ, 6.
[124] Erub. 4:1, 3; 5:7.
[125] Num. R. 2:9; Erub. 41b.
[126] Erub. 4:1.
[127] Horayoth 1:3; Shab. 7:4-8:7; 9:5-7; 10:1-5.
[128] Shab. 17:1-8; 18:1, 2.
[129] Erub. 4:7.
[130] Shab. 73a and 11:1.
[131] Hruby, *op. cit.*, pp. 449-451.
[132] Erub. 1:1.
[133] Mek. Vayassaᶜ 3.
[134] Betzah 5:2.
[135] Hagigah 1:8.
[136] Erub. 10:15.
[137] Mek. Shabbata 1.
[138] Cf. M.T. Aboth de Rabbi Nathan 27a.
[139] Pesikta Rabbati 23:3.
[140] Lev. R. 34:16; Pesikta Rabbati 23:3.
[141] Mek. Bachodesh 8.
[142] Sanhedrin 7:4, 1.
[143] Mek. Shabbata 1; Sanhedrin 7:4; 7:8.
[144] Makkoth 13a, b.
[145] Kerithoth 1:1.

[146] Sanhedrin 7:8.
[147] Shab. 11:6.
[148] Kerithoth 3:10.
[149] Shab. 72b.
[150] Kerithoth 4:1.
[151] Shab. 10b.
[152] Mek. Bachodesh 7; Pesikta Rabbati 23:1; et cetera.
[153] Shebuoth 20b.
[154] Gen. R. 9:14 advocates adding an extra hour to Sabbath, taken from Friday.
[155] Mek. Bachodesh 7.
[156] Taanith 1:6; Midrash on Psalm 92:3.
[157] Pesikta Rabbati 23:6, 7; Peshahim 99b.
[158] Shab. 118b; Lev. R. 30:1.
[159] Mek. Vayassa^c 5; Shab. 118a.
[160] Gen. R. 100:7; Shab. 12b.
[161] Shab. 113a; Gen. R. 11:2; Num. R. 10:1; Pesikta Rabbati 23:1.
[162] Ruth R. 5:12.
[163] Lam. R., Proem 17.
[164] Nedarim 8:6; 3:10; Baba Kama 82a; Niddah 38a, b; Kethuboth 62b. The expression "eat garlic," used in some of these references, is generally taken to be an euphemism.
[165] Kethuboth 5:9, interpreted in Kethuboth 65b.
[166] Shab. 23b, 25b.
[167] Shab. 35b. Since one should not bear burdens on the Sabbath, and the last blast of the *shofar* marked the beginning of the Sabbath, a quandary arose: What did the *chazzan* do with his *shofar* after the six blasts? Rabbi Jose ben Hanina said he allowed time to carry it home, blowing it a little early, but the rest of the rabbis said he "had a hidden place on the top of his roof, where he placed his *shofar*, because neither a *shofar* nor a trumpet may be handled on the Sabbath" (touching musical instruments violated the Sabbath *muktzeh* laws). Others said that the instruments may be moved as part of a ceremonial duty (Shab. 36a).
[168] Mek. Bachodesh 7.
[169] Shab. 35b.
[170] On the history of this custom, see Lauterbach, *op. cit.*, pp. 454-470. On Exodus 13:22 there is a Rabbinic comment: "This passage suggests that you can learn from the Torah what the proper custom on the eve of the Sabbath should be. The pillar of fire should shine forth while the pillar of the cloud is still present" (Mek. Beshallach, 1), meaning that the Sabbath lights should be kindled on Friday when there is still daylight. (For more details about Sabbath ritual, with references, see the works by Segal, Millgram, and Schauss.)
[171] Mek. Bachodesh 7.
[172] Pesikta Rabbati 23:6.
[173] Shebuoth 20b.
[174] Midrash on Psalm 92:3.
[175] Shab. 119b.
[176] Midrash on Psalm 29:2.
[177] Pesikta Rabbati 23:8.
[178] Gen. R. 11:4; Shab. 119a.
[179] Lev. R. 15:4.
[180] Pesikta Rabbati 23:9.
[181] Mek. Shabbata 1.

CHAPTER 5

The Sabbath in the New Testament

Walter F. Specht

CHRISTIANS accept the New Testament as normative for belief and life. It is therefore of importance to examine what the New Testament has to say about the Sabbath. This is especially important since the majority of Christians today regard the Sabbath as Jewish and believe that Jesus and/or His apostles changed the day of rest from the seventh to the first day, the day on which Christ arose from the dead.

Sabbaton, the Greek word for "Sabbath," is found sixty-seven times in the critical text of the Greek New Testament. The plural of this word, *sabbata,* may be regarded as a transliteration of the Aramaic, *shabbeta,* the emphatic state of the singular noun, meaning "the Sabbath."[1] In its Greek transliteration it was apparently taken as a plural, and hence the singular *sabbaton* was constructed from it. Another possible explanation is to regard the singular as a transliteration of the Hebrew *shabbath,* whereas the plural came from the Aramaic.[2]

Lexicographers recognize two clearly differentiated meanings for *sabbaton* in the New Testament: (1) Sabbath, the seventh day of the week, and (2) the period of seven days between Sabbaths, i.e., *week.*[3] The second meaning is demanded when *sabbaton* or *sabbata* is used in a genitive construction with a numeral: a clear example is found in Luke 18:12, where the Pharisee boasts, "I fast twice a week," *dis tou sabbatou.* It would obviously not make sense to translate: "I fast twice on Sabbath." It is well known that the Pharisees fasted on Mondays and Thursdays. In seven passages (eight if the long ending of Mark is included),[4] the first day of the week is designated by the numeral "one" and the genitive of *sabbaton,* mostly in the plural.[5] The fact that the numeral is feminine indicates that the feminine noun "day" is to be understood. The regular Greek word for "week," *hebdomas,* which had been used in the Septuagint, is not found in the New Testament.

The idiom used for the days of the week occurs in the Greek titles of a few of the psalms in the Greek version. Psalm 24 (Psalm 23, Septuagint) is designated *tēs mias sabbatōn,* "for the first day of the week." Psalm 48 (Psalm 47, Septuagint) has in its title *deutera sabbatou,* "for the second day of the week." Psalm 94 (Psalm 93, Septuagint) is designated as *tetradi sabbatou,* "for the fourth day of the week" (Wednesday). Most probably these originally meant the first, second, and fourth days after the Sabbath. Friday, however, was known as *prosabbaton,* and Psalm 92 (Psalm 91, Septuagint) was, according to the title, used in the temple ritual for that day.

In the New Testament passages where *sabbaton* means "Sabbath," the word occurs forty times in the singular and nineteen times in the plural. But in most of the occurrences of the word in the plural, the context makes it clear that a single day is intended.[6] As a matter of fact, in the Gospels and Acts, the only clear instance in which *sabbata* is plural in meaning is in Acts 17:2, where the numeral "three" used with it demands that more than one Sabbath is meant. The Revised Standard Version, however, translates *sabbata* in this passage as "weeks." In passages where *sabbaton* clearly means Sabbath, there is no consistency in usage between the singular and the plural when a single day is intended. In the story of the plucking of heads of wheat on the Sabbath, Matthew uses the plural in chapter 12:1 and the singular in chapter 12:2. Luke's usage is in reverse with the singular in chapter 6:1 and the plural in chapter 6:2. In the story of the healing of the man with the withered hand, Matthew 12:10-12 and Mark 3:2-4 use the plural, whereas the parallel in Luke 6:6-9 has the singular.

Similarly in the Septuagint the plural is sometimes used where the original Hebrew has the singular, and where it is obvious that the reference is to a single day.[7] There may be a parallel here to the custom of using the Greek plural for festivals such as the Feast of Dedication (John 10:22), the Feast of Unleavened Bread (Mark 14:1), a marriage feast (Matt. 22:2), or a birthday celebration (Mark 6:21).[8]

The Sabbath in the Gospels

Of the sixty-seven occurrences of the term *sabbaton* in the Greek New Testament, fifty-six are found in the Gospels: eleven in Matthew, twelve in Mark, twenty in Luke, and thirteen in John. In six of these references *sabbaton* means "week." Five of these speak of the "first day of the week," the day on which our Lord arose from the dead. The remaining fifty refer to the Sabbath, the seventh day of the week.

The Sabbath Service in Nazareth.—According to the Gospel of Luke, Jesus, near the beginning of His Galilean ministry, visited His hometown of Nazareth. "And he came to Nazareth, where he had been brought up" (Luke 4:16).* Nazareth was the hometown of both Joseph and Mary, and following the return from the flight into Egypt of the holy family, they returned to this insignificant mountain village in Galilee (Matt. 2:23). It is called "their own city" (Luke 2:39), and became the childhood home of Jesus, where He lived till He was about 30 years of age (chap. 3:23). His return there after He began His public ministry was, consequently, a source of curious interest on the part of the villagers who had known Him so many years.

"And he went to the synagogue, as his custom was, on the sabbath day" (chap. 4:16). Two interpretations of the phrase "as his custom was" are given by commentators.[9] Some would restrict the reference to Jesus' teaching ministry in the Jewish synagogue (verse 15): "As his custom was," as a teacher, He entered the synagogue in Nazareth on the Sabbath day. Others understand the phrase as a

---

* Unless otherwise indicated, all Scripture references in this chapter are from the Revised Standard Version.

reference to the years Jesus lived in Nazareth. Alfred Plummer, for example, has written: "It had been 'His custom' during His early life at Nazareth to attend the synagogue every sabbath."[10] Ralph Earle states: "'As his custom was' (verse 16) points to a lifelong habit of attending the synagogue on the sabbath day."[11]

But whichever view is correct, it is evident that Jesus, as a loyal Israelite, was a Sabbath observer. Paul Jewett boldly states: "There can be little doubt, then, that Jesus, as a devout Jew, observed the Sabbath. To feature Him as the grand innovator, who swept it aside in the name of liberty, is to remake Jesus in the image of the Enlightenment."[12] On the occasion referred to in Luke 4, He stood up in the synagogue and read from Isaiah 61. Then He sat down to interpret the passage as a reference to Himself and His mission. His work is to be understood in terms of Isaiah's "Servant of Yahweh." Jesus proclaims that the prophetic scriptures find their fulfillment in Him as the Servant of God.

The Sabbath Controversies.—All four Gospels bear witness to the fact that the Sabbath was one of the main areas of conflict between Jesus and the Jews. It may be well to raise the questions: Why did these controversies take place? What were they about? Why did the Gospel writers regard them of sufficient importance as to record them for the instruction of the church?

A careful study of these controversies shows that the point at issue was not whether the Sabbath should be kept or not. Sampey was correct when he asserted: "There is no reason to think that Jesus meant to discredit the Sabbath as an institution."[13]

Jesus Himself asserted, as *The New English Bible* translates His words: "'Do not suppose that I have come to abolish the Law and the prophets; I did not come to abolish, but to complete'" (Matt. 5:17).

What then was the issue? Plainly it was the manner of Sabbathkeeping. The question was not Should the Sabbath be kept? Rather, it was How should the Sabbath be kept? The Pharisees insisted that it be kept according to the oral rules that the rabbis had developed down through the years. "Jesus did not reject the institution of the Sabbath as such, but only the tradition of the elders regarding Sabbathkeeping."[14] He refused to abide by the man-made rabbinical rules for Sabbath observance, by which the Sabbath had become a burden instead of a blessing.

One has only to read the tractate Shabbath in the Mishnah to realize the extent of these rules.* It seems that Jesus deliberately challenged these oral traditions. He sought to free the Sabbath from burdensome restrictions, and make it a day of spiritual freedom and joy.

The Evangelists regarded these conflicts as of sufficient importance for the church to include them in their Gospel accounts. The church was not to observe the Sabbath according to these rules, but rather as a day of helpful service after the pattern of the Master. It is lawful to do good on that day. He who observes the Sabbath merely as a legalistic requirement will never receive the blessing God intended it to bring. Thus the church did not reject the institution as such, but it did reject the man-made rules for observing it.

The Conflict Over Plucking Grain on the Sabbath.—The first Sabbath conflict that is recorded in all three of the Synoptics (Matt. 12:1-8; Mark 2:23-28;

---

* For some of the details, see chapter 4.

THE SABBATH IN THE NEW TESTAMENT

Luke 6:1-5) concerned the legality of the disciples' act in plucking heads of wheat on the sacred day. Jesus and His disciples were going through some grain fields on a Sabbath. The disciples were hungry (Matt. 12:1), and they plucked some heads of wheat and, after "rubbing them in their hands" (Luke 6:1), ate the grain. Thereupon the Pharisees accused them of an unlawful act. The legitimacy of plucking heads of grain from someone's field was not in dispute. The Old Testament law had provided: "When you go into your neighbor's standing grain, you may pluck the ears with your hand, but you shall not put a sickle to your neighbor's standing grain" (Deut. 23:25). But the Pharisees branded their act as unlawful because they were engaged in work on the Sabbath.

The Old Testament law forbade agricultural activity on the day of rest: "'Six days you shall work, but on the seventh day you shall rest; in plowing time and in harvest you shall rest'" (Ex. 34:21). As noted in chapter 4, the Mishnah specified thirty-nine main categories of work that were forbidden on the Sabbath.[15] These included reaping, threshing, winnowing, and grinding. The Pharisees evidently interpreted plucking as reaping, rubbing the heads in one's hands as threshing, and blowing away the chaff as winnowing. Hence, the disciples were working, even though a very small amount of grain was involved. The Mishnah declares that a person is guilty who takes "ears of grain equal to a lamb's mouthful."[16]

"Among the scribes it was assumed that a teacher was responsible for the behavior of his disciples."[17] Hence the Pharisees confronted Jesus with the challenge: "'Look, why are they doing what is not lawful on the sabbath?'" (Mark 2:24).

Matthew gives the challenge in the form of a statement: "'Look, your disciples are doing what is not lawful to do on the sabbath'" (Matt. 12:2). In Luke the challenge is given to the disciples: "'Why are you doing what is not lawful to do on the sabbath?'" (Luke 6:2).

Jesus, however, declared that they were guiltless (Matt. 12:7) in satisfying their hunger. In their defense He first of all cited the example of David: "'Have you never read what David did, when he was in need and was hungry, he and . . . those who were with him?'" (Mark 2:25). In his flight from Saul, David went to Ahimelech the priest,[18] and upon his request was given the sacred "bread of the Presence" to share with his men (1 Sam. 21:1-6), which only the priests were to eat (Lev. 24:9). The point here seems to be that David was the anointed of the Lord, with all that this implied. If it was right for the anointed David and his hungry companions to eat the holy bread belonging to the priests, how much more could the hungry disciples of the Son of David violate the scribal rules about the sacred Sabbath.

Most likely the bread that David received was not that which was in God's presence on the table in the holy place, but rather that which had been removed to be replaced by freshly baked loaves (1 Sam. 21:6). The day on which the exchange of the new for the old was made was the Sabbath. In the view of some rabbis, the day on which David received the loaves was the Sabbath.[19] The scripture does not state the day of the week, but if it was indeed the Sabbath, then the example of David would be even more apropros.

According to the Gospel of Matthew, Jesus also cited the example of the priests from the law itself as a precedent for the action of the disciples: "'Or have you not read in the law how on the sabbath the priests in the temple profane the sabbath, and are guiltless?'" (Matt. 12:5). On the Sabbath, as already noted, the old loaves of "the bread of the Presence" were removed and fresh loaves put on the table. There was incense to be offered, and the daily burnt offerings were doubled on the Sabbath (Num. 28:9, 10). Hence there were animals to be slain, wood to be prepared and placed on the altar, et cetera. Thus, as Maimonides put it centuries later, there was "no Sabbatism in the Temple."[20] The priests actually worked harder on the Sabbath than on any other day of the week. But their work was not sinful, because it was in the service of God. Their priestly service was justifiable work, because it was sacred, not secular.

The argument based on this example rests on a famous principle of hermeneutics termed *qal wahomer,* that is, "the light and weighty," applied to an actual precept of the law.[21] The Christological statement in Matthew 12:6 is indeed significant: "'I tell you, something greater than the temple is here.'" It is an assertion that our Lord is superior to the Jewish regulations of worship. He is greater than the Temple and its cultus. It was to Him and His work as both priest and sacrifice that the Temple services pointed forward. He came to earth as the Redeemer of the world. His disciples were associated with Him in the great work of redeeming mankind, a work that was sacred, not secular. Hence it was right for them to satisfy their physical hunger to receive strength to carry on their work further.

The real nature of the Sabbath was often gravely misunderstood. Mere cessation of labor was not the essence of the Sabbath. It was never God's intention that the Sabbath be made a day of useless inactivity. The Sabbath was to be a day when man forsook his secular pursuits and devoted the day to worship and to the service of God.

According to Matthew, Jesus also referred to some well-known words of the prophet Hosea: "'And if you had known what this means, "I desire mercy, and not sacrifice," you would not have condemned the guiltless'" (Matt. 12:7). Jesus had come to establish the rule of the kingdom of God. In the eyes of a gracious God, mercy is of far more importance than a legalistic obedience to the law. Hence on another occasion our Lord accused the scribes and Pharisees of neglecting the weightier matters such as "'justice and mercy and faith,'" while meticulously tithing "'mint and dill and cummin'" (chap. 23:23).

In Mark's account (chap. 2:27), Jesus then raised the issue of the purpose of the Sabbath. The Sabbath was not an end in itself. "The sabbath was made for man, and not man for the sabbath." It was designed to be a blessing to man, a day of physical rest, but also a day devoted to spiritual exercises. The Pharisees treated the day as though man were created to serve the Sabbath, rather than the Sabbath meeting the needs of man. R. Shim'on ben Menasya about A.D. 180 made a similar statement: "The Sabbath is given over to you but you are not surrendered to the Sabbath."[22] E. Lohse asserts: "But in such sayings the rabbis are not in any way attacking the Sabbath commandment. They are simply saying that in exceptional cases the Sabbath may be infringed to save human life. In Mark 2:27, however, man and his needs are said to be of greater value than the commandment."[23]

All three of the Synoptic Gospels record the concluding statement, "The Son of man is Lord even of the sabbath" (Mark 2:28; Matt. 12:8; Luke 6:5). This statement asserts Christ's sovereignty over the Sabbath. He, after all, was with our heavenly Father when the Sabbath was made (John 1:1-3). Therefore He, rather than the scribes and Pharisees, has the authority to state what is lawful and not lawful to do on the day of rest. It was not the Sabbath law itself that Jesus' disciples had violated, but the man-made pharisaical regulations regarding Sabbath observance. Jesus on more than one occasion completely ignored the oral law so dear to the Pharisees.

The text of Codex Bezae, the leading representative of the so-called "western" type of text, varies strikingly from that of most New Testament manuscripts. The saying regarding the lordship of Christ over the Sabbath (Luke 6:5) is placed after verse 10. Between verses 4 and 6 this manuscript reads: "On the same day, seeing one working on the Sabbath day, he said to him, 'Man, if you know what you are doing, you are blessed; but if you do not know, you are accursed and a transgressor of the law.'" Thus this manuscript adds another Sabbath incident to the series. Although this verse has little claim to be a part of the original text of Luke, Bruce Metzger thinks that "it may well embody a first-century tradition." [24]

Healings on the Sabbath.—Mark and Luke describe the healing of a demoniac who interrupted the synagogue service on a Sabbath in Capernaum (Mark 1:21-28; Luke 4:31-37). Jesus was teaching in the synagogue, and the people were astonished at His teaching. When the man "who had the spirit of an unclean demon" (Luke 4:33) cried out in the service, Jesus commanded the demon: "'Be silent, and come out of him!'" (verse 35). Thereupon after convulsing the man, the demon came out. The reaction of the worshipers was: "'What is this? A new teaching! With authority he commands even the unclean spirits, and they obey him'" (Mark 1:27). Evidently the issue of healing on Sabbath was not raised on this occasion. Later, apparently on the same Sabbath, Jesus healed Peter's mother-in-law of a high fever in Peter's house in Capernaum (Matt. 8:14, 15; Mark 1:29-31; Luke 4:38, 39). There is no record of a controversy connected with either of these healings.

However, the Synoptic Gospels record another healing on the Sabbath that did give rise to controversy: the healing of the man with the withered hand (Matt. 12:9-14; Mark 3:1-6; Luke 6:6-11). Perhaps by this time the scribes and Pharisees were fully aware that Jesus did not allow the Sabbath to interrupt His healing ministry, and they were ready for a confrontation.

Later Jesus again entered the synagogue at Capernaum and began teaching. A man was present whose right hand (Luke 6:6) was withered, indicating some kind of paralysis. According to the Mishnah, a sick or injured person could be treated on the Sabbath only if life was actually in danger: "Whenever there is doubt whether life is in danger this overrides the Sabbath." [25] The case of the man was obviously not covered by this provision, since the withered hand presented no immediate threat to life. Hence the scribes and Pharisees were watching closely to see what Jesus would do, in order to have a case against Him. According to Matthew (12:10), they in fact asked Him, "Is it lawful to heal on the sabbath?" (Interestingly, the apocryphal Gospel according to the Hebrews, as stated by Jerome, presents the man as pleading: "I was a mason, seeking a living with my hands; I beg you, Jesus, restore my health to me, so that I need not beg for my food in shame." [26])

What should Jesus do in such a situation? He first of all had the man stand up so that all could see him. Matthew relates that He then answered the question of the Pharisees by asking a counterquestion that required an affirmative answer: "'What man of you, if he has one sheep and it falls into a pit on the sabbath, will not lay hold of it and lift it out?'" (Matt. 12:11). While there were rabbis who would not allow an animal to be rescued on the Sabbath, they at least allowed it to be made comfortable in the pit.[27] Should one be more considerate of an animal than a human being? "'Of how much more value is a man than a sheep!'" (verse 12).

According to the accounts in Mark and Luke, Jesus confronted the Pharisees with the question: "'Is it lawful on the sabbath to do good or to do harm, to save life or to kill?'" (Mark 3:4).[28] They could not, of course, say that it was lawful to do harm, and they would not say it was lawful to do good. Hence they remained silent. C. E. B. Cranfield is correct in asserting: "To omit to do the good which one could do to someone in need is to do evil."[29] To leave a man with a withered hand "in his deformed condition was to destroy him insofar as a full, complete life was concerned. . . . So simply to do nothing for the poor man was to do evil, to destroy him."[30]

Jesus then "looked around at them with anger, grieved at their hardness of heart" (verse 5). Gustav Stählin gives two reasons for this anger: "It is first the wrath of the merciful Lord at legalists who will not accept the new way of mercy and salvation, and who thus allow themselves to be carried away by mercilessness and even mortal enmity (verse 6). It is secondly the wrath of love, which seeks to win even the Pharisees for the kingdom of mercy and which encounters only hate because they want law, not love. There is thus mixed with holy wrath a divine pity for their piety which is so far from God."[31]

Jesus then commanded the man to stretch out his hand. When he did so, it was restored. This led the Pharisees to conspire with the Herodians as to how to do away with Jesus. Thus while they were unwilling to see a man with a deformed hand restored on the Sabbath, they felt no compunctions about plotting the death of one they hated. Thereby they gave their answer to the question: "'Is it lawful on the sabbath to do good or to do harm, to save life or to destroy it?'" On the other hand Jesus set forth the principle "It is lawful to do good on the sabbath" (Matt. 12:12). F. F. Bruce summarizes Jesus' position:

"Instead of following the sabbath law as expounded in the schools of Hillel or Shammai, Jesus insisted that, since the sabbath was given to men for their relief and well-being, any action which promoted that end was specially appropriate to the sabbath day. The rabbis would have agreed that, in an urgent case of life or death, medical attention might be given on the sabbath day, but if the patient could without danger wait until the next day, then the healing action should be postponed. Jesus argued on the contrary that the sabbath was a pre-eminently suitable day for the performance of such works of mercy, whether the case was urgent or not, since such works were so completely in keeping with God's purpose in giving the day. On the other hand, anything that tended to make the sabbath law burdensome conflicted with that purpose."[32]

Sabbath Healings Peculiar to Luke.—The Gospel of Luke records two other Sabbath healings, which also provoked controversy. One of these, given in Luke 13:10-17, was the healing of "a woman who had had a spirit of infirmity for eighteen years; she was bent over and could not fully straighten herself." The statement that she had "a spirit of infirmity" suggests that her illness was a result of the power of demons. Jesus immediately healed her by announcing to her that she was cured and by laying His hands upon her. As contrasted with the previous controversy, in this instance the healing came first and the debate followed.

The opposition originated with the "ruler of the synagogue," who was angry with Jesus but scolded the congregation instead: "'There are six days on which work ought to be done; come on those days and be healed, and not on the sabbath day'" (verse 14). Jesus called this man and all who accepted his interpretation "'You hypocrites!'" He proceeded to show how they had concern for the well-being of animals on Sabbath, but no genuine concern for the welfare of people. Are animals more important than people? The values of an institution such as the Sabbath were not to be placed above human values. T. W. Manson interprets: "You undo the bonds of your draught animals to refresh them, and you feel that this is no infringement of the holy day, but you protest against the release of a human creature, a daughter of Abraham, from which Satan—the source of the evil spirit—has clamped upon her not for a day but for eighteen years!" [33]

The woman's illness was not the will of God. She was bound by Satan. Should not God bring her freedom even on Sabbath? W. F. Arndt calls attention to the powerful antithesis in Jesus' *a fortiori* argument: "a daughter of Abraham—animals; eighteen years of suffering—thirst for one day; a bond of Satan—a mere physical lack." [34] Not only should such a woman be allowed liberation on Sabbath, she ought to be freed. Where there is power to free such a one, there is the obligation to do so.

On this occasion Jesus won the controversy: "All his adversaries were put to shame; and all the people rejoiced at all the glorious things that were done by him" (Luke 13:17).

The other Sabbath healing recorded only in Luke was that of the healing of a man with the dropsy (chap. 14:1-4). The miracle occurred in the home of a "ruler who belonged to the Pharisees" where Jesus was a Sabbath dinner guest. The presence of a man suffering from dropsy presented Jesus with a challenge. He grasped the initiative by asking, "'Is it lawful to heal on the sabbath, or not?'" These lawyers and Pharisees "could not answer yes or no without appearing either lax in their attitude to the Law or harsh and unsympathetic towards suffering." [35] Hence they gave no answer. Jesus then proceeded to heal the man.

He then asked: "'Which of you, having an ass or an ox that has fallen into a well, will not immediately pull him out on a sabbath day?'" The Old Testament law laid down the obligation of helping an animal in need that belonged to a brother or even an enemy.[36] But nothing is said about rendering such help on the Sabbath day, and the rabbis varied in their interpretation.[37] Apparently, Jesus was on common ground with His theological opponents in approving humane action to animals in need.[38] But if an animal can be helped, why not a man? Neither the host nor the guests had an answer to that question.

Sabbath Healings Peculiar to John.—Two Sabbath healings that brought Jesus into sharp conflict with the Jews are recorded exclusively in the Gospel of John. One was the healing of the lame man at the pool of Bethesda (John 5:1-9). While Jesus was in Jerusalem at "a feast of the Jews" He saw a chronic invalid of thirty-eight years lying in one of the porticoes surrounding the pool, waiting for the troubling of the waters. The pool apparently was fed by an intermittent spring. A popular superstition explained this natural phenomenon as a supernatural troubling of the water by an angel.[39] Jesus asked the unfortunate man, "'Do you want to be healed?'" Then He commanded, "'Rise, take up your pallet, and walk.'" By faith the man set his will to obey the command, and in doing so received healing and restoration. He demonstrated the reality and completeness of his cure by walking and carrying home the pallet on which he had been lying.

It is only at the conclusion of the account of the miracle that John informs us that it occurred on the Sabbath (verse 9b). It was an open challenge to the rabbinical rules of Sabbathkeeping. The man who was healed was not in acute danger of losing his life, and could, therefore, have waited for healing until after the Sabbath.[40]

In addition the healed man violated one of the thirty-nine principal kinds of labor forbidden on the Sabbath by carrying his pallet.[41] The Jews lost no time in reminding him that by carrying this mat he was doing something unlawful on the Sabbath. The man, however, in his new-found health, felt no compunctions of conscience in obeying Christ's command. Since Jesus was the source of life and wholeness to him, why should He not also be the source of proper laws? When the Jews learned that the healer was indeed Jesus, as they had suspected, they began to take hostile action against Him (verse 16). The Greek suggests that this was not because of a single violation, but because it had become a habit. *The New English Bible* rendering is: "It was works of this kind done on the Sabbath that stirred the Jews to persecute Jesus."

Jesus' defense of His action rests on two basic premises: (1) His intimate relationship with God the Father; and (2) the fact, admitted by the Jews, that God continued to work on the Sabbath. "'My Father is working still, and I am working'" (verse 17). He thus claimed the example of His Father for doing these miracles of mercy. C. H. Dodd aptly observes: "This puts the controversy at once on the highest theological level."[42] The designation "My Father" significantly points to Jesus' consciousness of a special relationship to God. The continuous, round-the-clock activity of God in the universe constitutes an example for Jesus. He works like the Father.

Thoughtful Jewish exegetes had difficulty in understanding God's resting referred to in Genesis 2:2. How to interpret God's rest was the subject of much discussion. It was generally recognized that God could not rest even for a moment from the moral governance of the universe. Even on the Sabbath day God continues to give life and to judge men, they concluded.

It would indeed be tragic for the universe and for man if God ceased even for a moment to govern the universe. God is ceaselessly at work in the operations of the natural world. He is also constantly engaged in the work of redemption. From such work there is no rest, no Sabbath. Sabbaths have never hindered the work of God. Neither must they, Jesus asserted, hinder the work of God's Son. He regarded His work as equally sacred, and of the same character as the work of the Father.

John 5:18 indicates that the Jews well understood the high claims that Jesus made for Himself, but they rejected these claims as unjustified. They regarded His claim to a unique relation to God as nothing less than blasphemy. Jesus, however, replied (verse 19) that He did not work independently of God. He did only the things He saw His Father doing. He worked not only like the Father but with the Father. He did the same works because He was of the same nature as the Father. The fact that His statement is introduced with the words "truly, truly" implies a finality and authority to His saying. He speaks in the name and with the authority of God. With the question of that authority the rest of the chapter is concerned.

The argument is resumed in John 7:19-24. Ever since the Sabbath healing of the impotent man at the pool, the Jews in Jerusalem were intent on Jesus' destruction (chaps. 5:18; 7:1). How could they claim to keep the Mosaic law while they cherished hatred and murder in their hearts? How could they justify their interpretation that circumcision overrides the Sabbath while they regarded healings as violating it?

The "one deed" to which reference is made in John 7:21 was the healing at the pool, which caused the multitude to marvel, but which also resulted in a long discussion related in chapter 5. Jesus called attention to the Pharisaic interpretation that circumcision overrides the Sabbath. The Mosaic law required that a baby boy be circumcised on the eighth day (Lev. 12:3). Rabbi Jose had declared: "Great is circumcision which overrides even the rigour of the Sabbath."[43] Whatever was necessary for this rite could be done on the Sabbath.[44] Circumcision was regarded as completing man's perfection. Abraham was not regarded as perfect until he was circumcised.

Jesus argued, "'If on the sabbath a man receives circumcision, so that the law of Moses may not be broken, are you angry with me because on the sabbath I made a man's whole body well?'" (John 7:23). It is an argument *a minori ad maius*, from the lesser to the greater.

Leon Morris has stated: "Had they understood the significance of what they were doing they would have seen that a practice which overrode the sabbath in order to provide for the ceremonial needs of a man justified the overriding of the sabbath in order to provide for the bodily healing of a man. This is a most important point for an understanding of the sabbath controversy between Jesus and His legalistic opponents. He was not arguing simply that a repressive law be liberalized. Nor did He adopt an anti-sabbatarian attitude, opposing the whole institution. He pointed out that His action fulfilled the purpose of the original institution. Had they understood the implications of the Mosaic provision for circumcision on the sabbath they would have seen that deeds of mercy such as He had just done were not merely permissible but obligatory."[45]

The other Sabbath miracle found only in John is that of the healing of a man born blind (chapter 9). The method used in giving the man sight is unusual: "He spat on the ground and made clay of the spittle and anointed the man's eyes with the clay, saying to him, 'Go, wash in the pool of Siloam'" (verses 6, 7). Perhaps Jesus used this method deliberately to challenge the rabbinical rules of Sabbath observance. As pointed out earlier, healing on Sabbath was itself forbidden unless human life was in mortal danger. By making the clay as He did, Jesus violated one of the thirty-nine main categories of prohibited work, viz., kneading,[46] and probably also another, mixing.[47] Furthermore, a person was allowed to anoint his eyes only with what was used for the same purpose on weekdays.[48]

In the view of some of the Pharisees Jesus was not of God, "'for,'" they said, "'he does not keep the sabbath'" (verse 16). A man could be regarded a Sabbathkeeper only if he obeyed the Pharisaic rules of Sabbathkeeping. If He violated these, they concluded that He was not from God. Others, however, were deeply impressed by the giving of sight to a man born blind, and they asked, "'How could such signs come from a sinful man?'" (verse 16, N.E.B.). So different men took different sides in relation to Jesus.

Lohse has well said: "Here, too, Jesus' act on the Sabbath is an expression of His work as the One whom God has sent and who is the φῶς τοῦ κόσμου [light of the world], John 9:5; 8:12. Face to face with Him the decision is made as to who is blind and who sees, John 9:39-41. Thus the works of God are manifest in the healings of Jesus on the Sabbath, John 9:3. Church and Synagogue are separated from one another by confession of Him on the one side and on the other a passionate rejection of His work which sets aside the Law."[49]

The Meaning of Matthew 24:20.—In His eschatological discourse to the twelve apostles on the Mount of Olives (Matt. 24:4-36; Mark 13:5-37; Luke 21:8-36) our Lord plainly foretold the destruction of Jerusalem. "'When you see Jerusalem surrounded by armies,'" He warned, "'then know that its desolation has come near. Then let those who are in Judea flee to the mountains, and let those who are inside the city depart'" (Luke 21:20, 21). Christians were to save their lives by immediate flight not only from the doomed city but from Judea, as well. In view of this, according to the Gospel of Matthew, He urged them, "'Pray that your flight may not be in winter or on a sabbath'" (Matt. 24:20). The parallel in Mark has only, "'Pray that it may not happen in winter'" (Mark 13:18). Why not in winter? Because the cold and rainy weather would make it more difficult to flee as well as to find shelter.[50]

The additional phrase "'or on a sabbath,'" found only in Matthew, has been variously interpreted. Some commentators have denied that these words were uttered by Jesus.[51] There can, however, be no doubt that they were a part of the original text of Matthew.[52] Were they simply put in by the author of the first Gospel in harmony with his Jewish predilections, as some have concluded?[53] W. C. Allen has suggested that they may well have come from the logia of Jesus and were known by the author of the first Gospel from Jewish sources.[54] We can see no valid reason for rejecting them as a genuine part of the logion. Accepting them as such, what is their significance?

In the interpretation of many commentators the injunction "'Pray that your flight may not be . . . on a sabbath'" is to be understood as a reference to the prohibition of traveling beyond a "Sabbath-day's journey," which was about three fifths of a mile. It is clear that the Israelites, during their wilderness wanderings, were forbidden to go long distances on the seventh day. The command was: "'Remain every man of you in his place, let no man go out of his place on the seventh day'" (Ex. 16:29). This command had specific reference to going out from the camp on the Sabbath to gather manna, which lay "on the face of the wilderness" "round about the camp" on six days of the week (verses 13, 14, 26, 27). "His place," however, was subject to various interpretations. Most likely, as just suggested, it meant the camp of the Israelites.[55] The Septuagint translators, on the other hand, took it as meaning one's house, and this idea is reflected in several modern translations, such as *The New English Bible:* "'No one may stir from his home on the seventh day.'" However, this interpretation would not harmonize with the designation of the Sabbath as "'a holy convocation,'" "a sacred assembly,'" or a "religious gathering" (Lev. 23:2-4).

The prohibition regarding traveling no more than a "Sabbath-day's journey" was a post-Exilic Rabbinic regulation. Inasmuch as Jesus ignored other such man-made rules of Sabbathkeeping, it is doubtful that He would have endorsed this one. Some think that He was here merely recognizing the conscientious scruples of Jewish Christians about fleeing on the Sabbath. A Sabbath-day's journey would not have carried them far enough to reach a place of safety. Hence, pray that your flight will be on a different day. But even the rabbis recognized that to save one's life might be regarded as justifying flight on the Sabbath.[56]

Many students of the New Testament see in Matthew 24:20 an indication that the Christian community for which Matthew writes was still observing the Sabbath.[57] Furthermore, if this is a genuine dominical saying, it indicates that our Lord expected His followers to regard the Sabbath as sacred as late as the destruction of Jerusalem in A.D. 70. He instructed them to pray that at that time of crisis they would not find it necessary to flee on the Sabbath. But the implication is that conditions could be such as to make instant flight necessary even on the day of rest.[58]

But the fear, bustle, and confusion that a hasty flight on Sabbath would bring were not in harmony with the worship, peace, and joy that should characterize the sacred day of rest. Hence, Jesus' followers were urged to pray that the flight would occur on a different day of the week.

The Sabbath in the Passion Narratives.—In all four Gospels the day on which our Lord was crucified and died is designated as *paraskeuē*, "preparation."[59] *Paraskeuē*, Mark explains, is *pro-sabbaton*, "fore-sabbath," i.e., the day before the Sabbath (Mark 15:42). In Luke 23:54 Codex Bezae similarly reads, "It was the day before the sabbath," instead of "It was the day of Preparation." It is evident that the "Preparation" had become a technical term for "the Preparation for the sabbath."[60] At the time of the giving of the manna, the Israelites were instructed to prepare their food for the Sabbath on the sixth day of the week (Ex. 16:5, 23). By New Testament times, *paraskeuē* had become the technical name for Friday.[61] This is shown not only by Josephus' linking it with the Sabbath[62] but also by its use absolutely in the *Didache*[63] and the *Martyrdom of Polycarp*.[64] It is the name for Friday in ecclesiastical Latin and in modern Greek.[65]

In John 19:31 the connection of "the day of Preparation" with the Sabbath is also clear. The Deuteronomic law forbade that the body of a criminal that had been hung on a tree be allowed to remain there overnight (Deut. 21:22, 23). Hence, the Jews followed the custom of removing the body of a crucified victim from a cross before evening on any day of the week,[66] but even more so when the Sabbath was about to begin, especially when the Sabbath was a "high day." The Sabbath evidently was regarded as a "high day" when it fell within the Paschal season. At such a time, desecration must be more scrupulously avoided than on any other Sabbath.

In John 19:42 the close connection of the "Jewish day of Preparation" with the Sabbath is also clear. Inasmuch as it was late on that day of Preparation, and the tomb of Joseph of Arimathea was nearby in a garden, they quickly buried Jesus there. It is obvious that the approaching Sabbath called for haste.

John 19:14, however, speaks of the day of Jesus' death as "the day of Preparation of the Passover." This designation is peculiar to John. The Synoptic Gospels do not associate *paraskeuē* with the Passover.[67] Commentators are divided on the interpretation of the phrase "the day of Preparation of the Passover." Some take the genitive *tou pascha* as an objective genitive and interpret the phrase as meaning "Preparation *for* the Passover."[68] A. Milligan and W. F. Moulton, however, point out that there is no evidence that the day before the Passover was ever called "the preparation of the Passover."[69] Hence, it is perhaps better to interpret the genitive "of the Passover" as a possessive genitive, meaning the preparation that belonged to the Paschal season or Friday of the Passover week.[70] This interpretation is given by G. B. Winer: "But in John 19:14 παρασκευὴ τοῦ πάσχα [*paraskeuē tou pascha*] does not mean the day of preparation *for* the Passover, but simply and naturally the resting-day of the Passover (the day of rest belonging to the Paschal festival)."[71]

The term "Passover," while originally used to designate the Paschal lamb or Paschal sacrifice,[72] came to be applied to the entire festival extending from the fourteenth to the twenty-first day of the month Nisan.[73] In this general sense it is used in the New Testament.[74] Hence, the *paraskeuē tou pascha* may be interpreted as the preparation belonging to the Paschal week. T. Zahn points out that John unites the idea of Friday as the preparation day with the time of the Passover, and he interprets: "It was Friday at the time of the Passover, and about the sixth hour."[75]

The Synoptic Gospels call attention to a group of Galilean women who carefully observed the death and burial of Jesus on that day of preparation.[76] These women, along with the twelve apostles, had traveled with their Lord in Galilee. They had used their means to support Him and His band of disciples. They had followed Him to Jerusalem and remained loyal to Him to the very end. Among them were Mary Magdalene, Mary the mother of James the younger and Joseph, and the mother of James and John. Now they watched as Joseph of Arimathea, a secret disciple, removed the body of the Master from the cross, wrapped it in a linen shroud, and laid it in his own tomb. By this time it was late in the afternoon of the day of preparation, and the Sabbath, Luke tells us, was about to begin.[77] The Greek verb *epephōsken* means, literally, *was dawning*. But how can one speak of dawning at sunset? Lohse explains, "The reference is obviously to the shining of the first star as the Sabbath comes."[78]

Luke's narrative continues: "The women who had come with him from Galilee followed, and saw the tomb, and how his body was laid; then they returned, and prepared spices and ointments. On the sabbath they rested according to the commandment. But on the first day of the week, at early dawn, they went to the tomb, taking the spices which they had prepared" (Luke 23:55-24:1, R.S.V.).[79]

The recognition of the relation of these women to Jesus and His Messianic ministry makes this simple account very significant. Next to the twelve apostles they were among Jesus' most intimate and most devoted followers. They risked their lives to follow Him to the cross. Their devotion is shown by their hasty purchase of spices and ointments to anoint the body of their Lord.

Even so they felt that they could not violate the Sabbath even to give honor to their dead Master. The spices and ointments were purchased for use when the Sabbath was over. Sundown was too near to think of using them on the day of preparation. "On the sabbath they rested according to the commandment." If we ask, According to what commandment? the answer is obvious: They rested according to the commandment that has to do with the Sabbath. They rested "in obedience to the commandment."[80] The accusative, *to sabbaton*, indicates that they rested "all through the sabbath" (Goodspeed). The conjunctive particle *men* before *sabbaton* of the last clause of Luke 23:56 corresponds to the adversative conjunction *de* of chapter 24:1, indicating that chapters 23:56 and 24:1 are one sentence. At the close of chapter 23 there should be only a comma, for the *de* carries the story on without a break.[81] They rested for the duration of the Sabbath, but at early dawn on the first day of the week they went to the tomb to continue their work.[82]

They were greatly disturbed when they found the tomb empty. But an angel informed them: " 'I know that you seek Jesus who was crucified. He is not here; for he has risen, as he said. Come, see the place where he lay' " (Matt. 28:5, 6). Jesus, too, had rested from His great work of redemption, but now He was alive forevermore.[83]

Luke plainly refers to three distinct days in this Passion narrative: the day of preparation, the Sabbath, and the first day of the week. On the first of these He was crucified, on the second He rested in the tomb, on the third He rose from the tomb. His most devoted followers also rested on the Sabbath in obedience to the commandment.

The Nature of the Gospels.—The significance of what the Gospels record concerning the Sabbath can be better understood and appreciated when one considers the purposes for which these documents were written. It is generally recognized today that they are not histories as such, though they contain historical facts.[84] Nor are they primarily biographies of Jesus. They are rather church books written for the purpose of promoting the Christian faith (Luke 1:1-4; John 20:31). They were written by committed Christians to aid in spreading the good news of what God has done in Jesus Christ. They are primarily theological handbooks of the early church.[85]

The Gospels record much of what Jesus said and did. We may well ask, Why? The answer is apparent: because what Jesus said and did is normative for the Christian. He is the church's Messiah and Lord. Therefore what He *said* is binding on those who profess to follow Him. And what He *did* is also normative. He is the standard of belief and practice.

In the light of this, what Jesus said and did with reference to the Sabbath has great significance. He did not speak words abolishing the Sabbath. Although He performed miracles of healing on that day, these acts were holy deeds in harmony with the spirit of the Sabbath. He did, however, endeavor to free the day from the interpretative restrictions that the Jewish oral law had placed upon it. He made it a day of spiritual freedom and helpful service.

It must further be recognized that when the Gospels recorded the sayings and doings of Jesus, they also reflected the faith and practice of the early church. The accounts in the book of Acts likewise give evidence of early Christian faith and practice, and to this book we now turn.

The Sabbath in the Book of Acts

The Greek word for "Sabbath," *sabbaton*, occurs ten times in the Greek text of the book of Acts. In the King James Version it is translated as "Sabbath" nine times,[86] and "week" once.[87] In the Revised Standard Version these figures become "Sabbath" eight times and "week" twice.[88]

The first occurrence of "Sabbath" in the Acts of the Apostles is in chapter 1:12. This passage merely asserts that the Mount of Olives, where the Ascension took place, "is near Jerusalem, a sabbath day's journey away." This is the only place in the Bible where the phrase "sabbath-day's journey" is found. It referred to the distance a Jew could travel on the Sabbath according to the regulation laid down by the scribes. The Mishnah gives the distance as 2,000 cubits,[89] the distance that was to separate the ark from the Israelites in their march around Jericho (Joshua 3:4). The pasture lands for a distance of 2,000 cubits outside the city walls of Levite cities were also assigned to these cities. Furthermore, the camp of Israel, the place out of which no Israelite was to go on the Sabbath (Ex. 16:29), was held to extend 2,000 cubits beyond the tabernacle. There is no evidence that Jesus felt bound by this scribal interpretation.

With the exception of the mention of the Sabbath by James at the Jerusalem Conference (Acts 15:21), the remaining references to this day in the Acts are all connected with Paul's missionary work. The Sabbath is associated with the founding of churches in Pisidian Antioch (chap. 13:13-52), Philippi (chap. 16:11-15), Thessalonica (chap. 17:1-9), Corinth (chap. 18:1-4), and, according to the Western text, Ephesus (verse 19d). As a loyal Jew (chaps. 24:14; 28:17) Paul kept the Sabbath. He entered the synagogues not only to teach but to worship on that day. Nor is there any hint that he regarded the Gentile Christians as free to observe some other day, such as Sunday, as the weekly day of rest.

The Sabbath Services in Pisidian Antioch.—The Gospels make it clear that Jesus began His public ministry of preaching and teaching in the Jewish synagogues.[90] According to the book of Acts the apostle Paul and his associates followed the same practice in their missionary work in the Gentile world.[91] Immediately after their ordination at Antioch on the Orontes River, Paul and Barnabas sailed for Cyprus. There, "when they arrived at Salamis, they proclaimed the word of God in the synagogues of the Jews" (Acts 13:5). It is worthy of note that frequently in the book of Acts, synagogue preaching and the Sabbath are linked together.[92] The earliest specific mention of this connection is the account of Paul's and Barnabas' mission to Pisidian Antioch in the lake district of southwest Asia Minor (verse 14ff.). This city evidently had a large Jewish community, and on the Sabbath that followed their arrival the missionaries "went into the synagogue and sat down."

As devout Jews they participated in the synagogue worship service. When the time came for the sermon, "after the reading of the law and the prophets," the visiting missionaries were invited to speak a "'word of exhortation,'" evidently a synagogue term for a homily.

The address that Paul gave in response to that invitation, along with several given by Peter, was used by C. H. Dodd to reconstruct the *Kerygma,* or preaching message, of the early church.[93] We cannot enter into a study of the content of Paul's address here, but we must note the kind of audience the apostle had, and the reaction to his message. It is evident that the worshipers in the synagogue consisted not only of Jews, either by birth or conversion, but also of devout Gentiles who were attracted by the monotheistic theology and high ethical principles of Judaism. Paul addresses his audience as "'men of Israel, and you that fear God'" (verse 16). Again he refers to them as "'brethren, sons of the family of Abraham, and those among you that fear God'" (verse 26). These God-fearers,

THE SABBATH IN THE NEW TESTAMENT

who are mentioned a number of times in Acts,[94] were Gentiles who attended the synagogue with varying degrees of attachment to Judaism, but who had not been circumcised as a mark that they had fully taken on the yoke of the Jewish law. It is among these devout Gentiles that Paul's missionary preaching enjoyed the greatest success, as the remainder of the chapter suggests.

The presence of these Gentile worshipers in the Jewish synagogue on the Sabbath is very significant. Lohse has correctly observed: "Beyond the circle of the Jewish communities which everywhere in the Diaspora sanctified the Sabbath to the God of Israel many god-fearers and proselytes also kept the Sabbath as a day of rest."[95] Even in Old Testament times the Gentile "sojourner" *(gēr)* who dwelt with the Hebrews was commanded to keep the Sabbath.[96] The God-fearers of Paul's day, of course, lived in a vastly different social environment. Nevertheless they found their way to the synagogue on the Sabbath.

At the conclusion of the Sabbath service at Pisidian Antioch the people on their way out begged that Paul continue his subject on the following Sabbath (verse 42). The King James Version, based on the *Textus Receptus,* states that this request came from "the Gentiles." But the better Greek manuscripts do not have the addition of *ta ethnē* at this point, and we may safely assume that there were both Jews and Gentiles among the people who made this request. Verse 43, then, tells us that "many Jews and devout converts to Judaism followed Paul and Barnabas." There is some uncertainty regarding the meaning of the Greek phrase translated as "devout converts to Judaism." Does this refer to "God-fearers" or to full proselytes to the Jewish faith? Probably the latter is intended. Paul and Barnabas urged those who were especially interested in Christianity "to continue in the grace of God."

"The next Sabbath almost the whole city gathered together to hear the word of God" (verse 44). Evidently the Gentiles who had attended the service on the previous Sabbath spread the word to their neighbors with remarkable results. It is doubtful that the synagogue could hold such a crowd, and perhaps some Jews were unable to get into their own synagogue. In any case, their animosity was aroused and they strongly opposed the teaching of the Christian missionaries. Paul and Barnabas told them plainly that since they were rejecting their necessary opportunity, the message would now be presented directly to the Gentiles (verse 46). As a result many Gentiles became Christians, "and the word of the Lord spread throughout all the region" (verse 49).

In a short time the apostles were expelled from that area and made their way to Iconium, where they again "entered together into the Jewish synagogue, and so spoke that a great company believed, both of Jews and of Greeks" (chap. 14:1). There is no mention of the Sabbath in the record, but it may nevertheless well have been on the day of rest when this occurred.

The Sabbath Day in Philippi.—On Paul's second missionary tour he had Silas as his associate. They were working in Asia Minor and had come to Troas when Paul had a vision of a man from Macedonia pleading, " 'Come over to Macedonia, and help us' " (chap. 16:9). This vision was interpreted as a call from God to leave the narrow confines of Asia Minor and open up the continent of Europe to the spread of the gospel: "And when he had seen the vision, immediately we sought to go on into Macedonia, concluding that God had called us to preach the gospel to them" (verse 10). It is to be noted that in relating the story Luke changes from the third person to the first person plural, suggesting that he joined the band of missionaries at Troas and accompanied them to Philippi.[97]

The missionaries recognized the urgency of the call and responded immediately. They set sail from Troas for the island of Samothrace and from there sailed to Neapolis, the seaport of Philippi in Macedonia. When they arrived in Philippi, they spent some days in this "leading city of the district of Macedonia, and a Roman colony" (verse 12). When the Sabbath came, they found the place where a group of devout Jews and God-fearers met for worship and joined them. The King James Version states: "And on the sabbath we went out of the city by a river side, where prayer was wont to be made" (verse 13). The word translated "prayer" *(proseuchē)* can mean not only the act of prayer but also a place of prayer. Hence, another translation is possible, as in the Revised Standard Version: "where we supposed there was a place of prayer."

There is no consensus among New Testament students regarding what this place of prayer was. Some hold that it was a synagogue.[98] But the fact that only women are mentioned as attending the service, apart from the missionaries, makes this interpretation extremely doubtful. It may have been a house,[99] or perhaps an informal meeting place in the open air.[100] There the missionaries sat down "and spoke to the women who had come together" (verse 13).

Paul's first convert in Europe was Lydia from Thyatira, a dealer in purple woolen cloth. She is described as "a worshiper of God," which suggests that she was a God-fearing Gentile. She and her household (probably including employees and servants) were baptized, and she insisted on entertaining the missionaries in her home. It is possible that Euodia and Syntyche, mentioned in Philippians 4:2, may also have become converts at this time. It is again worthy of note that Gentiles join Jews in worshiping on the Sabbath.

Three Sabbaths in Thessalonica.—From Philippi Paul and Silas followed the great military road, the *Via Egnatia* to Thessalonica, "where there was a synagogue of the Jews" (Acts 17:1). In his Gospel Luke mentions that when Jesus arrived at Nazareth, "where he had been brought up," he entered the synagogue on the Sabbath "as his custom was" (Luke 4:16). Exactly the same expression is used of Paul, who went into the synagogue "as was his custom" (Acts 17:2). For three *sabbata* he discoursed with the Thessalonians "from the scriptures, explaining and proving that it was necessary for the Christ to suffer and to rise from the dead, and saying, 'This Jesus, whom I proclaim to you, is the Christ'" (verses 2, 3).

Sabbata in verse 3 is translated as "weeks" in the Revised Standard Version, with "sabbaths" in a footnote. "This is the only certain New Testament example of the use of σάββατα [*sabbata*] as plural in meaning as well as in form."[101] Most likely it should be translated "Sabbaths" here, though the word can indicate the period of time between Sabbaths, i.e., weeks.[102] But it is evident that Paul labored in Thessalonica for a longer period than three weeks.[103] Furthermore, in his Philippian letter Paul declares that this Christian community sent help to him at Thessalonica "once and again."[104] Hence, the account in Acts seems to refer only to his labor in the synagogue. As the result of that labor some of the Jews accepted Christianity, "as did a great many of the devout Greeks and not a few of the leading women" (verse 4). The first Thessalonian letter confirms the conclusion that the Christian community in Thessalonica was largely Gentile (1 Thess. 1:9).

The first contact Paul made with Gentiles was in the Jewish synagogue on the Sabbath.

Berea.—While the Sabbath is not mentioned in connection with Paul's work in Berea, there is a reference to his entry into the synagogue. Many of the Jews in this city accepted Christ, "with not a few Greek women of high standing as well as men" (Acts 17:12).

The Sabbath in Corinth.—After a disheartening experience at Athens, Paul arrived at Corinth, where he sought lodging and remunerative labor. He found both in the home of Aquila and Priscilla, for they and he were "tentmakers," or, as many expositors interpret, "leather-workers," or "saddlers" (Acts 18:1-3).[105] During the week, then, he toiled with these Jewish converts. But on every Sabbath he preached in the synagogue, "and persuaded Jews and Greeks" (verse 4). The Western text of this verse reads: "And going to the synagogue every Sabbath he argued and introduced the name of the Lord Jesus, and persuaded not only Jews, but also Greeks."

When Silas and Timothy arrived with financial support, Paul was able to devote his full time to his missionary work. His strong emphasis on Jesus as the Messiah aroused opposition on the part of the unbelieving Jews. He therefore found it necessary to leave the synagogue and carry on his work in the house of Titius Justus, next door to the synagogue (verses 6, 7). Among the Jews who became converts to Christianity was Crispus, "the ruler of the synagogue" (verse 8). Paul remained in Corinth for a year and a half (verse 11).

On his way to Palestine he made a brief stop at Ephesus, where he "went into the synagogue and argued with the Jews" (verse 19). The Western text includes the words "and on the Sabbath."

On his third missionary journey Paul again visited Ephesus. The record states: "And he entered the synagogue and for three months spoke boldly, arguing and pleading about the kingdom of God" (chap. 19:8). After that he withdrew from the synagogue and carried on his work in "the hall of Tyrannus" for two years (verses 9, 10). The result was "that all the residents of [the province of] Asia heard the word of the Lord, both Jews and Greeks" (verse 10).

Although Paul found it expedient to withdraw from the synagogue on a number of occasions, it is evident that the Christians did not at first completely separate themselves from the synagogues. Before he became a Christian, Paul himself went to the high priest to get letters to the synagogues of Damascus, authorizing him to arrest the Christians he found in those synagogues, whether men or women, and to bring them bound to Jerusalem (chap. 9:1, 2). Christians did not yet constitute a separate group independent of the Jewish synagogue congregations (compare chaps. 22:19; 26:11). Of course, the time did come when they were forced to leave the Jewish synagogues.

The Sabbath and the Jerusalem Conference.—As more and more Gentiles joined the Christian movement, the question of what should be expected of them came to the fore. Must a Gentile first become a Jew before he could be a bona fide Christian? What was to be the basis of fellowship between Jewish and Gentile Christians? Many Jewish Christians, particularly those with a Pharisaic point of view, maintained that Gentiles who wanted to be Christians should take on the whole yoke of the Jewish law. Their message to Gentile converts was: "'Unless you are circumcised according to the custom of Moses, you cannot be saved'" (chap.

15:1). Circumcision was emphasized because it was the mark of submission to the whole Jewish law—oral as well as written (verse 5; Gal. 5:3). Paul and Barnabas, however, maintained that Gentiles should not be saddled with the yoke of the Jewish law.[106]

The Jerusalem Conference was called to consider the matter and to arrive at a decision. Representatives from the Gentile churches went up with Barnabas and Paul to the apostles and elders in Jerusalem (Acts 15:2). After considerable debate Peter set forth the argument that the fundamental principle had already been settled by the Holy Spirit, who had come with equal power on uncircumcised Gentiles and circumcised Jews, indicating that they were on the same level. God had accepted the Gentiles and cleansed their hearts by the Holy Spirit as soon as they put their faith in Jesus. Should the Christian community go beyond what God required (verses 7-11)?[107]

Barnabas and Paul then rehearsed the story of the miraculous signs and wonders that God was performing among the Gentiles (verse 12). These miracles were an attestation of God's acceptance of the mission among Gentiles. Finally, James the leader of the Jerusalem church proposed the following decision: " 'My judgment is that we should not trouble those of the Gentiles who turn to God, but write to them to abstain from the pollutions of idols and from unchastity and from what is strangled and from blood' " (verse 20). This solution was accepted by "the apostles and the elders, with the whole church" (verse 22, R.S.V.).

How should these prescriptions for Gentile converts laid down by the conference be regarded? Are we to conclude that these were the only ethical or moral standards required of Gentile Christians? W. Gutbrod has aptly pointed out that "the decree should not be regarded as in any sense a minimal ethics, an abstract of the Law which in a kind of compromise tries to make at least the fundamentals of the Law obligatory in place of the whole Law."[108] What the Jerusalem Council laid down was the terms for fellowship between Jewish and Gentile Christians.[109] "These requirements did not provide the ground of salvation or of church membership but of a working agreement for Gentile and Jewish converts."[110]

Practices that would scandalize Jews were singled out. Prohibitions were laid down that the Jewish world held to be binding upon all men. Gentiles were to avoid the pollution of idols, i.e., to abstain from eating the flesh of animals slain for pagan sacrifices (verse 29), which might imply a sharing in pagan polytheistic worship.[111] Second, they were to abstain from blood, which symbolizes life, which belongs to God alone.[112] They were also to abstain from the eating of the flesh of strangled animals, inasmuch as the blood remained in them.[113] Finally, unchastity was forbidden, which included any form of illicit sexual intercourse or marriage of closely related persons.[114]

Though the text underlying the Revised Standard Version is to be preferred to the "Western" text, the latter of Acts 15:20, 29 is of great interest. It omits the words "and from what is strangled" and at the end adds a negative form of the golden rule: "and not to do to others what they do not wish done to them." To abstain from blood can be interpreted as forbidding bloodshed, i.e., murder. Thus the decrees can be interpreted as forbidding the three cardinal sins in Jewish eyes: idolatry, fornication, and murder. These plus the addition of the golden rule (in negative form) transform the prohibitions into purely ethical demands.

THE SABBATH IN THE NEW TESTAMENT

After setting forth these principles, James added: "'For from early generations Moses has had in every city those who preach him, for he is read every Sabbath in the synagogues'" (verse 21). The significance of this statement has been variously interpreted. One explanation given is that since Jews are in every city, the Gentiles should respect these principles so as not to cause constant offense.[115] In every city there are synagogues where Moses is read.

A second explanation is that Moses would suffer no loss by not requiring the Gentiles to observe the whole Jewish law, for these Gentiles had never been adherents of Judaism.[116] Another is that the yoke of the Jewish law is not to be placed on Gentiles, for there are enough preachers of Moses already in the synagogues every Sabbath. A fourth interpretation is that there is ample opportunity for Gentiles to know these basic principles, for Moses' writings are read every Sabbath.

As pointed out earlier, the early Gentile Christians came from "God-fearers" who were already worshiping in the synagogues on the Sabbath. It is evident also that Christians did not immediately sever all connections with the synagogue. Hence, the best explanation, in our view, is that the Jerusalem Council is not enjoining anything new or strange, but that with which the Gentiles would already be familiar, through the reading and exposition of the Mosaic law in the synagogues.[117]

It is significant that the matter of Sabbathkeeping is not mentioned as an issue at this conference. Had there been a movement on foot to do away with the Sabbath or to change the day of worship to Sunday, there would no doubt have been considerable debate and bitter contention on the part of the large number of Jewish Christians who were "'zealous for the law'" (chap. 21:20). Gentiles were not admonished to respect the scruples of their Jewish brethren with reference to the Sabbath. The silence of the conference on this subject eloquently testifies to the continual observance of the Sabbath by both Jewish and Gentile Christians.

NOTES

[1] A different explanation of the final −α is offered in F. Blass, A. Debrunner, and Robert W. Funk, *A Greek Grammar of the New Testament and Other Early Christian Literature* (Chicago, 1961), par. 141 (3): "Σάββατα = שבת + α to make it pronounceable in Greek."
[2] A. T. Robertson, *A Grammar of the Greek New Testament in the Light of Historical Research* (Nashville, 1934), pp. 95, 105.
[3] See such standard Greek lexicons as Henry George Liddell and Robert Scott, *A Greek-English Lexicon*, rev. and augm. by Henry Stuart Jones (Oxford, 1940), p. 1579; Joseph Henry Thayer, *A Greek-English Lexicon of the New Testament* (New York, 1889), pp. 565, 566; Walter Bauer, *A Greek-English Lexicon of the New Testament and Other Early Christian Literature*, rev. and augm. by William F. Arndt and F. Wilbur Gingrich (Chicago, 1957), p. 746; and G. Abbott-Smith, *A Manual Greek Lexicon of the New Testament*, 3d ed. (Edinburgh, 1937), pp. 399, 400.
[4] A brief summary of the evidence regarding the problem of the ending of Mark is given in Bruce M. Metzger, *A Textual Commentary on the Greek New Testament* (London, 1971), pp. 122-126.
[5] Matt. 28:1; Mark 16:9; Luke 24:1; John 20:1, 19; Acts 20:7; 1 Cor. 16:2.
[6] Matt. 12:1, 5, 10, 11, 12; 28:1; Mark 1:21; 2:23, 24; 3:2, 4; Luke 4:16; 6:2; 13:10; Acts 13:14; 16:13.
[7] Ex. 16:25, 26; 20:8, 10; 35:3; Num. 15:32; Deut. 5:12.
[8] Robertson, *op. cit.*, p. 408; James Hope Moulton and Nigel Turner, *A Grammar of New Testament Greek* (Edinburgh, 1963), 3:26, 27.
[9] See Wolfgang Schrage, "συναγωγή," *TDNT*, 7:831, n. 216.
[10] Alfred Plummer, *A Critical and Exegetical Commentary on the Gospel According to S. Luke*, 5th ed., ICC (Edinburgh, 1922), p. 118.
[11] Ralph Earle, "Luke," *Wesleyan Bible Commentary*, 4:233.
[12] Paul K. Jewett, *The Lord's Day* (Grand Rapids, 1971), pp. 34, 35.
[13] John Richard Sampey, "Sabbath," *International Standard Bible Encyclopaedia* (Grand Rapids, 1939), 4:2631.
[14] Jewett, *loc. cit.*
[15] Mishnah Shabbath 7:2 (Danby).
[16] Shabbath 7:4.
[17] William L. Lane, *The Gospel According to Mark*, NIC (Grand Rapids, 1974), p. 115.

THE SABBATH IN SCRIPTURE AND HISTORY

[18] Mark 2:26 speaks of Abiathar as the priest, but 1 Samuel 21:1, 2 names the priest as Ahimelech. Abiathar succeeded to the office after his father Ahimelech's death (1 Sam. 22:20-23).
[19] Hermann L. Strack and Paul Billerbeck, *Das Evangelium nach Matthäus Erläutert aus Talmud und Midrasch, Kommentar zum Neuen Testament* (Munich, 1922), 1:619; Eduard Lohse, "σάββατον," *TDNT*, 7:22, n. 170.
[20] Maimonides Pesach 1, quoted in Frederick W. Farrar, *The Life of Christ* (Portland, Oreg., 1960), p. 333. For earlier rabbinical statements expressing the same point of view, see Strack and Billerbeck, *op. cit.*, pp. 620-622.
[21] W. D. Davies, *The Setting of the Sermon on the Mount* (Cambridge, 1964), pp. 103, 104; David Daube, *The New Testament and Rabbinic Judaism* (New York, 1956), p. 68.
[22] Mekilta, Ex. 31:12-17, tractate Shabbata (Lauterbach); cf. Lohse, *op. cit.*, p. 14.
[23] *Ibid.*, p. 22.
[24] Bruce M. Metzger, *The Text of the New Testament* (New York, 1968), p. 50.
[25] Mishnah Yoma 8:6.
[26] Burton H. Throckmorton, Jr., ed., *Gospel Parallels* (New York, 1957), p. 51, n. Matt. 12:10.
[27] Lohse, *op. cit.*, p. 25, n. 198.
[28] In the last clause Luke 6:9 has "'to save life or to destroy it?'"
[29] C. E. B. Cranfield, *The Gospel According to Saint Mark* (Cambridge, Eng., 1959), p. 120.
[30] Herschel H. Hobbs, *The Exposition of the Gospel of Luke* (Grand Rapids, 1966), p. 112.
[31] Gustav Stählin, "ὀργή" (E), *TDNT*, 5:428.
[32] F. F. Bruce, *New Testament History* (London, 1969), pp. 173, 174.
[33] T. W. Manson, *The Gospel of Luke* (New York, 1930), pp. 164, 165.
[34] William F. Arndt, *The Gospel According to St. Luke* (St. Louis, 1956), p. 329.
[35] G. B. Caird, *The Gospel of St Luke, Pelican Gospel Commentaries* (Baltimore, 1963), p. 175.
[36] Ex. 23:5; Deut. 22:4.
[37] Strack and Billerbeck, *op. cit.*, 1:629.
[38] Bruce, *op. cit.*, p. 105. The Sabbath regulations of the Qumran community were even stricter than those of the strictest Pharisees. With reference to humane treatment of animals on Sabbath the "Damascus Rule" specifically states: "No man shall assist a beast to give birth on the Sabbath day. And if it should fall into a cistern or pit, he shall not lift it out on the Sabbath" (CD xi., G. Vermes, *The Dead Sea Scrolls in English* [Baltimore, 1962], p. 113).
[39] Most textual critics are agreed that John 5:3b, 4, about the angel troubling the water, is not an original part of the Gospel of John but was most probably a marginal gloss that crept into the text. It is not found in the earliest and best Greek manuscripts of the Gospels ($P^{66,75}$ ABC* DW$^{supp.}$ 33). Nor does it occur in several Old Latin manuscripts, the true text of the Vulgate, nor the Curetinian Syriac or the Coptic versions. More than twenty manuscripts that do contain it mark it with asterisks and obeli as being suspect. Furthermore, it contains a number of non-Johannine words and expressions, three of which are found only here in the entire New Testament.
[40] See Yoma 8:6; Strack and Billerbeck, *op. cit.*, 1:623-639; 3:533ff.
[41] Shabbath 7:2; Strack and Billerbeck, *op. cit.*, 2:454-461.
[42] C. H. Dodd, *The Interpretation of the Fourth Gospel* (Cambridge, 1953), p. 320.
[43] Mishnah Nedarim 3:11.
[44] Shabbath 18:3; 19:2.
[45] Leon Morris, *The Gospel According to John, NIC* (Grand Rapids, 1971), pp. 408, 409.
[46] Shabbath 7:2.
[47] Shabbath 24:3.
[48] Cf. Shabbath 14:4.
[49] Lohse, *op. cit.*, p. 28.
[50] Floyd V. Filson, *A Commentary on the Gospel According to St. Matthew* (London, 1960), p. 255.
[51] See Alexander Balmain Bruce, "The Synoptic Gospels," in *The Expositors' Greek Testament*, ed. W. Robertson Nicoll (Grand Rapids [1942?]), 1:293.
[52] The only variants listed for the verse in the critical apparatus of Kurt Aland's *Synopsis Quattuor Evangeliorum* (Stuttgart, 1964) are the substitution of the genuine singular (DLQ 047^{al}), or plural (094 e) for the dative case of "Sabbath," and the addition of ἐν (on) before "Sabbath" (EFGH 565 1424).
[53] For example, J. C. Fenton, *The Gospel of St Matthew, Pelican Gospel Commentaries* (Baltimore, 1963), p. 387.
[54] Willoughby C. Allen, *A Critical and Exegetical Commentary on the Gospel According to S. Matthew, ICC* (Edinburgh, 1912), pp. lv (n. 1), 256.
[55] Lohse, *op. cit.*, p. 13.
[56] Strack and Billerbeck, *op. cit.*, 1:953.
[57] Sherman E. Johnson on Matt. 24:19, 20, *IB*, 7:547; Filson, *loc. cit.*; A. W. Argyle, *The Gospel According to Matthew* (Cambridge, Eng., 1963), p. 183; Alfred Plummer, *An Exegetical Commentary on the Gospel According to S. Matthew*, 2d ed. (London [1960?]), pp. 333, 334; Lohse, *op. cit.*, p. 29; Strack and Billerbeck, *op. cit.*, pp. 952, 953.
[58] Filson, *loc. cit.*
[59] Matt. 27:62; Mark 15:42; Luke 23:54; John 19:14, 31, 42.
[60] Morris, *op. cit.*, p. 816.
[61] James Hope Moulton and George Milligan, *The Vocabulary of the Greek Testament* (Grand Rapids, 1959), p. 490; Morris, *op. cit.*, p. 776, n. 97.
[62] Josephus *Antiquities of the Jews* 16. 6. 2.
[63] *Didache* 8. 1.
[64] *Martyrdom of Polycarp* 7. 1.
[65] W. E. Vine, *Expository Dictionary of New Testament Words* (London, 1940), 3:204.
[66] Josephus *War of the Jews* 4. 5. 2.
[67] Edwin A. Abbott, *Johannine Grammar* (London, 1906), pp. 92, 93.
[68] For example, see Brooke Foss Westcott, *An Introduction to the Study of the Gospels*, 4th ed. (London, 1872), p. 340; Plummer, *The Gospel According to S. John* (Cambridge, Eng., 1923), p. 379, and many others.
[69] William Milligan and William F. Moulton, *The Gospel According to John* (New York, 1883), p. 388.
[70] A. T. Robertson, *Word Pictures in the New Testament* (Nashville, 1930-1933), 5:299. See the illuminating article "The Origins of the Eucharist" by A. J. B. Higgins in *New Testament Studies*, 1 (1954-55), especially pp. 206-208.
[71] George Benedict Winer, *A Grammar of the Idiom of the New Testament*, 7th ed. (Andover, Mass. [1869]), p. 189.

THE SABBATH IN THE NEW TESTAMENT

[72] Ex. 12:11, 21; Num. 9:2-6; 2 Chron. 30:15, Septuagint.
[73] Deut. 16:2-4; 2 Chron. 30:1ff., Septuagint.
[74] Acts 12:3, 4; Luke 22:1; Mark 14:1; Matt. 26:17; John 2:13, 23; 6:4; 11:55; 12:1.
[75] Theodor Zahn, *Introduction to the New Testament* (Grand Rapids, 1953), 3:296.
[76] Matt. 27:55, 56; Mark 15:40, 41; Luke 23:49, 56.
[77] Luke 8:1-3.
[78] Lohse, *op. cit.*, p. 20, n. 159.
[79] *Epephōsken*, according to Robertson *(Grammar*, p. 885), is a conative imperfect.
[80] Luke 23:55-24:1.
[81] The accusative case in expressions of time indicates extent or duration of time. A. T. Robertson and W. Hersey Davis, *A New Short Grammar of the Greek Testament* (New York, 1933), par. 345(c); Robertson, *Grammar*, p. 495; William Webster, *Syntax and Synonyms of the Greek Testament* (n.p., 1864), p. 63, quoted in H. E. Dana and Julius R. Mantey, *A Manual Grammar of the Greek New Testament* (New York, 1955), p. 91.
[82] Henry Alford, *The Greek Testament*, 6th ed. (Boston, 1872), 1:664.
[83] Rev. 1:18.
[84] See, e.g., George Eldon Ladd, *A Theology of the New Testament* (Grand Rapids, 1974), pp. 174, 175.
[85] Ralph P. Martin, *New Testament Foundations* (Grand Rapids, 1975), 1:10.
[86] Acts 1:12; 13:14, 27, 42, 44; 15:21; 16:13; 17:2; 18:4.
[87] Chap. 20:7.
[88] The change was made from "sabbath" to "week" in Acts 17:2.
[89] Mishnah, Erubin 4:3-8.
[90] Matt. 4:23; 9:35; 12:9; 13:54; Mark 1:21, 39; 6:2; Luke 4:15, 16; 6:6; 13:10; John 6:59; 18:20.
[91] Acts 9:20; 13:5, 6, 14; 14:1; 17:1; 18:4, 19; 19:8, et cetera.
[92] Chap. 13:14; 16:13; 17:2; 18:4, 19d.
[93] C. H. Dodd, *The Apostolic Preaching and Its Developments* (New York [1944]).
[94] In addition to Acts 13, see: Acts 10:1, 22; 16:14; 17:4, 17; 18:7.
[95] Lohse, *op. cit.*, p. 18.
[96] Ex. 20:10; 23:12.
[97] The reading of the "Western text" as given in Codex Bezae is: "Having awakened, then, he related the vision to us, and we recognized that the Lord had called us to evangelize those in Macedonia."
[98] Heinrich Greeven, "προσεύχομαι," *TDNT*, 2:808.
[99] Karl Heinrich Rengstorf, "ποταμός," *TDNT*, 6:602.
[100] Bauer, Arndt, and Gingrich, *op. cit.*, p. 720.
[101] F. F. Bruce, *The Acts of the Apostles* (Chicago, 1952), p. 324.
[102] Cf. Lev. 23:15; 25:8.
[103] 1 Thess. 2:9; 2 Thess. 3:7-10.
[104] Phil. 4:16.
[105] Wilhelm Michaelis, "σκηνοποιός," *TDNT*, 7:393, 394.
[106] The Western text of verse 2 after the words "no small dissension with them" adds "for Paul insisted that they should remain just as they were when they believed."
[107] Verse 12 in the Western text begins. "And when the elders had consented to the words spoken by Peter..."
[108] W. Gutbrod, "νόμος," *TDNT*, 4:1067.
[109] Johannes Weiss, *Earliest Christianity* (New York, 1959), 1:312.
[110] George Eldon Ladd, *The Young Church* (London and New York, 1964), p. 61.
[111] See Lev. 17:7-9; 2 Cor. 8:1ff.; 10.
[112] Gen. 9:4; Lev. 17:10ff.; Deut. 12:23.
[113] Lev. 17:13.
[114] Lev. 18:6-18.
[115] Bruce, *The Acts of the Apostles*, pp. 300, 301.
[116] Richard Belward Rackham, *The Acts of the Apostles* (London, 1951; reprinted Grand Rapids, 1964), p. 254.
[117] A. C. Hervey, *Acts of the Apostles, The Pulpit Commentary* (London and New York [1913]), 2:4.

CHAPTER 6

Sunday in the New Testament

Walter F. Specht

MANY Christians honestly believe that Jesus and/or His apostles changed the day of rest from the seventh-day Sabbath to the first day of the week, i.e., Sunday. Hence, after examining the passages where the term "Sabbath" occurs in the Gospels and Acts, fairness demands that notice also be taken of the passages in the New Testament that speak of the first day of the week. Obviously the designation "Sunday" is not used in the New Testament. Rather, the days are designated by number after the manner of Judaism.

There are seven or eight passages in the New Testament that speak of the first day of the week. The exact number depends on whether one accepts the long ending of Mark (16:9-20), found in a large number of manuscripts, as a genuine part of the second Gospel. All but two[1] of the passages that mention the first day of the week are in the Gospels and refer to the same first day—namely, the day on which our Lord rose from the dead.

According to the testimony of all four Gospels, the devoted Galilean women who accompanied Jesus to Jerusalem were the first to receive the good news of the Resurrection. C. E. B. Cranfield points out that the prominence of women in all four Gospels "goes a long way toward authenticating the story as a whole . . . ; for this is a feature which the early Church would not be likely to invent."[2] In Jewish culture women were ineligible to bear a credible witness.[3]

The First Day of the Week in Mark

Inasmuch as Mark is usually regarded as the earliest of the Gospels, it seems logical to begin with its account of the empty tomb (Mark 16:1-8). Concerning this account Cranfield remarks: "The naturalness of the first part (esp. verse 3), the simplicity and restraint of verses 5-8, and the surprising feature of the women's silence all point to its authenticity. It reads like an eyewitness's account, not a dramatization of a religious conviction."[4]

Mark specifically names three women as among those who had followed Jesus in Galilee and ministered to Him: Mary Magdalene; Mary, the mother of James the Younger and Joses; and Salome[5] (chap. 15:40, 41). These three, along with many other women, witnessed the Crucifixion, and the two Marys also observed

Jesus' burial: they "saw where he was laid" (verse 47). This tragic day is identified as "the day of Preparation, that is, the day before the sabbath" (verse 42). The fact of Jesus' burial became a part of the central truth of the gospel as Paul preached it (1 Cor. 15:4).

"When the sabbath was past,"[6] the two Marys and Salome purchased aromatic oils to anoint the body of Jesus. This purchasing was evidently done on Saturday evening after sunset. They were unable to complete their service of love to their beloved Teacher on Friday before sunset, and so had to wait until after the Sabbath. This was intended to be their final act of love and devotion. It is evident that they regarded Jesus' death as the end. They did not expect Him to rise from the dead. To anoint one who had lain in the tomb that long must have been unusual. Cranfield explains: "Love often prompts people to do what from a practical point of view is useless."[7]

"Very early on the first day of the week they went to the tomb when the sun had risen" (Mark 16:2). There is some confusion regarding the meaning of the temporal expressions used. "Very early" normally refers to the period of the fourth watch, i.e., from three to six o'clock, but this would not agree with the expression "when the sun had risen." H. B. Swete suggests that they left their abodes "just before daybreak and arrived just after sunrise."[8] At any rate, they seem to have come as early as possible to complete the rites of burial. On their way to the tomb they wondered how they would get the stone rolled back from the opening.[9] But when they arrived, they found it had already been rolled back. Inside they saw "a young man" clothed in dazzling apparel who said to them, "'Do not be amazed; you seek Jesus of Nazareth, who was crucified. . . . He is not here; see the place where they laid him'" (verse 6). Thus the great news of the Resurrection was made known to them, but they could not believe their ears and fled in terror and amazement from the tomb.

These momentous historical events took place on the first day of the week.[10] But, though Mark's Gospel was written more than a quarter of a century after the events took place, there is no hint that the day on which they occurred had acquired any sacred character whatever. It is not called a day of rest or a holy day.

Mark 16:9 also contains a reference to the first day of the week. Unfortunately, it is not possible today to determine how the Gospel originally ended. The famous uncial codices Vaticanus and Sinaiticus, and the Sinaitic form of the Old Syriac and some others conclude with verse 9. The Old Latin manuscript, Codex Bobiensis, contains a shorter ending that seems to have originated about the middle of the second century or early part of the third. Four Greek uncials have this ending followed by the longer ending (verses 9-20). A large number of Greek manuscripts have this longer ending, but some of these indicate uncertainty about it by marking with asterisks, obeli, or a critical note. The Freer Gospels of the fourth and fifth centuries contain an expansion of the long ending by inserting a substantial addition (the Freer Logion) between verses 14 and 15. The language, form, and style of all these additions is non-Markan. Furthermore, the connection of verses 9-20 with what precedes is not smooth.

This ending consists of three parts: (1) three post-Resurrection appearances of Jesus (verses 9-14); (2) the commission to the apostles to preach the gospel (verses 15-18); and (3) an account of the ascension of Jesus to God's right hand (verses 19, 20). The three appearances evidently took place on the first day of the week (verse 9).¹¹ Verse 9 in the Revised Standard Version* reads: "Now when he rose early on the first day of the week, he appeared first to Mary Magdalene, from whom he had cast out seven demons." Grammatically the temporal phrase "on the first day of the week" may be construed with either "rose" or "appeared," but probably the R.S.V. is correct in taking it with "rose." The word "first" in the clause "he appeared first" can be taken in an absolute sense, or as first in relation to the three appearances mentioned. Mary hastened to bear the news of this Christophany to "those who had been with him [the apostles, cf. chap. 3:14], as they mourned and wept" (verse 10). But her report that "he was alive and had been seen by her" was met by incredulity (verse 11).

The second appearance seems to be an abbreviation of the story of the walk to Emmaus by two disciples (not of the twelve) recorded in detail by Luke (chap. 24:13-35). Jesus appeared to them in "another form." But when they returned to the eleven to tell what they had seen, their report, too, was met with unbelief (Mark 16:12, 13).

Finally, He appeared "to the eleven themselves as they sat at table; and he upbraided them for their unbelief and hardness of heart" (verse 14). This appearance seems to be identical with the one mentioned in Luke 24:36-53 and/or John 20:19-29.

This longer ending of Mark seems to have been known by the middle of the second century, and verse 19 is cited by Irenaeus.¹² But this passage again gives no hint that there is anything sacred about the first day of the week or that Christians were meeting for worship on that day.

The First Day of the Week in Matthew

According to the Gospel of Matthew "many" Galilean women who had accompanied Jesus to Jerusalem observed His crucifixion and death "from afar" on that awful Friday (Matt. 27:55). The Mosaic law forbade that one who had suffered a criminal's death be allowed to remain hanging on a tree overnight; the body was to be buried the same day.¹³ Josephus confirms that the Jews in New Testament times removed those who had been crucified and buried them "before the going down of the sun." ¹⁴ This was even more essential on a Friday, when the Sabbath was about to begin.

Joseph of Arimathea, "a rich man" and "a respected member of the council" (Mark 15:43), obtained permission from Pilate to perform this service for Jesus. He followed the first-century Jewish custom of burial in a white linen shroud.¹⁵ Jesus was buried in Joseph's own tomb, cut in the rock, which had not been previously used, and the entrance was secured by rolling a large stone in front of it. To all of this Mary Magdalene and the other Mary were witnesses. There is then no question about their ability to identify the right tomb two days later. As a gesture of their grief they were sitting "opposite the sepulchre" (Matt. 27:61).¹⁶

The account of the sealing of the tomb and the stationing of a guard is peculiar to Matthew (chap. 27:62-66). Permission for this was granted by Pilate to the "chief priests and Pharisees" on the next day, "that is, after the day of preparation," i.e., the Sabbath. The delegation from the Sanhedrin suddenly recalled that Jesus had predicted that after He was put to death He would rise

---

*Unless otherwise noted, all Scripture references in this chapter are from the Revised Standard Version.

again " " "after three days." " " They therefore wanted the tomb guarded until " 'the third day.' " They expressed fear that the disciples would steal His body and then claim He rose from the dead.

Pilate replied sharply and peremptorily, "Take a guard [i.e., of Roman soldiers, not mere Temple police],[17] and make it as secure as you can." So they sealed the tomb and stationed a guard of Roman soldiers. But the precautions they employed only provided further evidence of the resurrection of our Lord.

The earthquake and the descent of an angel to roll away the stone, as connected with that resurrection, are described in Matthew 28. The timing of these events is given in verse 1. Unfortunately, however, all Bible students are not agreed on the interpretation of the temporal expressions given in the verse. The chief difficulty lies in harmonizing the phrase *opse sabbatōn* ("late on the Sabbath") with the expression that follows, "at the [hour] dawning toward the first day of the week." The first might be taken to mean toward sunset Saturday night, whereas the second suggests toward sunrise on Sunday morning.

Opse de sabbatōn is rendered as "now late on the Sabbath day" in the Revised Version, the American Standard Version, and the New American Standard Bible (omits day). The Latin Vulgate translates it as *vespere autem sabbati*, "however on sabbath evening." Those who follow these renderings are forced to interpret "as it began to dawn toward the first day of the week" as meaning when the first day of the week was about to begin on Saturday evening. The verb *epiphoskein*, to dawn, must then mean "to dawn on," as in Luke 23:54. There are two main objections to this. First, to interpret *opse de sabbatōn* as meaning "late on the Sabbath" is to make Matthew contradict the other Gospel accounts, all of which have the women visit the tomb early Sunday morning. Second, the whole course of the narrative in Matthew 28 indicates that the events there recorded occurred in the daytime, not in the evening. The women hastened from the empty tomb to tell the disciples that they had seen an angel who informed them that Jesus was alive (verses 5-8). While this was going on (verse 11) some of the soldiers from the Roman guard went into the city and reported to the chief priests the startling news of the Resurrection. The chief priests quickly assembled the Sanhedrin, which offered a sum of money as a bribe to the soldiers to tell the falsehood that Jesus' disciples had come by night while the guards were asleep and had stolen their Master's body. The Jewish authorities offered protection to the soldiers should this word reach Pilate. The clear implication is that these things were happening in the daytime.

How then can the two temporal expressions in Matthew 28:1 be harmonized? *Opse* is primarily a temporal adverb that usually denotes late in, or the last of, the period of time in question; hence, in Mark 4:35 it means "late in the day," i.e., in the evening.[18] But it can also be used as an improper preposition, signifying "after"—a well-attested meaning in Greek papyri. Hence, the Revised Standard Version and most recent translations render *opse sabbatōn* as "after the Sabbath." [19] Lohse asserts that *opse sabbatōn* corresponds to the Rabbinic *Motzaey Shabbath*, "the termination of the Sabbath," and "thus means the night from the Sabbath to the first day of the week or the first day of the week itself." [20]

From the standpoint of grammar by itself, one may translate either "late on the Sabbath" or "after the Sabbath." But the analogy with the other Gospels, plus the context and the phrase "at the [hour] dawning into the first [day] of the week," decide the matter in favor of the latter.

The two Marys came early in the morning "to see the sepulchre." According to Mark and Luke, they came to complete the work of anointing Jesus' body with spices and perfumes as a final tribute of love. But in Matthew's Gospel they are depicted as coming to see the tomb. The Jews in Jesus' day observed two periods of mourning for a deceased loved one: the first period was between the death and burial, and the second was the period following interment. Does Matthew's account suggest that we are to connect this early-morning visit with the second period of mourning? This is possible. At any rate, the apocryphal Gospel of Peter has them say, "Even if we were not able to weep and lament him on the day in which he was crucified, yet let us now do so at his tomb" (chap. 12:52).

The Gospel of Matthew is variously dated from the late sixties to around A.D. 80. That Gospel was the most popular one in the early church. It was quoted more frequently by early Christian writers than any other, and was regarded as the teaching Gospel and as the church's Gospel. Does it reflect even a hint that the first day of the week was now to be observed by Christians rather than the seventh day? We have found no evidence of such a change in Matthew.

It is true that Jesus appeared to the women as they departed from the tomb "with fear and great joy" (chap 28:8). They "took hold of his feet and worshiped him" (verse 9). However, this had to do not with the day of the week but with the tremendous impact of the risen Lord upon these devoted followers. Matthew knew nothing of the observance of Sunday as a day of worship.

The First Day of the Week in Luke

The Gospel of Luke is usually dated about the same time as Matthew, or perhaps a little later. William M. Ramsay considers Luke as one of the greatest of historians.[21] He was a man of culture, with a trained mind and literary charm. In his prologue (Luke 1:1-4), he claims to have accurately[22] traced the course of the "Jesus-event" and to have written an "orderly account"[23] of what happened. Hence it is of special interest to note how carefully he presents the sequence of the events of Jesus' death, burial, and resurrection.

The day of Jesus' death and burial was "the day of Preparation," when the Sabbath was about to begin (Luke 23:54). All through the Sabbath[24] the devoted women who had prepared to perform the last rites "rested according to the commandment" (verse 56). But at early dawn on the first day of the week they came with their spices to complete their work (chap. 24:1). The passage from Luke 23:55 to 24:1 is in reality but one sentence in the Greek. The adversitive conjunction *de* of Luke 24:1 corresponds to the conjunctive particle *men* of Luke 23:56. It is unfortunate that the chapter division was made in the midst of a sentence, for the story goes on without a break: the women rested on the Sabbath, but on the first day of the week they did not rest.[25]

When they arrived at the tomb "at early dawn," they found the stone rolled away[26] from the mouth, and no corpse inside. They did, however, see two men, evidently angels, "in dazzling apparel," who asked, "'Why do you seek the living among the dead?'"[27] These angels recalled to their minds Jesus' own prediction, repeated three times,[28] that He would not only suffer and be crucified but would rise from the dead "'on the third day'" (chap. 24:4-8). Jesus' followers ought to have clung to His words and expected a resurrection: "'Remember what he told you'" (N.E.B.). These devoted women were not only led to recall His words but to lay hold of them in faith, and they hurried to bring the good news to the apostles and other followers of Jesus. But the apostles regarded the report as nonsense, and refused to accept it (verses 9-11).

An exquisite story, peculiar to Luke, follows; it stresses the truth that the death of Jesus was not a meaningless tragedy but a fulfillment of the plans and purposes of God. On the very same day mentioned in verse 1, two disciples were walking to Emmaus, a village about seven miles from Jerusalem. As they walked and talked of the startling events that had transpired in Jerusalem, the risen Lord, disguised as a stranger, joined them and asked, "What are these words that you are exchanging with one another as you walk?"[29] In response to His question they told of Jesus the Nazarene, who was recognized by His miracles and teachings as a prophet but who had suffered a violent death at the hands of the chief priests and rulers. His followers had been hoping that He would prove to be more than a prophet—the Messiah, who would deliver Israel from the yoke of Rome—but now their hopes seemed to be doomed to disappointment.

At the same time, these two individuals seemed to have been aware of Jesus' prediction regarding a resurrection on the third day, for they added, "Yes, and besides all this, it is now the third day since this happened" (verse 21).[30] Moreover, they knew of the report of the women that the tomb was empty and that angels had declared that Jesus was alive. Some of their company had even checked the report of the empty tomb and found it to be accurate (verses 22-24).

Then the Divine Teacher, still disguised as a stranger, reproved their spiritual dullness. The sufferings of the Messiah were a necessary fulfillment of Old Testament prophecies (verse 25ff.): "And beginning with Moses and all the prophets, he interpreted to them in all the scriptures the things concerning himself" (verse 27). They felt their hearts strangely warmed as He expounded the Scriptures. Then at the end of their walk, they pressed Him to stay with them. When He sat down at the table with them, He assumed the position of host: He blessed the bread, broke it, and offered it to them. Suddenly their eyes were opened. They recognized Him, but then immediately He vanished from their sight.

Later that same evening the apostles and other Christians were startled and frightened by the sudden appearance of the risen Christ in their midst. How He got there or where He came from, no one knew. He had to assure them that He really was their beloved Master. "'See my hands and my feet, that it is I myself,'" He urged. "'Handle me, and see'" (verses 39, 40). But even this was insufficient to allay their doubts and fears. Hence He asked for food and was given a piece of broiled fish, which He ate before them (verses 42, 43).[31] Jesus then attempted to teach them the significance of Old Testament scriptures as interpreted in the light of the cross and resurrection. "'Thus it is written,'" He told them, "'that the Christ should suffer and on the third day rise from the dead'" (verses 46, 47).

It is a marvelous story and full of deep significance. But though Luke wrote several decades after the events portrayed and wrote his Gospel specifically to teach Theophilus about the Christian faith (chap. 1:4), we fail to detect even a hint that the Sabbath was now to be laid aside and that Christians were to observe the first day of the week.

The First Day of the Week in John

The testimony of the Gospel of John regarding the Sabbath and the first day of the week is of special interest for two reasons: (1) its late date and (2) its apostolic authority. Although this Gospel cannot be dated precisely, the majority of New Testament scholars opt for a date around the end of the first century. There is no conclusive evidence that this is the case, but such a date would harmonize with the testimony of early Christian writers.[32] If the Gospel is indeed that late, its testimony regarding the Christian day of worship is very significant.[33]

Furthermore, although the Gospel as it stands is anonymous, there are good grounds for regarding its testimony as originating from John the apostle, an eyewitness of Jesus. This view has the support of early Christian writers, and the Gospel itself appears to affirm it. The next-to-last verse of the postscript (chapter 21) declares: "This is the disciple who is bearing witness to these things, and who has written these things; and we know that his testimony is true" (verse 24). The "we" of this verse is an unidentified group, consisting perhaps of contemporary church leaders capable of certifying the authorship and authority of the Gospel. To what disciple are they referring? Verse 20 identifies him as "the disciple whom Jesus loved, who had lain close to his breast at the supper." This statement refers back to the announcement by Jesus of His betrayal in John 13:23ff. The fact that the disciple referred to was present at the Last Supper indicates that he was one of the twelve. His place of honor next to Jesus suggests that he was one of the inner circle (Peter, James, and John).[34] The disciple whom Jesus loved was later standing near the cross and accepted from Jesus the sacred charge of caring for His mother (chap. 19:25-27). He witnessed the awful end and saw the streams of water and blood issuing from Jesus' pierced side. "He who saw it has borne witness—his testimony is true, and he knows that he tells the truth—that you also may believe" (verse 35).

According to John 18:15, 16, Peter and another disciple followed Jesus to the court of the high priest. He was sufficiently known to secure access not only for himself but for Peter as well. John 20:2 seems also to identify "the other disciple" with the disciple whom Jesus loved. Support for the conclusion that this disciple was John is found, too, in the fact that neither James nor John is named in the Gospel. The two, however, are mentioned in John 21:2 as "the sons of Zebedee."

We conclude that it is John's authority that lies behind the fourth Gospel. The fact that he was one of Jesus' closest followers adds great weight to his testimony. Just as Jesus is in the bosom of the Father (John 1:18), so John the Beloved lay close to the breast of Jesus at the Last Supper.

John's Gospel pictures Mary Magdalene as coming to the tomb "on the first day of the week," "early, while it was still dark" (chap. 20:1). When she found the stone removed from the door of the tomb, she concluded that the body of Jesus had been removed, and she ran to report this to Simon Peter and John.

These two disciples began running together to the tomb, but John outran Peter and arrived first (verses 2-10). Although he looked into the opened tomb, he did not enter it until after Peter arrived and had gone in. What John saw in the tomb convinced him that this was no grave robbery. The condition of the graveclothes, with the napkin carefully rolled up, had meaning for him. "He saw and believed" (verse 8).

Apparently Mary had followed Peter and John back to the tomb at a slower pace, and remained behind after they "went back to their homes" (verse 10). In her deep grief she looked into the tomb, where she saw "two angels in white, sitting where the body of Jesus had lain, one at the head and one at the feet. They said to her, 'Woman, why are you weeping?'" Then turning around, she saw Jesus, whom she supposed to be the gardener, and requested, "'Tell me where you have laid him'" (verse 15). In His familiar way He spoke her name, "'Mary.'" She sprang forward to embrace Him, but Jesus said to her, "'Do not hold me'" (verse 17). Then she hastened to the disciples with the news, "'I have seen the Lord.'"

The following evening the risen Christ appeared to the eleven disciples, apart from Thomas. This happened "on the evening of that day, the first day of the week" (verse 19). Evidently the Gospel is here using the Roman method of reckoning time (from midnight to midnight) rather than the Jewish (from sunset to sunset). The reference is to the evening after the first day (i.e., Sunday night), not the evening that began it, as in Jewish reckoning.

For what purpose had the disciples gathered together? Was it to celebrate the Resurrection? This could not be, for they did not at this time believe that Jesus had risen from the dead.[35] Was it to worship or hold religious services on the first day of the week? John gives no evidence of any such service. He gives no hint that the first day has any importance to the disciples. He asserts, rather, that they had gathered together behind locked doors for self-protection. The place where they were gathered was perhaps the same upper room where the Last Supper had been celebrated, and where they were apparently staying.[36] The doors[37] were closed and locked "for fear of the Jews" (verse 19). Jesus stepped into their midst and gave them the Semitic salutation "'Peace be with you.'" As evidence that He was indeed the risen Lord, He "showed them his hands and his side" (verse 20). Then He commissioned them with the words "'As the Father has sent me, even so I send you.'" And, as an anticipation of Pentecost, "he breathed on them, and said to them, 'Receive the Holy Spirit'" (verses 21, 22). Did Jesus give them any indication that the first day of the week was now to be substituted for the Sabbath? John's Gospel knows nothing of any such thing.

Thomas, the disciple who for some reason was absent, later refused to accept the testimony of the ten that they had indeed seen the risen Christ. "'Unless I see in his hands the print of the nails, and place my finger in the mark of the nails, and place my hand in his side, I will not believe,'" he insisted (verse 25).

About a week later Jesus again entered the locked room when Thomas was present (verses 26-29). The Revised Standard Version gives the time as "eight days later." Literally, the Greek reads, "after eight days." This is no doubt an idiom, meaning on the eighth day, just as the prediction of Jesus' resurrection "after three days" in Mark (chaps. 8:31; 9:31; 10:34) means "on the third day" (see Matt. 16:21; 20:19; Luke 9:22; 18:33). The Jews used the inclusive method of reckoning time. The specific day of the week is not indicated, though it is usually taken as meaning the following Sunday. Apparently John did not see any special significance in the day.

The specific purpose of Jesus' appearance was evidently to give Thomas the kind of evidence he demanded in order to believe. Jesus therefore invited the doubting Thomas to put his finger in the nailprints and his hand in Jesus' side. Thomas was overwhelmed and exclaimed, "'My Lord and my God!'" (John 20:28).

The final post-Resurrection appearance of Jesus to the disciples occurred on the shore of the "Sea of Tiberius" (chap. 21:1-8). Seven disciples (Peter, Thomas, Nathanael, James, John, and two others, possibly Andrew and Philip) had gone fishing. At daybreak, after an unsuccessful night on the lake, a lone figure called to them, "Have you caught anything?" Their answer was No. "Well, cast your net on the right side of the boat and you will catch some." They did so, and as a result caught 153 fish. John immediately recognized that the one responsible for the catch was the risen Lord. The impulsive Peter then left the net, the fish, the boat, and his companions, plunged into the sea, and swam to shore.

The chief purpose of this manifestation of their Lord was to reinstate Peter as a legitimate member of the apostolic band after his tragic betrayal of the Master. The day on which this revelation was made is not stated. The day itself apparently had no significance.

John, like the other Gospel writers, gives no support to the idea that the day of rest and worship had been changed from the Sabbath to Sunday. This is indeed surprising if such a change was supposedly made in the first century. If John's Gosepl is to be dated around the end of the first century, his silence about any such change is certainly striking.

The First-Day Meeting at Troas

The book of Acts gives the only explicit New Testament account of a public religious gathering on "the first day of the week" (Acts 20:7-12). On his way to Jerusalem Paul stopped for seven days at Troas, a town situated near the site of the ancient city of Troy. On the final day of his stay there, the Christian believers gathered together "to break bread." Luke states that this gathering took place on "the first day of the week," which would correspond roughly with the day we call Sunday. This passage is, consequently, repeatedly cited as evidence that Christians were now observing Sunday as a day of worship. It is therefore important to look closely at the passage to discover the nature of the evidence set forth.

There are several questions that need to be asked regarding this gathering: Was this a regular weekend meeting? Or was it occasioned by the presence and the imminent departure of the apostle Paul? And specifically when, in relation to our present Sunday, did the gathering occur? The reference to the use of lights and to the prolongation of the service past midnight, even till daybreak, plus the deep sleep of Eutychus, make it obvious that this was a night gathering. But on what night in relation to Sunday—the night before Sunday or the night after?

Furthermore, what is meant by the breaking of bread? Was this a fellowship dinner, the Lord's Supper, or perhaps a combination of the two?

Unfortunately, some of these questions cannot be answered with certainty.

To begin with, there is no evidence that this gathering was a regular weekend service, as it is often assumed to have been. The context would rather suggest that this was a special farewell meeting for the apostle Paul, who was leaving the following morning. The fact that this meeting was held on "the first day of the week" does not make it evident that the Christians of Troas habitually met on that day.[38]

Evidence has already been cited to indicate that this was a night meeting. F. F. Bruce suggests that this timing was for the convenience of the members who may have had to work during the daytime.³⁹ Be that as it may, all commentators agree, and it is clear from the text, that this was a night meeting. But on what night in relation to the first day of the week? Does Luke use the Jewish method of reckoning a 24-hour day from sundown to sundown,⁴⁰ or the Roman method of reckoning from midnight to midnight? There is an honest difference of opinion on this matter.

If Luke is using the Jewish method of reckoning, the meeting was held on what we call Saturday night, extending to early Sunday morning. This was the view held by Conybeare and Howson in their classic work on Paul: "It was the evening which succeeded the Jewish sabbath. On the Sunday morning the vessel was about to sail."⁴¹ This interpretation is reflected in a number of recent English translations of the New Testament.⁴² Foakes-Jackson was in agreement with this view when he wrote: "Paul and his friends could not, as good Jews, start on a journey on the Sabbath; they did so as soon after it as was possible, viz. at dawn on the 'first day'—the Sabbath having ended at sunset."⁴³ If the gathering took place on Saturday night, it would afford little support for Sundaykeeping.

However, there are other Bible students who argue that this gathering was held on Sunday night rather than on Saturday night. MacGregor takes this view and argues that "on the morrow" means the morrow after the first day of the week, i.e., Monday.⁴⁴ Bruce asserts: "Luke is not using the Jewish reckoning from sunset to sunset but the Roman reckoning from midnight to midnight."⁴⁵ Lake and Cadbury also defend this point of view.⁴⁶ In the face of such an honest difference of opinion it would not be safe to be dogmatic about the specific night of the week designated. If, however, the meeting was on Sunday night, the breaking of bread, which took place after midnight, must have been on Monday morning. Hence, though it could have been the Eucharist, it would afford little evidence for Sundaykeeping.

The purpose of the night gathering, Luke declares, was "to break bread." It had become customary in Palestine to break bread with the hands rather than to cut it with a knife. The host at the table, after the offering of thanks, broke the loaves and distributed them to his guests.⁴⁷ Hence, this preliminary action became the name for common meals in the early Christian communities,⁴⁸ even in the Gentile world. The act of breaking the bread was reminiscent of the days when Jesus as the host broke bread for His followers.⁴⁹ Table fellowship, therefore, gave expression to the spirit of unity and communion that prevailed. The memory of Jesus and the spirit of *koinonia* gave a religious character even to a common meal.

"To break bread," however, could also refer to the Lord's Supper,⁵⁰ a meal dedicated to the memory of Him who "took bread, blessed and broke it, and gave it to the disciples"⁵¹ as a symbol of Himself. Consequently, many regard the breaking of bread at Troas as a celebration of the Lord's Supper. It would be natural to expect such a celebration in connection with Paul's visit at Troas. However, there are features of the account that militate against this view. One is that the breaking of bread occurred after midnight, which appears to be strange if the purpose of the gathering in the evening was to celebrate the Lord's Supper. Furthermore, verse 11 speaks only of Paul as eating bread, not the entire congregation. Also there is no mention of a cup nor of any prayers.

Thus, this often-cited passage affords no real evidence for Sundaykeeping in New Testament times. There is not even certainty regarding the night involved:

Was it Saturday-Sunday or Sunday-Monday? In either case, the gathering was exceptional—a farewell gathering for the great missionary and his traveling companions. Nor is it certain that the Lord's Supper was celebrated. The expression "to break bread" could refer to the beginning of a farewell supper. But granting the possibility that this was more than a farewell fellowship meal, there is no evidence that this had become a weekly practice.

Indeed, there are numerous examples in the book of Acts of religious gatherings on the Sabbath in which the apostle took part. But there is no evidence whatever that regular assemblies for worship took place on the first day of the week.

Moreover, the book of Acts repeatedly pictures Paul as telling the Jews that he was true to the basic religion of their fathers as laid down in the law and the prophets (Acts 24:14). After his arrest he boldly asserted: "'Neither against the law of the Jews, nor against the temple, nor against Caesar have I offended at all'" (chap. 25:8). In the presence of Agrippa he declared: "'And so I stand here testifying both to small and great, saying nothing but what the prophets and Moses said would come to pass'" (chap. 26:22). Finally, in Rome he called together the Jews of that city and asserted that he had done nothing against the Jews or the customs of their fathers (chap. 28:17). How could he possibly make such assertions, which were not challenged, if he had taught the Gentiles to forsake the Sabbath and observe another day as the day of worship?

The Collection on the First Day of the Week

The chronologically earliest reference to the first day of the week in the New Testament documents is in 1 Corinthians 16:1, 2,[52] where Paul gives instruction concerning the relief offering "for the saints." These "saints" were the Jewish Christians of Jerusalem and Judea. Earlier in his career as a Christian, Paul with Silas had been sent to Jerusalem with funds from Antioch in a time of famine (Acts 11:29, 30). Now the great apostle was planning for a major love offering from the churches of Macedonia and Achaia for these poverty-stricken brethren. This was a matter that loomed large in Paul's mind and was one of the objects of his third missionary tour.[53] He looked upon this offering as a sign and pledge of the unity in Christ between the Gentile and Jewish Christians. And to the Corinthians he gave directions regarding it similar to those he had previously given the Galatian churches: "On the first day of every week, each of you is to put something aside and store it up, as he may prosper, so that contributions need not be made when I come" (1 Cor. 16:2).

Paul urged every member of the Corinthian Christian community to take part in this contribution. Every week each Christian was to contribute from his week's earnings, laying aside this weekly offering "on the first day of the week."

Why did Paul select the first day of the week as the day when these monies were to be laid aside? Many see in this an indication that Sunday had already acquired a religious significance. Leon Morris comments: "This is the first piece of evidence to show that Christians habitually observed that day."[54] Ralph Martin writes: "This is undoubtedly an allusion to the Church's holy day, the day of Christian fellowship in commemoration of the Lord's Resurrection . . . and the day of the Supper-meal."[55] Steven Barabas declares: "Paul directed the Corinthian

Christians to bring their weekly offering to the charities of the Church on the first day of the week."[56]

But a careful examination of the passage leads us to ask whether such conclusions are inherent in the text, or whether they are simply a reading back into the New Testament of developments that came later? No sacred character whatever is ascribed to the first day of the week by the apostle Paul in this text. Nor does the passage say anything about going to church or bringing a weekly offering to the church's charities on that day.

The first day of the week is rather spoken of as a fitting time for an examination of accounts, and the putting aside of funds from the week's profits. "The reference," Grosheide concedes, "is not to the church services but to a personal assignment which everyone had to perform."[57] "Each of you is to put something aside and store it up, as he may prosper" is the direction.

The American Standard Version gives a literal rendering: "Let each one of you lay by him in store, as he may prosper." "Lay by him" *(par heautō tithetō)* means to put aside *at home*.[58] Grosheide comments: "Paul trusts the Corinthians: he does not ask them to hand in their collection on a weekly basis, they are allowed to keep the collected money and thus little by little a significant amount will be saved up."[59] And Craig explains, "Paul's exhortation called for regularity in saving rather than for faithful attendance upon the assemblies."[60] If these Christians were meeting for public worship on the first day, one may well ask why they were admonished to put aside funds privately at home on that day.

No reason is indicated for the selection of the first day of the week. Deissmann has suggested the possibility that the first day of the week may have been payday in the Imperial period.[61] The same suggestion is made by J. Hering in his commentary on 1 Corinthians.[62] If this is so, the reason for the choice of the day has nothing to do with any supposed sacredness now attributed to that day. The act of reviewing the course of Providence and the prosperity experienced may be, of course, a deeply religious one, but that does not mean that the day on which it is done is therefore sacred. Long ago Neander correctly observed: "All mentioned here is easily explained, if one simply thinks of the ordinary beginning of the week in secular life."[63]

The beginning of the week may well have been designated, furthermore, so that the offering could be given the priority it deserved. Before the demands of secular life could absorb the week's earnings, they were admonished to plan for this special offering.

This passage sets forth valuable suggestions for systematic and regular fund raising. But to extract from it evidence of a change in the day of worship is to give a forced interpretation.

The Lord's Day in Revelation 1:10

In addition to the New Testament references to the "first day of the week," which have been examined, there remains to be considered the reference to "the Lord's day" in the opening chapter of the Apocalypse. The passage reads: "I John . . . was on the island called Patmos on account of the word of God and the testimony of Jesus. I was in the Spirit on the Lord's day, and I heard behind me a loud voice like a trumpet" (Rev. 1:9, 10).

This is the only passage in the Bible where the exact Greek phrase here translated "the Lord's day" is found. Unfortunately, there is no indication in the context to guide us in knowing what day is referred to. Nor do contemporary Christian writers help us, for there is no unequivocal use of the phrase in any authentic document for nearly a century after John. Nevertheless, the vast majority of commentaries interpret this as an undoubted reference to Sunday.

There is, of course, no question that Sunday became known as the Lord's day at a somewhat later time. *Kuriakē* by itself, in fact, became the name for Sunday in later Greek, and remains so in the modern form of the language. The Latin equivalent *Dominica dies*, found in the Vulgate of the passage, became the name for Sunday in ecclesiastical Latin. In fact *Dominica* is reflected in the name for Sunday in the Romance languages, e.g., *domenica* in Italian, *domingo* in Spanish, and *dimanche* in French.

But the question at issue is whether Sunday was known as "the Lord's day" in the late first century, and whether John meant Sunday by the phrase in Revelation 1:10. There is no specific evidence of either. It must further be pointed out that John's Gospel is usually dated later than the Apocalypse. Yet, as noted above, the Gospel refers to Sunday simply as "the first day of the week," which seems strange if it was then known as "the Lord's day."

A few commentators interpret "the Lord's day" in Revelation 1:10 as equivalent to the Old Testament "Day of the Lord," i.e., the eschatological day of judgment.[64] Although the Old Testament phrase *Yom Yahweh*[65] (Day of Yahweh) is not translated as *kuriakē hemera* in the Septuagint, but as *hē hēmera tou kuriou*, using the genitive rather than the adjective, it may be argued that there is little difference in meaning between the two.[66] The genitive may well have been used by the Septuagint translators in imitation of the Hebrew, which has a dearth of adjectives and frequently supplies the lack by the use of a genitive construction. Those who interpret "the Lord's day" in Revelation 1:10 as the future "Day of the Lord" argue that John in vision was transported to that day, and beheld its events being unfolded. According to this view, Revelation 1:10 means: "In my trance I found myself at the day of judgment."

Charles H. Welch, in advocating this view, writes: "The book of Revelation is taken up with something infinitely vaster than days of the *week*. It is solely concerned with the day of the LORD. To read that John became in spirit *on* the Lord's day (meaning Sunday) tells us practically nothing. To read in the solemn introduction that John became in spirit *in* the Day of the Lord, that day of prophetic import, is to tell us practically everything."[67]

But does the context of the phrase "the Lord's day" in Revelation 1:10 permit this kind of interpretation? I think not. The vision that John beheld after being caught up by the Spirit was not of events that belong to the eschatological "Day of the Lord." Rather it was a vision of the glorified Christ walking among the seven lampstands, representing the seven churches, as a minister to them in the present age. In Revelation 1:9, 10, the prophet gives the place and time when he received the vision, rather than implying that in his vision he was transported to the final day of judgment: "I John . . . was on the island called Patmos. . . . I was in the Spirit on the Lord's day."

A third interpretation, which has not been given adequate attention by most New Testament students, is that "the Lord's day" refers to the Christian Pascha, the annual celebration of Christ's resurrection, which later came to be called

"Easter." It is entirely possible that the earliest references in postcanonical writers to "the Lord's day" do not refer to a weekly observance at all, but to a yearly Resurrection-day celebration. This annual Lord's day was an appropriate time for the baptism of catechumens and the celebration of the Eucharist.[68] Dugmore suggests that there could be no more fitting time for John to have a vision of the risen and glorified Christ than on the anniversary of the Resurrection.

A basis for such an annual celebration might well be seen in Paul's first letter to the Corinthians, where the Lordship of Christ is especially emphasized. Was Paul suggesting such a celebration when he wrote: "For Christ, our paschal lamb, has been sacrificed. Let us, therefore, celebrate the festival" (1 Cor. 5:7, 8)? The fact that Christ arose on the day when the offering of first fruits was presented by the Jews seems to form the background of a later statement: "But in fact Christ has been raised from the dead, the first fruits of those who have fallen asleep" (chap. 15:20).

Finally, if one interprets the phrase "the Lord's day" according to the analogy of Scripture, a case can be made for regarding it as a reference to the seventh-day Sabbath. The Sabbath was set apart for sacred use at Creation (Gen. 2:2, 3). The intermediate agent in that creation, according to several New Testament passages,[69] was the Lord Jesus Christ. The fourth of the famous Ten Words describes the seventh day "as a sabbath to the Lord your God" (Ex. 20:10ff.). In the book of Isaiah God calls it "'my holy day'" and "'the holy day of the Lord'" (Isa. 58:13). All three of the Synoptic Gospels quote Jesus saying, "'The Son of man is lord even of the sabbath'" (Mark 2:28; cf. Matt. 12:8; Luke 6:5).

This view may also have the support of an interesting reference to the Lord's day in the apocryphal Acts of John: "And on the seventh day, it being the Lord's day . . ." It is not possible to be certain that the author refers to the seventh day of the week. He may possibly mean the seventh day of the journey, but the former seems probable.

But if John means the Sabbath in Revelation 1:10, why should he refer to it as "the Lord's day"? The book of Revelation has as its background the conflict between the "Lord Caesar" and the "Lord Christ." Christians were facing persecution and the threat of martyrdom because of their refusal to recognize Caesar as lord. For them there was but one Lord, Jesus Christ (1 Cor. 8:5, 6). Deissmann has shown that there were special days devoted to the Roman emperor. Would it not be appropriate under such circumstances to exalt Jesus Christ as "the ruler of kings on earth" (Rev. 1:5), and to refer to the Sabbath as the real "Lord's day"?

In conclusion, one may say that there is not sufficient data given in the book of Revelation to be certain of the correct interpretation of the phrase "the Lord's day" in Revelation 1:10. The popular attempt to equate it with Sunday does not rest on evidence supplied by the Scriptures but upon postapostolic usage of the phrase, long after John's time. The view that the phrase refers to the eschatological day of judgment is doubtful. More attention should be given to the possibility that the phrase refers to an annual resurrection celebration. And study could well be given to the idea that what is meant is in reality the seventh-day Sabbath.

THE SABBATH IN SCRIPTURE AND HISTORY

NOTES

[1] The exceptions are Acts 20:7 and 1 Corinthians 16:1, 2.
[2] C. E. B. Cranfield, *The Gospel According to Saint Mark* (Cambridge, Eng., 1959), p. 463.
[3] Mishnah Rosh ha-Shanah, 1. 8. (Danby).
[4] Cranfield, *loc. cit.*
[5] Cf. Matt. 27:56, "the mother of the sons of Zebedee."
[6] *Diagenomenou tou sabbaton* means "the Sabbath having intervened."
[7] Cranfield, *op. cit.*, p. 464.
[8] Henry Barclay Swete, *The Gospel According to St. Mark* (Grand Rapids, 1951), p. 395.
[9] The Old Latin manuscript Codex Bobiensis (k) adds a description of the Resurrection after "'from the door to the tomb'" in verse 3: "Suddenly, at the third hour of the day, there was darkness over the whole earth, and angels descended from heaven, and rising in the splendor of the living God they ascended together with him, and immediately it was light" (see William L. Lane, *The Gospel According to Mark*, NIC [Grand Rapids, 1974], p. 582, n. 3).
[10] In the phrase the "first day," the Greek uses the cardinal numeral "one."
[11] In contrast to verse 2, the ordinal numeral *prōtē* is used for "first," and "week" *(sabbatou)* is singular.
[12] Irenaeus *Against Heresies* 3. 10. 5 (ANF 1:426); cf. the possible reference to Mark 16:17, 18, in 2. 20. 3 (p. 388).
[13] Deut. 21:22, 23.
[14] Josephus *War of the Jews* 4. 5. 2 (Whiston).
[15] W. Michaelis, "λευκός," *TDNT*, 4:244, 245.
[16] Carl Schneider, "κάθημαι," *TDNT*, 3:443.
[17] Robertson, *Word Pictures in the New Testament* (Nashville, 1930-1933), 1:239.
[18] Walter Bauer, *A Greek-English Lexicon of the New Testament and Other Early Christian Literature*, rev. and augm. by William F. Arndt and F. Wilbur Gingrich (Chicago, 1957), p. 606.
[19] See the *Good News Bible* (T.E.V.), Goodspeed, *The Jerusalem Bible*, Weymouth's translation, et cetera; cf. *The New English Bible* and *The Modern Language Bible*.
[20] Eduard Lohse, "σάββατον," *TDNT*, 7:20, n. 158.
[21] W. M. Ramsay, *The Bearing of Recent Discovery on the Trustworthiness of the New Testament* (Grand Rapids, 1953), p. 222.
[22] Greek *akribōs*.
[23] Greek *kathexēs tini graphein*, "write something for someone in correct chronological order," Bauer, Arndt, and Gingrich, *op. cit.*, p. 389.
[24] The accusative case, *to sabbatōn*, indicates duration of time.
[25] Alfred Plummer, *A Critical Exegetical Commentary on the Gospel According to S. Luke*, ICC (Edinburgh, 1922), p. 543.
[26] The stone at the entrance of the tomb would be difficult to remove. An interesting addition to Luke 23:53 in Codex Bezae, the Old Latin manuscripts, and the Sahidic dialect of the Coptic read: "And when he had laid him, he placed a great stone on the sepulchre which twenty men could scarce have rolled."
[27] The words "He is not here, but has arisen," found in numerous manuscripts, are omitted from the Revised Standard Version, *The New English Bible*, and other English versions, because they are absent from the "western" manuscripts (Codex Bezae and the Old Latin manuscripts), and are therefore regarded as, to use a Westcott and Horte designation, a "western noninterpolation." Whether they are genuine or not, the question "'Why search among the dead for one who lives?'" (N.E.B.) clearly implies the Resurrection.
[28] Luke 9:22, 44; 18:31-33; and parallels in Matthew and Mark.
[29] Luke 24:17; see A. T. Robertson, *A Translation of Luke's Gospel* (New York, 1923), p. 133.
[30] The Greek of this sentence contains an idiom that is difficult to put into English. There is no general agreement among philologists regarding its translation. The meaning of the verb *agei* has been variously given as "keep," "spend" (G. Abbott-Smith, *A Manual Greek Lexicon of the New Testament*, 3d ed. [Edinburgh, 1937], p. 8; Joseph Henry Thayer, *A Greek-English Lexicon of the New Testament* [New York, 1889], pp. 9, 10); "observe," "pass" (Henry George Liddell and Robert Scott, *A Greek-English Lexicon* [Oxford, 1940], p. 18); "carry out" or "complete" (Hermann Cremer, *Biblico-Theological Lexicon*, 4th ed. [Edinburgh, 1895], p. 61). But the chief matter of disagreement is whether this verb should be taken impersonally (Plummer, *op. cit.*, p. 554; John Martin Creed, *The Gospel According to St. Luke* [London, 1960], p. 296; C. F. D. Moule, *An Idiom Book of New Testament Greek* [Cambridge, Eng., 1953], p. 27), i.e., "one passes" or "one is keeping" (or "spending") this third day or "we are at the third day"; or whether "Jesus" or "He" should be supplied as the subject, i.e., "Jesus is spending the third day" (Bauer, Arndt, and Gingrich, *op. cit.*, p. 14) or "He is already spending the third day" (F. Blass and A. Debrunner, *A Greek Grammar of the New Testament*, trans. and ed. by Robert W. Funk [Chicago, 1961], par. 129) or "He has already allowed three days to pass" (James Hope Moulton and Nigel Turner, *A Grammar of New Testament Greek* [Edinburgh, 1963], 3:291).
[31] The addition "and from a honeycomb" is found in later manuscripts. It is doubtful that this was part of the original text. Metzger explains this as an interpolation: "Since in parts of the ancient church honey was used in the celebration of the Eucharist and in the baptismal liturgy, copyists may have added the reference here in order to provide scriptural sanction for liturgical practice."—Bruce M. Metzger, *A Textual Commentary* (London and New York, 1971), p. 188.
[32] E.g., Irenaeus *Against Heresies* 3. 1; Clement of Alexandria according to Eusebius *Ecclesiastical History* 6. 14. 5-7; and the Antimarcionite Prologues.
[33] Archeological evidence shows that a date in the latter part of the second century, as was advocated by F. C. Baur and others, is untenable. The Edgerton Papyrus #2, dated A.D. 140-160, contains Gospel narratives that borrowed from all the Gospels, including John. The Rylands Papyrus 457 (p^{52}) is a small fragment of the gospel from central Egypt dated *c.* A.D. 125, indicating the gospel was known there at that time. The discovery of a gnostic library at Nag Hammadi, and the Qumran scrolls have shed light on the language and background. Albright and others have also shown that the author of John was well acquainted with Palestinian topography, Jewish customs, et cetera. See W. F. Albright, "Recent Discoveries in Palestine and the Gospel of St John," in *The Background of the New Testament and Its Eschatology*, ed. by W. D. Davies and D. Daube (Cambridge, Eng., 1956), pp. 153-171.
[34] See Mark 9:2; 14:33; and parallels.
[35] Luke 24:36-43; cf. Mark 16:9-13.

36 Acts 1:13.
37 The plural suggests that both the outer gate leading to the courtyard and the inner door opening into the room were both secured.
38 See Josef Maria Nielen, *The Earliest Christian Liturgy* (St. Louis, Mo., and London, 1941), p. 346.
39 F. F. Bruce, *Commentary on the Book of the Acts, NIC* (Grand Rapids, 1956), p. 408.
40 Gen. 1:5, 8; Lev. 23:32; cf. Mark 1:32.
41 W. J. Conybeare and J. S. Howson, *The Life and Epistles of the Apostle Paul* (New York, n.d.), p. 520.
42 See the Catholic edition of the Revised Standard Version, *The Jerusalem Bible, The New English Bible*, the *Good News Bible*, and Ronald Knox's, J. B. Phillips', and William Barclay's translations.
43 F. J. Foakes-Jackson, *The Acts of the Apostles, Moffatt New Testament Commentary* (London, 1931), p. 187.
44 G. H. C. MacGregor, Exegesis of "The Acts of the Apostles," *IB*, 9:267.
45 Bruce, *loc. cit.*
46 F. J. Foakes-Jackson and Kirsopp Lake, eds., *The Beginnings of Christianity*, part 1: *The Acts of the Apostles*, 5 vols. (London, 1920-33), vol. 4: Kirsopp Lake and Henry J. Cadbury, *English Translation and Commentary*, p. 255.
47 Johannes Behm, "κλάω," *TDNT*, 3:728, 729.
48 *Ibid.*, p. 729; Acts 2:42, 46.
49 Matt. 14:19; 15:36; Mark 8:6, 19.
50 1 Cor. 11:20.
51 Matt. 26:26.
52 1 Corinthians is usually dated c. A.D. 57.
53 Rom. 15:25-27; 2 Corinthians 8, 9; Acts 24:17.
54 Leon Morris, *The First Epistle of Paul to the Corinthians* (Grand Rapids, 1958), p. 238; cf. Oscar Cullmann, *Early Christian Worship* (London, 1953), pp. 10, 11.
55 Ralph P. Martin, *Worship in the Early Church* (London, 1964), p. 79.
56 Steven Barabas, "Sabbath," *The Zondervan Pictorial Bible Dictionary* (Grand Rapids, 1963), p. 736.
57 F. W. Grosheide, *Commentary on the First Epistle to the Corinthians, NIC* (Grand Rapids, 1953), p. 398.
58 Bauer, Arndt, and Gingrich, *op. cit.*, pp. 823, 615.
59 Grosheide, *op. cit.*, p. 398.
60 Clarence Tucker Craig, Exegesis of "The First Epistle to the Corinthians," *IB*, 10:256.
61 Adolf Deissmann, *Light From the Ancient East* (New York [1922]), p. 361.
62 Jean Hering, *The First Epistle of Saint Paul to the Corinthians* (London, 1962), p. 183.
63 Augustus Neander, *General History of the Christian Religion and Church* (Boston, 1854-1870), 1:239.
64 Examples include: F. J. A. Hort, *The Apocalypse of St. John I-III* (London, 1908), p. 15; J. B. Smith, *A Revelation of Jesus Christ*, ed. by J. Otis Yoder (Scottdale, Penn., 1961), pp. 319-324; J. A. Seiss, *The Apocalypse*, 7th ed., 3 vols. (New York, 1900); Charles W. Welch, *This Prophecy* (Banstead, Eng., 1950), p. 49.
65 Isa. 2:9; Amos 5:18-27; Joel 2:11, 31; Seph. 1:7, 14; 2:2, 3; 3:8, et cetera.
66 Werner Foerster, "κύιος," *TDNT*, 3:1096. In 1 Corinthians 11:20 Paul speaks of the Lord's Supper, using the adjective *kuriakon* (the only place other than Revelation 1:10 where the adjective is found in the New Testament), while in 1 Corinthians 10:21 he speaks of the Lord's table, using the genitive *tou kuriou*.
67 Welch, *loc. cit.*
68 C. W. Dugmore, "Lord's Day and Easter," *Neotestamentica et patristica*, supplement to *Novum Testamentum* (Leiden, 1962), 6:272-281. Lawrence T. Geraty, "The Pascha and the Origin of Sunday Observance," *AUSS* 3 (1965):85-96. Kenneth A. Strand, "Another Look at 'Lord's Day' in the Early Church and in Rev. I. 10," *New Testament Studies* (1966-1967), 13:74-181.
69 John 1:1-3; Col. 1:15-17; Heb. 1:1, 2.

Sabbath and Sunday in Christian History
PART II

CHAPTER 7

The Rise of Sunday Observance in Early Christianity

Samuele Bacchiocchi

THE question of the origin of Sunday observance in early Christianity has in recent years aroused great interest on the part of scholars of differing religious persuasions. Numerous scientific and scholarly studies on the subject have appeared over the past two decades and are clear evidence of renewed interest in finding a more satisfactory answer to the ever-intriguing question of the time, place, and causes of the origin of Christian Sundaykeeping.[1]

Jerusalem and the Origin of Sunday

The tendency in these recent studies has been to attribute to the apostles, or even to Christ, the initiative and responsibility for the abandonment of Sabbathkeeping and the institution of Sunday observance in its place. This thesis that the institution of Sunday observance goes back to the very first community of Jerusalem rests on several assumptions.

It is assumed by some students, for instance, that since Paul could hardly have pioneered the observance of Sunday inasmuch as he is the only New Testament writer who warns against the observance of days (Col. 2:16; Gal. 4:10; Rom. 14:5, 6), Sunday observance must have first begun in the primitive community of Jerusalem, prior to Paul's Gentile mission. It is pointed out that if Paul had been the promoter of Sunday observance, he would have met and answered objections from a Judaizing opposition, as was the case with regard to circumcision. The absence of any trace of a Sabbath-Sunday controversy between Paul and the Judaizing party is, therefore, interpreted as indicating that worship on the first day of the week is an original apostolic institution that Paul found well established and thus accepted as a *fait accompli*.[2]

It is also presumed by some that since the events of the Resurrection and/or the appearances of Jesus occurred in Jerusalem on a Sunday, the apostles must then have instituted Sunday observance in the city to commemorate these very events by a distinctive Christian day and with a unique Christian liturgy. This action was allegedly encouraged by the immediate necessity felt by the earliest Christians in Jerusalem to have a special time and place for their worship, since they "no longer felt at home in Jewish sabbath worship."[3] Moreover, it is argued that only the apostolic authority exercised in Jerusalem—the mother church of Christendom—could have legitimately changed the day of worship and enforced it on Christians at large.

These arguments appear persuasive, but their validity must be tested in the light of the historical information provided by both the New Testament and the early patristic literature regarding the theological orientation of the Jerusalem church: Do the earliest documentary sources suggest that the first Christians "no longer felt at home in Jewish sabbath worship"[4] and consequently abandoned at once its regular worship time and places? Did the primitive church of Jerusalem break immediately and radically from the Jewish religious traditions and services? Are there evidences that the resurrection of Christ was first commemorated in Jerusalem on a Sunday through the celebration of the Lord's Supper? Owing to the limited scope of the present chapter, only brief answers can be provided here, with reference in the notes to my more extensive treatment.

The Resurrection.—The widely accepted view that "the event of the resurrection has determined the choice of Sunday as the day of worship"[5] rests more on speculation than on facts. Are there any sayings in the New Testament enjoining the commemoration of Christ's resurrection on the actual day on which it occurred? No!

Is Sunday ever called in the New Testament the "Day of Resurrection"? No! It is consistently denominated "first day of the week."[6] Was the "Lord's Supper" celebrated exclusively on Sunday to commemorate Christ's resurrection? No! The New Testament suggests that it was celebrated at *indeterminate* times and on various days (cf. 1 Cor. 11:18, 20, 33, 34). Moreover, the rite proclaims, primarily, "the Lord's *death* till he comes" (verse 26),* not the Resurrection.[7]

Is Christ's resurrection presented in the earliest documents as the primary theological motivation for Sunday worship. No! Both Barnabas and Justin Martyr, who provide the earliest record of Sundaykeeping, mention the Resurrection as the secondary or additional reason for its observance, though this is not to deny the fact that the Resurrection later became the dominant reason for Sunday observance.[8]

The foregoing indications suffice to discredit the claim that Christ's resurrection determined the origin of Christian Sunday worship during the lifetime of the apostles.

The Jerusalem Church in the New Testament.—The book of Acts, which provides the earliest historical account of the Jerusalem church, gives no hint that the acceptance of the Messiah caused converted Jews to abandon immediately the regular worship time and places of their own people. Peter and John, for example, after the Pentecost experience, went up to the Temple at the hour of prayer (Acts 3:1). There are ample indications that attendance at the Temple and synagogue was still continued by Christ's followers, though complementary private meetings were conducted too. The synagogue is, in fact, the place of worship most

---

* Unless otherwise indicated, all Scripture references in this chapter are taken from the Revised Standard Version.

frequently mentioned as attended not only by Christ and His disciples but also by Christian converts. Paul, for example, met regularly in the synagogue on the Sabbath with "Jews and Greeks" (Acts 18:4, 19; 13:5, 14, 42, 44; 14:1; 17:1, 10, 17). Apollo, likewise, when he arrived at Ephesus, met with the believers in the synagogue (chap. 18:24-26).*

Close attachment to Jewish religious traditions and services is particularly noticeable in the early Jerusalem church. Its membership was composed mostly of converted Jews (chaps. 2:41; 4:4; 5:14), characterized as "'zealous for the law'" (chap. 21:20). Luke reports (in Acts) that "a great many of the priests were obedient to the faith" (chap. 6:7). Presumably these converted priests became the "elders" who together with James administered the Jerusalem church.[9] The very choice of James, "the Lord's brother" (Gal. 1:19), rather than an apostle as leader of the church, indicates how Jewishly oriented the new leadership and "Christian priesthood" in Jerusalem really were by placing emphasis on blood relationship with Christ. Several works of Judeo-Christian origin reveal more explicitly than does the New Testament that in choosing the leaders of the church, the matter of blood relationship was regarded as more important than any other kind of previous relationship with Christ.[10]

Certain events reported in Acts corroborate this conclusion. For instance, the Jewish persecution reported in Acts 6-8 was apparently not against the whole church but primarily against the "Hellenists," a nonconformist group. According to Acts 8:1, the church was "all scattered... except the apostles." That the apostles were allowed to remain in the city suggests that they did not share the radical ideas of the Hellenists, but maintained an allegiance to basic Jewish traditions.[11]

Several additional matters reported in Acts further establish this fact. First, we may notice that at the earliest Christian ecumenical council, held in the city of Jerusalem (about A.D. 49-50), James, the presiding officer, proposed that the Gentiles who became Christians were to be exempted from circumcision, but at the same time they were "'to abstain from the pollutions of idols and from unchastity and from what is strangled and from blood. For from early generations Moses has had in every city those who preach him, for he is read every sabbath in the synagogues'" (Acts 15:20, 21). The inclination toward traditional Jewish practices is obvious.[12] Second, in the account of Paul's last visit to Jerusalem (A.D. 58-60), the facts that Paul "was hastening to be at Jerusalem, if possible, on the day of Pentecost" (chap. 20:16) and that Paul's company had spent the days of "Unleavened Bread" at Philippi (verse 6) suggest that Christians still regulated their lives by the normative Jewish liturgical calendar.

Finally, more enlightening still is the account of what happened in Jerusalem itself. James and the elders not only informed Paul that the many thousands of converted Jews were "'*all zealous for the law*'" (chap. 21:20) but these leaders even confronted the apostle with the rumor that he dissuaded *Jewish* believers from practicing ancestral customs such as circumcision.[13] To discredit the malicious accusation and to prove that he himself "*live*[*d*] *in observance of the law*" (verse 24), Paul underwent a rite of purification in the Temple.

In such a climate of profound attachment to Jewish religious observances, is it conceivable that a longstanding and cherished custom such as Sabbathkeeping

---

* For a discussion of the Sabbath and Sunday in the New Testament, see the preceding two chapters.

had been abrogated and that a new day of worship had been introduced in its place? Hardly!

The Jerusalem Church After A.D. 70.—Because of indications such as the foregoing, some scholars prefer to place the beginning of Sunday observance no earlier than A.D. 70.[14] It is argued that the flight of the Christians from Jerusalem to Pella and the destruction of the Temple might have encouraged Palestinian Christians to break away from Sabbathkeeping at that time.

Undoubtedly, the exodus from and the destruction of Jerusalem had decisive effects on the relationship between Christianity and Judaism. There are, however, significant historical indications that exclude the possibility that the Judeo-Christians of Palestine introduced Sunday observance as early as the year A.D. 70 or soon thereafter.

The historians Eusebius (c. A.D. 260-340) and Epiphanius (c. A.D. 315-403) both inform us that the church of Jerusalem up to the siege of Hadrian (A.D. 135) was composed of, and administered by, converted Jews.[15] Eusebius describes a group of them, known as Ebionites, as being "zealous to insist on the literal observance of the Law."[16] Epiphanius adds that those Jewish Christians who fled from Jerusalem became known as the sect of the Nazarenes, who "fulfill till now Jewish rites as circumcision, the Sabbath, and others."[17] The fact that the Nazarenes, who represent "the very direct descendants of the primitive community"[18] of Jerusalem, retained Sabbathkeeping as one of their distinguishing marks for centuries after the destruction of Jerusalem shows persuasively that this was the original day of worship of the Jerusalem church and that no change from Sabbath to Sunday occurred among Palestinian Jewish Christians immediately after the destruction of the city in A.D. 70.

Another indirect indication of the survival of Sabbath observance among Palestinian Jewish Christians is provided by the curse of the Christians *(Birkath-ha-Minin)*, which the rabbinical authorities introduced (A.D. 80-90) in the daily prayer.[19] It has been conclusively shown that this was a test designed to bar the Christians from presence and/or participation in the synagogue service.[20] The fact that many Jewish Christians in Palestine still considered themselves essentially as Jews, keen to attend the Sabbath services at the synagogue, discredits any attempt to make them responsible at this time for the introduction of Sunday observance.[21]

It was not until the year A.D. 135 that a radical change took place in the church of Jerusalem. At that time Emperor Hadrian destroyed the city, expelled both the Jews and the Jewish Christians, and prohibited categorically the practice of the Jewish religion, especially Sabbathkeeping and circumcision.[22] In accordance with the emperor's edict, the city was repopulated by foreigners, and only Gentile Christians were allowed to enter.[23] The latter differed from Jewish Christians not only racially but presumably also theologically, since Epiphanius suggests that they provoked a controversy by introducing Easter Sunday.[24] A significant minority of Christians apparently refused to accept the innovation occasioned by the new imperial repressive measures taken against Jewish religious practices.[25]

The foregoing historical data discredits any attempt to make the Jerusalem church prior to A.D. 135 the champion of liturgical innovations such as Sunday observance. We have found that this church was both racially and theologically the closest and most loyal to Jewish religious traditions. After A.D. 135, however, radical changes took place in the Jerusalem church as a result of Hadrian's decree that prohibited the practice of the Jewish religion and particularly the observance of the Sabbath. But the new small Gentile church that became established in the city no longer enjoyed religious prestige or authority. In fact, for the second century nothing is known of the Jerusalem church, with the exception of a few uncertain names of bishops.[26] It would be futile, therefore, to probe further into the origin of Sunday observance among the new insignificant Gentile church in Jerusalem.

Since the adoption of new religious feast days and their enforcement on the rest of Christendom could presumably be accomplished only by a church that severed her ties from Judaism *early* and that enjoyed wide recognition, the church of the capital of the empire appears to be the most likely birthplace of Sunday observance. Several religious, social, and political conditions that prevailed both in the city of Rome and in the Christian church in that city substantiate the validity of this hypothesis.

Rome and the Origin of Sunday

The ancient Christian church in Rome, contrary to most Eastern churches, was composed primarily of a Gentile Christian majority (Romans 11 and 13) and a Judeo-Christian minority (Romans 14). Paul in his Epistle to the Romans explicitly affirms: "I am speaking to you Gentiles" (chap. 11:13).[27] The predominance of Gentile members and their conflict with the Jews, inside and outside the church, resulted, as stated well by Leonard Goppelt, in "a chasm between the Church and the Synagogue . . . unknown in the Eastern churches." [28]

Early Differentiation.—It is a recognized fact also that Christians were early distinguished from the Jews in the capital city. The latter, in fact, seemingly influenced Nero (through the Empress Poppaea Sabina, a Jewish proselyte) to relieve himself of the charge of arson by putting the blame on the Christians.[29] According to Tacitus, Nero "fastened the guilt [i.e., arson] and inflicted the most exquisite tortures on . . . Christians." [30] The fact that in Rome the Christians were clearly differentiated from the Jews more quickly than was the case in Palestine suggests the possibility that the abandonment of the Sabbath and adoption of Sunday as a new day of worship could have occurred first in Rome as part of this process of differentiation from Judaism. Additional significant factors present in the Church of Rome enable us to verify the validity of this hypothesis.

Anti-Judaic Feelings and Measures.—Following the death of Nero, the Jews experienced a setback. Military, political, fiscal, and literary repressive measures were taken against them on account of their resurgent nationalism, which exploded in violent uprisings in many places. Militarily, the statistics of bloodshed provided by contemporary historians, even allowing for possible exaggerations, are most impressive. Tacitus (*c.* A.D. 33-120), for instance, reports having heard that 600,000 Jews were besieged in the A.D. 70 war.[31] Dio Cassius (*c.* A.D. 150-235), states that in the Barkokeba war of A.D. 132-135, some 580,000 Jews were killed in action, besides the numberless who died of hunger and disease.[32]

Politically, under Vespasian (A.D. 69-79) both the Sanhedrin and the high priesthood were abolished; and under Hadrian, as we noted earlier, the practice of the Jewish religion and particularly Sabbathkeeping were outlawed.[33]

THE RISE OF SUNDAY OBSERVANCE IN EARLY CHRISTIANITY

Also, fiscally, the Jews were subjected to a discriminatory tax, the *fiscus judaicus*, which was introduced by Vespasian and intensified first by Domitian (A.D. 81-96) and later by Hadrian.[34]

Literarily, a new wave of anti-Semitic literature surged at that time, undoubtedly reflecting the Roman mood against the Jews. Writers such as Seneca (died A.D. 65), Persius (A.D. 34-62), Petronius (died *c.* A.D. 66), Quintilian *(c.* A.D. 35-100), Martial *(c.* A.D. 40-104), Plutarch *(c.* A.D. 46-after 119), Juvenal (died *c.* A.D. 125), and Tacitus *(c.* A.D. 55-120), who lived in Rome for most of their professional lives, reviled the Jews racially and culturally.[35] Particularly were the Jewish customs of Sabbathkeeping and circumcision contemptuously derided as examples of degrading superstition.

These repressive measures and hostile attitudes prevailing toward the Jews were particularly felt in the capital city. Titus, for example, because of the mounting hostility of the populace against the Jews, was forced, though "unwillingly" *(invitus)*, to ask Berenice, Herod the Younger's sister (whom he wanted to marry), to leave Rome.[36] The Jewish problem became particularly acute by Hadrian's time as a result of that emperor's policy of radical suppression of the Jewish religion.

Such circumstances apparently encouraged Christians, too, to produce a whole body of anti-Jewish literature, which began appearing at that time.[37] A "Christian theology" of separation from, and contempt for, the Jews was developed. Characteristic Jewish customs, such as circumcision and Sabbath-keeping, were particularly condemned.

The Church of Rome and the Sabbath.—Though denunciations of Sabbath observance can be found in the writings of Church Fathers from many geographical areas, it is in the Church of Rome that we find evidence of the earliest concrete measures to wean Christians away from veneration of the Sabbath and to urge Sunday observance exclusively. Justin Martyr, for instance, writing from Rome about the middle of the second century, presents a most devastating and systematic condemnation of the Sabbath, as well as giving the earliest explicit account of Christian Sunday worship services. He empties the Sabbath of all its theological significance, reducing it to a temporary ordinance derived from Moses, which God imposed solely on the Jews as "a mark to single them out for punishment they so well deserve for their infidelities."[38] He refers, on the other hand, to Sunday as "the day on which we all hold our common assembly, because it is the first day on which God, having wrought a change in the darkness and matter, made the world; and Jesus Christ our Saviour on the same day rose from the dead."[39]

Justin's negative view of the Sabbath is reflected also in the early introduction of the Sabbath fast by the Church of Rome, in spite of the opposition of Eastern Christianity and of several Western churches. That the Church of Rome was the champion of the Sabbath fast and anxious to impose it on other Christian communities is well attested by the historical references from Bishop Callistus (A.D. 217-222), Hippolytus *(c.* A.D. 170-236), Pope Sylvester (A.D. 314-335), Pope Innocent I (A.D. 401-417), Augustine (A.D. 354-430), and John Cassian *(c.* A.D. 360-435).[40] The fast was designed not only to express sorrow for Christ's death but also, as Pope Sylvester emphatically states, to show "contempt for the Jews" *(execratione Judaeorum)* and for their Sabbath "feasting" *(destructiones ciborum)*.[41]

How would fasting on the Sabbath serve to avoid "appearing to observe the Sabbath with the Jews," to use the words of Victorinus of Pettau (died c. A.D. 304)?[42] The answer is to be found in the fact that for the Jews the Sabbath was definitely not a day of fasting or of mourning. Even the strictest Jewish sects objected to fasting on the Sabbath. The rabbis, though they differed in their views regarding the time and number of the Sabbath meals, agreed that food on the Sabbath ought to be abundant and good.[43]

That the early Christians adopted this Jewish custom is implied, for instance, in Augustine's rhetorical remark in which, when referring to the Sabbath, he says: "Did not the tradition of the elders prohibit fasting on the one hand, and enjoin rest on the other?"[44] Further support can be seen in the opposition to the Sabbath fast by Christians in the East and in some important Western areas, such as in Milan at the time of Ambrose (died A.D. 397), and in certain churches and regions of North Africa.[45]

A strict Sabbath fast would naturally preclude also the celebration of the Lord's Supper, since partaking of its elements would be regarded as breaking the fast. Consequently, as reported by several Fathers, the Sabbath was made in Rome not only a day of fasting but also a day in which no Eucharistic celebration and no religious assemblies were allowed.[46] The transformation of the Sabbath from a day of feasting, joy, and religious celebrations to a day of fasting, mourning, and no religious assembly represents concrete measures taken by the Church of Rome to force Christians away from the veneration of the Sabbath. On the other hand, this practice enhanced Sunday, a day of rejoicing and feasting when the Sabbath fast was over.

When did the Church of Rome introduce the weekly Sabbath fast? The historical genesis of religious customs cannot always be established with certainty, and this is true regarding Sabbath fasting. That it was introduced early in Rome, however, is clearly implied by the following statement of Hippolytus (written in Rome between A.D. 202 and 234): "Even today (Καὶ γὰρ νυν) some . . . order fasting on the Sabbath, [a practice] of which Christ has not spoken, dishonoring the Gospel of Christ."[47] Though it is difficult to establish whether Hippolytus was referring to Bishop Callistus' decretal enjoining a seasonal Sabbath fast or to some Marcionites against whom he wrote a treatise (possibly to both?), the expression "even today" clearly presupposes that the custom had been known for some time.

It has been suggested that the weekly Sabbath fast originated as an extension of the annual Holy Saturday of the Easter season, when all Christians fasted.[48] This view appears altogether plausible, since, for instance, Tertullian and Augustine associated the two. Tertullian specifically approved the annual paschal Sabbath fast and condemned the weekly Sabbath fast that Rome and a few Western churches practiced. "You sometimes continue your Station [i.e., fast] even over the Sabbath,—a day never to be kept as a fast except at the passover season."[49] An additional indication of a connection between the two customs is provided by the fact that the annual paschal Saturday fast, like the weekly one, was designed to express not only sorrow for Christ's death but also contempt for the perpetrators of His death, namely the Jews. The *Didascalia Apostolorum* (c. A.D. 250), for instance, enjoins Christians to fast on Easter Friday and Saturday "on account of the disobedience of our brethren [i.e., the Jews] . . . because thereon the People killed themselves in crucifying our Saviour."[50]

THE RISE OF SUNDAY OBSERVANCE IN EARLY CHRISTIANITY

Our investigation so far has established that the change in the day of worship seems to have been encouraged, on the one hand, by the social, political, military, and literary anti-Judaic imperial policies that made it necessary for Christians to sever their ties with the Jews, and, on the other hand, by the very conflict existing between Jews and Christians. The Church of Rome, whose members, mostly of pagan extraction, experienced a break from the Jews earlier than in the East, and where the unpopularity of the Jews was particularly felt, appears to have played a leading role in inducing the adoption of Sunday observance, as well as in downgrading the Sabbath by the weekly Sabbath fast.

Sun Worship and the Origin of Sunday

Why, it may now be asked, was Sunday rather than another day of the week (such as Friday, the day of Christ's passion) chosen to evidence the Christian separation from Judaism? Anti-Judaism explains the necessity that arose to substitute a new day of worship for the Sabbath, but the reasons for the specific choice of Sunday must be found elsewhere. Significant indications suggest that Sun worship with its "Sun-day" was influential in determining the choice of Sunday.

Sun Worship and the Planetary Week Prior to A.D. 150.—To establish a possible causal relationship between Sun worship and the Christian adoption of Sunday observance, it is crucial to verify the contemporaneous existence by the end of the first century of both a widespread Sun worship and a common use of the planetary week with its "sun-day—dies solis." * Only if the planetary week was in use in the Greco-Roman world already in the first century of our era and the Sun was being venerated on Sunday does the possibility exist that Christian converts from paganism, facing the necessity to worship on a day that would be different from the Jewish Sabbath, were oriented toward the day of the Sun.[51]

Gaston H. Halsberghe has persuasively demonstrated in his recent monograph, *The Cult of Sol Invictus*, that Sun worship was "one of the oldest components of the Roman religion." As a result of the penetration of Eastern Sun cults, Halsberghe concludes that "from the early part of the second century A.D., the cult of *Sol Invictus* was dominant in Rome and in other parts of the Empire."[52] The identification and worship of the emperor as Sun-god, encouraged by the Eastern theology of the "King-Sun," and by political considerations, undoubtedly contributed to the diffusion of a public Sun cult.[53]

Did the planetary week also with its *"dies solis*—day of Sun" already exist in the first century A.D. in the Greco-Roman world? Only in such a case could the predominant Sun cults have enhanced the day of the sun and consequently influenced Christians to adopt this day for their weekly worship after reinterpreting its symbolism in the light of the Christian message.[54]

Several testimonies from such ancient writers as Horace (*c.* 35 B.C.), Tibullus (*c.* 29 B.C.), Petronius (died *c.* A.D. 66), Frontinus (*c.* A.D. 35-103), Plutarch (*c.* A.D. 46-after 119), Philostratus (*c.* A.D. 170-245), and Dio Cassius (*c.* A.D. 130-220) clearly attest the existence and common use of the planetary week already in the first century A.D.[55] Mural pictures and inscriptions of the planetary gods and days uncovered in Pompeii and Herculaneum, as well as the so-called *"indices*

---

* See the account of the planetary week given by S. Douglas Waterhouse in appendix A, pp. 308-322.

nundinarii" and three stone calendars (presenting in the right column the eight letters from A to H of the Roman *nundinum* market week and in the left column the seven letters from A to G of the planetary week, and to be dated no later than the time of Tiberius, A.D. 14-37), erase all doubt of the common use of the planetary week in ancient Rome from at least the beginning of the Christian Era.[56]

The prevailing Sun worship and the contemporaneous existence of the planetary week caused a significant development. The day of Saturn, which originally was the first day of the planetary week (as clearly evidenced by the *indices nundinarii* and by the mural inscriptions found in Pompeii and Herculaneum, where the days of the week are given horizontally starting with the day of Saturn), was in time supplanted by the day of the Sun, which moved from second place to first place in the week.

It is difficult to determine the exact time when the primacy and the prestige of the day of Saturn was transferred to that of the Sun. That this had occurred already by the middle of the second century is clearly indicated by the famous astrologer Vettius Valens. In his *Anthology,* composed between A.D. 154 and 174, he explicitly states: "And this is the sequence of the planetary stars in relation to the days of the week: Sun, Moon, Mars, Mercury, Jupiter, Venus, Saturn."[57] Statements from Justin Martyr and Tertullian, as well as several Mithraea and two constitutions of Constantine (March 7 and July 3, A.D. 321), confirm that the day of the Sun occupied the dominant place in the sequence of the days of the week.[58]

Since the emergence of the day of the Sun over that of Saturn occurred apparently in the early part of the second century in concomitance with the Christian adoption of Sunday observance in place of the Sabbath, one may ask, Is the latter related to the former? Did the advancement of the day of the Sun to the position of first day of the week possibly influence Christians, who desired to differentiate themselves from the Sabbath of the Jews, to adopt and adapt such a day for their weekly worship?

Several kinds of evidence support this hypothesis. It is a fact, first of all, that Christian converts from paganism were constantly attracted toward the veneration of the Sun. This is indicated not only by the frequent condemnation of this practice by the Fathers but also by significant reflexes of Sun worship in the Christian liturgy.[59] In early Christian art and literature, for instance, the image of the Sun was often used to represent Christ, the true "Sun of righteousness."[60] In the earliest known Christian mosaic (dated *c.* A.D. 240), found below the altar of St. Peter in Rome, Christ is portrayed as the Sun *(helios)* ascending on the quadriga chariot with a nimbus behind His head from which irradiates seven rays in the form of a T (allusion to the cross?).[61] Thousands of hours have been devoted to drawing the sun disk with an equal-armed cross behind the head of Christ and of other important persons.

Another significant indication of the influence of the Sun cults on early Christian worship is provided by the change in orientation for prayer from Jerusalem to the East.[62] Some of the reasons advanced by the Fathers to justify the adoption of the eastward position for prayer are that the Orient represents the birth of light, the orientation of "the ancient temples," God's paradise and/or Christ's coming.[63] Apparently, Christians who previously, as pagans, had venerated the Sun, when faced with the necessity of dissociating themselves from the Jews, not only abandoned the orientation toward Jerusalem for prayer but also reverted to the direction of sunrise, reinterpreting its meaning in the light of the Christian message. Would not the *daily* praying toward the Sun encourage Christians to worship also *weekly* on the day of the Sun?

Perhaps the most explicit example of Sun worship's influence on the Christian liturgical calendar is the adoption of the pagan feast of the *dies natalis Solis Invicti*—the birthday of the Invincible Sun—which was celebrated on December 25. That the Church of Rome introduced and championed this date (as in the case of Easter Sunday) is accepted by most scholars.[64] Mario Righetti, for instance, a renowned Catholic liturgist, writes: "After the peace the Church of Rome, to facilitate the acceptance of the faith by the pagan masses, found it convenient to institute the 25th of December as the feast of the temporal birth of Christ, to divert them from the pagan feast, celebrated on the same day in honor of the 'Invincible Sun' Mithras, the conqueror of darkness."[65]

These few examples evidence sufficiently the influence of Sun cults on Christian thought and liturgy. A more direct indication of the influence of the pagan veneration of the day of the Sun on the Christian adoption of the very same day is provided by the frequent use of the symbology of the day of the Sun to justify Sunday observance.

Justin Martyr (*c.* A.D. 100-165) emphasizes that Christians assemble "on the day called Sunday . . . because it is the first day on which God, having wrought a change in the darkness and matter, made the world."[66] Is the nexus between the day of the Sun and the creation of light on the first day a pure coincidence? It hardly seems so, not only because Justin himself in his *Dialogue with Trypho* explicitly compares the devotion that pagans render to the Sun with that which Christians offer to Christ, who is "more blazing and bright than the rays of the sun,"[67] but also because the coincidence between the creation of light on the first day and the veneration of the Sun on the selfsame day is clearly established by several Fathers. Eusebius (*c.* A.D. 260-340), for instance, refers explicitly to the motifs of the light and of the day of the Sun to justify Sunday worship: *"In this day of light,* first day and *true day of the sun,* when we gather after the interval of six days, we celebrate the holy and spiritual Sabbaths. . . . In fact, it is on this day of the creation of the world that God said: '*"Let there be light";* and there was light.' It is also on this day that the Sun of Justice has risen for our souls."[68]

Such testimonies and others that could be cited clearly reveal that the choice of the day of the Sun was not motivated by the desire to venerate the Sun-god on his day, but rather by the fact that such a day provided a fitting symbology that could efficaciously commemorate and explain to the pagan world two fundamental events of the history of salvation—*creation* and *resurrection.*[69] Jerome well expresses this point: "If it is called day of the Sun by the pagans, we most willingly acknowledge it as such, since it is on this day that the *light of the world has appeared* and on this day the *Sun of Justice has risen.*"[70]

Undoubtedly, the existence of a rich Judeo-Christian tradition that associated the Deity with the sun and light facilitated and encouraged such an amalgamation of ideas.[71] It appears, therefore, that the ingredients necessary to influence the Christian choice of the pagan day of the Sun were already present when the latter made its appearance in Rome. Various Sun cults were dominant in ancient Rome by the early part of the second century, and their symbology soon found counterparts in Christian literature, art, and liturgy. Furthermore, the valorization of the day of the Sun over that of Saturn (which we found to be concomitant with the Christian adoption of Sunday observance in place of the Sabbath) seemingly influenced the Christian choice of the same day, since its rich symbology was conducive to worship of the true Sun of Righteousness, who on the day "divided light from darkness and on the day of the resurrection separated faith from infidelity." [72]

The Early Theology of Sunday

A brief survey of the basic theological motivations advanced by the early Fathers to justify both the choice and the observance of Sunday will enable us to test the validity of the conclusions emerging from our study.

Resurrection.—We noticed earlier that the New Testament gives no hint that the apostles instituted a weekly or yearly commemoration of the Resurrection on Sunday. It is noteworthy, in fact, that both Barnabas and Justin, who lived at the very time when Sunday worship was rising, present the Resurrection as the second of two reasons, important but not predominant.[73] Nevertheless, the resurrection of Christ eventually emerged as the primary reason for the observance of Sunday. Augustine perhaps provides the most explicit enunciation of this when he writes: "The Lord's day was not declared to the Jews but to the Christians by the resurrection of the Lord and from that event its festivity had its origin." [74] Several liturgical practices such as the prohibition to fast and to kneel on Sunday, as well as the celebration of a Sunday-morning Lord's Supper, were introduced to honor specifically the memory of the Resurrection.[75] Since, however, Christ's resurrection initially was not the exclusive or preponderant justification for Sunday worship, we need to recognize and evaluate the role played by other theological motives as well.

Creation.—The commemoration of the anniversary of the creation of the world is a justification frequently adduced by the Fathers for observing Sunday.[76] We cited earlier Justin, Eusebius, and Jerome, who mention the creation of light on the first day as a reason for Sundaykeeping.[77] Apparently this justification was intended primarily for pagans to whom Christians wished to explain that on the day of the Sun they did not venerate the Sun-god but rather celebrated the creation of light and the rise of the Sun of Righteousness, events occurring on the first day.

In the polemic with Sabbathkeeping Christians, however, the Creation argument was used in a modified form to show the superiority of Sunday over the Sabbath. In the *Syriac Didascalia* (c. A.D. 250) the terms of the dispute are most explicit: "Cease therefore, beloved brethren, you who from among the People have believed, yet desire (still) to be tied with the bonds, and say that the Sabbath is prior to the first day of the week because that the Scripture has said: *In six days did God make all things; and on the seventh day he finished all his works, and he sanctified it.*

"We ask you now, which is first, Alaf or Tau? For that (day) which is the greater is that which is the beginning of the world, even as the Lord our Saviour said to Moses: *In the beginning God created the heaven and the earth.*" [78]

A similar reasoning appears, though in a more refined form, in the treatise *On the Sabbath and Circumcision,* found among the works of Athanasius (c. A.D. 296-373), but probably spurious: "The Sabbath was the end of the first creation, the Lord's day was the beginning of the second in which He renewed and restored the old. In the same way as He prescribed that they should formerly observe the Sabbath as a memorial of the end of the first things, so we honor the Lord's day as being the memorial of the new creation. Indeed, He did not create another one, but He renewed the old one and completed what He had begun to do."[79]

This notion of the Sabbath as herald of the end of the first and of the beginning of the second creation is totally foreign to the Scriptures and apparently was devised to refute the Sabbathkeepers' claim of the superiority of the Sabbath as the memorial of Creation.

The Eighth Day.—Another valuable arsenal of apologetic techniques to defend the superiority of Sunday over the Sabbath was provided by the symbology of the eighth day. As a designation for Sunday, this term first appears in anti-Judaic polemical writings, such as the *Epistle of Barnabas* and the *Dialogue with Trypho*. It was widely employed in Christian literature of the first five centuries.[80]

Such a designation apparently derives from chiliastic-eschatological speculations on the seven-day Creation week (sometimes called "cosmic week") prevailing in Jewish and Jewish Christian circles.[81] The duration of the world was subdivided into seven periods (or millennia), of which the seventh (identified with the Sabbath) generally represented paradise restored. At the end of the seventh period the eternal new eon would dawn, which eon came to be known as "the eighth day" since it was the successor to the seventh.

In the polemic with Sabbathkeepers, the symbology of the eighth day was applied to Sunday to prove the superiority of the latter over the Sabbath. A wide range of arguments were drawn not only from apocalyptic literature but also from the Scriptures, philosophy, and the natural world. As the eighth eschatological day, Sunday was defended as the symbol of the new world, superior to the Sabbath, which represented only the seventh terrestrial millennium.[82] Also, as the Gnostic ogdoad, Sunday was presented as a symbol of the rest of spiritual beings in the supercelestial eternal world, found above the sevenness of this transitory world.[83] Moreover, Sunday could be prestigiously traced back to the "prophecies" of the Old Testament, by means of the Biblical number eight, which the Fathers found in several references from the Old Testament, such as the eighth day for circumcision; the eight souls saved from the Flood; the fifteen cubits (seven plus eight) of the Flood waters above the mountains;[84] the superscription of Psalms 6 and 11 ("for the eighth day");[85] the fifteen (seven plus eight) gradual psalms;[86] the saying "give a portion to seven, or even to eight," of Ecclesiastes 11:2;[87] the eighth day when Job offered sacrifices; and others.[88] Invested with such "prophetic" authority, the eighth day could "legitimately" represent the fulfillment of the reign of the law, allegedly typified by the Sabbath, and the inauguration of the kingdom of grace supposedly exemplified by Sunday. Jerome expressed this view by saying that "the number seven having been fulfilled, we now rise to the Gospel through the eighth."[89]

The polemic use of the symbolism of the eighth day that developed out of apocalyptic, Gnostic, and Biblical sources to prove the superiority of Sunday over the Sabbath corroborates again that Sunday worship arose as a controversial innovation and not as an undisputed apostolic institution. Indeed, when the Sabbath-Sunday controversy subsided, the very name "eighth day" and its inherent eschatological meaning (used first by Barnabas and afterward by numerous Fathers) were formally and explicitly repudiated as a designation and motivation for Sundaykeeping! John Chrysostom (c. A.D. 347-407), Bishop of Constantinople, provides a most explicit confirmation of this development. After explaining that the eighth day represents exclusively the future life, he affirms categorically: "It is for this reason that no one calls the Lord's day the eighth day but only first day."[90]

This brief survey of the various early Christians' motivations for Sunday observance suggests that the new day of worship was introduced in a climate of controversy and uncertainty. It appears that because of the exigency that arose to separate Christians from the Jews and their Sabbath, Gentile Christians adopted the venerable day of the Sun, since it provided an adequate time and symbolism to commemorate significant divine events that occurred on that day, such as the creation of light and the resurrection of the Sun of Justice. This innovation provoked a controversy with those who maintained the inviolability and superiority of the Sabbath. To silence such opposition, we found that the symbolism of the first day and of the eighth day was introduced and widely used, since they provided valuable apologetic arguments to defend the validity and superiority of Sunday. As the first day, Sunday could allegedly claim superiority over the Sabbath, since it celebrated the anniversary of both the first and the second creation, the latter inaugurated by Christ's resurrection. The seventh day, on the other hand, could claim only to commemorate the completion of Creation. As the eighth day, Sunday could claim to be the alleged continuation, fulfillment, and replacement of the Sabbath, both temporally and eschatologically.

Conclusion

The picture that has emerged in this chapter is that the origin of Sunday was the result of an interplay of Jewish, pagan, and Christian factors. Judaism, we found, contributed negatively to the rise of Sunday by creating the Christian desire for a radical separation from Jewish observances such as the Sabbath. It also contributed positively by providing the cosmic millenarian week and the consequent possibility of defending Sunday as the eighth day representing the eternal new world.

Paganism suggested to those Christians who had previously known the day and the cult of the Sun the possibility of adopting the "venerable day of the Sun" as their new day of worship, since its rich symbology was conducive to the worship of the true Sun of Righteousness.

Christianity, lastly, gave theological justification to Sunday observance by teaching that the day commemorated important events such as the inauguration of Creation, the resurrection of Christ, and the eschatological hope of the new world to come. It appears, therefore, that Jewish, pagan, and Christian factors, though of differing derivation, merged to give rise to an institution capable of satisfying the exigencies of many Jewish and pagan converts.

Our study has also shown (we hope persuasively) that the adoption of Sunday observance in place of the Sabbath did not occur in the Jerusalem church by virtue of the authority of Christ or of the apostles, but rather took place several decades later, evidently in the Church of Rome during the second century. It was solicited by external circumstances.

We found, too, that the earliest theological justifications do not reflect an organic Biblical-apostolic teaching, but rather differing polemic argumentations.

THE RISE OF SUNDAY OBSERVANCE IN EARLY CHRISTIANITY

Those Biblical *testimonia* that were drawn from the Old Testament (references to the numbers eight and one) to prove the legitimacy and superiority of Sunday were eventually abandoned, since they were based on faulty, questionable, *and questioned,* Biblical hermeneutics.

This means, to state the matter frankly, that Sunday observance does not rest on a foundation of Biblical theology and/or of apostolic authority, but rather on later contributory factors to which we have briefly alluded above. Any attempt, therefore, to formulate a Biblical theology of Sunday to help solve the pressing problem of its widespread profanation is doomed to fail. More hopeful results could be expected from educating our Christian communities to rediscover and accept those permanent values and obligations of the Sabbath commandment that are still relevant to Christians today.

Ed. Note: *Although various items of importance regarding the Sabbath and Sunday from the second through fifth centuries* A.D. *are noted at random within the broader contexts of chapters 8-10, a more systematic and comprehensive treatment of the subject is provided in appendix B at the end of this volume. It may also be noted here that the topic of "The 'Lord's Day' in the Second Century" is treated in appendix F.*

NOTES

[1] Among the more recent and significant studies are Willy Rordorf, *Sunday* (Philadelphia, 1968); C. S. Mosna, *Storia della domenica dalle origini fino agli inizi del V secolo,* Analecta Gregoriana 170 (Rome, 1969); Francis A. Regan, "Dies Dominica and Dies Solis: The Beginnings of the Lord's Day in Christian Antiquity" (S.T.D. dissertation, Catholic University of America, 1961); and Paul K. Jewett, *The Lord's Day* (Grand Rapids, 1971). See Samuele Bacchiocchi, *From Sabbath to Sunday* (Rome, 1977), for additional bibliography.

[2] These assumptions and conclusions are explicitly presented by Jewett, *op. cit.,* pp. 56, 57. Rordorf also excludes the possibility that the observance of Sunday is a Pauline invention, first because Paul had "been so strong in his polemic against any kind of devotion to particular days," and second because "he would have answered the objections of a Judaizing opposition." He interprets the silence over the Sabbath-Sunday issue as "the most eloquent proof that the observance of Sunday had been recognized by the entire apostolic Church and had been adopted by the Pauline churches."—*Op. cit.,* pp. 218, 219. J. A. Jungmann, *The Mass of the Roman Rite* (New York, 1950), 1:20, 21, argues that the replacement of the Sabbath with Sunday occurred between the martyrdom of Stephen and the persecution of the year A.D. 44 as a result of the Jewish persecution. Mosna also reasons that the Christians in Jerusalem detached themselves very early from the Temple and synagogue because of the persecution from the religious leaders (*op. cit.,* pp. 179, 180). This view is discredited by the fact that the first Jewish persecution was apparently directed, not against the whole church, but primarily against a nonconformist group known as "Hellenists." This is suggested by Acts 8:1, where it is reported that while the Hellenists "were scattered," the apostles were allowed to remain in the city, undoubtedly because they did not share their bold views (see p. 134). Moreover, as we shall note, the Jerusalem church was deeply attached to Jewish observances until A.D. 135.

[3] Rordorf, *op. cit.,* p. 218; cf. Mosna, *op. cit.,* p. 53.

[4] Rordorf, *op. cit.,* p. 218.

[5] Mosna, *op. cit.,* p. 44. For other advocates of this view, see note 2.

[6] S. V. McCasland cogently states that "to say that Sunday is observed because Jesus rose on that day is really a *petitio principii,* for such a celebration might just as well be monthly or annually and still be an observance of that particular day."—"The Origin of the Lord's Day," *JBL* 49 (1930):69.

[7] In 1 Corinthians 11 Paul takes pains to instruct the Corinthians concerning the *manner* of celebrating the Lord's Supper, but on the question of the *time* of the assembly he repeats no fewer than four times, "when you come together," συνερχουμ ένον (verses 18, 20, 33, 34), implying *indeterminate* days. Moreover, the fact that Paul employs the adjective "Lord's," κυριακός, to describe only the nature of the Supper and not Sunday (the latter he calls by the Jewish designation "first day of the week" [chap. 16:2]), especially when mention of the sacredness of the time could have strengthened the apostle's plea for a more worshipful attitude during the partaking of the Lord's Supper, hardly suggests that Sunday was already known as the "Lord's day" or that the Lord's Supper was celebrated exclusively on Sunday. The latter view is defended strenuously by Rordorf (*op. cit.,* pp. 221-228). His arguments, however, are rightly rejected by Mosna, *op. cit.,* p. 52, and by O. Betz in his review of Rordorf's book (*JBL* 83 [1964]:81-83). Concerning the meaning of the Lord's Supper, the allusion to Christ's sacrifice is clear also in the Synoptic account of the Last Supper (Matt. 26:28; Mark 14:22-25; Luke 22:17-20). The *Didache* (dated between A.D. 70 and 150), though it devotes three chapters (9, 10, 14) to the Lord's Supper and lists many reasons for expressing thanks over the cup and bread, makes no allusion to Christ's resurrection. The same is true of Clement's *Epistle to the Corinthians* (dated about A.D. 95). The Roman bishop employs several symbols (chaps. 24-27) to reassure the Christians of Corinth that "there shall be a future resurrection, of which He has rendered the Lord Jesus Christ the first-fruits" (*ANF* 24:1), but omits the mention of the Lord's Supper and Sunday worship. This omission is certainly surprising if the Eucharist was already celebrated on Sunday and had acquired the commemorative value of the Resurrection.

8 The crucial passages of Barnabas and Justin are examined at length in Samuele Bacchiocchi, *Anti-Judaism and the Origin of Sunday* (Rome, 1975), pp. 94-116, and in *idem, From Sabbath to Sunday*, pp. 218-233.

9 B. Bagatti suggests that the converted priests naturally "continued to exercise their ministry" *(The Church From the Circumcision* [Jerusalem, 1971], p. 67). Their ministry may well have been needed, since, according to Luke, there were "many thousands . . . among the Jews of those who have believed" (Acts 21:20). F. F. Bruce advances the hypothesis that "there may well have been seventy of them [i.e., elders], constituting a sort of Nazarene Sanhedrin, with James as their president."—*Commentary on the Book of the Acts* (Grand Rapids, 1954), p. 429. The same view is held by Charles W. Carter and Ralph Earle, *The Acts of the Apostles* (Grand Rapids, 1959), p. 322.

10 For a concise survey of the exaltation of James in the Judeo-Christian literature, see Bagatti, *op. cit.*, pp. 70-78; cf. Bacchiocchi, *From Sabbath to Sunday*, pp. 142-145.

11 This view is persuasively defended by O. Cullmann, "Courants multiples dans la communauté primitive," in *Judéo-christianisme* (Paris, 1972), p. 58; *idem*, "Dissensions Within the Early Church," *Union Seminary Quarterly Review* 22 (1967):83-87. In the charge made against Stephen, there is a generic reference to the Temple, law, and customs; but there is no specific allusion to the Sabbath. If, as some speculate (cf. Rordorf, *op. cit.*, pp. 127, 217), the Hellenists promoted Sunday observance, they would have stirred up a sharp controversy, especially in view of their "'vocal' missionary activity" and of the loyal adherence to Jewish customs of the Jerusalem church. The fact that no echo of such a polemic can be detected in Acts suggests that no change in the day of worship had yet occurred.

12 Several points are noteworthy in the proposal of James, a proposal approved by "the apostles and the elders" (verse 22). 1. The exemption from circumcision was granted *only* "'to the brethren who are of the Gentiles'" (verse 23), there being no concession in this regard for the Jewish Christians, who continued to circumcise their children. This is indicated both by the existence after the Council of a circumcision party, apparently supported by James (Gal. 2:12), and by the concern of the leaders of the Jerusalem church to silence the rumor that Paul was teaching Jews "'not to circumcise their children or observe the customs'" (Acts 21:21). 2. Moreover, of the four provisions of the decree noted in Acts 15:20, one is moral (abstention "'from the pollution of idols . . . and from what is strangled and from blood'"). This undue concern for ritual defilement and food laws is reflective of the great respect prevailing for the ceremonial law. 3. Finally, the statement that James made to support his proposal is also significant: "'For from early generations Moses has had in every city those who preach him, for he is read every sabbath in the synagogues'" (verse 21). Though James's remark has been variously understood, interpreters generally recognize that both in his proposal and in its justification James reaffirms the binding nature of the Mosaic law, which was customarily taught every Sabbath in the synagogues. The manifestation of such an excessive respect by this Jerusalem Council for the Mosaic ceremonial law excludes categorically the hypothesis that the Jerusalem church had already broken away from Sabbathkeeping and pioneered the adoption of Sunday worship.

13 It is possible, as suggested by R. C. H. Lenski, that "these Jewish believers in Palestine suffered because of false rumors regarding Paul."—*The Interpretation of the Acts of the Apostles* (Columbus, Ohio, 1944), p. 878. The concern of the leaders of the church to see Paul demonstrate publicly his respect for ancestral customs reveals, as stated by Lenski, that "they retained their Jewish way of living, circumcised their children, ate kosher, kept the Sabbath, etc."—*Ibid.*

14 This hypothesis is advanced by Regan, when he writes: "Can one point to any one event in particular in which the decisive break occurred between the Sabbath and that day we now call Sunday? A most likely date would probably be the year A.D. 70 with the destruction of the Temple of Jerusalem."—*Op. cit.*, p. 18.

15 Eusebius *Ecclesiastical History* 4. 5. 2-11 *(NPNF/2* 1:176, 177); Epiphanius *Adversus haereses* 70. 10 *(PG* 42:355-358).

16 *Eccl. Hist.* 3. 27. 3 (LCL). On the question of the liberal wing of the Ebionites who observed Sunday in addition to the Sabbath, see the discussion in Bacchiocchi, *From Sabbath to Sunday*, pp. 153-156.

17 *Adversus haereses* 29. 7 *(PG* 41:401).

18 M. Simon, "La migration à Pella: Légende ou réalité," in *Judéo-christianisme*, p. 48. J. Daniélou also views the Nazarenes as the descendants of the Aramaic-speaking Christians who fled to Transjordan and who "separated from the rest of the Church because they regarded the Jewish observances of Sabbath and circumcision as still of obligation" *(The Theology of Jewish Christianity* [London, 1964], p. 56). A similar assessment is given by Bagatti, *op. cit.*, pp. 31-35.

19 The date A.D. 80-90 for the introduction of the malediction is accepted by practically all scholars. For an extensive bibliography, see W. Schrage, "ἀποσυνάγωγος," *TDNT*, 7:848.

20 See especially the study of M. Simon, *Verus Israel* (Paris, 1964; reprint of 1948 ed.) p. 235.

21 James Parkes remarks, "The fact that the test was a statement made in the synagogue service shows that at the time of making it the Judeo-Christians still frequented the synagogue."—*The Conflict of the Church and the Synagogue* (London, 1934), p. 78.

22 The following is a sample of statements often occurring in the Talmud regarding Hadrian's anti-Jewish policies: "The Government of Rome had issued a decree that they should not study the Torah and that they should not circumcise their sons and that they should profane the Sabbath" (B. Talmud, Rosh ha-Shanah 19a [Soncino]). J. Derenbourg, who provides a well-documented treatment of Hadrian's war and policies, writes: "The government of Rome prohibited, under penalty of death, circumcision, the observance of the Sabbath and the study of the law."—*Essai sur l'histoire et la géographie de la Palestine* (Paris, 1867), p. 430.

23 Eusebius reports: "When the city had been emptied of the Jewish nation and had suffered the total destruction of its ancient inhabitants, it was colonized by a different race. . . . And as the Church there was now composed of Gentiles, the first one to assume the government of it after the bishops of the circumcision was Marcus."—*Eccl. Hist.* 4. 6. 4 *(NPNF/2* 1:177,178).

24 *Adversus haereses* 70. 10 *(PG* 42:355, 356): "The controversy arose [ἐταρόχφη—literally, "was stirred up"] after the exodus of the bishops of the circumcision [A.D. 135] and it has continued until our time." The bishop makes specific reference to the fifteen Judeo-Christian bishops who until A.D. 135 observed the Quartodeciman Passover. For a discussion of Epiphanius' text, see Bacchiocchi, *From Sabbath to Sunday*, pp. 161, 162, and *idem, Anti-Judaism and the Origin of Sunday*, pp. 45-52.

25 Bagatti *(op. cit.*, p. 10) is of the opinion that the Passover controversy in Jerusalem was provoked by the return of Judeo-Christians to the city, since about sixty years later Narcissus, Bishop of Jerusalem, facing opposition from Quartodecimans, appealed for help to his teacher Clement of Alexandria *(PG* 9:1480). This hypothesis does not exclude the possibility that even among the new Gentile membership some refused to accept the new Easter Sunday date, since the latter was by no means universally accepted by all. On the extent of the observance of Easter Sunday,

see the lengthy treatment in Bacchiocchi, *From Sabbath to Sunday*, pp. 198-204, especially nn. 97, 101, 102.

[26] On the Gentile bishops of Jerusalem, see Eusebius *Eccl. Hist.* 5. 12 *(NPNF/2* 1:226).

[27] That the majority of the members in Rome were pagan converts is clearly indicated also by Paul's statement in Romans 1: "I am eager to preach the gospel to you also who are in Rome" (verse 15). "I have often intended to come to you . . . in order that I may reap some harvest among you *as well as among the rest of the Gentiles*" (verse 13).

[28] Leonard Goppelt, *Les Origines de l'Église* (Paris, 1961), p. 203.

[29] Several authors suggest this possibility. See, for instance, A. von Harnack, *The Mission and Expansion of Christianity in the First Three Centuries* (New York, 1908), 1:51, 400; J. Lebreton and J. Zeiller, *The History of the Primitive Church* (New York, 1944), 1:372; Ernest Renan, *Antichrist* (Boston, 1897), p. 109; Pierre Batiffol, *Primitive Catholicism*, (London, 1911), p. 19.

[30] *Annales* 15. 44.

[31] *Historiae* 5. 13; Josephus *War of the Jews* 6. 9. 3 specifies that 97,000 Jews were taken captive and 1.1 million either were killed or perished during the siege.

[32] *Historiae* 69. 13.

[33] See note 22 above. Some scholars maintain that sacrifices still continued at the Temple after A.D. 70, though in a reduced form; cf. K. W. Clark, "Worship in the Jerusalem Temple after A.D. 70," *New Testament Studies* 6 (1959-1960):269-280.

[34] According to Suetonius *(c.* A.D. 70-122), the *fiscus judaicus* was excised for the temple of *Jupiter Capitolinus* even from those "who without publicly acknowledging that faith yet lived as Jews" *(Domitian* 12 [LCL]). Under Hadrian (D.D. 117-138), according to Appian, a contemporary historian, the Jews were subjected at that time to a "poll-tax . . . heavier than that imposed upon the surrounding peoples" *(Roman History, The Syrian Wars* 50 [LCL]).

[35] Quotations from these and other Roman authors are cited in Bacchiocchi, *From Sabbath to Sunday*, pp. 173-177.

[36] Suetonius' expressive *invitus invitam (Titus* 7) indicates that the separation was difficult for both of them.

[37] The following list of significant authors and/or writings, which defamed the Jews to a lesser or greater degree, may serve to make the reader aware of the existence and intensity of the problem: *The Preaching of Peter, The Epistle of Barnabas,* Quadratus' lost *Apology,* Aristides' *Apology, The Disputation between Jason and Papiscus concerning Christ,* Justin's *Dialogue with Trypho,* Miltiades' *Against the Jews* (unfortunately lost), Apollinarius' *Against the Jews* (also perished), Melito's *On the Passover, The Epistle to Diognetus, The Gospel of Peter,* Tertullian's *Against the Jews,* Origen's *Against Celsus.* For a brief analysis of these works, see Bacchiocchi, *From Sabbath to Sunday*, pp. 178-185. An excellent survey of the Christian anti-Jewish literature of the second century is provided by F. Blanchetière, "Aux sources de l'anti-judaïsme chrétien," *Revue d'Histoire et de Philosophie Religieuses* 53 (1973):353-398.

[38] *Dialogue with Trypho* 21. 1. See also 23. 3; 29. 3; 16. 1. These and other texts of Justin Martyr are quoted and discussed in Bacchiocchi, *From Sabbath to Sunday*, pp. 223-233, and in *idem, Anti-Judaism and the Origin of Sunday*, pp. 101-114.

[39] *Apology* 1. 67 (ANF 1:186).

[40] The *Liber Pontificalis* under the name of Bishop Callistus records as the only act of his pontificate the institution of a seasonal Sabbath fast: "He established a Sabbath fast to be observed three times a year [at the time of the harvest], of the wheat, of the grapes and of the oil" *(Le Liber Pontificalis, text, introduction et commentaire,* ed. by L. Duchesne [Paris, 1955], vol. 1, p. 141). For further information on the relationship of the Roman church to the Sabbath feast, see Bacchiocchi, *Sabbath to Sunday*, pp. 185-198, where ancient sources are cited.

[41] S. R. E. Humbert *Adversus Graecorum calumnias* 6 *(PL* 143:937). The text is quoted and discussed in Bacchiocchi, *From Sabbath to Sunday*, pp. 194, 195.

[42] Victorinus *De fabrica mudni* 5 *(CSEL* 49:5). The full passage reads: "On the seventh day, He rested from all His works. On this day we are accustomed to fast rigorously so that on the Lord's day we may go forth to our bread with giving thanks. We must fast even on Friday in order that we might not appear to observe the Sabbath with the Jews, of which the Lord of the Sabbath Himself, the Christ, says by His prophets that His soul hateth."

[43] For a good treatment of the Sabbath meals, see Nathan A. Barack, *A History of the Sabbath* (New York, 1965), pp. 100, 101, 182, n. 70; cf. J. Talmud, Shabbat 15:3; Judith 8:6; Jubilees 50:10, 13; CD 11:4, 5; Hermann L. Strack and Paul Billerbeck, *Kommentar zum Neuen Testament* (Munich, 1922), 1:611, 612.

[44] *Epistle to Casulanus* 36. 6 *(NPNF/1* 1:267).

[45] The fact that in Milan Christians did not fast on the Sabbath is attested by the advice Ambrose gave to Monica, Augustine's mother: "When I am here [i.e., in Milan] I do not fast on Saturday; but when I am at Rome I do."—Augustine *Epistle to Casulanus* 36. 32 [*NPNF/1* 1:270]; cf. *idem, Epistle to Januarius* 54. 3; Paulinus *Vita Ambrosii* 38. A similar dichotomy existed in North Africa in the time of Augustine. In fact, the bishop writes: "It happens, especially in Africa, that one church, or the churches within the same district, have some members who fast and others who do not fast on the seventh day."—*Epistle to Casulanus* 36. 32 [*NPNF/1,* 1:270]; for an analysis of the Sabbath fast in early Christianity, see Kenneth A. Strand, *The Early Christian Sabbath* (Ann Arbor, Mich., 1979), pp. 9-15, 25-42.

[46] Pope Innocent I (A.D. 401-417) established that "as the tradition of the Church maintains, in these two days [i.e., Friday and Saturday] one should not absolutely *(penitus)* celebrate the sacraments" *(Ad Decentium* 25. 4. 7 [*PL* 20:555]); Socrates *(c.* A.D. 439) confirms the situation in Rome when he reports that "although almost all churches throughout the world celebrate the sacred mysteries on the sabbath of every week, yet the Christians of Alexandria and at Rome, on account of some ancient tradition, have ceased to do this" *(Eccl. Hist.* 5. 22 [*NPNF/2* 2:132]); Sozomen *(c.* A.D. 440) refers exclusively to religious assemblies, saying that while "the people of Constantinople, and almost everywhere, assemble together on the Sabbath, as well as on the first day of the week," such a "custom is never observed at Rome or at Alexandria."—*Eccl. Hist.* 7. 9 *(NPNF/2* 2:390).

[47] *In Danielem commentarius* 4. 20. 3 *(GCS* 1:234).

[48] Rordorf observes that since "the whole of western Christendom by this time [i.e., Tertullian's time] fasted on Holy Saturday, . . . it would have been easy to have hit upon the idea of fasting on every Saturday (just as every Sunday was a little Easter)."—*Op. cit.,* p. 143.

[49] *On Fasting* 14 *(ANF* 4:112); Augustine similarly associates the weekly Sabbath fast with the annual paschal Sabbath fast, explaining that while the former was kept *only* by "the Church of Rome, and some churches in the West, . . . once in the year, namely at Easter, all Christians observe the seventh day of the week by fasting."—*Epistle to Casulanus* 36. 31 *(NPNF/1* 1:270). The same prohibition to fast on the Sabbath with the exception of the annual paschal Sabbath fast is found in the *Apostolic Constitutions* 5. 15, 18, and in the *Apostolic Canons* 64.

[50] *Didascalia Apostolorum* 5. 14, 19 (Connolly, pp. 184, 190). In the *Apostolic Constitutions*, a related document, in a

THE SABBATH IN SCRIPTURE AND HISTORY

similar vein Christians are enjoined to fast on Easter Friday and Saturday because "in these days . . . He was taken from us by the Jews, falsely so named, and fastened to the cross."—5. 18 *(ANF* 7:447); cf. 5. 15 *(ANF* 7:445). Epiphanius also refers to an alleged apostolic ordinance, which established: "When they [i.e., the Jews] feast, we should mourn for them with fasting, because in that feast they fastened Christ on the Cross."—*Adversus haereses* 70. 11 *(PG* 42:359, 360).

⁵¹ The chief objection against the possible influence of Sun worship with its "Sun-day" on the Christian choice of Sunday is of chronological nature. It is generally argued that Christian Sunday worship originated before the existence of the planetary week. Thus, for instance, Mosna reasons: "To be able to speak of influence [of Sun worship] on Sunday, one should demonstrate that the day dedicated to the Sun already existed in the earliest times of the Christian community as a fixed day that recurred regularly every week, and that it corresponded exactly to the day after the Sabbath. For this, one should demonstrate the existence of the planetary week before Sunday."—*Op. cit.,* p. 33. Rordorf expresses the same view even more emphatically. He maintains that "since the earliest evidence for the existence of the planetary week is to be dated towards the end of the first century A.D.," at a time when he claims "the Christian observance of Sunday was . . . a practice of long standing" *(op. cit.,* p. 37, cf. p. 181), any influence of Sun worship on the origin of Sunday is to be categorically excluded. Rordorf's argument falls short on two counts. Not only does he fail to demonstrate that the origin of Christian Sunday observance is prior to the introduction of the planetary week, but he also attributes to the latter (perhaps intentionally?) an obvious late date in order to defend the earlier existence of Christian Sunday observance.

⁵² Gaston H. Halsberghe, *The Cult of Sol Invictus* (Leiden, 1972), pp. 26, 44. Halsberghe cites A. von Domaszewski *(Abhandlungen zur Römischen Religion* [1909], p. 173) as an earlier advocate of the view that the Sun was an autochthonous god in ancient Rome.

⁵³ This point is expressed by Franz Cumont, *The Mysteries of Mithra* (New York, 1956), p. 101.

⁵⁴ Before the existence of a weekly "Sun-day," the Sun was venerated every morning. Regarding Sun worship in India, Persia, Syria, and in the Greco-Roman world, see F. J. Dölger, *Sol Salutis* (Münster, 1925); for Palestine, see *Realencyklopädie für protestantische Theologie und Kirche* (1863 ed.), s.v. "Sonne bei den Hebräern," by W. Baudissin; *Lexikon für Theologie und Kirche* (1964 ed.), s.v. "Sonne," by H. Baumann; that the sun cult was widespread even among the Hebrews before and Josiah's reform is well established by passages such as 2 Kings 23:11; Ezekiel 8:16; Wisdom 16:28; Philo *(De Vita contemplative* 3. 27) reports that the Therapeutae prayed at sunrise, seeking for heavenly light.

⁵⁵ Horace alludes to the day of Jupiter (Thursday) when describing the vow of a superstitious mother *(Satirae* 2. 3. 288-290). Tibullus in one of his poems explains that he could have excused himself for staying in Rome with his beloved Delia by claiming that "the sacred day of Saturn held him back" *(Carmina* 1. 3. 15-18). The day of Saturn was regarded as an unlucky day *(dies nefastus).* Sextus Propertius speaks, for instance, of "the sign of Saturn that brings woe to one and all" *(Elegies* 4. 1. 84 [LCL]. Petronius in his novel *The Banquet of Trimalchio* describes a stick calendar affixed on the doorpost with the number of the days on the one side and "the likenesses of the seven stars" on the other. A knob was inserted in the respective holes to indicate the date and the day *(Satyricon* 30). Frontinus reports that Vespasian "attacked the Jews [A.D. 70] on the day of Saturn, on which it is forbidden for them to do anything serious, and defeated them" *(Strategemata* 2. 1. 17). Plutarch raises the question, "Why are not the days which have the names of the planets arranged according to the order of the planets but the contrary?"—*Symposiacs* 4. 7., *Plutarch's Complete Works* (New York, 1909), 3:230. Unfortunately only the title of this dialogue has come down to us. Dio Cassius mentions that as early as 37 B.C., when Jerusalem was captured by Sosius and Herod the Great, the Sabbath was "even then called the day of Saturn" *(History* 49. 22). For an extensive survey of documents related to the planetary week, see Robert Leo Odom, *Sunday in Roman Paganism* (Washington, D.C., 1944), pp. 54-124; cf. Bacchiocchi, *From Sabbath to Sunday,* pp. 241-247.

⁵⁶ In the light of these and other indications, the archeologist Attilio Degrassi at the Third International Congress of Greek and Roman Epigraphy (1957) stated: "I wish to insist on my conviction that this planetary week . . . did not become known and commonly used, as generally believed, only in the first half of the first century A.D., but *already in the first years of the Augustan era* [27 B.C.-A.D. 14]. . . . This is a conclusion that appears inevitable after the discovery of the calendar of Nola."—"Un nuovo frammento di calendario Romano e la settimana planetaria dei sette giorni," *Atti del Terzo Congresso Internazionale di Epigrafia Greca e Latina* (Rome, 1957), p. 103. (Italics supplied.) The same article is included by the author in his *Scritti vari di antichita* (Rome, 1962), pp. 681-691. For a source collection of the various stone planetarian calendars, paintings, and inscriptions of the planetary gods and days see *Corpus Inscriptionum Latinorum,* ed. A. Reimer (Berlin: apud G. Reimerum, 1863-1893), 1:218, 220, 342; 4:515, No. 4182; 582, No. 5202; 712, No. 6779; 717, No. 6338. Several stone planetarian calendars are reproduced also by A. Degrassi in his recent edition of *Inscriptiones Italiae* (Rome, 1963), 3:49, 52, 53, 55, 56.

⁵⁷ *Anthologiarum* 5. 10 (Kroll). The date is established by Otto Neugebauer and Henry B. Van Hoesen, *Greek Horoscopes* (Philadelphia, 1949), p. 177. Robert L. Odom, "Vettius Valens and the Planetary Week," *AUSS* 3 (1965): 110-137, provides a penetrating analysis of the calendations used by Vettius Valens and shows convincingly that "Vettius Valens, who undoubtedly was a pagan, used the week of seven days, [and] reckoned the seven-day week as beginning with the day of the Sun (Sunday) and ending with 'the sabbatical day' (Sabbath day)" (p. 134); H. Dumaine, "Dimanche," *DACL* 4:912 defends the same view on the basis of different evidences; cf. W. H. Roscher, "Planeten," *Allgemeines Lexikon der griech und röm Mythologie* (1909), col. 2538.

⁵⁸ Justin Martyr implies the preeminence of Sunday by his threefold reference to it in his *I Apology* 67; Tertullian replies to the taunt that Christians were Sun worshipers because they made "Sunday a day of festivity," saying, "It is you, at all events, who have even admitted the sun into the calendar of the week; and you have selected its day [Sunday], in preference to the preceding day [Saturday], as the most suitable in the week for either an entire abstinence from the bath, or for its postponement until the evening, or for taking rest and for banqueting."—*Ad nationes* 1. 13 *(ANF* 3:123). On the dominant position of the sun in the *Mithraea* of the Seven Portals, of the Seven Spheres and on the Bononia relief, see Leroy A. Campbell, *Mithraic Iconography and Ideology* (Leiden, 1968), pp. 300-307, figs. 19, 20; cf. Cumont, *op. cit.,* p. 167; the text of Constantine's Sunday law of March 7, 321, is found in *Codex Justinianus* 3. 12. 3 and that of July 3, 321, in *Codex Theodosianus* 2. 8. 1.

⁵⁹ For a concise survey of the influence of astrological beliefs on early Christianity, see Jack Lindsay, *Origins of Astrology* (London, 1971), pp. 373-401; cf. Bacchiocchi, *From Sabbath to Sunday,* pp. 252, 253.

⁶⁰ For examples of literary application of the motif of the sun to Christ, see, e.g., *Dialogue with Trypho* 121 *(ANF* 1:109); Melito *On Baptism* 2. 5 (ed. by J. B. Pitra, *Analecta Sacra Spicilegio Solesmens* [1884]; Clement of Alexandria

THE RISE OF SUNDAY OBSERVANCE IN EARLY CHRISTIANITY

Protrepticus 11. 114 *(ANF* 2:203); *Stromateis* 7. 3 *(ANF* 2:528); Origen *In Numeros homilia* 23. 5; *In Leviticum homilia* 9; Cyprian *De oratione* 35 *(CSEL* 60, 1/2:292); Ambrose *In Psalmos* 118, *Sermo* 19. 6 *(CSEL* 62:425); Dolger, *op. cit.* (esp. chapters 20 and 21), provides an extensive documentation of the influence of Sun worship on Christian liturgy. Cf. Bacchiocchi, *From Sabbath to Sunday*, pp. 253, 254.

61 See E. Kirschbaum, *The Tomb of St. Peter and Paul* (London, 1959), pp. 35, 36; P. Testini, *Archeologia Cristiana* (Bologna, 1958), p. 167; cf. an artistic reproduction of Christ portrayed as *Sol Invictus* in F. Cumont, *Textes et monuments figures relatifs aux mysteres de Mythra* (Brussels, 1899), 2:434, No. 379.

62 That praying toward Jerusalem was customary among the Jews is indicated by Daniel's practice and by Solomon's prayer at the dedication of the Temple (Dan. 6:11; 2 Chron. 6:34ff.); the practice was continued by the Judeo-Christian sect of the Ebionites, who, according to Irenaeus, "prayed toward Jerusalem as if it were the house of God" *(Adversus haereses* 1. 26 [*anf* 1:352]).

63 See, for instance, *Stromateis* 7. 7; *De oratione* 32; *Apostolic Constitutions* 2. 57 *(ANF* 7:421); *Didascalia* 2. 57 (Connolly, p. 119); Hippolytus *De Antichristo* 59 *(ANF* 5:216); Cyril *Catechesibus* 1. 9; Basil *De Spiritu Sancto* 27. 64 *(PG* 32:189, 192); Gregory of Nyssa *De oratione Domini* 5 *(PG* 44:1184); Augustine *De sermone Domini in monte* 2. 5. 18 *(PL* 34:1277).

64 Halsberghe, *op. cit.*, p. 174, states: "The authors whom we consulted on this point are unanimous in admitting the influence of the pagan celebration held in honor of Deus Sol Invictus on the 25th of December, the *Natalis Invicti,* on the Christian celebration of Christmas. This influence is held to be responsible for the shifting of the 25th of December of the birth of Christ, which had until then been held on the day of the Epiphany, the 6th of January." For additional references and discussion see Bacchiocchi, *From Sabbath to Sunday*, pp. 256-261.

65 Mario Righetti, *Manuale di storia liturgica,* 4 vols. (Milan, 1950-1956), 2:67. Cullmann similarly comments: "The Roman Church intentionally opposed to this pagan nature cult its own festival of light, the festival of the birth of Christ."—*The Early Church* (Philadelphia, 1956), p. 30.

66 *I Apology* 67 *(ANF* 1:186); the passage is analyzed in Bacchiocchi, *From Sabbath to Sunday*, pp. 230-232.

67 *Dialogue with Trypho* 121.

68 *Commentaria in Psalmos* 91 *(PG* 23:1169-1172; italics supplied); in his *Life of Constantine* Eusebius similarly states that "the Savior's day . . . derives its name from light, and from the sun" (4. 18 [*NPNF*/2 1:544]).

69 Maximus of Turin *(c.* A.D. 400-423) views the designation of the "day of the Sun" as a proleptic announcement of the resurrection of Christ: "We hold the day of the Lord to be venerable and solemn, because on it the Saviour, like the rising sun, conquered the darkness of the underworld and gleamed in the glory of the resurrection. This is why the same day was called the day of the sun by the pagans, because the Sun of Justice once risen would have illuminated it."—*Homilia* 61 *(PL* 57:371). Gaudentius, Bishop of Brescia *(c.* A.D. 400), *Sermo* 10, *In Exodi lectione octavus (PL* 20:916), and *Sermo* 1, *De Exodo lectione primus (PL* 20:845), explains that the Lord's day became first in relationship to the Sabbath, because on that day the Sun of Righteousness has appeared, dispelling the darkness of the Jews, melting the ice of the pagans and restoring the world to its primordial order; cf. Hilary of Poitiers *Tractatus in Psalmos* 67. 6 *(CSEL* 22:280); Athanasius *Expositio in Psalmos* 67. 34 *(PG* 27:303); Ambrose *Hexaemeron* 4. 2. 7 *(PL* 14:203); and *Epistola* 44 *(PL* 16:1188).

70 *In die dominica Paschae homilia corpus Christianorum, Series Latina* (Turnholti: Typographi Brepols Editores Pontificii, 1953—) 78. 550. 1. 52; the same in Augustine *Contra Faustum* 18. 5 *(PL* 42:346); in *Sermo* 226 *(PL* 38:1099) Augustine explains that Sunday is the day of light because on the first day of Creation "God said, 'Let there be light.' And there was light. And God separated the light from darkness. And God called the light day and the darkness night."

71 Malachi, for example, predicted that "the Sun of righteousness [shall] arise with healing in his wings" (chap. 4:2, K.J.V.). Zechariah, the father of John the Baptist, announced the coming of Christ, saying that the sunrising (ἀνατολή) "from on high hath visited us, to give light to them that sit in darkness" (Luke 1:78, 79, K.J.V.); cf. Ps. 84:11; 72:17; Isa. 9:2; 60:1-3; Zeph. 3:8; John 1:4, 5, 9; 5:35; 8:12; 9:4, 5; 12:34; Rev. 22:4, 5.

72 Dionysius of Alexandria *Analecta sacra spicilegio solesmensi* 4 (ed. by J. B. Pitra, 1883, p. 421).

73 See note 8.

74 *Epistula* 55. 23 *(CSEL* 34/2:194); in another epistle Augustine similarly states that "the Lord's day has been preferred to the Sabbath by the faith of the resurrection."—*Epistula* 36. 12 *(CSEL* 34/2:40).

75 Augustine explicitly explains that on Sunday "fasting is interrupted and we pray standing, because it is a sign of the resurrection."—*Ibid.*, 55. 28 [*CSEL* 34/2:202]); cf. *De Spiritu Sanctu* 27. 66 *(SC*, p. 236); in the *Apostolic Constitutions* it is stated: "We pray thrice [on Sunday] standing in memory of Him who arose in three days" (2. 59 [*ANF* 7:423]); Cyprian declares: "Though partaken by Christ in the evening . . . we celebrate it [i.e., the Lord's Supper] in the morning on account of the resurrection of the Lord."—*Epistula* 63. 15 *(CSEL* 3/2:714).

76 In a hymn of praise to Sunday, attributed to Ambrose, it says: "On the first day the blessed Trinity created the world or rather the resurgent Redeemer who conquered death, liberated us" (M. Britt, *The Hymns of the Breviary and Missal* [New York, 1948], p. 91); cf. Gregory of Nazianzus *Oratio 44. In novam Dominicam* 5 *(PG* 36:612): "As the first creation began on the Lord's Day (this is clearly indicated by the fact that the Sabbath falls seven days later, being repose from work), so the second creation began on the same day"; *Analecta sacra spicilegio solesmensi* 4 (Pitra, p. 421): "God Himself has instituted Sunday the first day both of creation and also of resurrection: on the day of creation He separated light from darkness and on the day of the resurrection He divided belief from unbelief"; the author known as the Ambrosiaster *(Liber quaestionum veteris et novi testamenti* 95. 2 [*CSEL* 50:167]) proposes a variation on the same theme: "In fact the world was created on Sunday and since it fell after creation, again it was restored on Sunday. . . . In the same day He both resurrected and created."

77 See notes 66, 68, 70.

78 *Syriac Didascalia* 6. 18 (Connolly, pp. 233, 234); other interesting arguments are also submitted to prove the superiority of Sunday over the Sabbath.

79 *De sabbatis et circumcisione* 4 *(PG* 28:137).

80 See *The Epistle of Barnabas* 15; *Dialogue with Trypho* 24, 41, 138; for a survey of the use of the "eighth day" in the Fathers, see Bacchiocchi, *From Sabbath to Sunday*, pp. 278-301.

81 In the Slavonic *Secrets of Enoch* (an apocrypha of the Old Testament interpolated by Jewish Christians toward the end of the first century) we find not only the seven-days-millennia scheme, but also the first explicit designation of the new eon as "the eighth day" (Enoch 33:1, *APOT*, 2:451).

82 Origen, e.g., explains: "The number eight, which contains the power of the resurrection, is the figure of the

world to come, just as the number seven is the symbol of this present world" *(Selecta in Psalmos. Psal.* 118 [*PG* 12:1624]); cf. *Syriac Didascalia* 6. 18; for Victorinus of Pettau the seventh day bespeaks of the duration of the present world, of the consummation of the humanity of Christ and of the "seventh millenary of years, when Christ with His elect shall reign." The eighth day, on the contrary, "is indeed the eighth day of that future judgment, which will pass beyond the order of the sevenfold arrangement" *(On the Creation of the World* [*ANF* 7:342]); cf. Bacchiocchi, *From Sabbath to Sunday*, pp. 287-300, for additional patristic references and discussion.

   83 See, for example, Clement of Alexandria *Excerpta ex Theodoto* 63; *Stromateis* 4. 25. *(ANF* 2:438); 6. 16. *(ANF* 2:512, 513); Origen *Contra Celsum* 6. 22; especially Irenaeus *Adversus haereses* 1. 5. 3.

   84 Justin interprets arbitrarily the eighth day of the circumcision, the eight persons saved from the Flood, and possibly the fifteen cubits (seven plus eight) of the Flood waters that rose above the mountains (see Danielou, "Le Dimanche comme huitième jour," p. 64) as prefiguration and justification for the observance of Sunday *(Dialogue with Trypho* 41; 138; Asterius of Amasa *Homilia* 20 *(PG* 40: 444, 445, 448, 449): "Inasmuch as the first resurrection of the race after the flood happened to eight persons, the Lord has begun on the eighth day the resurrection of the dead"; cf. Gregory of Nyssa *De beatitudinibus, Oratio* 8 *(PG* 44: 1292); *Epistola* 26 *(PL* 16:1088, 895, 896).

   85 Victorinus *On the Creation of the World* (*ANF* 7:342).

   86 Hilary interprets the fifteen gradual psalms as "the continuation of the seventh day of the Old Testament and the eighth day of the Gospel, by which we rise to holy and spiritual things" *(Tractatus super Psalmos* [*CSEL* 22:14]). See also *Epistola* 26. 10 *(PL* 16:1088).

   87 See *Epistola* 26. 8 *(PL* 16:1088); Gregory the Great *Moralium* 35. 8. 17 *(PL* 76:759); Jerome *Commentarius in Ecclesiasten* 11. 2 *(PL* 23:1157).

   88 Gregory the Great, referring to the eighth day when Job offered seven sacrifices after the feasting of his sons and daughters, explains, "The story truly indicates that the blessed Job when offering sacrifices on the eighth day, was celebrating the mystery of the resurrection."—*Moralium* 1. 8. 12 *(PL* 75:532).

   89 *Commentarius in Ecclesiasten* 11. 2 *(PL* 20:1157). See also *Epistola* 26. 9 *(PL* 16:1088).

   90 *De compunctione* 2. 4 *(PG* 47:415).

CHAPTER 8

The Sabbath in Asia

Werner K. Vyhmeister

THE present chapter will examine the main sources dealing with Sabbath and Sunday observance in Asia from approximately the fourth to the seventeenth centuries. After an introductory survey of the situation in Near Eastern Asia, and an examination of the anti-Judaistic literature of the period, a brief account will be given of what is known about Sabbath-Sunday observance among the Nestorians (including China and India) and the Armenians.[1]

Sabbath and Sunday in Asia in the Early Centuries

By the second half of the fourth century, the practice of keeping both Sabbath and Sunday was widespread in Christian Asia, as witnessed by several documents. For example, the so-called *Constitutions of the Holy Apostles,* composed in Syria c. A.D. 375, reflect what probably was the most generalized attitude toward Sabbath-Sunday observance in the Eastern Church at that time: "But keep the Sabbath, and the Lord's day festival; because the former is the memorial of the creation, and the latter of the resurrection."[2] The Sabbath is never supposed to be a day of fasting (except on Easter, on account of Christ's burial).[3] Even slaves would work only five days so that "on the Sabbath-day and the Lord's day" they could "go to church for instruction in piety."[4]

The sixteenth canon of the synod of Laodicea (c. A.D. 364) prescribes: "The Gospels are to be read on the Sabbath, with the other Scriptures."[5] As will be noticed later, canon 29 tells Christians not to Judaize on the Sabbath day. But then, canons 49 and 51 recognize the special nature of both Sabbath and Sunday during Lent.[6]

The Christian editor (from Antioch-Syria?) who at about the same time expanded the Ignatian Epistles states: "Therefore let us no longer observe the Sabbath in a Judaistic way and rejoice in idleness. . . . But each of you should observe Sabbath in a spiritual way, rejoicing in study of laws. . . . And after keeping the Sabbath, let every lover of Christ celebrate the festival of the Lord's Day—the resurrection day, the royal day, the most excellent of all days."[7]

Socrates Scholasticus indicates (c. A.D. 440) that "almost all churches throughout the world celebrate the sacred mysteries on the sabbath of every

151

week."[8] Essentially the same is reported by Sozomen (*c.* 450) when he states that the "people of Constantinople, and almost everywhere, assemble together on the Sabbath, as well as on the first day of the week."[9] Both Socrates and Sozomen, in the tests quoted in part above, single out only Rome and Alexandria as places where there was no Sabbath assembly. Socrates also states that even Arians in Constantinople congregated on "Saturday and Lord's day—in each week."[10]

Bishop Asterius of Amasea of Pontus in Asia Minor (*c.* 400) says in one of his homilies: "It is beautiful to Christians and to the industrious that the team of these two days comes together; I speak of the Sabbath and the Lord's day, which time in its course brings around weekly. For as mothers and nurses of the church they gather the people, set over them priests as instructors, and lead both disciples and teachers to have a care for souls."[11]

Sunday observance, along with Sabbath observance, had become so well accepted, according to Syrian bishop Theodoret of Cyrrhus (*c.* 393-*c.* 458), that even the Ebionites kept both days.[12] However, there were several dissenting voices.[13] Furthermore, even in those areas where Sabbath was being observed, Sunday had already become the important liturgical day of the week.[14] Slowly in some places, rather quickly in others, the Sabbath became something like a fossilized festivity for many Eastern Christians. They refused to follow the example of Roman Christianity of fasting on the Sabbath day.[15] But, eventually, the Sabbath ceased to be a day of rest, while it was still considered, officially, as a day of festivity.

The Eastern Orthodox Church is perhaps the best example of this evolution in the practice of Sabbath observance. Even as late as the seventeenth century Samuel Purchas (*c.* 1577-1626), listing the beliefs and practices of the Greek Church of the Constantinople patriarchate, states that "they solemnize Saturday (the old Sabbath) festivally, and eat therein flesh, forbidding as unlawful, to fast any Saturday in the yeere, except Easter Eve."[16] So, the distinguishing mark of Sabbath was not rest but festivity heightened by the absence of fasting.

The situation of the Maronite Church was for a while similar. The Maronites, writes Purchas, do not "fast on the Lords day, nor on the Sabbath."[17] This and other practices were abandoned by them when, under the Crusaders' influence, an agreement was made with the Roman Church in 1182; but an anti-Roman reaction led to the revival of the recently abandoned practices. However, the national synod of 1596 resulted in the final submission of the Maronites to the Roman See.[18] Here again, Sabbath observance was in essence the absence of fasting.

It should probably be briefly added that Sunday observance was not at first understood as necessarily meaning complete cessation of work on that day. Constantine's Sunday law of March 7, 321, although recommending Sunday rest, also expressly indicated that "persons engaged in agriculture may freely and lawfully continue their pursuits."[19] In his Sunday law of July 3, 321, Constantine added that "all men shall have the right to emancipate and to manumit on this festive day, and the legal formalities thereof are not forbidden."[20]

Jerome (*c.* 345-*c.* 419), referring to nuns in Bethlehem, wrote that "on the Lord's day only they proceeded to the church beside which they lived, each company following its own mother-superior. Returning home in the same order, they then devoted themselves to their allotted tasks, and made garments either for themselves or else for others."[21] However, later legislation,[22] together with persistent and growing church pressure, succeeded eventually in making Sunday also a day of rest.

How can we explain the growing emphasis on Sunday to the detriment of Sabbath observance in Asia during the early Middle Ages? Several factors appear to have been working, such as: (1) the obvious prestige of a day whose observance was required by imperial laws, since Constantine I; (2) the relation between Sunday and Christ's resurrection, emphasized repeatedly by Christian writers, with Sunday being made to appear more meaningful to Christians than was the memorial of Creation (the Sabbath); (3) persisting anti-Judaism; and (4) to a much lesser degree, the influence of the Roman Catholic Church.[23]

The impact of factors 1 and 2 in favor of Sunday observance is so obvious that no additional comment is necessary. The importance of anti-Judaism as a factor in the rather fast abandonment of Sabbath observance has been noted in chapter seven, but deserves some further attention here because of the further developments during this later period.

Anti-Judaism in Church Canons and Byzantine Legislation

Canon 29 of the synod of Laodicea (c. 364) reads: "Christians must not judaize by resting on the Sabbath, but most work on that day, rather honouring the Lord's Day; and, if they can, resting then as Christians. But if any shall be found to be judaizers, let them be anathema from Christ."[24]

The *Apostolic Canons,* later incorporated as part of book 8 of the *Apostolic Constitutions,* came from the same period (c. 381). Of special interest are canons 65, 70, and 71:

"65. If any one, either of the clergy or laity, enters into a synagogue of the Jews or heretics to pray, let him be deprived and suspended. . . .

"70. If any bishop, or any other of the clergy, fasts with the Jews, or keeps the festivals with them, or accepts of the presents from their festivals, as unleavened bread or some such thing, let him be deprived; but if he be one of the laity, let him be suspended.

"71. If any Christian carries oil into an heathen temple, or into a synagogue of the Jews, or lights up lamps in their festivals, let him be suspended."[25]

Christian-Jewish contacts seem to have been frequent, or at least easy. Even some of the clergy were, evidently, participating in some Jewish ceremonies and festivals. There was the risk of losing sight of the uniqueness of the Christian gospel. As canon 62 implies, some "of the clergy for fear of men, as of a Jew, or a Gentile, or an heretic" went so far as to "deny the name of Christ."[26]

Jewish influence was indeed strong. Laws were enacted by the Byzantine emperors to keep Jews from proselytizing among Christians,[27] though the laws also guaranteed the status of Judaism as a lawful religion. However, the laws also established that the Jews should not insult the Patriarch (396),[28] nor should they mock the cross at Purim (408).[29] Possession of Christian slaves by Jews was at first regulated (417),[30] and later forbidden (sixth century).[31] Emperor Leo the Isaurian (c. 680-741) reiterated that Jews could not possess Christian slaves.[32] No new synagogues could be built (423, 438).[33] Jews were to be exiled for circumcising non-Jews (423) and punished with death for proselytizing (438).[34] Justinian I (483-565) revised a law of Honorius (409 or 412) that commanded that Jews should be left undisturbed on Sabbaths and feast days, by adding that on their feasts Jews were not entitled to summon Christians.[35] Leo the Isaurian, about two to three centuries later, insisted that proselytizing to Judaism and apostasy to Judaism were to be punished.[36]

Canon 11 of the Quinisext Council (692) warns Christians: "Let no one in the priestly order nor any layman eat the unleavened bread of the Jews, nor have any familiar intercourse with them, nor summon them in illness, nor receive medicines from them, nor bathe with them; but if anyone shall take in hand to do so, if he is a cleric, let him be deposed, but if a layman let him be cut off."[37]

Anti-Jewish Christian Literature From the Fourth to Fifteenth Centuries

To the foregoing evidences of Christian anti-Judaism should be added the fact that between the fourth and the ninth centuries more than twenty Eastern Christian writers prepared one or more works against the Jews.[38] Some of these works were written with the purpose of winning Jews to Christianity. But, as A. P. Hayman comments in the introduction to one of these books, "the Church's anti-Jewish polemic was motivated, not by any abstract theological considerations, but by a very real threat to its position."[39]

Writing about anti-Jewish documents written by Near Eastern monks from the seventh through eleventh centuries, A. Lukyn Williams suggests that "not a few" of them "give the impression of being written by those who had indeed Jews around them, and therefore feared the influence of Jews on others if not on themselves, yet never came into any close intellectual contact with Jews. They wrote in the hope that their words would provide weapons for their brethren who did meet them, and would also answer difficulties about the relation of the New Testament and the Church to the Old Testament and the Synagogue. The former reason must not be eliminated, or even unduly minimised, although the latter was more successful in the results attained."[40]

The real problem underlying John Chrysostom's eight *Homilies against the Jews* (387-389) is "that of Christians participating in Jewish festivals, with some getting circumcised. This time, however, it is specifically Gentile Christians who are involved."[41]

Isaac of Antioch (fifth century A.D.), in his *Homily Two against the Jews,* "witnesses to the fact that the same state of affairs existed in his days as had existed in those of John Chrysostom; his homilies inveigh against Christians who practice circumcision and celebrate Jewish festivals."[42]

Jacob of Serug (*c.* 450-521), in his three *Homilies against the Jews,* "appears to be dealing with real difficulties raised in the minds of his congregation by their Jewish neighbours."[43] The same happens with Pseudo-Ephraim's *De Fine et Admonitione,*[44] and with Jerome of Jerusalem (eighth century A.D.). Commenting on Jerome's work, Williams suggests that, after all, "the Christian Church was even in the eighth century exposed to danger from Jewish influence, and felt bound to argue with Jews according to its opportunities and knowledge."[45]

The early centuries of Byzantine history clearly show a "progressively increasing hostility between the Jews and their Christian neighbours."[46] The vitality of Judaism appeared as a permanent threat to the Christian Church.

What did this anti-Judaism mean in terms of Sabbath observance? One indication is given in Aphrahat's *Homilies* (336-345), written, from all appearance, "to provide Christians with arguments with which to combat Jews, and to strengthen the faith of Christians who were weakening in the face of Jewish attacks."[47] His thirteenth homily deals specifically with the Sabbath *(De Sabbato).*[48]

The Jews boast that they live by the Sabbath, suggests Aphrahat, and he counters that the Sabbath was not given to distinguish between life and death, righteousness and sin. Its purpose, he says, was not to be the great test of obedience to God, but to provide physical rest; and its observance is useful for health but not for salvation. Otherwise, he continues, it would have been established from the beginning of the world, and for all creatures, whereas the patriarchs, in spite of the fact that they were among God's elect, did not keep the Sabbath. Domestic animals, he further posits, observe the Sabbath as men do in spite of the fact that there is no commandment or divine remuneration for them; and thus it is clear that the Sabbath corresponds to a physical need, not to a religious duty. In view of this, Aphrahat concludes that it has been and still is permissible, when deemed necessary, not to observe the Sabbath, for instance, in time of war, as in the cases of Joshua and the Maccabees. Furthermore, Jews should not pride themselves in its observance; it does not give them any merits. However, the institution is nevertheless good, desired by God. If *He* rested, how much more should we! The Sabbath should be observed in God's way, and for failure to do so properly, the Jews were scattered abroad.

It seems clear that in Aphrahat's community[49] the Sabbath was observed along with Sunday, as the *Apostolic Constitutions* prescribe. Some of the believers kept the Sabbath in the same manner as the Jews. Aphrahat himself does not dare to eliminate Sabbath observance entirely, but he tries to eliminate what he considers its Jewish character, which, to him, empties the Sabbath of religious significance.[50]

A somewhat later writer, Pseudo-Gregory of Nyssa, in his *Selected Testimonies from the Old Testament against the Jews* (*c.* 400), declares that the Sabbath was given to the Jews to stop their desire for money. When they came out of Egypt, he says, they did not have anything except what the Egyptians had given them, and they were eager to make money by continuous toil. Therefore God limited their labor to six days only.[51]

There is also some documentary evidence showing that converted Jews were required to abandon completely their Sabbath observance. In a long profession of faith of uncertain Eastern origin, attached to the *Clementine Recognitions,* a converted Jew states, in part: "I renounce the whole worship of the Hebrews, circumcision, all its legalisms, unleavened bread, Passover, the sacrificing of lambs, the feasts of Weeks, Jubilees, Trumpets, Atonement, Tabernacles, and all the other Hebrew feasts, their sacrifices, prayers, aspersions, purifications, expiations, fasts, Sabbaths, new moons, foods and drinks. And I absolutely renounce every custom and institution of the Jewish laws."[52] A similar, but shorter, profession of faith from the church of Constantinople also specifies abandonment of the Sabbath.[53]

Byzantine emperor Heraclius (610-641), as part of his efforts to unify his empire when it was threatened by Moslem invaders and by other forces, compelled many Jews to be baptized "from fear, or even by direct physical compulsion."[54] The church, knowing that the newcomers had not been instructed, drew up treatises with that purpose. One of these treatises is *The Teaching of Jacob*

(634),[55] which declares that the Israelites, before Moses, had neither commandments nor Sabbath observance. But once the law of Moses came, they were told to keep the Sabbath and all the commandments. After Jesus Christ, the Sun of Righteousness, came, one should not abandon Him and go the way of the Sabbath.[56] The section is fittingly entitled "The uselessness of Sabbath."

If, as it appears, *The Teaching of Jacob* reflects the official position of the Orthodox Church in the Byzantine Empire, by 634 (and perhaps somewhat earlier) the Sabbath had ceased to have any significance for that church as a day of physical rest. Nevertheless, by force of tradition the Sabbath still retained a small degree of liturgical importance.

About a century later, John of Damascus (*c.* 675-*c.* 749), the last of the great Eastern Fathers, writing in Moslem-ruled Syria-Palestine, prepared a document entitled "Against the Jews, Concerning the Sabbath."[57] And *The Disputation of Sergius the Stylite against a Jew* appears to belong to the same century (*c.* 730-*c.* 770). Its geographical setting is somewhere between Homs (Emesa) and Antioch, in Syria, and its purpose was "to strengthen Christians" who were "in danger of apostatizing to Judaism."[58] Chapter 22 starts with the following interesting remark: "The Jew said: Then, when I approached you, I approached inadvisedly, for I was unaware that you (Christians) had all this knowledge. But now I am amazed how, after knowing (all) this, there are among you some Christians who associate with us in the synagogue, and who bring offerings and alms and oil, and at the time of the Passover send unleavened bread (and), doubtless, other things also. They are not entirely Christians, and some of our men had said that, if they were truly Christians, they would not associate with us in our synagogue and in our law. And now, because of this, we are all the more scandalized."[59] Regarding the Sabbath, the author repeats some of the well-known arguments, closing with the statement "Also God does not cease work on the Sabbath."[60]

Sergius, in trying to explain why some "weak and feeble" Christians "give oil or bring unleavened bread to your provocative synagogue," suggests that these are "doubters . . . the children of heathen and their mind has not yet been cleansed from the fear of their fathers' idols. Or they are the children of Hebrews, and the former custom still prevails over them."[61]

"Anastasius," in his *Dissertation against the Jews* (*c.* 1050),[62] briefly restates the well-known anti-Sabbath position. The Sabbath rest was given to the Jews in Old Testament times, he says; but when Jesus came, the Jews crucified Him on the grounds that He had broken the law and done away with the Sabbath. Had He? Would not the Jews save a beast on Sabbath, and not a man? And they also circumcised on the Sabbath.[63] After quoting Psalm 95:8-11, he develops the idea of a new kind of rest as follows:

"Therefore another *[heteros]* sabbatism *[sabbatismos]* and another *[hetera]* rest has been left, which is (the) faith in Christ, as (the) Lord said through Jeremiah the prophet: 'Behold (the) days are coming, and I will establish with the house of Israel and with the house of Judah a new covenant' [Jer. 31:31]. When he says new, he makes the first one old."[64]

Dionysius Bar Salibi (died 1171), Jacobite metropolitan of Amid (Diabekr) in the upper Tigris valley, 100 miles north of Edessa, was the author of several commentaries on Biblical books, and of a work entitled *Against the Jews*. As late as the thirteenth century the Jacobite Church felt the need to promulgate canons that "forbid the participation of bishops and other clerics in the Jewish Passover celebrations, enjoin the faithful to work on the sabbath and not to observe it in the Jewish manner, and . . . forbid Christians to receive unleavened bread from the Jews."[65]

The anti-Jewish writings continued into the fourteenth and fifteenth centuries, but these Jacobite canons appear to be the latest source where the Sabbath occupies a prominent place.

Two Marginal Christian Groups Considered to Be Influenced by Judaism

Two marginal groups are mentioned by several authors as Sabbathkeepers, with no reference to Sundaykeeping on their part. The first one seems to have originated as a result of the schism created within Novatianism by Sabbatius, during the reign of Theodosius I (379-395). Socrates Scholasticus calls Sabbatius "a converted Jew . . . who nevertheless continued to retain many of his Jewish prejudices."[66] A catalog of heresies, attributed to Maruthas, Bishop of Maipherkat (died c. 420), gives the following description of the Sabbatians:

"They say that the sacrifice should be offered on Sabbath, and not on Sunday; that the *Torah* should be read to the people, and not the Gospel. Circumcision has not been abolished, nor the commandments of the Law eliminated. The (Jewish) Passover must be observed because the New Testament is not opposed to the Old. Holding unto the Law, they still pretend to be Christians."[67]

Purchas (c. 1625) describes the second group as follows: "There are others, continuing from ancient times under divers Lords, Romanes, Greekes, Saracens and Christians, called Surians, unfit for Warre, men for the most part Unfaithfull, Double-dealing, Lyers, Inconstant, Fortunefawners, Traytors, Gift-takers, esteeming Theft and Robbery for nothing, Spyes to the Saracens, imitating their Language and Condition. . . . They keepe Saturday holy, nor esteeme Saturday Fast lawfull but on Easter Eeven. They have solemne Service on Saturdayes, eate flesh, and feast it bravely like the Jewes."[68]

Purchas does not state where this group was located. But the context suggests either Syria, or less probably, Asia Minor. There is no way of knowing whether there was any connection between these "Surians" and the "Sabbatians."

The Nestorians

In 424 the hostilities between Persia and Rome led to the severance of the ties between the East Syrian Church (in Persian territory) and the faraway patriarchal see of Antioch (under Roman control), and in 486 Nestorianism was officially adopted by the Persian Church.[69] This Nestorian "Church of the East" had its patriarchal see in Seleucia-Ctesiphon until c. 762, when it was moved to Baghdad. In 1258 it moved to Mosul and, finally, after 1400, to Maragha, east of Lake Urmia.[70]

The Nestorians distinguished themselves as missionaries, A. Mingana referring to them as "the most missionary church that the world has ever seen."[71] They spread from Persia to Arabia, India, Turkestan, Siberia, and China, with their greatest expansion being reached in the thirteenth century.[72] Since separate sections below are devoted to China and India, the rest of the present section will deal with the information available on Sabbath-Sunday observance in the other areas reached by the Nestorians.

A canonical letter written by Nestorian patriarch Ishu'-Yab (c. 585) discusses Sunday observance at some length: "In regard to the Lord's day, the holy first day of the week.... Since the kingdom of heaven has been announced, the day of the bodily resurrection of the Son of God has been given to the children of the house (the Christians) in place of God's day of rest; and the day in which the general renewal has been figuratively accomplished and will really be accomplished, in place of the day of rest that benefits men and animals; the day that begins the week, in which this transitory world began, and in which also the future world will begin, that will have a beginning but no end, in the place of the day in which the week ends.... In the first day of the week, our Lord broke and opened the Sheol by means of His resurrection, laid the foundation of the Church and preached the Kingdom of heaven. That is why the children of the doctrine of life must keep, from evening to evening, the day in which these marvels were accomplished.... Some of the faithful abstain themselves, during the first day of the week, of working or traveling until the church (service) has finished. But others, be it because of an emergency stronger than their good will, or because of their own disdainful, rebellious and froward will, like disobedient children, treat the Lord's day, the first day of the week, as they treat the sabbath or the second day of the week, and they do not honor it at all, that is, they do not want to honor themselves that day by performing divine works and justice. This is inadmissible. They work out of love of the money that leads to sin and does not last."[73]

This interesting text clearly shows that, officially, the day of worship for the sixth-century Nestorian church was Sunday. Sabbath rest seems to have been so completely abandoned that individuals who did not honor Sunday at all were accused of treating that day as if it were as secular as Sabbath or Monday. On the other hand, those who worked or traveled on Sunday after the church services were over were not condemned. Further on in this same letter (addressed to the Christians in the island of Daraī, who had pearl fishing as one of their main occupations), the patriarch deals with the special situation of the pearl divers who often had to dive on Sunday. If they can come to church, he declares, let them come; if not, it would be necessary to find a solution to protect them both from sinning and from financial loss.[74]

From the sixth century on, Sunday is the only day of rest that we have been able to find in Nestorian sources, and in descriptions of Nestorian practices by Western medieval travelers.[75] The only remnant of Sabbath observance seems to be the persistent obligation to refrain from fasting on that day.[76]

By the sixteenth century the Nestorians had retreated to the only place that still seemed safe for them, the roughly triangular area between Lake Urmia, Lake Van, and Mosul (in what is today northwestern Iran, eastern Turkey, and northern Iraq). Very little is known of their history during the next two centuries. After the Nestorian schism of 1551, the Roman Catholic Church entered the scene, and two Uniate patriarchates eventually developed, both recognized by the Papal See.[77] However, when at the beginning of the nineteenth century the Protestants learned of the existence of these Christians, they found them "anti-popish" with "neither icons nor crucifixes in their churches, only a simple and symbolic Cross."[78] Sunday was still being kept, quite strictly among the mountain dwellers, but not so strictly in the plains.[79]

China

The first reliable information on the presence of Christianity in China dates from the T'ang dynasty (618-907).[80] It is found in the imperial edicts of 638, 745, and 845, in the famous Nestorian Monument, uncovered near Hsi-an-fu in 1623 or 1625, and in other Nestorian records discovered in China during the first half of the twentieth century.

The Nestorian Monument, erected in 781, describes the arrival in Ch'angan of Bishop Alopen (635) and gives some information on the "propagation of the Luminous Religion" in China. It also has a description of the beliefs and practices of the Nestorian Christians in China that includes the following information: "Seven times a day they meet for worship and praise, and earnestly they offer prayers for the living as well as for the dead. Once in seven days, they have 'a sacrifice without the animal' (*i.e.*, a bloodless sacrifice). Thus cleansing their hearts, they regain their purity."[81]

Jean Vuilleumier (1864-1959) takes this text as a proof of Sabbath observance in seventh- and eighth-century China.[82] On the other hand, P. Y. Saeki, a Japanese expert on the Nestorian Monument and other Nestorian documents and relics in China, states on linguistic grounds that the text refers to Sundaykeeping.[83]

In some of the other Nestorian documents discovered in China there are a few hints that seem to support Saeki's position. First of all, it is puzzling to discover that no mention of a weekly day of rest is found in a rather lengthy exposition-paraphrase of the Ten Commandments that appears in the "Jesus-Messiah Sûtra," written probably between 635 and 638, just after Alopen's arrival. The other commandments are mentioned, the first three in an oblique way, the last six in a very clear manner.[84] Was the author afraid to be clear about the weekly rest because of the Nestorians' recent arrival?

In June of 1905 Dr. A. von Le Coq discovered several Syriac manuscripts in Kao-ch'ang, Chinese Turkestan. One of these manuscripts is a portion of a Nestorian church book "giving the names of proper Anthems, etc., to be used on Sundays and the Church Festival days" for the whole year. It belongs to the ninth or the tenth century, at the latest.[85] Line 16 states, "First I say this that on a Sunday shall the Church be consecrated"; and line 23 refers to Sunday's "evening service."[86]

Another set of Syriac manuscripts, discovered at the imperial palace in Peking between 1925 and 1926, are "a portion of the Nestorian Hymns in the Nestorian Service Book . . . used on Sunday throughout the year."[87] They were written in the twelfth or the thirteenth century, or earlier.[88] An interesting reference is made in one of the hymns to the Sunday of the martyrdom of two "blessed martyrs."[89] Although these documents are not in themselves compelling proofs regarding the day of worship, the little information they provide on the weekly day of rest basically harmonizes with what is already known about the Nestorian practice in other areas of Asia.

It may be added that under the Mongol emperors of the thirteenth century, Rabban Sawma, a Nestorian monk, traveled all the way from Peking to Western Europe, and that throughout the book that records his life and travels, Sunday appears to be the normal day of worship. There is not even a hint of Sabbath-Sunday tension in the detailed account of his contacts with the Roman Catholic Church. In Rome he celebrated the Eucharist on a Sunday, with full papal approval, and the pope even invited him to stay with him in Rome.[90]

Thus, in China during this period we do not find any evidence of Christian Saturday observance. There are several documents that, on the contrary, suggest that as early as the seventh century Sunday was the only day of weekly rest among Christians there.[91]

India

It is not known when Christianity originally reached India. The first possible traces of its existence there are from the third century,[92] and clear evidence begins with the fifth century.[93] The Christian church in India was subordinated to the Nestorian patriarchate of Seleucia-Ctesiphon, and Syriac was its liturgical language. Although eventually Christianity spread widely throughout India,[94] when Vasco da Gama arrived in India in 1498 he found the vast majority of the remaining Christians living on the Malabar Coast in southwest India. According to a contemporary Nestorian Indian source, 30,000 families lived there.[95]

There are no known references to Sabbath observance by the church in India before the arrival of the Portuguese. During the synod of Diamper (1599), Roman Catholic Archbishop Aleixo de Menezes succeeded in getting the approval of a decree requiring that all the books written in the Syriac tongue be turned over to Jesuit Father Francisco Roz, to be "perused and corrected, or destroyed."[96] Julius Richter, commenting on this decree, writes: "It is to this vandalism that we must attribute the scarcity of reliable information concerning the earlier history of the Thomas Church."[97] However, it is difficult to imagine that *all* the books were located. On the other hand, the absence of documentary evidence gives us no special freedom to speculate; and both Stephen Neill and John Stewart assume that before the arrival of the Portuguese the Malabar Christians kept Sunday.[98]

The same Nestorian Indian document referred to above, written in Syriac possibly in the first decade of the sixteenth century, describes the first landing of the Portuguese in India and some of the Nestorians' initial contacts with them. The author tells how he met these Portuguese, for the first time, in the town of Cananore and stayed with them for two and a half months. Then he continues: "They ordered us one day to say mass. They have prepared for themselves a beautiful place, like a chapel, and their priests say their mass in it every day, as is their custom. On the Sunday, therefore, of *Nusardail* [the sixth Sunday after Trinity], after their priest had finished his mass, we also went and said mass, at which they were greatly pleased with us."[99]

In 1505, a Roman Catholic Italian traveler, Ludovico di Varthema, left the following comments about the Thomas Christians he met at Kayamkulam (north of Quilon): "In this city we found some Christians of those of St. Thomas, some of whom are merchants and believe in Christ, as we do. . . . These Christians keep Lent longer than we do: but they keep Easter like ourselves and *they all observe the same solemnities that we do*. But they say Mass like the Greeks."[100] No further details are given, but the implications seem quite clear that Sunday alone, not both Saturday and Sunday, was the weekly day for worship.

The detailed descriptions of the customs and of the religious practices of the Thomas Christians, when they first came in contact with the Portuguese, mention only Sunday observance.[101] However, "Sunday labor was not infrequent."[102] Wednesday and Friday were the weekly days of fasting,[103] with no fasting on the

Sabbath[104] nor on Sunday.[105] Sundays and the days of fasting were kept from sundown to sundown.[106]

Relations between the Thomas Christians and the Portuguese were friendly for a few years. However, tension began to rise when some Roman Catholic priests started penetrating into the local churches, insisting on saying mass according to the Latin rite. The Roman Catholic Church entered more and more into the affairs of the Thomas Christians, until it finally succeeded in bringing them to the Roman fold in the synod of Diamper (1599).

The acts and decrees of this synod are the best witness to the effort of the Roman Catholic Church to "straighten out" the Thomas Christians in almost incredible detail regarding their religious beliefs and practices.[107] Everything that was supposedly wrong seems to have been mentioned in the decrees.

The synod decided that it was wrong to eat flesh on Saturdays, making Saturday, along with Friday, a day of fasting.[108] It was also wrong to fast or keep the festivities from evening to evening. These had to be kept from midnight to midnight, to be in harmony with the "Holy Mother Church."[109] Thus, "the Obligation of ceasing from labour begins at the midnight of the said day [Sunday], and ends at the midnight of *Monday.*"[110] Sunday is mentioned many times as the only day of weekly rest.[111] No Sabbath-Sunday tension is detected in any of the many decrees.[112]

There is, however, some evidence regarding observance of the Sabbath toward the end of the seventeenth century. About 1673, C. Dellon, a Frenchman, was imprisoned by the Inquisition while traveling in India. After his release, about two years later, he wrote a book, *The Inquisition at Goa,* and in his account he refers to people accused before the Inquisition of "assisting at the Jewish Sabbath."[113] The accusation of Judaizing included "having conformed to the ceremonies of the Mosaic law; such as not eating pork, hare, fish without scales, &c., of having attended the solemnization of the sabbath, having eaten the Paschal Lamb, &c."[114]

At least two writers[115] have concluded from Dellon's account that there were many Sabbathkeepers among the Christians in India at that time.[116] How can this be so, inasmuch as there was no known Sabbathkeeping before the synod of Diamper in 1599? Dellon himself seems to provide the answer. Before he deals in detail with the treatment of the Judaizers by the Inquisition, he gives an account of the force conversion, in Portugal, of many Spanish and Portuguese Jews who came to be classified as "New Christians." The "New Christians" had a very difficult time being accepted by the "Old Christians." Most, if not all, of their business dealings and social contacts were with other "New Christians." Their conversion was not always believed to be true. They were under constant suspicion of secretly practicing Jewish ceremonies, including Sabbath observance.[117] Many of them, undoubtedly, went to the Portuguese colonies with the hope of escaping the rigidities of life in Portugal.[118]

When the Inquisition asked Dellon to mention the names of his accusers, he finally had to name some of his brethren, the only ones that knew of his Sabbathkeeping because they had, together with him, been keeping the Sabbath. The "New Christians . . . look for their accusers and accomplices in a certain class."[119] It seems clear, in the context, that the "certain class" refers to the "New Christians." It is not impossible, as happened with Judaizing Christians in other areas of the world, that some Christians of Indian origin were attracted by the ceremonies practiced by "New Christians" who were still Jews at heart. However, Dellon's account seems to have only "New Christians" in mind. These are the only known Sabbathkeeping Christians in India before the nineteenth century.[120]

Armenia

Christianity entered Armenia apparently by the beginning of the third century.[121] After the synod of Vagharshabad (491), in which the Armenian Church condemned the Council of Chalcedon, the Armenians adhered to the strict Monophysite doctrine.[122] Tension arose with their Greek Orthodox neighbors, and Monophysitism lost ground when Armenians and Byzantines united under Emperor Heraclius (610-641). In 652, when Emperor Constans II (641-688) appeared at Dewin (Tevin), " the decisions of Chalcedon were solemnly proclaimed on Sunday in the main church."[123]

Both the Sabbath and Sunday seem to have been kept in Armenia, probably from the fourth century on. In the seventh century, the fathers attending the Quinisext Council (692) acknowledged that they had "learned that in the regions of Armenia and in other places certain people eat eggs and cheese on the Sabbaths and Lord's days of the holy lent." The council decided that "the whole Church of God which is in all the world should follow one rule," that is, the Greek Orthodox rule.[124]

Some years later, in 719, probably as a reaction, the Armenians at the synod of Dewin (Tevin) tried to draw a more marked line between themselves and the Greeks. They decided, among other things, to abstain from fish, oil, eggs, and butter during Lent, except on Sundays and Saturdays.[125]

In the Council of Manazkert in 728, attended by all the Armenian bishops and also by some Jacobite bishops, "Chalcedon was repudiated afresh . . . the five days' preliminary fast before Lent restored, Saturday as well as Sunday made a day of feasting and synaxis [religious gathering]."[126] This action suggests that the Sabbath rest had been at least partially forgotten. The Sabbath had probably become just a day without fasting, not intended for religious meetings, as was the case with the other Eastern churches. The council restored the significance of the Sabbath as a day both of feasting and religious gathering.

Manazkert's importance is indicated in F. C. Conybeare's comment that in general, "these rules have been observed in the Armenian church ever since."[127]

Contacts between the Armenians and the Roman Catholic Church during the Crusades resulted, eventually, in the establishment of the Armenian Uniates, or United Armenians, who severed ties with their church and attached themselves to Rome.[128] Among them was the Lousinian dynasty of the last independent Armenian kingdom of Cilicia, including Leo VI, who gave himself up to the Egyptian Mamelukes in 1375.

Earlier in the fourteenth century, an Ethiopian monk and founder of a new monastic house, Eustathius (c. 1273-1352), who had left his country because he could not keep Sabbath there unmolested, had arrived in Armenia after stopping in Cairo, Jerusalem, and Cyprus (see pp. 176, 177). Did he, perhaps, choose to spend his last fourteen years in Armenia because he could keep the Sabbath there as he thought he should?

It seems that from early times the Armenians had a church order of a similar nature to, but still different from, the *Didascalia Apostolorum*. Several manuscripts of this Armenian *Didascalia* are known today. Five of them, examined in some detail by Abraham Terian of Andrews University, were copied from the thirteenth to the eighteenth century. In all except one, there is a clear injunction for Sabbath observance.[129] The following translation, made by Terian, is from an eighteenth-century manuscript:

"The apostles ordered and firmly established that on the Sabbath day there should be feast and worship in all the world; there should also be a memorial (service) for all martyrs. On that day the priests should offer the eucharist and recite the Psalms joyfully, for they announce the coming of the Great King. It behooves all saints to rejoice in the presence of Christ."

These manuscripts are not a compelling proof that Armenians continued to keep the Sabbath during the latter part of the Middle Ages and early modern times. However, the discovery in the nineteenth century that the Armenian Church still had a special regard for the Sabbath suggests that Sabbath and Sunday were kept by this church, at least to a certain extent, all through these centuries.[130]

Summary and Conclusions

The observance of Sabbath together with Sunday was widespread in Christian Asia during the second half of the fourth century, and continued to be so for approximately another century. However, there is no clear documentary evidence that after the year A.D. 500 Sabbath *and* Sunday were observed together by the main Christian churches in Asia, the only exception being the Armenian Church, plus some "New Christians" in India, who also observed the Saturday Sabbath. Nevertheless, a certain respect for the Sabbath was shown, and continues to be shown, by the Eastern churches in general by their refusal to make the Sabbath a day of fasting. But even this vestige of the Sabbath's former status was lost among such Christians as the Maronites and the United Armenians when they came into communion with Rome.

As in earlier Christian history, anti-Judaism continued to be, from the sixth century onward, one of the most important factors in accelerating the process of abandonment of Sabbath observance. The church often felt threatened by the synagogue, and several Christian preachers and writers did their best to show that Sabbath observance was only one more Jewish practice, of no value for Christians if not definitely anti-Christian. However, their very concern in trying to discourage Sabbath observance shows that the practice persisted or reappeared for centuries with varying intensity, in different areas of Near Eastern Asia, and in open defiance to the official teaching of the Orthodox, the Nestorian, and the Jacobite churches.

NOTES

[1] We will be limited to a rather succinct presentation of the documents that deal with Sabbath-Sunday observance, giving only the historical background that is indispensable to understanding each document. The sources we have been able to locate give only fragmentary information on Sabbath-Sunday observance in Asia.

[2] *Constitutions of the Holy Apostles* 7. 2. 23 (*ANF* 7:469). Cf. 2. 7. 59; 5. 3. 20 (*ANF* 7:423, 449).

[3] *Ibid.*

[4] *Ibid.*, 8. 4. 33 (*ANF* 7:495). It should probably be mentioned here that Ephraem the Syrian *(c.* 306-373), the great classical writer of the Syrian Church who died in Syria about the time when the so-called *Constitutions of the Holy Apostles* were taking final shape in that country, clearly preached in favor of Sunday observance. Trying to impress on his listeners the importance of Sunday, he said that Sunday had taken from Sabbath the birthright, as Jacob did, and as was done with Ephraim. He calls for a more careful observance of Sunday, not only as a day of physical rest *(Sermon*

pour l'office de nuit de la résurrection du Seigneur, in Willy Rordorf, *Sabbat et dimanche dans l'Église ancienne* [Neuchâtel, Switzerland, 1972], p. 185).
⁵ *The Canons of the Synod Held in the City of Laodicea (NPNF/2* 14:133).
⁶ *Ibid.,* 14. 155, 156.
⁷ Pseudo-Ignatius *Magnesians* 9:3, 4, ed. by Funk-Diekamp, quoted in A. Kraft, "Some Notes on Sabbath Observance in Early Christianity," *AUSS* 3:24. See also *Trallians* 9:5-6 (Kraft, *op. cit.,* p. 24, n. 19).
⁸ Socrates Scholasticus *Ecclesiastical History* 5. 22 *(NPNF/2* 2:132).
⁹ Sozomen, *Ecclesiastical History* 7. 19 *(NPNF/2* 2:390).
¹⁰ Socrates Scholasticus *Eccl. Hist.* 6. 8 *(NPNF/2* 2:144).
¹¹ Asterius of Amasea, Homily 5, on Matt. 19:3 *(PG* 40:225).
¹² Theodoret of Cyrrhus *Haereticarum Fabularum* 2. 1 *(PG* 83:389). Cf. Eusebius *Ecclesiastical History* 3. 27 (in The Loeb Classical Library [Cambridge, Mass., 1949] 1. 263).
¹³ Epiphanius *(c.* 315-402), bishop of Salamis, Cyprus, in his *Medicine Box* (374-377) against heresies *(Panarion)* considers that the "little" weekly Sabbath has been superseded by Christ, "the great Sabbath," of whom it was a type. *Panarion Haereseon* 30, 32, 6-9 (K. Holl, *GCS* 25, 1915), quoted in Rordorf, *op. cit.,* pp. 45, 55. Epiphanius adds, in *De Fide* (377) 24, 7 (Holl, *GCS* 37, 1933): "In certain places, religious services are celebrated also on the Sabbath days, but not everywhere." See Rordorf, *op. cit.,* pp. 54, 55. Gregory of Nyssa (331?-396?) opposed the attitude of some Christians who dishonor the Sabbath day but keep Sunday, when he tells them: "Do you not know that these days are sisters."—*De Castigatione (PG* 46:309). More will be said on this point later in this chapter when the anti-Jewish Christian literature of the fourth and the fifth centuries is discussed.
¹⁴ John Cassian *(c.* 360-c. 433) in his *Institutes of the Coenobia* 3. 11 *(NPNF/2* 11:218), mentions that on Sunday morning in "the Lord's communion, they use a more solemn and a longer service of Psalms and prayers and lessons. . . . And hence it results that . . . an indulgence over other times seems to be granted to the brethren out of reverence of the Lord's resurrection . . . and, by reason of the difference which is interposed, *it makes the day to be looked forward to more solemnly as a festival,* and owing to the anticipation of it the fasts of the coming week are less felt." (Italics supplied.)
¹⁵ Cassian explains that Rome kept the Sabbath fast because tradition said that Peter fasted on Sabbath before his encounter with Simon Magus. But this fast was not intended to be canonical. If Peter had had to fast on Sunday, we would have done it too, for that one occasion, as "a matter of necessity," but "no canonical rule of fasting would have been made general from this."—*Institutes* 3. 10 *(NPNF/2* 11:218). Cassian reiterates that Sabbath is not a day of fasting in the East. We "are charged to give to both days—that is, to the seventh and eighth equally—the same share of the service." The dispensation of fasting is not Jewish, but for the benefit of the wearied body. If throughout the whole year we fast five days a week, our body "would easily be worn out and fail, unless it were revived by an interval of at least two days."—*Ibid.,* 3. 9.; cf. chap. 12 *(NPNF/2* 11:217, 218).
¹⁶ Samuel Purchas, *Hakluytus Posthumus or Purchas His Pilgrimes* (New York, 1965), 1:350. Cf. B. J. Kidd, *The Churches of Eastern Christendom* (London, [1927]), pp. 70, 74, 130, 131, 470; Charles Joseph Hefele, *A History of the Christian Councils* (Edinburgh, 1896), 2:320. The Quinisext Council (692), under Greek Orthodox control, decided "that also in the Church of the Romans the canon shall immovably stand fast which says: 'If any cleric shall be found to fast on a Sunday or Saturday (except on one occasion only) he is to be deposed; and if he is a layman he shall be cut off' " (canon 55). Canon 56 requires that "on the Sabbaths and Lord's days of the holy lent" all Christians, Armenians included, should "abstain from everything which is killed," and also "from eggs and cheese" *(NPNF/2* 14:391). See also R. L. Odom, "The Sabbath in the Great Schism of A.D. 1054," *AUSS* 1 (1963):74-80.
¹⁷ Purchas, *op. cit.,* p. 387.
¹⁸ *Ibid.;* A. A. Stamouli, "Maronites," *Schaff-Herzog* 7:189.
¹⁹ *Codex Justinianus* [hereinafter cited as *CJ*] 3. 12, 3, trans. in Philip Schaff, *History of the Christian Church* (Grand Rapids, 1957), 3:380, n. 1.
²⁰ *Theodosian Code* [hereinafter cited as *CT, Codex Theodosianus*] 2. 8. 1, translated by Clyde Pharr (Princeton, N.J., 1952), p. 44.
²¹ *The Letters of St. Jerome,* Letter 108, to Eustochium, sec. 20 *(NPNF/2* 6:206).
²² For instance, Sunday laws by: (a) Emperors Gratian Valentian and Theodosius I, of November 3, 386, forbidding litigation on the "Lord's Day" *(CT* 11. 7. 13, trans. in Pharr, *op. cit.,* p. 300); and (b) Emperor Theodosius II of the Eastern Roman Empire, of February 1, 425, forbidding public spectacles—circus, theater—on Sunday *(ibid.,* 15. 5. 5, in Pharr, *op. cit.,* p. 433). See note of M. A. Kugener and Egd. Triffaux on the effect of Theodosius II's law on the preaching of patriarch Severus of Antioch (512-518), in *Les Homiliae Cathedrales de Sévère D'Antioche,* in *Patrologia Orientalis* [hereinafter cited as *PO*] (Paris, 1922), vol. 16, p. 862.
²³ As Sozomen and Socrates Scholasticus record it, Rome's position against Sabbath observance was well known in the fifth century. It undoubtedly had some influence on the practice of Eastern Christians. However, Roman Catholic influence on the Maronite Church and on a segment of the Armenian Church is more clearly seen much later in the Middle Ages (beginning with the Crusades).
²⁴ As translated in *NPNF/2* 14:148. Cf. Marcel Simon, *Verus Israel* (Paris, 1964), pp. 382, 383, 422, 423.
²⁵ *The Ecclesiastical Canons of the Same Holy Apostles (ANF* 7:504).
²⁶ *Ibid.,* 7:503, 504.
²⁷ For a detailed listing of these laws, see James Parkes, *The Conflict of the Church and the Synagogue* (Cleveland, 1961), pp. 379-391. The laws cited in notes 28 to 36 are taken from this source.
²⁸ *CT* 16. 8. 11, of April 24, 396 (Pharr, *op. cit.,* p. 380); cf. *CT* 16. 8. 22, of Oct. 20, 415 (Pharr, *op. cit.,* p. 381).
²⁹ *CT* 16. 8. 18, of May 29, 408 (Pharr, *op. cit.,* p. 381).
³⁰ *CT* 16. 9. 4, of April 10, 417 (Pharr, *op. cit.,* p. 381).
³¹ *CJ* 1. 3. 54 and 1. 10. 2 (Schaff, *op. cit.,* p. 387).
³² Ecloga, App. 6. 26 (p. 388).
³³ *CT* 16. 8. 25, of Feb. 15, 423; *CT* 16. 8. 27, of June 8, 423; Novella 3 of Theodosius II, of Jan. 31, 438 (p. 381).
³⁴ *Ibid.;* cf. Ecloga, App. 6. 30 of Leo the Isaurian stating that circumcision of a Christian should be punished (p. 388).
³⁵ *CJ* 1. 9. 13 (Schaff, *op. cit.,* p. 387).
³⁶ Ecloga, App. 4. 24, 16 (p. 388).
³⁷ *The Canons of the Council in Trullo (NPNF/2* 14:370).
³⁸ The following incomplete list has been compiled from A. Lukyn Williams, *Adversus Judaeos* (Cambridge,

1935), pp. 93-203; Parkes, *op. cit.*, pp. 271-306; Simon, *op. cit.*; and A. P. Hayman, trans., *The Disputation of Sergius the Stylite against a Jew* (Louvain, 1973), pp. 1-77. Most of the anti-Jewish literature in the Near East during the period under consideration was written in Greek. The Syriac writers will be specifically indicated.
 1. Aphrahat (Syriac), *Homilies* (336-345).
 2. John Chrysostom, *Eight Homilies Against the Jews* (387-389), *A Demonstration to Jews and Greeks that Christ is God* (c. 386).
 3. Pseudo-Chrysostom, *Against Jews and Greeks (i.e. Heathen) and Heretics*; and *Against Jews, with reference to the Brazen Serpent* (dates unknown).
 4. Pseudo-Gregory of Nyssa, *Selected Testimonies from the Old Testament against the Jews* (c. 400).
 5. Marootha (Syriac), *Book of Evidences* (before 420).
 6. Isaac of Antioch, *Homily Two against the Jews* (first half, fifth century).
 7. Mana (Syriac), *Against the Jews* (457-484).
 8. Jacob of Serub (Syriac, c. 450-521), three *Homilies against the Jews*.
 9. *The Discussion of Archbishop Gregentius with the Jew Herban* (c. 480).
 10. *Questions addressed to Antiochus the Dux* (sixth century?).
 11. John, a Nestorian (Syriac), wrote a treatise against the Jews (sixth century).
 12. Pseudo-Ephraim (Syriac), *De Fine et Admonitione, Rhythm against the Jews delivered upon Palm Sunday*, and *Rhythm 44* (fourth, fifth, and sixth centuries).
 13. *The Teaching of Jacob* (Sargis d'Aberga) (634).
 14. Leontius, *Against the Jews* (c. 660?).
 15. *The Trophies of Damascus* (681).
 16. Stephen of Bostra, *Against the Jews* (c. 700?).
 17. Jerome of Jerusalem, *A Dialogue concerning the Holy Trinity, the Discussion of a Jew with the Christian* (c. 730).
 18. John of Damascus, *Against the Jews, concerning the Sabbath* (c. 740).
 19. *The Disputation of Sergius the Stylite against a Jew* (c. 730-c. 770).
 20. "Anastasius," *Dissertation against the Jews* (c. 1050).
 21. Dionysius bar Salibi (Syriac), *Commentaries*, and *Against the Jews* (A.D. 12).
 22. Andronicus of Constantinople, *A Dialogue against the Jews* (1310?).
 23. Gennadius, *A Refutation of error of the Jews* (c. 1455).
There is a corresponding wealth (about thirty-eight writers) of anti-Jewish literature among Latin and Spanish authors (fourth to fifteenth centuries). See Williams, *op. cit.*, pp. 206-418.
 [39] Hayman, *op. cit.*, p. 75; cf. Simon, *op. cit.*, pp. 354-393.
 [40] Williams, *op. cit.*, pp. 159, 160.
 [41] Hayman, *op. cit.*, p. 75; cf. *PG* 48:843-942. Williams, *op. cit.*, p. 133, n. 2, comments: "Chrysostom's hatred of the Jews is not confined to these eight Homilies, as may be seen from the countless references to them scattered throughout his works."
 [42] Hayman, *op. cit.*, p. 74.
 [43] Parkes, *op. cit.*, p. 279.
 [44] Williams, *op. cit.*, p. 104.
 [45] *Ibid.*, p. 169.
 [46] Parkes, *op. cit.*, p. 305.
 [47] Hayman, *op. cit.*, pp. 75, 76, based on Jacob Neusner, *Aphrahat and Judaism* (Leiden, 1971), pp. 124, 125, 144, 149, 168, 171; cf. Williams, *op. cit.*, p. 102.
 [48] Aphrahat, *De Sabbato*, in *Patrologia Syriaca* [hereinafter cited as *PS*], ed. by R. Graffin, part 1 (Paris, 1894), 1:540-571.
 [49] For several years Aphrahat was bishop and abbot of the monastery of Mar Mathai, on the eastern side of the Tigris (under Persia), a few miles northeast of Mosul. He died c. 350.
 [50] Simon, *op. cit.*, pp. 375, 376; cf. Williams, *op. cit.*, pp. 97, 98; Aphrahat, *De Fide*, in *PS* 1:43; idem, *De Caritate*, in *PS* 1:78, 962, 1019.
 [51] *Delecta Testimonia Adversus Judaeos* 13 (*PG* 46:222); Williams, *op. cit.*, pp. 125, 128, 129.
 [52] *PG* 1:1456, trans. in Parkes, *op. cit.*, p. 398.
 [53] Assemani *Cod. Lit.* 1. 105, quoted in Parkes, *op. cit.*, p. 397.
 [54] Williams, *op. cit.*, pp. 151, 152.
 [55] The name in Greek is *The Teaching of Jacob*. In Ethiopic the name is *Sargis d'Aberga* (Williams, *op. cit.*, p. 152). The Ethiopic text with French translation is in *PO* 3:555-643, and 13:5-109.
 [56] *PO* 3:612.
 [57] John of Damascus *De Fide Orthodoxa* (*PG* 94:1201-1206).
 [58] Hayman, *op. cit.*, p. 74 (cf. *Disputation* 2. 8, 3. 5, and most of chap. 22).
 [59] *Disputation* 22. 1; cf. *Disputation*, 4. 12 (*ibid.*, p. 72).
 [60] *Disputation*, 4. 103 (*ibid.*, p. 9).
 [61] *Disputation*, 22. 1. 12. 5 (*ibid.*, pp. 72, 76, 73).
 [62] Attributed to Anastasius of Sinai (seventh century), but not his work, according to Williams, *op. cit.*, p. 175, based on internal evidence. Text in *PG* 89:1203-1282.
 [63] *PG* 89:1241-2480.
 [64] *Ibid.*, 89:1252. Cf. col. 1249; Williams, *op. cit.*, pp. 177, 178, 180.
 [65] Hayman, *op. cit.*, p. 76, and n. 99: "Summarized in Kawerau, *Die jakobitische Kirche*, p. 106, from Bar Hebraeus' *Nomocanon*. Cf. also Kazan, *Isaac of Antioch's Homily, OC* [*Oriens Christianus* (Leipzig-Wiesbaden)], 49:69." Perhaps a very brief note on the Syrian Jacobites should be added here. The few references we have found about their weekly day of rest mention only Sunday observance (manuscripts of 824, 1084, 1214, 1539, and also information on their customs in the twentieth century). See H. W. Codrington, *Studies of the Syrian Liturgies* (London, [c. 1937]), pp. 44-47; see also *Sept Menologes Jacobites*, in *PO* 10:125-130 (manuscripts of 1210 and 1465), 92, 134. Cf. *infra*, section 6 (Armenia) on the presence of a few Jacobite bishops in the Council of Manazkert (728), where Sabbaths as well as Sundays were made days of feasting and religious gathering. See note 127.
 [66] Socrates Scholasticus *Eccl. Hist.* 5. 21 (*NPNF*/2 2:129); cf. 7. 5, 12 (*NPNF*/2 2:155, 156, 158); Sozomen, *Eccl. Hist.*, 7. 18 *NPNF*/2 2:388, 389). Canon 7 of the Council of Constantinople (381) mentions the Sabbatians together

with several other heretical groups *(NPNF/*2 14:185). Cf. also Joannes Dominicus Mansi, *Sacrorum Conciliorum Nova et Amplissima Collectio* (Graz, 1960), 3:564. With some modifications, this canon is incorporated in the Quinisext Council (692), canon 95 *(NPNF/*2 14:405). The Sabbatians are not mentioned. Had they disappeared already by 692?
67 As quoted by E. Amann, "Sabbatiens," *Dictionnaire de Théologie Catholique* (Paris, 1939), 14:431; cf. Mansi, *op. cit.,* 2:1056, 1057. See also E. Tisserant, "Marouta de Maypherqat," *Dictionnaire de Théologie Catholique* (1928), 10:147-149. *The History of Barhadbešabba 'Arbaia,* written at the end of the sixth century, gives a description that is very similar to the one attributed to Marutha. The Sabbatians are called Simbatianists (and Sabbetâyê, in Syriac). *PO* 23:181, 187, 188. The Sabbatians are also mentioned in the book entitled *Lamp of Darkness* (La Lampe des Ténèbres), written in Egypt by Priest Sams ar-Ri' qsah Abûl-Barakât (died 1320-1327), in which, among a similar list of heresies, the "Sabbatéens" (French) are described as "rests of the Jews who had embraced Christianity with an unclean heart. They thought that the Sabbath day deserved more than Sunday to be honored and that on it offerings should be made."—*PO* 20:682, 683. *Lamp of Darkness* was an encyclopedia of ecclesiastical science of the Coptic Church. These Sabbathkeepers are mentioned as having existed, but not necessarily as a group. There is no connection between these Sabbatians and the Sabbatian movement within Judaism of the seventeenth century, with Sabbatai Tsevi. See Gershom Scholem, *Sabbatai Sevi: the Mystical Messiah 1626-1676* (Princeton, N.J.: 1973).
68 Purchas, *op. cit.,* 8:73.
69 G. A. Maloney, "Eastern Churches," *NCE* 5:16; M. J. Costelloe, "Nestorian Church," *NCE* 10:344; Kidd, *op. cit.,* p. 418; Kenneth Scott Latourette, *A History of the Expansion of Christianity* (New York, 1937), 1:230.
70 John Stewart, *Nestorian Missionary Enterprise* (Edinburgh: 1928), p. 102; Aziz S. Atiya, *A History of Eastern Christianity* (London: 1968), p. 277.
71 As quoted by Stewart, *op. cit.,* p. 139; cf. Latourette, *op. cit.,* 2:265.
72 Arthur Vööbus, *History of the School of Nisibis* (Louvain, 1965), p. 3; *The Journey of William of Rubruck,* in *The Mongol Mission,* ed. by Christopher Dawson (New York, 1955), pp. 79-220; A. Mingana, *The Early Spread of Christianity in India* (Manchester, 1926), p. 34; Codrington, *op. cit.,* p. 60; Stewart, *op. cit.,* p. 196.
73 "Iš 'yahb patriarch Nestorianus," Epistula canonica ad Iacobum episcopum (c. 585) 19," in *Das Buch de Synhados,* ed. by O. Braun (1900), cited in Rordorf, *op. cit.,* pp. 226-229.
74 Rordorf, *op. cit.,* p. 229, n. 5. Rordorf adds: "The spiritual Letters of monk John (died 530), ed. S. Vailhe, Echos d'Orient 8, 1905, p. 156f. show exactly the same tolerant position."
75 R. H. Connolly, *The Liturgical Homilies of Narsai* [died c. 502] (Cambridge: 1909), p. 23; Vööbus, *op. cit.,* p. 298; Iso-'iab of Hadiab *(c.* 650) "arranged the service book for the Sundays of the whole year"; Martyrius (Sahdona) [*c.* seventh century], *Oeuvres Spirituelles* (Louvain: 1965), 3:18, 19; *ibid.,* vol. 4, p. 9; Rubruck *(c.* 1250), in Dawson, *op. cit.,* pp. 163, 172, 174, 177, 178, 180. (Rubruck, writing about some of the Nestorians "who are with the Tartars" accuses them of having "several wives like them." Then he adds: "When they enter a church they wash their lower members like the Saracens; they eat meat on Fridays and have feasting on the day after the Saracen custom."—Dawson, *op. cit.,* p. 145; cf. Purchas, *op. cit.,* 11:68.) E. A. Wallis Budge, *The Monks of Kûblâi Khân Emperor of China* [thirteenth century] (London, 1928), pp. 156, 305. Most interesting is the detailed description and defense of "the truth of Christianity" entitled *The Jewel,* written by Mar Abd Yeshua, Nestorian metropolitan of Nisibis and Armenia, in 1298, included as appendix B in George Percy Badger, *The Nestorians and their Rituals* (London, 1852), 2:380-426. Sunday is presented as "the holy first day of the week" that should be hallowed by all. The "Apostles ordained, that on the first day of the week Christians should suspend all worldly occupations, and engage in prayer to GOD, in reading the Holy Scriptures, and in meditating on the life of CHRIST" (p. 415). Friday is also mentioned, as a day of fasting (pp. 416, 417). Sabbath is not mentioned at all, not even where fasting is discussed (pp. 416-418). It is necessary to remember that the Nestorians and the Roman Catholic Church exchanged some friendly letters during the thirteenth and early fourteenth centuries (1247, 1288, 1304, et cetera). But the schism that led to the creation of the Uniate Patriarchate of the Chaldeans took place in 1551. K. Kessler, "Nestorians," *Schaff-Herzog* 8:121, 122; cf. Atiya, *op. cit.,* pp. 277, 278.
76 Badger, *op. cit.,* pp. 187, 188; see also p. 416. Cf. Rubruck, in Dawson, *op. cit.,* p. 164.
77 Atiya, *op. cit.,* pp. 278, 279.
78 *Ibid.,* p. 280.
79 Asahel Grant, *The Nestorians* (London, 1841), pp. 60-63, 184, 185. A. H. Lewis, *A Critical History of the Sabbath and the Sunday in the Christian Church* (Plainfield, N.J.: 1903), pp. 219-221, contends that Dr. Grant's statements refer to Saturday observance. A careful reading of Grant's book, and especially of page 185, where it is said that the "preparation before the Sabbath" begins "about three hours before sunset on Saturday," makes Lewis' interpretation completely untenable. Cf. Codrington, *op. cit.,* pp. 82-85. Kessler *(op. cit.,* p. 122) states that the nineteenth-century Nestorians kept both Sabbath and Sunday. No details are given on what is meant by Sabbath observance. It may well have been just the absence of a Sabbath fast, as Nestorians kept on fasting on Wednesdays and Fridays. See Lewis, *op. cit.,* p. 219. There are about 30,000 Nestorians in the Near East today. About 8,000 live in Syria. "The rest live around Baghdad and Mosul, shepherded by one metropolitan and a single bishop."—Atiya, *op. cit.,* p. 286; cf. Costelloe, *op. cit.,* p. 346.
80 Kenneth Scott Latourette, *A History of Christian Missions in China* (New York, 1929), p. 51.
81 As quoted by P. Y. Saeki, *The Nestorian Monument in China* (London, 1916), pp. 164, 165. Cf. Charles F. Horne (director of editorial staff), *The Sacred Books and Early Literature of the East* (New York, 1917), p. 384; John Foster, *The Church of the T'ang Dynasty* (London, 1939), p. 138.
82 Jean Vuilleumier, *Le jour du repos à travers les âges* (Dammarie-les-Lys (S. and M., 1936), p. 166.
83 P. Y. Saeki, *The Nestorian Documents and Relics in China* (Tokyo, 1951), pp. 45, 46, 49, 50; cf. pp. 68, 101, and also Saeki, *Nestorian Monument,* p. 202, n. 33.
84 Saeki, *Nestorian Documents,* pp. 114-116, 134-136; cf. also pp. 125-133.
85 *Ibid.,* pp. 334, 335.
86 *Ibid.,* p. 346.
87 *Ibid.,* p. 316.
88 *Ibid.,* p. 317.
89 *Ibid.,* p. 330.
90 Budge, *op. cit.,* pp. 190, 191, 209, 216, 226, 232, 254, 268. Cf. pp. 267, 289, where Sabbath is mentioned in the context of nonreligious activities (local tension, and a massacre) in which Christians were involved.
91 The T'ai P'ing rebellion (1848-*c.* 1864), which featured Sabbath observance "by strict suspension of work and business and by three services" (Latourette, *China,* p. 297), does not belong to our period. Their Sabbath observance

THE SABBATH IN ASIA

was Bible based, as were several of their other practices, but their theology was syncretistic. There is no historical connection between them and the Christian churches that worked in China in earlier centuries. *Ibid.*, pp. 295-299. Cf. Franz Michael, *The Taiping Rebellion* (Seattle, 1966), 1:24-34.

[92] Mingana, *op. cit.*, pp. 8, 9, 16-18, 26, 27, 63, 64; Stewart, *op. cit.*, pp. 85-88; L. W. Brown, *The Indian Christians of St. Thomas* (Cambridge, 1956), pp. 66-68.

[93] Mingana, *op. cit.*, pp. 27-30; Stewart, *op. cit.*, pp. 88, 89; Latourette, *Expansion*, 1:231-233; Stephen Neill, *The Story of the Christian Church in India and Pakistan* (Grand Rapids, 1970), pp. 17, 18; Brown, *op. cit.*, pp. 68, 69.

[94] Mingana, *op. cit.*, pp. 53-56.

[95] Nestorian document, written in Syriac, in *ibid.*, p. 38; cf. p. 55. George Mark Moraes, *A History of Christianity in India* (Bombay, 1964), p. 175, speaks of 100,000 Christians in that area at that time.

[96] *A Diocesan Synod of the Church and Bishoprick of Angamale* (Conimbra, 1606), action 3, decree 16, quoted in Michael Geddes, *The History of the Church of Malabar* (London, 1694), p. 172.

[97] Thomas Church is another name used for the Church of India, or, in a narrower sense, the Church of Malabar. Julius Richter, *A History of Missions in India* (Edinburgh, 1908), p. 82.

[98] Neill, *op. cit.*, p. 19; Stewart, *op. cit.*, p. 123. Stewart writes: "They were particular and devout in their Sabbath attendance." But he evidently means first-day sabbath (Sunday). He also refers to an old Sanscrit fable, "The Jackal and the Deer," where the jackal uses the words: "The snares are made of sinew; how can I to-day, on the Lord's Day, touch these with my teeth?"—Page 94. The fable may have been written before the tenth century A.D. According to Stewart, the words "the Lord's Day" may "reflect Christian influence."

[99] As quoted in Mingana, *op. cit.*, p. 41.

[100] G. P. Badger, ed., *The Travels of Ludovico di Varthema . . . A.D. 1503-1508* (London, 1863), p. 180, quoted in Brown, *op. cit.*, pp. 84, 85. (Italics supplied.)

[101] Moraes, *op. cit.*, pp. 188, 189, 198; P. Placid J. Podipara, *Die Thomas-Christen* (Würzburg, 1966), p. 77; Richter, *op. cit.*, p. 78.

[102] Richter, *op. cit.*, p. 78.

[103] Podipara, *loc. cit.*; Richter, *op. cit.*, p. 78.

[104] Richter, *op. cit.*, p. 78.

[105] Moraes, *op. cit.*, p. 199.

[106] Podipara, *op. cit.*, p. 77; Moraes, *op. cit.*, p. 188.

[107] Geddes devotes 347 pages of his book just to the transcription of the acts and decrees (pp. 97-443).

[108] Geddes, *op. cit.*, p. 357 (action 8, decrees 15, 16). Curiously enough, the obligation to fast on Wednesdays was lifted (decree 15); cf. p. 351 (action 8, decree 10).

[109] *Ibid.*, pp. 357, 358 (action 8, decree 16).

[110] *Ibid.* Notice that the *night*, following Biblical usage, precedes the *day*.

[111] *Ibid.*, pp. 253-255 (act. 5, dec. 11-13), 297, 298 (act. 7, dec. 6, 8), 323 (act. 8, dec. 3), 331 (act. 8, dec. 9), 347 (act. 8, dec. 9), 352 (act. 8, dec. 10), 354 (act. 8, dec. 11), 357-359 (act. 8, dec. 16, 17), 367 (act. 8, dec. 24), 393 (act. 9, dec. 5), 413 (act. 9, dec. 25), 418, 420 (conclusion).

[112] In one of the several not-so-friendly encounters between Archbishop Aleixo de Menezes (Roman Catholic) and Archdeacon George (Thomas Christian) in the months preceding the synod of Diamper, the Archdeacon challenged the Archbishop to persuade them that "none can be saved out of the Obedience of the Roman Church." He mentioned, then, a letter of Pope Caius where he stated that "he had nothing to do with the Church of Babylon" (Nestorian), and another letter "wherein the same Truth is affirmed." This letter "is called in our Books the Letter of the Lord's-day, because it is said upon that day to have fallen down from Heaven" (Geddes, *op. cit.*, pp. 69, 70). The title of this letter would suggest that the Thomas Christians had a special regard for Sunday, and did not seem to feel any contradiction between their keeping that day and their desire to stay independent from Rome.

[113] *Dellon's Account of the Inquisition at Goa* (Hull, 1812), p. 53.

[114] *Ibid.*, p. 56; cf. also pp. 57-60, 64, 67.

[115] Christian Edwardson, *Facts of Faith* (Nashville, 1943), pp. 156-158; Lewis, *op. cit.*, pp. 225, 226.

[116] By 1673 the Thomas Christians were split into two factions: one allied with Rome, the other (after the Koonen cross gathering of 1652) faithful to the old Eastern traditions and hostile to Rome. Neill, *op. cit.*, p. 36.

[117] Dellon, *op. cit.*, pp. 53-63; cf., on the "New Christians" and the Inquisition in Portugal, Georg Schurhammer, *Francis Xavier* (Rome, 1973), 1:622-654.

[118] Assumed in Dellon, *op. cit.*, pp. 53-63. Other Jews had been living in India for centuries before the arrival of the Portuguese. See, for instance, *The Travels of Marco Polo* (New York [1931]), p. 279. The Portuguese expelled the Jews "from their original settlement in Cranganore" in 1566, but the Jews "were given shelter in Cochin by the Raja of Cochin where their small settlement now exists. That Jewish colonies were established near the Syrian Christian colonies is not in doubt."—S. G. Pothan, *The Syrian Christians of Kerala* (New York, 1963), p. 33.

[119] Dellon, *op. cit.*, p. 61.

[120] The only reference that we have found to real *Christian* Sabbathkeepers in India before the arrival of Sabbathkeeping missionaries in the nineteenth century comes from c. 1806. Anglican Claudius Buchanan, *Christian Researches in Asia* (Philadelphia, 1813), p. 143, writes: "The Armenians in Hindostan . . . maintain the solemn observance of Christian worship, throughout our Empire on the seventh day; and they have as many spires pointing to heaven among the Hindoos as we ourselves."

[121] Latourette, *Expansion*, 1:105.

[122] H. Gelzer, "Armenia," *Schaff-Herzog*, 1:292.

[123] *Ibid.*, pp. 292, 293.

[124] Canon 56 *(NPNF/2* 14:391). Cf. note 16.

[125] E. F. K. Fortescue, *The Armenian Church* (New York, 1872, 1970), p. 24. These decisions were not followed "for a time" by the Armenians of "Lesser Armenia," more influenced by the Greeks *(ibid.)*.

[126] Frederick Cornwallis Conybeare, "Armenian Church," *The Encyclopaedia Britannica*, 11th ed. (New York, 1970), 2:571.

[127] *Ibid.*

[128] The United Armenians number about 100,000. Gelzer, *op. cit.*, p. 294; Endre von Ivánka, Julius Tyciak, Paul Wiertz, *Handbuch der Ostkirchenkunde* (Düsseldorf, 1971), p. 758. The Gregorian Armenians number about 1.6 million. Maloney, *op. cit.*, pp. 16, 17.

[129] Manuscripts 58, 100, 256, 297, and 1118 of the Librairie des P. P. Mechitharistes (Vienna). These have been examined and partially translated by Abraham Terian of Andrews University. See James J. C. Cox, "Studies in the Determination and Evaluation of the Dominical Logoi as Cited in the Original Text of the Greek Didascalia Apostolorum" (Ph.D. dissertation, Harvard University, 1973), 1:7, n. 7. Terian has seen other similar manuscripts in the Armenian Convent of St. James, in Jerusalem, and thinks that there are more copies in the Maštoc' Library (Maštoc' Matenadaran) in Erevan, Soviet Armenia.

[130] As noted above, under "India" (cf. note 120), Buchanan states that the Armenians in India kept the seventh day. He also mentions that the Armenians "are to be found in every principal city of Asia," including "all the principal places of India, where they arrived many centuries before the English," Central Asia and, in general, "from Canton to Constantinople" (Buchanan, *op. cit.*, pp. 141, 142). It is assumed that wherever they went, they kept the Sabbath. Fortescue, *op. cit.*, p. 53, writes: "It must not be forgotten that throughout the East Saturday is looked on as a second Sunday. The Armenians keep Saturday as a day in honour of Almighty God, the Creator of all things, and Sunday in commemoration of the New Creation brought about by the Resurrection of our Blessed Lord JESUS CHRIST." What kind of Sabbath observance is meant here? John Mason Neale (1818-1868) in his *A History of the Holy Eastern Church* (London, 1850), 2:795, quotes Ricaut, who, complaining of the difficulty in understanding the system of Armenian fasts, says of the Armenian priests that their "learning principally consists in knowing the appointed times of fasting and feasting; the which they never omit on Sundays to publish unto the people." It can be inferred that the day when the people were available in church for such announcements was Sunday. Neale comments: "There is, in truth, no great difficulty in the Armenian fasts; at the same time, there are great difficulties in the Calendar, arising from the Saturday commemorations fixed as such, and the translation of festivals from a fast to a following Saturday."—*Ibid.* On 2:731, after stating that the "observation of the Saturday is, as every one knows, a subject of bitter dispute between the Greeks and Latins; the former observing it as a festival, the latter as a day of abstinence," Neale adds: "Among both Greeks and Armenians Saturday is viewed in the light of a second Sunday; the Liturgy is then celebrated even when on other days of the week it is not; communions are more frequent; and in the daily offices, as we shall see, the troparia, etc., are varied, as for a day of peculiar solemnity." Neale's equating Sabbath observance by the Armenians with Sabbath observance by the Greeks (cf. Fortescue, *op. cit.*, p. 53), helps us to understand that the Sabbath received some special consideration, particularly marked by increased liturgical activity. But, as the quotation from Ricaut suggests, Sunday was the great day when the whole congregation came to church. Even today special mass is said on Sabbath in some Armenian churches (cf. the Cathedral of St. James, in Jerusalem, as reported by A. Terian). But today Sunday appears to be the only weekly day of rest and worship for the people. However, as some of the above quotations seem to imply, Sabbath observance (with Sunday) was still a meaningful experience among the Armenians of the nineteenth century.

CHAPTER 9

The Sabbath in Egypt and Ethiopia

Werner K. Vyhmeister

ONE of the most fascinating examples of persisting observance of the seventh day of the week as the Sabbath, up to the twentieth century, is found in Ethiopia. Although closely linked to Egypt in ecclesiastical affairs from the fourth century on, Ethiopia had a mind of its own when it came to Sabbath observance. This chapter presents first the available evidences for Sabbath-Sunday observance in Egypt, beginning with the fourth century. Then, the major portion of the chapter is devoted to Ethiopia.

Egypt

The evolution of Sabbath-Sunday observance in Egypt is quite similar to that which has already been noticed in the preceding chapter for other Near Eastern countries, with the exception of Armenia. In A.D. 306, Archbishop Peter of Alexandria (died 311), wrote in canon 15 of his *Canones Poenitentiales:*[1] "Wednesday is to be fasted, because then the Jews conspired to betray Jesus; Friday, because, he then suffered for us. We keep the Lord's Day as a day of joy, because then our Lord rose. Our tradition is, not to kneel on that day."[2] But nothing is said about the Sabbath, even though the Eastern tradition of fasting only on Wednesdays and Fridays is clearly present. Moreover, since later Christian writers refer to Sabbath observance in Egypt, the mention of Sunday alone in this short canon may be taken as an indication that Sunday was considered at that time as the most important day of weekly worship, but not necessarily as the only day.

In (Pseudo) Athanasius' *Homilia de Semente* (fourth century)[3] we read:
"On the Sabbath day we gathered together, not being infected with Judaism, for we do not lay hold of false Sabbaths, but we come on the Sabbath to worship Jesus, the Lord of the Sabbath. For of old there was among the ancients the honorable Sabbath, but the Lord changed the day of the Sabbath to the Lord's day, and not we alone despise the Sabbath, but the prophet is the one who cast it aside and said, 'Your new moons and Sabbaths my soul hates.'"[4]

The Sabbath, this source indicates, was being kept, but not as the Jews kept it. The homily goes on to discuss the occasion when Christ's disciples began plucking heads of grain and eating them—this as a clear example of the Jews' perverting the meaning of Sabbathkeeping by forbidding to be done on the Sabbath what even God had not forbidden.[5]

Another pseudo-Athanasian work discusses other aspects of the Sabbath-Sunday question: "Therefore, after the first creation, God rested. For that reason that generation [the Jews] has observed the Sabbath on the seventh day. But the second creation has no end. For that reason he [God] has not rested, but he *still works*. So, we do not observe a Sabbath day as in the times of the first (creation); but our hope is in the coming Sabbath of sabbaths, when the new creation will have no end, but it will be revealed and will celebrate a perpetual feast. The Sabbath was given to the first people for the following reason: that they would know equally well the end of (the old) creation and the beginning (of the new). . . .

"It is not because of the physical rest that (God) gave the Sabbath, but so that they [the Jews] would recognize the end of the (first) creation. . . . He wanted, precisely, that in knowing its end, they would search for the beginning of the following (creation). Then, the end of the first creation was the Sabbath; the beginning of the new one is the Lord's day, when he has renewed and begun anew the old one."[6]

Even circumcision, performed on the eighth day, anticipated "the spiritual rebirth of all after the seventh day":[7] "As the Lord's day is the beginning of creation and the end of the Sabbath, so, having regenerated man, it has put an end to circumcision. These two things are, in fact, accomplished on the eighth day: the beginning of creation and of regeneration of man. For this reason the eighth day has abolished the Sabbath, and not the Sabbath the eighth day."[8]

(Pseudo) Athanasius clearly states that Christ changed "the day of the Sabbath to the Lord's day," and that the Sabbath was abolished by Sunday. But at the same time, he reports that in the fourth century, Christians in Egypt still came "on the Sabbath to worship Jesus, the Lord of the Sabbath."

Timotheus I, archbishop of Alexandria (*c.* 381), says that since communion was administered on Sabbaths and Sundays Christians should abstain from marital relations on these two days in order to be in condition to partake of "the spiritual sacrifice."[9]

Palladius (*c.* 363-425), in his *Historia Lausiaca* (419/420), referring to the Egyptian monks who followed the rule of Pachomius (292-346), says that they partook of communion on Sabbath and on Sunday.[10] In the same work he mentions Taor, a virgin who had already spent thirty years in a monastery. Every Sunday, while the other virgins went to church for the communion service, Taor stayed, clothed in rags, working.[11]

John Cassian *(c.* 360-c. 433) in his *Institutes of the Coenobia* (425-430) also refers to customs of the Egyptian monks when he states: "Wherefore, except Vespers and Nocturns, there are no public services among them in the day except on Saturday and Sunday, when they meet together at the third hour for the purpose of Holy Communion."[12] The third hour corresponds to 9:00 A.M.

Cassian mentions also an old monk who lived alone in his cell and never partook of food by himself alone. Even if "for five days running none of the brethren came to his cell he constantly put off taking food until on Saturday or Sunday he went to church for service and found some stranger whom he brought" to his cell to eat with him.[13]

THE SABBATH IN EGYPT AND ETHIOPIA

Cassian adds that "throughout the whole of Egypt and the Thebaid"[14] in the evening and nocturnal worship services, there is the option of reading two lessons, one from the Old and one from the New Testament. "But on Saturday and Sunday they read them both from the New Testament."[15]

In Cassian's *Conferences* (written between 426 and 428) he argues against the practice of some monks who considered the sacraments so holy that they did not dare to partake of them more than once a year. "It is much better to receive them every Sunday for the healing of our infirmities."[16] The omission of Sabbath could be an indication of the greater importance attributed to Sunday, even when Sabbath was still kept to a certain extent.[17]

After Cassian, church historian Socrates Scholasticus (c. 440) refers to Sabbath and Sunday observance in Egypt in the following terms:

"Although almost all churches throughout the world celebrate the sacred mysteries on the sabbath of every week, yet the Christians of Alexandria and at Rome, on account of some ancient tradition, have ceased to do this. The Egyptians in the neighborhood of Alexandria, and the inhabitants of Thebaïs, hold their religious assemblies on the sabbath, but do not participate of the mysteries in the manner usual among Christians in general: for after having eaten and satisfied themselves with food of all kinds, in the evening making their offerings they partake of the mysteries."[18]

Sozomen (c. 400-c. 447), in the parallel passage of his *Ecclesiastical History*, writes:

"The people of Constantinople, and almost everywhere, assemble together on the Sabbath, as well as on the first day of the week, which custom is never observed at Rome or at Alexandria. There are several cities and villages in Egypt where, contrary to the usage established elsewhere, the people meet together on Sabbath evenings, and, although they have dined previously, partake of the mysteries."[19]

Some years earlier, Cassian had written that communion was celebrated in Egypt at the third hour (9:00 A.M.) on Sabbath and Sunday. Socrates Scholasticus and Sozomen mention now a Sabbath-evening celebration of the Eucharist, after a meal. They consider this practice "contrary to the usage established elsewhere" by Christians. Could it be that since the time of Cassian's sojourns in Egypt about A.D. 400 the Sabbath celebration had, in a matter of three to four decades, been reduced to this evening communion service in the country, and completely eliminated in Alexandria?

Striking in the accounts of Socrates Scholasticus and Sozomen is their mention of Rome and Alexandria as the places where Christians did not assemble on the Sabbath day. The reasons are not clearly given. Reference to an "ancient tradition" is made by Socrates. It is well known that Rome had begun keeping Sunday in the second century. One of the strong factors that prompted Rome's decision was the Christians' desire to disassociate themselves from Judaism. Indeed, the church in Rome went so far as to convert the Sabbath into a day of fasting.*

Alexandrian Christianity, too, had early adopted Sunday observance. However, in harmony with Eastern Christianity, it had also kept the Sabbath as a

---

* See chapter 7, p. 137.

day of worship and a festival. Did the strong Jewish population of Alexandria have any part in the decision made by the church in that great city to eventually abandon Sabbath observance completely?

It is a well-known fact that at least since the *Epistle of Barnabas* (early second century) there was tension between Christianity and Judaism in Alexandria. Socrates Scholasticus, discussing Alexandrian history, says that the Jews "are always hostile toward the Christians."[20] He also mentions that Alexandrian Jews, "being disengaged from business on the Sabbath, and spending their time, not hearing the Law, but in theatrical amusements,"[21] increased the existing tension during the time of Cyril, archbishop of Alexandria (412-444). The Jews burned a church and killed many Christians. Cyril reacted with his characteristic bellicosity and expelled the Jews from Alexandria in spite of the opposition of the prefect Orestes. "Thus the Jews who had inhabited the city from the time of Alexander the Macedonian were expelled from it, stripped of all they possessed."[22]

It seems to be more than coincidental that Sabbath services disappeared from the Alexandrian churches apparently during the time of Archbishop Cyril.[23] It is interesting to notice that, according to Socrates Scholasticus and Sozomen, "in the neighborhood" of the city and elsewhere in Egypt, Sabbath services continued. However, as noted above, these services were confined to Sabbath evening. Was the rest of Christian Egypt trying to reach a compromise between its respect for the Sabbath and Alexandria's strong reaction against it?

Among several homilies written in the late fifth or early sixth century and attributed to Eusebius of Alexandria,[24] is one (Homily 16) entitled "On the Lord's Day."[25] This homily purports to be an answer to the following questions asked by an individual named Alexander to Eusebius at the close of a Sunday service: "Why do we need to keep the Lord's day without working in it? What is our reward if we do not work?" The long answer includes the following ideas and comments: 1. The "holy day of the Lord" is a memorial of the Lord. It is called the Lord's day because it is the lord of all days. It is the beginning of creation, of resurrection, and of the week; and these three "beginnings" allude to the beginning of the most holy Trinity.[26] 2. God has given us six days to work and one to pray, to rest, and to make our evil actions disappear. So, one should go early to the church on the Lord's day, and should not depart before the end of the service.[27] 3. There is no reason to observe the Lord's day unless, besides ceasing from work, we go to church. 4. "Woe to all who, in the Lord's day, play the zither, dance, litigate, work, take oath or make others take oath, because they will be condemned to the eternal fire, *and their lot will be with the hypocrites.*"[28] 5. It is not right even to try to help the poor people with their work on Sundays. Slaves, hired men, oxen, all need the Sunday rest.[29]

A Coptic fragment, probably of the sixth century,[30] is very similar to Eusebius' instructions on how Sunday should be kept: "I instruct you to not do anything on the holy Sunday, and to not get involved in disputations, or in lawsuits, or in acts of violence, but to give your attention to the holy Scriptures, and to give bread to the needy.... Cursed be the one who does anything on the holy Sunday, except what benefits the soul or what is necessary to take care of the animals."[31] This appears to be the first instance when a curse was pronounced for working on Sunday.[32]

Zacharias Scholasticus (*c.* 465-after 536), church historian and bishop of Mytilene, in his *Life of Severus,* patriarch of Antioch, mentions that on Sundays in

THE SABBATH IN EGYPT AND ETHIOPIA

Alexandria people congregated at the time of the celebration of the Eucharist, and he refers to Sunday as the day of Christ's resurrection.[33]

Beginning with the sixth century, there are no known references to Sabbath observance among the Egyptian Coptic Christians.[34] The change from Sabbath *and* Sunday observance to *only* Sundaykeeping led to some tensions between the Ethiopian Church and Alexandria, as will be shown later in this chapter. Furthermore, if Alexander Ross (1590-1654) is to be trusted, by the seventeenth century the Egyptian Copts kept "no Lords day, nor Feasts except in Cities." [35]

It should also be mentioned, however, that some aspects of the earlier dual observance of Sabbath and Sunday were remembered for centuries in Egypt by the copyists and readers of the so-called *Egyptian Church Order* and other similar works. The *Egyptian Church Order* is identified as a version of the *Apostolic Tradition* of Hippolytus. The Greek text of the *Apostolic Tradition* was translated to Sahidic (a Coptic dialect) probably not before the latter part of the fifth century.[36] It was later translated into Arabic.[37] The following statute is found in the Sahidic version: "Let the servants (of the Lord) work five days; on the Sabbath *(Sabbaton)* and the Lord's day *(Kyriakē)* let them rest for the church that they may be instructed in piety. The Sabbath because God Himself rested on it when He completed all the creation. The Lord's day because it is the day of the resurrection of the Lord." [38]

Among *The 127 Apostolic Canons,* found in several Arabic manuscripts,[39] there is one canon that strictly forbids fasting on Sabbath and Sunday, except for Easter Sabbath.[40] There is another canon stating that even sick persons should be encouraged to participate in the Easter Sabbath fast.[41]

Thus, the Sabbath was not entirely forgotten. However, there is no evidence available to show that the statute on Sabbath and Sunday rest for servants (slaves) was obeyed in medieval Egypt.[42] Sunday appears to have been the only day of weekly rest in Christian Egypt after the year 500.

Ethiopia

Pre-Christian Ethiopia.—Christianity reached the kingdom of Aksum, the forerunner of present-day Ethiopia, in the first half of the fourth century. Previous to this the country had for centuries received merchants and seafarers from southwest Arabia who had established commercial and military posts and, later on, mingled with the existing Cushitic population. As they settled farther inland, these immigrants "no doubt reproduced in the highlands of Africa the type of social, political, and cultural organization which they had left behind in Arabia." [43]

Was the seventh-day Sabbath known in the Aksumite kingdom before the arrival of Christianity? Edward Ullendorff, who has carefully researched what he calls "Hebraic-Jewish Elements in Abyssinian (Monophysite) Christianity," strongly contends that before Christianity arrived in Aksum, many Aksumites had already been influenced by Jewish beliefs and practices. When Christianity was accepted, most of these Jewish elements were kept and have persisted even until today. How could we otherwise, he queries, explain the presence of Sabbath observance, circumcision on the eighth day, food laws, an "ark of the covenant," and other "Jewish" elements?[44]

Ullendorff further notes: "In the Semitic culture which the immigrants from South Arabia had transplanted across the Red Sea into the Aksumite kingdom the

Jewish ingredient must have been fairly prominent. That was due not only to the undoubted presence of some Jews and Jewish proselytes among the immigrant traders and settlers, but also to the notable Hebraic-Jewish admixture in South Arabian civilization at that period."[45] However, he has to admit that "for the history of the carriers of those influences we lack nearly all genuine and trustworthy source material."[46]

The strict Sabbathkeeping Falashas ("emigrants"), mistakenly considered by some as black (or Ethiopian) Jews, are, according to Ullendorff, from "all the evidence available," "descendants of those elements in the Aksumite Kingdom who resisted conversion to Christianity."[47] They were discovered in the sixteenth century, and live now to the north of Lake Tana.[48] Unfortunately, there is no way of knowing when they first came into contact with Judaism.

Maxime Rodinson takes a dim view of Ullendorff's arguments and suggests that before stating that certain Jewish practices entered the Aksumite kingdom prior to Christianity's arrival there, it is necessary to study these practices one by one and try to establish the probable dates of the historical appearance of each one of them in the Aksumite kingdom. Rodinson also points out that in modern times "the imitation of the Old Testament, even to the point of identification with Israel, is a frequent phenomenon in countries colonized by Europe."[49] This could have happened in old Ethiopia after Christianity was accepted. Moreover, it appears uncontrovertible that Judaizing Christianity was well represented in Arabia; and thus, in time, its influence could have reached Ethiopia.[50]

It seems clear that at present there is no way of proving that Sabbath observance was known and practiced in Aksum before the arrival of Christianity.[51]

The First Ten Centuries of Sabbath and Sunday Observance (Fourth to Thirteenth).—According to several Greek and Roman Church historians, Christianity entered Aksum in the first half of the fourth century. Its apostle was a Christian from Tyre named Frumentius, who, as a youth, together with Edesius, was captured by the Aksumites when their boat touched at an Aksumite port. Frumentius eventually became the king's secretary and Edesius the king's cupbearer. Their influence was used to protect Christian merchants and to spread Christianity. After several years, Frumentius and Edesius were granted permission to leave Aksum. Edesius went back to Tyre. Frumentius went to Alexandria, Egypt, and requested from Bishop Athanasius (c. 296-373) the appointment of a bishop for the Christians in Aksum. Athanasius consecrated Frumentius, who thus became the first *Abuna* ("Our Father"), a title used later by the Ethiopian metropolitan.[52] About the year 340, the conversion of King Ezana marks the official beginning of Aksum (and Ethiopia) as a Christian kingdom.[53]

No document is available with information on Sabbath observance in the early history of Christian Aksum. However, since Frumentius was a Syrian Christian, and the Aksumite Church was so closely connected with Egypt from its very beginning, we can assume that the current Egyptian and Syrian practice of keeping both Sabbath *and* Sunday was followed.[54]

Christianity's influence was strengthened in the Aksumite kingdom with the arrival, at the end of the fifth century, of groups of Syrian missionaries. The church grew rapidly, thanks to their missionary zeal. They established schools and translated at least parts of the Bible and other religious books into Ethiopic.[55]

THE SABBATH IN EGYPT AND ETHIOPIA

However, while Sabbath and Sunday were both generally observed, it is well known that already in the fourth century there was a growing anti-Sabbath sentiment in Egypt and in other areas of the Near East. As has been noted in the first part of this chapter, Alexandria and most probably all Egypt had by the year 500 abandoned any semblance of Sabbath observance.

What effect did the new Alexandrian position on Sabbathkeeping have in the Aksumite kingdom? There is no documentary evidence from this early period. It is possible that the Alexandrian position was not at first forced upon Ethiopia. But the steady line of Egyptians who were consecrated as metropolitans of Ethiopia made the Alexandrian influence felt to some extent in the following centuries. The earliest known hint of tension comes from the eleventh century. In a report on Ethiopia, Bishop Sawiros requested Patriarch Cyril II (1077-1092) of Alexandria to write to the Ethiopians "forbidding them to observe the customs of the Old Testament." [56] The Sabbath is not specifically mentioned. But in 1238, Ibn al-Assal completed his Collection of Canons for the benefit of Coptic Christians in Egypt where "the observance of the Sabbath is clearly rejected as a Jewish custom." [57] "At least from this period onwards, it is quite evident that the Egyptian bishops were determined to impose the official Alexandrian line on the Ethiopians." [58]

The Collection of Canons was translated into Ethiopic (Ge'ez), transformed and adapted to local conditions. It is known as the *Fetha Nagast* ("Legislation of the Kings"), and "has retained its value and practical importance in Ethiopia to the present day." [59] In chapter 19 the authorities for Sabbath observance are given. The first one is canon 29 of the Council of Laodicea, which clearly tells Christians to work on the Sabbath day. It is followed by canon 20 of the Council of Nicea: "And do not keep the Sabbath as the Jews." [60] But then, based on the *Didascalia*, Christians are urged to observe the Sabbath in the same way as Sunday is observed. The example of Jews and heathen is even used as a reproof.[61]

The *Fetha Nagast* quotes, further on, from the Qalementos,[62] indicating that servants should work five days and go to church on both Sunday and Sabbath to be instructed in godliness. Finally, in closing, the *Didascalia* is quoted again in a passage urging the believers to receive the Eucharist every Sabbath and Sunday (except on Easter Sabbath).[63]

The *Fetha Nagast*, as a collection or compilation, has provided some source material both in favor of and against Sabbath observance. But the real power behind the attempt to eliminate Sabbath observance in Ethiopia was the Alexandrian patriarch. King Zara Yaqob (1424-1468), describing the situation that obtained in the fourteenth century, has written: "The observance of the Sabbath was not in force in the kingdom, and the Sabbath was abolished in the realms of the patriarchs [of Alexandria]. They considered it just like the other five working days [of the week]. They also considered all those who observed the Sabbath as Jews, they excommunicated them, and did not give them permission to enter the churches." [64]

It is possible that the apparently sudden and strong drive to do away with Sabbath observance in Ethiopia was connected with a dispute between the patriarchs of Alexandria and Antioch that broke out during the first half of the thirteenth century. Before that time it had been conventional for Antioch to appoint the Jacobite bishop for Jerusalem. However, Patriarch Cyril III

(1235-1243) of Alexandria "seems to have used the growing military and political superiority of Egypt in appointing an Alexandrian bishop for the Jacobite church of Jerusalem."[65] Ignatius II, patriarch of Antioch, retaliated by appointing an Ethiopian pilgrim, Abba Thomas, as metropolitan of Ethiopia.[66]

There is no way of knowing whether Abba Thomas ever went back to Ethiopia. However, letters written by the Ethiopian kings to the Alexandrian patriarchs in the second half of the thirteenth century make clear that Ethiopia was having difficulties getting new metropolitans from Alexandria. Some clerics of Syrian origin had arrived with uncertain credentials, but were accepted by the king without full consensus of the Ethiopian Church. There were "Syrian metropolitans" still living in Ethiopia in 1290, but the opposition against them was on the increase. Finally the king decided to write (1290) to the Alexandrian patriarch and to the sultan of Egypt asking for a metropolitan. His request was not honored.[67]

At the same time, during the second half of the thirteenth century, Egyptian monks went to Ethiopia—so writes E. A. Wallis Budge—"and having profited by the reform of the Coptic Church in Alexandria, they devoted themselves . . . to the restoration of the decayed Church of Abyssinia."[68] That "restoration" most probably included the Sabbath question.[69]

To the Syrian and Egyptian influences we need to add the effect of a strong monastic revival after the middle of the thirteenth century—a revival produced perhaps in part by these influences. It is possible that out of loyalty to Alexandria, and as a reaction against the "Syrian metropolitans," the Alexandrian rejection of the Sabbath was soon accepted by this revived monasticism, and by the country at large. The fact is that the great Sabbath controversy of the fourteenth and fifteenth centuries seems to have originated with a monastic leader, Eustathius (Ewostatewos), who did not want to give up Sabbath observance.

From Eustathius to Zara Yaqob (c. 1300-1468).—Eustathius *(c.* 1273-1352) had established his own monastery in Sära'é.[70] Many students joined him, and he taught them until the arrival in Ethiopia of the new Egyptian Abuna, Ya'iqob, whom he met on his way to the king's court *(c.* 1337). Soon after this, he left the country as a result of religious controversies. A rival group of clergy made an attempt on his life immediately before his departure. In Cairo fellow Ethiopian pilgrims accused him, before the patriarch, of observing the Sabbath as well as Sunday.

Eustathius admitted that the Sabbath was central in the conflict. But he defended his position by referring to the Ten Commandments and to the *Apostolic Canons.*[71] He told the patriarch: "I came to your country . . . so that I may die for the word of God, for I have found no rest in this World. In Ethiopia they said to me, 'Break the Sabbath and the [other] rest Days like us,' and I refused. And here you say to me 'Be one with us in prayer' while you do not observe the rest Days."[72]

Eustathius and his disciples left Cairo for Jerusalem. On the way, at the monastery of Scete, he is said to have been put in fetters. These "cruel people opposed him for the Law and Commandments (of God)."[73] He went from Palestine to Cyprus, and finally to Armenia, where he died fourteen years later. After his death, several of his disciples returned to Ethiopia and joined hands with the disciples who had stayed behind. Planting monasteries mainly in the northern provinces of the kingdom, they gave birth to the "house" of Eustathius, opposed to the "house" of Takla-Haymanot, which followed the official, Alexandrian, line.[74]

Eustathius had taught against the Alexandrian position on the Sabbath. His disciples made the Sabbath their rallying point. They grew rather rapidly in numbers, to the great alarm of the anti-Sabbath party. The Abuna personally led the campaign against the followers of Eustathius. Fortunately for them, the metropolitan see was vacant from 1388-1398/9; and this became the period of their greatest advance. When Bishop Bartholomew finally arrived, he asked King Dawit (1380-1412) for help "in bringing the recalcitrant 'house' of Éwostatéwos back to strict Alexandrian discipline." [75]

King Dawit summoned Abba Filipos and other Eustathian leaders for a theological discussion on the Sabbath. As a result, Filipos and some of his colleagues were imprisoned. During his four years of detention, from 1400 to 1404, Filipos won many allies among the attendants and clergy of the royal court. Upon his release, the king commanded the disciples of Eustathius "to observe both Sabbaths" [76] (that is, both the Sabbath and Sunday). However, at the same time, the Alexandrian opposition to Sabbath observance was supposed to be maintained in the non-Eustathian churches and at the royal court.

Protected by the royal decree, the Eustathian "house" experienced widespread growth in the country, and it also began gaining ground at the royal court. For instance, an increasing number of monastic communities readopted the Sabbath, and at the royal court a pro-Sabbath clergyman assayed to give religious instructions to the princes.[77]

When Zara Yaqob (1434-1468) came to the throne, he seemed to have had clear pro-Sabbath convictions, and he found a vigorous "house" of Eustathius opposed by a politically weak anti-Sabbath party. He immediately set out to unify his country, but the Egyptian bishops, Mikael and Gabriel, were opposed to any official change. Finally the king convened the Council of Däbrä Miṭmaq (1450), concerning which the king himself wrote: "And God . . . revealed the honours of the two Sabbaths to our fathers, the reverend bishops Mika'él and Gäbri'él. He had not made this revelation to the [Egyptian] bishops of Ethiopia who came before them. . . . And our fathers Abba Mika'él and Abba Gäbri'él . . . agreed with us on the observance of the two Sabbaths, and they declared this in their own handwriting." [78]

The religious unification of the country having been achieved, numerous decrees were passed to regulate the religious conduct of the people. Christians were not to perform "on Saturday and Sunday, any kind of labor," but were to come "together in the churches for the study of the service of God and the Holy Spirit." [79] If some Christians lived too far from a church, a priest had to be sent to them on Friday, and spend the weekend there, giving religious instruction.[80]

To Zara Yaqob's time corresponds the final redaction of the *Maṣhafa Berhān* ("Book of Light"), whose major concern is Sabbath observance. The authorship of this book has been generally attributed to King Zara Yaqob himself. However, more recently, Ephraim Isaac has come to the conclusion that the book "is a composite work based on a pre-fifteenth-century original homiletical discourse composed in honor of the Sabbath." [81]

The *Maṣhafa Berhān (MB)* strongly enjoins both Sabbath and Sunday observance. In order to avoid confusion, Saturday is often called "the first Sabbath." The first book of the *MB* consists of six readings for "the first Sabbath."

The second reading includes a rather lengthy list of works that should not be done "on Sabbath and on Sunday": "agricultural work (farming), plowing, cutting of grain or grass, cutting of wood, grinding, fermenting of beer, fermenting of grapes or mead, reaping or threshing ripe grain, cutting vegetables (near or far) and cutting of trees, watering of farmland and garden [trees] and vegetables, washing of clothes, hunting wild animals, catching birds, fishing, covering [roofs of] houses, being on a road, collecting sheaves [of grain] so as to make one heap, carrying grain into the houses from the field, building a fence, writing a book, tanning the vellum, smithing iron, clay-work, making muddays for food, weaving of cloth, sewing of cloth, weaving cotton or wool (spinning), weaving of baskets and the like, making palm leaf [hats] and the like, punishing of men-servants and maid-servants, binding of all men, let them not do any worldly work and all that is like it; and coming near to a woman. . . . And drawing water is desecrating the Sabbath." [82]

The list of prohibited works is followed immediately by "that which can be done on the first Sabbath and Sunday: slaughtering of animals, cooking of food and the like, preparing of waṭ [Ethiopian sauce of special spicy and hot flavor] and the like. Whoever wants can eat meat which is slaughtered on the first Sabbath and on Sunday either roasted or boiled." [83] The reason given to justify these seemingly liberal rules is that if the people were not allowed to do this, Sabbath and Sunday would be days of sadness, and not of joy as they are supposed to be.

Although the *MB* enjoins the observance of both Sabbath and Sunday, it is obvious that it was written with the purpose of defending Sabbath observance over against the ones who said that the Sabbath had been abolished. Matthew 5:18, 19, is quoted several times to remind the readers of the unchangeable character of God's law. The *Iota* that is mentioned there represents, in fact it is, the Ten Commandments. These cannot change. On the other hand, the "beginning of the name of Jesus is 'Iota,' by number, ten." [84] The Ten Commandments and Jesus are thus very closely connected. The author continues: "Regarding him who abolished the honor of the first Sabbath, behold he uprooted the foundation of the church. He cast her out because he has abolished one major word from the Decalogue upon which the church is founded. . . .

"Whosoever strikes out one word from the Decalogue, behold he has stricken out the name of Jesus. . . .

"And if one strikes out of the name of Jesus, behold he has stricken out the name of the Trinity. And if one struck out one from the Trinity, he has indeed cancelled out his Christianity." [85]

In order to make absolutely sure that there is no misunderstanding, the text of the Decalogue is repeated in full both in reading two and in reading six.[86] The following paragraph summarizes quite well the main thrust of book one of the *MB*:

"The keeping of the first Sabbath is [equal to] the keeping of Sunday. If [therefore] the first Sabbath is not kept, [it is indeed as if] Sunday is not kept; for the honor of the first Sabbath is written in the *Orit* [the Law], the prophets, and the gospel, and the *Sinodos* of the apostles. He who honors it [also] honors God who wrote with his own hand and commanded that one should honor it. And God honors him who honors it." [87]

Scattered through several of the other five books of the *MB* there are more references to the law and the Sabbath. In book two "we find a special effort that was made to criticize those who breach the Sabbath. In an elaborate section the gospel stories are called upon to show that Jesus did not desecrate the first Sabbath. . . ."[88]

Zara Yaqob was helped, in his efforts in favor of Sabbath and Sunday observance, by some pseudo-apostolic writings and other works that had been translated into Geᶜez, apparently during the fourteenth century, as part of the literary revival that accompanied monastic renewal. Some of them, such as the *Didascalia,* were known earlier in Arabic translation.

In the Ethiopic *Didascalia* Sabbath and Sunday observance is strongly enjoined, as the following fragments clearly show: Chapter 29: "We ought not to fast on the Sabbath, except the one day (the Sabbath) of the Passion. . . . But the other Sabbaths let us honour because our Lord rested from His work on the Sabbath." Chapter 30: ". . . and honour the Sabbath being gathered together in the Church with joy and gladness." Chapter 38: "O Lord Almighty, who didst . . . appoint the Sabbath, and rest thereon from all Thy work, and hast commanded us to rest (on it) from all the work of our hands." ". . . and didst command them to rest on the Sabbath day, that they might give Thee humble thanks, and be safe from all evil. . . . Wherefore He hath commanded us to rest on every Sabbath day, because on the Sabbath day our Lord rested from all His work. . . . And greater than all these is (the day of) His holy resurrection which our Lord and Saviour and Creator, God the Word, hath taught us (to observe)."[89]

Another work that appears to have influenced Zara Yaqob's prescriptions on practices connected with Sabbath observance is the so-called *Egyptian Church Order.* This work is based on Hippolytus' *Apostolic Tradition,* found, with many adaptations, as part of Book 8 of the *Apostolic Constitutions (c.* A.D. 375). One of its canons, in the Ethiopic version, prescribes: "[*And on the sabbath and*] on the first day of the week the bishop, if it be possible, shall with his own hand deliver to all the people, while the deacons break the bread." A few lines further it becomes very clear that Sabbath and Sunday were considered to be different from the "other days."[90]

Zara Yaqob also used the Kidan, an Ethiopic version of *The Testament of our Lord,* as an authority prescribing Sabbath *and* Sunday observance.[91]

The *Sinodos* is another important work that was translated during the fourteenth century. Together with the *Didascalia* it orders the religious life of the Ethiopians even today.[92] King Zara Yaqob sent a copy of it to the Ethiopian community in Jerusalem (1442) with the message: "I hereby send you this book of *Sīnodos* so that you may get consolation from it on the days of the First Sabbath and on Sundays."[93]

The *Apostolic Canons* are an integral part of the *Sinodos.*[94] Canon 66 reads: "And we have ordered in our writings [that] you, your slaves, and your servants should work five days, and [that] on the Sabbath and on Sunday you should rest."[95] There is also in the *Canons* a homily that repeats the idea that on Sabbath and Sunday both master and slave should have the opportunity to go to church and be instructed in the Christian religion. Among the Biblical texts used are Genesis 2:2, Exodus 31:13, and Isaiah 56:4-7. Interestingly enough, the Old Testament prophets are credited with having ordered that the "Sabbaths" (i.e., Sabbath *and* Sunday) should be kept.[96]

There are other texts from this period, or earlier, that deal directly with Sabbath and/or Sunday observance. Among these are the Ethiopic *Athanasius Anaphora* (a glorification of the "holy Sabbath of the Christians," i.e., Sunday), prayers for the Sabbath day, and a homily about the Sabbath.[97]

Zara Yaqob's chronicler gives us what is probably the best summary of the king's efforts to restore Sabbath observance when he writes: "The Ethiopian people had . . . neglected the precepts of their faith and the manner of the keeping of the Sabbath and feast days. I have myself witnessed, in my youth, that the Sabbath was profaned and that everyone worked on that day.

"It was only beginning from the ninth hour *(i.e., 3:00 P.M.)*, when the trumpet was sounded, that all activity ceased and that the people, starting their rest, would say, 'It is now that the Sabbath begins.' Other feast days were no better observed. The King re-established them and prescribed that the Sabbath should be as holy as Sunday, without any distinction, according to the prescriptions of the holy apostles. . . . All these beliefs and practices, as well as others of a similar nature, were expounded by our King who ordered them to be taught to all men and women by calling them all together in every locality every Sabbath and feast day."[98]

First Contacts With Rome and Portugal *(c. 1482-c. 1600)*.—Francisco Alvarez (died *c.* 1540), in his *Narrative of the Portuguese Embassy to Abyssinia*, testifies of the observance of both the Sabbath and Sunday. In a passage that seems to refer to the Sabbath controversy around the year 1400 he refers to a king "who commanded that Saturday should not be observed"; this monarch was opposed by Abba Philip with his friars, who "undertook to show how God had commanded that Saturday should be kept . . . and he made it good before the King. Therefore they say that he was a Saint for making Saturday to be kept."[99]

Later in the century, probably in 1482, under King Iskindir (1478-1494), Franciscan monk Ioane de Calabria arrived in Ethiopia with a lay companion, Giovanni da Imola. Many Europeans were in the country at that time.[100] After years of waiting, Ioane de Calabria was apparently allowed to see the young king. When Francisco Alvarez himself visited Ethiopia (1520-1526?), Egyptian Bishop Marqos told him that King Iskindir had tried, about that time, to change the traditional practices of the Ethiopians, especially concerning the Sabbath and food laws.[101]

Alvarez was one of the members of the exploratory mission sent by the king of Portugal in answer to a request for help sent by Queen Helena of Ethiopia in 1507. Ethiopia felt threatened at that time by the Moslems of the Red Sea littoral.[102] The mission arrived in 1520. Alvarez apparently succeeded in winning the confidence of King Lebna Dengel (1508-1540) and of the Abuna, to the point of discussing the possibility of doing away with Sabbath observance and food laws.[103]

After about six years of stay in Ethiopia the mission left for Portugal, taking along an Ethiopian envoy, Saga za-Ab (Zaga Zabo), and leaving behind physician Joao Bermudez.[104]

At some time between 1527 and 1534,[105] Saga za-Ab is reported to have explained in Lisbon the following about Sabbath observance in Ethiopia (in the context of a report on other beliefs and practices, as well): "We are bound by the Institutions of the Apostles to observe two days, to wit; the Sabbath and the Lord's-day, on which it is not lawful for us to do any work, no, not the least. On the

THE SABBATH IN EGYPT AND ETHIOPIA

Sabbath-day, because God, after he had finished the creation of the world, rested thereon; which day, as God would have it called the *Holy of Holies,* so the not celebrating thereof with *great honor and devotion* seems to be plainly contrary to God's will and precept, who will suffer heaven and earth to pass away sooner than his word; and that especially, since Christ came not to dissolve the law, but to fulfill it. It is *not, therefore, in imitation of the Jews,* but in *obedience to Christ and his holy apostles,* that we observe that day, the favor that was showed herein to the Jews, being transferred to us, Christians. . . . We do observe the Lord's-day after the manner of all other Christians in memory of Christ's resurrection." [106]

Meanwhile, in the East, the Moslem military leader Ahman ibn Ibrahim (nicknamed Grañ, the "left-handed"), of the sultanate of Adal, had started his raids and incursions that brought ruin, devastation, and misery upon Christian Ethiopia. As early as 1529 he inflicted a major defeat on Lebna Dengel. In desperation the king sent Joao Bermudez to Europe in 1535 to summon help. Trying to enlist the sympathy and support of Portugal and of other Christian powers, the king made it be known that he was willing "to bring the monophysite Church, without changing its character or doctrine, under the supreme jurisdiction of the Church of Rome." [107]

Bermudez' embassy eventually resulted in the arrival at the Red Sea port of Massawa (1541) of 400 Portuguese soldiers with firearms, sent by Portugal from Goa (India) under the leadership of Cristovao da Gama, younger brother of Vasco. Meanwhile young Claudius (Galawdewos, 1540-1559) had succeeded his father on the Ethiopian throne. With the decisive help of the Portuguese firearms he succeeded in defeating, and in finally killing, Grañ (1543). For all practical purposes the Moslem menace had ended. Now the country needed to be rebuilt.

Confrontation with the Roman Catholic Church began soon after the above-mentioned decisive military victory. Bermudez was back in Ethiopia and insisted that the Roman rite be enforced throughout the country. Claudius refused, and, according to the royal chronicler, finally (*c.* 1545) had Bermudez "exiled to the country of Gafā. . . . Claudius disliked the religion of the Franks." [108]

Wishing to convert Ethiopia to the Roman faith, Pope Julius III appointed a Patriarch of Ethiopia (1554). In order to prepare the way for him, Gonçales Rodriguez and two other Jesuits went to Ethiopia first (1555). The king treated them kindly, but firmly rejected their pressure to abandon the faith of his ancestors. In 1557 Jesuit Bishop André de Oviedo arrived in Ethiopia.[109] The royal chronicler comments: "The object of this voyage . . . was to criticize the true faith which was brought to Ethiopia from Alexandria and openly to proclaim the false belief which issued from Rome." [110]

Claudius explained to Oviedo that he already had a monophysite Abuna. He argued with him and his companions, "defeated them in argument and confounded their falsehoods." [111] Out of these disputes came what is known as Claudius' "Confession of Faith." The Jesuits, as others before them, had accused the Ethiopian Church of observing several Jewish customs and laws. Claudius refutes these charges in the context of a fairly comprehensive confession of faith. In regard to Sabbath and Sunday observance he writes:

"But as far as our celebration of the Sabbath day is concerned, we do not celebrate it as the Jews do, who have crucified Christ, saying: Let His blood (fall) over us and over our children. For these Jews neither draw water nor kindle a fire nor cook any food, nor bake bread, neither [do] they go from house to house.

"But we celebrate it in bringing the offering [i.e., the Sacrament] on it and in keeping the agape, as our fathers, the apostles, have commanded us in the *Didascalia*. We do not celebrate it in the way that Sunday is celebrated, which is the new day, about which David said: On this day which the Lord has made, let us be glad and full of joy."[112]

Claudius follows very closely Zara Yaqob's position of a century earlier. Sunday seems to be preferred, but he is far from ready to give up the Sabbath. The contrast between the Jewish and the Christian (Ethiopian) ways of observing the Sabbath is sharply drawn.

Soon afterward, in 1559, Claudius was killed in battle. His brother Minas (1559-1563) succeeded him. After the victory over Grañ, 100 or 150 surviving Portuguese soldiers had settled in Ethiopia and had become an integral part of the population.[113] In the words of A. Jones and E. Monroe, "Claudius had allowed the Abyssinian wives and slaves of the Portuguese to adopt the Roman faith, and had permitted the Abyssinians to attend the Roman churches. Minas forbade this, and when Bishop Oviedo defied him, he was barely restrained from killing the Jesuit with his own hands."[114]

About this time the *Mashafa Tomar* ("Book of the Letter") appeared, translated from the Arabic. According to tradition, the original "came down from heaven in the Church of Saints Peter and Paul in Rome in December, A. Gr. 1050, in the presence of all the principal priests and a very large congregation."[115] "The letter deals with Christian doctrines in the broadest sense, but directs particular attention to the importance of Sabbath observance."[116]

Minas was succeeded by his son Sartsa Dengel (1563-1597), who reversed his father's policy, protected Oviedo, tolerated the Roman priests, and was even accused by the native clergy of having asked the pope to send missionaries to Ethiopia. His chronicler records the baptism *en masse* of a newly conquered heathen people, performed on a Sabbath and the immediate Sunday, in the twenty-fifth year of his reign.[117]

The Ephemeral Triumph of the Anti-Sabbath Party (1604-1632).—Some years later, in 1603, Spanish Jesuit Pero F. Paez arrived in Ethiopia. A man of extraordinary ability, he mastered Geʿez in one year. His "common sense, shrewdness and discretion"[118] appealed to all classes. He established a school in the monastery of Fremonat (near Aksum), to which both Ethiopian and Portuguese children were admitted, and were taught the Roman faith. The fame of Paez as a teacher soon reached the royal court. In April, 1604, he was received by the new king, Za Dengel (1603-1604). The king "both favourably and patiently" listened to "several Disputes . . . about Controversies in Religion. . . . Mass was also said after the *Roman* manner, and a Sermon Preach'd; with which *Zadenghel* was so taken, that . . . he resolv'd to submit himself to the Pope."[119]

Za Dengel's decision to join the Roman Catholic Church became clear to his subjects when he set forth an edict *"That no Person should any longer observe the Sabbath as a Holy day."*[120] Letters followed from him to both Pope Clement VIII and King Philip III of Spain and Portugal, asking for artisans, soldiers, and more Jesuit fathers to instruct his subjects.[121]

The reaction in Ethiopia was fast and violent. Peter, the Abuna, released the people from their oath of allegiance to the king, and excommunicated Za Dengel.

Only once before had a king been excommunicated (for incest). A successful military revolt ended with the defeat and death of the king, only months later, in October of 1604, in spite of his being supported by about 200 Portuguese soldiers with firearms.[122]

To Za Dengel's reign belongs the *Sawana Nafs* ("Refuge of the Soul"), a letter written to the king by Newaya Masqal from the latter's place of exile in Egypt. It is an attempt to convince the king to hold firm to the Alexandrian faith. In chapter 2 the author tells the king that in yielding to the Jesuits and rejecting the Sabbath he has ignored both the law of the Creator and the canons of the apostles. Then, turning against the "innovators" who argue that the Jews crucified Jesus because He broke the Sabbath, he quotes John 5:18, and concludes that if the charge of His breaking the Sabbath is enough to justify abolishing Sabbath observance now, then the belief in God as Jesus' Father should also be abandoned. Newaya Masqal's logic could be charged with *ignoratio elenchi*, but he is one more clear example of the deep concern for Sabbath observance shown so many times by Ethiopians.[123]

After some three years of a war of succession, the throne was finally made secure in the hands of Susenyos (1607-1632). The king "was an educated man and . . . was favourably impressed by the intelligence and learning of the Jesuit priests."[124] He eased the restrictions against the Roman faith and permitted proselytizing. Letters were sent to the pope and to the king of Spain requesting assistance.[125]

By 1612 Susenyos had privately decided to become a Roman Catholic. There were several public disputes on the two natures of Christ, a key point of disagreement between the Alexandrian (monophysite) and the Roman faith. The Jesuits won every time. Encouraged by these results, the king published an edict giving liberty to all his subjects to embrace Roman Catholicism.[126]

Ethiopian Metropolitan Simeon, several of the nobility, and many of the clergy decided to rebel. The rebels were defeated by Susenyos (1617), who in the year 1620 published another edict forbidding Sabbath observance as Jewish and repugnant to Christianity. An anonymous reply to this edict so incensed the king that, according to Ludolf, he "renew'd the Edict about the Sabbath, and commanded the Husbandmen to Plough and Sow upon that Day, adding as a Penalty upon the Offenders, for the first Fault the Forfeiture of a weav'd Vestment to the value of a *Portugal* Patack; for the second, Confiscation of Goods, and that the said Offence should not be prescribed to Seven years; a certain form usually inserted in their more severe Decrees."[127] Ludolf could not hide his admiration for the piety of the Ethiopians "since they were thus to be compell'd to the Neglect of the Sabbath by such Severe Laws, when we can hardly be induc'd by stricter Penalties to observe the Lord's-Day."[128]

To make sure that the decree would be obeyed, a general, accused of having refused to work on the Sabbath, was "beaten with rods, and publicly degraded,"[129] and in trying to explain his position to the chief nobles and commanders of the army, Susenyos expressed his surprise at the accusation that he had changed the religion of the country. He had only reformed it. Christ, in fact, had two natures, he added. *"In the next place he had abrogated the Observation of the Sabbath Day, because it became not Christians to observe the Jews Sabbath."*[130]

The armed rebellion against the "Prophanation of the Sabbath," as it was called by some, spread.[131] But the king was able to defeat the rebels. Encouraged by his victories, in 1622 he issued a proclamation to his subjects giving the reasons why he had abandoned the Alexandrian faith and accepted the Roman. He urged them to follow his example. But the rebellion continued.[132]

Having received a reply from Paul V, Susenyos answered in a letter dated January 31, 1623, promising to obey him as universal pastor of the church, and asking for a Patriarch.[133] More Jesuits came in 1623. Then, in 1624 or 1625, Alphonso Mendez, the new Patriarch, arrived. He is described as "a brave and a bold man, but rigid, uncompromising, narrow-minded and intolerant."[134] Mendez "made Sūsenyōs and his sons and officials and priests make a new confession of the Roman Faith in February 1626, and to swear solemnly by the Gospel an oath of obedience to His Holiness the Pope;" and he introduced sweeping changes.[135] Saturday became a day of fasting.[136]

The changes so abruptly introduced soon began to turn the tide against the king, and he was confronted with a growing opposition to the religious civil war that was ruining the country. In response to argumentation by enemies of the Jesuits, King Susenyos finally yielded slightly.[137] An edict was published that permitted again the exercise of all the ancient ceremonies that were not repugnant to the faith. When Mendez protested, suggesting that a new edict be published with the help of one of the Jesuits, the king complied. But the new edict specified in article 2 "That the Festivals should be observ'd according to the ancient Computation of Time," and in article 3 that whoever wanted to do so could fast on the fourth day of the week instead of on the Sabbath.[138]

After one more military victory against the rebels, Susenyos, pressed by his son Fasiladas and others to stop the carnage of his own subjects, proclaimed religious freedom in June, 1632.[139] Thus ended the most decided attempt to modify the religious faith of Ethiopia, the Sabbath included, since Christianity had entered the country in the fourth century A.D.

Susenyos died a Roman Catholic in September of the same year. The new king, Fasiladas (1632-1667), ordered the Jesuits out of the country (1633), and then started "burning all the Catholic books he could find, and . . . beheading and hanging every priest, whether Jesuit or Capuchin, and all who were associated with them."[140] His son, Yohannes I (1667-1682), went even further by expelling all Roman Catholics from Ethiopia (1669).[141]

Ethiopia had now entered a new period of relative isolation. Sabbath observance (together with that of Sunday) has continued uninterrupted since the seventeenth century until today.[142] However, the quality of Sabbath observance is, by far, not uniform in all parts of the country.[143]

Summary and Conclusions

Both the Sabbath and Sunday were observed in fourth-century Egypt. However, Sunday was the preferred day. Communion was administered in Alexandria (c. 385) only on these two days, and the Sabbath was never supposed to be a day of fasting, except on Easter Sabbath. Moreover, until c. 400 there were no public services in the Egyptian monasteries—except for Vespers and Nocturns—other than on the Sabbath and Sunday.

It appears that during the first half of the fifth century, Christians in Alexandria stopped assembling together and celebrating the "sacred mysteries" on the Sabbath. However, the churches in the neighborhood of Alexandria and elsewhere in Egypt participated in the "mysteries" on Sabbath evening. It is possible that the Alexandrian change of posture can be traced to the anti-Jewish outbreak under Archbishop Cyril (412-444) that resulted in the expulsion of the Jews from Alexandria. Christian-Jewish relations had been less than cordial in Alexandria at least since the second century A.D.

The available documents also suggest that from approximately the year 500 Egypt abandoned all semblance of Sabbath observance.

Christianity entered the kingdom of Aksum in the fourth century. It is assumed that Sabbath *and* Sunday were from the outset observed as days of rest, following the practice of the church of Alexandria to which the church of the Aksumite kingdom was closely attached. Beginning, apparently, with the eleventh century, the Alexandrian See began exerting pressure on the Ethiopian Church to follow its example in abandoning Sabbath observance. By the second half of the thirteenth century, Ethiopia was well on her way toward following Alexandria.

An increasingly strong pro-Sabbath reaction was championed by Eustathius and his followers beginning in the first half of the fourteenth century. It culminated with the full legal reinstatement of Sabbath as a day of rest (along with Sunday) by King Zara Yaqob during the first half of the fifteenth century.

In the last quarter of the fifteenth century, the first Roman Catholic priests entered Ethiopia. In 1541 a force of 400 Portuguese soldiers arrived in answer to King Lebna Dengel's desperate plea for help against the Moslem invaders. After victory, Bermudez first, then Oviedo a few years later, unsuccessfully exerted pressure on kings Claudius and Minas to submit to the Roman Church, and to abandon, among other beliefs and practices, the observance of the seventh-day Sabbath.

Jesuit P. F. Paez was successful in attracting King Za Dengel to the Roman Catholic faith. This monarch issued an edict forbidding Sabbath observance (1604). After the king was killed in the ensuing revolt, Paez won over King Susenyos, who became a Roman Catholic. Susenyos issued harsh edicts commanding the people to work on the Sabbath and crushed almost all armed opposition. But after Paez's death (1622), Patriarch Alphonso Mendez's rigid, uncompromising ways strengthened the anti-Jesuit party. The king, after a final military victory, decreed complete religious freedom and abdicated. His son Fasiladas expelled the Jesuits. Later King Yohannes (1669) expelled all Roman Catholics from his kingdom.

Since the seventeenth century, Ethiopia has kept, undisturbed, both Sabbath and Sunday. However, real Sabbath observance today, as far as the Coptic Church is concerned, is confined mostly to the rural areas in the northern provinces.

NOTES

[1] Canons later approved by name—not quoted—as binding, in canon 2 of the Quinisext Council in 692. *Notitia Historio-Litteraria* (introductory notes to the works of St. Peter; *PG* 18:449, 450).

[2] *Sancti Petri Episcopi Alexandrini et Martyris Epistola Canonica* trans. in *NPNF*/2 14:601.

[3] The *Homilia de Semente* is only attributed to Athanasius, bishop of Alexandria (*c.* 296-373). It is considered of dubious authenticity *(PG* 28:7).

[4] S. P. N. Athanasii *Homilia de Semente* (PG 28:144); see English version in *SDABSSB*, No. 1422.

[5] *Ibid.* (PG 28:144, 145).

[6] S. P. N. Athanasii *De Sabbatis et Circumcisione* (PG 28:133, 137). (Italics supplied.) French version in Willy Rordorf, *Sabbat et dimanche dans l'Eglise ancienne* (Neuchâtel, Switzerland, 1972), p. 91.

[7] *Ibid.* (PG 28:140); French version in Rordorf, *op. cit.,* pp. 185, 187.

[8] *Ibid.* (PG 28:141); Rordorf, *op. cit.*, p. 187. See also a clearly spurious work attributed to Athanasius, *Syntagma Doctrinae ad Monachos, Omnesque Christianos tam Clericos quam Laicos* (PG 28:837). The author classifies Sabbath

observance together with actions such as saying "raka" to a brother, or dealing with magic and incantations, as something that a Christian should not do (col. 839). However, Sabbath and Sunday are singled out as days when fasting should not take place, except for Easter Sabbath (col. 840).

⁹ *The Canonical Answers of Timothy, the Most Holy Bishop of Alexandria, Who Was One of the CL Fathers Gathered Together at Constantinople, to the Questions Proposed to Him Concerning Bishops and Clerics*, Question XIII, in *NPNF/2*, 14 (Appendix IX):613. See *PG* 33:1305. See also Rordorf, *op. cit.*, pp. 103, 105.

¹⁰ Palladius *Historia ad Lausum* 38 (*PG* 34:1099). Cf. 7 (*PG* 34:1020), and chaps. 15, 16 (*PG* 34:1036). See also Rordorf, *op. cit.*, p. 87. Rordorf, *op. cit.*, p. 85, quotes *Vita I sancti Pachomii* 28 as follows: "He [Pachomius] prescribed: the superintendent of the monastery will arrange for three (sessions of) instruction: one on the Sabbath and two on Sunday." According to Rordorf, the Coptic text of Pachomius' rule is not that clear. It states that the "instruction had to take place, obligatorily, twice a week."—*Ibid.*, n. 3.

¹¹ *Ibid.*, 138 (*PG* 34:1236). See Rordorf, *op. cit.*, p. 207.
¹² John Cassian *The Institutes of the Coenobia* 3. 2 (*NPNF/2* 11:213).
¹³ *Ibid.*, 5. 26 (*NPNF/2* 11:243).
¹⁴ *Ibid.*, 2. 4 (*NPNF/2* 11:206).
¹⁵ *Ibid.*, 2. 6 (*NPNF/2* 11:207).
¹⁶ John Cassian, *Conferences* 23. 21 (*NPNF/2* 11:531).
¹⁷ Cf. chap. 8, nn. 14, 15.
¹⁸ Socrates Scholasticus *Ecclesiastical History* 5. 22 (*NPNF/2* 2:132).
¹⁹ Sozomen *Ecclesiastical History* 7. 19 (*NPNF/2* 2:390).
²⁰ Socrates Scholasticus *Eccl. Hist.* 7. 13 (*NPNF/2* 2:159); cf. Marcel Simon, *Verus Israel* (Paris, 1964), p. 382.
²¹ *Ibid.*
²² *Ibid.*
²³ Cf. Cassian's witness (*c.* 400), with Socrates Scholasticus' and Sozomen's statements (*c.* 440).
²⁴ Rordorf, *op. cit.*, p. 208, and p. 209, n. 4; G. Krüger, "Eusebius of Alexandria," *Schaff-Herzog*, 4:208.
²⁵ Text in *PG* 86/1:413-421. French version in Rordorf, *op. cit.*, pp. 209-219.
²⁶ *Ibid.*, col. 416.
²⁷ *Ibid.*
²⁸ *Ibid.*, cols. 419, 420.
²⁹ *Ibid.*, cols. 420, 421.
³⁰ Rordorf, *op. cit.*, p. 219, n. 3, explains that the fragment has been attributed to Peter of Alexandria (died 311). But Rordorf argues that the "Sunday legislation" in the fragment "seems impossible at the beginning of the fourth century...." On the other hand, the contents are strikingly similar to Eusebius of Alexandria's homily 16.
³¹ (Pseudo) Petrus Alexandrinum, *Fragmentum*, in *Texte und Untersuchungen zur Geschichte der altchristlichen Literatur*, vol. 20, ed. by C. Schmidt (1901), quoted in Rordorf, *op. cit.*, pp. 219-221.
³² Rordorf, *op. cit.*, p. 221, n. 1.
³³ Zacharie le Scholastique *Vie de Sévère* (*PO* 2:32).
³⁴ See in *PO* 14:344, a reference to "the holy night of the Lords Day" in *The Life of Abba John Khamé*. John Khamé was a Syrian who lived in Egypt (sometime between 700 and 800). There are references to several consecrations done on Sunday in the thirteenth century, in Moufazzal Ibn Abil-Fazail, *Histoire des Sultans Mamlouks*, *PO* 14:447-451.
³⁵ Alexander Ross, *Pansebeia: or, A View of all Religions in the World* (London, 1655), p. 494.
³⁶ Gregory Dix, ed., *The Treatise on the Apostolic Tradition of St Hippolytus of Rome* (London, 1968), p. lviii.
³⁷ *Ibid.*, p. lix.
³⁸ Wilson B. Bishai, "Sabbath Observance from Coptic Sources," *AUSS* 1 (1963):27; cf. a parallel text in *Les "127 Canons des Apôtres,"* 1:65, trans. from Arabic to French by Jean Périer and Augustin Périer, in *PO* 8:649.
³⁹ The Arabic version was made from the Coptic before 1295. There are several manuscripts. In *PO* 8:567-570, manuscripts are mentioned from the years 1339, 1348, 1353, 1641, 1664, and 1730.
⁴⁰ *Ibid.*, 2. 45 (*PO* 8:684).
⁴¹ *Ibid.*, 1. 40 (*PO* 8:612).
⁴² Cf. p. 175 in this same chapter on the impact that Ibn al-Assal's *Collection of Canons* (1238), prepared for the benefit of Coptic Christians in Egypt, had on Ethiopia.
⁴³ Edward Ullendorff, *The Ethiopians*, 2d ed. (London, 1965), p. 49.
⁴⁴ *Idem*, "Hebraic-Jewish Elements in Abyssinian (Monophysite) Christianity," *Journal of Semetic Studies* 1 (July, 1956):216-256; *idem*, *Ethiopia and the Bible* (London, 1968), pp. 15-30.
⁴⁵ *Idem*, *Ethiopia*, p. 23.
⁴⁶ *Ibid.* There is a late Ethiopian tradition according to which in pre-Christian days part of the population followed the Jewish religion, and the other part worshiped the "serpent." See *idem*, *Ethiopians*, p. 97; E. A. Wallis Budge, *A History of Ethiopia* (London, 1928), 1:148. Cf. with the also late tradition (legend?) of the queen of Sheba, Solomon, and Menelik I that, for all practical purposes, was treated as historical fact when it was included in the 1955 Constitution. Ullendorff, *Ethiopians*, pp. 64, 65, 143, 144, 194; Budge, *op. cit.*, pp. 194-200, 220-227, et cetera.
⁴⁷ Ullendorff, *Ethiopians*, p. 111.
⁴⁸ Maxime Rodinson, "Sur la Question des 'Influences Juives' en Ethiopie," *Journal of Semetic Studies* 9 (Spring 1964):12. Their number has been variously estimated at between 15,000 and 60,000. Among the works they have written we find the "Commandments of the Sabbath." Ullendorff, *Ethiopians*, pp. 111, 154. See also Ernst Hammerschmidt, *Stellung und Bedeutung des Sabbats in Athiopien* (Stuttgart, 1963), pp. 66-69.
⁴⁹ *Ibid.*, pp. 18, 19.
⁵⁰ *Ibid.*, p. 19.
⁵¹ See Taddesse Tamrat, *Church and State in Ethiopia: 1270-1527* (Oxford, 1972), pp. 218, 219. It should probably be mentioned at this point that the Ethiopian eunuch baptized by Philip (Acts 8:26-39) was not an Aksumite subject, but a minister of one of the Candaces of Nubia, whose capital was at Meroë, 130 miles north of Khartum (in present-day Sudan).
⁵² Since that time, and until June 29, 1959, the Ethiopian Church depended on Alexandria for her metropolitan. Almost without exception the Abuna was an Egyptian. G. A. Maloney, "Ethiopian Rite," *NCE* 5:587; G. Krüger, "Abyssinia and the Abyssinian Church," *Schaff-Herzog*, 1:19; B. J. Kidd, *The Churches of Eastern Christendom* (London, 1927), pp. 448, 449.

53 Budge, *op. cit.*, p. 258; Ullendorff, *Ethiopians*, pp. 100, 101.
54 Cf. chap. 8, pp. 151, 152, and chap. 9, pp. 173, 174. Kidd, *op. cit.*, p. 453, writes: "Conservative because of their age-long isolation, the Abyssinians have retained customs once prevalent in early days—the communion of infants from the chalice, the observance of Sabbath as well as Sunday, and the celebration of the Agapé."
55 Tamrat, *op. cit.*, pp. 23-25.
56 *History of the Patriarchs of Alexandria* 2. 3. 330, quoted in Tamrat, *op. cit.*, p. 209.
57 Tamrat, *op. cit.*, p. 209.
58 *Ibid.*; cf. pp. 218, 219.
59 Ullendorff, *Ethiopians*, p. 153; see also pp. 138, 185.
60 "Und beobachtet nicht den Sabbat wie die Juden." Hammerschmidt's *(op. cit.*, p. 60) translation from Geʿez.
61 *Ibid.* The *Didascalia* was written in Syria during the third century A.D. It was incorporated, with adaptations, in the *Apostolic Constitutions* as books 1-6.
62 The pseudo-Clementine work known as "Teaching of the Apostle Peter to Clement," translated from the Arabic into Ethiopic at the end of the fourteenth century, or early fifteenth century (not later than 1425). *Ibid.*, p. 42, and n. 214.
63 *Ibid.*, pp. 60, 61.
64 Zärʾa-Yaʾiqob *Mäṣhafä Birhan* ["Book of Light"] 2 (hereafter cited as *MB*), quoted in Tamrat, *op. cit.*, p. 210.
65 Tamrat, *op. cit.*, p. 70.
66 *Ibid.*
67 *Ibid.*, *op. cit.*, pp. 69-72; cf. Budge, *op. cit.*, p. 154.
68 Budge, *op. cit.*, p. 154.
69 Tamrat, *op. cit.*, p. 209.
70 *Ibid.*, p. 206.
71 *Ibid.*, p. 207.
72 *Gädlä Ēwostatēwos*, ed. by B. Turaiev in *Monumenta Aethiopiae Hagiologia*, fasc. iii (Petropoli, 1905), p. 91, quoted in Tamrat, *op. cit.*, p. 207. Cf. Rudolf Kriss and Hubert Kriss-Heinrich, in *Volkskundliche Anteile in Kult und Legende äthiopischer Heiliger* (Wiesbaden, 1975), p. 112. They state that Ewostatewos (Eustathius) was the founder of the teaching on the sanctification of the Sabbath. Somehow they seem to forget that on page 15 they have referred to a miracle of Gabra Manfas Qeddus on a woman who was in trouble because, among other things, she did not honor the Sabbath (Saturday). The miracle is supposed to have happened several decades before Eustathius' birth (cf. p. 9). As Ephraim Isaac has clearly stated, "By and large there is now scholarly agreement that keeping Saturday Sabbath is an ancient Ethiopian custom."—*A New Text-Critical Introduction to Maṣḥafa Berhān, with a Translation of Book I* (Leiden, 1973), p. 67; cf. p. 68.
73 *Gädlä Ēwostatēwos*, p. 96, quoted in Tamrat, *op. cit.*, p. 207, n. 6.
74 Tamrat, *op. cit.*, pp. 109, 209.
75 *Ibid.*, p. 213.
76 Zärʾa-Yaʾiqob *MB* 2. 82, quoted in Tamrat, *op. cit.*, p. 216.
77 Tamrat, *op. cit.*, pp. 217-219.
78 *MB* 1. 2, in Tamrat, *op. cit.*, p. 230.
79 *MB* 1. 1 (annotated translation by Isaac, *op. cit.*, p. 83).
80 Tamrat, *op. cit.*, p. 238; cf. Hammerschmidt, *op. cit.*, pp. 30, 31.
81 Isaac, *op. cit.*, p. 27.
82 *MB* 1. 2 (Isaac, *op. cit.*, pp. 90, 91).
83 *Ibid.* (Isaac, *op. cit.*, p. 91).
84 *MB* 1. 3 (Isaac, *op. cit.*, p. 108). Cf. Isaac, *op. cit.*, pp. 95-98, 108-111; see also pp. 133, 134.
85 *Ibid.* (Isaac, *op. cit.*, pp. 109, 110).
86 *MB* 1. 3, 6 (Isaac, *op. cit.*, pp. 96, 97, 145, 146).
87 *Ibid.* (Isaac, *op. cit.*, p. 141).
88 Isaac, *op. cit.*, p. 34.
89 J. M. Harden, *The Ethiopic Didascalia*, Translations of Christian Literature, Series 4: Oriental Texts (London, 1920), quoted in Hammerschmidt, *op. cit.*, pp. 37, 38.
90 Dix, *op. cit.*, pp. 43, 44. See also Hammerschmidt, *op. cit.*, pp. 42-47; J. Quasten, "Apostolic Constitutions," *NCE*, vol. 1, pp. 689, 690. It should be noted that the phrase "and on the Sabbath and" does not appear in the corresponding text of the *Canons of Hippolytus*, a fifth- or sixth-century drastic recasting of the *Apostolic Tradition* done in Egypt. Dix, *op. cit.*, pp. lxxvi, lxxvii, 43, esp. n. 1. It seems to be an Ethiopic interpolation, underlining the Ethiopian Church's deep concern for Sabbath observance. Cf. another instance of an interpolated "Sabbath" in the Ethiopic version of the *Egyptian Church Order* (that does not appear in the Sahidic and Arabic versions) in Kenneth A. Strand, "A Further Note on the Sabbath in Coptic Sources," *AUSS* 6 (1968):154, 155.
91 Hammerschmidt, *op. cit.*, pp. 39-42.
92 Ullendorff, *Ethiopians*, p. 145. "The *Sinodos* is the Ethiopian translation of the canons of the Apostles and the apostolic constitutions taken from the Alexandrian Church, plus the canons of the ecumenical Council of Nicaea I . . . and the canons of the six local synods of Ancyra, Neocaesarea, Gangres, Sardica, Antioch, and Laodicea."—G. A. Maloney, "Ethiopian Rite," *NCE* 5:587.
93 H. Ludolf, *Commentarius ad Suam Historiam Aethiopicam* (Frankfurt, 1691), p. 303, quoted in Tamrat, *op. cit.*, p. 229.
94 *The Apostolic Canons* are sometimes called *Statutes of the Apostles*, or *Canones Ecclesiastici*. They are part of book 8 of the *Apostolic Constitutions (ANF* 7:500-505); Hammerschmidt, *op. cit.*, p. 47; cf. Maloney, *op. cit.*, p. 587.
95 G. Horner, *The Statutes of the Apostles* (London, 1904), p. 68, quoted in Hammerschmidt, *op. cit.*, p. 47.
96 Hammerschmidt, *op. cit.*, pp. 47, 48 (information taken from Horner, *op. cit.*, pp. 68-70). The Sabbath is called "holy," "blessed," "honoured," and "pure."
97 *Ibid.*, p. 62, n. 322.
98 Richard K. P. Pankhurst, ed., *The Ethiopian Royal Chronicles* (Addis Ababa, 1967), pp. 39, 40.
99 Francisco Alvarez, *Narrative of the Portuguese Embassy to Abyssinia (1520-1527)* (London, 1861), pp. 23, 34, quoted in *SDABSSB*, No. 1462.
100 Tamrat, *op. cit.*, pp. 290, 291.

101 *Ibid.*, p. 291; cf. Ullendorff, *Ethiopians*, pp. 3, 4, 71, 72.
102 Ullendorff, *Ethiopians*, p. 71; Budge, *op. cit.*, pp. 330, 331.
103 A. H. M. Jones and Elizabeth Monroe, *A History of Ethiopia* (Oxford, 1960), pp. 76, 77. See also Bekele Heye, "The Sabbath in Ethiopia" (research paper, Andrews University [1970]), pp. 24, 25.
104 Ullendorff, *Ethiopians*, p. 4; Budge, *op. cit.*, pp. 331, 332.
105 According to Budge (*op. cit.*, p. 332), in 1527 or 1533; according to *SDABSSB*, No. 1463, *c.* 1532; and in 1534 according to A. H. Lewis, *A Critical History of the Sabbath and the Sunday in the Christian Church*, 2d ed. (Plainfield, N.J., 1903), p. 212.
106 Michael Geddes, *Church History of Ethiopia* (London, 1696), pp. 34, 35, quoted in Lewis, *op. cit.*, pp. 212, 213. See also *SDABSSB*, No. 1463; Jean Vuilleumier, *Le jour du repos à travers les âges* (Dammarie-les-Lys, 1936), p. 165.
107 Ullendorff, *Ethiopians*, p. 74. Heye (*op. cit.*, p. 30) apparently quoting from the letters sent with Bermudez both to John III of Portugal and to Pope Paul III, gives the following paragraph taken from Tekletsadik Mekuria, *A History of Ethiopia from Lebna Dengel to Tewodros* (Addis Ababa, 1953), pp. 194, 195: "We are willing to subject our faith and our Church to the Holy See at Rome. We are willing to recognize the sovereignty of Portugal over our Empire. We and the peoples of our Empire are willing to become Portuguese and Roman Catholic subjects. To make this effective we have given the bishopric to Bermudez." Cf. Budge, *op. cit.*, p. 335; John Mason Neale, *A History of the Holy Eastern Church* (London, 1847), 2:347, 348. It should be mentioned that the historicity of Bermudez's consecration as bishop (Abuna) of Ethiopia is still disputed. See Heye, *op. cit.*, pp. 35, 36; Hammerschmidt, *op. cit.*, p. 49. Budge (*op. cit.*, p. 332) states that Zaga za-Ab had already (1534) presented to Pope Clement VII a letter from Legna Dengel acknowledging the supremacy of the pope. Cf. Neale, *op. cit.*, p. 348, who states that the "letters" were delivered by "chaplain Álvarez."
108 From the chronicle of the fifth year of Claudius, as quoted in Budge, *op. cit.*, 2:352; cf. Heye, *op. cit.*, pp. 35, 36. Ever since the Crusades, "Franks" was a common gentillic for West Europeans in general, in the Middle East.
109 Budge, *op. cit.*, 2:345-347; Ullendorff, *Ethiopians*, p. 77; Hammerschmidt, *op. cit.*, pp. 49, 50. Nuñez Barreto had been originally appointed Patriarch of Ethiopia, but he stayed behind, in India. When he died, Andre de Oviedo, who already was in Ethiopia (since 1557), became Patriarch (1561). Budge, *op. cit.*, 2:373.
110 Pankhurst, *op. cit.*, p. 76.
111 *Ibid.*
112 As quoted by Hammerschmidt, *op. cit.*, p. 51; see also pp. 48-53; cf. Job Ludolphus [Hiob Ludolf], *A New History of Ethiopia* (London, 1682), p. 247; Budge, *op. cit.*, 2:354; Pankhurst, *op. cit.*, p. 78.
113 Ullendorff, *Ethiopians*, p. 77.
114 Jones and Monroe, *op. cit.*, p. 90.
115 Budge, *op. cit.*, 2:573. This is apparently a quotation from the book.
116 Ullendorff, *Ethiopians*, p. 151.
117 Budge, *op. cit.*, 2:373, 374; Pankhurst, *op. cit.*, pp. 88, 89.
118 Budge, *op. cit.*, 2:377; cf. Ludolf, *op. cit.*, p. 326.
119 Ludolf, *op. cit.*, p. 326.
120 *Ibid.*, p. 327; cf. Budge, *op. cit.*, 2:378; Hammerschmidt, *op. cit.*, p. 54.
121 *Ibid.*; Budge, *op. cit.*, 2:378.
122 Budge, *op. cit.*, 2:378-380; Hammerschmidt, *op. cit.*, p. 54.
123 Hammerschmidt, *op. cit.*, pp. 54, 55. It was thought, before, that it had been written during Claudius' reign. See Budge, *op. cit.*, 1:155; Ullendorff, *Ethiopians*, p. 151.
124 Budge, *op. cit.*, 2:388.
125 Ullendorff, *Ethiopians*, p. 78; Ludolf, *op. cit.*, p. 328. An attempt will be made to follow a clear chronological sequence of the events during Susenyos' reign. It is quite difficult, at times, to see this sequence in Ludolf's *History*.
126 *Ibid.*, pp. 328-330.
127 *Ibid.*, pp. 332, 333. A detailed study of Portuguese intervention in Ethiopia contains several items of interest: Daniel Augsburger, "Le sabbat en Ethiopie et les écrivains portugais du XVIe et XVIIe siècles" (Diplôme Licencié thesis, Séminaire Adventiste, Collonges-sous-Salève, France, 1970).
128 Ludolf, *op. cit.*, p. 333.
129 C. F. Rey, *The Romance of the Portuguese in Abyssinia* (London, 1935), p. 253, cited by Heye, *op. cit.*, p. 54. See also Ludolf, *op. cit.*, p. 333; Budge, *op. cit.*, 2:391.
130 Ludolf, *op. cit.*, pp. 333, 334.
131 *Ibid.*, p. 334.
132 *Ibid.*, p. 335; Budge, *op. cit.*, 2:389.
133 Ludolf, *op. cit.*, p. 328. Metropolitan Simeon had been killed in an armed confrontation. *Ibid.*, p. 332; Budge, *op. cit.*, 2:389.
134 Budge, *op. cit.*, 2:390.
135 *Ibid.*; cf. Heye, *op. cit.*, pp. 57, 58; Ullendorff, *Ethiopians*, p. 78.
136 Ludolf, *op. cit.*, p. 351.
137 For the arguments used, see Ludolf, *op. cit.*, p. 350.
138 *Ibid.*, p. 351.
139 See Budge, *op. cit.*, 2:393, 395; cf. Ludolf, *op. cit.*, p. 357; Ullendorff, *Ethiopians*, p. 78.
140 Budge, *op. cit.*, 2:401, 402.
141 Pankhurst, *op. cit.*, p. 102.
142 On witnesses to Sabbath observance in Ethiopia (with Sunday) in the seventeenth century, see: *SDABSSB*, Nos. 1464, 1465; Ullendorff, *Ethiopia*, p. 110 (cf. n. 7); Ludolf, *op. cit.*, pp. 299-302; Ross, *op. cit.*, p. 495; Samuel Purchas, *Hakluytus Posthumus or Purchas His Pilgrimes*, 20 vols. (New York, 1965), 1:376, 408. For witnesses from the eighteenth to the twentieth century, see: Ullendorff, *Ethiopia*, pp. 112, 113; idem, *Ethiopians*, p. 105; Lewis, *op. cit.*, p. 214; Hammerschmidt, *op. cit.*, pp. 1, 2; Harry Middleton Hyatt, *The Church of Abyssinia* (London, 1928), pp. 224-282; Adrian Fortescue, *The Lesser Eastern Churches* (London, 1913), p. 319.
143 Ethiopian Heye writes: "In the northern provinces, especially in the Governorate General of Godjam, which is the stronghold of the Coptic Church, the Seventh-day Sabbath is still strictly observed. This is also true in most parts of the Governorate General of Eritrea, Tigre, and Begemdir. A traveler can see the farmers threshing wheat during the harvesttime, on Sundays, especially on Sunday afternoons. But, no work of any sort is done on the Sabbath by the

THE SABBATH IN EGYPT AND ETHIOPIA

strict Copts. Housewives draw their water on Friday and all their cooking is done on the preparation day just as it was in the Old Testament time. Even though this does not appear in the Ethiopian Government Revised Constitution, Sabbathbreakers are accused from time to time and are brought to the local chiefs where they receive their punishment for breaking the law of God." Then Heye mentions (*op. cit.*, pp. 66, 67) that he went as part of a delegation that in March of 1968 interviewed the bishop of West Ethiopia, in Lekempti. Regarding the position of the Ethiopian Orthodox Church on the seventh-day Sabbath, the Bishop "told us plainly that the Coptic Church has never given up Sabbath observance. He referred to Matthew 5:17-18 and said that the Decalogue is still binding."—Page 65.

Hammerschmidt (*op. cit.*, p. 2) mentions an interview with Patriarch Bāselyos, who told him that Sabbath is still "celebrated" today. But he also points out that in Addis Ababa people work until 1:00 P.M. on Sabbath, and that the activity in the market reaches its high point on Sabbath. On the other hand, in rural areas Sabbath is kept much more strictly.

CHAPTER 10

The Sabbath and Lord's Day During the Middle Ages

Daniel Augsburger

THE early Middle Ages as a whole accepted without questioning the Lord's day of the great Church Fathers and their spiritualized interpretation of the Sabbath rest. This concept of the Lord's day was expressed clearly by Augustine (A.D. 350-431), who became the tutor of the medieval theologians.

The Spiritual Interpretation of the Fathers and Early Medieval Period

According to Augustine, the first day of the week is the glorious memorial of the resurrection of the Lord and His victory over evil. It celebrates the spiritual rest that He acquired for us. Man, therefore, must observe it, not by ceasing from work but by ceasing from sin, and live in a perpetual Sabbath. Augustine said, in a sermon on the Gospel of John: "The Jews taking the observance of the Sabbath in a carnal sense, fancied that the Lord had, as it were, slept after the labor of framing the world, even to this day.... Now to our fathers of old there was ordained a sacrament of the Sabbath, which we Christians observe spiritually, in abstaining from every servile work, that is from every sin (for the Lord saith, 'Everyone that committeth sin is the servant of sin') and in having rest in our heart, that is spiritual tranquillity. And although in this life we strive after this rest, yet not until we have departed this life shall we attain to that perfect rest."[1]

This was also the view of the Eastern Church. In his great exposition of the orthodox faith, John of Damascus *(c.* 675-*c.* 749) explained that the fourth commandment must be understood mystically by the spiritually minded: "Yea we shall celebrate the perfect rest of human nature, I mean the day after the resurrection, on which the Lord Jesus, the author of life and our Saviour, shall lead us into the heritage promised to those who serve God in the Spirit.... What belongs to us, therefore, who walk by the Spirit and not by the letter, is the complete abandonment of carnal things, the spiritual service and communion with God.... The Sabbath, moreover, is cessation of sin."[2]

In Judeo-Christian controversies this spiritual understanding of the Sabbath was a major argument of the Christians. Isidore of Seville *(c. 560-636)*, whose *Etymologies* remained the encyclopedia of knowledge of medieval man, appealed to that concept in his *Contra Judaeos,* which he wrote to try to win by persuasion the Jews whom the Visigoth kings, recently won over to Roman Orthodoxy, were attempting to convert by persecutions. In the second book of that work he stated that it could not be a sin to work on the Sabbath since God Himself is active in the universe every day of the week. Thus the keeping of the Sabbath must be spiritual: " 'Bear no burden on the Sabbath day.' Hear the mystery of prophecy. He bears burdens on the Sabbath, whom the day of judgment will find with his transgression; he bears burdens on the Sabbath who, though he believes in Christ, does not cease from sin."[3]

Among the Church Fathers the day of the Lord was also called the eighth day, the glorious day of the eternal rest of God. Originally that notion came from a blend of Gnostic speculation and neo-Pythagorean cosmology that emphasized the distinction between the seven spheres where the evil angels are kept and the eighth one where God dwells. As it was applied to Sunday, it signified reality and eternity in contrast with the seven days of the week, which were symbolic of time and illusion. In the West, the concept acquired a millenarist dimension in which the seventh day became typical of the last earthly millennium that precedes the eternal eighth day of bliss.

The idea of the eighth day appealed greatly to Augustine, who was so fond of number symbolism. According to him, the eighth day typifies the heavenly rest prepared by God for His children, which he describes so glowingly in the last page of the *City of God:* "The seventh shall be our Sabbath, which shall be brought to a close, not by an evening, but by the Lord's Day as an eighth and eternal day, consecrated by the resurrection of Christ, and prefiguring the eternal repose not only of the spirit, but also of the body. There we shall rest and see, see and love, love and praise."[4] Thus, the eighth day stands for a better rest.

We must, therefore, not be surprised to find Gregory the Great (540-604), the first Western medieval theologian, saying that "seven days represent the present time, the eighth day designates life eternal, which the Lord revealed to us through the resurrection."[5]

It is at that time also, especially in Judeo-Christian controversies, that Christian writers begin to claim that even in Scriptures the first day of the week is much holier than the seventh one. While the Sabbath was hallowed once, Sunday was hallowed repeatedly. Isidore of Seville, for instance, writes: "It is clear that [Sunday] was already very solemn in the Holy Scriptures. It is indeed the first day of the world, the day when the angels were created; the day when Christ was resurrected; the day when the Holy Spirit fell upon the apostles; the day when the manna was given for the first time in the wilderness. . . . Is not the sabbath the seventh day which follows Sunday? It must be, therefore, on Sunday that manna fell for the first time. For the Jews already then our Sunday was greater than Sabbath."[6]

This statement of Isidore had a lasting influence on later writers. It was copied verbatim, as we shall see, by Bede, Rabanus Maurus, and Alcuin. The double justification of Sundaykeeping by the historical fact of the resurrection of the Lord and by the Biblical evidence of the Sunday hallowings was used by most of the theologians who dealt with that problem later on. But one must not forget that for Isidore of Seville, Sunday ranked low among church festivals. In his *Etymologies* he states that the first of all the Christian holidays is Easter. Then come Pentecost, the Epiphany, Palm Sunday, Maundy Thursday, and finally Sunday.[7]

Steps Toward Making Sunday a Rest Day

To understand the development of the day of rest during the medieval period, we must not forget that in the early church, Sunday was not a day of total rest from physical labor. A strong effort was made to draw a sharp distinction between the wicked idleness of the Jewish day of rest and the spiritual delight of Sunday. In a sermon Augustine said, "You must keep the Sabbath spiritually, not in carnal idleness like the Jews. They want to have free time for their frivolities and their pleasures. It would be far better for the Jew to do something useful in his field than to spend time shouting in the stadium. And their wives would be better off spinning on the Sabbath than dancing shamelessly on their terraces."[8]

It was only in the fourth century that Sunday celebration ceased being an early-morning festivity. Later on, when religious services began to be held in the middle of the morning, work stopped only at the time of the divine offices.[9] Jerome wrote that the nuns at Bethlehem went to church and resumed their sewing afterward.[10] The Benedictine rule stated clearly that all monks at Mount Cassino should be active on Sunday, preferably reading, but if they were unable to read, they should tend to manual activities.[11]

Mention should be also made regarding the reaction of Licinianus, bishop of Carthagena about 582, to what he heard from his friend Bishop Vincentius about the *Letter from Heaven*. This letter, as we shall see later, advocated a sabbatizing of Sunday with complete abstention from work on that day. Licinianus reminded his correspondent that under the new law there was no prohibition of labor on the day of the Lord. In fact, he added, if the faithful do not go to church on that day, it is far better for them to do something—gardening, spinning, hiking, or some other useful activity.[12]

There was so little thought of stopping work on Sunday that the Council of Orleans in 538 expressed grave concern about the fact that some encouraged idleness on the first day of the week.[13] At Rome at the end of the sixth century Pope Gregory the Great was greatly distressed because some "Jewishness" was seeping into the church. Some people advocated the prohibition of work, even necessary work, on Sunday. He had also heard that some went as far as forbidding any bathing. This appeared to Gregory as a return to legalism. He showed that one should distinguish between bathing for cleanliness and bathing for pleasure and lust. To stop working is meaningless, since true Sundaykeeping is rest from sin, a "sabbath" that is found in Christ alone.[14]

During that period, Christians refused to see any identity between the Old Testament rest and Sunday because they associated the seventh day with idleness and foolishness while they looked upon Sunday as a day for worship and useful activities. Augustine proclaimed loudly that Sunday is not for the Jews: "The day of the Lord is not for the Jews, but because of the resurrection of the Lord, set apart for the Christians."[15] For that reason the Christians saw no reason to draw from the prescriptions of the fourth commandment norms for the observation of Sunday.[16] That sharp distinction between the two days was vividly symbolized at Rome and in some other places by the fact that Saturday was a day of fasting and

Sunday a day of rejoicing, upon which it was utterly wrong to mourn.[17]

While the desire to distinguish Sabbath from Sunday was very strong, one must note, however, that in their legislation the Christian emperors had attempted to secure cessation of certain activities. They applied to Sunday, it appears, the traditional norm followed in the observation of pagan holidays: *Licet quod praetermissum noceret,* "One may do what would cause harm if it were omitted." Thus rural labors that could be postponed, trials in court that had to do with the quest for gain, and entertainments were forbidden.[18]

In order to encourage public worship, the church also began soon to condemn certain types of labor. At the Council of Orleans, which had opposed Judaizing tendencies, the people were told not to plow, prune vines, erect fences, plant posts, et cetera, that "one may have leisure more easily to attend church and take part in prayers."[19] Although Pope Gregory had upheld a spiritual rest, he demanded that all secular activities should stop to allow the people to devote their time to prayer.[20] This is the reason why he was so critical of Januarius, bishop of Cagliari, who used his Sundays for harvesting crops.[21]

Some went even further in sabbatizing the day of the Lord. As we have seen, the Council of Orleans refers to Christians who wanted to prohibit the preparation of food and the use of farm animals, and Gregory the Great knew some who reproved bathing on Sunday. The most curious witness of that tendency is the famous *Letter from Heaven,* to which allusion has already been made. It appeared first in Spain but enjoyed an immense success both in the West and in the East. In some places in the East it still enjoys credence today.[22]

The text of this letter to which Bishop Licinianus referred has not been preserved, and he mentions only prohibition of food preparation and walking. However, it is interesting to see what was included in later versions.[23] The letter began with a preface telling the story of the document—how it was found at one of the most famous shrines of Christianity, at Jerusalem or on the main altar of St. Peter at Rome, and how it was written not by an angel but by Christ Himself, with His own blood or with letters of gold.

The letter itself demanded the strictest Sabbatarianism: "Do not sit in the forum on the Lord's day and judge idle matters or go hunting and gathering game on this day. Do not milk cattle on this day either, but rather be occupied with the poor. Do not send your oxen to work on this day. . . . You must not wash your clothes nor wash or cut your hair. . . . Truly I say to you, be very faithful in keeping the day of the Lord, not even gathering vegetables from your gardens on the day of the Lord."[24]

According to the letter, the day should be consecrated to pious purposes, for going to church, for visiting the sick, for comforting the worried, and for making peace with others. It uttered a frightful curse against those who were irreverent in church: "I advise you by this letter that there must be no one in my churches, man or woman, who dares to talk and chit-chat, or to sit down or to go out during mass before the solemn rites are finished."

Natural and supernatural disasters were threatened against the transgressors. To famines, locusts, and sicknesses were added such things as burning stones and poisonous flying snakes. Women who dare to work in the garden were warned that "I will send upon you winged snakes to beat and devour your breasts."

The epistle made much use of the Old Testament. It grounded the duty to keep Sunday on the Sabbath commandment, and called for careful observation from sunset on Saturday night, "from the ninth hour of the sabbath until the first hour of the second day." [25]

This concept of the Lord's day must have been shared by some of the Arian rulers, for the Visigoths suffered a telling defeat by the Romans in 543 because the attack was made on Sunday and the Goths would not fight.[26]

The Saturday Sabbath in the Early Period

There were Christians who kept the seventh day, probably along with the first day of the week. Gregory the Great writes in the epistle that has already been quoted: "It has been reported to me that men of a perverse spirit have spread among you some despicable doctrines that are completely opposed to our holy faith, teaching that all work must be interrupted on the Sabbath. Whom could I call them but preachers of the Antichrist? Is it not Antichrist who shall come and force all to keep Sabbath and Sunday?" [27] In the beginning of the seventh century, therefore, we have at Rome people who advocated total rest on the seventh day, and it is interesting that the pope calls that day "Sabbath."

Finding people at Rome who advocate keeping both Sabbath and Sunday should not be a great surprise, since we have witnesses to that practice in other parts of the Empire. In the *Apostolic Constitutions* (compiled in the later half of the fourth century), for instance, we are told: "But keep the Sabbath and the Lord's day festivals; because the former is the memorial of the creation and the latter of the resurrection.... I, Peter, and I, Paul, have ordained: let the slaves work five days; but on the Sabbath day and the Lord's day let them have leisure to go to church for instruction in piety: on the Sabbath in regard to the creation; on the Lord's day in regard to the resurrection." [28] Gregory of Nyssa *(c. 330-c. 395)* explains: "With what eyes can you behold Sunday, if you desecrate the Sabbath? Don't you know that these days are brethren? He who esteems the one, disregards also the other." [29] John Cassian *(c. 360-435)* states concerning Egyptian monks that they "had no public assemblies on other days, besides in the morning and at evening, except on the Sabbath or on the Lord's day, when they met at the third hour to celebrate the communion." [30]

Augustine noted a great flexibility toward worship requirements: "In some places the communion takes place daily, in some only on the Sabbath and the Lord's day, and in some only on the Lord's day." [31] The tension concerning the keeping of both Sabbath and Sunday is reflected in a homily given at a Sabbath meeting, but opposing Sabbatarian idleness and proclaiming the superiority of Sunday over the seventh day.[32] It is that variety of uses that Socrates Scholasticus (died 445) describes in his *Ecclesiastical History:* "Although almost all churches throughout the world celebrate the sacred mysteries on the Sabbath of every week, yet the Christians of Alexandria and at Rome on account of some ancient traditions have ceased to do this." [33]

The Sabbath in the Celtic Church

Certain scholars have assumed that the Celtic Church kept the seventh day of the week.[34] A study of the available evidence shows first that for the Irish, the Sabbath was distinct from the Lord's day. According to Columba's biographer Adomnan (late seventh century), the saint said on his deathbed: "Truly this day is for me a Sabbath, because it is my last day of this present laborious life. In it after my toilsome labours I keep Sabbath; and at midnight of this following venerated Lord's Day, in the language of the Scriptures I shall go the way of the fathers."[35] In the same work we are told that it was the custom in Ireland to go to church and celebrate mass on the Lord's day: "[Columba] obeyed their command and on the Lord's Day according to custom he entered the church, along with them, after the reading of the gospel.... While the rites of the Mass were being celebrated on the Lord's Day according to the custom."[36] Columba's *Rules* for his monks (early seventh century) contain references only for a Lord's day public worship.

The Sabbath seems to have received some special recognition. In Columba's directions for the choir office, the singing of more psalms was ordained for the nights of Sabbath and Sunday than for the other nights of the week. "On the most holy nights, namely on those of the Lord's Day or the Sabbath, three times the same number is performed at morning, that is, with thrice ten and six psalms."[37] St. David's followers "from the eve of the Sabbath until the light shines in the first hour after the break of the Sabbath, employ themselves in watchings, prayers and genuflexions, except one hour after morning service on the Sabbath."[38] These special vigils remind us of the practices commanded by John Cassian.[39] The monks' diet was improved on Sabbath and Sunday. On those days they could add a little cheese boiled in water to their slim fare.[40]

Some texts may well indicate some recognition of the seventh day also. The ancient law Senchus Mor states that "every seventh day of the year" was to be devoted to the service of the Lord.[41] In a letter attributed to Columba but whose real authorship is unkown we find a passage that might indicate a spiritualized Sabbathkeeping. "We are bidden to work on six days but on the seventh day which is the Sabbath, we are restrained from every servile labour. Now by the number six the completeness of our work is meant, since it was in six days that the Lord made heaven and earth. Yet on the Sabbath we are forbidden to labour at any servile work, that is sin, since he who commits sin is a slave to sin, so that, when in this present age we have completely fulfilled our works, not hardening our hearts, we may deserve to reach that true rest."[42]

It is not clear whether the Lord's day was kept in the early Celtic Church in a Sabbatized way, that is, according to the Old Testament laws. In the *Life of Patrick* by Muirchu, we are told that St. Patrick, resting on the Lord's day, heard pagan laborers building earthworks nearby. The saint forbade them to work on the Lord's day. In another passage of the same work it is said that "it was [Patrick's] custome not to travel between vespers of the Lord's night and the dawn of the second day of the week."[43] In Admonan's *Life of Columba*, however, we find that saint helping wayfarers to be ferried across the strait and to be received at Iona on a Sunday. He also refers to a monk fishing on a Sunday with other men.[44] We find in that *Life* no threat against violators of Sunday rules, similar to those that abound in later documents.

The "Judaizing Craze"

This attitude toward the Sabbath and to the Sabbatizing of Sunday must be considered in the broader setting of a strong current of interest in, and reverence for, Judaism and the Old Testament, which Marcel Simon calls "the judaizing craze."[45] It had very deep and ancient roots, and its powerful attraction was felt particularly strongly by the Christians of Syria. John Chrysostom delivered eight homilies at Antioch in 386 and 387, probably to warn the faithful against the allurements of the synagogue. He was moved to action by the large number of Christians who had no intention of leaving the church but who attended Jewish services not only as observers but as enthusiastic participants.[46] The great orator was especially exercised because the great Jewish holidays were imminent and he knew that Christians would find their way *en masse* to the synagogue. Many went there because they believed that the Jewish ceremonies were solemn and holy.[47] In fact, another Church Father, Jerome, talks about Christians who thought that those rituals were holier than those of the Christians.[48]

The same current reappeared later in some parts of the West, where we find nuclei of Christians isolated in time and space who wanted to keep the gospel and observe Jewish precepts at the same time. Many of them lived in the Visigothic realm. Isidore of Seville speaks of many who are neither truly Jews nor truly Christians.[49] Another document informs us that late in the seventh century in Septimania there was a disquieting amount of "judaizing."[50] The Visigothic rulers were led to enact the death penalty for Christians who practiced Jewish rituals.[51] This must not have been enforced successfully, since Pope Hadrian I in 794 wrote a letter to the Spanish bishops to complain that nothing was being done about Christians who fraternized with Jews in pleasures and beliefs.[52] Christian authors often speak of Christians partaking in Jewish Sabbath banquets.[53] The popularity of Judaism may have been because many Christians were convinced that the Jews preached far better than the priests.[54]

The same situation is reported elsewhere. The anonymous author of a commentary on Deuteronomy from the middle of the eighth century knew Christians who held to the gospel and to the Jewish precepts.[55] Rabanus Maurus (776-856), the great abbot of Fulda, mentions "Jews and Judaizers in our time,"[56] a group to which Fulbert of Chartres (*c.* 960-1028) also referred in his sermons.[57] The words "Judaizer" and "Judaizing" were used, it is true, very loosely—sometimes for very minor deviations from orthodoxy. While recognizing this fact, B. Blumenkranz, one of the leading authorities in this domain, concludes his study of Judaizing currents by saying, "In a conscious, determined way, Christians accepted Jewish practices, influenced as they were either by the reading of the Old Testament alone, or by real contact with Jews, above all in observing the Sabbath rest or in accepting some of the food precepts."[58]

According to the thirteenth canon of the Council of Frioul in Northern Italy held in 796 or 797 there were farmers who kept the Sabbath.[59] The fact that the recently converted Bulgarians wrote Pope Nicholas I to ask whether they should stop their work on the Sabbath indicates that the Sabbath rest was still a live matter in that region in the tenth century.[60] A council at the end of the ninth century urged the people to keep Sunday rather than Sabbath and drew stern measures against Judaizing.[61] The very frequent repetition of the anti-Sabbath canon of Laodicea in medieval councils shows the persistence of Sabbatizing.[62]

The anti-Sabbath attitude of the Western Church was an important factor in the Great Schism of 1054.[63] The Easterners were very critical of the Western practice of fasting on Saturday because it contravened the canons of so many councils. The Westerners felt that the word of the pope should be sufficient to settle that matter and demanded the prompt submission of the Byzantines.[64] The quarrel embittered itself as the Catholics accused the Christians of Constantinople of Judaizing with the Jews and Christianizing with the Christians, while genuine believers should look upon the Jews and their Sabbath with execration. "The Easterners, Cardinal Humbert wrote, "chose to observe the Sabbath with the Jews." [65] After the schism, the patriarch of Constantinople, Michael Cerularius, wrote the patriarch of Antioch an account of the tragic event and said, "For we are commanded also to honor the Sabbath equally with the Lord's day and to keep it and not to work on it." [66]

The desire to have a Sabbath-type holiday was also affected by the ever-increasing use of the Old Testament by the church itself in its liturgy and laws. It was easy to draw analogies between the Aaronic priesthood and the Catholic hierarchy, the Paschal lamb and the sacrifice of the mass, the Passover and Christian Easter. In Gaul and in Spain the Old Testament became a creative pattern for Christian ritual.[67] The influence was not always as obvious as with regard to the Paschal lamb, which was blessed by the priest on Easter Day and eaten at dinner immediately after, but it was reflected in countless usages, as Chydenius has shown in his book *Medieval Institutions and the Old Testament*.[68]

This popularity of the Old Testament made it the model, as well, for courtly ceremonials, especially in Carolingian times. Inasmuch as the Christian rulers were considered to be the proper successors and imitators of the Old Testament kings, it became customary for the popes, for instance, to address the Carolingian kings as "Novus David." [69] Thus both church and state exalted the use of the Old Testament.[70]

The Decalogue as a Basis for Sunday Observance by the Barbarians

The decline of learning that accompanied the victory of the barbarians led to a greater reliance upon the Mosaic law in general. As the new conquerors developed their own legislation they attempted to include the Biblical ideals, rather than Roman law, in their codes. "The further a law removes itself from Roman law," writes Verdam, "the more it seeks support in Mosaic law, at least in so far as Christianized peoples are concerned." [71] This was true until the revival of Roman law in the twelfth and thirteenth centuries.

With that great influence of the Old Testament pattern it comes as no surprise that the church turned to the Decalogue in its efforts to secure the observance of Sunday by the barbarians. Asking the new converts to keep a special day for worship was not an easy endeavor. Even in an ancient Christian center such as Arles in the sixth century, if we believe the sermons of Caesarius of Arles, Sundaykeeping left much to be desired. He describes the people who leave before mass is finished; he talks of others who still rest on Thursday in honor of Jupiter, but would do any work on the day of the Lord.[72] Late in the sixth century in Spain, Martin of Braga also contrasted the zeal of the pagans for the day of Jupiter with the carelessness of the Christians.[73]

Although references to Sundaykeeping by the barbarians are very scanty, one can see that church attendance must have been extremely sparse by the exiguity of the places of worship and the repeated laments of ecclesiastical writers about the inattention, the noise, and the constant babbling during mass.[74] As Chelini points out, the laymen were hardly to blame: "Spectators of a drama in which they have no role, witnesses of a banquet of which they are not guests, their interest wears off quickly."[75] There was practically no participation of the people. They could hardly follow the service since it was held in a foreign tongue and even the practice of bringing offerings had been lost. Very few people took communion. Bonifacius advised them to participate "per tempora" (from time to time).[76] Egbert in England noted the difference between the Eastern Church, where everyone had to commune on Sunday under penalty of excommunication, and the church in the West, where no effort was made to enforce participation.[77]

To enforce Sundaykeeping among the barbarians, the church used different methods. It enacted ecclesiastical legislation derived from the Mosaic laws, enlisted state support of its efforts, and even appealed to the superstition and credulity of the flock. It is interesting to note that as a result there developed gradually a new perspective that emphasized outward interruption of physical activities rather than the primitive spiritual rest from sin. The major Sabbath development during the Middle Ages is that the sharp distinction between the Sabbath and Lord's day faded away, and Sunday became the Christian Sabbath to be kept according to the fourth commandment.[78]

The connection between Sundaykeeping and the Decalogue rest was clearly established at the Second Council of Macon in 585, which justified by the Old Testament a strong call for complete ceasing of work on the Lord's day. In the canons of that council, Sunday was exalted as the day when the Lord freed us from all sins, as the eternal day of rest foreshadowed by the rest of the seventh day of the law and the prophets. For that reason, Christians should interrupt all their activities and spend the day in prayer and tears at the nearest church.[79]

A few years later the prohibition of work was extended to all, Christians and non-Christians. At the Council of Narbonne (589) it was decided that "all, whether child or slave, Goth or Roman or Syrian or Greek or Jew, must cease from all work on the Day of the Lord." Only one exception was contemplated: an emergency trip that required the hitching of the oxen; but otherwise, anyone caught transgressing the law would be punished—the freeborn by a fine of six solidi, the slave by one hundred blows.[80] Thus Sundaybreaking became a punishable offense.

It is interesting to note that civil support for the Sabbatarian Sunday came quickly. The canons of the Council of Macon were upheld by an edict of King Gunthram (Nov. 10, 585), which stated clearly that those who did not heed the priestly exhortations would have to face the severity of the judges.[81] The decisions of Narbonne were soon backed by a law of Childebert II that also prohibited any Sunday work under threat of heavy fines.[82]

Along with these ecclesiastical and civil efforts to enforce Sunday observance, we must not forget the effect upon the barbarian tribes of the tales of miraculous punishments for transgression of Sunday rest. Many of those stories were already recorded by Gregory of Tours (540-594). He tells us, for instance, that in Limousin a large group of people working in the fields on Sunday were consumed by fire.[83] There was also a man who insolently started to plow on Sunday but whose hands were set solidly to the handle of the plow when he touched it to make an adjustment.[84] Another man who neither respected nor feared the day of the Resurrection went to a grain mill. After grinding his wheat, he tried to take his hand off the handle of the mill but found that his hand was stuck to it.[85] And the same punishment came to that same man again the following year. Similar misfortunes fell on one who tried to set up a post, to a woman who was putting bread in the oven, even to a girl who was combing her hair.[86]

Some were crippled in the attempt to break Sunday, Gregory of Tours tells us. The fingers of a worker who was making a key contracted together and never opened again.[87] The limbs of a woman who was baking bread after sunset on Saturday night withered away. At Bourges there was someone whose hands became completely deformed because he had tried to fence his field on Sunday.[88] Even emergencies failed to protect the transgressors. A man of Bourges who feared that rain would spoil his hay went to load it on his cart, but he felt fire burning his leg. After returning home, he tried to resume his labor after mass, only to feel his eyes hit by sharp thorns.[89] It is by such tales that the sanctity of Sunday was impressed upon the common people.

Sundaykeeping Casuistry and Extreme Sabbatarianism

In the following centuries there developed an ever-increasing casuistry concerning Sundaykeeping. The prohibitions became more and more encompassing. The acts that were prohibited and those that were allowed were defined with greater and greater detail. The trend was greatly accelerated by the generalization of private confession, which led to the use of penitential books in which sins and penances were carefully catalogued.[90]

By now Sunday had become an institution in its own right, a duty required from all, since transgression would bring the danger of divine punishment individually and collectively. Indeed, Sunday legislation took an increasingly important place in the statutes of the barbarian states. The right of all persons to have Sunday rest was solemnly affirmed and supported by severe punishments for those who interfered with it. Even the tasks required from the serfs had to stop on that day. Feudal lords could not require them to work in their fields or to use their animals for the cartage of goods.[91] As for the freemen who persistently transgressed Sunday, in some places they eventually lost their freedom and became serfs, for as the *Bavarian Laws* (744) state: "Let him lose his freedom and become a servant, since he did not want to be free on the holy day."[92]

The appeal to the Sabbath commandment of the Decalogue became more and more definite. In the *Laws of the Alemani* (725), we are told that abstention from physical labor is commanded by human and divine law.[93] In the *Bavarian Laws* the proper way of keeping the first day of the week was, for the first time perhaps, derived directly from the Decalogue. One must not harvest on Sunday nor travel by chariot or by boat, they declare, because the Lord has said, "You shall not do any work, you or your manservant or your maidservant, or your ox, or your donkey or any of those under your command."[94] At the Roman Council of 826, over which Pope Eugene II presided, it was agreed that it is important to secure Sunday rest through great threats lest the people, forgetting the word of God, might engage in secular activities, since God made the heavens and the earth and all that therein is.[95]

The *Letter from Heaven* enjoyed an immense influence at that time and was circulated widely. New and more striking stories of heavenly punishments for Sundaybreakers were told. Lists of Sunday hallowings showing the glory of Sunday grew longer and longer, not now to persuade the Jews, but to instill in Christians the duty to rest on that day. Pirmin, the founder of the monastery of

Reichenau, saw Sunday in all the great events of salvation history: "The day of the Lord was created first. It was then that darkness was dispelled and light shone. On that day the elements of the world and the angels were created. The people of Israel left Egypt on Sunday as if it had gone through a baptism through the Red Sea. On the same day the manna, the food from heaven, was given for the first time. It is concerning that day that the prophet exclaims, 'This is the day that the Lord has made, let us rejoice in it.' It is also on that day that Christ was raised from the dead; that the Holy Spirit came from heaven upon the apostles. It is called therefore Day of the Lord that we might abstain from earthly activities and the indecencies of the world, devoting ourselves to the divine offices." [96]

The extreme limit of Sabbatarianism was reached, perhaps, in Ireland, where, as we have seen, there was a long tradition of veneration for the Mosaic teachings. A feeling of the unique importance of Sunday observance among the Irish is reflected in the list of the four laws of the Irish in the Felire of Oengus (eighth century), where the rule of the Lord's day is included with Patrick's rule not to kill clerics, Adaman's rule not to slay women, and Daire's rule not to steal oxen.[97] It is also interesting to observe that the *Liber ex Lege Moysi*, a collection of Mosaic commands, which may be dated perhaps as early as the seventh century, includes several passages on the importance and manner of Sabbathkeeping.[98] In Ireland we find also an extraordinary number of accounts of miraculous punishments of Sundaybreakers.[99]

No document expresses better the Irish Sabbatarian ideal than the *Cain Domnaig*, or Law of Sunday, where are found together a *Letter from Christ* on Sundaykeeping, a group of miraculous punishments against the contemptors of the day of rest, and the *Cain Domnaig* itself, a Sunday legislation.[100] The opening of the *Letter from Jesus* sets the tone. It is the dramatic account of the sending of the letter, an event that caused the whole earth to tremble from the rising to the setting of the sun. Stones and trees were thrown up into the air, and the tomb of Peter was opened at that time. Obviously the author wanted the reader to place that event on the same rank as the Resurrection. For him "whatsoever plague and trouble has come into the world, it is through the transgression of Sunday that it has come." [101]

With such a beginning we must not be surprised by the supernatural woes that, according to the letter, befall Sundaybreakers. In the East, monstrous *bruchae*, whose hair is made of pins of iron, have been known to go out into the vineyards, cut the branches, and roll over the fruit. Iron-winged locusts eat through the wheat they encounter. If that example is not enough, it is added that tears of blood will fill the eyes of those who have forced others to desecrate the holy day. What the supernatural animals have left will be destroyed by terrible tempests, hailstorms, and flying serpents. Pagan invaders will come and enslave the wretched sinners and offer them as sacrifices to their gods.

The day must be kept holy not only because it is commanded by Jesus Christ but also for all the wonderful things that have happened on it. Then in the Irish *Letter from Heaven* comes the longest list of Sunday hallowings found anywhere: the beginning of Creation, the resting of the ark on Mount Ararat, the appearance of the rainbow after the Flood, the crossing of the Red Sea, the gift of the manna, the conception of Jesus in the womb of Mary, the birth of Jesus, the adoration of the Magi, the baptism of Jesus, the feeding of the multitude, the Transfiguration, the triumphal entry, the victory of Christ at the Temptation, the first teaching of

THE SABBATH AND LORD'S DAY DURING THE MIDDLE AGES

Jesus in the Temple, the changing of water into wine, John's vision that is recorded in the book of Revelation, the Resurrection, and Pentecost. Sunday wonders have not ceased, for the day of judgment and the renewal of all things will come on Sunday.

The list of prohibited activities reminds the reader of the detailed Jewish Sabbath regulations. "This is what I forbid," saith the Lord. "On Sunday there shall be no dispute, or lawsuit, or assembly, or strife, or bargain, or horse-driving, or sweeping the floor of a house, or shaving, or washing, or bathing, or washing clothes, or grinding in mill or quern, or cooking, or churning, or yarn-weaving, or adultery, or journeying by anyone beyond the border of his own territory, or racing, or shooting with spear or arrow, or riding on horse or ass, or boiling food, or swimming, or horse-riding, or splitting firewood, or [going on a boat] coracle on water, or anything involving wrong." [102]

Very severe punishments are threatened against Sundaybreakers by the author of the letter, usually heavy fines, with the loss of the animal or the serf involved on the occasion, or the destruction of the tool used for the transgression. A few dispensations are given: fleeing before pagans, warning the people of the coming of raiders, going to the help of someone—but on the condition of not returning before the end of Sunday. It is lawful to seek someone to give Communion, but not to baptize. Animals can be helped, fires fought, cattle protected from the wolves, crops saved from plunder, and of course, the sick may be assisted. [103]

However, the Sabbatarian trend was not welcome everywhere. The Council of Les Estinnes *(c. 743)* took a strong stand against a Jewish understanding of Sunday: "We who are Christians must not observe the Sabbath according to the letter. Christians must observe the Sabbath in this manner: by abstaining from dishonesty, fraud, perjuries, blasphemies, and all illicit things." [104] The same attitude appeared at the Council of Cloveshore (747), where the cultic significance of the holy day was emphasized. [105]

That latent theological conflict may also have been at the root of the very hostile reception given at that time by the leaders of the Franks to the preaching of the *Letter from Heaven*. In the *Admonitio generalis* (789), the letter is called "worst and most false," not to be believed or read but to be burned, lest by such writings the people might be led into error. [106] It was condemned also at a synod at Rome in 745. [107]

Civil Enforcement of the Sabbatarian Sunday

The Carolingian rulers were, just the same, zealous defenders of Sundaykeeping. Pepin the Short, Charlemagne, and their successors attempted to enforce Sunday rest. Strangely, the *Admonitio generalis,* which condemned the *Letter from Heaven,* may well mark the triumph of the Sabbatarian Sunday. In that document we find detailed instructions given in chapter 81: "We order, what the Lord has also prescribed in his law, that no physical work be performed on the day of the Lord as my father of good memory prescribed in his synodal edicts, that is, that men should not work in the fields, that they should not cultivate the vineyards, or plow in the fields, or harvest the grain or make hay, or erect fences, or clear forest lands or fell trees. They must not break stones on roads, build houses or do garden work. Only three uses of the wagons are permissible on

Sunday: to drive to war, to fetch foodstuff or take a body to the cemetery in an emergency.... Women shall not do their weaving either or cut garments, or sew or embroider. It is not allowed for them to card wool, or beat hemp or wash garments publicly or shear sheep, so that the honor and the rest of the Day of the Lord may be preserved in every way. Let all go to church for the mystery of the masses and let them praise God for all his blessings on that day." [108]

The *missi dominici*, Charlemagne's representatives, were instructed to pay close attention to the manner in which Sunday was kept everywhere they went,[109] and the effort only increased during the dark years toward the end of his reign. In 813, for instance, the prohibition of servile labor was repeated at the five reforming synods of Arles, Reims, Mainz, Chalon sur Saone, and Tours. The holding of public markets on that day was especially decried because so many people loafed through them rather than going to church.[110]

The same zeal toward stopping all servile work on Sunday was manifested by the newly converted rulers. When King Stephan of Hungary attempted to Christianize his realm in 1016, he issued Sunday edicts. "If a priest, or a nobleman, or anyone else finds one working on Sunday, let him drive him away from his work. If that man works with oxen, [the official] may take the ox and give it to the people for food. If he works with a horse, let the horse be confiscated, which the owner may redeem with an ox, that shall be also given to the people for food. If he works with tools, let those and the garments be confiscated, which he may redeem with his skin [a flogging]." [111] Harsh Sunday legislation was also enacted by King Knud (died 1035) in Denmark, where Christianity had now triumphed.

Sunday as the Christian Substitute for the Sabbath

From a theological standpoint, it is interesting to compare a few passages on the Sabbath from the Carolingian period: chapter 51 in the *Education of the Clergy* (819) by Rabanus Maurus, the learned abbot of Fulda; canon 50 of the Synod of Paris (829); Theodulf of Orleans' *Capitula;* and chapter 26 of the *Capitula* of Rudolf of Bourges, which reveals clearly Theodulf's influence.[112] This will help us to evaluate some of the changes that took place between Isidore's time and that of Rabanus.

All these writings ground the origin of Sunday in the resurrection of Christ; all justify its keeping by the tradition or the custom of the apostles, although the canon of the Parisian synod reveals some doubt concerning this by saying *"ut creditur"* ("as generally believed"), and by adding, "but very certainly by the authority of the church." All four documents bolster the claims of Sunday sacredness by references to essentially the same Sunday hallowings (the creation of light, the resurrection of Christ, the coming of the Holy Spirit, and the gift of the manna). All four urge cessation from secular activities, and they insist on the superiority of the Christian institution over the Jewish one. Although the references to Sunday hallowings are taken from Isidore, the urging to stop secular activities on that day is new. Of special interest is that for the first time we begin to sense a clear consciousness of a substitution of Sunday for Sabbath—a change justified by the authority of tradition rather than scriptural command.

Beyond these essential agreements, we discover some interesting differences of emphasis. The passage in Rabanus, copied verbatim from Isidore, presents the main ideas of the patristic Sundaykeeping, the importance of spiritual rest, the glory of the first day that is also the eighth day, and the radical difference between the sinful idleness of the Jews and the festal spirit of the Christian day.

The canon of the Synod of Paris is preoccupied with the general desecration of the Lord's day. It is clearly a pastoral utterance that uses both religion and superstition, containing especially numerous stories of miraculous punishments of Sunday desecrators. It appeals to all priests, rulers, and lay people to show reverence for the Lord's day.

We find a strong Sabbatizing spirit in the passages of Theodulf of Orleans and Rudolf of Bourges. Theodulf provides for some travel or navigation on the Lord's day if it does not interfere with church attendance. Rudolf expands that to a long list of twenty-five specific Sabbath activities on the farm or in the home that are totally prohibited on Sunday. Both authors emphasize that the day must be spent in holy activities with family and friends.

The ecclesiastical origin of Sunday is unequivocally stated by Henry of Auxerre (died *c.* 880): "The Sabbath day was held very sacred and solemn indeed by the ancient ritual; all work stopped and all devoted themselves to prayer and to meals. That observation has been transferred most fittingly by Christian custom to Sunday because of reverence for the resurrection of the Lord." [113]

Sunset-to-Sunset Celebration of Sunday

During the Carolingian period there was also a strong effort to enforce a sunset-to-sunset keeping of Sunday. The Synod of Frioul (796 or 797), presided over by the patriarch of Aquileia, the friend and the theological adviser of Charlemagne, specified in canon 13 that the Lord's day began at nightfall.[114] At the Synod of Rouen, held in the middle of the ninth century, it was stated very clearly that holy days had to be celebrated from evening until evening.[115] Practically the same wording is found in the famous *Sermo Synodalis*, about whose authorship there is much debate but which appears to date from the middle of the ninth century: "Let the priest teach that Sundays and other holidays must be celebrated from evening until evening."[116] In the homily of Rabanus Maurus already cited, we read, "Let us keep the Day of the Lord and let us hallow it, as the lawgiver formerly commanded of the Sabbath day: 'From evening unto evening shall ye keep the Sabbath.' Let us therefore be careful that our rest shall not be vain, but from Sabbath evening unto Sunday evening let us stay away from our work in the fields and from all business and let us devote ourselves to divine worship."[117]

It is to that practice of Saturday vespers that we owe a beautiful Christian hymn, *Hymn for Saturday Vespers*, by Peter Abelard, the famous scholastic doctor:

O what their joy and their glory must be,
Those endless Sabbaths the blessed ones see!
Crown for the valiant; to weary ones rest;
God shall be all, and in all ever blest.

What are the Monarch, his court, and his throne?
What are the peace and the joy that they own?
Tell us, ye blest ones, that in it have share,
If what ye feel ye can fully declare.

Truly "Jerusalem" name we that shore,
"Vision of peace," that brings joy evermore!
Wish and fulfillment can severed be ne'er,
Nor the thing prayed for come short of the prayer.

We, where no trouble distraction can bring,
Safely the anthems of Zion shall sing;
While for thy grace, Lord, their voices of praise
Thy blessed people shall evermore raise.

There dawns no Sabbath, no Sabbath is o'er,
Those Sabbathkeepers have one and no more;
One and unending is that triumph song
Which to the angels and us shall belong.

Now in the meanwhile, with hearts raised on high,
We for that country must yearn and must sigh,
Seeking Jerusalem, dear native land,
Through our long exile on Babylon's strand.

Low before Him with our praises we fall,
Of whom, and in whom, and through whom are all;
Of whom, the Father; and through whom, the Son;
In whom, the Spirit, with these ever One.

Sunday an Ecclesiastical Institution

By the twelfth century, Sunday had become quite fully the church substitute for the seventh day. The rest began at sunset and lasted until the next sunset. All secular work was strictly prohibited under stern ecclesiastical and civil penalties, for nothing except very stringent necessity was allowed to interfere with church attendance (though dispensations could be granted by ecclesiastical authority). This concept of Sundaykeeping was spelled out clearly by the great decretalists. In his collection of 1234, Gregory IX, for instance, collated a decree from the Synod of Mayence from the early part of the ninth century and a letter from Pope Alexander III to the Archbishop of Trondheim in Norway teaching how Sunday must be kept. Although those were local documents, they acquired a much greater authority when they were included in a major canonic collection.

The lines that follow from the canon law summarize the final stage of Sundaykeeping in the Middle Ages: "We command that all Sundays must be observed with the greatest veneration from sunset until sunset and that all must abstain from any unlawful work.... Although the seventh day has been devoted in a very special way to human rest by the pages of the Old and the New Testaments and the church has commanded to observe it and the days devoted to the Supreme Majesty as well as the birthdays of the holy martyrs by refraining from all secular work, we to whom has been entrusted the rule of the church by the ruler of all must make for the faithful a fair application to those things which necessity requires. Thus, the Apostolic See comes with its usual mercy to the relief of those who do not look for an excuse for servile works, that is to say, sinful works, but for the possibility to provide the necessities of food and garment. Knowing by the reports of many that your region does not abound in fruits and that the sea which traditionally provided your people with much of their food has been less generous than usual, by Peter's and our own authority we grant that except on the great feasts of the years, your parishioners may devote themselves to fishing on Sundays or other holidays, when the herrings come toward the land because of the urgent necessity of the catch of those fish. This is granted, however, with the requirement that a fair portion of the catch be given to nearby churches and to the poor of the Lord."[118]

The theology of the medieval Christian Sunday received its final elaboration in the works of the great scholastic theologians of the thirteenth century. The change from the seventh to the first day was authorized by making the Sabbath a Jewish ceremony and the fourth commandment a ceremonial law. This, however, raised the problem of a ceremonial command in the midst of the moral law. It was Alexander of Hales (died 1245) who attempted to solve that problem by finding the common ground of Sabbath and Sunday in natural law. Although man should be free for communion with God at all times (since he is His creature), this is impossible because of temporal necessities. Thus God claims a specific amount of time. God in the law of Sinai appointed the seventh day, and the church chose the day of the Lord's resurrection. The command to rest is a command of nature, hence a moral command that all Christians must obey, while the seventh day was a Jewish and a ceremonial law that is no longer binding upon Christians.[119]

This new approach to the fourth commandment reflects a deep change in Christian thought that marks what has been called the second feudal age. Through the Crusades, the increase of trade, the discovery of Aristotle, and the study of Roman law spurred by the long struggle between papacy and empire, the horizon of medieval man was greatly broadened. A new approach to knowledge was developed, based on trust in the rational capacity of man to discover the secrets of the universe. The world is a world of order, ruled by secondary natural cause, ordained by the great first cause, God. This order is the *lex aeterna* that can be discovered in all branches of learning. Through reason pagans, Moslems, and Christians can equally well discover that divine order in the moral makeup of man. It is that natural law that provides the foundation for all moral systems, all judicial codes, all social institutions. That natural law is the essence of the Decalogue, and therefore, of the Sabbath commandment.[120] Sunday is the practical application, the positive Christian interpretation, of the natural duty to have communion with God, which is recognized by all men.

Thus, we have now arrived at the concept of Sunday as a purely ecclesiastical institution. It is a cultic institution primarily, and the church may determine what is permissible and what may not be done on that day. Thomas Aquinas expressed that thought very clearly:

"In the New Law the keeping of the Sunday supplants that of the Sabbath, not in virtue of the precept of the law, but through determination by the church and the custom of the Christian people. Furthermore this practice does not stand as a figure as did that of the Sabbath in the Old Law, and so the prohibition of work on Sunday is not as strict as it was on the sabbath; some works are allowed on Sunday which were forbidden on the sabbath, cooking and the like, for example. Even with regard to works that are forbidden, dispensation by reason of necessity is easier in the New Law than in the Old Law, the reason being that a figure belongs to the proclaiming of a truth, no detail of which may be set aside. But observances considered absolutely can be changed according to circumstances of time and place." [121]

Thomas is preoccupied with the problem of either why what appears to be a ceremonial command is included in the Decalogue or why God did not enunciate also other prescriptions concerning worship such as prayer and devotion. He answers: "Taken in its literal sense the commandment to keep the sabbath is partly moral, partly ceremonial. It is moral in that man should set aside some time in his life for concentration upon the things of God. For man is connaturally predisposed to set aside a portion of his time for every affair of necessity—for bodily refreshment, for example. . . . Wherefore it is in accord with a dictate of natural reason that a man reserve some time for spiritual nourishment. . . . But it is a ceremonial precept on the grounds that in this commandment a particular time is determined in order to signify creation. It is also ceremonial in its allegorical sense, i.e., as it was a sign of Christ's repose in the tomb on the seventh day; likewise in its moral sense, i.e., as symbolizing desisting from every act of sin and resting in God; in this sense, too, it is in a way a general precept. It is also ceremonial in its anagogical sense, i.e., as it prefigures rest in the enjoyment of God in heaven." [122]

In Thomas, Augustine's ideas had become joined with the subsequent development of Sunday observance. The spiritual value of Sabbath was linked with the absolute requirement of rest for the worshiper. By the use of the typically medieval "four-senses" interpretation of Scriptures, the literal historical meaning of the fourth commandment was replaced by the allegorical, the moral, and the anagogical meanings.[123] Sabbath, it was asserted, should lead the Christian to think of Christ's rest in the tomb, of the moral duty to desist from sin, and of the future blessedness in heaven. The bond with Creation had been totally lost.

By his distinction between the way Mosaic judicial and ceremonial commands had become void, Thomas made the literal keeping of the Sabbath commandment a very grievous sin. The judicial provisions are dead, he claimed, but not deadly. A ruler could very properly revive them in his territories. Ceremonial prescriptions, on the other hand, are dead and deadly for those who keep them after Christ has come, for they are a rejection of Christ's sacrifice on the cross.[124]

It is interesting to observe that this new theological understanding of Sunday was soon reflected in Jewish-Christian controversies over the Sabbath commandment. In his *Scrutinium Scripturarum,* one of the most comprehensive and learned manuals of Christian apologetics against the Jews, Paul of Burgos (1350-1435), a converted Jewish rabbi, justifies the Christian discarding of the Sabbath rest by reasoning that the Sabbath's being a moral command, it is not tied to any day of the week. Since the original Sabbath was just as much a sign of redemption and freedom as a memorial of Creation, he indicates, it is perfectly proper for Christians to commemorate the great redemption that they find in Jesus.[125]

With Sunday considered as an ecclesiastical institution, it was up to the church to define the proper way of keeping it; and the last step in the medieval theological development of Sunday was made by the casuists, among whom were Raymond de Pennefort (died 1275) and Guillaume de Rennes (13th century). Such casuists attempted to define for the faithful what were mortal and what were venial sins in the transgression of Sunday. What, for instance, if a person should go to a market on Sunday? This was not a mortal sin if it was not done regularly or if one went to take care of necessities. It was a mortal sin if one went because of greed or if the market had been forbidden by the bishop. Another example of a mortal sin was for students to write their lessons on Sunday unless they could not learn otherwise.[126]

Such casuistry—this effort to classify and distinguish what is right and wrong—is reflected in John Huss's commentaries on the fourth commandment.[127] As he does with all the other commands, Huss considers the Sabbath precept from three different perspectives. First he shows the general significance of the day of rest, then he presents its special meaning, and finally he concludes with a discussion of its deepest value.

The Sabbath command of the Decalogue urges us first to remember, and Huss hastens to show how vital it is to do so. A woman, he tells us, who forgot and joined a procession on a day when she had had sexual relations with her husband was publicly dragged and tormented by the devil. He proceeds to warn us that drunks and dancers run a great risk of transgressing that command, and with the casuist's skill he defines for us when drunkenness and dancing on Sundays are sins and when they are not. Then he takes us to a higher level, the sanctification of the day of rest. He does so negatively, by pointing out how the command can be broken in four different ways: by manual work, attending markets, seeking secular pleasure, and pleading in justice. He provides a list of works that can be justified on the day of the Lord.

The third level is the most meaningful to Huss. The command, he declares, tells us to contemplate the spiritual realities, an experience that brings three goods to the contemplator: spiritual seeds, which normally would be crushed by the daily routine, germinate and bloom; secular thoughts become totally insipid and worthless; and the hard flesh that holds us captive melts away in the light of Him who is the true Sabbath.

As Sunday became an ecclesiastical institution, its significance as the feast of the Resurrection was blurred. Instead, each Sunday was individualized and dedicated to some particular feast, most commonly with the Trinity.[128] On the other hand, Saturday became the day of the virgin Mary[129] Peter Damian endorsed warmly the dedication of Saturday to Mary.[130] At the Council of Clermont in 1095 it was decreed that all Christians should "recite the office of the Blessed Virgin every Sabbath day."[131] Because the relationship with the Old Testament was lost, the sunset-to-sunset observance was slowly discarded. In the fifteenth century Nicholas Siculus (died 1445) expressed the view that all weekly holidays should begin at sunset except Sunday, lest the people might Judaize.[132] Beginning Sunday at midnight became general in the sixteenth century.[133]

The Saturday Sabbath

What was the fate of the Sabbath as a day of rest during the late Middle Ages? In some documents there are references to the *insabbati*, a popular name for the Waldenses, which some have taken as evidence that they were a Sabbathkeeping sect.[134] This interpretation appears to be incorrect as far as the sect in general is concerned. The documents reveal what the main grievances against those people were. They took the "conversatio apostolica" very seriously. They believed that

Jesus commanded His followers to give up their possessions and to go to preach the gospel. When ecclesiastical authorities denied them the right of preaching the gospel, they felt it was a matter of obeying God rather than men, and they defied the church.

In his attack against the Waldenses, Alan of Lille says: "They are called Waldenses after their heresiarch, who was named Waldes. He, by the prompting of his own spirit, not sent by God, invented a new sect in that, without the authority from a prelate, without divine inspiration, without knowledge, without learning, he presumed to preach; a philosopher without thought, a prophet without vision, an apostle without a mission, a teacher without a tutor. . . . [His followers] dare to preach to fill their bellies rather than their minds and, because they do not wish to work with their own hands to obtain food, they make the evil choice of living without employment, preaching falsities so that they may buy food." [135]

Alan added the grievance that women were allowed to preach also: "These persons resist the Apostle in that they have women with them and have them preach in the gatherings of the faithful, although the Apostle says in the first epistle to the Corinthians, 'Let women keep silence in the churches.'" [136]

Undaunted by the papal order to stop such practices, the Waldenses went into clandestinity and spread their ideas under the garb of pilgrims, cobblers, barbers, harvesters, et cetera.[137] The Waldenses' major crime, in the eyes of their contemporaries, was insubordination. Sabbathkeeping was not an issue. Ebrard of Bethune in his *Liber Antiheresis* indicates that they were in agreement with the church on the reading of the gospels, respect for Sunday, and the practice of fasting and prayer.[138]

In his description of the Waldenses, Peter of Vaux-de-Cernay adds a detail that clarifies the name *insabbati:* "But to pass over many points of their unbelief, their error consisted chiefly in four things: to wit, in the wearing of sandals after the apostles; in their refusal, under any circumstances, to swear an oath; [their refusal] to take life; and in their claim that any one of them in case of necessity, so long as he is a sandal wearer, may perform the sacrament of the Eucharist, even though he may not have been ordained by a bishop." [139]

The Latin word for *sandal* is *sabbatum,* the root of the Spanish *zapato* and the French *sabot.* The sandals were an outward sign of their being imitators of the apostles in living the *vita apostolica* and the justification of their preaching the gospel. The wearing of the sandals seems to have indicated a certain standing in the sect, as is also shown by Anselm of Alessandria: "Also the sandal-wearers among them, whom they call priests, carry only one cloak and either go barefooted or wear shoes or sandals cut away at the top." [140]

In view of the foregoing, one can understand why Pope Innocent III wrote to Durand of Huesca, who had recanted his Waldensian faith, that he should stop wearing sandals: "Therefore, we admonish, we advise, we exhort those of you who have not yet adopted this fashion or those who shall be associated with you in the future not to bind themselves to the custom of wearing sandals open at the top nor to wear such footgear, so that thus the scandal may entirely disappear." [141]

The Sabbath was not totally forgotten as a day of rest, however, and it is interesting to note that instances of Sabbathkeeping occur where the Waldenses had preached with the greatest success. In northern Italy we find the sect of the Passagini in the twelfth and the thirteenth centuries.[142] Their beliefs are described and attacked in the *Summa contra Haereticos*, the authorship of which is often attributed to Praepositinus of Cremona.[143] While the Waldenses took Jesus as their sole authority and emphasized the Sermon on the Mount, the Passagini attempted to uphold the whole of the Old and the New Testaments. For that reason they observed the Mosaic precepts, even circumcision and the distinction of clean and unclean meats. Because the Sabbath was instituted long before the Law was proclaimed on Sinai, they observed that day as their day of rest and worship.[144]

In northern France, the secret meetings of a group of Sabbathkeepers were denounced to the authorities in 1420.[145] Sixteen or eighteen persons of Douai were arrested with the preacher, a man from the nearby town of Valenciennes, and judged by the tribunal of the Inquisition for denying that the Father, the Son, and the Holy Ghost are one Person; for disrespect of the sacraments; for denial of the perpetual virginity of Mary; for keeping Saturday as their Sabbath; and for stating that the masses for the dead have no value whatsoever. The second folio of that collection of judgments of heresy records the death of a priest, Hennequin of Langle, "for keeping his Sabbath on Saturday and other reasons." On the last folio we are told that the preacher of the group, Bertoul Thurin, was executed "for keeping Saturday as his Sabbath."

Was there any relationship between those people and the Bohemian "Picards" mentioned in several late medieval and Reformation era documents?[146] According to the *Summarium impiae et pharisaicae picardorum religionis*, some of them were Sabbathkeepers. While their real place within the heresies of the late Middle Ages has not been fully determined, it is clear that they stood very close to the Waldenses, whose thirst for the *conversation evangelica* they shared.[147] According to the accounts of their opponents, they showed little respect for church authority, explained the gospel at private meetings, and gave the sacraments very differently from the Catholics. They condemned prayers for the dead and the teaching of purgatory, and they scoffed at processions and other traditional rituals. The *Summarium* explains also that they omitted the festivities in honor of Mary and the saints, keeping Sunday only. In fact, it added, "some celebrate Sabbath with the Jews."[148] They may well be the "new kind of Jews" to whom Erasmus alluded in his *De Amabili ecclesiae concordia* in 1533.[149]

In England the Lollards also insisted on the right of lay people to possess and preach the Word.[150] They were followers of John Wycliffe, who proclaimed the supreme authority of Scriptures, far above that of popes, Church Fathers, or councils. His translation of the Bible into the vernacular, opening the sacred writings to the common people, was considered as a form of blasphemy by the clergy.[151] The Lollards did not manifest the greatest veneration for Sunday. Sir Lewis Clifford, a former sympathizer of theirs, gave a report to Archbishop Arundel that "they did not hold any day as hallowed or holy, not even Sunday, but that every day they were equally free to work, to eat and to drink."[152] We even have a record of the recantation in October, 1402, of a man who had already abjured several heresies but still maintained that the Sabbath of the Old Testament was to be observed until good reason should be shown him to the contrary.[153]

Sabbathkeepers were reported in the Scandinavian lands at that time. In Norway Bishop Aslak Bolt, in the year 1435, called together a provincial council at Bergen, in order to put a stop to "Saturday observance," which, he said, was being practiced in a number of places in the land.[154] Bishop Bang, a Danish prelate, believed that the revival of Sabbathkeeping may have been a result of the wording of the two first catechisms written in Nordic countries. In one of them the commandment was worded: Remember to keep the seventh day holy," and in the other, "Do not forget to keep the seventh day holy."[155]

There arose a strong Judaizing movement at Novgorod in Russia. The origin of that group is commonly attributed to the teachings of Lithuanian Jews between 1470 and 1475. Because of their importance in political and economic circles, there was a large degree of tolerance for the Jews in Muscovy. Those Judaizers questioned the Trinity, the efficacy of the sacraments, and the authority of the writings of the early Church Fathers. On the other hand, they asserted the primacy of the Mosaic law, the singleness of the Godhead, and the sanctity of the Sabbath. These assertions brought about a series of harsh persecutions by the Orthodox Church and the end of the era of toleration for the Jews in that region.[156]

Conclusion

As we conclude this chapter, we may say that the history of the Sabbath and the Lord's day during the Middle Ages is extremely interesting and significant. We see the evolution of the Lord's day from a spiritual rest, totally independent of the Mosaic precept, to a day of physical rest defined completely in terms of the Old Testament. Sunday, a day that in the beginning had relatively little importance, became an ecclesiastical institution protected by religious and civil sanctions. To that degree the "Sabbatical rest" survived during the Middle Ages. But also, all throughout that period there were groups of people who, either through the example of the Jews or because of their study of the Scriptures, attempted to keep the day that Jesus and the apostles had kept. For obvious reasons we know little about their number or their names, but their presence shows that in every age there were some who attempted to place the Word of God above the traditions of men.

NOTES

[1] *Tractate on the Gospel of John* 20 (*NPNF*/1 7:132-133).
[2] *Exposition of the Orthodox Faith* 4. 23 (*NPNF*/2 9:96).
[3] Quoted in A. Lukyns Williams, *Adversus Judaeos: A Bird's Eyeview of Christian Apologiae until the Renaissance* (Cambridge, 1935), p. 291.
[4] 22. 30 (*NPNF*/1 2:511). On the eighth day, see H. Dumaine, "Dimanche," *DACL* 4/1:879-884; J. Daniélou, *Bible et Liturgie* (Paris, 1958), pp. 349-354; J. Gaillard, "Dimanche," *Dictionnaire de la spiritualité* (1957), 3:952-959; S. Bacchiocchi, *From Sabbath to Sunday* (Rome, 1977), pp. 278-300.
[5] *Moralium libri* 25. 8 (*PL* 76:759).
[6] *De ecclesiasticis officiis* 1. 25. 3.
[7] 6. 18 (*PL* 82:250, 251); on the medieval use of Isidore of Seville's Sunday statement, see P. Heylyn, *History of the Sabbath*, 2d ed. (London, 1636), 2:137-142.
[8] *Serm.* 9. 3 (*Corpus Christianorum* 41:110). The "shamelessly" refers probably to barefooted dancing.
[9] Joseph Jungmann, "Die Heiligung des Sonntags im frühchristentum und im Mittelalter," in *Der Tag des Herrn* (Vienna, 1958), p. 62.
[10] *Epist.* 108. 20 (*CSEL* 55:335).
[11] "Idleness is an enemy of the soul. Because this is so, the brethren ought to be occupied at specified times in manual labour, and at other fixed hours in holy reading. . . . On Sunday also, all, save those who are assigned to various offices, shall have time for reading. If, however, any one be so negligent or so slothful as to be unwilling or unable to read or meditate, he must have some work given him, so as not to be idle. For weak brethren, or those of delicate constitutions, some work or craft shall be found to keep them from idleness, and yet not such as to crush them by the heavy labour or to drive them away."—Rule 48 in Marshall Baldwin, ed., *Christianity Through the Thirteenth Century* (New York, 1970), pp. 90, 91. The great opposition of the medieval church to idleness, as one of the major vices, colored significantly the attitude toward the Sabbatic rest.
[12] ("If only Christians when they do not go to church on that day would do something useful and not dance! It

THE SABBATH AND LORD'S DAY DURING THE MIDDLE AGES

would be much better for a man to do some gardening, to go for a trip, and for the woman to use her distaff and not, as they say, to jump around and dance and sprain limbs created by God and shout loudly one's longing for lust by cheap songs!")—*Epist. . . . Contra eos qui credebant epistolas de caelo cecidisse*, R. Priebsch, ed., in *Letter from Heaven on the Observance of the Lord's Day* (Oxford, 1936), p. 2.

[13] Canon 28 (*MGH Concilia* 1:82), trans. in J. N. Andrews and L. R. Conradi, *History of the Sabbath* (Washington, D.C., 1912), p. 485.

[14] "We, therefore, accept spiritually and hold spiritually this which is written about the Sabbath. For the Sabbath means rest. But we have the true Sabbath in our Redeemer Himself. . . . We introduce, then, no burden through the gates on the Sabbath day if we draw no weights of sin brought to my knowledge; namely, that it has been preached to you by perverse men that no one ought to wash on the Lord's day. And indeed if any one craves to wash for luxury and pleasure, neither on any other day do we allow this to be done."—*Epist*. 13. 1 (*PL* 77:1253, 1254).

[15] *Epist. ad Januarium* 55. 23 (*NPNF*/1 1:310).

[16] This was the general attitude toward Jewish laws. "In general we can say of the first centuries that on the whole Christianity did not feel attracted towards Mosaic law."—P. J. Verdam, *Mosaic Law in Practice and Study throughout the Ages* (Kampen, 1959), p. 18.

[17] See K. Strand, *The Early Christian Sabbath: Selected Essays and a Source Collection* (Worthington, Ohio, 1979); idem, "Some Notes on the Sabbath Fast in Early Christianity," *AUSS* 3 (1965):171-173; F. Cabrol, "Jeûnes," *DACL* 7/2:2498; Bacchiocchi, *op. cit.*, pp. 185-198.

[18] Macrobius *Saturnalia* 1. 16. 11 (trans. Bornecque [Paris (n.d.)], 1:153-155); Dumaine, *op. cit.*, pp. 947, 948. E. Dublanchy, "Dimanche," *Dictionnaire de théologie catholique* (Paris, 1911), 4/1:1311, 1312; Biondi Biondi, *Il diritto romano cristiano* (Milan, 1952), 2:162-167.

[19] See note 16.

[20] "On the Lord's day, however, there should be a cessation of earthly labor (*a labore terreno cessandum est*), and attention given in every way to prayers, so that if anything is done negligently during the six days, it may be expiated by supplications on the day of the Lord's resurrection."—*Epist*. 13. 1, note (*PL* 77:1254, 1255).

[21] *Ibid.*, 9. 1 (*PL* 77:939).

[22] In his article "Christ (lettre du) tombée du ciel" (*DACL* 3/1:1534-1546), E. Renoir gives an excellent survey of our knowledge of the manuscripts and the whereabouts of that letter both in Eastern and Western Christianity. The letter had an immense success in the East. There are Greek, Armenian, Syriac, Arabic, and Ethiopic translations of the letter. Different texts of the letter can be found in Etienne Baluze, *Capitularia regum francorum* (Paris, 1780), 2:1369-1399); Johann A. Febricius, *Codex Apocryphi Novi Testamenti* (Hamburg, 1719), pp. 310-314; Priebsch, *op. cit.*, pp. 36-39; and J. G. O'Keefe, "Cain Domnaig: I, The Epistle Concerning Sunday," *Eriu*, 2 (1905):189-211, who gives the text of an Irish version. English translations of the letter are provided in O'Keefe's article, in Andrews and Conradi, *op. cit.*, p. 497, and in C. Mervyn Maxwell's "Collection of Papers for the Class on History of Sabbath and Sunday" (Andrews University, 1978), pp. 478-481. See also J. Michl, "Briefe, apocryphe," *Lexikon für Theologie und Kirche*, 2d ed. (1958), 2:689; R. Kottje, *Studien zum Einfluss des Alten Testamentes auf Recht und Liturgie des frühen Mittelalters* (6-8 Jahrhundert), (Bonn, 1964), pp. 52-56; A. de Santos Otero, "Der apocryphe sogennante Sonntagsbrief," *Studia Patristica* (Berlin, 1961), 3:290-296. The text of Licinianus' letter to Valentinius is found in *PL* 72:699-700. On that letter, see more particularly J. Madoz, *Liciniano de Cartagena y sus cartas*, Estudios onienses, 1/4 (Madrid, 1948). Renoir tends to accept C. Schmidt's belief in an Eastern origin of the letter. "Fragment einer Schrift des Martyrer Bishofs Petrus von Alexandrien," *Texte und Untersuchungen* (Berlin, 1920), 20:4-46. Priebsch is quite critical of that view. He believes (p. 33) that Baluze's text lies quite close to the text considered at the Synod of Rome in 745. Kottje claims that the text included in the Irish *Cain Domnaig*, which can be dated from the beginning of the eighth century, may well be our earliest Latin text (p. 54).

[23] I quote from Maxwell's translation.

[24] Maxwell, *op. cit.*, pp. 458, 461.

[25] "de hora nona usque lucescente die lune feriatis," manuscripts *L* and *V*, Priebsch, *op. cit.*, pp. 7, 8.

[26] Heylyn, *op. cit.*, pp. 115, 116. Priebsch (passim) shows that the Sabbatizing of Sunday went from West to East, from the Visigothic realms to the Franks and on.

[27] *Epist*. 13. 3 (*PL* 77:1253, 1254; *NPNF*/2 13:92, 93).

[28] 7. 21 (*Didascalia et constitutiones apostolorum*, ed. by F. X. Funk [Paderborn, 1905], p. 409; *ANF* 7:469).

[29] *De castigatione* (*PG* 46:310).

[30] *De coenobiorum institutis* 3. 2 (*CSEL* 17:34); cf. 3. 9 (*CSEL* 17:43, 44). Cassian adds concerning the Saturday-night and Sunday-night vigils, "We are charged to give both days—that is, to the seventh and the eighth equally—the same share of service, as it says, 'Give a portion to the seventh and the eighth equally,' Ecc. 11:2." The author adds, however, "This dispensation from fasting must not be understood as a participation in Jewish festivals by those above all who are shown to be free from all Jewish superstitions."

[31] *Epist*. 54. 2 (*CSEL* 24/2:160; *Fathers of the Church* 12:253).

[32] *De semente* (*PG* 23:144).

[33] *Ecclesiastical History* 5. 22 (*PG* 67:635; *NPNF*/2 2:132). Sozomen states also in his history: "The people of Constantinople and several other cities assemble together on the Sabbath, as well as on the next day, which custom is never observed at Rome or at Alexandria."—*Hist. eccles*. 7. 19 (*PG* 67:1478). See Marcel Simon, *Verus Israel* (Paris, 1964), pp. 374-376.

[34] W. T. Skene (*Celtic Scotland* [Edinburgh, 1876], 2:349, 350) asserted that the Celtic Church kept the seventh day, and his assertion was repeated by many later writers. G. A. Keough studied the evidence used by Skene and showed that it was a misunderstanding of the texts. ("An Inquiry into the Days of the Week Observed as Holy Days by the Celtic Church" [M.A. thesis, SDA Theological Seminary, 1946], pp. 84-88). In his *Celtic Church in Britain* (London, 1972), Leslie Hardinge presents limited evidence for some recognition of the seventh day in the Celtic Church.

[35] *Adomnan's Life of Columba*, ed. by A. O. Anderson and M. O. Anderson (London, 1961), p. 523.

[36] *Ibid.*, pp. 501, 519.

[37] *Sancti Columbani Opera*, ed. by G. S. M. Walker (Dublin, 1957), p. 181; cf. p. 159.

[38] *Second Life of St. David* in *Lives of Saints from the Book of Lismore*, ed. by W. Stokes (Oxford, 1890), p. 430.

[39] See note 30.

[40] *Life of Brendon of Clonfert* in *Vitae Sanctorum Hiberniae*, ed. by Ch. Plummer (Oxford, 1910), 1:117; *Book of St. David* in *Councils and Ecclesiastical Documents Relating to Great Britain and Ireland*, ed. by A. W. Haddan and William Stubbs, 3 vols. (Oxford, 1869-1878), 1:113. There were also stories of release from the pains of hell on Saturday.

THE SABBATH IN SCRIPTURE AND HISTORY

Tripartite Life of St. Patrick, ed. by W. Stokes, 2 vols. (London, 1887), 1:117. Dom Louis Gougaud states that "in the Celtic churches Saturday bore something of a festive character, which was expressed by greater length and solemnity in the liturgy and also in the monasteries by a less rigorous diet."—*Christianity in Celtic Lands* (London, 1932), p. 323. Cf. W. Phillipp, ed., *History of the Church of Ireland* (London, 1933).
   [41] *Ancient Laws of Ireland*, ed. by W. N. Hancock and others (Dublin, 1865-1901), 3:41.
   [42] *Columbani opera*, p. 203. On the text itself, see Hardinge, *op. cit.*, p. 83.
   [43] *Muirchu's Latin Life of Patrick*, in the *Book of Armagh*, 1. 25; 2. 3, quoted in Hardinge, *op. cit.*, pp. 79, 80.
   [44] *Adomnan's Life of Columba*, pp. 271, 535. The editors of that work conclude: "It seems to follow that the sabbatical Sunday had not yet been accepted by Adomnan or in Iona at the time when Adomnan wrote."—Page 29. They date the writing of *Adomnan's Life* between 688 and 692, about a century after the death of Columba (p. 96).
   [45] "La polémique anti-juive de Saint Jean Chrysostome et le mouvement judaïsant d'Antioche," in Marcel Simon, *Recherches d'histoire judéo-chrétienne* (Paris, 1962), p. 144.
   [46] *Hom.* 1 (PG 48:844). These homilies have been translated and studied by C. Mervyn Maxwell, "Chrysostom's Homilies against the Jews" (Ph.D. dissertation, University of Chicago, 1966), and also appear in *Discourses against Judaizing Christians*, trans. Paul W. Harkins (Washington, D.C., 1979).
   [47] *Hom.* 1 (PG 48:847).
   [48] *In Ezech.* 33:33 (PL 25:326). Cf. Augustine's *Epistle* 196. 4 *Ad Asellicum de cavendo judaismo* (PL 33:898, 899). Marcel Simon discusses the popularity of the seven-branched candlestick in early Christian art and sees there a manifestation of the attraction of Judaism. "Le chandelier à sept branches," *Recherches*, pp. 181-187.
   [49] *Quaest. adv. Jud., Praef.* in *Liber de variis quaestionibus*, ed. by P. A. C. Vega and A. E. Anspach (Escurial, 1940), quoted in B. Blumenkranz, *Juifs et chrétiens dans le monde occidental* (Paris, 1960), p. 62. Much of the information on medieval Judaizers is drawn from that work.
   [50] Julian of Toledo, *Insult. in tyr. gall.* 2 (PL 96:797).
   [51] The rubric of the law is *De iudaizantibus christianis*, *Leges Visigothorum* 12. 2. 16 *(MGH LL* 1:424).
   [52] *PL* 98:385. See also P. A. C. Vega, "Una herejia judaizante de principio del siglo viii en Espana," *Ciudad de Dios* 153 (1941): 57.
   [53] "Idle and resting on the Sabbath, they do not plow, harvest or do any usual work but celebrate and go banqueting, while their servants and cattle rest."—Card. Humbert of Montmoutier, *Adversus calumnias Graecorum*, 6 *(PL* 143:936); see Blumenkranz, *op. cit.*, pp. 172-175.
   [54] "It has reached the point where the ignorant Christians say that the Jews preach better to them than our priests."—Agobard *De insol. jud.* 5 (PL 104:74, 75). "So that they say that [the Jews] preach better than our priests—so that they sabbatize with them, they work on the Lord's day."—Aniolon *Lib. contra Iud.* 41 (PL 116:170). This matter is discussed in Blumenkranz, *op. cit.*, p. 58. On Spanish Judaizers, see Marcelino Menendez-Pelayo, *Historia de los heterodoxos españoles*, edicion national de las obras completas (Madrid, 1946), 2:462-478.
   [55] Pseudo-Bede *Quaest. super Deuter.* 6 (PL 93:411). Blumenkranz, *op. cit.*, p. 63. The same thing happened in the East, as the following passage illustrates. "In his folly he thinks thus: If Christianity is good, behold I am baptized as a Christian. But if Judaism is also useful, I will associate partly with Judaism that I might hold on to the Sabbath."—*The Disputation of Sergius the Stylite against a Jew*, 22. 15 (trans. by A. P. Hayman, *Corpus Scriptorum christianorum orientalium* 339, *Scriptores Syri* [Louvain, 1973], 153:77). See also p. 72.
   [56] *Exp. Ierem.* lib. 6, cap. 13 (PL 111:912).
   [57] See B. Blumenkranz, "A propos du (ou des) *Tractatus c. Iudaeos* de Fulbert de Chartres," *Revue du moyen age chrétien* 8 (1952):51-53.
   [58] Blumenkranz, *Juifs et chrétiens*, p. 63; cf. p. 243.
   [59] Mansi 13:852. The condemnation of the literal Sabbathkeeping at the Council of Les Estinnes may well stem from the same problem. *Ibid.*, 12:378.
   [60] *Epist.* 97 (99).10 (PL 119:984). In his answer the pope relied heavily upon Gregory's epistle.
   [61] Karl Hefele, *Histoire des conciles*, trans. H. Leclercq (Paris, 1907-), 3/2:1224. "For it is not proper for Christians to Judaize and be idle on the Sabbath but they should rather work on that day, giving greater veneration to Sunday if they want to rest, as Christians do."
   [62] See Blumenkranz, *Juifs et chrétiens*, p. 176, n. 66, for several instances.
   [63] See R. L. Odom, "The Sabbath in the Great Schism of 1054," *AUSS* 1 (1963):74-80.
   [64] Cf. Leo IX, *Epist.* 103 *(PL* 143:777-781).
   [65] Card. Humbert of Montmoutier, *op. cit. (PL* 143:936, 937).
   [66] *Epist.* 1. 24 *(PG* 120:778).
   [67] Johan Chydenius, *Medieval Institutions and the Old Testament* (Helsinki, 1965), p. 37. Cf. C. F. Atchley, *A History of the Use of Incense in Divine Worship* (London, 1909), pp. 160, 161; Kottje, *op. cit.*, pp. 11, 12.
   [68] *The Bobbio Missal* 559, ed. by E. A. Lowe. (London, 1917-1924), 2:170. The analogy between Easter and the Passover had been carefully drawn by Isidore of Seville. *De eccl. off.* 1 *(PL* 83:776).
   [69] In a letter, Pope Stephen II writes to Peppin: "What else can I call you but New Moses and splendid King David?"—*MGH Ep* 3:505; his successor Paul also called Peppin "New Moses and new David," *MGH Ep* 3:552; see Chydenius, *op. cit.*, p. 48.
   [70] See E. Kantorowicz, *The King's Two Bodies* (Princeton, N.J., 1957), p. 77; K. F. Morrison, *The Two Kingdoms: Ecclesiology in Carolingian Political Thought* (Princeton, N.J., 1964), p. 26, n. 1; W. Ullmann, "The Bible and Principles of Government in the Middle Ages," in *La Bibbia nell'alto medioevo* (Spoleto, 1963), pp. 188-196; Percy E. Schram, "Das Alte und das Neue Testament in der Staatslehre und Staatssymbolik des Mittelalters," in *ibid.*, pp. 229-255.
   [71] Verdam, *op. cit.*, p. 19.
   [72] *Serm* 135, in C. Morin, *Etudes, textes et découvertes*, Anecdota maredsolana 3/2 (Maredsous, 1897). On the problems of the authorship of the sermons of Caesarius, see Dumaine, *op. cit.*, p. 940, n. 6.
   [73] *De correctione rusticorum*, in *Martini episcopi Bracarensis opera omnia*, ed. by C. W. von Barlow (London, 1950), pp. 202, 203.
   [74] Jean Chélini, "La pratique dominicale dans l'église franque," *Revue d'histoire de l'église de France* 42 (1956):165.
   [75] *Ibid.*, p. 173.
   [76] *Ser.* 5 *(PL* 89:854); Ser. 15 *(PL* 89:870).
   [77] Penitential, art. 35 *(PL* 89:410).
   [78] See M.-D. Chenu, *Nature, Man and Society in the Twelfth Century*, sel. and trans. by J. Taylor and L. K. Little (Chicago, 1968), p. 160.

[79] Canon 1 *(MGH Conc.* 1:165, 166).
[80] Canon 4 *(Mansi* 9:1015).
[81] *MGH Cap.* 1:11, 12.
[82] *Ibid.,* 17.
[83] *Lib. Histor.* 10, 30 *(MGH SS* 1:525).
[84] *Lib. de virt. S. Iuliani* 11 *(MGH SS* 1:569).
[85] *Lib. de virt. S. Martini* 3. 3 *(MGH SS* 1:633).
[86] *Ibid.,* 3:39; 3:56 *(MGH SS* 1:633); *Liber Vitae patrum* 7. 5 *(MGH SS* 1:690).
[87] *Lib. de virt. S. Martini* 3. 7 *(MGH SS* 1:633).
[88] *Ibid.,* 3. 45 *(MGH SS* 1:643).
[89] *Ibid.,* 4. 45 *(MGH SS* 1:660).
[90] On those books, see G. LeBras, "Pénitentiels," *Dictionnaire de theologie catholique* 12/1:1160-1179; H. Leclercq, "Pénitentiels," *DACL* 14/1:215-251; C. Vogel, *Le pécheur et la pénitence au moyen age* (Paris, 1969).
[91] *PL* 97:181.
[92] *Lex Baiwariorum* 7. 3 *(MGH L* 5:350).
[93] *Leges alamannorum (MGH L* 5:98).
[94] *Lex Baiwariorum* 7. 4 *(MGH L* 5:350, 351).
[95] *MGH Conc.* 2/2:557.
[96] Quoted by G. Jecker, *Die Heimat des Hl. Pirmin, des Apostels der Alamannen* (Münster in Westfalen, 1927), p. 57. See J. Daniélou, "La typologie biblique traditionnelle dans la liturgie du moyen âge," in *La Bibbia nell'alto medioevo,* pp. 154-160; Robert McNally, "Dies dominica, Two Hiberno-Latin Texts," *Medieval Studies* 22 (1960):355-361; Dumaine, *op. cit.,* pp. 985-990.
[97] D. MacLean, *The Law of the Lord's Day in the Celtic Church* (Edinburgh, 1926), p. 16. Cf. Kottje, *op. cit.,* p. 52.
[98] A brief summary is found in Hardinge, *op. cit.,* pp. 208-216; See also P. Fournier, "Le *Liber ex lege Moysi,*" *Revue celtique* 30 (1909):221-234.
[99] Kottje, *op. cit.,* pp. 49-89; Hardinge, *op. cit.,* pp. 88, 89.
[100] MacLean, *op. cit.,* pp. 3-15; O'Keefe, *loc. cit.*
[101] O'Keefe, *op. cit.,* p. 193.
[102] *Ibid.,* pp. 201-203.
[103] See MacLean, *op. cit.,* pp. 6-9. Very similar ideas are found in the *Cain Domnaig,* the law of Sunday. Even Sunday washing, bathing, or shaving are strictly prohibited. Some dispensations are given in both documents. One may travel to go to Communion or to baptism, to see the sick and dying. One may run to arrest a thief or pursue a prisoner. For the sake of Christ one may prepare food for guests. A farmer may go to capture a swarm of bees and bring a bull to a cow. Cattle can be protected from the wolves. The law threatens the witness of Sunday desecrator who remains silent as much as the Sundaybreaker.
[104] *Mansi* 13:378.
[105] *Ibid.,* 12:399, 400.
[106] *Cap.* 78 *(MGH Cap.* 1:60).
[107] *Boniface's Epist.* 59 *(MGH Ep. sel.* 1:115, 116). These decisions did not put an end to the use of the *Letter from Heaven* in the West. In 1200 a certain Eustace from Normandy came to England to advocate Sunday rest. He read to the people a letter from heaven. See A. H. Lewis, *A Critical History of the Sabbath and the Sunday in the Christian Church* (Plainfield, N.J., 1905), pp. 182-184. He also spoke of pagan invasions of monstrous animals with heads of lions, hair of women, and tails of camels that would devour the desecrators of the holy days. Later in that century the flagellants struck the imagination of the common people by their self-inflicted lacerations and used a letter from heaven to call for hallowing the Lord's day. See Gordon Leff, *Heresy in the Later Middle Ages,* 2 vols. (Manchester, 1967), 2:485-488.
[108] *Cap.* 81 *(MGH Cap.* 1:61). See Rosamund M. Kitterick, *The Frankish Church and the Carolingian Reform, 789-895* (London, 1977).
[109] *Cap.* 46 *(MGH Cap.* 1:105); *Cap.* 11 *(MGH Cap.* 1:146); *Cap.* 13 *MGH Cap.* 1:152).
[110] *MGH Conc.* 2:252, 256, 270, 283, 292.
[111] *Mansi* 19:370, 371.
[112] Rhabanus Maurus *(PL* 107:355); Synod of Paris *(MGH Conc.* 42:643, 644); Theodulf of Orleans *(PL* 105:198, 199); Rudolf of Bourges *(Mansi* 14:955).
[113] *Hom.* 181 *(PL* 95:1424). The passage is sometimes attributed to Alcuin. See Hans Huber, *Geist und Buchstabe der Sonntagsruhe* (Salzburg, 1958), p. 190, n. 266, for the evidence.
[114] *MGH Conc.* 2:194, 195. Priebsch *(op. cit.,* pp. 7-9) shows that the emphasis on sunset-to-sunset keeping of Sunday came during the Carolingian period.
[115] Hefele-Leclercq, 3:287, 288.
[116] *Mansi* 14:889-898.
[117] *PL* 110:76-78. Rudolf of Bourges wrote: "Conveniendum est sabbato die cum luminaribus ad ecclesiam."—*Mansi* 14:955, 956. Pope Nicholas I also ordered sunset-to-sunset keeping of the Lord's day. *Epist.* 63 *(PL* 119:1004). See also Kottje, *op. cit.,* p. 46; Gaillard, *op. cit.,* pp. 961, 962.
[118] *Corpus juris canonici, pars secunda, Decretalium Collectiones,* ed. by E. Friedberg (Leipzig, 1881), c. 1, x *de feriis,* ii, 9 and c. 3, x *de feriis,* ii, 9.
[119] 3. 2. 3, sect. 1 *De tertio precepto, Summa theologica* (Ad Claras Aquas, 1924-1948), 4:490-504. On the place of the Old Testament in medieval theology, see Chenu, *op. cit.,* pp. 146-161.
[120] The implications of that philosophical development for natural law and Decalogue are described in Michel Villey, *La formation de la pensée juridique moderne* (Paris, 1968), pp. 114, 115.
[121] *Summa theologiae* 2a2ae. 122. 4 ad 4. In 1a2ae. 100.5 Thomas gives a feudal dimension to Sundaykeeping: The first three commandments (the second commandment is omitted in Catholic catechisms) define the duties to the Lord: fidelity, reverence, and service.
[122] *Ibid.,* 2a2ae. 122. 4 and 1.
[123] On the fourfold sense of Scriptures, see *Summa theologiae* 1a1ae, 10. See also Henri de Lubac, *Exégèse médiévale* (Paris, 1961), 2d part, 1:403-415; Beryl Smalley, *The Study of the Bible in the Middle Ages* (1952 reprint ed.; Notre Dame, Ind., 1964), pp. 242-263.
[124] *Summa theologiae* 1a2ae. 104. 3.
[125] See Williams, *op. cit.,* p. 272, 273.

[126] St. Thomas had carefully distinguished between different types of *opera servilia*. On the development of Sunday casuistry see Dublanchy, *op. cit.*, cols. 1320-1322; Huber, *op. cit.*, pp. 195-200; Vincent J. Kelly, *Forbidden Sunday and Feast Day Occupations* (Washington, 1943).
[127] *Expositio Decalogi*, ed. by Wenzel Flajshaus, in *Opera Omnia* (1903; reprint ed. Osnabrück: 1966), I/1:14-17.
[128] See Gaillard, *op. cit.*, col. 962b; also *idem*, "Le dimanche et le culte de la Sainte Trinité," in *Le Huitième Jour, Vie Spirituelle* 76 (1947):640-652.
[129] Odom, *op. cit.*, pp. 79, 80, n. 58a.
[130] *Opusculum* 33. 3, 4 (*PL* 145:564-567).
[131] *Mansi* 20:821.
[132] Dublanchy, *op. cit.*, col. 1321.
[133] *Ibid.*
[134] Several excellent studies on the Waldenses have appeared abroad, but there is unfortunately no recent scholarly work in English; read especially Jean Gonnet and Amedeo Molnar, *Les Vaudois au Moyen Age* (Turin, [1974]); A. Molnar, *Storia dei Valdesi*, vol. 1; *Dalle origini all'adesione alla Riforma* (Turin, 1974); Kurt-Victor Selge, *Die ersten Waldenser* (Berlin, 1967); R. Manselli, *Studi sulle eresie del secolo XII* (Roma, 1953); E. Dupré-Theseider, *Introduzione alle eresie medioevali* (Bologna, 1953). For collections of source material: J. Gonnet, ed., *Enchiridion fontium valdensium* (Torre Pellice, 1958); Walter L. Wakefield and Austin P. Evans, *Heresies of the High Middle Ages: Selected Sources Translated and Annotated* (New York, 1969).
[135] *De fide catholica* in Wakefield and Evans, *op. cit.*, pp. 217, 218. Joachim of Fiore made the same accusation in the *De articulis fidei*. See Gonnet and Molnar, *op. cit.*, p. 51.
[136] Wakefield and Evans, *op. cit.*, p. 219. Cf. Stephen of Bourbon, *Tractatus*, in *ibid.*, p. 209.
[137] Stephen of Bourbon, *Tractatus*, in *ibid.*, p. 210.
[138] "In reading the gospel, in keeping Sunday, in fasting, in prayer you are one with us," in Gonnet and Molnar, *op. cit.*, p. 152.
[139] *Hystoria albigensis*, in Wakefield and Evans, *op. cit.*, pp. 240, 241. "They are called *insabbati* because ever since they began the Waldensian spiritual perfects have been wearing a sign in the shape of a shield on the top of their sandals."—*Akten der Inquisition zu Carcassone*, in *Beiträge zur Sektengeschichte des Mittelalters*, vol. 2 of *Dokumente*, ed. by I. von Dollinger (1890; reprint ed. New York, n.d.), p. 7. On the use of the name *insabbati* ("sandal wearers"), see Selge, *op. cit.*, 1:139; 270, n. 118; Gonnet and Molnar, *op. cit.*, pp. 140, 141; J. Gonnet, *Le confessioni di fede valdesi prima della Riforma* (Torino, 1967), s.v. "*sandaliati*"; W. Earle Hilgert, "Religious Practices of the Waldenses and Their Doctrinal Implications," (M.A. thesis, SDA Theological Seminary, 1964), pp. 49-56. The Waldenses were also called *sandaliati* and *sotularii* (from *sotularis:* shoe). The documents show clearly the significance that was attached to the wearing of sandals. The misunderstanding of the word *insabbati* was compounded by the fact that Puritan translators of the Waldensian chronicles translated the Latin *dies dominica* and the French *dimanche* by Sabbath. See Hilgert, pp. 56-58.
[140] *Tractatus de hereticis*, in Wakefield and Evans, *op. cit.*, p. 371.
[141] (July 8, 1209) in Wakefield and Evans, *op. cit.*, p. 228. It is unlikely that Sabbathkeeping would appear among the Albigenses since they tended to disparage the Old Testament and its laws. See A. Schmidt, *Histoire et doctrine de la secte des Cathares ou Albigeois* (Paris, 1849), 2:294; Christine Thouseler, "Controverses vaudoises cathares iv: Loi mosaïque," in *Hérésie et hérétiques* (Rome, 1969), pp. 129-152. The text of Durand of Huesca where he attacks the Cathars' views on the Mosaic law is found in Selge, *op. cit.*, 2:161-193.
[142] On the Passagini, see Ch. Molinier, "Les Passagini: Etude sur une secte contemporaine des Cathares et des Vaudois," *Mémoires de l'Académie de Toulouse*, 82 série, 10:428-458; Paul Alphandéry, *Les idées morales chez les hétérodoxes latins au début du XIIIe siècle* (1903; reprint ed. Frankfurt a/Main, 1976), pp. 168-173; Raoul Manselli, "I Passagini," *Bulletino dell'Istituto Storico Italiano per il Medio Evo e Archivio Muratoriano* 75 (1963):189-210. Their name appears first in the canons of the Council of Verona in 1184 and last in a list of heresies by Pope Nicholas IV in 1291.
[143] Ed. by James A. Garvin and James A. Corbett (Notre Dame, Ind., 1958).
[144] *Ibid.*, pp. 130, 131.
[145] The fate of that group is studied in Paul Beuzart, *Les hérésies pendant le Moyen Age et la réforme jusqu'à la mort de Philippe II, 1598 dans la région de Douai, d'Arras et au pays de l'Alleu* (Paris, 1912). I have used the article by Denis Romain, "Condamnés à mort ... pour avoir fait le sabbat en samedy," *Revue adventiste*, March, 1976, pp. 7-9, where a picture of the folio of the original document is included.
[146] Little is known concerning the Picards. Some documents, including the *Summarium*, are included in the second volume of Dollinger's *Beiträge*; see also Frederick G. Heymann, *John Zizka and the Hussite Revolution* (Princeton, N.J.), pp. 209-213; Howard Kaminsky, *A History of the Hussite Revolution* (Berkeley, Calif., 1967), pp. 353-359.
[147] On the influence of the Vaudois in northern France, see Paul Leutrat, *Les Vaudois* (Paris, 1966), chaps. 3-6. Leff refers to the presence of the Vaudois at Douai in *Heresy*, 2:481. The name *picard* was practically synonymous with *Waldenses* in the later Middle Ages, M. Martini, *Pierre Valdo* (Paris, 1961), p. 132. On the Waldensians' presence in Central Europe, see Leff, *op. cit.*, pp. 452-485, esp. p. 477; Gonnet and Molnar, *op. cit.*, pp. 154-158; Kaminsky, *op. cit.*, pp. 173-180; Heymann, *op. cit.*, p. 210, n. 19.
[148] Döllinger, *op. cit.*, p. 662. Leff reports the presence of Waldenses in Poland who had their day of prayer on the seventh day. *Op. cit.*, p. 464.
[149] In *Opera Omnia*, ed. by J. Leclerc, 10 vols. (1703-1706; reprint ed. Hildescheim, 1962), 5:505. Luther and Calvin knew also about the Bohemian Sabbatarians. Luther, *Lectures on Genesis*, LW 2:361. Calvin, *De vera participatione in sacra coena, corpus Reformatorum* 9:590. On the activities of the Sabbatarians in Hapsburg lands, see J. K. Zeman, *Anabaptists and the Czech Brethren in Moravia*, (The Hague, 1969) passim.
[150] On the Lollards, see James Gardner, *Lollardy and the Reformation in England*, 4 vols. (London, 1908). J. A. T. Thompson, *The Later Lollards, 1414-1520* (Oxford, 1965); Leff, *op. cit.*, pp. 559-605; M. E. Aston, "Lollardy and Sedition, 1381-1431," *Past and Present*, No. 17 (April, 1960):1-44.
[151] For the Lollards and Scriptures, see Gardner, *op. cit.*, 1:100-118.
[152] Walsingham's *Historia Anglicana*, ed. by H. T. Riley, 2 vols. (London, 1869), 2:252-253, quoted in Gardner, *op. cit.*, p. 48.
[153] Gardner, *op. cit.*, p. 54.
[154] A. C. Bang, *Luther's Katekismus Historia*, 2 vols. (Christiana, 1893-1899), 2:87.
[155] *Ibid.*
[156] Henry C. Huttenbach, "The Judaizing Heresy and the Origins of the Muscovite Anti-Semitism," in *Studies in Medieval Culture*, IV/3 (Kalamazoo, 1974), pp. 496-506.

CHAPTER 11

Sabbath and Sunday in the Reformation Era

Kenneth A. Strand

THE Reformation Era inherited the religious traditions and practices of the Middle Ages, but in certain respects the Protestant Reformers made significant changes. With regard to the chief weekly day for Christian worship services, such major Reformers as Luther, Zwingli, and Calvin continued the pattern of Sunday observance, though with changes in rationale for keeping the day and in attitude toward abstinence from work. Certain Reformation groups, however, moved further away from medieval tradition by reverting to the ancient pattern of observing the seventh day of the week (Saturday) as the Sabbath of the Lord. On the other hand, some Reformers tended to retain a good deal of the medieval "Sabbatarian" attitude toward Sunday.

The present chapter will provide a brief overview of Sabbath-Sunday attitudes, discussions, and practices during the Reformation Era. Treatment herein will be limited to the European continent, inasmuch as a later chapter will deal with the Sabbath and Sunday in connection with the English Reformation.

Sabbath and Sunday in Germany and Northern Switzerland

As noted in the preceding chapter, medieval Roman Catholicism had set forth a twofold basis for weekly Sunday observance; namely, (1) that the Sabbath commandment of the Decalogue was still fully binding on Christians, and (2) that the day of the week for such observance (which included refraining from regular work) had been transferred from Saturday to Sunday by the authority of the Catholic Church.[1] (This line of argument, incidentally, received significant Catholic reaffirmation during the Reformation Era itself by the Counter-Reformation Council of Trent, which concluded its work in 1563.)[2]

In general, the major Protestant Reformers, including Martin Luther and his colleagues at Wittenberg, broke quite radically with this Roman Catholic twofold basis for Sunday observance. In their emphasis on salvation through faith and in their rejection of religious legalism, the Reformers quite naturally tended to remove the medieval "Sabbatarian" restrictions that had become attached to Sunday observance. They also quite naturally rejected, of course, the idea that their own practice of observing Sunday for worship services was in any way the creation of the Roman Catholic Church.[3]

Luther, as early as 1520 in his famous *Address to the Christian Nobility of the German Nation,* explicitly encouraged a reduction in the numerous ceremonies and festival days inherited from medieval Catholicism, stating that "all festivals should be abolished, and Sunday alone retained."[4] His mention of Sunday as an exception is significant, and the German Reformer continued throughout his career to feel that Sunday was useful as the main weekly day for Christian worship. His attitude in this respect, however, was not based on any belief that Sunday was especially appointed by God as the day for this purpose. "Although all days are free and open, one like another," he once declared, "it is nevertheless useful, good, and necessary to observe one, be it Sabbath, Sunday, or any other day, because God wants to rule the world orderly and peacefully."[5] Interestingly enough, he followed up this statement with a reference to the Sabbath commandment in the Decalogue, indicating that God "gave six days over to labor" but required rest for servants and even for working animals on the seventh day.[6]

In various of his writings Luther also had a good deal to say about the Sabbath of the Old Testament and about the Sabbath commandment itself.[7] He believed that the day on which Adam and God's children in Old Testament times had rested was the seventh day of the week, the day now called Saturday. In Eden, Adam had kept the Sabbath as a day for reflection on the works of God and for bestowing honor on the Creator; and after the Fall he continued to keep it. Abraham kept it too. Indeed, the Decalogue itself was pre-Mosaic, with only "those ceremonials that pertain to definite persons" being Mosaic.[8] But curiously enough, in polemical context Luther could also classify both the ban on images and the Sabbath commandment as ceremonial.[9]

In addition to believing that God's children in Old Testament times had literally observed the Sabbath on each seventh day of the week, Luther conceived of the seventh-day Sabbath as a prefiguration of either eternity itself or an era of "sleeping" prior to the eternal age (patterned after Christ's resting in the tomb on the Sabbath and resurrection on Sunday). Prior to this were six ages that would take the world from Adam to the second coming of Christ.[10] However, Isaiah 66:23—"from one new moon to another, and from one sabbath to another, shall all flesh come to worship before me, saith the Lord"—receives allegorization of a different sort. This means, says Luther, that "there shall be a daily sabbath in the New Testament, with no difference as to time."[11]

With respect to the Sabbath commandment itself, it appears that Luther looked upon it as having both moral and ceremonial aspects—God's command to rest being moral, and the specific day of the week being ceremonial. In this way he was able to justify his position that Christians could keep any day, just so long as they did keep one. Quite emphatically in a sermon at Torgau in 1544 Luther explained, "Since our Lord has come, we have the liberty, if Sabbath or Sunday does not please us, to take Monday or another day of the week and make a Sunday out of it."[12] Moreover, Luther felt that the observance must be in a totally nonlegalistic manner.

Undoubtedly, Luther's position regarding Sabbath and Sunday was also held by his Wittenberg followers generally. Nevertheless, certain refinements of that position may be seen among them. Luther's close associate Philip Melanchthon, for example, stressed the concept that the Sabbath commandment in the Decalogue was ordained of God to provide for preaching and public worship; and in this respect it was a commandment binding on all men.[13] This particular purpose or intent of the Sabbath commandment, he felt, was still fully applicable to Christians; but the *specific day* designated in the commandment (the seventh day of the week) pertained, in his opinion, only to ancient Israel, with Christians now observing Sunday instead. Thus, Melanchthon somewhat heightened Luther's treatment of the Sabbath commandment.

Luther's older colleague Andreas Carlstadt of Bodenstein also heightened Luther's emphasis on keeping the Sabbath commandment.[14] Carlstadt's major treatise on the subject, *Concerning the Sabbath and Commanded Holy Days*, appeared in 1524, two years after a breach had occurred between him and Luther. A major portion of this treatise deals with the nature of the Sabbath and the manner of Sabbath observance, and includes a protest against such activities as personal entertainment, joy riding, normal menial tasks (for example, a cook's lighting of a fire), and making horses and oxen work on the Sabbath. Finally, in the tenth chapter Carlstadt raises the question of the proper day to keep. He refers to Sunday as a day "which men have established"; and as for the seventh day of the week, Saturday, he simply indicates that this is a disputed question.[15]

Interestingly enough, Luther responded in the following way to Carlstadt's brief and rather noncommittal discussion of the proper day: "Yes, if Karlstadt were to write more about the sabbath, even Sunday would have to give way, and the sabbath, that is, Saturday, would be celebrated. He would truly make us Jews in all things, so that we also would have to be circumcised, etc."[16]

This type of reaction was also displayed by Luther toward real Sabbath-keepers who appeared in such places as Moravia and Austria. He said, for example, "In our time there arose in Moravia a foolish kind of people, the Sabbatarians, who maintain that the Sabbath must be observed after the fashion of the Jews. Perhaps they will insist on circumcision too, for a like reason."[17] Somehow, the German Reformer tended to classify any Christian emphasis on Saturday observance as part of a reversion to a Judaistic way of life, whether this was with respect to Christian Sabbathkeeping groups of which he had heard or whether it was with regard to suspicions about his own former close colleague Carlstadt.

In northern Switzerland at Zurich, Huldreich Zwingli (1484-1531) fostered a reform program from 1519 onward. His attitude toward Sunday was quite similar to that of Luther.[18] At approximately the same time Martin Bucer (1491-1551), who advanced the Reformation cause in Strassburg in southwestern Germany with an attitude generally more tolerant than the other contemporary Reformers, placed a strange emphasis on strict Sunday observance—an emphasis that was reminiscent, in fact, of Roman Catholic practice in this regard.[19]

Indeed, Bucer went so far as to state, "It must be a matter of special concern for those who wish the Kingdom of Christ to be restored among them that Sunday religious observance be renewed and established."[20] As for the manner of keeping "religious days singularly consecrated to God" (Sunday was, of course, primarily intended), Bucer declared that "no one [is to] do unnecessary corporal works with impunity on such days, ... much less be absent from the sacred gatherings and do works of the flesh." Among these "works of the flesh" were such activities as "making shameful gains, disturbing the religious spirit of brethren by demanding repayment of debts," et cetera. Sports and other personal pleasures were also to be set aside.[21]

Furthermore, in November of 1532, Bucer and his colleagues went so far as to request from the civil authorities in Strassburg that on Sundays an interdiction be placed on all works beyond those strictly necessary for bodily needs. By 1534 the city adopted an ordinance in this regard, sanctioned by heavy financial penalties.[22]

Before concluding our discussion of Bucer, we should add that in spite of all of his emphasis on strict Sunday observance, this Reformer had written in his commentary on Matthew 12 that it was a "superstition" to condemn work on Sunday as being sin—a statement that seems puzzling in view of his other remarks and especially in view of his efforts toward politically enforced Sunday "Sabbatarianism."[23] In any event, it appears evident that among the various Protestant Reformers on the European continent, Bucer's attitude was the most akin to that of the later strict Puritan Sabbatarians in England, who might well have drawn from him in this respect.

The Question of Sabbath and Sunday in Southwestern Switzerland

The Protestant reform movement swept southwestern Switzerland within two decades after its appearance in Wittenberg, Zurich, and Strassburg. The main reform center in this region was Geneva, and the chief reform leader was John Calvin (1509-1564). Calvin's reform career in Geneva spanned the years from 1536 to 1564, with an interim spent in Strassburg from 1538 to 1541.[24]

Earlier in the 1530s the Reformation had been carried to the southwest regions of Switzerland from the Protestant canton of Bern, with Guillaume Farel being among the first preachers to evangelize Geneva. By May of 1536, the city had declared itself Protestant, and it was but two months later that Farel urged Calvin to help him organize the religious institutions there. Before turning to an analysis of Calvin's own Sabbath-Sunday attitude, it will be well to notice certain discussions involving Farel and other Protestant preachers who had preceded Calvin to Geneva, such as Pierre Viret and Jacques Bernard.

One of the methods utilized by the Protestant Reformers in spreading the gospel was that of public debate, called "disputation." Interestingly enough, in several of the disputations in Geneva and neighboring Lausanne, the question was raised as to whether the Protestants were consistent in worshiping on Sunday and rejecting other institutions claimed by the Catholic Church, as has recently been called to attention by Daniel Augsburger.[25]

In 1534, for example, there was a disputation between Farel and a Catholic Dominican monk, Guy Furbity, a doctor of the Sorbonne.[26] When the Protestant representatives stated that man could not introduce any ordinance into the church, Furbity responded that God ordered the Jews to keep Saturday, "but the church through the power given to her has changed Saturday into Sunday because of the resurrection of the Lord." He added that "we celebrate Sunday because of a commandment and law of the church, not because of the commandment of God," and that a person following God's command literally "should rest on Saturday." [27] The Protestant preacher responded that all days are equally sacred, and that Christians rest on Sunday to hear God's Word and to give rest to their neighbor. To this, the Dominican monk replied that if the keeping of one day in seven were sufficient, a person could rest on any day of the week, with the result being dreadful confusion. And once again he emphasized that the Bible specifies the keeping of Saturday, with Sunday observance being based solely on the authority of the Catholic Church.[28]

During May and June of 1535, a further disputation was held in which the Catholic representatives Pierre Caroli and Jean Chappuis debated the Protestant leaders Farel, Viret, and Bernard.[29] The line of argumentation relating to Sabbath and Sunday was basically similar to that used in the earlier debate, but the Protestants entered a further point to the effect that resting on the seventh day (by which in this instance they meant Sunday) was, to use Augsburger's paraphrase, "no more a command of the church than are the words of someone telling somebody else to help his neighbor who is experiencing great necessity." [30] In both cases, they claimed, there was human need; and thus, in the sense of ethical concerns, both could be considered commandments of God.[31] Needless to say, such an analogy had little weight with the Catholic opponents in view of the Reformers' otherwise strong appeal to *Sola Scriptura*.

A still further disputation in which the Sabbath-Sunday question was raised was held in the city of Lausanne in October of 1536, after Calvin had joined Farel in reformation work in Geneva.[32] Farel was again central in the debate from the Protestant side, and he was assisted by Viret. A Dominican monk, Dominique de Monbouson, held forth for the Catholics. In a portion of the debate during which Viret was representing the Protestant side, the question arose as to why the Protestants observed Sunday rather than the Saturday Sabbath, if it were not because the Catholic Church had authority to make an ordinance beyond and outside Scripture. Said Dominique de Monbouson, "If you refuse to make any change in Scripture and must stop at the words and the letter [of Scripture], you ought to keep Sabbath like the Jews!" [33]

Viret responded by endeavoring to prove that Sunday observance was in the final analysis drawn from a Biblical base. But as Augsburger has aptly pointed out, "Viret had asserted that a spiritual observation was more important than a literal observation and that practical considerations (need of time to assemble together, duty to provide rest for the labors) could be taken into account in justifying a practice that did not agree fully with the words of the law." [34] There was inconsistency in this kind of an approach, as Augsburger has further pointed out, for "when it came to images, for instance, which the defenders of Rome argued were set up only to facilitate a spiritual worship and provide a simple and practical means to communicate some religious notions to the uneducated people, or even when it involved the fasts and Lent which were intended to curb sensuality, they objected." [35]

The three disputations do not indicate any observance of the seventh-day Sabbath on either side, of course; but they do give evidence of an interesting issue raised by the Catholics as to whether the Protestants were really being consistent when they observed Sunday and rejected other festivals claimed on the authority of the Catholic Church.

We now come directly to a consideration of the attitude of John Calvin himself regarding Saturday and Sunday.[36] Before his arrival in Geneva, Calvin had already clarified his basic position regarding the two days in the first edition of his *Institutes of the Christian Religion,* published in Basel in the spring of 1536. Here he set forth three basic considerations with regard to the Sabbath commandment: (1) the Sabbath is a moral institution vitally significant for spiritual growth; (2) it is the anchor for public worship; (3) it has great social value in guaranteeing rest for servants. As Augsburger has pointed out, "these three ideas constitute the structure of Calvin's thought on the Sabbath. In later works we may find fuller expositions, slight shifts in emphasis, efforts to meet objections, but he never altered these essential viewpoints." [37]

In his early work Calvin, much like Luther, emphasized that the choice of the particular day was rather unimportant. But even after Calvin's close association with Bucer in Strassburg from 1538 to 1541, he continued a similar attitude. For example, in his commentary on Colossians 2:16 (written some five or six years after his return from Strassburg to Geneva) he states that "we do not by any means observe days, as though there were any sacredness in holy days, or as though it were not lawful to work on them," adding that the observance "is done for government and order, not for the days." [38]

Although Calvin had a good deal to say at various times throughout his career about Sabbath (or Sunday) observance, we must come quickly to what is to be considered the Genevan Reformer's definitive treatment of the question in his 1559 edition of the *Institutes*.[39] Here he reiterates, though with slight shift in emphasis, the three basic considerations he first set forth in 1536.[40] He clarifies, however, that there is no connection between the Sabbath commandment and the observance of the Christian Sunday. Thus he rejected the views of both the Catholic scholastic theologians and Luther regarding a moral versus a ceremonial distinction in that commandment as laying the foundation for observance of another day than Saturday.[41]

Even though a Sabbatarian type of Sunday observance was, in Calvin's opinion, going "thrice as far as the Jews in the gross and carnal superstition of sabbatism," [42] the Geneva Reformer nevertheless also indicated, as he had in his commentary on Colossians, the need for observance of discipline and order. He has aptly summed up his position as follows:

"It was not, however, without a reason that the early Christians substituted what we call the Lord's day for the Sabbath. The resurrection of our Lord being the end and accomplishment of that true rest which the ancient Sabbath typified, this day, by which types were abolished, serves to warn Christians against adhering to a shadowy ceremony. I do not cling so to the number seven as to bring the church under bondage to it, nor do I condemn churches for holding their meetings on other solemn days, provided they guard against superstition. This they will do if they employ those days merely for the observance of discipline and regular order." [43]

Anabaptists and the Sabbath

We now turn to the so-called "Radical Reformation," in contrast to the magisterial reform parties. Our attention goes especially to the Anabaptists, who for the most part used Sunday as their weekly day of worship, but among whom were groups observing the seventh day of the week, Saturday. The basic study of these Sabbatarian Anabaptists of the sixteenth century has been done by Gerhard F. Hasel.[44]

The Anabaptists consisted of many groups scattered widely throughout the European continent, and were given their name by their enemies because of their belief in adult baptism. Actually the Anabaptists did not consider themselves to be "rebaptizers" (as the term "Anabaptists" signifies), for they simply did not accept infant baptism as being any baptism at all. As to their other beliefs and practices, these varied from group to group. For the most part, the Anabaptists seemed to have been pacifistic, but a few segments took up the sword and created violence that gave the Anabaptist name undue and generally ill-deserved notoriety.[45]

In several lists of sects compiled both by Catholics and by Protestants in the latter half of the sixteenth century, Sabbatarian Anabaptists (observers of Saturday) are mentioned among other groups. Such Sabbatarians certainly were not in the majority of Anabaptists, but they were still sufficiently numerous and well enough known to be noted by compilers of lists of sects and by writers who produced polemical works against them.[46]

Among the early leaders of Sabbatarian Anabaptists, the names of Oswald Glait and Andreas Fischer stand out prominently. About 1527 and 1528 these two individuals accepted Saturday as being the Lord's Sabbath. They traveled about considerably, but one of their chief centers was at Nikolsburg in Moravia. Both Glait and Fischer wrote books regarding the Sabbath, but unfortunately their books are no longer extant. Nevertheless, we are able to determine the basic content of those books from answers given by their opponents.

The most significant source for determining Glait's Sabbath doctrine is a response written by Casper Schwenkfeld.[47] It seems from this response that Glait's chief argument for the necessity of keeping the seventh day as the Sabbath was the Decalogue itself. Says Schwenkfeld, "The strongest argument of Oswald [Glait] is the number of the Ten Commandments.... He holds irrevocable the thought that God did not give eight or nine but ten commandments, which he wants everyone to keep." Moreover, according to Schwenkfeld, Glait "wants to make it understood that either the Sabbath must be kept too or all the other nine commandments must be rejected."[48]

The following are among several further points of interest that emerge in Schwenkfeld's response to Glait: (1) Glait believed that the Sabbath had been commanded and kept from Creation, with God's having commanded Adam in Paradise to celebrate the Sabbath; (2) Glait felt that although circumcision began with Abraham, the Sabbath and other laws existed from the beginning of the world; (3) Glait further believed that the children of Israel's keeping of the Sabbath earlier than at Sinai, as evidenced in Exodus 16, was proof that the Sabbath did not originate at Sinai.[49]

With regard to Fischer, knowledge of his Sabbatarian doctrine is derived mainly from a polemical treatise against it written by Valentine Crautwald.[50] Crautwald, in fact, refers to some sixteen points by Fischer that he endeavors to critique. Basically, the line of Fischer's argument goes somewhat like this: The Ten Commandments are ten covenant words that include the Sabbath, so that if the Sabbath is not kept, one breaks the commandments of God. Moses, the prophets, and the New Testament command the observance of the Ten Commandments, and therefore the Sabbath is included. When the law is referred to by James and Paul, it is the law that includes the Sabbath. Moreover, faith establishes the law, and therefore it also establishes the Sabbath. Paul and the other apostles held meetings on the Sabbath; and Christ, the apostles, and all the early Church Fathers kept the Sabbath holy. Pope Victor and Emperor Constantine were the first to order that Sunday should be kept. The Ten Commandments are eternal.

Fischer's eleventh point is especially worth noting because of its personal reflection on Scripture evidence: "The Scriptures speak so often about the Sabbath; if I would have as many texts and passages about Sunday as there are about Sabbath, I would keep Sunday instead of Sabbath."[51]

In concluding, it would be well to quote here Hasel's summary paragraph regarding Glait and Fischer: "Because of the nature of the sources, a comparison of the Sabbatarian teachings of Glait and Fischer is most difficult. It is certain, however, that both leaders of Sabbatarian Anabaptism based their teachings on the *sola scriptura* principle of the Reformers. It is, therefore, not surprising that this Reformation approach provided them with a powerful basis of argumentation and that their proclamation of Sabbatarianism met with considerable success. Both men regarded the Old and New Testaments as inseparable and indivisible. In this view they were far in advance of their time. Biblical scholars have in recent decades more and more recognized this inherent unity. There is close proximity of thought and presentation in the teachings of Glait and Fischer. This may be expected of propagators who associated together, uniting their efforts in common missionary activity, and who through circumstances were forced to defend together their Sabbatarianism."[52]

The Seventh-Day Sabbath in Spain

Reform movements in Spain unfortunately have received relatively little attention, taking a subordinate place to the more dramatic and widespread Reformation activities to the north. However, in 1972 Mario Veloso brought to light some truly intriguing aspects of the Reformation in Seville.[53] Among the Reformers to whom Veloso calls attention is Constantino Ponce de la Fuente, who attended the universities of Alcala and Seville and subsequently became quite famous as a preacher. To his preaching fame, which he had achieved by 1536, he added distinction as a writer during the 1540s. In 1548 he was invited by Prince Philip to serve as chaplain for a trip of that prince throughout various lands of Europe. It was not until 1555 that Constantino returned to Seville, where he was almost immediately attacked by inquisitorial forces. He finally died in prison in February, 1560.

As Veloso points out, Constantino was a representative of an independent reformation, rather than having connections with Lutheranism. He had actually learned his doctrine from two earlier Spaniards, Valer and Egidio.[54] It is interesting to note that even while Constantino was on trial and during his imprisonment, the staunchly anti-Lutheran Emperor Charles V was sympathetic to him.[55] The particular aspect of Constantino's doctrine that interests us here is his attitude toward Sabbathkeeping. This falls within the framework of his doctrine of righteousness and perfection. He states, for example, "You must keep the Ten Commandments if you do not wish to be an enemy of God."[56] Moreover, as Veloso points out, to Constantino perfection was possible for the Christian "only because his life lies in Christ and because Christ's works are done in his life." In Constantino's own words, "Works are only pieces and leftovers of the riches of Jesus Christ, and all is attributed to Him and has value through Him, and in Him do we put our trust."[57]

Not only did Constantino declare the importance of obedience to the Ten Commandments lest we "be an enemy of God," but he specifically pointed out that observance of Saturday was part of that obedience to the Decalogue. And he also explained the Sabbath commandment and the meaning of "servile work" that should not be done on the Sabbath day. Servile work, he states, is the kind in which "one works or causes another to work corporally, without being necessary or for charitable purposes." This work, he continues, was forbidden by God on Saturday, not that at the time of the giving of the Decalogue such work was evil in itself, nor that "it should be so now; but that man should find himself unencumbered for the true spiritual sanctification of the holy day."[58]

Regarding the significance of God's instituting of the Sabbath, Constantino declares that "God appointed a stated day to be offered to Himself as a tithe, on which, unencumbered by other cares man should offer, inwardly and outwardly, acknowledgement to the Lord who created him, who sustains him in this world, and who has promised him great and eternal benefits." The day, says Constantino, is one in which according to God's provision "man should meet with other members of the church where he should be as a living evidence that he, together with them, gives tribute [to God] with the same kind of obedience as theirs."[59]

Constantino's references specifically to the Saturday Sabbath are from two of his works referred to by Veloso. The references are brief but nonetheless telltale. It appears that Constantino planned to elaborate on the Sabbath in a later work, a work that apparently was never produced or published.[60]

In summarizing the thrust of Constantino's remarks on the Saturday Sabbath, Veloso has aptly stated: "These references to Sabbath-keeping on the seventh day seem to be unique among the major theologians of the Reformation and imply a concept of the Sabbath that did not develop to any great extent until the rise of the Sabbatarian Anabaptists, the Seventh Day Baptists, and especially, in the nineteenth century, the Seventh-day Adventists."[61]

Other Sabbathkeepers in the Reformation Era

Although space will not permit a survey of all European Sabbathkeeping groups in evidence during the Reformation Era, at least brief notice should be made of the fact that observers of Saturday sprang up quite widely throughout the Continent, and a few illustrations will be given relating to such groups.[62]

As one example, in Transylvania toward the end of the sixteenth century Andreas Eössi, a wealthy nobleman influenced by Judaistic teachings of one Francis Dávid, inaugurated a Sabbath movement.[63] Eössi began intensive personal study of Scripture after the death of his wife and two sons, and among convictions that he gained from this study was that Saturday, the seventh day of the week, was God's true Sabbath day. Through writing and other contacts he raised up a sizable number of converts who were observing the Saturday Sabbath by the last decade of the century.

Although Eössi himself died about 1600, some prominent colaborers, including Simon Pechi, an adopted son, continued to promulgate the Sabbath doctrine in the early seventeenth century. During the first two decades of that century, Pechi himself advanced politically until he became chancellor of state; but loss of favor led him to an imprisonment. During some nine years in prison, he devoted time to preparation of a commentary on Genesis and to composing a number of hymns, many of which specifically honored the seventh-day Sabbath.[64] Apparently, after severe pressure in 1638 and 1639, he eventually repudiated his Sabbath observance, at least outwardly.[65]

In spite of the fact that various persecutions were inaugurated against these Transylvanian Sabbathkeepers (they underwent various severe persecutions beginning about the year 1595), their number at first increased. In 1618, when a reformed bishop with 300 soldiers attacked the Sabbatarians and arrested their ministers, some twenty-two of their church buildings were confiscated. The very number of church buildings thus confiscated is, as J. N. Andrews and L. R. Conradi aptly note, "an evidence of the extent of the Sabbath movement" in that region of Transylvania (the Szekler district).[66]

From about 1538 to 1540, stern measures against the Sabbathkeepers, including confiscation of personal property and imprisonment until death, virtually destroyed their existence in Transylvania, though some remnants of these Sabbathkeeping Christians continued on. In fact, one might think that there had been somewhat of a resurgence of Sabbath observance by 1668 in that Prince Apafy at the Besztercze Diet in January of that year complained that through "secret devices," "Judaism" (the reference was apparently to Christian Sabbatarianism) was daily increasing. In any event, however, interrogations two years later revealed only six Sabbatarian towns—a considerable reduction from earlier times.[67]

The persecutions, especially those of 1638-1640, had the effect of spreading the Transylvanian Sabbatarian influence beyond Transylvania itself, as some Sabbatarians managed to escape and carried their doctrines and practices to distant places, including Constantinople. Moreover, the Sabbatarian writings of such leaders as Eössi and Pechi apparently spread far and wide. For instance, a copy of Pechi's Genesis commentary of 1634 had reached Maros-Vasarhely in Hungary, where it was personally seen by Conradi in the year 1890.[68]

In Norway, Finland, and Sweden there were also extensive groups of observers of the Saturday Sabbath.[69] Evidence is available of such groups during the late Middle Ages through the action of Catholic councils against them, including the councils held in Bergen, Norway, in 1435 and in Oslo (Christiania), Norway, the following year. These councils forbade abstention from work on Saturday.[70] It appears that in the early years of the sixteenth century, before the Protestant Reformation reached Scandinavia, there were two kinds of observance of the Saturday Sabbath in Norway—one wherein Roman Catholic priests caused the common people to hallow Saturdays in a fashion similar to Sundays under penalty of fine to the bishop, and another kind that was outlawed by the Catholic Church.[71] Possibly the difference involved varying ecclesiastical attitudes in different geographical locations more than it did any significant divergences in practice, but this we cannot tell for certain from the document that stipulates the required Sabbath observance. That document unfortunately is only fragmentary and obscure, but it at least alerts us to the curious fact that somewhere in Norway in the early sixteenth century there were Roman Catholic authorities ordering that Saturday be observed as well as Sunday.[72]

Further evidence regarding Sabbath observance in Norway comes from the period after Lutheranism reached Scandinavia. There is, for example, an edict of Christopher Huitfeldt, "lord of Bergen, Stavanger, and Vardoe," dated 1544, which among other things refers to the fact that "some of you, especially in Aardal, in Sogn, contrary to the warning given you last year, keep Saturday." His edict imposed a fine of ten marks on anyone found keeping Saturday.[73]

A decade later, in 1554, evidence of Saturday observance in Finland is afforded through a letter of Swedish King Gustavus I Vasa, who had fostered the Lutheran Reformation in his lands, which included Finland as well as Sweden. In this letter he earnestly commands that any of these folk in Finland who have fallen into what he calls "such error" should forsake it immediately.[74]

The main evidence regarding observance of the Saturday Sabbath in Sweden arises somewhat later, toward the end of the sixteenth century and in the early part of the seventeenth century, with some evidence at least as late as 1667.[75] There appears to have been in Sweden at this time two types of Sabbath observance, as had been the case in Norway about a century earlier. But whereas the specifics in Norway are unclear, the types in Sweden are quite clearly distinguished as a Judaistic Sabbathkeeping (on the part of converts to Judaism) and a genuinely Christian Saturday observance. The latter frequently, but not necessarily always, entailed a continuing observance of Sunday as well.[76] King Gustavus II Adolphus (died 1632) was especially forceful in his activity against Sabbathkeepers.[77]

In addition to Transylvania and the Nordic countries, there are evidences of observance of the Saturday Sabbath from the Netherlands, France, Russia, and elsewhere in Europe, as Andrews and Conradi point out.[78] However, it should be borne in mind that in some cases the Sabbathkeeping may have been on the part of Jews or Christian converts to Judaism, rather than by Christians themselves. Nevertheless, that there was indeed *Christian* observance of Saturday by groups spread widely throughout all sections of Europe seems clear from the sources. And it may be noted that in England, as well as on the Continent, there were some who observed this day during the sixteenth century, prior to the Puritan Sabbathkeepers, who will be treated in the next chapter.[79]

It must not be assumed, however, that the people who kept Saturday were by any means in the majority of the Christians or that they were even a large minority of them. The medieval tradition of Sunday as the day for Christian worship continued throughout Christian Europe as the main one observed by Protestant groups as well as by Roman Catholics. However, it is interesting to note that in many places, sizable communions of sincere Christians who had studied Scripture faithfully did decide to honor their Lord on the seventh day of the week because they felt that this was in harmony with God's command.

Summary

We have now very quickly traced the question of Sabbath and Sunday in the Reformation Era. Basically, the major Protestant Reformers continued to utilize the day of worship hallowed by the Roman Catholic Church throughout the Middle Ages. However, in their effort to avoid legalism, and with their strong emphasis on justification by faith, the major Reformers tended to shy away from anything like a "Sabbatarian" approach to Sunday observance. In fact, most of

THE SABBATH IN SCRIPTURE AND HISTORY

them in Germany and Switzerland felt that Sunday was not necessarily the day to be observed, just so long as one day in seven was set aside for special religious purposes. Martin Bucer seems to have been an exception in that he tended to give a "Sabbatarian" emphasis to Sundaykeeping. Such an emphasis did not come into vogue as a widespread Protestant practice until taken up by certain Puritans in England during the seventeenth century, a matter treated in chapter 12.

The Protestant Reformers in southwestern Switzerland actually found themselves in somewhat of a dilemma when facing their Roman Catholic adversaries on the matter of Sunday observance. In several disputations in Geneva and Lausanne the Roman Catholic representatives chided the Reformers with inconsistency for rejecting Catholic ceremonies in general, while adhering to Sunday as a weekly day for worship services.

However, there were certain Reformation Era Christians who endeavored to go beyond the major Reformers in reform measures taken. These included the Anabaptists, among whom were at least some Saturday-observing groups. Adherents of the Saturday Sabbath included also an important Spanish Reformer of Seville, Constantino Ponce de la Fuente; and Saturday-observing Christians, although always in the minority during the Reformation Era, were actually rather numerous among various groups. Moreover, such Sabbathkeepers were quite widely dispersed throughout Europe in the sixteenth and early seventeenth centuries.

NOTES

[1] See pp. 204-206 in chapter 10. Especially noteworthy in this connection is the line of argument of Thomas Aquinas, *Summa Theologica*, 2:2, quest. 122, art. 4 (American ed. by Benziger Brothers, 1947).

[2] For a discussion of "The Third Commandment" (fourth commandment), see *The Catechism of the Council of Trent* (pp. 352-362 in the Baltimore ed., 1829).

[3] A basic study of Luther's attitude toward the seventh-day Sabbath has been provided by William M. Landeen, *Martin Luther's Religious Thought* (Mountain View, Calif., 1971), pp. 191-199, in a chapter entitled "Sabbath."

[4] This is his point 18 under the section "Proposals for Reform." *The Address* is available in a number of English translations (as well as in German editions, including the standard Weimar ed.). See, e.g., my *Reform Appeals of Luther and Calvin* (Ann Arbor, Mich., 1974), col. 46. The translation here is that of *LW* 44:182.

[5] Weimar ed., 16:478-479, Engl. trans. in Landeen, *op. cit.*, p. 196.

[6] See Landeen, *op. cit.*, pp. 196, 197.

[7] For a summary, see Landeen, *op. cit.*, pp. 191-197.

[8] *LW* 5:20.

[9] This appraisal is found, e.g., in both *Von Zwilling und Karlstadt* and *Wider die himmlishchen Propheten*.

[10] See, e.g., *LW* 2:129-130, 3:141-142, and 8:67, as well as the discussion in Landeen, *op. cit.*, p. 194.

[11] *LW* 40:93.

[12] This translation from the Erlangen ed. of Luther's works is that of J. N. Andrews and L. R. Conradi, *History of the Sabbath and First Day of the Week*, 4th ed. (Washington, D.C., 1912), p. 605. In his "Larger Catechism" of 1529, Luther had voiced a similar type of sentiment in a statement noted in *LW* 40:93.

[13] Melanchthon's position has been briefly but adequately summarized by Daniel Augsburger, "Calvin and the Mosaic Law" (Th.D. dissertation, University of Strasbourg, 1976), 1:253, 254.

[14] Details regarding Carlstadt are given by Augsburger, *op. cit.*, pp. 248, 249. See also Andrews and Conradi, *op. cit.*, pp. 652-656. Carlstadt's treatise may be found in Erich Hertzsch, *Karlstadts Schriften aus den Jahren 1523-25* (Halle [Saale], 1956), 1:23-47. Discussions of Carlstadt's attitude toward the Sabbath commandment are given by Gordon Rupp, *Patterns of Reformation* (Philadelphia, 1969), pp. 123-130, and by R. Willard Wentland, "The Teaching of Andreas Bodenstein von Carlstadt on the Seventh Day Sabbath" (M.A. thesis, SDA Theological Seminary, 1947).

[15] Text in Hertzsch, *op. cit.*, p. 41. Regarding Sunday, Carlstadt declares that it is "vynheymlich" that men have instituted it. Wentland (*op. cit.*, p. 33) translates this as "one is alarmed that men have instituted it," and Andrews and Conradi (*op. cit.*, p. 604) render the clause as "one feels uneasy because men have instituted it." *Vynheymlich* in this context undoubtedly carries the idea of "open," "clear," "known" (cf. Hertzsch, *op. cit.*, p. 100: "vynheymlich = bekannt"); thus we might translate, "Concerning Sunday, it is known that men have instituted it."

[16] *LW* 40:94.

[17] *LW* 2:361. Cf. Landeen, *op. cit.*, p. 198. Also noteworthy are other references by Luther to Sabbathkeepers as provided in Andrews and Conradi, *op. cit.*, p. 640.

[18] Zwingli's position is briefly treated by Augsburger, *op. cit.*, p. 255.

[19] Bucer's position has been carefully noted by Augsburger, *op. cit.*, pp. 254, 255, and the description given below is a summary of the account given there.

[20] Wilhelm Pauck, ed., *Melanchthon and Bucer*, LCC, 19:252.

[21] *Ibid.*, pp. 280, 281.
[22] See Augsburger, *op. cit.*, p. 255.
[23] Referred to by Augsburger, *op. cit.*, 2:81, n. 37, and also quoted in Andrews and Conradi, *op. cit.*, p. 606. The statement comes from Bucer's *Commentary on Matthew*, chap. 12. In presenting this statement, Andrews and Conradi seem to have been unaware of Bucer's other statements and actions with regard to Sunday. The apparent conflict of this statement by Bucer with the other evidence regarding him has not, to my knowledge, been adequately explained, and it seems as yet to defy solution.
[24] Numerous accounts of the historical background are available. Perhaps the best *relatively brief* summary in English is that given by Williston Walker, *John Calvin: The Organiser of Reformed Protestantism (1509-1564)* (New York, 1906; now available in Shocken pb. ed., 1969, with excellent introductory bibliographical essay by John T. McNeill), pp. 159-181.
[25] The first adequate treatment of these disputations from the point of view of the Sabbath-Sunday issues is the excellent article by Daniel Augsburger, "Sunday in the Pre-Reformation Disputations in French Switzerland," *AUSS* 14 (1976):265-277.
[26] *Ibid.*, pp. 267-270, gives the account of this first disputation.
[27] Augsburger's translation in *ibid.*, p. 269.
[28] *Ibid.*, p. 270.
[29] *Ibid.*, pp. 270-272, gives the account of this second disputation.
[30] *Ibid.*, p. 272.
[31] *Ibid.*
[32] *Ibid.*, pp. 273-276, gives the account of this third disputation.
[33] Augsburger's translation in *ibid.*, p. 275.
[34] *Ibid.*, p. 276.
[35] *Ibid.*
[36] Augsburger, "Calvin and the Mosaic Law," 1:256-284, has given a detailed treatment of Calvin's position throughout the Reformer's career, analyzing the various statements found in editions of the *Institutes of the Christian Religion*, in commentaries, and in other source materials. Space limits here forbid even a summary of this extensive and excellent treatment, and only a cursory overview of Calvin's basic position can be noted.
[37] Augsburger, "Calvin and the Mosaic Law," 1:257.
[38] The quotation is as given in the new Edinburgh edition of *Calvin's Commentaries: The Epistles of Paul the Apostle to the Galatians, Ephesians, Philippians and Colossians*, trans. by T. H. L. Parker (Edinburgh, 1965), p. 337. Parker notes in his introduction, p. v, that Calvin had begun his work on these books by October of 1546 and that the preface was dated February of 1548. Thus, it is apparent that Calvin's comments here noted must have been written approximately five or six years after his return to Geneva from Strassburg in September, 1541.
[39] The *Institutes*, 1559 ed., are available in several English translations, including two volumes of *LCC* and a two-volume Edinburgh ed. With regard to the references given herein, volume and page numbers will be those of the Edinburgh ed. as reprinted in Grand Rapids, Michigan, by William B. Eerdmans Pub. Co., 1957. The "Fourth Commandment" is treated in the *Institutes* 2. 8. 28-34 (1:339-344).
[40] Prior to his more detailed discussion of these three considerations, Calvin simply summarizes them, in *ibid.*, par. 28 (1:339).
[41] Although he does refer in *ibid.*, par. 31 (1:341) to "the ceremonial part of the commandment" as being abolished by the advent of Christ, he decries the claim of there being a ceremonial part that has been abrogated and a moral part that remains—the moral part being "viz. the observance of one day in seven" (par. 34 [1:343]). This sort of distinction he characterizes as being "nothing else than to insult the Jews, by changing the day, and yet mentally attributing to it the same sanctity; thus retaining the same typical distinction of days as had place among the Jews" (par. 34 [1:343, 344]).
[42] *Ibid.*, par. 34 (1:344).
[43] *Ibid.*, par. 34 (1:343).
[44] Gerhard F. Hasel, "Sabbatarian Anabaptists of the Sixteenth Century," *AUSS* 5 (1967):101-121, and 6 (1968):19-28.
[45] Historical surveys of the Anabaptists are available in virtually all major textbooks dealing with the history of the Reformation Period. Various valuable works specifically on the Anabaptists have been produced in recent years by such scholars as Harold S. Bender, Abraham Friesen, Hans Hillerbrand, Leonard Verduin, and others; these have tended to present the Anabaptists in a more favorable (and accurate) way than has often been the case. The available works by these and other recent writers on the subject are too numerous to note here, but attention may be called, e.g., to Verduin's book, *The Reformers and Their Stepchildren* (Grand Rapids, 1964). Also, from the standpoint of presenting the "Radical Reformation" in a broader perspective, the excellent standard work by George H. Williams, *The Radical Reformation* (Philadelphia, 1962) is worth consulting. Williams has provided, too, an excellent selection of documents in volume 25 of *LCC*, entitled *Spiritual and Anabaptist Writers*.
[46] For treatment of the lists, note the discussion by Hasel, *op. cit.*, 5:101-106.
[47] *Ibid.*, pp. 116, 117.
[48] *Ibid.*, p. 118 (translation is basically Hasel's, with occasional variation in wording; this will be the case throughout this section).
[49] These and other important points in Glait's belief are treated in *ibid.*, pp. 117-121.
[50] The details given herein are based again on Hasel's excellent presentation. Fischer is treated in *ibid.*, 6:19-28.
[51] *Ibid.*, p. 26.
[52] *Ibid.*, p. 28.
[53] Mario Veloso, "The Reformation in Seville, 1530-1560" (M.Div. thesis, Andrews University, 1972). See especially chap. 6, "The Famous Preacher: Constantino Ponce de la Fuente," pp. 88-117, and chap. 7, "Independent Theology of Constantino Ponce de la Fuente," pp. 118-157. Translations given herein will follow closely those given by Veloso, with possible variation in exact wording at times.
[54] *Ibid.*, p. 116. Actually, as stated by Veloso, the line of influence was as follows: "Through the teaching of Doctor Egidio, Constantino de la Fuente received the 'Gospel of Christ' preached earlier by Rodrigo Valer in Seville."
[55] *Ibid.*, pp. 113-115.
[56] *Ibid.*, p. 142. The quotation comes from Constantino's *Primer Salmo*.
[57] *Ibid.* The quotation is from Constantino's *Suma de Doctrina Christiana*.

[58] *Ibid.,* p. 144. The quotation is from Constantino's *Suma.*
[59] *Ibid.,* p. 145. The quotation is from Constantino's *Suma.*
[60] *Ibid.,* p. 143. Constantino's works referring specifically to the Sabbath are the *Doctrina Christiana* and the *Suma.*
[61] *Ibid.,* p. 145.
[62] The brief summary given herein is drawn largely from Andrews and Conradi, *op. cit.,* pp. 632-684, supplemented by several other sources indicated in the notes below.
[63] *Ibid.,* pp. 659-663. Considerable further detail is furnished by József Pokoly, *Az erdélyi református egyház története* (History of the Transylvanian Reformed Church), 3 vols. (Budapest, 1904), especially vol. 2. Also of some interest is Ladislaus M. Pákozdy, *Der siebenbürgische Sabbatismus* (The Transylvanian Sabbatarianism) (Stuttgart, 1973). These works were called to my attention by Lewis Laszlo Szerecz, who as a seminarian at Andrews University presented to Professor Daniel Augsburger a research paper entitled "Sabbatarians in 16th and 17th Century Transylvania" (1977), in which he surveys rather extensively the pertinent material presented by Pokoly.
[64] *Ibid.,* pp. 661-663.
[65] See Pokoly, *op. cit.,* 2:140, quoted in Szerecz, *op. cit.,* p. 15.
[66] Andrews and Conradi, *op. cit.,* p. 660.
[67] Details regarding the Besztercze Diet and subsequent events are given by Pokoly, *op.cit.,* pp. 273-276.
[68] Andrews and Conradi, *op. cit.,* pp. 661, 662.
[69] See Andrews and Conradi, *op. cit.,* pp. 672-683; Roald Martin Guleng, "The Marian and Sabbatarian Observance in Norway during the 15th and 16th Centuries" (M.A. thesis, SDA Theological Seminary, 1951); Arne Sandström, "Du temps où, en Suède, les observateurs du sabbat étient exécutés," *Revue adventiste,* Juillet-Août, 1976, pp. 10, 11. Sandström quotes from the useful works by L. A. Anjou, *Svenska Kyrkans Historia ifrån Upsala Möte År 1593 till Slutet af Sjuttonde Århundradet* (Stockholm, 1866), and Theodor Norlin, *Svenska Kyrkans Historia efter Reformationen* (Lund, 1864), whose titles and specific citations are unfortunately lacking in the aforementioned French version of Sandström's material.
[70] Andrews and Conradi, *op. cit.,* pp. 672, 673.
[71] See Guleng, *op. cit.,* pp. 48, 49, 52.
[72] The pertinent parts of the document are quoted in *ibid.,* pp. 48, 49.
[73] Andrews and Conradi, *op. cit.,* p. 675 (the translation is theirs).
[74] *Ibid., op. cit.,* pp. 676-679.
[75] See Sandström, *loc. cit.*
[76] See Guleng, *op. cit.,* pp. 56, 57, and Sandström, *op. cit.,* p. 10, col. 3.
[77] See Sandström, *op. cit.,* p. 11, col. 1.
[78] See Andrews and Conradi, *op. cit.,* pp. 632-672, especially pp. 649, 650 (Netherlands and France) and 663-672 (Russia). Although not dealing specifically with Sabbathkeepers, a very useful source from which to obtain further insight as to historical developments as reflected in the chronicles with regard to treatment of "heretics" and "schismatics" in Russia is Ned P. Maletin, "Dissent and Reform in Russian Orthodox Church History from the 11th through the 16th Centuries," *AUSS* 8 (1970):51-64.
[79] Andrews and Conradi, *op. cit.,* p. 650.

CHAPTER 12

The Sabbath in Puritanism

Walter B. Douglas

THE controversies and discussions surrounding the Sabbath respecting the day, time, and manner of its observance in England during the late sixteenth and throughout the seventeenth centuries arose more from doctrinal and practical considerations than from theological or philosophical ones. The terms "Sabbath" and "Sabbatarianism" were descriptive of the majority of Puritans in the seventeenth century and referred to the excessive and rigorous adherence of Sunday as the day of rest and sanctification. As such, these Puritans felt that Sunday as the "Sabbath" was obligatory on all Christians and that it was never intended to be set aside or profaned. Then there was the small group of Puritans who argued for a contrary position, basing their views entirely on the authority of Scripture. These believed that the seventh day of the fourth commandment of the Decalogue was never changed and that obedience to God's law requires the proper observance of Saturday as the Sabbath.

On the other side of the controversy was the established church, which through its clergy and scholars argued against both positions that were held by the Puritan opponents. These Anglicans, with royal sanction, provided what they thought to be reasoned arguments based on church history for not accepting the Puritan teaching about the Sabbath. They believed that the Puritans were fanatical in their insistence on proper observance of the Sabbath, irrespective of the day, and argued against them from the point of view of an imposition on religious freedom. They maintained that in observing Sunday in a more "liberal" vein, they were in the tradition of the ancient church and the practice of the Fathers.

It should be noted that among the Anglicans and the Puritans were men of sincerity and integrity who believed truly in the rightness of their positions. These were usually individuals of deep learning, acuteness, and piety who were seeking the truth of God as revealed in Holy Scripture.

Although this chapter is principally interested in the Puritans and the Sabbath in the seventeenth century, it is worth remembering that the events of this century, in some respects, had their antecedents in the sixteenth century and that the Sabbath was one of several critical issues that the Reformation left vague.

THE SABBATH IN SCRIPTURE AND HISTORY

From the time of Elizabeth's refusal to support a thorough Reformation on the model of the continental reformed churches, there was a widening gap in the Church of England between those who strove for an Elizabethan settlement (that is, an Erastian ecclesiastical settlement with a theology that was substantially reformed and a liturgy that was substantially Catholic) and those who insisted on reforms beyond those that the queen and her successors were willing to initiate.

During Elizabeth's reign, as A. H. Lewis points out, those Puritans who based their observance of Sunday on the fourth commandment pleaded at first "for a better observance of Sunday as a part of the general work of civil and religious reform. As they continued to seek for higher life and greater purity, the Sabbath [Sunday] question grew in importance. This was not fortuitous. Men never come into closer relations with God without feeling the sacredness of the claims which his law imposes; and no part of that law stands out more prominently than the Fourth Commandment. . . . As these men threw off the shackles of church authority, and stood face to face with God, recognizing him as their only lawgiver, they were compelled to take higher ground concerning the Sabbath."[1]

The general attitude toward the Sabbath during the time of Elizabeth, and one that was of deep concern to the Sabbatarian Puritan, was summarized in an admonition issued in 1580 by the government and enjoined to be read as a homily during divine service. A portion of the homily describes the conditions concerning the Sabbath in the following words: "The Sabbath days and holy-days, ordained for the hearing of God's word to the reformation of our lives, . . . are spent full heathenishly in taverning, tippling, gaming, playing, and beholding of bearbaiting and stage-plays; to the utter dishonor of God, impeachment of all godliness, and unnecessary consuming of men's substances, which ought to be better employed. The want of orderly discipline and catechising hath either sent great numbers, both old and young, back again into papistry, or let them run lose into godless atheism."[2]

As the controversy raged over the strictness or laxity of Sabbathkeeping, the Puritans grew increasingly apprehensive about what they described as the "spiritual well-being of the nation." This feeling of apprehension and concern was, of course, consistent with their belief that England was to become God's holy commonwealth, and that they were God's chosen people.

But at this time, the late sixteenth century, the "covenanted people of God" lacked the political as well as ecclesiastical influence and authority to force the issue of the Sabbath to the forefront of national consciousness. Such power and authority was to come years later, as we shall soon see. In the meantime, despite the opposition and protest of the Sabbatarians, Sunday was still the favorite time for theatrical presentations and sports. In fact, when in 1585 Parliament attempted to pass a law "for better and more reverend observance of the Sabbath," the queen used her veto power against it "because she would suffer nothing to be altered in matters of religion or ecclesiastical government."[3]

The rapid march of events in both church and state soon found the Puritans gaining strength and support in the popular mind for their Sabbatarianism. One of the most remarkable influences in preparing the way was Nicholas Bownd's *The Doctrine of the Sabbath, plainely layde forth and soundly proved* . . . , which appeared in 1595. Bownd's presupposition was that England was to be God's holy commonwealth and Englishmen were to be His chosen people; but unless society was to be thoroughly demoralized (largely through the abuse of its day of rest), the mode of observing the Sabbath must be radically changed.

In the development of his ideas on the Sabbath, Bownd argued that although the Lord's day (meaning Saturday) had been changed, its manner of observance was still to be seen in the Old Testament. The moral and perpetual nature of the Sabbath puts beyond doubt the total sovereignty of God that extends to the whole of life. Consequently, not only labor, but every form of recreation should be given up on the Christian Sabbath (Sunday).[4]

The foundation of his argument was laid in Scripture, the Fathers, and the Reformers. He provoked the ecclesiastical wrath of both the monarch and bishops by stating that the Sabbath was neither a bare ordinance of man nor merely a civil or ecclesiastical constitution appointed only for polity, but that it was an immortal commandment of God and therefore binding on men's consciences. Bownd first argues the antiquity of the Sabbath, that it appears "in the story of Genesis, that it was from the beginning, and that the seventh day was sanctified at the first, so soon as it was made"; then he concludes that "as the first seventh day was sanctified so must the last be, and as God bestowed this blessing upon it in the most perfect estate of man, so must it be reserved with it till we be restored to his perfection again."[5]

Upon this premise Bownd proceeds to prove that while the ceremonies of the law, which made a difference between Jew and Gentile, are taken away by the gospel, the Sabbath commandment remains still in full force and is binding for all nations and sorts of men as before. The most important principle enshrined in the stipulation of the rest day was that God should be worshiped. The people were admonished to attend public services where the Word of God was plainly read and purely preached, the sacraments rightly administered, and prayer made in a known tongue to the edifying of the people, and in attending upon these things from the beginning to the ending.[6]

When Bownd's first volume appeared, it created an extraordinary sensation. One historian, Thomas Fuller, points out that "throughout England, began the more solemn and strict observation of the Lord's day" and that "it is almost incredible how taking this doctrine was, partly because of its own purity, and partly for the eminent piety of such persons as maintained it; so that the Lord's day, especially in corporations, began to be precisely kept, people becoming a law to themselves, forbearing such sports as yet by statute permitted; yea, many rejoicing at their own restraint herein." Fuller goes on to state that learned men were nevertheless "much divided in their judgments about these sabbatarian doctrines," some embracing them and others opposing them.[7]

It should be noted that the opposition to the publication and to the reading of Bownd's book came largely from the established church party. Many of the bishops took a firm stand against what they thought to be a "Jewish yoke" and the restriction of "the liberty of Christians."[8] Many other Anglican ministers seemed convinced that if the teachings enunciated in the book were adopted, the results would be distasteful to Anglicans, who would not relinquish their inherited forms of worship. They found support for their view from Parliament and the queen.

These Anglican ministers denounced the doctrine as tending to weaken the authority of the church in appointing other holy days and of giving an unequal luster to Sunday, and an attempt was made to suppress the book. In 1599,

Archbishop Whitgift "issued orders for all persons having copies of the book to give them up, and, in 1600, Chief Justice Popham reissued these orders from the bench."[9] But the suppression of the book was not to be; in 1606, after Whitgift's death, a new edition was published, and thenceforth the Puritans were distinguished by their rigid observance of the Sabbath (Sunday).

James I and the Puritans

When Elizabeth's successor, James I, became king of England in 1603, the problem of dissenters and the proliferation of sectarianism were already evident. Among the different religious groups, three only were at that time powerful enough to contend for James's support: the Roman Catholics, Erastians, and Puritans. The Puritans, who already had a reputation for advocating renewal and reform in worship, submitted to the king the Millenary Petition, which embodied the essentials of their most immediate reform measures. For more than thirty years before this, the Puritans had been agitating for a renewal of church life both in worship and discipline. They expressed their grievances over the laxity in Sabbath observance and the strictness with which ceremonials were enforced. They vigorously urged more and better preaching by competent ministers and insisted on a simplification of ritual and vestments.

There was no lack of men of sufficient breadth to articulate and defend the Puritans' position on the Sabbath against the established church. But their representations and expectations did not bring the king to their side. Indeed, James himself had no deep affection for the Puritans, mainly because of his speculations as to their political persuasion and the harsh treatment that he and his mother had received from the Scottish Presbyterians, with whom, he assumed, the Puritans now shared a similar political philosophy.

But neither did the Roman Catholics fare any better with the king than did their Puritan rivals. They, of course, looked forward to a change in attitudes. However, they were soon to discover that once the king was able to rule from a position of strength, he no longer needed "the Papists."[10]

Then there was the group who came into royal favor by showing their willingness to support the crown. This group represents virtually the whole official class in England, who acknowledged James I's indefeasible hereditary right to the throne of England. It was to these persons that the king looked, and along with them he reaffirmed his intention to maintain the Elizabethan settlement.[11]

At the Hampton Court Conference (1604), the king dealt very cautiously with the Puritans. John Reynolds, a member of the Puritan party, expressed on behalf of his colleagues their disappointment in the king's proclamation made for the reformation of the abuses and profanation of the Sabbath.[12] They earnestly pleaded for a thorough reform of Sunday observance that would reflect the practice of the primitive Christian church and the harmony of the scriptural injunctions enjoined upon all Christians.

In opposition to this strong Puritan plea for a thorough reformation of Sunday observance, James in 1618 published the famous, or infamous, *Book of Sports*.[13] The document claimed to be an explanation rendered necessary by the calumnious misrepresentations of papists and Puritans in Lincolnshire, but in its title page it is addressed to all his majesty's subjects.

THE SABBATH IN PURITANISM

The *Book of Sports* was, in fact, a condemnation of Sabbatarianism "and gave full legal sanction to the continental Sunday in England." [14] This view is confirmed by the Anglican clergyman Peter Heylyn. According to Heylyn, the *Book of Sports* "was the first blow, in effect, which had been given, in all his time, to the new Lords-day-Sabbath, then so much applauded." [15] With the death of James I and accession of Charles I in 1625, the Puritans became even more apprehensive of affairs in both church and state. Archbishop George Abbot's rival and successor to the See of Canterbury, William Laud, demanded absolute conformity; and he rigorously prosecuted those who for reasons of tender consciences, both public and private, chose not to conform. Laud demonstrated in his personal life and through legislation a marked preference for a sacramental rather than a doctrinal approach in religious matters. His rule is described by some as notorious and highhanded, but R. H. Tawney does not fully agree and presents Laud as a man who was possessed by a fundamental conviction that the oneness of the church and state must not be sacrificed to any personal motive or divergent religious or social movement.[16]

The Puritans' advocacy of the Sabbath (Sunday) and of cessation of all labor and recreational activity on that day grew in importance and eventually took on religious as well as political significance. This was certainly one of the chief reasons why so many Puritans were persecuted under Laudian prelacy. So severe was the persecution that it is not surprising that several of the bishops declared their opinions against it. Laud had succeeded in getting Charles I to renew the declaration of the *Book of Sports*. Thus, it was the studied plan of the archbishop to subdue as far as possible the influence of the Puritan teachings on the Sabbath. But within five years into his reign, the Puritans had greatly increased their number and influence; and side by side with this growth were the persecutions against them. Thus, the separation and eventual ejection of the Puritans from the Anglican Church during the reigns of Charles I (1625-1649) and of his son Charles II (1660-1685), were inevitable.

The Puritan Concept of the Covenant and the Sabbath Controversy

The vigor of the Puritan position that brought them into conflict was rooted in their concept of the covenant and their self-estimation as the chosen people of God. One prominent scholar has pointed out that "the Covenant was not, for the Puritans, one idea or concept among others. It was the fundamental motif running throughout the whole of their life to shape their understanding, and their feeling for existence. It pervaded and held together their views of religion, politics, and ethics; it shaped their whole approach to marriage, church, and society." [17]

The systematic articulation of this fundamental condition of Christian experience was in the law of God. That law, declared Richard Baxter, is a signification of God's will and constitutes the subjects' due. Obedience to God's law, therefore, is not an option but a duty that when done reflects His glory and graciousness.[18]

The point to which we must draw attention, and one that carries considerable weight, is that not only is the Sabbath rooted in the law of God but it is based on a covenant between God and man, and itself has the nature of a covenant.[19] Precisely for this reason, the Puritans opposed those sectarians who advocated the "hellish" doctrine that the law of God was no longer binding on Christians.

The essential claim made by the Puritans was that the law rendered intelligible all of their experience, even those aspects not manifestly religious. The law was as much binding after Calvary as it had been before. Theophilus Brabourne, an "able defender" of the Sabbath, although differing from his colleagues respecting the seventh day (as will be noted shortly), was in full agreement with mainstream Puritan thought when he argued that the New Testament revelation reinforces the continuing relevance and the necessity of obedience to the law.[20] Both he and his colleagues readily agreed that this obedience was not intended and should not become a slavish conformity to authority. They understood the relation between law and grace, and insisted that the sinful heart cannot delight in God's law; but when that heart is regenerated, then the works of the law are carried out in perfect freedom.[21] This helps to pinpoint for us the prominence the Puritans gave to the concept of the covenant. Strictly speaking, the law was not the covenant. When God handed down the law at Sinai, He did not give a list of stipulations whose successful accomplishment by man would bring man into relationship with Him. What God did do, the Puritans were quick to point out, was to prepare the law with a statement of the covenant relation He already had with His people because of His mighty acts: "I am the Lord thy God, which have brought thee out of the land of Egypt, out of the house of bondage" (Ex. 20:2). Thus, the sovereignty of God was clearly established, and the appropriate response to such graciousness was an unconditional obedience to the terms of the covenant.[22]

Another point must be noted regarding the Puritans' understanding of the covenant and its relationship to the Sabbath: One who through justification in Christ Jesus comes into relationship with God will necessarily be inclined toward the Sabbath, since it is the most visible sign of God's creative authority and rule by law.[23]

The Controversy Respecting the Change of the Sabbath

Thus far, our discussion of the history of the Sabbath in seventeenth-century England has been confined to the question of its sanctification and observance, and the divergence of opinions between the Sabbatarians and the established church party, the latter being supported in large measure by the Crown.

When it comes to the question of the precise day and time for observance, we begin to witness a disintegration in the otherwise cohesive Puritan movement. By far, the largest number of Puritans contended for the change of the day from Saturday to Sunday; and it will be useful to trace, very briefly, the historical development of what came to be known as the "transfer theory" as it pertains to England.

Historically, the discussion in England about the change of the Sabbath came into prominence through the influence of Thomas Cranmer (1485-1556). When the church in England rejected the authority of the Roman Church, it became necessary for English Christianity to develop a liturgy that would reflect its own teachings and practices. Cranmer, Archbishop of Canterbury from 1533 to 1556, produced the official service book (1549 and 1552) and included in its litany the Ten Commandments. The fourth commandment in particular was the nub of the problem, for when the minister repeated it, the people responded with the words:

"Incline our hearts to keep this law." The question of the observance of the Sabbath then became one of crucial importance. Did the people's response mean that the church was obligated to keep the Sabbath of the Ten Commandments?

There were those of evangelical spirit who argued in the affirmative and insisted that to deny the truth of the seventh-day Sabbath (Saturday) was to make mockery of the "plain Word of God." Others maintained that this statement was a general recognition of God's authority and a call to worship Him and to set aside a portion of one's time to His glory. Peter Heylyn, the High Church historian, gives notice of the fact that neither the archbishop nor any of the other reformers had any intention of introducing the Jewish Sabbath when they included it in the litany.[24] Perhaps he is right. The fact still remains, however, that for many Anglicans the question as to whether they were really following the teaching of the Bible or the authority of the Church of Rome still provoked their consciences.

In the scramble for the control of church authority, the Catholics claimed that since the Roman Church "had displaced without question the Sabbath day, therefore its authority was supreme, and it could make other laws."[25] As a rejoinder to this challenge, Cranmer pointed out that the Sabbath commandment consists of two parts, a physical and a spiritual, and that the spiritual aspect of the Sabbath cannot be changed.[26] This gave rise to the concept of a "transfer theory," which meant that the Sabbath as a sacred institution was not necessarily related to a particular day.[27]

But it was not Cranmer's influence that led the Puritans to their acceptance and advocacy of Sunday as the Sabbath rest. Undoubtedly, the decisive influence upon them came from Nicholas Bownd, to whom we have already made reference. We deem it necessary to reintroduce him at this point in our discussion, because his propagation of the transfer theory was of decisive importance for discussion of the Sabbath in the 1630s and the 1640s. In this connection, Bownd advocated that "as it [the Sabbath] came in with the first man, so it must not go out but with the last man," that our Lord and all the apostles "established it by their practice,"[28] that if "Adam needed the Sabbath before the Fall, the world lost in sin needs it much more."[29]

He builds what seems to be a convincing and solid argument for the Biblical Sabbath (Saturday), stating, "Now, as we have hitherto seen, that there ought to be a Sabbath-day, so it remaineth that we should hear upon what day this Sabbath should be kept, and which is that very day sanctified for that purpose. For I know it is not agreed upon among them that do truly hold that there ought to be a Sabbath, which is that very day upon which the Sabbath should always be." Bownd then goes on to show that the Lord in His mercy did not leave man in any doubt regarding the specific day on which the Sabbath is to be kept. It is clear both in Genesis 2:3, where God "blessed the seventh day, and sanctified it," and in Exodus 20:10, where He declares that "the seventh day is the sabbath of the Lord thy God." So then, "it must needs be upon that day, and upon none other; for the Lord himself sanctified that day, and appointed it for that purpose, and none but it."[30] In the light of such plain teaching on the Sabbath, Bownd concludes that it is unreasonable for anyone to keep any other day and still expect to receive that blessing from God that He bestows by virtue of His special promise to those who reverence His Sabbath.

After decrying the endless controversies surrounding the issue of the day that is to be kept, Bownd exclaims further, "Therefore we must needs acknowledge it to be the singular wisdom and mercy of God toward his church, thus by sanctifying the seventh day, to end the strife. For, as we in God's service, when men go away from his Word, there is no end of devising that which he alloweth not; and they fall upon everything, saving upon that they should; so in appointing the day if we be not ruled by the Word, we shall find by experience that every day will seem more convenient to us than that, at leastwise we shall seem to have as good reason to keep any other as the seventh."[31]

It is quite clear that for Bownd, the Word of God was the only authoritative source for any change or transfer of the Sabbath to any other day of the week. And since, as he explains, to deviate from the sure Word could lead to mishandling of the Sabbath, it is both safe and right to remain faithful to what God Himself has ordained. He concludes that "thus we learn that God did not only bless it, but bless it for this cause and so we see that the Sabbath must needs still be upon the seventh day, as it always hath been."[32]

Nevertheless, in spite of such statements as the foregoing, Bownd sincerely advocated and taught that Sunday was the seventh-day Sabbath rather than Saturday.[33] Here is his decisive statement in this regard: "But now concerning this very special *seventh day* that we now keep in the time of the gospel, that is well known, that it is *not* the *same* it was from the beginning, which *God* himself did *sanctify*, and whereof he speaketh in this commandment, for it was the day going before *ours*, which in Latin retaineth its ancient name, and is called the *Sabbath*, which we also grant, but so that we confess it must always remain, never to be changed any more, and that all men must keep holy *this* seventh day, and none other, which was unto them not *the seventh*, but the first day of the week, and it is so called many times in the New Testament, and so it still standeth in force, that we are bound unto the seventh day, though not unto *that* very *seventh*. Concerning the time, and persons by whom, and when the day was changed, it appeareth in the New Testament, that it was done in the time of the apostles, and by the apostles themselves, and that together with the day, the name was changed, and was in the beginning called the *first day of the week*, afterwards the *Lord's-Day*."[34]

The foregoing is a very crucial statement, because it shows the sincerity with which Bownd articulated his convictions about the change of the Sabbath. Notwithstanding his piety, one cannot avoid noticing how far he himself had moved away from his own norm, namely, the Word of God; and it is of considerable interest to note that in his complete argument for the change (too lengthy to incorporate here) he relied more on church history than on Scripture. Only two scriptural references appear in support for his Sunday advocacy, whereas he cites copiously from the doctors of the church and early Christian sources to substantiate his position.

Despite what one says or how one wishes to judge Bownd's work, it is beyond dispute that his treatise on the Sabbath represents an entirely new position in the history of the Sabbath in England and that it colored the whole question of Sabbath reform for more than three hundred years. The book was adopted by the majority of the Puritans and became a source for their arguments against those of their number who believed in and advocated the seventh-day Sabbath.

Among prominent sixteenth- and seventeenth-century advocates of Sunday Sabbatarianism in England were Richard Greenhorn, Richard Baxter, Richard

Bernard, and John Wallis. These and others proclaimed the "transfer theory" proposed by Bownd. On the whole, they were sincere individuals who took it to be their duty not only to guide and instruct in the proper worship of the true God but also to rebuke and discipline persons who, in their opinion, failed in this respect—as, for instance, by not properly observing Sunday as the Sabbath. Their determination led them at times to extreme measures that opened them to severe criticism from their contemporaries. It should also be noted that like Bownd, these later advocates of a Sunday Sabbatarianism tended to use history, rather than Scripture alone, in their efforts to support the "transfer theory."[35]

Some Representative Puritan Advocates of Saturday as the True Sabbath

We must now turn our attention to the other group of Puritans who believed and kept the seventh-day Sabbath (Saturday). This group, as we have already noted, represented a minority among the Puritans. Nevertheless, they held firmly to their position that the Decalogue was still obligatory for all men, and that the difference between the Old and New Covenants did not effect any change in the original day of rest.

One of the earliest Puritan advocates of the Saturday Sabbath was John Trask (*c.* 1583-*c.* 1636). When he applied for orders in the Church of England, he was refused because of his advanced evangelical views. Trask left the established church and began preaching as a Puritan minister. Along with Hamlet Jackson, he studied the Bible and became convinced that the fourth commandment refers to the true and lasting Sabbath of God. Trask was successful in attracting a small group of followers who accepted the Saturday Sabbath. Because of imprisonment brought about as a result of his acceptance and preaching of the Sabbath, Trask for a short period forsook his Sabbathkeeping practices. But so firmly grounded were his church members that his departure did not affect their belief in the Sabbath.[36]

A radical answer to the divisiveness within the Puritan camp came from Theophilus Brabourne, who has been called "an able exponent of Sabbath truth." When in 1628 the Puritans were being forced away from the established church through the influence of William Laud, there appeared in print a definitive defense of the seventh-day Sabbath (Saturday) by Brabourne.[37] This was the beginning of almost a lifework of study and writing on the Sabbath. In the space of thirty years, he produced four volumes defending the Sabbath of the fourth commandment. His second volume, which was dedicated to Charles I, was entitled *A Defence of that most Ancient, and Sacred Ordinance of Gods, the Sabbath Day*.

In his *Church History of Britain*, Thomas Fuller assigns the beginning of the revival of the Sabbatarian controversy to 1632 and represents Brabourne as having "sounded the first trumpet to this fight."[38] James Gilfillan declares that this publication "blew a blast in the ear of royalty itself, which compelled attention, and provoked immediate as well as lasting hostilities."[39] After establishing that the fourth commandment is simply and entirely moral, containing nothing legally ceremonial in whole or in part, Brabourne defends the position that Saturday, the seventh day of the week, must be an everlasting holy day in the Christian church, and that Christians are obliged to observe it. "I am tied in conscience," he delcares, "rather to depart with my life than with this truth; so captivated is my conscience and enthralled to the law of my God."[40]

Shortly after this expression of confidence in his view of the Sabbath, Brabourne was brought before the Court of High Commission, and there was asked to recant. According to Bishop Francis White, who wrote against Brabourne at the command of Laud, "there was yielded unto him a deliberate patient and full hearing, together with a satisfactory answer to all his main objections."[41] Although it appears that at that time Brabourne personally returned to the orthodox Anglican position (though all of his followers did not accompany him in this), one thing stands out clearly: Whatever may have happened at the hearing before the court, Brabourne believed and preached that if the Sabbath is indeed moral and perpetually binding, the seventh day ought to be sacredly kept. From his first publication in 1628 to the appearance of his last volume during the negotiations for the restoration of Charles II (1660), Brabourne was always, at least in heart, a firm and consistent champion of the Saturday Sabbath. His last book attested to this fact by the very title that it bore: *Of the Sabbath day, which is now the highest controversy in the Church of England, for of this controversy dependeth the gaining or losing one of God's Ten Commandments, by the name of the Fourth Command for the Sabbath day.*

Another outstanding spokesman for the seventh-day Sabbath was Thomas Bampfield. He cites New Testament passages such as Matthew 5:17 and Mark 12:28-30 to prove that these passages shed light on the truth of the Old Testament teaching about the fourth commandment. These texts provided the hermeneutical principles that enabled him and his colleagues to interpret the vaguely worded sections referring to the first day of the week. Bampfield also cites Acts 20:7, and argues that rather than proving the sanctity of Sunday, it clarifies the fact that Paul started preaching on Saturday evening and continued into the early part of Sunday.

In dealing with such passages as Colossians 2:14 and Ephesians 2:15, 16, he endeavored to show that these refer not to the Sabbath of the Decalogue, but to ceremonial Levitical Sabbaths. For Revelation 1:9, 10, three alternative interpretations were provided. Here "Lord's day" could refer either to an annual day observed by the early church in commemoration of Christ's birth, or to an annual remembrance of His resurrection, or to an eschatological day of religious observance. If the last were true, there were two alternatives: either Sunday, being supported by tradition, or Saturday, being supported by Scripture.[42]

Bampfield cast doubt upon the common assumption that tradition is veritably unanimous in favoring Sunday observance. To support his reservations and to show that Saturday was observed by many during the early Christian centuries, he quotes from such authorities as Ambrose, Chrysostom, Ischius (Presbyter of Jerusalem), and Lucius' *Ecclesiastical History*.[43]

The critical and decisive point in Bampfield's argument, and the one that created further alienation between the two parties, is found in his drawing attention to the fact that the belief in the Sabbath should be based on two basic Puritan doctrines: first, that Christians should obey the will of Christ; and second, that the will of Christ is revealed in the Bible. Therefore, the conclusion regarding the proper day for the Sabbath must be decided on the basis of the Bible only, and not on *tradition*.[44]

The logic in this argument caused mainstream believers some difficulties, for they relied mainly, although not exclusively, on tradition for any *concrete* proof, and their theological arguments were mostly *secondary* implications taken from their basic beliefs.[45]

As one might have already gathered, the Sunday advocates, by sheer majority, won the support for the Sunday Sabbath. The minority who defended the Saturday Sabbath were branded as radicals and reactionaries, and many among them were treated as heretics, even though some of their accusers confessed that "the words of the law . . . seem to favour their opinion."[46]

In this brief survey we have been able to take only a quick glance at a few of the more outstanding proponents of the seventh-day Sabbath in Puritan England. Recent research by Bryan W. Ball has uncovered the fact that observers and advocates of Saturday as the weekly day for Christian rest and worship were much more numerous and widespread in seventeenth-century England than has commonly been assumed.[47] And thus it may be said that although these Saturday Sabbathkeepers were a minority, they were nonetheless a significant minority.

The Sunday "Sabbath" in the New World

We must now proceed to a consideration of the developments regarding the Sabbath, and the surrounding controversies, in the New World. The religious and political situation in England in the seventeenth century forced many Puritans away from the established church and their homeland. Many of them first sought a new home in the Netherlands, but they soon found it difficult there to advocate their views with the freedom they were seeking and for which they had left England. At the same time they became fearful of the apparent laxity in Sabbath (Sunday) observance that was creeping into their ranks. Determined to seek a home in the New World, a group reached America in 1620 and settled at New Plymouth. In 1629 another large group of these "persecuted saints" came to America to join those who were now settled at New Plymouth. With these migrations came the beginnings of New England and the planting of Puritanism and the Sabbath (Sunday) in America. Thus, "recalling the place of the Puritan in the establishment and development of this Republic reminds us that the keeping of the Sabbath Day holy is one of its mighty corner stones."[48]

One of the deepest concerns of the Pilgrim Fathers and the Puritan dissenters who followed them after 1620 was that a strict Sundaykeeping would become a vital part of their New World experience. Thus, according to Herbert Richardson, "It is one of the peculiarities of Christian history that the American Puritans attempted to reestablish an institution which the Church, in its continuing opposition to Judaism, had rejected."[49] For them, the sanctification of the Lord's day and its proper observance were not negotiables. With an attractive eagerness of interest they looked to the time when Sunday Sabbatarianism would flourish in its new environment. Indeed, in one of the earliest accounts by the Dutch colonists in New York, there are several notices regarding the stringent regulations employed by these Puritans "to guard the infant community against the demoralizing tendencies of Sabbath [Sunday] profanations."[50]

Wherever the Sabbatarian Puritans established themselves in the New World, their observance of Sunday was indubitable. But despite their great effort, there arose the unsettled state of affairs among some of the early settlers who were opposing the strictness and regularity of this observance. "These were libertines, Familists, Antinomians, and enthusiasts, who had brought these wicked opinions out of Old England with them, where they grew under prelacy."[51]

From the 1630s, we find several Puritan ministers in correspondence with one another over the questions of the day and the manner of keeping Sunday. One of the leading defenders of the Sunday position in America was Thomas Shepard, who arrived in 1635, after suffering under Archbishop Laud. In his *Theses Sabbatica,* he presented his views on the morality, the change, the beginning, and the sanctification of the Sunday Sabbath. His activities brought him to Harvard College in 1649, where he preached a series of sermons on the subject.

By a consensus in 1648, the circuit of churches in the New England area accepted the Westminster Confession of Faith as their *modus operandi* and in harmony with its principles continued to maintain its Sabbath teaching. Thus John Eliot, the apostle to the Indians, taught his converts that they must "remember the Sabbath day [meaning Sunday] to keep it holy"[52] as long as they lived.

Sunday Sabbatarianism and the Seventh-Day Sabbath in the New World

In the Colonies there was Sunday legislation against the desecration of the Lord's day, and the penalties for the violations of Sunday laws were quite often heavy and severe. For example, Massachusetts in 1629 decreed that all labor should cease at three o'clock on Saturday so that preparation for the Lord's-day observance would be duly carried out. In 1650, Connecticut passed a code of laws relative to Sunday observance and the prohibitions of certain activities that were considered to be out of harmony with genuine Sabbatarianism, and in 1656 instituted the death penalty for certain violations. In 1658, the Plymouth legislators ruled against the carrying of any load on Sunday and attached a penalty of twenty shillings for such violation. In 1665, they declared that those who slept in church should be admonished, and if they persisted should be punished by being placed in stocks.[53]

But as in England, so also in the New World the Puritan camp was divided not so much on the question of the manner of sanctification and observance of the Sabbath as on the question of whether it should be kept on Sunday or on Saturday. Whether or not the stringency of Sunday legislation forced the majority of the American Puritans to accept and honor Sunday as the Sabbath is a matter of dispute. It is clear, however, that those who defended Saturday represented a minority viewpoint and were quite often considered as radicals and heretics. They nevertheless held firmly to the belief that their course of action was based on the Word of God and was the logical outcome of its teaching. Therefore, for them to agree that the Sabbath was moral and eternal but that it was changed from the seventh day to the first was to constitute a willful disobedience to God's law.

Historically, the Seventh Day Baptists appear to have been the first group of English Puritans who maintained the Saturday Sabbath position in America. Some of them had come to America on the *Mayflower.* Indeed, for more than a century and a half, both in England and in the Colonies, Baptists played an important role in the development of American Christianity and the teaching of the Sabbath. Inasmuch as their story will be given in the next chapter (pp. 244-263), only a brief outline will be presented here.

In 1664, Stephen Mumford arrived in Newport, Rhode Island, from England and "brought with him the opinion that the Ten Commandments as they were delivered from Mount Sinai were moral and immutable, and that it was an anti-Christian power which changed the Sabbath from the seventh to the first day of the week." Mumford soon found response to the propagation of his Sabbath views among the Baptist congregation at Newport. Many members of this church accepted his teaching, and this led to some degree of divisiveness. Finally there was a split in the congregation, as followers of Mumford separated themselves in 1671 to establish the first Seventh Day Baptist Church in America.[54]

For many years after its organization, this Seventh Day Baptist Church at Newport was the center for nearly all those who kept the Sabbath in Rhode Island and Connecticut; and the church grew both by the coming of Seventh Day Baptists from England and by conversions to the Sabbath in the Rhode Island colony.[55] Among its members were several prominent public figures, one of whom was Richard Ward, governor of Rhode Island.

The Seventh Day Baptists became the main early champions of the Saturday Sabbath in the New World. The second branch of that church was also planted by emigration from England. In 1684, Abel Noble, a Seventh Day Baptist minister from London, settled in Philadelphia, becoming the chief advocate of seventh-day Sabbatarianism in Pennsylvania.[56]

Summary

The attitude of the American Puritans toward the Sabbath is instructive for the present day, for it pinpoints clearly the grave dangers inherent in civil authority's attempting to legislate laws for the protection and proper observance of Sunday. The harshness and severity with which the Puritans sought to enforce Sunday observance were reminiscent of the religious intolerance that they themselves had suffered under Laudian prelacy. Life was uncomfortable not only for those who did not believe in any Sabbath but also for those who, because of "tender conscience," felt obliged to keep Saturday as the true Sabbath. The controversy and the sharpness with which the Puritans battled for the sanctity of Sunday has a special value even beyond their time, since it gives to us a spontaneous and unconscious revelation of the Puritan mind as it wrestles with its problems practical and theoretical, in an effort not merely to justify a policy and battle down opposition, but to arrive at truth and agreement. To the Puritan mind, there was a direct relationship between proper Sabbath observance and civil obedience. The sanctification of the Sunday, they argued, acted as a corrective against the worldliness of the masses while at the same time producing an able ministry that encouraged families to bring up their children in a Christian way. A multitude of gross sins would be prevented and the discipline that Sunday observance required would help to produce not only good Christians but also exemplary citizens.

In summarizing our discussion, one central point must be noted regarding the Puritans' attitude toward an understanding of the Sabbath. Both in England and the early American colonies, the essential claim made by the Puritans was that they kept the Sabbath not to earn salvation but to honor and please God and experience the blessings that a covenant relationship with Him gave. We have tried to show that for them their basic beliefs found their focus in their understanding of the covenant, law, the authority of the Word of God, and personal piety. All of these according to the Puritans held a direct relationship to the Sabbath.

We may not agree with all their teachings and practices about the Sabbath (we have seen that they did not agree among themselves on these matters), but their sincerity of purpose and their determination to make relevant the command of God to keep the Sabbath should be taken with great seriousness. It was to them a matter of supreme practical importance, and not a subject for mere philosophical or theological debate.

NOTES

[1] A. H. Lewis, *A Critical History of the Sabbath and the Sunday in the Christian Church*, 2d ed. (Plainfield, N.J., 1903), p. 273.
[2] John Strype, *Annals of the Reformation* (Oxford, 1824), 2:668.
[3] *Ibid.*, p. 296. It should be noted that Parliament was driven to pass this law because of a disaster that occurred on a Sunday in 1583 in which many were killed. This was interpreted as an act of God against the willful desecration of His day of rest.
[4] Bownd and two to three hundred other ministers were suspended by the Anglican Church, through the instigation of the queen and some eminent bishops, for their views on the Sabbath. Their license to preach was taken away and they were prohibited from conducting religious services in any other congregation. In addition to his Sabbatarian teaching, he also refused to subscribe to Archbishop Whitgift's three articles. These were: "1. That the Queen was supreme head of the Church; 2. That the Ordinal and the Book of Common Prayer contained nothing contrary to the Word of God; and, 3. That the Thirty-Nine Articles of the Church of England were to be admitted as agreeable to the Holy Scriptures."—James Gilfillan, *The Sabbath Viewed in the Light of Reason, Revelation, and History* (New York [1862]), p. 66.
[5] Nicholas Bownd, *The Doctrine of the Sabbath, plainely layed forth, and soundly proved* . . . (London, 1595), pp. 5, 6.
[6] *Ibid.*, pp. 2, 3.
[7] Thomas Fuller, *The Church History of Britain* (London, 1868), 3:158-160. Some of the more learned men who endorsed Bownd's position were Babington, Perkins, and Dod. These writers maintained their views on the Sabbath, which before the publication of Bownd's Treatise they had published, and which in their essentials were in harmony with his. See Gervase Babington, *Works* (1596); William Perkins, *A Golden Chain* (1597); and John Dod, *An Exposition of the Ten Commandments* (1604).
[8] This is language used in Fuller's description, summarized above. See note 7.
[9] Douglas Campbell, *The Puritan in Holland, England, and America*, 4th ed. (New York, 1892), 2:159.
[10] Maurice Ashley, *The Seventeenth Century* (London, 1958), p. 25.
[11] In 1603 and even as late as 1625, we still find clear evidence of the performance of plays and other public entertainment on Sundays.
[12] Peter Heylyn records that on the seventh of May, 1603, James so far yielded to the Puritans as to issue a proclamation; not that the king's purpose was "to debar himself of lawful Pleasures on that day; but to prohibit such disordered and unlawful Pastimes, whereby the Common people were withdrawn from the Congregation."—Peter Heylyn, *The History of the Sabbath*, 2d ed. (London, 1636), p. 257, Heritage Room, James White Library, Andrews University, Berrien Springs, Mich.
[13] Perhaps it is not too well known that the Bishop of Durham, Thomas Morton, had a considerable share in the drafting and eventual execution of this document. According to John Barwick, Morton's biographer, the king consulted with the bishop over the profanity and licentiousness that were done on the Sabbath. "The bishop thereupon, retiring from the court at Haughton Tower to his own lodging at Preston, considered of six limitations or restrictions, by way of conditions, to be imposed upon every man that should enjoy the benefit of that liberty, which he presented to the King in writing the next day, and which the King did very well approve of, and added a seventh; saying only, he would alter them from the words of a bishop to the words of a King." See John Barwick, *Life of Bishop Morton*, p. 80, quoted in Gilfillan, *op. cit.*, p. 84.
[14] A. H. Lewis, *Spiritual Sabbathism* (Plainfield, N.J., 1910), p. 171.
[15] Heylyn, *op. cit.*, p. 261.
[16] R. H. Tawney, *Religion and the Rise of Capitalism* (New York, 1926), pp. 145, 146.
[17] Gordon Harland, "American Protestantism: Its Genius and Its Problem," *The Drew Gateway* 34 (Winter 1964): 73, 74.
[18] Richard Baxter, *A Holy Commonwealth* (London, 1659), p. 320, rare book collection, University of Toronto Archives.
[19] John Owen, *Exercitations Concerning the Name, Original Nature, Use and Continuance of a Day of Sacred Rest* (London, 1671), p. 221, Heritage Room, James White Library, Andrews University.
[20] Theophilus Brabourne, *A Defence of that most Ancient, and Sacred Ordinance of Gods, the Sabbath Day* (1632), pp. 8ff.
[21] Richard Baxter, *Life of Faith* (London, 1649), p. 388; Thomas Shepard, *Theses Sabbaticae* (London, 1650), p. 90, rare book collection, University of Toronto Archives.
[22] Shepard, *op. cit.*, p. 87.
[23] James D. Packer agrees with this point of view and claims that it was most noticeable in Baxter's teachings on the redemption and restoration of man. See James D. Packer, "The Redemption and Restoration of Man in the Thought of Richard Baxter" (D.Phil. thesis, Oxford University, 1954), pp. 332, 333. Used by permission.
[24] Heylyn, *op. cit.*, pp. 239-241.
[25] Ahva John Clarence Bond, *Sabbath History—I. Before the Beginning of Modern Denominations* (Plainfield, N.J., 1922), p. 42.
[26] Lewis, *Sabbath and Sunday*, p. 257.
[27] Bond, *op. cit.*, p. 43.
[28] Bownd, *op. cit.*, pp. 6, 9.
[29] Lewis, *Sabbath and Sunday*, p. 276.

[30] *Ibid.*, p. 277.
[31] *Ibid.*, p. 278.
[32] *Ibid.*, p. 279.
[33] It is believed that Bownd and several others advocated the change from Saturday to Sunday because of their prejudices against what they called Judaism.
[34] Bownd, *op. cit.*, pp. 35, 36.
[35] Richard Baxter, *The Divine Appointment of the Lords Day Proved: as a Separated Day for Holy Worship; Especially in the Church Assemblies. And consequently the cessation of the seventh day sabbath* (London, 1671); Richard Barnard, *A Threefold Treatise of the Sabbath* (London, 1641), rare book collection, University of Toronto Archives; John Wallis, *A Defense of the Christian Sabbath: In Answer to a Treatise of Mr. Thomas Bampfield, Pleading for Saturday-Sabbath* 2d ed. (Oxford, 1693).
[36] J. Lee Gamble and Charles H. Greene, "The Sabbath in the British Isles," in *Seventh Day Baptists in Europe and America* (Plainfield, N.J., 1910), 1:107-109.
[37] Theophilus Brabourne, *A Discourse upon the Sabbath Day* (London, 1628).
[38] Fuller, *op. cit.*, p. 419.
[39] Gilfillan, *op. cit.*, p. 125.
[40] Brabourne, *A Defence of that most Ancient, and Sacred Ordinance of Gods, the Sabbath Day*, p. [i].
[41] Francis White, *A Treatise of the Sabbath-Day Containing a Defence of the Orthodoxall Doctrine of the Church of England Against Sabbatarian-Novelty* (London, 1636), p. [xxiv], Heritage Room, James White Library, Andrews University, Berrien Springs, Michigan.
[42] Thomas Bampfield, p. 29.
[43] *Ibid.*, p. 85.
[44] *Ibid.*, p. 2.
[45] Lawrence Allen Turner, "The Puritan Sabbath," pp. 75, 14, personal files of author. Used by permission.
[46] George Walker, *The Doctrine of the Holy Weekly Sabbath* (London: 1651), rare book collection, Thomas Fisher Library, University of Toronto.
[47] B. W. Ball, *The English Connection* (Cambridge, 1981), pp. 138-158.
[48] J. C. Broomfield, "The Day Through the Ages," in *The Day of Worship*, ed. by W. W. Davis (New York 1932), p. 140.
[49] Herbert W. Richardson, *Toward an American Theology* (New York, 1967), pp. 112, 113.
[50] Gilfillan, *op. cit.*, p. 150.
[51] *Ibid.*
[52] John Eliot source.
[53] Lewis, *Spiritual Sabbathism*, pp. 177, 178; The First Code of Laws, 1650, and The New Haven Code, 1655, in *The True-Blue Laws of Connecticut and New Haven*, ed. by J. Hammond Trumbull (Hartford, Conn., 1876); *Records of the Colony at New Plymouth in New England—Laws: 1623-1682*, ed. by David Pulsifer (Boston, 1861).
[54] Lewis, *Sabbath and Sunday*, p. 364.
[55] L. A. Platts, "Seventh-day Baptists in America Previous to 1802," in *Seventh Day Baptists in Europe and America* (Plainfield, N.J.: 1910), 1:126.
[56] Arthur E. Main, "The Seventh-day Baptist General Conference, 1802 to 1902," in *Seventh Day Baptists in Europe and America* (Plainfield, N.J.: 1910), 1:149, 150.

CHAPTER 13

The Sabbath in the New World

Raymond F. Cottrell

FIRST to observe the seventh-day Sabbath in the New World were Jews who had been compelled by the Inquisition in the Old World to convert to Christianity. These "New Christians," who were still Jews at heart and who continued to practice their own religion in secret, sailed with Columbus and other explorers on their voyages of discovery to the New World more than a century before the first Christian Sabbathkeepers arrived. In 1502 one group of Crypto-Jews, fugitives from the Inquisition in Portugal, applied for a commission to migrate to Brazil and became the first Jewish settlers in the Western Hemisphere. In 1521 others accompanied Cortes on his conquest of Mexico, and it is said that by 1550 there were more Spanish Crypto-Jews in Mexico City than Spanish Catholics. Jewish immigrants entered Argentina soon after 1580.[1] The first Jewish congregation in the New World, Mikveh Israel, was formed in Curaçao, Netherland Antilles, in 1651.[2] In Mexico, Brazil, and elsewhere in Latin America, Crypto-Jews who had reverted to Judaism or who were under suspicion of practicing their own religion in secret were burned at the stake.[3]

When the Portuguese took Brazil from the Dutch, in 1654, twenty-three Jewish refugees fled the country and found refuge in New Amsterdam (later renamed New York), where they established the first congregation in North America, Sherith Israel.[4] Erelong synagogue communities were founded in such cities as Newport, Rhode Island; Philadelphia, Pennsylvania; Charleston, South Carolina; and Savannah, Georgia. At the time of the American Revolution about 2,500 Jews resided in the thirteen Colonies. By 1850 seventy-seven congregations had been formed in twenty-one States.[5] Permanent settlements were established in Halifax about 1750 and in French Canada in 1759.[6]

The total Jewish population of the Americas in 1967 was approximately 6,952,000. Eighty-five percent of these lived in the United States, half of them in New York City. In 1978 there were 6,115,000 American Jews.[7]

There are three main branches of American Judaism—Orthodox, Reform, and Conservative. Orthodox Jews preserve the theology and traditions of Old World Jewry. Adhering strictly to the Torah and faithfully observing the dietary laws and the traditional holy days and festivals, including the Sabbath, they are the

THE SABBATH IN THE NEW WORLD

fundamentalists of Judaism. Reform Judaism, liberal in belief and practice, recognizes only the Torah as normative, but is ready to adapt it to modern requirements: for example, shorter synagogue services and use of the vernacular instead of Hebrew in the ritual. Reform Jews no longer believe in a personal Messiah but still look forward to a Messianic Age. In belief and practice Conservative Judaism is midway between Orthodox and Reform Judaism.

Many modern Jews are practicing or crypto-atheists or -agnostics. For them being a Jew is more a matter of race, culture, and ethics than religion. Many attend synagogue for the major religious festivals, and perhaps on Friday night or Sunday morning rather than the Sabbath. In some synagogues such as Temple Beth Immanuel in New York City, largest in the United States, Sunday services are much better attended than those on the Sabbath. With approximately 3,000 congregations, Orthodox Judaism is the largest of the three groups. Conservative and Reform Judaism have about half that number, almost evenly divided between them.[8]

First Christian Sabbatarians in the New World

As noted in the preceding chapter (p. 240), Christian observance of the seventh day of the week as the Sabbath came to the New World with the arrival in Newport, Rhode Island, of Stephen Mumford, of the Bell Lane Seventh Day Baptist church of London, in about 1664. Finding none of his own faith, he united with the Newport Baptist church, and soon other members of the congregation joined him in observing the Sabbath. Church leaders preached against the practice and denounced those who observed Saturday as "heretics and schismatics." Two families gave up the Sabbath as the controversy waxed sharp and bitter, and eventually those who persisted in its observance were summoned before the church in an open trial and charged with teaching and practicing error. Convinced at last that they could not keep the Sabbath if they remained members of the Baptist Church, seven withdrew and, a few days later—December 23, 1671—entered into solemn covenant with one another as the First Seventh Day Baptist church of Newport. William Hiscox, one of Mumford's first converts, was their first pastor.[9]

In 1684 another English immigrant, Abel Nobel, settled in Bucks County, Pennsylvania, twenty-five miles north of Philadelphia. Coming in contact with a Seventh Day Baptist from Connecticut, he accepted the Sabbath and persuaded a number of his neighbors to join him in observing it. In 1702 Edmund Dunham, a deacon and licensed Baptist preacher of Piscataway, New Jersey, discovered the Sabbath and was influential in leading several others to acknowledge its claims. In 1705 this group established the First Seventh Day Baptist church of Piscataway, with seventeen members.

About the same time still other Seventh Day Baptist communities grew up in the vicinity of Philadelphia, Pennsylvania. In 1708 a Sabbathkeeping group migrated from Newport to Westerly (later Hopkinton), on the mainland, and formed a new congregation there. The first Seventh Day Baptist congregation in New York State was organized in Renselaer County, in 1780, by folk from Rhode Island, and the first in Connecticut in 1784, at New London. It was from these early centers in Rhode Island, Pennsylvania, and New Jersey that the Sabbath followed the tide of American migration westward.[10]

245

As in England, Seventh Day Baptists in the New World suffered the displeasure of most other Christians because of the seventh-day Sabbath, and were subjected to fines and imprisonment for their faith.[11] This was true to some extent even in Rhode Island, where freedom of belief presumably prevailed.[12] During the Revolutionary War, on the other hand, loyalty to the Sabbath protected the sanctuary of the mother congregation in Newport when British troops were being billeted in church buildings. Upon entering the Newport Seventh Day Baptist church with this objective in mind, the British commander noticed the Ten Commandments on the wall of the sanctuary and ordered his men to retire. He would not desecrate a house in which the sacred laws of God were written and honored, he explained.[13]

The General Conference of Seventh Day Baptists

A yearly meeting of Seventh Day Baptist churches, convened first at Newport as early as 1696, was later transferred to Westerly. Delegates attending the annual meeting of September 11, 1801, at Hopkinton (Westerly), Rhode Island, reported seven congregations and a dozen settlements of Sabbathkeepers in four States, and a membership of 1,031. This session adopted the designation General Conference and issued an urgent invitation to all of the "churches, branches and people of the same faith and order in the States of America" to meet with them one year later. The name Seventh Day Baptist was adopted in 1818.[14]

The primary objective motivating organization of the General Conference was "the growing conviction among the active membership of the churches that the time had come when all Seventh-day [sic] Baptist churches should be united in active and aggressive missionary work," meaning, specifically, propagation of the Sabbath message.[15] It was not until the sessions of 1817 and 1818, however, that definite steps were taken to implement concerted evangelism. A Board of Trustees and Directors of Missions was appointed, and local congregations were encouraged to constitute themselves missionary societies in order to witness more effectively to the Sabbath, each in its own vicinity. By this time there were 2,173 members in 14 churches.[16] In 1821 *The Seventh-day Baptist Missionary Magazine* was launched, with the objective of disseminating information about the Bible Sabbath, and in 1830 the *Protestant Sentinel*. In 1844 these were replaced by *The Sabbath Recorder,* which has continued publication to the present time. In 1824 the General Conference voted to publish a series of tracts, and in 1828 established the American Seventh Day Baptist Missionary Society. The result of these missionary activities was an increase of membership to 3,400 in 27 churches by the close of the decade.[17]

In 1835 the Seventh Day Baptist General Tract Society was organized, and the following year a three-man committee was commissioned to write and procure manuscripts for a series of missionary tracts on the Sabbath. In 1838 six of these tracts were issued, in an edition of 2,000 each. In 1843 the name was changed to General Sabbath Tract Society, and in 1844 to American Sabbath Tract Society, which has continued to the present. In 1843 approval was given for a special appeal to Baptists, urging them to accept the Sabbath. Twenty thousand copies of the appeal were printed, and the little tract was later incorporated into the Sabbath tract series. By 1850 there were seventeen titles in the series, and six books on the subject had been published.[18]

THE SABBATH IN THE NEW WORLD

First Sabbatarian Adventists

The 1843 session of the General Conference of Seventh Day Baptists appointed November 1 of that year as a day of fasting and prayer for the proclamation of the Sabbath truth. A year later the 1844 session (September 11 to 15) rejoiced in an unprecedented, "deeper and wider-spread" interest in the Sabbath and in the accession of converts to the Sabbath, "including several ministers."[19] Among these converts were Frederick Wheeler, a Methodist-Adventist minister whose circuit included the Washington, New Hampshire, Christian church, and several members of his congregation. Two editorials in the Millerite paper *The Midnight Cry* (September 5 and 12, 1844) noted that "many persons have their minds deeply exercised respecting a supposed obligation to observe the seventh day," and mentioned the Seventh Day Baptist agitation of the issue. "We love the seventh-day brethren and sisters," the editor said, "but we think they are trying to mend the old broken Jewish yoke, and putting it on their necks."[20] Nothing was to be permitted to distract attention from the anticipated return of Christ in only a few weeks.

Conducting the communion service one Sunday morning early in 1844, Frederick Wheeler, the Methodist-Adventist minister of the Washington, New Hampshire, Christian church, stressed the importance of obeying God's commandments. Present was a middle-aged woman, Mrs. Rachel Oakes, a Seventh Day Baptist, who later married Nathan Preston. In a subsequent conversation with Pastor Wheeler she witnessed to her belief in the seventh day of the week as the Bible Sabbath, with the result that a few weeks later, in March, he kept his first Sabbath and preached a sermon on the subject. By early 1845 many of his Washington parishioners, including several members of the Farnsworth family, had begun keeping the Sabbath, and eventually Rachel Preston became an Adventist.[21] Frederick Wheeler was thus the first Adventist to observe the Sabbath, and she the first Sabbathkeeper to become an Adventist. These Sabbathkeeping Adventists in Washington became the first Sabbatarian Adventist congregation, and eventually purchased the church building.[22]

During the years prior to 1844, many Seventh Day Baptists had listened approvingly to the Millerite proclamation of an imminent Advent, and sought to share with the Adventists their own conviction with respect to the Sabbath. One such Seventh Day Baptist, who had listened to the Advent Message in 1844 but did not accept it until October, 1851, was Roswell F. Cottrell, of Mill Grove in western New York. He had always "believed in the personal appearing of Christ," which he believed "was near," as he later wrote James White, a founder of the Seventh-day Adventist Church. But being deeply committed to the seventh-day Sabbath, Cottrell "saw the proclaimers of the Advent in darkness in regard to the commandments of God, and bowing to an institution of Papacy." It was the discovery of a group of Sabbathkeeping Adventists, through *The Second Advent Review and Sabbath Herald* early in its first year of publication (1850-1851), that led him to unite with the Adventists.[23] Many other Seventh Day Baptists, such as W. A. Spicer, later followed his example, often doubtless for the same reason.[24]

Seventh Day Baptists could not conscientiously unite with Sundaykeepers, and the Millerite leaders, on their part, resented any diversion of attention from the Advent to the Sabbath, which to them was an unimportant side issue. Thus relatively few Seventh Day Baptists became Millerite Adventists, or vice versa.[25]

THE SABBATH IN SCRIPTURE AND HISTORY

Emergence of Sabbatarian Adventism

Acceptance of the seventh-day Sabbath in 1844-1845 by Adventists such as Frederick Wheeler and many of his fellow parishioners in Washington, New Hampshire, proved to be a local phenomenon. Sabbathkeeping did not spread thence to other Adventist individuals or groups, at least to any extent sufficient to become a matter of record. Acceptance of the Sabbath by a significant number of the early Adventists, scattered and without communication with one another, came gradually over the next four or five years. It was not until 1849 that a small but identifiable group of Sabbatarian Adventists began to emerge. "The Sabbath cause did not advance with us but little up to 1849. At that time it began to rise, and its progress has been steady and firm till the present," James White wrote in 1853.[26]

The second Millerite Adventist minister to adopt the seventh-day Sabbath was Thomas M. Preble, in the summer of 1844. Publication of his article on the Sabbath in *The Hope of Israel* as *A Tract Showing that the Seventh Day Should Be Observed as the Sabbath* in March, 1845, was of major importance in bringing the Sabbath to Adventists generally.[27] A few weeks later Joseph Bates read both the article and the tract, studied the matter carefully himself, and then visited Frederick Wheeler specifically to learn more about the Sabbath. It proved to be largely through Bates's dedicated witness among his fellow Adventists that they adopted the Sabbath. Asked "What is the news?" by a friend the day following his visit to the home of Frederick Wheeler, Bates replied, "The news is that the seventh day is the Sabbath of the Lord our God." Bates devoted the remainder of his life to proclaiming that news. A year later, in August, 1846, he published his own tract, *The Seventh-day Sabbath a Perpetual Sign*.[28] Also that year he called the Sabbath to the attention of Hiram Edson, James White, and Ellen Harmon (soon to become Ellen White), thereby preparing the way for the crystallization of Sabbatarian Adventism.*

This, Ellen Harmon's first encounter with the seventh-day Sabbath, took place during the course of a visit to New Bedford, Massachusetts, in the summer of 1846 for the purpose of encouraging Advent believers in that city. Bates urged the Sabbath upon her, but she did not at that time see its importance, thinking that he erred in dwelling upon the fourth commandment more than the others. A few days later, on August 30, she and James White were married, and soon thereafter they studied Bates's pamphlet together, and in the autumn began to observe the Sabbath.[29]

In a vision late the following winter, "a few months" after their marriage, she saw Jesus raise the cover of the ark in the sanctuary in heaven, and within the ark she saw the tables of stone inscribed with the Ten Commandments. She was surprised to see "a soft halo of light encircling" the fourth command, and was shown "that if the true Sabbath had been kept, there would never have been an infidel or an atheist." In response to the proclamation of the message of the third angel of Revelation 14, "many would embrace the Sabbath of the Lord." This vision, emphasizing the perpetuity of the law of God, including the Sabbath, confirmed her and her husband in its observance.[30] The prediction that "many would embrace the Sabbath" was soon to become a reality.

---

* Joseph Bates's part in the earliest formulation of Adventism's distinctive Sabbath theology was especially important. Hence, his special contributions, plus an overview of later trends, are given further attention in appendix G.

THE SABBATH IN THE NEW WORLD

The "Sabbath Conferences"

In response to invitations, James and Ellen White attended six (or seven, according to some reckonings) important "general meetings" in Connecticut, New York, Maine, and Massachusetts between April 20 and November 18-19, 1848. Participants spoke of them as "general meetings" in view of the fact that Advent believers and interested friends in the general vicinity of each meeting were invited to attend. They were also referred to as "conferences" (later "Sabbath conferences"), but they were not conferences in the usual sense of the term. Their purpose was to instruct those who attended on major points of doctrine already determined, not to confer in order to determine doctrine. Those in attendance "'were not all fully in the truth'"; "hardly two agreed"; "some were holding serious errors, and each strenuously urged his own views"; others "loved the truth, but were listening to and cherishing error."[31]

James and Ellen White and Joseph Bates were the principal speakers, their main subjects being the Sabbath, the third angel's message (Rev. 14:9-12) in relation to the Sabbath, and last-day events in prophecy. This was the "present truth" in which these meetings established the scattered Advent believers. "Truth gained the victory," Ellen White wrote. "Our brethren renounced their errors and united upon the third angel's message, and God greatly blessed them and added to their numbers."[32] It was in the setting of the third angel's message that the Sabbath became relevant to many Adventists and began to take hold of them as a group.

At each of the meetings differences of opinion and discord gave way to harmony, and these scattered believers in New England and New York began to feel a bond of unity and fellowship. Sabbathkeeping Adventists, James White wrote in 1853, had come from various denominations "holding different views on some subjects; yet, thank Heaven, the Sabbath is a mighty platform on which we can all stand united. And while standing here . . . all party feelings are lost."[33] Arthur Spalding estimates that there were at that time, all told, no more than one hundred of these Sabbathkeeping Adventists, who formed the nucleus of what later became the Seventh-day Adventist Church.[34]

The Present Truth and *The Advent Review*

In November, 1848, Ellen White told her husband that he should begin publishing a small paper to advance the cause of present truth. In response, James White brought out the first issue of *The Present Truth* in July, 1849. He later wrote that it had not been his intention to "issue more than two or three numbers," but eventually there were eleven, the last dated November, 1850.[35]

Articles on the Sabbath, filling nearly two thirds of the space in the eleven issues (865 of 1408 column inches), traced the Sabbath back to Creation and presented its immutability. It had not been changed, could not be changed, and was therefore still binding. The first two issues dealt exclusively with the Sabbath; later issues touched also on Christ's ministry in the heavenly sanctuary, the third angel's message, and the "shut door." The article on the sanctuary presented the Sabbath of the fourth commandment in that setting, while that on the third angel's message presented the Sabbath as the great test that would signify God's loyal people prior to the return of Jesus, which was considered very imminent.[36] This particular article was addressed specifically to first-day Adventists. Two years later

James White wrote that "in the fulfillment of the prophecy of Rev. xiv, 6-14, in the Second Advent movement, the 'commandments of God' hold a place, as the last great testing truth, just before the Son of man takes His place on the white cloud to reap the harvest of the earth." [37]

Introducing the first number of *The Present Truth*, James White said that for several months he had been "burdened with the duty of writing, and publishing the *present truth* for the scattered flock" of Advent believers. He identified "the keeping of the fourth commandment" as *all-important present truth*." In the same sentence he hastened to add that "this alone, will not save anyone." [38] The title of the little journal, together with the fact that it was devoted primarily—and in its first two issues exclusively—to the seventh-day Sabbath, tacitly identifies the Sabbath as uppermost in the minds of James and Ellen White as "present truth" for that time. The Sabbath was still "news," as Joseph Bates had described it three years before.

The influence of the Sabbath conferences and *The Present Truth* in uniting the Advent believers is also evident in letters from readers. Some of these letters were from persons ministering to the "little flock scattered abroad." Others were from some who had accepted present truth—the Sabbath and the third angel's message. There were also announcements of further "conferences," in 1849 and 1850, in various parts of New England and New York.

In a letter from North Paris, Maine, dated October 16, 1849, and published in *The Present Truth* in December of that year, J. N. Andrews wrote that "the Conference recently held in this place, resulted in much good." "Erroneous" and "painful" views had long separated "the brethren" in that vicinity, but the conference had united them "in the great and important truths of God." He concludes: "How important it is, beloved brethren, in this, our final struggle with the dragon, that we be found UNITED in *'the commandments of God and the testimony of Jesus Christ.'"*

On the same page of that issue, another correspondent in Vermont writes of being "very much encouraged in view of what is being done by the late publications"; he tells of neighbors embracing the Sabbath as a result of reading "your little paper." [39] Another reader reported that "the present state of the cause in this part of the State is cheering. Our last conference, held April 20 and 21, was one of the best I ever attended. The brethren all seemed to be very firm on the truth." Another group in Camden, Maine, he says, "have lately embraced the Sabbath." They had been "scattered and torn" by various errors, but recent efforts have produced "a strong union" among them. [40]

The Sabbath doctrine proved to be the catalyst needed to unite the scattered Advent believers and to weld them together as a coherent, cohesive group. Prior to 1848 Sabbath observance among them had been a matter of personal conviction and practice on the part of a few individuals. By late 1849 it had become the accepted norm among those Adventists who later adopted the name *Seventh-day Adventist*.[41] In 1851 Ellen White wrote: "God's people are coming into the unity of the faith. Those who observe the Sabbath of the Bible are united in their views of Bible truth. But those who oppose the Sabbath among the Advent people are disunited and strangely divided." [42] In the final issue of *The Present Truth* she spoke of that as being the "gathering time" in which God purposed to "recover the remnant of His people." For this reason they should be "united and zealous in the work" of spreading the truth. Also for this reason "it . . . [was] necessary that the truth should be published in a paper, as [it had been] preached."[43] This "gathering" and unification was largely accomplished through the Sabbath conferences of 1848 to 1850 and publication of *The Present Truth*.

The Sabbath was thus, in a very real sense, the unifying factor around which the Seventh-day Adventist Church came into being, and it is still a potent force that binds together the Adventist people around the world, transcending all barriers of nationality, race, language, political ideology, and economic status. It levels all barriers and makes the most diverse people one in Christ as has nothing else in the history of the world.

Curiously, between Numbers 10 and 11 of *The Present Truth*[44] James White brought out the five regular issues and two extras of another periodical, *The Advent Review*. The fact that he did not incorporate its articles into further issues of *The Present Truth* points to the unique role he conceived for each journal, one as a harbinger of the Sabbath and the other of the fact that *these* ardent *Sabbatarians* were still dedicated *Adventists*. They "were now carrying forward the torch of prophetic truth once held aloft by the entire body of Adventists prior to and immediately following the great disappointment," he wrote.[45] Thus, publication of *The Advent Review* at this juncture brought these two major facets of Sabbatarian Adventist belief back into balance.

This was the prelude to White's publication of volume 1, Number 1, of the *Second Advent Review and Sabbath Herald* (now the *Adventist Review*), in November, 1850, the same month in which the final numbers of both *The Present Truth* and *The Advent Review* appeared. That must have been a busy month for James White. This merger of the Sabbath and the Advent in one publication made *seventh-day* Adventism a permanent entity on the religious scene. It found expression also, eleven years later, in the choice of the name "Seventh-day Adventist." Prior to 1861 those who adopted the name identified themselves, and were spoken of by others, variously as "the little flock," "Second Advent Sabbath Keepers," "Seventh-day Advent people," and "Sabbath-keeping Adventists."[46]

Deserving of special mention among the multiplicity of Adventist publications on the Sabbath was J. N. Andrews' classic *History of the Sabbath*, first published in 1861 and revised and reprinted repeatedly for more than half a century (the fourth edition was coauthored by L. R. Conradi). This volume represented the more mature development of his series of articles in the *Review* in April and May, 1853.[47] In January, 1854, James White announced his intention to publish a series of twelve to fifteen Sabbath and Advent tracts of 32 to 100 pages each. The first four of these were ready in August.[48]

Determining When to Begin the Sabbath

Sabbathkeeping Adventists were agreed on the binding force of the Sabbath command and the proper mode of Sabbath observance. Examining the Scriptures for themselves, they concluded that the Seventh Day Baptists were right on these matters and followed their example in everything except the point of when to begin the Sabbath. The latter observed the Sabbath from "even to even," which they defined as from sunset to sunset.[49] "With the Seventh Day Baptists," wrote James White, "we agree on the institution, design, and perpetuity of the Sabbath."[50] But a majority of Adventists, in accepting the Sabbath from the

Seventh Day Baptists, had evidently missed the definition of "even" as "sunset." Thus it had been with Joseph Bates, through whom the Sabbath came to most Adventists and who began the Sabbath at six o'clock Friday night. Other Adventists were beginning it at sunset, and still others at midnight or at sunrise Saturday morning.[51]

Obviously this diversity of practice on so important a matter could not continue indefinitely without affecting the unity of the fledgling church, which, *mirabile dictu,* the Sabbath had brought about. Fearing such a division unless the issue "could be settled by good testimony," in August, 1855, James White asked J. N. Andrews to make a thorough investigation of the matter and prepare an article on the subject for the *Review.* Andrews was already recognized as a careful Bible scholar.[52]

Andrews' review of the evidence appeared at length (72 column inches) in the *Review* for December 4, 1855. In the *Review* for June 2, 1851, he had advocated a six o'clock Sabbath, but now, following a detailed examination of the Biblical evidence for sunset as marking the beginning and end of each day, and thus also of the Sabbath, he concluded that there is no Biblical evidence whatever for six o'clock as "even," in the expression "from even unto even, shall ye celebrate your sabbath." Citing *Putnam's Hand Book of Useful Arts* that clocks and watches were invented in 1658, he commented with typical New England logic that if six o'clock were indeed the proper time to begin the Sabbath, then "for nearly the whole space of 6,000 years the people of God have been without the means of telling when the Sabbath commenced." Impeccable logic!

In an accompanying note Andrews announced that for him "the result of the investigation is the firm conviction that the commencement and close of each day [and thus of the Sabbath] is marked by the setting of the sun." "The Seventh Day Baptists have always held to this doctrine," he explained, "but I have never happened to meet with their views. Had I done so, I should not have remained in error on this subject." "Besides this, as I now learn, a considerable number of our brethren have long been convinced that the Sabbath commences at sunset." [53]

Later Contacts With the Seventh Day Baptists

During the thirty-five years from 1844 to 1879 a more or less friendly relationship prevailed between Seventh-day Adventists and Seventh Day Baptists. The first official contact between the two groups came with a letter from J. C. Rogers, "corresponding secretary" of "the Seventh Day Baptist Central Association," to James White as editor of the *Review* dated July 28, 1853. He had been commissioned "to correspond with the Seventh-day Advent people, and learn their faith." James White published his response to Rogers' letter in the *Review* two weeks later.[54]

In 1869 a friendly overture from the Seventh-day Adventist General Conference, then in its sixth year, elicited "a fraternal reply" from its Seventh Day Baptist counterpart, which in turn appointed one of its number as "a delegate to the next meeting of that body." In 1870 Roswell F. Cottrell reported in the *Review* that he attended their General Conference session in Little Genesee, New York, and had been "courteously invited by vote to take part in their deliberations." At the same session they voted "co-operation with the Seventh-day Adventists, but without compromising distinctive principles," but tabled "a motion to send a delegate to the Adventist Conference."[55] Over the next ten years Seventh-day Adventist leaders such as John Nevins Andrews, Uriah Smith, James White, and J. H. Waggoner were commissioned as representatives to the annual Seventh Day Baptist General Conference sessions, where they were always cordially welcomed and seated as delegates. The Seventh Day Baptists reciprocated, and their delegates were as cordially received and welcomed by the Adventists. Reports of the "prosperity" attending the work of the Adventists were met with Baptist resolutions "expressing fraternal joy."[56] This interchange of delegates has continued intermittently to the present time.

Certain unfortunate incidents, however, involving a few overzealous Adventists acting on their own initiative, gradually drove a wedge of sorts between Seventh Day Baptists and Seventh-day Adventists. The years 1850 to 1880 witnessed relatively rapid growth of Seventh-day Adventists, and an occasional loss of Seventh Day Baptist members to the Adventists. "This loss might have been sustained with a minimum of misunderstanding" except for several instances of the traumatic breakup of a Seventh Day Baptist congregation by Adventists whose crude tactics aroused distrust and resentment that lingered for many years.[57]

The most blatant such episode occurred one winter day in 1855 when an Adventist, D. P. Hall, appeared at the Hayfield, Pennsylvania, Seventh Day Baptist church and challenged all comers to a rousing debate. The result was a split in the Hayfield church that left bitter feelings on both sides. Several Seventh Day Baptist congregations were thus weakened by a loss of members to the Adventists, and some disbanded altogether. It was often the case, however, that a church was already weak as the result of internal strife or a lack of leadership or doctrinal cohesiveness. Articles about "sheep stealing" appeared in the journals on both sides.[58]

A number of years later, James White included the following reflection: "'We deeply regretted the havoc made in some of the S. D. Baptist churches in Pennsylvania, more than twenty years since, by men who do not now stand with us. For while that work weakened the S. D. Baptists, it brought but very little strength to our cause.'"[59]

White expressed the sentiment of responsible Adventists when he wrote: "'Both bodies have a specific work to do. God bless them both in all their efforts for its accomplishment. The field is a wide one. And we further recommend that Seventh-day Adventists in their aggressive work avoid laboring to build up Seventh-day Adventist churches where Seventh Day Baptist churches are already established. If ministers or members from the Seventh Day Baptists regard it their duty to come to us, under the impression that they can serve the cause of God better, we shall give them a place with us. But we see no reason why there should be any effort put forth on the part of our people to weaken the hands of our Seventh Day Baptist brethren, in order to add to our numbers from those who were before us in revering the ancient Sabbath of the Lord."[60]

The Seventh Day Baptists in Later Years

During the second half of the nineteenth century the Seventh Day Baptists continued to experience a gradual increase in membership until, by the centenary of their General Conference, in 1901, it stood at 9,257; since then it has slowly declined, and in 1978 stood at 5,139.[61] During the nineteenth century they operated a number of seminaries, colleges, and one university—Alfred University—but these educational institutions have been either discontinued or secularized.[62]

The Sabbath is the only significant point of belief on which Baptists and Seventh Day Baptists differ. One contemporary Seventh Day Baptist author refers to it as the "only just reason for our denominational existence, separate from other Baptists."[63] Their zealous endeavor, especially over the past century and a half, to inspire among fellow Christians of other faiths an appreciation of the seventh-day Sabbath is worthy of commendation. But their dwindling membership over the past eight decades suggests that the Sabbath alone does not provide sufficient incentive to attract members and to maintain a separate denominational existence. Only as one important facet of Bible truth along with other truths can the Sabbath be understood and appreciated in its true perspective and so win minds and hearts on any significant scale.[64] Their 1801 membership of slightly more than 1,130 peaked a little more than a century later at something more than 9,300[65]—an average gain of approximately eighty members per year, far below the growth rate of either the United States or the world. Since the turn of the century their membership has decreased back to approximately its 1840 level.[66] Perhaps the major success of their three centuries and more of dedicated denominational witness in the New World was the acceptance of the Sabbath by a few Millerite Adventists during the 1840s.

Other Sabbathkeeping Sects

Distinct both historically and administratively from regular Seventh Day Baptists are about 150 German Seventh Day Baptists, the remnant of a group organized in 1728 (they established themselves in Ephrata, Pennsylvania, in 1732), with roots in the Old World. In belief they are similar to the Dunkards, with whom their founder was associated prior to that time. They practice communism and celibacy.[67]

A number of small Christian denominations or groups observe the seventh day of the week as the Sabbath. Two of these grew out of the Second Advent Movement of 1844—the Seventh Day Church of God (Denver), with about 8,000 members, and the Church of God (Salem, West Virginia), with about 2,000. The former originated about 1900 and the latter in 1933. Related to the West Virginia group is the so-called World Headquarters of the Church of God in Jerusalem, Israel, led by the late A. N. Dugger. Based in Portsmouth, Virginia, is the Church of God and Saints in Christ, which was established in 1896 and in 1980 had a membership of about 38,000.[68]

A more recent group that observes the seventh day of the week as the Sabbath is Herbert W. Armstrong's Worldwide Church of God. Originally a Quaker, he united with the Church of God in Oregon, and in 1934 began a radiobroadcast, later incorporating under the name Radio Church of God. In 1968 the name was changed to Worldwide Church of God. With headquarters in Pasadena, California, membership has been reported variously as between 30,000 and 100,000. (In 1978 Armstrong's son, Garner Ted, broke away to found the Church of God, International.)[69]

The Strangite Church of Jesus Christ of Latter-day Saints, organized in Wisconsin in 1844, in 1980 had perhaps 300 members. It claims to be "the one and original Church of Jesus Christ of Latter-Day Saints" and that its founder, James J. Strang, is the only legitimate successor to Joseph Smith. In several respects, including observance of the seventh-day Sabbath, Strangites differ from other Mormons.[70] According to the *Book of Mormon* the seventh day is the Sabbath, but the Mormon Church explains that it is impractical to observe Saturday in the modern world.

Finally, there is a seventh-day Pentecostal group of about 25,000 with headquarters in Brazil known as the Adventist Church of Promise, organized in 1932 and consisting of some 500 congregations in various countries of South America.[71]

Adventist Indebtedness to the Seventh Day Baptists

The extent of Adventist indebtedness to the Seventh Day Baptists for an understanding of the Sabbath is evident from the constant use made of Seventh Day Baptist publications, especially their Sabbath Tract Series, during the early years of the church. "The writings of the Seventh Day Baptists have been a great comfort and strength to us," wrote James White in 1853.[72]

On page 7 of volume 1, Number 1, of *The Second Advent Review and Sabbath Herald* (November, 1850) appeared the editorial note: "We call special attention of the brethren to the articles, in this number from the publications of the Seventh-day Baptists [sic]. They are clear, comprehensive, and irrefutable. We intend to enrich the columns of the *Review and Herald,* with extracts from their excellent works on the Sabbath.

"We also design to get out a large pamphlet, containing the same material from their publications, that we publish in this paper. Such a work, judiciously circulated, will certainly do a great amount of good." [73]

The first number of the *Review* contains four such reprints, which fill 124 of its 166 column inches, fully three fourths of the space. The second issue, in December, contains one Seventh Day Baptist article on the Sabbath, and one each by J. N. Andrews and Joseph Bates.[74] The twelve issues of volume 1 devoted 769 column inches to the Sabbath, or 38.5 percent of the space. Of this, 399 column inches were from Seventh Day Baptist sources and 370 by Adventist authors, or 20 and 18.5 percent of the total, respectively. This clearly reflects the extent to which pioneer Adventists were indebted to the Seventh Day Baptists for their understanding of the Sabbath.

On the front page of Number 6 is a poem of seven stanzas, "'It's Jewish,'" in defense of the Sabbath, by former Seventh Day Baptist Roswell Fenner Cottrell.[75] At the same time Cottrell had sent *Review* editor James White a copy of an eight-page tract he had written about the Sabbath—*A Letter to the Disciples of the Lord.* Of this tract James White wrote in the same issue of the *Review:* "We think it is *very good,* and hope to be able to publish it entire, soon." It appeared two weeks later in Number 8, six months before the author became an Adventist.[76] Over the next forty years Cottrell contributed 1,692 articles and other items to the paper and was listed as a member of the original "Publishing Committee," with J. N. Andrews and Uriah Smith, and later as a "corresponding editor." [77] Many of his articles dealt with the Sabbath, which ever remained a precious treasure to him. Repeatedly, through the columns of the *Review,* he appealed to his "dear" former Seventh Day Baptist "brethren" to espouse the Advent hope, as he had done.[78]

The Sabbath in Adventist Theology

Consideration of possible alternatives to the events of history—a contrast between what actually happened and what might have happened—is one useful way by which to estimate the meaning and importance of those events. Without the Sabbath there obviously would not be a Seventh-day Adventist Church. What would have become of the mid-nineteenth-century Millerite Adventists who became Sabbatarians had they not accepted the Sabbath? And what would have become of the Seventh Day Baptists had they, as a body, accepted the hope of an imminent Advent? Answers to these hypothetical questions can be inferred from the relative success, over the years, of Sabbatarian Adventism, non-Sabbatarian Adventism, and non-Adventist Sabbatarianism—that is, from a theological perspective, of the Advent and the Sabbath in a symbiotic relationship, and of each apart from the other. More important than either of these questions, however, is the meaning and importance of the Advent and the Sabbath to each other in Seventh-day Adventist theology, and thus to the church in its life, mission, and witness.

Sabbatarian Adventists emerged as a discrete, identifiable group in 1849, and the relative strength of the three religious groups in that year is taken as a basis for comparing their relative viability over the intervening years, as determined by membership growth. Other significant factors have, of course, been involved, especially (1) prophetic guidance in the life and work of the church and (2) the Adventist concept of world mission.

Post-1844 Millerite Adventists who did not accept the Sabbath eventually coalesced into three groups extant in 1980—The Advent Christian Church, with approximately 30,000 members; the Church of God (Abrahamic Faith), with about 6,500; and the Primitive Advent Christian Church, with 600 or so—a total of some 37,000 members.[79] This total represents slightly more than one percent of the 3-million-plus worldwide membership of Seventh-day Adventists.[80] From this we might conclude that Adventism *with* the Sabbath has been approximately one hundred times more effective than it has proved to be *without* the Sabbath.

The significant theological difference between Seventh-day Adventists and Seventh Day Baptists is, of course, emphasis on the imminence of the Advent. The 1849 Seventh Day Baptist membership of 5,949 far outnumbered that of Sabbatarian Adventists, of whom there were about 100[81]—a ratio of better than 59 to 1. Or we might say that there were 0.017 times as many Sabbatarian Adventists as there were Seventh Day Baptists. In 1978 Seventh Day Baptist membership stood at 5,139 (810 *less* than in 1849),[82] and that of Seventh-day Adventists at more than 3 million, a ratio of 584 to 1. Accordingly, the Sabbath *with* the Advent has proved to be 30,647 times more effective than it has been *without* the Advent.

Thus on a strictly empirical, historical basis, the Sabbath and the Advent have proved to be of significant importance *to each other*. Evidently the merging of the Sabbath with the hope of an imminent Advent during the formative years 1846 to 1849 was a theological and religious event of the first magnitude, and a brief résumé of the interrelationship between the two in the formulation of Seventh-day Adventist theology during those years is of major importance to a study of the history of the Sabbath. It may, as well, point the way to an even more effective witness to the Sabbath in years to come.

To begin with, during those formative years Adventists tested the Seventh Day Baptist concept of the Sabbath by the Bible and adopted it as their own. In historic Seventh Day Baptist thought, the fourth precept of the Decalogue memorializes the Creator-creature relationship, which is of ultimate importance to our very existence. At first glance the Sabbath appears to be an arbitrary command, that is, an expression of the authority of the One who gave it and not one whose inherent moral quality is obvious, as with the prohibitions against murder, adultery, and theft. Recognition of the Sabbath is therefore an acknowledgment of God's authority as Creator, on an even higher level than compliance with the other nine. It is a test of a person's recognition of his Creator and his attitude toward Him. With this purpose in view, God intended the Sabbath for all mankind, for all time. God has never altered the Sabbath command, and it is, in fact, inherently unalterable. Any attempt to change it constitutes an overt challenge to the authority of the Creator. In Seventh Day Baptist thought the Sabbath is also destined to play a key role in the great future eschatological crisis when truth will be in the balance. Finally, "the rest of the holy Sabbath" is an "earnest to God's people, of the eternal rest, which is reserved for them in heaven," an earthly "type" of that heavenly "antitype."[83]

Adventist appreciation of, and reliance on, the extensive Seventh Day Baptist literature about the Sabbath available to them during the years 1846 to 1849 has already been documented. Those pioneer Adventists adopted the Seventh Day Baptist exposition of the Sabbath *in toto* and gratefully acknowleged their indebtedness to the Seventh Day Baptists. But the Sabbatarian Adventist concept of an imminent Advent meant that they could not be content to let matters rest there. In effect, Seventh Day Baptist theology of the Sabbath devoted most of its time to looking intently into the rearview mirror of history, while the Advent hope kept Adventist eyes fixed on the road ahead. Adventist conviction with respect to the fundamental validity of the 1844 experience despite the disappointment, a conviction that came as a result of their study of Christ's ministry in the heavenly sanctuary, led to a comprehensive and coherent theology of the Sabbath in relation to the Advent. They incorporated this theological stance at once into the title chosen for their publication, *The Second Advent Review and Sabbath Herald,* and a decade later into the name Seventh-day Adventist.

The first step in the theological departure of what were to become Seventh-day Adventists from the rest of their disappointed Advent brethren took place the morning following the bitter disappointment of October 22, 1844. Like a flash of light it came to Hiram Edson's mind that the "sanctuary" to be "cleansed" on that memorable day was not this earth, as the Millerites had supposed, but the sanctuary in heaven in which Christ, since His ascension, has been ministering to His people here on earth the benefits of His infinite sacrifice of love.[84] For several years after 1844 the other Adventists worked on the basis of the idea that the event they had anticipated—the literal appearing of Christ in the clouds of heaven—was correct, but that they had been mistaken in figuring the time aspect of the prophecies. As a result they set one date after another for Christ to come. With Crosier and those who accepted his explanation regarding the sanctuary in heaven, Millerite Adventists had been right with respect to the *time* but wrong as to the *nature* of the event, specifically with respect to the identity of the "sanctuary" that was to be "cleansed." Nowhere in the Bible could they find evidence suggesting that the sanctuary of Daniel 8:14 is this earth, whereas the New Testament, and most particularly the book of Hebrews, is replete with the concept of a *heavenly* sanctuary operating since Christ's ascension.

This concept of the sanctuary protected those who accepted it against further time setting, and drew a sharp line of distinction between them and other Adventists. But even more important, it directed their attention to the law of God and the Sabbath. In Ellen White's vision in the late winter or early spring of 1847, mentioned earlier, she saw Jesus standing by the ark in the heavenly sanctuary. Before her eyes He opened the folded tables of stone on which the Ten Commandments were inscribed, and a halo of light encircled the fourth.[85] She understood this emphasis on the fourth commandment as divine confirmation of the seventh-day Sabbath and was confirmed in her own acceptance of it. The Sabbath was thus linked to the sanctuary in heaven. In an editorial in the July 25, 1854, *Review* entitled "The Relation which the Sabbath sustains to other Points of Present Truth," Uriah Smith wrote:

"The sanctuary and the Sabbath are inseparably connected. Whoever admits the truth of the first must admit it also of the second: the sanctuary contains the ark, the ark contains the law, and the law contains the fourth commandment unabolished and unchanged." "No truth need be more clearly demonstrated than that the Sabbath of the Lord, instituted and given to man at Creation, is still binding upon the whole human family. Perhaps no truth can be more clearly demonstrated." "Especial attention should be called to this point in these last days."[86]

The imminence of the Advent gave point and urgency to the Sabbath as "present truth," which had been lacking in the Seventh Day Baptist witness to it. In 1850 Ellen White wrote: "I saw that the time for Jesus to be in the most holy place was nearly finished and that time can last but a very little longer. . . . The sealing time is very short, and will soon be over." "'Time is almost finished.' . . . Said the angel, 'Get ready, get ready, get ready.'"[87] It was this concept of a *very imminent* Advent that gave particular point and urgency to the Sabbath, and this was intensified by the discovery, a little later, of its relationship to the third angel's message of Revelation 14:9-12.

Adventists had already identified the proclamation of Christ's coming in 1844 with the fulfillment of the first angel's message of Revelation 14:6, 7, and the "midnight cry" during the summer of 1844 as the historical counterpart of the second angel's message in verse 8. The first angel summons all men everywhere to worship the Creator, whose work of creation the Sabbath memorializes, and the second warns against popular rejection of that message. But there was a third angel with a warning against the mark of the beast, which they understood to be the satanic counterpart of the seal of God. Identifying the seal of God with the Sabbath, they concluded that the mark of the beast must be Satan's counterfeit Sabbath. Furthermore, inasmuch as the first angel announced the hour of divine judgment, and inasmuch as John presented the coming of Christ as following immediately upon the proclamation of the message by the third angel, they concluded that the Sabbath was to be the great final test of loyalty to God immediately preceding Christ's coming, which they took to be very imminent.[88]

Those who accept these messages are said in verse 12 of the chapter to be keeping the commandments of God along with their faith in Jesus Christ as man's Saviour from sin. The Sabbath, they concluded, was thus implicit in both the first and third messages.

A few years later Ellen White wrote: "Separate the Sabbath from the [three angels'] messages, and it loses its power; but when connected with the message of the third angel, a power attends it which convicts unbelievers and infidels, and brings them out with strength to stand, to live, grow, and flourish in the Lord." Substitution of the laws of men for the law of God, she wrote, is to be the very last act in the drama of the great controversy between good and evil.[89] With the issue thus clearly drawn, all who sincerely love God will have received His seal of approval, and those who submit to human requirements opposed to the divine law will receive the mark of the beast foretold in Revelation 13 and 14. Eventually there will be a universal decree imposing the death penalty on those who persist in observing the Bible Sabbath instead of honoring the first day of the week.[90]

As indicated in the foregoing, the second advent of Christ and the Sabbath were bonded together in Adventist theology in an inseparable, symbiotic union in which each was dependent on the other. This union of the Advent and the Sabbath in the setting of the everlasting gospel (Rev. 14:6) and the imminent hour of divine judgment (verse 7) is the constitutive dynamic of Seventh-day Adventist theology. Adventists often refer to those who convert to the church as "accepting the third angel's message" or as "accepting the Sabbath"; both expressions are commonly used for becoming a Seventh-day Adventist. This understanding of Scripture made the Sabbath "present truth" during the years 1846 to 1849 in a supremely important sense, and gave it an ultimate importance it never had for Seventh Day Baptists. It is also an important factor in the phenomenal growth of Seventh-day Adventists and for their high level of dedication.

This emphasis on the eschatological significance of the seventh-day Sabbath explains its major role in Adventist theology. It was the catalyst that brought the scattered Advent believers of pioneer days together and that still today transcends all social, economic, racial, and national barriers, uniting Adventists around the world in a bond of loyalty to Christ and to one another. The name "Seventh-day Adventist" aptly expresses the *raison d'être* of the church and the reason for being a member of the church.

Relevance of the Sabbath: a Positive Perspective

Traditionally, and almost exclusively until recent years, it has been customary to emphasize observance of the Sabbath as man's proper response to a divine command, as an obligation. God commands; it is our duty to obey. Contemporary literature on the Sabbath, however, emphasizes its positive aspect, as a gracious provision by a wise Creator designed to meet an inherent need of created beings, even in a perfect world. From this perspective the Sabbath is the same, and man's duty with respect to it is the same. But instead of more or less rote compliance, of keeping it only, or primarily, because God requires it, there is emphasis on the Creator's purpose in giving man the Sabbath, on its intrinsic therapeutic value, and on an intelligent, appreciative observance of it. The balance in this new perspective has been aptly and tersely expressed by Ahva J. C. Bond: "It is God's Sabbath; He made it. . . . It is man's Sabbath; he needs it."[91]

Overemphasis on the traditional perspective of the Sabbath tends to reflect a distorted view of God as an arbitrary being who is pleased to burden created beings with restrictive requirements designed to impress them with the fact that He is God. Thus conceived, Sabbath observance tends to deteriorate into a works-righteousness device by which the Sabbathkeeper hopes to earn merit by impressing God with his dutiful obedience. Such observance thwarts the very purpose it was designed to serve. The new perspective of the Sabbath conceives of God as a gracious person infinitely concerned with the happiness and well-being of His creatures. Mature Sabbath observance requires an understanding of the Creator's purpose in consecrating it as holy time, and a choice to keep it, not only because man's creatureliness obliges him to do so but even more because as a rational, responsible being he purposes to enter fully into the Creator's beneficent purpose in giving him existence and being. This point of view makes the Sabbath even more important today because it provides an ideal therapeutic that enables modern man to cope with the frenetic rush of the materialistically oriented modern world.

Although more detail on this subject will be furnished in the three chapters in Part III of this volume, brief mention may be made here of several authors who in recent years have ably presented this new perspective of the Sabbath—a perspective whose newness consists more in emphasis than content.

Jewish rabbi Abraham Joshua Heschel has had considerable impact on Christian as well as Jewish thinking through his book *The Sabbath: Its Meaning for Modern Man*.[92] Inasmuch as Heschel will be discussed in great detail in a later chapter (see Branson, pp. 15-21), it will suffice here to say that his treatment stresses the Sabbath as *"holiness in time,"* and that he also refers to the Sabbath as "a sanctuary which we build, *a sanctuary in time."*[93]

A second writer deserving brief mention here, though he too will receive some further attention in a later chapter (see La Rondelle, pp. 25-27), is Seventh Day Baptist Herbert E. Saunders. This author, in his book *The Sabbath: Symbol of Creation and Re-Creation*,[94] refers to the Sabbath as a "perfect link between God and our race," a constant reminder of the Creator's interest in us and of our creatureliness in relation to Him as our Father.[95] For Saunders, the Sabbath stands at the apex not only of God's creative activity but also of His redeeming power, being a symbol of both.[96] Indeed, the Sabbath highlights the personal identity and worth of man, and frees him from the tyranny of the world.[97]

A third writer, whose recent work on the theology of both the Sabbath and Second Advent deserves somewhat more extended treatment here, inasmuch as he is not treated elsewhere in the present volume, is Seventh-day Adventist Sakae Kubo. In his *God Meets Man: A Theology of the Sabbath and Second Advent*,[98] Kubo discusses the Sabbath under three main headings: "The Sabbath and Creation," "The Sabbath as Redemption," and "The Sabbath as Future Rest."[99] He highlights, as does Heschel, the concept of holiness in time.[100] But particularly interesting is Kubo's treatment of the Sabbath in relationship to redemption. He tells us, for example, in connection with a chapter on "The Sabbath and Justification," that "when man ceases from his works, he must come to realize that they are not so important and that even though he stops them, the world still moves on without him or his works"; that "it is God and what He does that are vital." Kubo adds that "the Sabbath understood as that which strips us of our works

THE SABBATH IN THE NEW WORLD

and our autonomy before God provides no opportunity for self-justification" and is "truly the sign of God's grace and sovereignty, and of man's reception and dependence." [101]

When dealing with the Sabbath as "The Sign of Redemption," Kubo states that "the Sabbath has no meaning at all unless creative power accomplishes its results in the life of the one who observes the day. Holiness of being must match holiness of time." [102] And in dealing with the Sabbath in connection with sanctification, Kubo points out that "in our present world the Sabbath confronts us as God's challenge to our seriousness in accepting Christ. Since a large part of the world structures its life and business around Sunday as its rest day, observance of the seventh-day Sabbath today demands a radical, conscious, deliberate decision to follow Christ. Some such demand is always present in Christian conversion." [103]

Kubo recognizes that the "priority of justification is fundamental," stating that we "must ever keep in mind that man alone and in his own strength cannot do anything for his salvation. No amount of good works on his part can produce it. Yet it is just as important that we do not think of the Christian simply as lifeless matter on whom and for whom God does everything. God's initiative is basic, but unless man responds in faith, he has no salvation. And the life of loving obedience must follow the response." [104]

NOTES

[1] *Encyclopedia Judaica*, 2:808; 4:1322; 11:1454; 3:409.
[2] *Ibid.*, 12:993. Mikveh Israel means "the Hope of Israel."
[3] *Ibid.*, 2:808.
[4] Sherith Israel means "the Remnant of Israel." *Ibid.*, 12:1062, 1063; 15:1586.
[5] *Ibid.*, 15:1586, 1596; Frank S. Mead, *Handbook of Denominations in the United States* (Nashville, 1970), p. 102.
[6] *Encyclopedia Judaica*, 5:102.
[7] *Ibid.*, 13:895, 896; 15:1636; *Reader's Digest 1978 Almanac and Yearbook* (Pleasantville, N.Y., 1978), p. 705.
[8] Mead, *op. cit.*, pp. 105, 106.
[9] Lewis A. Platts, "Seventh Day Baptists in America Previous to 1802," in *Seventh Day Baptists in Europe and America* (Plainfield, N.J., 1910), pp. 122-126. (Hereinafter abbreviated *SDB*.)
[10] *Ibid.*, pp. 124-128, 133.
[11] [Seventh Day Baptist] *Missionary Magazine*, May, 1822, pp. 122, 123.
[12] Platts, *op. cit.*, p. 122.
[13] *Missionary Magazine*, May, 1822, p. 124.
[14] Arthur E. Main, "The Seventh Day Baptist General Conference, 1802-1902," in *SDB*, pp. 127, 150, 153, 169; *Missionary Magazine*, May, 1822, p. 128.
[15] Stephen Burdick, "Lessons of the Past," in *SDB*, p. 1289.
[16] *Ibid.*; Oscar U. Whitford, "The Seventh Day Baptist Missionary Society," in *SDB*, pp. 327-331; Main, *op. cit.*, p. 168.
[17] Arthur L. Titsworth, "The American Sabbath Tract Society," in *SDB*, p. 422; Edwin Shaw, "Catalog of Publications," in *SDB*, pp. 1328-1330; Whitford, *op. cit.*, pp. 335, 337.
[18] Titsworth, *op. cit.*, p. 429; Main, *op. cit.*, pp. 233, 234, 185; Burdick, *op. cit.*, p. 1291; Shaw, *op. cit.*, pp. 1341, 1342. For a list of the titles, see Gordon O. Martinborough, "The Beginnings of a Theology of the Sabbath Among American Sabbatarian Adventists, 1842-1850" (M.A. thesis, Loma Linda University, 1976), pp. 169, 170.
[19] Main, *op. cit.*, pp. 185-187.
[20] *The Midnight Cry*, Sept. 5 and 12, 1844, quoted in Arthur W. Spalding, *Origin and History of Seventh-day Adventists*, 4 vols. (Washington, D.C., 1961), 1:116, 117.
[21] Spalding, *op. cit.*, pp. 116, 397-400.
[22] *Ibid.*, pp. 115, 116, 399, 400; S. N. Haskell, "Our First Meeting-House," *General Conference Bulletin*, June 2, 1909, p. 290.
[23] Roswell F. Cottrell letter to the editor, *Advent Review and Sabbath Herald*, Nov. 25, 1851, p. 54; July 21, 1853, p. 38; Dec. 5, 1854, p. 125 (hereafter cited as *Review*); Spalding, *op. cit.*, p. 400.
[24] Don F. Neufeld, ed., *Seventh-day Adventist Encyclopedia* (Washington, D.C., 1976), s.v. "Spicer, William Ambrose."
[25] Spalding, *op. cit.*, p. 117; see *Review*, Aug. 11, 1853, p. 52.
[26] James White reply to letter from J. C. Rogers, *Review*, Aug. 11, 1853, p. 52.
[27] Spalding, *op. cit.*, pp. 117-119. An article in *Hope of Israel*, February 28, 1845, was revised and printed as a tract in March, 1845. An excellent point-by-point comparison of Preble's tract with extant Seventh Day Baptist literature and with Joseph Bates' 1846 pamphlet is given by Martinborough, *op. cit.*, pp. 179-184.
[28] Spalding, *op. cit.*, pp. 119-121, 123-125.

THE SABBATH IN SCRIPTURE AND HISTORY

29 Ellen G. White, *Life Sketches* (Mountain View, Calif., 1915), p. 95; idem, *Testimonies for the Church*, 9 vols. (Mountain View, Calif., 1948), 1:76; idem, *Spiritual Gifts*, 4 vols. (Battle Creek, Mich., 1860), 2:83.
30 Ellen G. White, *Early Writings* (Washington, D.C., 1882), pp. 32, 33; idem, *Life Sketches*, pp. 95, 96, 100.
31 Spalding, *op. cit.*, pp. 190-195; White, *Life Sketches*, pp. 107, 108, 110-112.
32 Spalding, *op. cit.*, p. 191; White, *Life Sketches*, p. 111.
33 *Review*, Aug. 11, 1853, p. 52.
34 Spalding, *op. cit.*, p. 197.
35 *Ibid.*, p. 195; White, *Life Sketches*, p. 125; *The Present Truth*, December, 1849, p. 47. Martinborough, *op. cit.*, pp. 185-189, lists the focus of each article in both *The Present Truth* and *The Advent Review*.
36 *The Present Truth*, August, 1849, pp. 21-23; April, 1850, pp. 65-69.
37 *Review*, Aug. 11, 1853, p. 53.
38 *The Present Truth*, July, 1849, pp. 1, 6. (Italics supplied.)
39 *Ibid.*, December, 1849, p. 39.
40 *Ibid.*, May, 1850, p. 80.
41 Cf. *Review*, Aug. 11, 1853, p. 52.
42 White, *Early Writings*, p. 68.
43 *The Present Truth*, November, 1850, pp. 86, 87.
44 May and November, 1850.
45 "Historical Setting of These Documents," *Facsimile Reproductions of The Present Truth and The Advent Review* (Washington, D.C., [1946]), p. 8.
46 *Review*, Jan. 24, 1854, p. 4; Aug. 11, 1853, p. 52; Dec. 5, 1854, p. 125; *The Present Truth*, April, 1850, p. 71.
47 John N. Andrews, *History of the Sabbath and First Day of the Week* (Battle Creek, Mich., 1861).
48 *Review*, Jan. 24, 1854, p. 4; Aug. 29, 1854, p. 21; Oct. 17, 1854, p. 80.
49 *Ibid.*, Dec. 9, 1852, p. 113, reprinted from *The Sabbath Recorder*.
50 *Review*, Aug. 11, 1853, p. 52.
51 *Ibid.*, May 26, 1853, p. 4; Dec. 4, 1855, p. 76.
52 *Ibid.*, Dec. 4, 1855, p. 78.
53 *Ibid.*, June 2, 1851, p. 92; Dec. 4, 1855, pp. 76-78.
54 *Ibid.*, Aug. 11, 1853, p. 52.
55 Main, *op. cit.*, pp. 198, 199; *Review*, Sept. 20, 1870, p. 109.
56 Main, *op. cit.*, pp. 200-205, 207-209.
57 Russel J. Thomsen, *Seventh Day Baptists—Their Legacy to Adventists* (Mountain View, Calif., 1971), p. 48.
58 *Ibid.*, p. 49.
59 James White, "Seventh Day Baptists and Seventh-day Adventists," *Review*, Dec. 4, 1879, p. 181.
60 *Ibid.*, p. 180.
61 Jesse E. Hutchins, "Statistics," in *SDB*, p. 1313; Constant H. Jacquet, *Yearbook of American Churches, 1978* (Nashville, 1978), p. 41.
62 James L. Gamble et al., "Denominational Schools: Alfred University, in *SDB*, pp. 487-528.
63 Herbert E. Saunders, *The Sabbath: Symbol of Creation and Re-Creation*, (Plainfield, N.J., 1970), p. 10, quoting A. H. Lewis, *The Sabbath Recorder*, July 3, 1890, p. 423.
64 White, *Testimonies*, 1:337.
65 Main, *op. cit.*, p. 233n.
66 Hutchins, *op. cit.*, p. 1312; cf. Mead, *op. cit.*, p. 38.
67 Mead, *op. cit.*, p. 39.
68 *Ibid.*, pp. 56, 57; Jacquet, *op. cit.*, p. 219, 44, 40, 218.
69 William C. Martin, "Father, Son, and Mammon," *The Atlantic Monthly*, March, 1980, pp. 58, 61.
70 Mead, *op. cit.*, pp. 111, 112.
71 Eugene Lincoln, in *The Sabbath Sentinel*, April, 1978, p. 6. Official monthly publication of the Bible Sabbath Association, Cleveland, Tennessee.
72 *Review*, Aug. 11, 1853, p. 53; Martinborough, *op. cit.*, pp. 179-184; see note 52.
73 *Review*, November, 1850, p. 7.
74 *Ibid.*, December, 1850, p. 10.
75 *Ibid.*, February, 1851, p. 41; reprinted Oct. 21, 1851, p. 41.
76 *Ibid.*, February, 1851, p. 48; April, 1851, pp. 59-61.
77 From a card count in the *Review* index.
78 For example, *Review*, June 10, 1852, p. 22.
79 Jacquet, *op. cit.*, pp. 22, 40, 41.
80 *Seventh-day Adventist Yearbook, 1980* (Washington, D.C., 1980), p. 4.
81 Hutchins, *op. cit.*, p. 1312; Spalding, *op. cit.*, p. 197.
82 Jacquet, *op. cit.*, p. 89.
83 Seventh Day Baptist General Conference, *An Appeal for the Restoration of the Bible Sabbath*; reprinted in S. D. *Advent Library* (Battle Creek, Mich., 1860) vol. 4, pp. 9-11, 21, 34; *Missionary Magazine*, August, 1821, p. 18; February, 1823, pp. 224-227; May, 1823, pp. 249-255.
84 Spalding, *op. cit.*, p. 101. Martinborough, *op. cit.*, pp. 95-121, provides a good discussion of the formation of the Adventist theology of the Sabbath.
85 White, *Early Writings*, pp. 32, 33; idem, *Life Sketches*, pp. 95, 96.
86 *Review*, July 25, 1854, p. 196.
87 White, *Early Writings*, pp. 58, 64.
88 *Ibid.*, p. 64.
89 Idem, *Testimonies*, 1:337.
90 Idem, *The Great Controversy* (Mountain View, Calif., 1911), pp. 615, 616.
91 Ahva J. C. Bond, "The Sabbath: God's and Man's," *The Sabbath Recorder*, Jan. 6, 1947, p. 6.
92 Abraham Joshua Heschel, *The Sabbath: Its Meaning for Modern Man* (New York, 1951).
93 *Ibid.*, pp. 10, 29.
94 See note 62.

[95] Saunders, *op. cit.*, p. 63.
[96] *Ibid.*, p. 74.
[97] *Ibid.*, pp. 8, 11, 16, 17, 87, 89.
[98] Sakae Kubo, *God Meets Man: A Theology of the Sabbath and Second Advent* (Nashville, Tenn., 1978).
[99] These are the main divisions of Kubo's "Part I: The Meaning of the Sabbath."
[100] Kubo devotes a full chapter to "Holiness in Time" in his section on "The Sabbath and Creation."
[101] Kubo, *op. cit.*, pp. 40, 43.
[102] *Ibid.*, p. 49.
[103] *Ibid.*, p. 54.
[104] *Ibid.*, pp. 55, 56.

Sabbath Theology
PART III

CHAPTER 14

The Sabbath in Modern Jewish Theology*

Roy Branson

A FEW Protestant groups, most notably the Seventh-day Adventists, observe the Sabbath on the seventh day of the week, as do Jews.[1] But because most Christians celebrate their Sabbath, or weekly day of worship, on Sunday, they often do not recognize or explore the theological resources within Judaism for deepening Christianity's appreciation of the weekly Sabbath. The present chapter surveys various of the more significant of these resources.

Divergence

Whether they stress law, reason, or history, Jewish thinkers are increasingly in agreement on the unique importance of the Sabbath experience; and it may safely be said that today the joy of the Sabbath suffuses all of Judaism.[2] But during the past 150 years it has not always been so. Ever since the end of the eighteenth century, and that gradual securing of civil liberties by European Jews called Emancipation, disputes within Judaism have extended to the Sabbath. If "it is Germany that must be credited with being the birthplace of modern Judaism," differences over the Sabbath must be considered part of the birthpangs.[3] In the complex interrelationships among prominent Jewish thinkers in Germany during the nineteenth and twentieth centuries, the Sabbath remained enmeshed in controversy.

One of the founders of what came to be called Reform Judaism,† Samuel Holdheim, established a temple in Berlin that worshiped on Sunday instead of the seventh day of the week. No doubt Holdheim was stating an extreme position when he said that Jews had an obligation to violate the Sabbath in order to show their commitment to work for the common good of the state, but Holdheim was

---

* Adapted from "Sabbath—Heart of Jewish Unity," *Journal of Ecumenical Studies* 15 (Fall, 1978):716-736. Used by permission.

† For an explanation of the three main branches of Judaism—Orthodox, Reform, and Conservative—see pp. 244, 245.

prominent in initiating the three great Reform rabbinical conferences held during 1844 and 1845 in the German cities of Brunswick, Frankfurt, and Breslau.[4] "How could the essential qualities of the Sabbath be saved in the modern environment?" According to one of its historians, "this was the question to which Reform addressed itself, a question which was extensively discussed at the third conference in Breslau in 1846."[5]

Some rabbis who had broken with many of the requirements of Orthodoxy were nevertheless outraged at the general trend of discussion at the conferences. Zechariah Frankel walked out of the second conference at Frankfurt and refused to attend the third at Breslau. By founding and editing two journals and becoming the first head of the Rabbinical Seminary in Breslau in 1845, Frankel assumed leadership of those who advocated what came to be called Conservative Judaism. While Conservatives did not insist on performance of minor ritual requirements, they sustained a respect for the central symbol of Jewish faith and practice and "were disturbed by the trend on the part of the radical Reform leaders in the 1870s to transfer the Sabbath to Sunday."[6]

Shortly after the last of the Reform conferences and just before Frankel became head of the Breslau Seminary, Samson Raphael Hirsch went in 1851 to Frankfurt, one of the centers of German Judaism. He started a program of preaching, teaching, and writing that was to give traditional Judaism (what others called Orthodoxy) its first carefully worked out rationale since Emancipation and the coming of the Enlightenment. His insistence that observing Jews should not be forced to contribute to Reform-dominated institutions that ignored requirements of Jewish law, such as Sabbath regulations, led to the first state-recognized split in what had always been in German cities a single Jewish community.

Conflicts begun in Germany continued in the United States. Radicals from Germany came to dominate Reform Judaism in the United States, culminating in the Pittsburgh Platform of 1885. It said that Reform Jews accept "only such ceremonies as elevate and sanctify our lives, but reject all such as are not adapted to the views and habits of modern civilization."[7] This position was propagated by young rabbis graduating from Hebrew Union College, founded a decade earlier in Cincinnati by Reform leaders. "Toward the turn of the century some fifty American Reform congregations had introduced Sunday services, and the whole issue was fervently debated at several conferences."[8]

Those American rabbis more in tune with Frankel and the historical school of the Breslau Seminary founded their own journal, *American Hebrew* (1879), which called for the encouragement of Sabbath observance. Their reaction to the Pittsburgh Platform was so strong that within two years they had organized a new seminary. A historian makes the judgment that "the coming of age of Conservatism may be dated from the beginning of instruction in the Jewish Theological Seminary of America."[9] There the importance of the Sabbath was never doubted.

For ten years, despite the massive influx to the United States during the 1880s of Eastern European Jews practicing an encompassing piety not seen by even German Orthodoxy, no separate American Orthodox movement was begun. The established congregations consisting of Orthodox Jews from Germany continued to find the graduates of Jewish Theological Seminary acceptable. Finally, however, in 1896 the Rabbi Isaac Elchanan Theological Seminary was founded to provide Eastern European Orthodox synagogues with rabbis trained in that tradition. As it became assimilated into Yeshiva University in 1915, its teachers became committed to the program Samson Raphael Hirsch and nineteenth-century German Orthodoxy had advanced, namely, traditional Rabbinic instruction combined with modern secular studies. The most revered teacher at Yeshiva epitomizes modern orthodoxy. Dr. Joseph B. Soloveitchik, acknowledged by many to be the foremost Talmudic scholar in the world, was tutored in his grandfather's "Brisker" method of Talmudic interpretation and then earned a doctorate in philosophy from the University of Berlin.

Will and Law

From Samson Raphael Hirsch in nineteenth-century Germany to Joseph Soloveitchik and his contemporary followers in America, thinkers in Orthodoxy have seen the Sabbath as a witness to the authority and freedom of God's will. The Sabbath is also a time when man realizes that his will is most free when it conforms with God's. Observing the Sabbath becomes the epitome of Orthodox existence: acting as God acts. In Hirsch's characteristically volitional framework, the Sabbath is the "symbol of God's rule and man's destiny."[10]

In trying to will and act as God does, the Jew has been given an advantage. To him has been revealed the law. By learning the basic principles guiding how the Jew should act on the Sabbath, he finds the meaning of the Sabbath. For example, Orthodox discussion of the Sabbath develops the historic, Talmudic concept of *melakhah*, "an act that shows man's mastery over the world by the constructive exercise of his intelligence and skill."[11] Such acts, encouraged during six days of the week, are prohibited on the seventh. The law clarifies by saying that either enhancement or exploitation of the external creation is *melakhah*. However, because there is no material production of man's skills, neither consumption of nature nor exertion in cultivation of internal sentiments or ideas is *melakhah*.[12] Says Hirsch, "Even if you tired yourself out the whole day, as long as you have *produced* nothing . . . you have performed no *melakhah*."[13]

To shape and form creation on Sabbath is to presume to add to what God has already completed. "Even the smallest work done on the Sabbath is a denial of the fact that God is the Creator and Master of the world. It is an arrogant setting-up of man as his own master."[14] Resting from work acknowledges that God is completely the Maker of creation. By conforming to God's rest after Creation, man also reveals his Godlikeness. Isidor Grunfeld, the English translator of Hirsch's works, explains that as God demonstrated His freedom by ceasing from His work of Creation, "freely controlling and limiting the creation He brought into being according to His will," so "by keeping Sabbath the Jew becomes," like God, "work's master, not its slave."[15] Emanuel Rackman, one of Soloveitchik's disciples, agrees. Man, by resting from subduing nature, "might, in a kind of imitation of God, catch a glimpse of that freedom which is the essence of God's nature."[16]

The Jew is not left by the law with only a negative understanding of the Sabbath—not performing *melakhah*. There is also the concept of *menuhah*, or rest. While negative understandings of this word are possible, Norman Lamm, another of Soloveitchik's students and president of Yeshiva University, stresses that in relation to the Sabbath, *menuhah* has a positive meaning—inner re-creation or self-transformation. On the Sabbath the Jew is involved with God in creating "a new and better identity." This is what tradition means when it says that "on Shabbat we receive a *neshamah yeterah,* an 'additional soul.' " [17]

Orthodoxy's discussion of the Sabbath emphasizes how conformity to the law brings man's actions into line with the will of the Creator. But conformity to God's will does not result in dreariness. On the contrary, for the Orthodox, as for all Jews, the Sabbath brings a sense of freedom and joyfulness. Because in the Sabbath God comes to all observing men, whatever their rank, no Jew has to think that he is ultimately in God's eyes inferior to any other man. Observance of the Sabbath frees the Jew from all hierarchies: "On the Sabbath servant and master meet as equals, as free human personalities.... Sabbath is thus a weekly-recurring divine protest against slavery and oppression. Lifting up his Kiddush-cup on Friday night, the Jew links the creation of the world with man's freedom, so declaring slavery and oppression deadly sins against the very foundation of the universe." [18]

Moreover, assured that following God's will has brought him equally into God's favor, Hirsch says that "the feeling of ecstasy which fills a Jew on a Friday night, when after a week of hard and honest labour he greets the Sabbath amidst his family with his cup raised unto God—no lips have yet found words for it." [19]

Reason and Ethics

For all the experimentation of nineteenth-century Reform rabbis with Sabbath services on the first day of the week, Hermann Cohen, who provided the foundation for Reform thinking in the early twentieth century, revered the Sabbath. Whereas Orthodoxy's understanding of the Sabbath emphasizes will and Jewish law, the Reform tradition stresses the relation of the Sabbath to intellect and a universal ethics.

According to Cohen, at least two aspects of Judaism demonstrate its adherence to a universal, rational ethics: first, the concern of the prophets in proclaiming that the love of a monotheistic God must be reflected in man's "social love for the fellowman";[20] and second, the prophets' proclamation of the Sabbath.

"The prophets' work for moral reform centers on the idea of the Sabbath which becomes the symbol of social morality," he states. "All men are equal, for all have been called upon to lead a moral life.... And it is his [Jeremiah's] concept of social justice that motivates him to advocate the sanctification of the Sabbath." [21] "For the prophets the Sabbath becomes the expression of morality itself." [22]

As much as Hirsch or any of the Orthodox writers, Cohen shares in the joy of the Sabbath, but for different reasons. Rather than praising the Sabbath as God's gracious way to form Jewish character, Cohen delights in the way the Sabbath has extended monotheism. "The Sabbath is given first to Israel. But the world has accepted it." [23]

Cohen believes that the Sabbath has preserved Judaism to fulfill its "mission of spreading monotheism over the earth.... In the Sabbath the God of love showed himself as the unique God of love for mankind." Indeed, Cohen refers to "the law of the *Sabbath*" as "the quintessence of the monotheistic moral teaching," and he also dares to hope that in universality of its celebration the Messianic Age has already dawned. "If Judaism had given only the Sabbath to the world, it would by this alone be identified as the messenger of joy and as the founder of peace among mankind. The Sabbath took the first step which led to the abolition of slavery, and the Sabbath also took the first step in showing the way to the abolition of the division of labor into manual and intellectual labor. The Sabbath is the sign of joy which will rise over men when all men are equally free and liable to service, and have an equal share in the teaching, in science, its inquiry and its knowledge, as well as in the labor for their daily bread. The conquest of the world which has been achieved by the Sabbath, does not permit one to abandon the hope, the confidence, that this joy is no empty illusion, and that the peace which radiates in this joy is, and will remain, a fundamental power of the human race." [24]

The same year that Cohen retired from his University of Marburg philosophy professorship, 1912, and went to Berlin to teach in the Academy for the Scientific Study of Judaism, Leo Baeck arrived to take the place of Berlin's ailing senior rabbi. Baeck, like Cohen more than thirty years before, received a doctorate in philosophy from the University of Berlin (for a dissertation on Spinoza), and Cohen assumed that Baeck would be his intellectual successor. Baeck's theology of the Sabbath does echo some of Cohen's themes. In spite of living through two world wars, Baeck sustained Cohen's faith in a universal moral order and regarded the Sabbath as its symbol. He considered the Sabbath one of Judaism's greatest contributions to mankind because "from this people the Sabbath made its way through many lands and times. As this people was blessed by it and is to remain blessed, so did it bless the peoples to whom it came." The Sabbath "points and reaches toward a world of harmony, toward a great peace." [25] For Baeck, as for Cohen, "the Sabbath is the image of the messianic." [26]

But Baeck's description of the Sabbath and Judaism removes him, more than Cohen, from his contemporary society. The Jew lives in the world, "yet is different." Judaism contributes to the good of society, and yet "it may well be its historic task to offer this image of the dissenter, who dissents for humanity's sake." [27]

What Baeck calls the Jewish "capacity to be different" is the result of the Sabbath's educating man's capacity to explore "the depth of life." In language that reaches beyond Cohen's identification of religion with rationality and ethics, Baeck also says that the Sabbath rest "is essentially religious, part of the atmosphere of the divine; it leads us to the mystery, to the depth." He says that "a life without Sabbath would lack the spring of renewal, that which opens the well of the depth again and again. An essential and fruitful aspect of Judaism would dry up in such a life; it could still be an ethical life, but it would lack that which defines the Jewish life." [28] Baeck does not restrict Judaism to the depths of religion, but he does say that what is unique about Judaism lies in that area, and the experience of the Sabbath draws us into just such realms of revivifying mystery.

Existence and History

By the time Baeck and Cohen came to Berlin, another philosopher, Martin Buber, had already emerged from the University of Vienna and from an intense study of Hasidism with ideas that would take Jewish theology even further in the direction that Baeck's comments on mystery and depth indicated. Interestingly, however, Buber's writings specifically on the Sabbath carry on some of the themes Baeck continued from Cohen, namely, the universality of the Sabbath and the Sabbath's ethical importance.

The Sabbath does not burst into view at Sinai, declares Buber; rather, the

Sabbath is "rooted in the very beginnings of the world itself." The "creation of the world . . . flow[s] into such a Sabbath." With such an origin, "the Sabbath week is really to articulate universal time." The Sabbath, for Buber, does not represent the unique, but the quotidian. "The Sabbath represents the equal measure, the regular articulation of the year. . . . [It represents] that which is valid at all times." Having rooted the Sabbath in something as universal as Creation, Buber emphasizes, like Cohen, that "the Sabbath is the common property of all, and all ought to enjoy it without restriction."[29]

For Buber, as for Cohen, God's Sabbath is a just peace. With the Sabbath in the Decalogue coming between initial commandments regarding worship of Yahweh and those respecting ethical obligations to fellow humans, it is clear that for Moses "the reign of his God and a just order between men are one and the same." In the coming of the weekly Sabbath to servants as much as to masters, and the restoration of debtors and slaves to full status during the Sabbatical year, one can see that " 'the idea of the equality of all creatures' is certainly characteristic of the Sabbatical year, as it is of the Sabbath itself."[30]

In spite of the fact that Franz Rosenzweig would, like Buber, take Jewish theology in a direction very different from Cohen's, it is not astonishing that he shared some of the same ideas about the Sabbath Buber held in common with Cohen. After all, Rosenzweig was Hermann Cohen's admiring student. The same year that Baeck and Cohen converged on Berlin, Rosenzweig finished his doctoral dissertation on Hegel at Freiberg. A few months later, in a small orthodox synagogue in Berlin, he made a dramatic recommitment to Judaism and immediately enrolled in Cohen's courses at the Berlin Academy for the Scientific Study of Judaism. He remained in touch with Cohen to the end of his life, and after Cohen's death he wrote an extended introduction to the great man's collected works. A few months after entering Cohen's classes, Rosenzweig met Martin Buber. The latter promptly asked Rosenzweig to contribute to a collection of essays he was editing, establishing a personal and professional relationship that was to result in Buber's replacing the ailing Rosenzweig (the University of Frankfurt's first choice) as the first professor of Judaism in a German university. Rosenzweig also joined Buber in translating the Hebrew Bible into German.

Rosenzweig begins his discussion of the Sabbath by relating it to Creation in terms that readers of Cohen and Buber would find familiar. The Sabbath represents that which is fundamental and enduring: "The very regularity in the sequence of Sabbaths, the very fact that . . . one Sabbath is just like the other, makes them the cornerstones of the year. . . . In the Sabbath the year is created, and thus the main significance of the Sabbath lies in the symbolic meaning of its liturgy: it is a holiday that commemorates creation."[31]

However, Rosenzweig's discussion of the Sabbath differs from his teachers' and friends' at points where his theology generally parts company with theirs. While Cohen, Baeck, and Buber stress the importance of the Sabbath for mankind and its significance for a universal ethics, Rosenzweig organizes his reflections on the Sabbath around the liturgical practice of the Jewish community. He begins his remarks on the Sabbath by discussing Creation because he believes the beginning of the Jewish Sabbath, the Friday evening celebration in the home, with its traditional use of the bread and wine, "the ennobled gifts of earth," particularly commemorates Creation.[32]

While Friday evening particularly honors Creation, "the morning celebrates revelation." In the morning, with the extensive reading from the Bible, "we find utterance of the people's awareness of being elect through the gift of the Torah." With the Afternoon Prayer of the Sabbath and the songs and dances of the "third meal," Jews "reel with the transport of certainty that the Messiah will come and will come soon." For Rosenzweig, who sees Creation, revelation, and especially redemption as the central themes of Judaism, the Sabbath is its epitome. Coming at the climax of the week, the Sabbath commemorates the goal of Creation—redemption. "In celebrating it we go, in the midst of creation, beyond creation and revelation." In fact, "on the Sabbath the congregation feels as if it were already redeemed."[33]

But the greatest impact of both Rosenzweig and Buber on understanding the Sabbath was not in their explicit statements on the Sabbath. It was in shifting the basis of Jewish theology from universal reason to personal existence. "The thinker," said Rosenzweig, as he launched his relentless attack on German idealism, "must proceed boldly from his own subjective situation."[34] The year that Rosenzweig asked Buber to take his place lecturing at the University of Frankfurt, Buber's *I and Thou* appeared. Its impact was such that rational idealism in Jewish theology has never fully recovered.

While Rosenzweig and Buber's development of the existentialist insights of men such as Kierkegaard and Nietzsche was notable, their appreciation of Hasidism was also significant for their Sabbath theology. Rosenzweig, after joining a congregation of Warsaw Hasidim in their celebration of the Sabbath "third mean," was furious at slurs against them. "I don't believe in all that talk about 'decadence'; those who now find all this decadent would have seen nothing but decadence even a hundred and fifty years ago," he exclaimed, later adding that "our craven chiming in with the chorus of obloquy against the Polish Jews is the most shameful of the many shameful things that make up Jewish life in Germany."[35]

It was Buber, of course, who had studied at the University of Berlin under professors such as Wilhelm Dilthey and Georg Simmel and written his dissertation in Vienna on German mysticism, who found in the Hasidic tradition within Judaism those subjective, personal qualities of existence treasured by his teachers and favorite writers. It is true that the Sabbath played a prominent part in some of the Hasidic tales he retold, but more significant for the place of the Sabbath in Judaism was his identifying his own ideas of dialogue and relationship with the Hasidim's religious experience. After Buber's discovery of the Hasidim, educated non-Orthodox Jews of Western Europe and the United States had options other than either Halachic observance of the law or espousal of some rational, universal morality. Jews could identify with a personal, communal enjoyment of a caring, responsive God. It was inevitable that acceptance of the emotional aspects of existence as a part of genuine Judaism would lead to renewed attraction for what Jews had always identified with joy—the Sabbath.

Passion and Symbol

In 1937, when he finally left Germany, Buber selected, as his successor to head both the Jewish Academy in Frankfurt established by Rosenzweig and the Central Office for Jewish Adult Education in Germany, a young Polish rabbi rooted in Hasidism and educated at the University of Berlin, Abraham Joshua Heschel. Heschel was to provide contemporary Judaism with a theology that drew from the full range of Jewish thinking and in the process was to write the most important book on the Sabbath since Emancipation.

Heschel's biography makes him appear destined to play his mediating role. His parents descended from early, illustrious Hasidic *rebbes;* his father from the Maggid of Mezhirech, the successor of the Baal Shem Tov, Hasidim's founder. After growing up immersed in the Hasidic interpretation of the Talmud and Kabbalah, Heschel broke away at 20 to enroll in the University of Berlin's philosophy department, where he studied phenomenology and wrote a dissertation on the phenomenon of prophetism. Immediately upon graduation he joined the faculty of the same Berlin academy for Jewish studies where Cohen and Rosenzweig had met and where Baeck was still teaching. After himself escaping Nazi Germany, Heschel first taught at the Reform Hebrew Union College in Cincinnati, then moved to New York and the Conservative Jewish Theological Seminary.[36]

Heschel took Jewish theology further in the direction that Buber and Rosenzweig had already started. His writing on the Sabbath was part of his lifelong preoccupation with religious experience, particularly the emotive aspects of characteristically Jewish experience. He insisted that "the employment of reason is indispensable to the understanding and worship of God." He also knew the importance of the will, stressing the significance of *mitzvoh*, or required deeds, saying that it was characteristic of Judaism to demand the "leap of action."[37] But more than his teachers or colleagues, Heschel drew Judaism beyond disputes over the law or reason to an appreciation of the passions, where man responds together with his other faculties to "the ineffable" with amazement, fascination, and awe.[38]

As he looked at the turbulent experience of the Biblical writers, particularly the prophets, he found the prophets' sympathy responding to God's pathos. "In the Biblical outlook, movements of feeling are no less spiritual than acts of thought." For the Biblical writers, "pathos, emotional involvement, passionate participation, is a part of religious existence." He was convinced that the "notion that God can be intimately affected, that He possesses not merely intelligence and will but also pathos, basically defines the prophetic consciousness of God." Heschel went so far as to say that "events and human actions arouse in Him joy or sorrow, pleasure or wrath." Conversely, human sympathy for God "is a feeling which feels the feeling to which it reacts.... In prophetic sympathy, man is open to the presence and emotion of the transcendent Subject. He carries within himself the awareness of what is happening to God." The phenomenologist from Berlin finds in religious experience all the passion and boldness of Hasidic piety.[39]

Heschel does not abandon his reason when discussing the Sabbath. Far from it. In terms reminiscent of the idealism Cohen admired, Heschel distinguishes the spiritual and material by emphasizing a parallel distinction between man's experience of time and space. Space is external to us, limited, manipulatable. Six days of the week we work and mold it. Time is internal, transcendent, sovereign: "It is both near and far, intrinsic to all experience and transcending all experience. It belongs exclusively to God."[40] To worship in time is to worship the God beyond us.

Heschel also associated the Sabbath with universality, a universality in time:

THE SABBATH IN SCRIPTURE AND HISTORY

"Every one of us occupies a portion of space. He takes it up exclusively. The portion of space which my body occupies is taken up by myself in exclusion of anyone else. Yet, no one possesses time. There is no moment which I possess exclusively. This very moment belongs to all living men as it belongs to me. We share time, we own space. Through my ownership of space, I am a rival of all other beings; through my living in time, I am a contemporary of all other beings."[41]

Thus, Heschel's view of the universality of the Sabbath differs from the emphasis of other Jewish writers. Not through its widespread practice (Cohen, Baeck), nor because of the recurringness it shares with all days (Buber, Rosenzweig), but from the character of our experience of time itself, Heschel recognizes in the Sabbath a fellowship encompassing all humanity.

Heschel also sees an aspect dear to the Reform Jews: the ethical importance of the Sabbath. A symbol in which one shares a day with all mankind is a day to remember one's common humanity. "The Sabbath is an embodiment of the belief that all men are equal and that equality of men means the nobility of men."[42] Heschel saw the relevance of the Sabbath experience to general experience. He acknowledged the Sabbath as "a day of armistice in the economic struggle with our fellow men and the forces of nature—is there any institution that holds out a greater hope for man's progress than the Sabbath?"[43]

However, Heschel did not so distinguish time and space as to oppose them. "The faith of the Jew is not a way out of this world, but a way of being within and above this world; not to reject but to surpass civilization. The Sabbath is the day on which we learn the art of *surpassing* civilization."[44]

But Heschel does not see the Sabbath as primarily a symbol of universal Creation. Like Rosenzweig, Heschel looks upon the temporal symbol of the Sabbath as ultimately a memorial of redemption: "The Bible is more concerned with time than with space. . . . It is more concerned with history than with geography. . . . To Israel the unique events of historic time were spiritually more significant than the repetitive processes in the cycle of nature." For Judaism, the Sabbath is a time to remember when it was chosen by God's mighty acts: "We remember the day of the exodus from Egypt, the day when Israel stood at Sinai; and our Messianic hope is the expectation of a day, of the end of days."[45]

More than his acknowledgment that "the Sabbath remains a concrete fact, a legal institution," and his defense of the rabbinic "system of laws and rules of observance" as a logical extension of "single-minded devotion of total love," it is Heschel's identification of the Sabbath with the particular, redemptive history of the Jews that makes his theology of the Sabbath, in some important sense of the word, orthodox.[46]

However, it is not *halachic* orthodoxy; Heschel's work on the Sabbath is traditional, but it is the tradition of *aggadah*. *Halachah* is the rationalism of the Orthodox, the codification of how the mind guides the will. Heschel respects and honors *halachah*, but "must halachah continue to ignore the voice of aggadah?" Must esoteric disputes over how the intellect can control the will ignore the emotions by which all may approach God? Heschel thought that "the utterances of the psalmist are charged with emotion," that in "reading the prophets we are stirred by their passion and enlivened imagination," and that for both, "their primary aim is to move the soul, to engage the attention by bold and striking images."[47] It is no wonder that his book, *The Sabbath*, with its metaphors, tales,

274

personifications, and poetry, is a work of *aggadah*.

For someone descended from both the Maggid of Mezhirech and Levi Isaac of Berdichev, how else could Heschel talk of the Sabbath but as "the exodus from tension," *"a sanctuary in time,"* "a palace in time with a kingdom for all"? How else could he describe observance of the Sabbath but as celebrating "the coronation of a day in the spiritual wonderland of time"?[48] And how could Heschel help but draw his readers into the very sense and atmosphere of the Sabbath he knows—into an awareness of the redemption that he and they know together?

"People assemble to welcome the wonder of the seventh day," he declares, "while the Sabbath sends out its presence over the fields, into our homes, into our hearts. It is a moment of resurrection of the dormant spirit in our souls. . . . Some of us are overcome with a feeling, as if almost all they would say would be like a veil. There is not enough grandeur in our souls to be able to unravel in words the knot of time and eternity. . . . A thought has blown the market place away. There is a song in the wind and joy in the trees. The Sabbath arrives in the world, scattering a song in the silence of the night: eternity utters a day. . . . When the Sabbath is entering the world, man is touched by a moment of actual redemption; as if for a moment the spirit of the Messiah moved over the face of the earth."[49]

Better than argue, Heschel will recreate within us those moments of yearning and sympathy for God that stirred the psalmist, the prophets, the pious ones of Israel. The experience of the Sabbath will reenact God's acts of revelation and redemption. Indeed, for Heschel, the Sabbath was a time when disputes over concepts and deeds could be transcended by the experience of feeling with God the joy that God feels.

Convergence

There is evidence that Heschel's hopes for the experience of the Sabbath are being fulfilled both in observance and theology. Among Reform Jews the issue of Sunday observance died after the turn of the century. Friday evening became the time for worship. Now, traditional liturgy is increasingly being introduced into the service. There has even been a call by one of Reform Judaism's best-known figures, W. Gunther Plaut, for a reformed *halachah* of the Sabbath, since "our 'mental health' approach to the Sabbath is a failure. The fact is that the rabbi's opinion of Sabbath observance as 'desirable' and 'good for the Jew' has not been convincing."[50]

The most dramatic evidence of greater appreciation within Reform Judaism for a more historic understanding of the Sabbath is the publication in 1975 of *Gates of Prayer—The New Union Prayerbook,* providing materials for Sabbath worship. Noting that the new prayer book "contains an impressive amount of traditional liturgical material, never before included in an American Reform ritual or in many a European Liberal or Reform prayerbook," Jacob J. Petuchowski, a professor of theology at Hebrew Union College, declares that "the publication of *Gates of Prayer* must be seen as a milestone not only in the history of Reform liturgy, but also in the history of American Reform Judaism itself."[51]

The accelerating trend toward traditional observance of the Sabbath coincides with renewed admiration for Heschel on the part of Reform Judaism's most respected theologians. With Emil L. Fackenheim having said of Heschel's theology in its most fully developed form, "It is perhaps the most profound religious thinking that has been offered to American Judaism in our time," and Eugene B. Borowitz's concluding an overview of contemporary Judaism with the statement that "no person of our time has so well epitomized the roundedness of Covenantal existence as did Abraham Heschel," it is certain that Heschel's invocation of the splendors of the Sabbath will meet with increasing response from Reform Judaism.[52]

While Reform Judaism wavered in its commitment to the Sabbath, Orthodoxy's strict observance of the Sabbath has continued uninterrupted by Emancipation. But there is virtually no public acknowledgment from its theologians of Heschel's emphasis on passionate experience of the Sabbath. However, one cannot help but think that even the few writings published in English by Orthodoxy's greatest living representative in America, Joseph R. Soloveitchik, reflects acquaintance with Heschel's theology.[53]

In conclusion, it must be stated that Heschel's greatness as a Jewish theologian must be measured by the boldness of his vision. His concerns reached beyond interfaith dialogue between Jews and Christians. His last book, completed the Friday afternoon he died, was a tribute to the Hasidic master most like the Gaon of Vilna, Reb Menahem Mendl of Kotzk. It ends with the words "Truth is alive, dwelling somewhere, never weary. And all of mankind is needed to liberate it."[54]

Moreover, Heschel's book on the Sabbath was surely not haphazardly titled: *The Sabbath: Its Meaning for Modern Man*. Was there ever a *rebbe* more daring? More than any thinker since Emancipation, Heschel launched Judaism on the venture of pursuing its most obvious particularity in the point of universality.[55] At a time when theories do not convince nor laws elicit reverence, Heschel has appealed to man's passions. Heschel has plunged to the very core of Jewish religious experience, certain that the radiance of Sabbath joy will inflame all men. From the heart of Judaism he will be a *tzaddik* to the world. As he says, in the final words of *The Sabbath*:

"There are few ideas in the world of thought which contain so much spiritual power as the idea of the Sabbath. Aeons hence, when of many of our cherished theories only shreds will remain, that cosmic tapestry will continue to shine."[56]

NOTES

[1] For information on present-day Sabbathkeeping groups, see chapter 13, pp. 253-255.
[2] Because this essay focuses on theology, it does not analyze rabbinic response regarding proper observance of the Sabbath. Also, the essay does not discuss contemporary Eastern European or Israeli writing. It concentrates, rather, on major writers of Jewish theology in the West.
[3] Simon Noveck, ed., *Great Jewish Personalities of Modern Times* (New York, 1960), p. 7.
[4] Mordecai M. Kaplan, *The Greater Judaism in the Making* (New York, 1960), pp. 227-231, quoted in Noveck, *op. cit.*, p. 63.
[5] W. Gunther Plaut, *The Rise of Reform Judaism* (New York, 1963), p. 185.
[6] Noveck, *op. cit.*, p. 130.
[7] Joseph L. Blau, *Modern Varieties of Judaism* (New York and London, 1966), p. 58.
[8] W. Gunther Plaut, *The Growth of Reform Judaism* (New York, 1965), p. 269.
[9] Blau, *op. cit.*, p. 107.
[10] Samson Raphael Hirsch, *Horeb: A Philosophy of Jewish Laws and Observances*, 2 vols. (London, 1962), 1:62.
[11] I. Grunfeld, *The Sabbath: A Guide to Its Understanding and Observance*, 3d ed. (Jerusalem and New York, 1972), p. 19.
[12] Hirsch, *op. cit.*, p. 65; cf. Emanuel Rackman, "Sabbath and Festivals in the Modern Age," in *Studies in Torah Judaism*, ed. by Leon D. Stitskin, (New York, 1969), p. 52.
[13] Hirsch, *op. cit.*, p. 64.
[14] *Ibid.*, p. 63.
[15] Grunfeld, *op. cit.*, pp. 4, 5.
[16] Rackman, *op. cit.*, p. 54.
[17] Norman Lamm, *Faith and Doubt: Studies in Traditional Jewish Thought* (New York, 1971), p. 204.

[18] Grunfeld, *op. cit.*, pp. 9, 10.
[19] Samson Raphael Hirsch, "The Jewish Sabbath," in *Judaism Eternal* (London, 1956), p. 152.
[20] Hermann Cohen, *Religion of Reason* (New York, 1972), p. 161.
[21] Hermann Cohen, *Reason and Hope: Selections from the Jewish Writings of Hermann Cohen* (New York, 1971), pp. 116, 117.
[22] Cohen, *op. cit.*, p. 157.
[23] *Ibid.*
[24] *Ibid.*, pp. 158, 155, 458.
[25] Leo Baeck, *This People Israel: The Meaning of Jewish Existence* (New York, 1964), pp. 137, 138.
[26] Idem, "Mystery and Commandment," in *Contemporary Jewish Thought*, ed. by Simon Noveck ([Washington], 1963), p. 202.
[27] Baeck, "Mystery and Commandment," p. 203.
[28] *Ibid.*, pp. 203, 202.
[29] Martin Buber, *Moses* (Oxford, 1946), pp. 85, 132, 133, 84.
[30] *Ibid.*, pp. 84, 85, 178.
[31] Franz Rosenzweig, *The Star of Redemption* (New York, 1971), pp. 310, 311.
[32] *Ibid.*, p. 312.
[33] *Ibid.*, pp. 312-315.
[34] Nahum Glatzer, *Franz Rosenzweig: His Life and Thought* (New York, 1953), p. 179.
[35] Glatzer, *op. cit.*, pp. 75, 78.
[36] Rabbi Seymour Siegel, who succeeded to the seminary's Simon Professorship in Jewish theology previously occupied by Heschel, and who has himself written on the Sabbath ("The Meaning of the Sabbath," unpublished manuscript), provided valuable criticism of the essay at this and other points.
[37] Abraham Joshua Heschel, *God in Search of Man: A Philosophy of Judaism* (New York, 1955), pp. 20, 283.
[38] *Ibid.*, p. 20.
[39] Abraham Joshua Heschel, *The Prophets* (New York and Evanston, 1962), pp. 259, 260, 224, 309. Commentary on Heschel's theology shows no sign of slackening. Some of the most helpful, in chronological order: E. La B. Cherbonnier, "A. J. Heschel and the Philosophy of the Bible," *Commentary* 27 (January, 1959):23-29; Zalman M. Schachter, "Two Facets of Judaism," *Tradition* 3 (Spring, 1961):191-202; Eliezer Berkovits, "Dr. A. J. Heschel's Theology of Pathos," *Tradition* 6 (Spring/Summer, 1964):67-104; Fritz A. Rotschild, "The Religious Thought of Abraham Heschel," *Conservative Judaism* 24 (Fall, 1968):12-14; Franklin Sherman, *The Promise of Heschel* (New York, 1970); Sol Tanenzapf, "Abraham Heschel and his Critics," *Judaism* 23 (Summer, 1974):276-286.
[40] Abraham Joshua Heschel, *The Sabbath* (New York, 1951), p. 99.
[41] *Ibid.*
[42] Heschel, *God in Search of Man*, p. 417.
[43] Heschel, *Sabbath*, p. 28.
[44] *Ibid.*, p. 27.
[45] *Ibid.*, pp. 6-8.
[46] *Ibid.*, pp. 16, 17.
[47] Heschel, *Prophets*, p. 258.
[48] Heschel, *Sabbath*, pp. 29, 21, 18.
[49] *Ibid.*, pp. 66-68.
[50] W. Gunther Plaut, "The Sabbath in the Reform Movement," in *Reform Judaism: A Historical Perspective*, ed. by Joseph L. Blau (New York, 1973), p. 244.
[51] Jacob J. Petuchowski, "Bookbinder to the Rescue!" *Conservative Judaism* 31 (Fall, 1975):12, 14.
[52] Emil L. Fackenheim, "Review of *God in Search of Man*," *Conservative Judaism* 16 (Fall, 1960):53; Eugene B. Borowitz, "God and Man in Judaism Today: A Reform Perspective," *Judaism* 23 (Summer, 1974):308.
[53] See Joseph B. Soloveitchik, "The Lonely Man of Faith," *Tradition* 7 (Summer, 1965):5-67. Soloveitchik, unlike Heschel has written relatively little for the public, but nevertheless has become highly revered for his knowledge and teaching of the Talmud. His aforementioned essay is subjective, the tale of a "personal dilemma"; in other words, it is *aggadah*. On the matter of Sabbath theology he is, like Heschel, interested in man's direct experience of time, not in abstract concepts. But he would undoubtedly differ considerably in tone from Heschel in any description he might give regarding man's awareness of redemption in the Sabbath "convenantal time experience." For further details on Soloveitchik, see pages 733-735 in my original article in the *Journal of Ecumenical Studies*. It seems to me that Soloveitchik's theological outlook has the potential for further developing certain creative aspects of Sabbath theology, and I would hope that he will allow himself to publish more extensively.
[54] Abraham Joshua Heschel, *A Passion for Truth* (New York, 1973), p. 323.
[55] See Borowitz, *op. cit.*, pp. 306-308.
[56] Heschel, *Sabbath*, p. 101.

CHAPTER 15

Contemporary Theologies of the Sabbath

Hans K. LaRondelle

THE present chapter surveys some contemporary theologies of the Sabbath (frequently used as a designation for Sunday), as held by four particular groups: the radical-critical school, neo-orthodoxy, evangelicals, and certain small denominations and sects. Space limitations necessitate that our treatment include only a few outstanding representatives of each group and that the Sabbath theologies of such individuals be summarized rather briefly.

Radical-Critical Concepts of the Sabbath

Radical-critical scholarship starts from the presupposition that the origin of the Sabbath remains a mystery and cannot be solved by any scientific verification. Several conflicting hypotheses of a possible origin have been proposed, such as the gloomy Babylonian-Assyrian taboo days, or the rest day of the Kenites (a tribe of smiths), or a feast day of the full moon, or an ancient market day, and various other theories.*,[1] Several conservative scholars have indicated the inconclusiveness and unlikeliness of such extra-Biblical origins of the Sabbath.[2] Especially the careful study of J. H. Meesters has shown conclusively that "all efforts to explain the origin of the Sabbath from extra-Israelite institutions or customs must be counted as a failure," so that only one conclusion remains: the Sabbath, just as the seven-day week, cannot be anything but a unique, Israelite creation, without a counterpart elsewhere at any time.[3] The same conclusion has been drawn by many other scholars, including Eduard Lohse, who states that the meaning and content of the Old Testament Sabbath "are exclusively controlled by Israel's faith in Yahweh."[4]

It is generally felt among critical scholars that the seventh-day Sabbath dates back to Mosaic times, but that the fourth commandment as found in the Decalogue of Exodus 20 or Deuteronomy 5 is the product of later redactors.

---

* For details, see chapter 1, pp. 21, 22.

CONTEMPORARY THEOLOGIES OF THE SABBATH

While it is acknowledged that the Sabbath is connected with Yahwism from the beginning, the motivation for the Sabbath celebration because of the Creation motif in Exodus 20:11 is thought to be a later addition around 500 B.C. by a redactor who was inspired by reading the priestly narrative of Creation in Genesis 1-2. The Exodus motif as motivation for the Sabbath commandment in Deuteronomy 5 is also taken as a later addition by the redactor of the book of Deuteronomy around 650 B.C.

Many have tried to reconstruct the so-called original Sabbath commandment, and a common conclusion is that it probably was formulated negatively: "You shall perform no work on the seventh day." Since 1930 the trend has been to date this so-called original Sabbath commandment early, during Israel's desert journey, or even to let it originate with Moses himself.[5] The Creation narrative with mention of the Sabbath, in Genesis 2:2, 3, however, is usually postulated as being written by priests *after* the codification of the Deuteronomic Decalogue, during the Babylonian exile. That is, on the basis of Genesis 2:2, 3, another redactor created the fourth commandment of Exodus 20:8-11 with its Creation motif.

In the field of New Testament studies Rudolf Bultmann and his followers have expressed some radical-critical concepts regarding the Sabbath that have been adopted also by some of the more conservative evangelical scholars. Bultmann considers the Sabbath story of Jesus and His disciples in the grainfield of Mark 2:23-28 (cf. Matthew 12:1-8) as a construction of the primitive church, molded by the post-Resurrection faith of the early Christians. He holds that the story represents the later theology by which the Christian church ascribed the justification of her Sabbath customs to Jesus. Also, he regards the expression "Son of man" (Christ) as coming from a later translator of the Aramaic, and concludes that *every* man is a "lord of the Sabbath" and therefore receives the liberty to disregard the Sabbath commandment.[6]

Ernst Käsemann agrees basically with Bultmann, but feels that the primitive church shrank back from so much freedom regarding the Sabbath, and therefore coined the phrase in Mark 2:28 that it was rather the "Son of man" who was the Lord of the Sabbath. And E. Lohse's position is similar.[7]

In a more historical study, Willy Rordorf, in *Sunday: The History of the Day of Rest and Worship in the Earliest Centuries of the Christian Church*, states: "It is a misunderstanding to hold that Jesus did not attack the sabbath commandment itself, but only the casuistical refinements of the Pharisees." He goes so far as to say that the Sabbath "had failed in its divine purpose, and as a consequence rebellion against it or disregard of it was no sin." He even states of the Sabbath commandment that "this commandment enslaved human beings": "For this reason he [Jesus] was not afraid of calling in question the commandment contained in the priestly tradition of the Old Testament." On this assumption Rordorf concludes that all of Jesus' healings on the Sabbath days were provocations to serve "the express intention of showing that for him the sabbath commandment had no binding force."[8]

Jesus' declaration that "'the sabbath was made for man, not man for the sabbath'" (Mark 2:27, R.S.V.) was therefore "throwing overboard the entire sabbath theology established by post-exilic Judaism." This is Rordorf's understanding of Jesus' Messianic consciousness "which knew no bounds," so that even the Sabbath commandment of the Old Testament "was simply annulled"[9] before the ceaseless activity of Jesus. The word of Jesus as transmitted in Matthew 24:20, "'Pray that your flight may not be ... *on a sabbath'*" (R.S.V.), is dismissed with the simple remark that this text "is a secondary, expanded version of Mark 13:18, where there is no mention of the sabbath ... it is usually said that this expansion derives from Jewish Christian circles strict in their observance of the law."[10]

Rordorf sharply separates the Christian Sunday from the "Jewish" Sabbath, deriving from three New Testament verses (1 Cor. 16:2; Acts 20:7; Rev. 1:10) "that Sunday clearly played an important role even in the Pauline churches."[11] He acknowledges that the New Testament nowhere announces the origin of the Christian observance of Sunday, but nevertheless concludes from the appearances of the risen Lord on Sunday evenings that the Christian worship around the Lord's Supper on Sunday reaches back to the apostles of Christ "and even to the intention of the risen Lord himself."[12]

In summary, radical-critical concepts concerning the Sabbath show neither trust in the historical reliability of the Biblical accounts and stories nor due respect for the transmitted text of Scripture.

Neo-Orthodox Theologies of the Sabbath

Undoubtedly the most profound theology on the Sabbath ever written is that by neo-orthodox theologian Karl Barth in his *Church Dogmatics*.[13] Barth is in basic agreement with John Calvin, who had stressed that the Sabbath commandment was regarded of supreme significance in the Old Testament. Calvin had noticed that the Sabbath was held in "singular estimation" "above all commandments of the law" because it is the distinctive sign of God's covenant of grace with Israel, as well as a foreshadowing of the spiritual and heavenly rest. Barth's Christological theology develops especially Calvin's concept that the Sabbath is a Creation ordinance and that the Creator aroused man's zeal to observe the Sabbath with greater piety by His own exemplary deed of resting on the seventh day of the Creation week.[14]

Taking the work of Creation in Genesis 1 theologically as "the external basis" of God's covenant of grace, Barth interprets God's *resting* on the seventh day in Genesis 2:2 as the "secret" beginning of God's covenant of redeeming man, because God's resting means that He has committed Himself to belong to man and this world. Barth is convinced that God's resting on the seventh day of the Creation week, in Genesis 2:2, signifies a specific Creation ordinance as a blessed gift for all mankind. Creation, with man at its head, would find its completion only in fellowship with God Himself and participation in His divine rest, joy, and freedom: "What is concretely revealed in the first and divine observance of the Sabbath, and in the implied invitation to the creation to observe it as well, is no more and no less than the meaning and intention of the covenant between God and man."[15]

Barth interprets this covenant between God and man, represented in Sabbath fellowship, as a covenant of grace and redemption to be fulfilled in Christ. Thus the Creation Sabbath speaks prophetically of Christ and must be understood Christologically from the beginning in Genesis 2. The Sabbath as the sign of the promised rest of grace really came not at the end but at the beginning of man's working week, since man was created on the sixth day. Man could therefore celebrate on the Sabbath only God's own works and merits.

CONTEMPORARY THEOLOGIES OF THE SABBATH

The fourth commandment, declares Barth, commands Israel to enter into the rest of divine grace and not to have the slightest trust in their own work or righteousness before God.[16] Israel was thus reminded weekly that the Creator was their Redeemer, their Justifier, and their Sanctifier. Moreover, Barth considers the Sabbath commandment as the comprehensive and fundamental command of all God's commandments, as the sum total of God's covenant of redeeming grace, because only in this commandment are law and gospel fully united!

Furthermore, he recognizes not only the *Christological* saving significance of the Sabbath but also an *eschatological* judging aspect. Appealing to Isaiah 58:13, 14, and Jeremiah 17:24-27, Barth observes a hidden relationship of the Sabbath with the day of the Lord as judgment day. That day will be, however, also the day of restored blessing, the day of the ultimate fulfillment of the promise given in the first Sabbath. Consequently, Barth is convinced "not without a certain awe, [of] the radical importance, the almost monstrous range of the Sabbath commandment."[17]

In Barth's theology of the Sabbath there can be sensed an unbearable tension between his idea that the Sabbath is a Creation ordinance and the sign of redeeming grace, on the one hand, and his conclusion that the resurrection of Christ has *terminated* the history of God's covenant of grace together with its sign, the Sabbath day, on the other hand. Barth tries to justify theologically the historic change of rest day from the seventh-day Sabbath to Sunday by the Christian church. He states—surprisingly—that the first advent of Christ, culminating in His resurrection from the dead on the first day of the week, meant the conclusion or "termination of the history of the covenant and salvation."[18] Therefore the first day "had to become" the day of rest of the new time. Barth seems to realize that the "necessity" of this switch of rest days is not obvious in such reasoning without scriptural legitimization. He presents two arguments for his Sunday theology that he feels must serve to solve "this apparent revolution against its divine order in creation."[19]

His first argument is an appeal to three controversial texts—1 Corinthians 16:2; Acts 20:7; Revelation 1:10—without any attempt at exegesis. He states only that early Christianity "began to keep the first day of the week instead of the seventh as a day of rest . . . as a debt of obedience."[20] One wonders *where* in Scripture Barth has read such a command, when neither Luther nor Calvin could find it!

But Barth then promises "also a direct proof." This consists in the Christian "discovery" that the original order set by God for man at Creation was the rest day first (on God's seventh day), followed by six working days: "The 'Lord's Day' was really his first day. Hence it ought always to have been his first day and not his seventh and last." Thus Barth tries to solve his dilemma by explaining that the "first day" rest was not really "an innovation but the discovery of the calculation which was already *hidden* in the calculation of Genesis 1."[21]

Barth admits that his so-called "direct proof" for the "Sunday Sabbath" is only an inference, since his proof is "hidden" in the calculation of the Genesis Creation account. But one may well ask: If the seventh-day Sabbath as the Lord's day really had been Adam's first day, thus symbolizing that man lives by God's initiating and maintaining grace, why the need for the church to change this "divine order in creation"?

281

In the final analysis, Barth's attempt to prove a Sunday Sabbath shows that he cannot accept an actual termination of the Sabbath and the Sabbath commandment in the new covenant of Christ. He even defends a basic continuity of the Sabbath when he concludes: "New Testament Christianity did not proclaim a particular annulment but, as it would appear from 1 Corinthians 16:2 and Acts 20:7 quite naturally began to celebrate this holy day on the first day of the week, it was not rebelling against the order of creation but was acting in profound agreement with what is said in Exodus 20:8f. and Genesis 2:1f. on the basis of the Sabbath commandment." [22]

It finally becomes clear *how* Barth can see the hallowing of Sunday in "profound agreement" with the Creation Sabbath of Genesis 2 and with the Sabbath commandment of Exodus 20: namely, by *dissecting* the Sabbath from the seventh day and by considering the Sabbath exclusively as the rest of grace. Then the Sabbath only hovers over the seventh day but *is* not the seventh day. This Docetic philosophical Sabbath concept is obviously a non-Biblical assumption. Also, Barth here reaps what he has sown in his position to accept the Creation account of Genesis 1 as a "saga" only, that is, not as historically real and authentic, but true in its "kernel." [23]

In his spiritualizing interpretation of the Sabbath, Barth returns somewhat to Calvin, who had already detached God's rest from the seventh day in his commentary on Genesis 2:3. Calvin had stated: "First, therefore, God rested; then he blessed this rest, that in all ages it might be held sacred among men." [24] In this respect Calvin and Barth do not allow Scripture to say what it actually says in Genesis 2:3: "So God blessed *the seventh day* and hallowed *it, because on it God rested* from all his work which he had done in creation" (R.S.V.). Scripture does not state that God blessed His rest, but that God blessed and hallowed "the seventh day," because He had rested on that day after six days of creative work. It is not the rest, but the rest *day*, that God blessed. This is emphatically repeated in the Decalogue, Exodus 20:11, with its pointed commission that the redeemed Israel should "remember the sabbath day, to keep it holy. . . . *The seventh day is a sabbath to the LORD your God*" (Ex. 20:8-10, R.S.V.).

Barth's dogmatic Sabbath theology would have become more consistently Biblical and less speculatively philosophical if he, as a Biblical theologian, could have seen that the resurrection of Christ and the seventh-day Sabbath are *not* in tension with each other, because the resurrected Christ *remains* the "faithful Creator" (1 Peter 4:19). Probably more than any theologian in recent Christian history, Barth has emphasized the gospel of God's free grace in the seventh-day Sabbath as the ordained sacrament of salvation. It is therefore hard to understand why he can conclude that Christ's resurrection was to *terminate* the very sign of God's everlasting covenant that He gave in the beginning to mankind, not just to Israel later.

Following in the footsteps of Barth, the German Old Testament scholar Ernst Jenni in 1956 developed his "theological foundations of the Sabbath commandment in the Old Testament" in a challenging study.[25] Jenni observes basically two kinds of foundations for the Sabbath commandment; one is in the Decalogue of Exodus 20 (verse 11), pointing back to God's rest in Creation, the other in the Decalogue of Deuteronomy 5 (verses 14, 15) pointing back to Israel's deliverance from Egypt. In Exodus 20 Jenni sees the typical "priestly" foundation represented and in Deuteronomy 5 the "Deuteronomic" one, although he thinks that both kinds of theological foundation were "certainly added to the commandment later." He even declares: "The original Sabbath commandment must have been formulated in shorter form and have contained no foundation.[26] That is, of course, a typical radical-critical concept.

In Deuteronomy Jenni sees a *redemptive-historical* foundation of the Sabbath established. The Sabbath is consecrated to Yahweh as the gracious Lord and Liberator of Israel. This counts for the cheerful character of the Sabbath in Israel before the Babylonian exile (Isa. 58:13).

The so-called priestly foundation of the Sabbath in Exodus 20:11 and 31:17, and Genesis 2:2, 3, transfers the Sabbath back to the creation of the world. Because the Sabbath is called a "perpetual covenant" (Ex. 31:16), the abiding obligation is stressed together with the grace character of Israel's redemptive institutions. Thus the holiness of the Sabbath is made independent from human achievement and astrological magic.[27]

In Genesis 2, Jenni distinguishes a threefold purpose of the Creation Sabbath. First, the Sabbath is "the goal of Creation," in the sense that the world is not created for itself or left to itself, but that on the Sabbath the whole cosmos, led by man, would praise God in worship. Second, the Creation Sabbath is the open door to make the history of God's covenant possible.[28] God's *hallowing* of the Sabbath makes room for cultic worship, separated from secular life. Third, the Sabbath rest of Genesis 2 implies a promise that points forward "to the perfect goal of creation, the perfect realization of the covenant. The sign becomes the presage of what is to come."[29]

The New Testament, Jenni says, teaches us that the Old Testament Sabbath, as a typological "witness of Christ," has been fulfilled in the coming of Jesus Christ (Matt. 11:28; 2 Cor. 1:20), although, according to Hebrews 4:9, Christ further guarantees a perfect rest that remains. "In this rest the promise of the earthly Sabbath will be fulfilled."[30]

Jenni's Sabbath theology allows the radical-critical concept of the origin of the Sabbath to deny the trustworthiness and historical reliability of the Creation narrative in Genesis 1-2. The Sabbath was in reality not inaugurated at the creation of the world, reasons Jenni, but later by Moses; and priests of Israel then projected the Sabbath of Israel back to the creation of the world in Holy Scripture. Consequently, the Sabbath becomes exclusively the sign of God's covenant of grace with Israel, implying the promise of a perfect rest as the goal of Creation at the end of history.

Although Barth and Jenni both emphatically unfold the redemptive and eschatological significance of the seventh-day Sabbath in the Old Testament, each theologian has a radically different interpretation of the Creation Sabbath in Genesis 2. While Barth stresses the Sabbath of Genesis 2 as an *ordinance of* Creation for mankind in the beginning, Jenni firmly rejects the Sabbath as a Creation ordinance. Accepting the periodic "market-day" of the heathen nations as the hypothetical origin of the Sabbath, Jenni believes that the religious seventh-day Sabbath is only an institution of Moses for the nation of Israel.

Consequently the justification of Sunday observance by the Christian church also diverges substantially with these two neo-orthodox theologians. Barth can see Sunday only as a *shifted Sabbath*. Jenni, on the other hand, believes in an *abrogated*

THE SABBATH IN SCRIPTURE AND HISTORY

Sabbath, based on the presupposition that the Sabbath is only a Jewish institution.

Diverging Evangelical Theologies of the Sabbath

The existing disunity and uncertainty in Protestant liberalism and neo-orthodoxy concerning a Biblical Sabbath theology are only aggravated by the confusion of conflicting Sabbath interpretations in evangelical circles. Two main streams of diverging Sabbath theologies can be discerned in contemporary evangelicalism.

The first stream accepts the seventh-day Sabbath as a divine Creation ordinance, based on Genesis 2:2, 3 and Exodus 20:8-11. It develops, however, a Sunday-Sabbath theology on the assumption that the resurrection of Christ actually *shifted* or transferred the Sabbath commandment to Sunday, the first day of the week. The final appeal is always to a trio of texts—Acts 20:7; 1 Corinthians 16:2; and Revelation 1:10—usually with little or no effort at real exegesis. Sunday is regarded as the "Lord's day" or the "Christian Sabbath."

The second stream rejects the Sabbath as a Creation ordinance, on the basis of a radical-liberal evaluation, and accepts the Sabbath merely as an Israelite and Jewish Sabbath intended as a covenant gift of God for the Jewish nation only. A Sunday theology is then developed on the assumption that Christ radically *abolished* the Sabbath as a holy day. Sunday observance by the church is often readily acknowledged as a postapostolic ecclesiastical institution, created for church order and in remembrance of the resurrection of Christ on the first day of the week. Yet frequently too, Sunday as a religious day of worship is piously regarded as authorized by the guidance of the Holy Spirit, possibly instituted by Christ or the apostles. But Sunday is not conceived as a Sunday Sabbath.

Not every evangelical theologian or writer can be classified clearly in one of these two main streams. Some intermingle various elements of both views or give interpretations of their own.

Evangelical Theology of the Transferred Sabbath.—The view that Sunday is the Christian Sabbath and that Christian Sunday observance really fulfills the fourth commandment of the Decalogue is basically the theological position of (1) the Roman Catholic Church as developed by Thomas Aquinas and explained in the Catechismus Romanus (A.D. 1567); (2) the English Puritans; and (3) the party of Jacobus Koelman in the Reformed State Church of the Netherlands in the so-called battle for the Sabbath in the second half of the seventeenth century.[31] The concern is not whether Saturday or Sunday should be kept as the day of worship, but rather on what grounds Sunday is to be kept as a holy day, how Sunday is to be related theologically to the Sabbath commandment in the Decalogue, and whether Christ or the apostles or the postapostolic church had initiated Sunday observance—in short, whether Sunday observance is of divine origin or based on mere ecclesiastical authority.

The Puritans and the Koelman party maintained that Sunday was the true Sabbath *by divine right* and the moral fulfillment of the Sabbath commandment. Their argument was based on the philosophical distinction of a separate moral and ceremonial precept *within* the fourth commandment, a concept introduced into Christian theology by Thomas Aquinas. To them, as to Aquinas, the perpetual *moral* precept would demand only one day chosen arbitrarily out of the week for worship, but the transitory *ceremonial* precept would demand the specific seventh day of the week, in commemoration of the creation of the world. Koelman insisted that Christ or the apostles by divine authority changed the Sabbath into Sunday rest, but that this change left the moral essence of the commandment untouched, since the change pertained only to the ceremonial aspect, the additional idea of the "seventh" day of the week.

Several prominent Dutch scholars, G. Voetius, Abraham Kuyper, W. Geesink, and G. Vos, have carried on in the Koelman tradition, with various refinements.

A. H. Strong, a Baptist, calls Sunday "the Christian Sabbath," which "commemorates... the new creation of the world in Christ, in which God's work in humanity first becomes complete." Appealing to Revelation 1:10, Acts 20:7, and 1 Corinthians 16:1, 2 (all without exegesis), Strong claims that "Christ's example and apostolic sanction have transferred the Sabbath from the seventh day to the first, for the reason that this last is the day of Christ's resurrection, and so the day when God's spiritual creation became in Christ complete." [32]

Strong immediately modifies this absolute statement by declaring, somewhat less assuredly, that the change "seems to have been due to the resurrection of Christ," [33] thus acknowledging that the "change" is a matter of a theological inference.

John Murray of Westminster Theological Seminary in Philadelphia has shown concern, in his *The Sabbath Institution,* to establish "the perpetuity of the principle embodied in the Fourth Commandment, namely, the divinely instituted sanctity of every recurring seventh day." Indeed, for Murray, Sunday observance stands or falls with the question of divine institution. Expediency "can never carry the sanction of law and it cannot bind the conscience of men." [34]

He affirms the Sabbath in Genesis 2 as a Creation ordinance, instituted before the Fall of man, and acknowledges clearly: "Sin does not abrogate creation ordinances and redemption does not make superfluous their obligation and fulfillment." [35]

Regarding the fourth commandment, Murray argues that "it would require the most conclusive evidence to establish the thesis that the fourth command is in a different category from the other nine. That it finds its place among the ten words written by the finger of God upon tables of stone establishes for this commandment and for the labour and rest it enjoins a position equal to that of the third or the fifth or the seventh or the tenth." And Jesus' words in Mark 2:27, 28, concerning His lordship over the Sabbath, do not mean any abrogation of the Sabbath but rather His sealing to man that which the Sabbath institution involves: "Our Lord Himself confirms its permanent relevance." [36]

However, Murray regards *Sunday* as the Christian Sabbath by the device of dissecting the "Sabbath" from the seventh day of the week and transferring that "Sabbath" to the first day of the week. Recognizing that the Sabbath as a Creation ordinance commemorated the completion of Creation, he says: "In the Christian economy the Sabbath is the Lord's Day and therefore the memorial of the completion of a work of God greater than that of creation." [37] Here an illegitimate contrast is introduced, which is utterly foreign to the Bible, namely that Christ as Redeemer would destroy a good memorial of a perfect work done by Himself as Creator. It contradicts also Murray's own statement that "sin does not abrogate creation ordinances and redemption does not make superfluous their obligation and fulfillment." [38]

Herbert W. Richardson has tried to elevate Sunday as the Sabbatical sacrament for "the American vision of holy worldliness, the sanctification of all things by the Holy Spirit." Richardson rejects the traditional theology that argues that the Sabbath commandment is not like the other nine but only a ceremonial shadow that Christ later abolished. He characterizes this argument as motivated by "anti-Jewish polemics." Opting basically for the position of the Puritans, he further acknowledges the fourth commandment as constituting "a universal moral law," and accepts the priority of the "creation interpretation" of Genesis 2 above the "redemption interpretation" of Deuteronomy 5.[39]

Harold Lindsell has placed a somewhat unusual twist to Sunday-Sabbath theology in his article "The Lord's Day and Natural Resources." After simply equating Sunday with the Sabbath of Holy Scriptures, he suggests that Christians should press for social Sunday legislation in order to enforce "outward Sabbath observance for unbelievers." As the reason for this objective, he offers the idea that only the church knows what is good for the world, because God's special revelation (Scripture) gives the insight into God's natural revelation (natural laws), which means in this respect that every man should obey "God's natural law of one day of rest in seven."[40]

On the basis of this philosophical abstraction Lindsell favors state legislation or political coercion of all the non-Christians in order to accomplish the objective of "the proper use of the Lord's Day, wholly apart from any religious implications," "to bring unredeemed men to the place where they will keep it also—but for different reasons."[41]

But we may well ask, Is it conceivable to keep the Sabbath "properly" without religion, without keeping the day holy? And is not this kind of externalizing compliance with regard to the Sabbath commandment a form of *secularization,* which Lindsell detests so much within the church? In an editorial of November 5, 1976, in *Christianity Today,* Lindsell surprisingly proposes, however, "that *Saturday* be set aside as the day of rest for all people," in order to help solve the national energy crisis. This argument includes an interesting admission: "Jews and other Sabbatarians would be well served by this decision. For Protestants and Catholics it should prove no theological hardship: apart from the fact that our Lord rose from the dead on the first day of the week, there is nothing in Scripture that requires us to keep Sunday rather than Saturday as a holy day."[42]

James P. Wesberry, editor of *Sunday* magazine of the Lord's Day Alliance of the United States, presents another interesting variation by stating: "Jesus did not abolish the old Sabbath, but he enlarged and ennobled it and merged it into the Lord's Day" and "The old Jewish Sabbath was buried in the grave with Jesus and when he arose it took on new dimensions."[43] "It is perpetuated by being transfigured."[44]

Editor Wesberry thus defends a *shifted* Sabbath, which was "transformed" by Christ into Sunday as the Lord's Day. Nevertheless, he frankly acknowledges: "There is no record of a statement on the part of Jesus authorizing such a change, nor is there recorded such a statement on the part of the apostles."[45]

Evangelical Theology of the Abrogated Sabbath.—A basically different school of Sabbath interpretation, which enjoys the favor of contemporary evangelical scholarship, was defended by the Dutch theology professor Johannes Coccejus during the Sabbath controversy in Holland in the seventeenth century.

He took the position that the seventh-day Sabbath was not a Creation ordinance but only a ceremonial, Mosaic institution that was abrogated by Christ. He further held that Sundaykeeping was a purely ecclesiastical institution. Focusing on the most serious point of debate, the origin and authority of Sunday as the day of the Lord, Coccejus shocked the Sundaykeeping churches with this penetrating question: "If it is moral to rest because God has rested, then it is also moral to rest on the day on which God rested. If we transfer the remembering of God's rest to another day of the week, we remove what God has given and instituted. If it has been ceremonial to keep the seventh day, why then is the keeping of one of the seven days moral?"[46]

The Reformed Evangelical Old Testament scholar, J. L. Koole, has stressed an inescapable theological consequence if the Sabbath must be accepted as a Creation ordinance. His point may be paraphrased thus: Just as we are presently not permitted to murder because the sixth commandment was already in force prior to the law of Moses, so we would not be free now to reject the Sabbath of the fourth commandment if the Sabbath was already in force prior to Moses' law.[47] In other words, if the Sabbath was actually instituted in the beginning in Paradise, then Christians also are under the obligation to observe the Creation Sabbath.

Defying the long Reformation and Puritan tradition, as well as the position of Kuyper, Geesink, and Bavinck, Koole urges the reader to think this through logically and consistently before accepting the Sabbath as a Creation ordinance. Koole does not hesitate to conclude that those who view Sunday rest as a renewed Sabbath, required by the fourth commandment, must, in the nature of the case, transfer that rest day back to Saturday. But because the Sabbath cannot be scientifically verified or proved to have been historically instituted in Paradise, Koole does not accept the Creation Sabbath as a fact.

Basically following Jenni, Koole regards Genesis 2:2, 3 merely as a vision of Moses concerning a heavenly reality of God's rest, of which Israel's Sabbath was the symbol and sign. Israel's Sabbath therefore had the nature of a sacrament, a real encounter between human and divine resting. The Sabbath rest was to Israel both a sign of the rest of grace, provided already in God's covenant with Abraham, and a memorial of their deliverance from Egypt (Deut. 5:15), and therefore a sign of redemption also.

Ignoring the foundation of the Sabbath in the fourth commandment in Exodus 20:8-11, Koole considers the Sabbath exclusively as the memorial of Israel's gracious deliverance from Egypt (Deut. 5:15), instituted for the first time during Israel's journey in the wilderness (Exodus 16). Then, by comparing Christ's resurrection from the dead with Israel's redemption from Egypt, he concludes that God's redemptive act in Christ is greater than that which He performed for Israel. On that basis he infers that Sunday should have precedence over the Sabbath for Christians. Sunday therefore is not and cannot be the Sabbath or a fulfillment of the fourth commandment.

In basic agreement with Koole's Sabbath and Sunday theology are the publications of P. Visser, a pastor of the Reformed Churches in the Netherlands. And another Dutch scholar, R. J. VanDerVeen, has gone so far as to deny even the legitimacy of any Sunday theology.[48]

Although Oscar Cullmann is not to be classified among the evangelicals, his influence on them has been such that brief notice of some of his exegetical comments on Jesus and the Sabbath is in order here. In his *The Christology of the New Testament* Cullmann interprets Jesus' saying in Mark 2:28, R.S.V. ("'So the Son of man is lord even of the sabbath'") to mean that Jesus had come to set man free from Sabbath observance. Cullmann accepts the possibility, based on the Aramaic expression *barnasha* behind both Mark 2:27 and 28, that Jesus may have announced that man in general has now received the authority to be lord of the Sabbath. In case Jesus did mean exclusively Himself by the expression "Son of man," as Mark clearly understood it, Jesus proclaimed that He had come with divine authority to abrogate all Sabbath observance. Cullmann sees the same sense expressed more explicitly in Jesus' words of John 5:17, "in which Jesus does give a Christological foundation for non-observance of the Sabbath."[49]

In fact, he even goes so far as to declare that Jesus' words "until now" in John 5:17 are "an allusion to the new day of rest of the community, the day of Christ's resurrection ἡμέρα του κυρίου [*hēmera tou kuriou*] (day of the Lord)." The designation "day of the Lord" in Revelation 1:10 he simply identifies with Sunday, and declares the following without any historical evidence: "In fact, in his time, the day of Christ's resurrection, called in Rev. 1:10 Κυριακὴ ἡμέρα [*kuriakē hēmera*], was already universally celebrated in Christian Churches."[50]

However, Cullmann does not claim, as Barth does, that Sunday celebration is basically an obedience to the fourth commandment. He bluntly proclaims that the idea of Jesus' words "until now" in John 5:17 "justifies the disobedience"[51] to the Old Testament Sabbath commandment.

Paul K. Jewett, professor of systematic theology at Fuller Theological Seminary in Pasadena, California, has presented a full-scale Sabbath theology in his *The Lord's Day: A Theological Guide to the Christian Day of Worship*. Jewett basically develops the position of Rordorf, Jenni, and Cullmann, but modifies it by his own interpretation. The Sabbath originated with Moses in Exodus 16, he declares, and therefore is not a Creation ordinance, only a "Jewish Sabbath." "Jesus, as a devout Jew, observed the Sabbath" and "did not reject the institution of the Sabbath as such, but only the tradition of the elders regarding Sabbathkeeping." Nevertheless, Jewett surprisingly draws from this the conclusion that Jesus' attitude toward the Sabbath convinced His disciples that their Master did not require them any longer to observe the Sabbath. He also comments: "It cannot be supposed that the fact of the resurrection as such could have brought about this change [to Sunday], apart from the authority and teaching of Jesus himself."[52]

In considering the apostolic writings, Jewett dismisses the idea that the apostle Paul would have innovated Sunday worship among the Gentile Christians. However, regarding Revelation 1:10, he states: "In all subsequent Patristic usage the term 'Lord's Day' refers to Sunday, and there is no reason to suppose Revelation 1:10 is an exception to this rule."[53] On this crucial point it becomes evident that Jewett ignores the *Sola Scriptura* principle, which Protestantism since Luther, Calvin, and Zwingli has established as the *sine qua non* of Protestant faith. Second, he ignores also the recognized principle of historical method, that an expression is to be interpreted only in terms of evidence that is prior to it or contemporary with it, not by historical data from a later period.[54] These two principles—the theological hermeneutic and the historical-scientific method—

must be responsibly applied before one interprets the unique expression the "Lord's day" in Revelation 1:10.*[55]

In his effort to reconstruct the origin of Sunday worship, Jewett opts for what he calls the "likely hypothesis" that Sunday worship originated in the custom of celebrating the Lord's Supper on the first day of the week right from the *first* Easter Sunday on. He appeals to a combination of texts—Acts 20:7, Luke 24:33-43, and John 20:19-23.[56]

Because Jewett has joined those who reject the Sabbath as a Creation Sabbath, he cannot maintain that the Christian Sunday is, in principle, obedience to the Creation rhythm of six days of labor followed by one rest day. But nevertheless, he seeks to ground Sunday worship on some divine foundation or scriptural support, doing so through a philosophical rationalism by which he can say *Sic* ("Yes") and *Non* ("No") at the same time to the fourth commandment: *Yes* to the Jewish weekly cycle, and *No* to the Jewish Sabbath.[57]

Basic to Jewett's Sunday theology is the assumption "We can only suppose that the early Christians, both Jews and Gentiles, accepted the weekly cycle of time as a divinely given institution."[58] Consequently, not in the seventh-day Sabbath, but in the week "as such"—the cycle of seven days—Jewett views the unity of redemptive history between Israel and the church, between the Old Testament and the New Testament.

Jewett even asserts that the apostles taught the Gentile Christians "to observe the Jewish week," "the sabbatical sequence of time, but rejected the Sabbath Day." This implies that Christians who gather for worship on the first day of the week "stand under the sign of the Sabbath in that they gather every seventh day." Furthermore, according to Jewett, by the nonobservance of the *seventh-day* Sabbath, Christians indicate the fulfillment of their redemptive rest in the Christ who has come, and by their observance of the *first day* they indicate their need and hope for the future, eternal rest when Christ will return. This is Jewett's theology of "the dialectic of fulfillment in hope."[59]

Jewett accuses the Reformers Luther and Calvin for their radical No to the fourth commandment and their equalizing of all days of the week for Christians. But he proceeds to condemn likewise all Christian Sabbathkeepers who say wholeheartedly Yes to the fourth commandment because of their presupposed "Judaism."[60]

Jewett disagrees, too, with those Reformed Evangelicals who try to identify Sunday as "Lord's day" with Sunday as a civil institution. Sunday rest is not obligatory for unbelievers. There simply cannot be a real Lord's day without faith, because "the Lord's Day rest is preeminently a soul rest, a spiritual experience." Nevertheless, the civil Sunday law is a fruit of the gospel in society and "a genuine boon to mankind."[61]

One step beyond Jewett we arrive in the circle of the Dispensationalists, such as L. S. Chafer. While Jewett still contends for "continuity, without identity" of Sabbath and Sunday, Dispensational theology radically opposes every continuity of Sabbath and Sunday. It regards the two rest days as the symbols *par excellence* of two absolutely unrelated and opposing dispensations of "pure law and pure grace."[62] Dispensational theology is promoted with modifications by the

---

* Regarding Revelation 1:10, see chapter 6, pp. 125-127.

radiobroadcasts and literature of Richard W. DeHaan of Grand Rapids, Michigan *(Why Christians Worship on Sunday)*, and of the Moody Bible Institute in Chicago, Illinois.

Sabbath Interpretations of Some Small Denominations and Sects

W. T. Purkiser, of the Church of the Nazarene, in his article "The Sabbath Question," makes the challenging assertion: "First off, let it be said that the Sabbath belongs to the New Testament as well as to the Old Testament." [63] Taking Jesus' words in Mark 2:27, 28, as "the most basic statement of the New Testament regarding the Sabbath," he concludes that the Sabbath "belongs not only to Moses, Isaiah, and Nehemiah, but it belongs to every person who acknowledges Jesus Christ as Lord and Saviour." Purkiser hastens to declare, however, that the equation of Sabbath with Saturday or the seventh day of the week is a false assumption: "No one has ever been authorized to add to the fourth commandment after the words 'the seventh day' the further words 'of a traditional weekly cycle, or Saturday.'" While calendars are "of man's contriving," God has only appointed "the Sabbath principle," and "that principle is always and simply, EVERY SEVENTH DAY BELONGS TO GOD!" [64]

Purkiser incorrectly calls the identification of the seventh-day Sabbath with our Saturday a mere Jewish tradition. Of Sunday he states: "It is the perpetual memorial of the resurrection of the Lord Jesus Christ from the dead" and tries to elevate Sunday into a new Sabbath by illegitimately translating Mark 16:2, "And very early the first of the Sabbaths" (cf. also Matt. 28:1). He declares that these texts at least hint "that one series of Sabbaths was ended, and a new series was beginning." [65] This is, of course, an irresponsible manipulating of the Greek text, and it defies the combined New Testament scholarship represented in the Authorized, Revised, and other standard translations.[66]

In the Sabbath theology of the Seventh Day Baptists we come into contact with a basically different approach in contemporary thought. The writings of A. H. Lewis, A. J. C. Bond, and H. E. Saunders, published by the American Sabbath Tract Society in Plainfield, New Jersey, represent a Protestant Sabbath reform movement that tries to lead Christians back to the Biblical Sabbath by bringing them to Christ as the Lord of the Sabbath.

Basing himself on the Holy Scriptures as God's special revelation, and guided by a Christological understanding of the Old Testament, Saunders develops a concise theology of the seventh-day Sabbath in his book *The Sabbath: Symbol of Creation and Re-Creation* (1970). His fundamental thesis is that the Sabbath stands not only as a memorial of Creation but also as a memorial of re-creation, redemption, and resurrection.[67] Saunders quotes Lewis, who states: "The Day of God leads to the House of God, to the Book of God, and to the Son of God." [68] However, in their enthusiasm for a Christo-centric theology of the Sabbath, Lewis and Saunders unfortunately shift the resurrection of Christ from the first day of the week to the Sabbath.

Acknowledging the ordinance of baptism as the symbol of re-creation—a once-in-a-lifetime experience—Saunders extols the Sabbath as the "symbol of the continuing baptism of the Holy Spirit." "The Sabbath stands at the heart of the message of reconciliation just as it stands at the heart of God's original purpose for man." The Sabbath is "the God-ordained symbol of his own presence in time and eternity," that is, of fellowship of the Creator and man.⁶⁹ Because men may behold God in clearer light in Jesus Christ and may experience God in a more intimate fellowship, "the Sabbath means infinitely more" since Christ.⁷⁰

Indeed, the Sabbath now represents the life of man restored in Christ: "It is a reminder that God is still in control and man is only redeemed and saved by an act 'in time' of the eternal God. What Christ did in redeeming the world was to restore man to his created place as an eternal being." This was the significance of Jesus' healing and forgiving on the Sabbath day. Thus Jesus made the Sabbath, the memorial of the creative power of God, "a sign of God's redeeming and sanctifying and upholding power in Christ." Jesus' death and resurrection did nothing to alter this fact: "instead it has made it all the more imperative that man 'remember the Sabbath Day to keep it holy.'"⁷¹

Seventh Day Baptists also envision that the Sabbath is the great "symbol for the unification of the peoples of the world under allegiance to the revelation that has come to man, and which Christians all accept."⁷²

The Church of Jesus Christ of Latter-day Saints (Mormon), as represented by James E. Talmage, teaches that Sunday "is the acceptable day for Sabbath observance, on the authority of direct revelation specifying the Lord's Day as such."⁷³ This "direct revelation" refers to a vision of the founder and prophet Joseph Smith on Sunday, August 7, 1831, which is published in *The Doctrine and Covenants*. In this passage Joseph Smith exhorts his fellow believers to worship on God's "holy day," also referred to as the "Lord's day."⁷⁴ There is no direct or explicit equation of "Lord's day" and Sunday, but this revelation is used by the Mormon leaders to settle the issue.⁷⁵

To those who are not satisfied with this settlement, the Mormon Church offers their reprint of the pseudoscientific Greek argumentation of the Methodist Samuel Walter Gamble, *Sunday, The True Sabbath of God* (1900),⁷⁶ whose reasoning is simply reiterated by K. F. Coombs, *The True Sabbath—Saturday or Sunday* (1948), and by Le Grand Richards, *A Marvelous Work and a Wonder* (1950).

The Mormon position is also represented by Presidents D. O. McKay and C. W. Penrose in their repeated exhortations to observe Sunday on the basis of the Sabbath commandment of Exodus 20.⁷⁷ Interestingly, the Mormon author B. H. Roberts, in examining the "first-day" texts in the New Testament, admits that the change of rest days by Christ or the apostles can only be called "probable."⁷⁸

Understandably, many Mormons have wondered from the very start whether a return to the Biblical holy day of the Lord is not the real restoration of true worship. One of these was Orson Pratt, one of the "Twelve Apostles," who wrote in 1850: "Again, must the seventh day or the first day of the week be kept holy unto the Lord? The New Testament does not clearly answer this question. There is rather more evidence in that book for keeping holy the Sabbath day or Saturday, than there is for keeping the first day or Sunday. The New Testament is very indefinite on this subject, and therefore it is an insufficient guide."⁷⁹

The International Bible Students Association (Jehovah's Witnesses) has developed a peculiar interpretation of the Sabbath of the Bible. The original seventh day of the Creation week in Genesis 2:2, the day of God's Sabbath, is calculated to last exactly 7,000 years. These are divided into 6,000 years of human history until Armageddon and 1,000 years of the "Kingdom Sabbath" under Christ in the future. In the publication *Let God Be True* we read: "Man being created toward the close of the sixth day, he was put on the earth toward the end of 42,000 years of earth's preparation. So in course of time the grand cycle of seven 'days' will add up to 49,000 years." [80]

Inasmuch as God's Sabbath is still proceeding, according to this group, "every day that Christians exercise faith and obedience through Christ, they are keeping Sabbath, God's Sabbath or rest." [81] Accordingly, no weekly day is recognized as a holy day or Sabbath day.

Summary and Conclusion

It is obvious that modern theologies of the Sunday "Sabbath" are quite divergent. With the rise of radical text criticism and modern evolutionism, the Sabbath was less and less accepted as a Creation ordinance, so that for various scholars the Sabbath commandment in the Decalogue was interpreted as a mere Jewish feast day and redemptive shadow of the old covenant. Rordorf, Cullmann, and Jewett, for instance, project Sunday observance back into apostolic times and exalt Sunday as the day of Christian worship according to the intention of the risen Lord Himself. Karl Barth's and Ernst Jenni's neo-Reformed Sabbath theologies surprisingly unfold neglected gospel dimensions of the Old Testament Sabbath with keen and refreshing insights. To them, the Sabbath is nothing less than the sacrament of grace. While Barth accepts the Sabbath as a Creation ordinance, he ends in virtually proclaiming Sunday as the Christian Sabbath "in profound agreement with" the fourth commandment. Jenni, however, rejects the Sabbath as a Creation ordinance, considering the Sabbath to be a Jewish shadow that was abrogated by Christ.

In Evangelicalism, two main streams of diverging Sabbath theologies have developed. The older Puritan stream maintains that the Sabbath was instituted by God as a Creation ordinance for mankind, was reinstituted for the people of Israel under Moses, and was transformed by Christ or His apostles into a "Sunday Sabbath." By way of this strange transfer theory, the fourth commandment is "in principle" applied to Sunday observance.

The newer stream of Evangelical Sabbath interpretation, however, drastically rejects both the Sabbath as a Creation ordinance and the Puritan theology of Sunday as a transferred Sabbath. The Sabbath is conceived merely as a redemptive shadow of the old covenant ritual, completely abolished by Christ Himself.

A recent combination of these two main streams is presented by Jewett, who proposes that Christian believers with their Sunday observance obey the principle of a Sabbatical-week rhythm as the abiding moral principle of the fourth commandment. For him Sunday is not a Christian Sabbath in any respect, only the believers' outward sign of having found their souls' rest in the resurrected Christ. Thus Jewett tries to combine law and gospel in his Sunday theology.

In Dispensationalism, with its dichotomy between law and gospel, all such attempts are considered futile because the Sunday of "pure grace" is in no way related any longer to the Old Testament Sabbath commandment of "pure law."

It becomes quite evident that any Sabbath theology whatsoever is inextricably connected, not only with a Biblical protology (doctrine of the beginning of all things) and eschatology (the end of things) but also with soteriology (doctrine of redemption) and the Biblical interrelationship of law and gospel. And it seems

CONTEMPORARY THEOLOGIES OF THE SABBATH

that a fully developed Biblical Sabbath theology must honor all the dimensions of the scriptural Sabbath, uniting Creation, redemption, and final perfection in one abiding sacrament of God's everlasting covenant, as presented in Hebrews 4. Weighed in the balances of this revealed unbreakable unity of God's work in Creation, redemption, and final restoration, all Sunday theologies are found wanting, in that they create an un-Biblical dichotomy between the work of the Creator and the work of the Redeemer, the Re-Creator.*

NOTES

[1] See the review in J. J. Stamm and M. E. Andrew, *The Ten Commandments in Recent Research*, 2d ed., (London, 1970), pp. 90-93.
[2] R. de Vaux, *Ancient Israel* (New York, 1961), 2:475-483; Robert North, "The Derivation of Sabbath," *Biblica* 36 (1955):182-201; Neils-Erik A. Andreasen, *The Old Testament Sabbath*, SBL Diss. Ser. 7 (Missoula, Mont., 1972), pp. 1-8.
[3] J. H. Meesters, *Op Zoek Naar De Oorsprong Van De Sabbat* (Assen, 1966), p. 82.
[4] Eduard Lohse, "σαββατον," *TDNT*, 7:3.
[5] Meesters, *op. cit.*, pp. 103-106, 162.
[6] Rudolf Bultmann, *The History of the Synoptic Tradition* (New York: 1963), p. 16.
[7] Lohse, *op. cit.*, p. 22. See also E. Käsemann, "Begründet der nt.liche Kanen die Einheit der Kirche?" *Evangelische Theologie* 11 (1951-1952):18.
[8] Willy Rordorf, *Sunday* (Philadelphia: 1968), pp. 62, 63, 66.
[9] *Ibid.*, pp. 62, 70, 71.
[10] *Ibid.*, p. 68.
[11] *Ibid.*, p. 215.
[12] *Ibid.*, p. 237.
[13] Karl Barth, *Church Dogmatics*, III/4, pp. 47-72; III/1, pp. 213-228.
[14] John Calvin *Institutes of the Christian Religion* 2. 8. 29-31.
[15] Barth, *op. cit.*, III/1, pp. 217, 218.
[16] *Ibid.*, III/4, pp. 54, 55.
[17] *Ibid.*, pp. 56, 57.
[18] *Ibid.*, p. 53.
[19] *Ibid.*, III/1, p. 228.
[20] *Ibid.*
[21] *Ibid.* (Italics supplied.)
[22] *Ibid.*, III/4, p. 53.
[23] See the incisive criticism on Barth's presuppositions in Genesis 1 by G. C. Berkouwer, *The Triumph of Grace in the Theology of Karl Barth*, (Grand Rapids, 1956), chap. 3.
[24] John Calvin, *Commentaries on the First Book of Moses* (Grand Rapids, 1948), 1:106.
[25] Ernst Jenni, *Die Theologische Begründung des Sabbatgebotes im Alten Testament* (Zurich, 1956).
[26] *Ibid.*, p. 5.
[27] *Ibid.*, pp. 18, 22.
[28] *Ibid.*, pp. 25-27.
[29] *Ibid.*, p. 35.
[30] *Ibid.*, p. 39.
[31] Thomas Aquinas, *Summa Theologica* 2a2ae. 122. 4; Westminister Confession 21. 7. (1646). See H. B. Visser, *De Geschiedenis van den Sabbatsstrijd onder de Gereformeerden in de Zeventiende Eeuw* (Utrecht, 1939), chap. 6.
[32] Augustus Hopkins Strong, *Systematic Theology* (Philadelphia, 1907), pp. 109, 110.
[33] *Ibid.*, p. 410.
[34] John Murray, *The Sabbath Institution* (London, 1953), pp. 3, 4.
[35] *Ibid.*, p. 5.
[36] *Ibid.*, pp. 6, 7.
[37] *Ibid.*, p. 14.
[38] *Ibid.*, p. 5.
[39] Herbert W. Richardson, *Toward an American Theology* (New York, 1967), pp. 112-115.
[40] Harold Lindsell, "The Lord's Day and Natural Resources," *Christianity Today*, May 7, 1976, pp. 9, 11.
[41] *Ibid.*, pp. 12, 9.
[42] Harold Lindsell, "Consider the Case for Quiet Saturdays," *Christianity Today*, Nov. 5, 1976, p. 42.
[43] James P. Wesberry, "Are We Compromising Ourselves?" *Sunday*, April-June, 1976, pp. 4, 5.
[44] James P. Wesberry. "The Case for Quiet Sundays," *Sunday*, January, 1977, p. 3.
[45] Wesberry, "Are We Compromising Ourselves?" p. 5.
[46] Johannes Coccejus (1658), quoted in Visser, *op. cit.*, p. 129.
[47] J. L. Koole, *De Tien Geboden* (Baarn, 1964), p. 75.
[48] P. Visser, *Zondagsrust en Zondagsheiliging* (Kampen, 1959); idem, *Decaloog en Zondag* (Kampen, 1967); R. J. VanDerVeen, "Het Vierde Gebod," in *De Thora in de Thora*, U.B.B. Series, No. 11 (Aalten, 1963), Deel I.
[49] Oscar Cullmann, *The Christology of the New Testament*, rev. ed. (Philadelphia, 1963), p. 152. Cullmann develops his exegesis of John 5:17 in the section "Jesus and the Day of Rest," added to his book *Early Christian Worship*, (London, 1969), pp. 88-93.

---

* The next chapter will provide a "Sabbath theology" that averts this sort of dichotomy and provides a positive approach to the subject.

50 Cullmann, *Early Christian Worship*, p. 91.
51 *Ibid.*, p. 92.
52 Paul K. Jewett, *The Lord's Day: A Theological Guide to the Christian Day of Worship* (Grand Rapids, 1971), pp. 34, 35.
53 *Ibid.*, pp. 56, 57, 59.
54 See *SDABC*, 7:735.
55 See Kenneth A. Strand, "Another Look at 'Lord's Day' in the Early Church and in Rev. 1. 10," *New Testament Studies* 13 (1966-1967):174-181.
56 G. E. Meuleman, among many, has concluded, however: "Nevertheless it cannot be proved whether they began to celebrate the first day consciously as a remembrance of the resurrection ..." in "De Zondag," *Geref. Weekblad*, 13e jrg. nr. 8.
57 Jewett, *op. cit.*, pp. 80, 117.
58 *Ibid.*, p. 79.
59 *Ibid.*, pp. 77, 80, 82, 81.
60 *Ibid.*, pp. 80-82.
61 *Ibid.*, pp. 160, 165, 146.
62 L. S. Chafer, *Grace: The Glorious Theme* (Philadelphia, 1922), p. 245.
63 W. T. Purkiser, "The Sabbath Question," *The Herald of Holiness;* reprinted in *Sunday*, September-October, 1973, p. 8.
64 *Ibid.*, pp. 9, 16.
65 *Ibid.*, pp. 17, 18.
66 This syntactical innovation is soundly rebuked by Wilbur Fletcher Steele, "Must Syntax Die That the Sabbath May Live?" *Methodist Review*, May, 1899, pp. 401-409, reproduced in Russel J. Thomsen, *Latter-day Saints and the Sabbath* (Mountain View, Calif., 1971), appendix. The author states that this particular translation of Matthew 28:1 (as "the first of the Sabbaths"): "rests upon the profoundest ... ignorance of a law of syntax" (p. 402). The established law of syntax referred to states that when a noun and an adjective belong together (*e.g.*, "first" and "Sabbaths"), they must agree in gender, number, and case. As the adjective "first" *(mian* in Matthew 28:1) is of a feminine gender, and the noun "Sabbaths" *(sabbaton)* is of neuter gender, the two do not belong in the same category. This fact forever excludes the translation "the first of the Sabbaths." The correct translation remains therefore: "the first (day) of the week." And New Testament scholarship concludes unanimously that the nouns *Sabbaton* (singular) or *Sabbata* (plural) mean only "week" in some contexts: Mark 16:9; Luke 18:12; 1 Corinthians 16:2; Matthew 28:1; Mark 16:2; Luke 24:1, John 20:1, 19; Acts 20:7.
67 Herbert E. Saunders, *The Sabbath: Symbol of Creation and Re-Creation* (Plainfield, N.J., 1970), pp. 54-80.
68 A. H. Lewis, "The Mission of the Sabbath," *The Sabbath Recorder*, April 26, 1943, pp. 273, 274, quoted in *ibid.*, p. 60.
69 Saunders, *op. cit.*, pp. 65, 74.
70 Ahva J. C. Bond, *The Sabbath* (Plainfield, N.J., 1925), p. 118, quoted in *ibid.*, p. 74.
71 Saunders, *op. cit.*, pp. 76, 78.
72 *Ibid.*, p. 78.
73 James E. Talmage, *A Study of the Articles of Faith* (Salt Lake City, 1942), p. 451.
74 Section 59:9-13.
75 See A. L. Crowley, *Statement of Beliefs of the Church of Jesus Christ of Latter-day Saints* (Salt Lake City: 1963), p. 121; Le Grand Richards, *A Marvelous Work and a Wonder* (Salt Lake City, 1950), pp. 287-294; Bruce R. McConkie, *Mormon Doctrine* 2d ed. (Salt Lake City, 1966), s.v. "Sabbath"; Joseph Fielding Smith, *Answers to Gospel Questions*, 2 vols. (Salt Lake City: 1957-1966), 2:58, 59. Thomsen claims, however, that there really is no revelation from God in Section 59 of *The Doctrine and Covenants* that elevates Sunday into the holy Sabbath (p. 19). "The basis for Sunday observance in the Mormon Church, as in the Roman Catholic Church, lies in tradition alone" (p. 53).
76 Samuel Walter Gamble, *Sunday, the True Sabbath of God* (Salt Lake City, 1954), pp. 154-171; Gamble had originally published his irresponsible Greek argumentation in the November, 1897, *Methodist Review* ("Saturdarianism: a Brief Review," pp. 867-883), which was soundly exposed by Steele (see note 66) as being "a monumental blunder" (p. 409).
77 See Thomsen, *op. cit.*, pp. 103, 104.
78 B. H. Roberts, "The Lord's Day," *Improvement Era* 1 (November, 1897):51.
79 *Orson Pratt's Works* (Salt Lake City, 1945), p. 170 (originally published between 1848 and 1851 in Liverpool, England), as quoted in Thomsen, *op. cit.*, pp. 20, 21.
80 *Let God Be True*, 2d ed. (New York, 1946), p. 168.
81 *Ibid.*, p. 179.

CHAPTER 16

Reflections on a Theology of the Sabbath

Raoul Dederen

THE Sabbath issue involves far more than the mechanics of keeping the right day as a holy day of rest and worship. Essentially, it is a matter of belief or disbelief in Jesus Christ as Creator and Redeemer, as revealed in the Scriptures; therefore it bears upon the future orientation of one's entire way of life.

In this chapter I wish first to consider briefly the basic theological significance of the Sabbath as it is conceived in Scripture, and second to discuss how this day of rest sheds light upon the pattern of man's basic posture in the presence of God and of his fellow men.

Although a brief treatment of this kind cannot provide satisfactory answers to all pertinent questions, I shall be quite satisfied if I can add to our mutual understanding of the theological dimension and practical implications of the question before us. For I think that one of our most imperative tasks is to uncover and to appreciate the implications of the Sabbath commandment for modern theological thought and practice in the church of today.

A Basic Affirmation About God

Let us first inquire into the meaning of the Sabbath rest as conceived in the Scriptures. It is now generally recognized that the weekly Sabbath was "certainly of great antiquity" and belongs to the earliest strata of Israelite religion.[1] And although various hypotheses regarding its origin have been proposed,[2] yet very little light has been added to the Biblical record that traces it back to the creation of the world.[3] The ordering of man's life to include rest on the seventh day is evidently a unique element in Israel's concept of time.[4]

By far the most frequently mentioned of all the days referred to in the Old Testament,[5] the Sabbath is a fundamental element of the religion of the Bible.[6] It is mentioned three times in connection with the creation of the universe: once in the Genesis narrative of Creation[7] and twice as foundation of the Sabbath commandment.[8] This is quite significant when one keeps in mind that the doctrine of Creation concerns the fundamental relationship between God and the world, a relationship that is at the very heart and center of the Christian gospel. The idea that God is Creator is indeed one of the basic affirmations about God that the Biblical writers,[9] and Christians after them, have regarded as the indispensable foundation upon which their other beliefs rest.[10] Interestingly enough, it is in the very first pages of the Bible, at the center of what the Biblical witness tells us about God as Creator, that we discover for the first time the concept of the Sabbath day. So considered, and because it is eminently a revelation of the nature of God and of His purpose,[11] the Biblical Sabbath yields *theology* in the strict sense of the term, i.e., it provides us with a doctrine of God, of God as Creator of heaven and earth, and of man's final goal in Him.

The Divine Rest—Its Implications

To clarify this, let us consider the Biblical statement itself. The Genesis account affirms that on the sixth day, after creating heaven and earth and man, God looked back with satisfaction upon His work of Creation. He saw that "everything that he had made" was good, even "very good."[12] Moses specifically indicates that it was at that point that God laid the foundation of the Sabbath by resting on the seventh day: "Thus the heavens and earth were finished, and all the host of them. And on the seventh day God finished his work which he had done, and he rested on the seventh day from all his work which he had done. So God blessed the seventh day and hallowed it, because on it God rested from all his work which he had done in creation."[13]

That God rested after His work of Creation is a fact underlined with equal clarity in the fourth commandment of the Decalogue: "'Remember the sabbath day, to keep it holy. Six days you shall labor, and do all your work; but the seventh day is a sabbath to the Lord your God; . . . for in six days the Lord made heaven and earth, the sea, and all that is in them, and rested the seventh day; therefore the Lord blessed the sabbath day and hallowed it."[14]

In both instances what is involved is not a divine decision to rest in the sense of leaving something undone. Nor are the ideas of tiredness and compensating recuperation to be connected with this divine rest.[15] The emphasis is on completion—completion of an activity, of a function. God's work and Creation were complete at the moment in which He took time to rest.[16] For although heaven and earth were indeed finished, God's work was not ended. The end came when He rested on the seventh day, thus making the Sabbath day a definite part of Creation. Only then was His work done.[17]

What are the implications of the idea of a divine rest on the seventh day of Creation? Let me briefly mention two of them. First and foremost, we are dealing here with the doctrine of God, with theology and not anthropology. What we have before us is no crude anthropomorphism, arguing back from man to God.[18] Nor is it an attempt to find a divine sanction for an already existing weekly rest by giving it fourth place in a set of ten commandments. The argument, definitely theological, is all the other way around, from God to man rather than from man to God. The Scriptures begin from the Creation account and from God's rest in which man is graciously commanded to share.

A most remarkable theological truth is thus stated, namely, that by resting on the Sabbath day God is making plain His desire to enter into a personal relationship with His creation. Far from being satisfied merely to create the world and man and then leave them to forge their own destiny, Himself retiring to the position of a detached spectator, God willed to coexist with man and expressed this in a most meaningful way, namely, by instituting the Sabbath and then inviting man to participate in His rest and blessedness.[19] Truly, this seventh day, blessed and sanctified by God, was "given in grace to the world."[20] It was "'made for man'" and given to him, as Christ Himself declared.[21] Gerhard von Rad correctly points out that this divine rest "is in every respect a new thing along with the process of creation."[22] God has come into man's world and He has come to stay.

Clearly, in the Scriptures Creation is not regarded as a timeless revelation that took place in the orderly course of nature, but as a historical work of God that launches history—history that itself is understood as a dialogue between God and man.

This points to a second theological implication in the Biblical concept of a divine rest at the end of the Creation process: God, because He is the God of history, is also the God of the covenant and of the promises. Man is the goal of Creation; but Creation, because it means fellowship, is also obedience, partnership in a covenant. This covenantal relationship, strongly emphasized in the Scriptures, affirms anew the astonishing proximity of the creature to the Creator. It testifies, on the one hand, to God's sovereign power in history,[23] His goodness and loyalty to His covenanted people,[24] while on the other it calls for man's allegiance—allegiance expressed, among other ways, in his grateful observance of the Sabbath rest, the "sign" of this covenant.[25] This underscores the religious character of the Sabbath, which is no longer merely God's gift,[26] but also a day "to the Lord,"[27] the Sabbath "of the Lord,"[28] a day "holy to the Lord"[29] and consecrated to Him. As Ellen G. White has expressed it, "Its observance was to be an act of grateful acknowledgment, on the part of all who should dwell upon the earth, that God was their Creator and their rightful Sovereign; that they were the work of His hands and the subjects of His authority."[30]

This is not to say that this day provides benefits for God or secures His rights. But on this day, set apart by Him, God's presence is particularly manifest. It belongs fully to Him, and comes entirely and in a particular way under His Lordship.[31] It is in the light of this relationship between God and man, between God and His people, that the Sabbath must be understood. It is this unfathomable intimacy of Creator and creature, Father and son, that gives this day the fullness of its significance.

Motivations for Sabbath Observance

But let us now turn our attention to the significance of the Sabbath rest and to the role it is to play in the belief and practice of Christian congregations. What are the basic motivations for observing the Sabbath day?

A Day of Rest.—In order to answer the question, I wish to consider the different formulations of the Biblical commandment regarding this particular day. In Exodus 20 the Sabbath day is connected with the Creation rest: "'Remember the sabbath day, to keep it holy. Six days you shall labor, and do all your work; but the seventh day is a sabbath to the Lord your God; in it you shall not do any work, . . . for in six days the Lord made heaven and earth, the sea, and all that is in them, and rested the seventh day; *therefore* the Lord blessed the sabbath day and hallowed it.' "³²

According to the fourth commandment, then, the Sabbath is first of all a day of rest. It is to be sanctified by demonstratively laying all work aside. Thus man will be reminded at least once every seven days of his creatureliness and of the fact that apart from God he is unable to understand himself or find the right relation to his work. The Sabbath day is a time during which man brings his work to a standstill, a day on which he ceases his toil to gain a livelihood and allows God's grace to be the first and last word in his life. This is the day on which he completely surrenders to God and places himself unreservedly and unconditionally at God's disposal.³³

For six days of every week the world belongs to us, as it were. For six days we may stamp our creative impress on things and make them the agents of our will. But on the seventh day we are to testify that, after all, the world is not ours but God's, that we are not its lord and master but merely God's vassals. Our observance of the Sabbath attests to the facts that we live and work only by God's grace, that He is our Lord and Master, and that we recognize Him as such. Our resting on that day is a demonstration of homage to God, proclaiming Him Creator and Master of the world and of ourselves.

Man needs a constant reminder of this relationship between the transcendent goodness and sovereignty of God and his own essential creatureliness.³⁴ For if God is not the center of our lives, our creaturely needs will drive us to make something else the center, and so devote our allegiance to a false loyalty.³⁵ Corresponding to the divine rest, the Sabbath rest does not connote recuperation after toilsome work, but a simple cessation and abstention from further work. On the Sabbath day man does not belong to his work; he renounces his autonomy and affirms God's dominion over him.

But although cessation of work is commanded, this is by no means all that is required. Consecrated to God as Creator, this day becomes a "tithe" on time, just as the tithe of one's earnings, the firstborn of the flock, and the first fruits of the harvest were a tithe of the work of the other days.³⁶ The Sabbath rest thus expresses the consecration of one's existence and time to God in the same way as the Temple in Jerusalem expressed the consecration of space.³⁷ Thus, while unquestionably requiring cessation of work, the Sabbath consists of something more than mere physical rest; it is a "holy" day, a day to be "kept holy." Its holiness derives from God's resting on that particular day of the Creation week and hallowing it.³⁸ Likewise, man is directed to keep it holy too. As the *imago Dei*, man knows and follows the will and example of his divine Father. The reality of the *imago Dei* implies the *imitatio Dei*.³⁹

A Day of Rejoicing.—There is a second basic motivation for observing the Sabbath day, namely as a day of joy, a memorial of redemption. Deuteronomy 5:15 attaches the Sabbath commandment to the memory of Israel's slavery in Egypt and subsequent salvation. After instructing Israel to " ' "observe the sabbath day, to keep it holy," ' "⁴⁰ the commandment adds: " ' "You shall remember that you were a servant in the land of Egypt, and the Lord your God brought you out thence with a mighty hand and an outstretched arm; *therefore* the Lord your God commanded you to keep the sabbath day." ' "⁴¹ Here the reason for observing the Sabbath day is the joyous affirmation that God delivered Israel from servitude in Egypt. On every Sabbath day Israel was to remember that God was her liberator, that He had put an end to her slavery. The Lord of the covenant, who suffers no other god and rules over the whole of creation, who as Creator commanded that His people observe the Sabbath day, was also the Emancipator of Israel. Since He redeemed them from Egypt, He "therefore" commanded them to keep the Sabbath day. The association of the Sabbath with redemption is unmistakable.[42]

The Deuteronomy statement does not mean that Moses considered Creation as insufficient reason for Sabbath observance, nor does it represent the addition of a foreign element to the memorial of the original Creation rest.[43] Moses simply introduces a further reason for God's right to summon Israel to keep the Sabbath. In Gary Cohen's words, "The original creation brought man forth unto God out of that which was nonexistent; redemption brought man forth unto God out of that which was lost!"[44]

The analogy for Christians is so obvious as not to require much elaboration. Suffice it to say that our redemption, as Christians, is of no lesser significance than was that of Israel of old. Delivered from the slavery of sin[45] and of the devil,[46] we are "a new creation."[47] We are invited to put on the new nature "created after the likeness of God,"[48] who created us, and with whom we enter into a new fellowship. In both Old and New Testaments we find an unbreakable unity between God's work in Creation and His work in redemption. This unity, unequivocal in the Deuteronomy passage, is expressed even more forcefully in Hebrews 4, where the apostle, in the context of the Creation Sabbath, exhorts his readers to enter into the believer's rest.[49]

Thus, as a memorial of Creation and a sign of redemption, the Sabbath becomes a symbol of God's dual activity as Creator, for it proclaims His creative power in the universe and His re-creative power in man's soul.[50] This unity of creation and redemption is clearly expressed in one of the most distinctive features of the New Testament witness in regard to Creation, namely, that Christ is declared to be the agent of both the first and the second creation: He is the creative Word through whom God created all things.[51] Sabbath observance, which keeps fresh in our minds the truth of the divine creative power, gives meaning and reality to those repeated New Testament declarations that all things were made through Christ and that without Him was not anything made that was made.

Once every seven days, on the Sabbath day, the Christian, like Israel of old, is specially invited to remember that God is a liberator who has put an end to all bondage and slavery. For the Christian, each Sabbath experience testifies to the fact that his Lord is Creator and that He has set him free—no longer to be conquered by any power, not even by death. In our proclamation and observance of the Sabbath there will, therefore, always be a strong and joyous affirmation of Creation: the affirmation that the world and human life are essentially good,[52] and the attestation that Jesus Christ is the living Lord of the church, the Lord of Creation, redemption, and consummation.

A Day of Hope.—This leads us to a third motivation for Sabbath observance. Though Genesis 1 and 2 make Creation the beginning of all things—and the Sabbath its memorial—belief in Creation is not reduced to a mere protology, to a mere doctrine of the origins of the world and man. Creation is also an act of the present instant, and it remains true to itself till the hour of the eschatological restoration. This is why the Sabbath day, a day of rest and rejoicing, is also a day of hope.

This day that signifies the basic fact that God is Creator and man is creature also remains the sign of the continuing presence of God in the life of man till the day comes when full fellowship with God will once again be realized. The weekly Sabbath is a reminder, then, of the other "day of the Lord,"[53] when our redemption shall be completed—when Christ, our Creator and Redeemer, will return as sovereign Lord and usher in the final consummation of the history of salvation. Thus the Sabbath, the memorial of Creation and deliverance, is also a sign of hope, of expectation of Christ the Lord coming in glory at the end of time. It is the sign of a hope that looks toward the complete freedom of the children of God in the future, a freedom and restoration awaited by the entire creation.[54] As such, it gives perspective, thrust, and depth to man's whole life—to his very being and to the work he does during the six days of his own time.[55]

But the Sabbath rest is even more than just a positive eschatological sign. It is also a sign that already grants participation in that to which it points, for even now it provides a foretaste of the future entrance into God's joyful rest. It is a sample, a taste, as well as a sign, of the eternal peace to come. Each Sabbath day is like a step or landmark in a long line of promises that runs through man's generations toward the eternal Sabbath—that day at the end of all days when all oppression and strife will cease and when man reaches the culmination of rest that is in the Lord.[56]

For this reason, while I fully side with Karl Barth in regard to the vital significance of the Sabbath as the symbol of continuity and unity between God's work in Creation and in redemption,[57] it is on quite different premises. Barth's position is based on a teleological interpretation of the first chapters of Genesis that absorbs Israel's protology in her soteriology and eschatology.[58] Denying Adam's original state of integrity, Barth cannot say that God was pleased with man as he functioned in his original historical reality.[59] God's rest on the original seventh day, therefore, must be interpreted teleologically and soteriologically too, i.e., as a prefiguration and inauguration of Christ's redeeming work.

While I gladly recognize the close relationship between Creation, redemption, and eschatology, I perceive them in the context of the historical reality of man's fall, redemption, and restoration.[60] In my view, the New Testament, like the Old, regards all three as intrinsic parts of the everlasting proclamation of the one Lord and Saviour Jesus Christ.[61] All three are rooted in the same God, who is Creator, Redeemer, and Lord.[62] The God of grace, being also the Lord of Creation and history, is thus the First and the Last. More specifically: When the New Testament considers the eschatological restoration of all things, it does not speak of this as the eventual realization of Creation but as the final restoration of God's initial Creation that was marred by sin. Creation, redemption, and restoration of all things belong together. When considered in the context of the Genesis account regarded as historical reality—a Creation marred by sin but to be restored on "that day"—the eschatological implications of the seventh-day Sabbath assume tremendous actuality.

Illumining the Whole of Man's Life

Considered in the context of its Biblical origin and its essential meaning and aim, the Sabbath day is a day of encounter with God. It is a day of remembrance, of joy, and of hope—a day in which the Christian believer receives anew all things

REFLECTIONS ON A THEOLOGY OF THE SABBATH

from God. Yet its import goes beyond even these.

It is indeed striking that the fourth commandment is found in the Decalogue exactly at the articulation of the commandments dealing with the service of God and those concerned with our fellow men and our daily life. The Sabbath seems to be the sign of what every other day ought to be, in that it defines and illumines man's attitude in all of his deeds. Man's actions—indeed, man's whole life—find their true meaning in the context of the fundamental attitude denoted by the Sabbath day as a day belonging to God. To many for whom it has become evident that faith and life, doctrine and practice, cannot be separated, the commandment enjoining Sabbath observance can be seen to be, in the words of Hans W. Wolff, "an archetypal model for our theology."[63]

There is little doubt, for instance, that at the heart of the Sabbath idea is the worship of the Christian community. This is not to say that the celebration of worship is that which sets this day apart and sanctifies it,[64] but rather that the Sabbath day is hardly conceivable apart from the celebration of divine worship.[65] To keep the Lord's day holy is also to gather together to hear and to study God's Word, to confess and to share the Christian faith, to offer prayer and praise to God.

Yet Sabbath worship is not to be conceived as an isolated act, one that removes man from his everyday world. On the contrary, it is the center from which every day of the week receives its meaning and light. This is so in at least two ways.

Relativization of Man's Work.—The Sabbath day involves rest—cessation of man's daily labor, as we noted earlier, and therefore also a recurring relativization of his labor. By this experience, man is repeatedly taught the lesson that God, and not his work, is the sum total of everything in his life. The Sabbath, and the cessation of work implicit in it, is God's corrective to man's ultimate confidence in his own toil. It is a warning against man's potential inebriation upon becoming aware of his own power and efficacy. The Sabbath serves to put man's labor in the right perspective, so that man turns to God as the only source of his existence. Transcending human labor, however impressive that labor may be, the Sabbath rest tells man in a very concrete manner, "It is not your work or activity that saves you, but it is God's perfect grace. Do not fret about tomorrow, neither become infatuated by your achievements. God grants as much to His beloved while they sleep. Seek first the kingdom of God and His righteousness and all these things shall be yours as well."

A theology of the Sabbath, therefore, is a theology of moderation and sobriety. It invites man to acquire the proper perspective toward his earthly achievements, and persuades him to refrain from putting his confidence in his work—that is, in himself. It is also a theology of grace and freedom. For when God commands man to rest on the seventh day, He restores in him the sense of belonging to God, thus freeing him again from the things of the created world.[66] And as man shares with his Maker the experience of the Sabbath rest in ceasing from daily toil, he becomes more aware of his spiritual freedom. Resting from work and freed from secular routine, man is given a rare opportunity to reflect upon and experience the divine love that created him and redeemed him.

There is in the Sabbath a quality of re-creation and relationship that cannot be found unless one discovers the potential with which God invested this particular day. Here we meet God on a plane not possible on any other day of the week,[67] for as Abraham Heschel points out, that into which we enter "is not a different state of consciousness but a different climate."[68] While it is true that we do not automatically realize this Sabbath quality by merely resting on the Sabbath day, there is a quality of Sabbath observance that cannot be found on any other day than God's own day, the day He "blessed."[69] Christians will never understand what it really means to keep *the Sabbath* until they try it—and try it not merely as a day of rest, but on the level of its full God-invested potential for divine-human fellowship.

The Positive Meaning of Man's Labor.—Man's labor, having thus been placed in correct perspective by the Sabbath rest and worship, acquires positive significance. The Sabbath actually becomes the basis for the formulation of a Christian ethic that calls on man in general to acknowledge the rule of God as experienced and celebrated in the life of the Christian community.

For this is indeed the day when God's people assemble to hear the Word of God, receiving it with gratitude, praise, and rejoicing. And the same gratitude, praise, and rejoicing are to characterize man's daily tasks. It is in worship that the true God is confessed and the Christian is called to live in God's truth. Here the Christian is not only challenged but is granted freedom to live the totality of his life in the responsibility offered him by the truth of God. Here man brings his offering and is called upon to live from what he earns, acknowledging that everything he owns belongs to God, in whose sight all men are equal.[70]

Now that he has felt the nearness of God, and has been renewed in the Lord's likeness, the Christian is free to encounter the world that God created. He is free to fulfill therein his daily labor, better equipped for the tasks of the coming week, indeed, better equipped for the whole task of living. As he starts a new week, he is not only a man who has experienced God's creative and redemptive love, but he is also a Christian "raised up" with Christ, sitting "in the heavenly places in Christ Jesus."[71] In this communion with God, all things are his, so that he may use them to the glory of God. God's grace has set him free, free from the fear of man and from the worship of things. It is this abiding, week-long presence, resulting from the calm and peace of the Sabbath day, that generates and emphasizes the ethical dimensions implied in the Sabbath rest.[72]

The "Arbitrariness" of the Sabbath

In an arbitrary manner God appointed that on the seventh day we should come to rest with His creation in a particular way. He filled this day with a content that is "uncontaminated" by anything related to the cyclical changes of nature or the movements of the heavenly bodies.[73] That content is the idea of the absolute sovereignty of God, a sovereignty unqualified even by an indirect cognizance of the natural movements of time and rhythms of life. As the Christian takes heed of the Sabbath day and keeps it holy, he does so purely in answer to God's command, and simply because God is his Creator. Thus, the Sabbath command comes nearer to being a true measure of spirituality than any other of the commandments, and, as in the days of Israel of old, it is often more of a test of loyalty to God than is any of the others.[74] To be willing on the Sabbath day to withdraw from the tyranny of the world of things in order to meet the Lord of heaven and earth in the quiet of our souls means to love God with all our hearts, souls, minds, and bodies.

Before concluding, I should like to make a cautionary distinction. It should be clear by now that the Sabbath does have significance for the twentieth-century man, and possibly more than for any previous man. This is primarily because the striking changes that have characterized modern man urgently require him to rediscover himself and to reestablish fellowship and communion with God and his fellow man. The increasing secularization of our culture, with its hectic activity, the disintegration of our social life, the impersonal connection of man with his God symbolized by such modern fads as the "God Is Dead" craze, has added to the confusion that dominates our contemporary Western world.[75]

In such an atmosphere, the Sabbath as a day of rest, kept holy unto God, has all too often become a traumatic experience, and this in many ways. For one, too many of us are tempted to secularize the Sabbath, to deprive it of its supernatural content and of any dimension of reality beyond empirical experience. Then, having deprived it of its intrinsic quality, we use it for our own selfish pleasure. Rather than a day of light that illumines the whole of man's time, it comes to be held as any other day lived by man in his newly found autonomy. By the same token, it loses its dimension of sanctification. However much we may choose to replenish it again with meaning, it remains for many an empty day, having lost its characteristic as the Sabbath day in the scriptural sense. It simply subsides to the inescapable tyranny and servitude of the weekdays.

But there are other ways of denying the basic meaning of the Sabbath day. Busy and preoccupied with the problems of a driving and complex daily life in a madly rushing, neurotic society, some tend to find in the Sabbath rest only boredom and uneasiness. Viewed as a day when all there is left is to wish for its hours to be gone, the Sabbath is to them a burden, an obligation, and Sabbathkeeping becomes a "job of religion."[76] This has little in common with the Biblical institution, for instead of being lived and experienced as a time of refreshment and renewal granted by a loving Creator, the Sabbath has become a burden, an empty time that man seizes to carry out his own plans and devices. Thus for those viewing it with this attitude, it has verily degenerated into a negation of God's covenant of grace.

Christ's uncompromising opposition to the Pharisees' erroneous understanding of Sabbathkeeping revolved precisely around this decisive factor.[77] "'The sabbath,'" said He, "'was made for man, not man for the sabbath.'"[78] In other words, the Sabbath was meant to be a *boon* to man, not a *burden*. It is not a day taken away from man by God in an exacting spirit, but a day given by God in love to man. To consider the Sabbath as a day of sorrow and gloom is a denial of its authentic meaning as a day of joy and delight, calling for man's free and grateful obedience as the necessary result of blessings received. It is this freedom and love that Christ affirms when reminding us that "'the Son of man is lord even of the sabbath.'"[79]

Conclusion

These few remarks must suffice to indicate that an authentic theology of the Sabbath is an invitation to keep the seventh-day holy in the spirit of joy and thankfulness to God the Creator for His gracious solicitude toward His creatures. The Sabbath is to be clearly distinguished from all working days, as well as from other free periods. It is not merely one of the free days but a holy day dedicated to the restoration of fellowship with God and fellow man, and thus particularly designed to build and strengthen the character of the believer. It is a constant reminder of our creatureliness and of our existence in time. Because He lays claim to the whole of man, God calls for men to keep the Sabbath day: It is a sign of grace; it is time that God has given us in His love, and which we fill with the celebration of the advent of that eternal freedom that, in part, is already ours, a freedom that comes from the living God Himself.

NOTES

[1] Roland de Vaux, *Ancient Israel* (London, 1961), p. 479. See also J. J. Stamm, "Dreizig Jahre Dekalogforschung," *Theologische Rundschau* NF 27 (1961):189-237, 281-305; Ernest Jenni, *Die theologische Begründung des Sabbatgebotes im Alten Testament*, Theologische Studien 46 (Zürich, 1956), pp. 10-13; H. H. Rowley, *Men of God* (London, 1963), pp. 1-36; J. J. Stamm and M. E. Andrew, *The Ten Commandments in Recent Research* (Napperville, Ill., 1967), pp. 22-35; J. Guillén, "Nuevas aportaciones al estudio del sábado," *Estudios Biblicos* 26 (1967):77-89.

[2] For useful surveys, see De Vaux, *op. cit.*, pp. 475-479; N.-E. A. Andreasen, *The Old Testament Sabbath*, SBL Diss. Ser. 7 (Missoula, Mont., 1972), pp. 1-16.

[3] Gen. 1:1-2:3.

[4] "Je mehr man sich in die Literatur über den Ursprung des Sabbats vertieft, desto eindrücklicher wird einem die Einzigartigkeit der israelitischen Institution des Sabbats," remarks Jenni in *Die theologische Begründung*, p. 10. See also E. G. Kraeling, "The Present Status of the Sabbath Question," *American Journal of Semitic Languages and Literatures*, 49 (1932-1933):218-228.

[5] It occurs about 50 times, according to Ernest Jenni, *Theologisches Handwörterbuch zum Alten Testament* (Munich, 1971), 1:710. "Das Wort 'Sabbat,'" precises Jenni, "begegnet im Alten Testament knapp über hundertmal."—*Die theologische Begründung*, p. 4.

[6] The Bible is more concerned with time than with space. It pays more attention to generations, events, countries, things, and history than it does to geography. In the Bible, time has a significance of its own, at least equal to that of space.

[7] Gen. 2:2, 3.

[8] Ex. 20:11; 31:17.

[9] For the Biblical doctrine of Creation, see Ps. 33:6-9; 89:11, 12; 90:1, 2; 146:5-7; 148:1-6; Isa. 40:26-31; 44:24-26; John 1:1-12; Acts 14:15-17; 17:22-31; Rom. 1:18-23; Col. 1:16-20.

[10] For a broader consideration of the issue, see Langdon Gilkey, *Maker of Heaven and Earth* (Garden City, N.Y., 1959), esp. chaps. 1 and 2.

[11] As admirably brought out by Karl Barth, *Church Dogmatics* (Edinburgh, 1956), esp. III/1, III/4, I/1, II/1, IV/1. I am indebted to Barth's profound study of the Sabbath for several basic concepts presented here. For an introduction to Barth's views on the subject, see James Brown, "Karl Barth's Doctrine of the Sabbath," *Scottish Journal of Theology* 19 (1966):pp. 409-425.

[12] Gen. 1:31. Scriptural quotations in this chapter are from the Revised Standard Version.

[13] Gen. 2:1-3.

[14] Ex. 20:8-11. The theme of God's rest is mentioned again in Exodus 31:17.

[15] That the Creator should weary and need rest is preposterous to the Biblical writers. See, for instance, Isa. 40:28. "He rested, not as one weary, but as well pleased with the fruits of His wisdom and goodness and the manifestations of His glory," remarks Ellen G. White in *Patriarchs and Prophets* (Mountain View, Calif., 1913), p. 47.

[16] The terms *finished* and *done* are used four times in connection with the Sabbath day in Genesis 2:2, 3.

[17] M. L. Andreasen, *The Sabbath: Which Day and Why?* (Washington, D.C., 1942), pp. 43-45.

[18] De Vaux, *op. cit.*, p. 481.

[19] Commenting on the Genesis statement that "God blessed the seventh day and hallowed it" (Gen. 2:3), Jenni points out that "on account of this blessing God puts living forces in this day. This is indeed the day when God wants to enter into fellowship with his creatures, and communion with God means life. On account of its being blessed, the day itself becomes in turn a blessing."—*Die theologische Begründung*, p. 29. Cf. Walther Zimmerli, *Die Urgeschichte, 1. Mose 1-11*, 1943, p. 102.

[20] G. C. Berkouwer, *The Providence of God* (Grand Rapids, 1952), p. 62.

[21] Mark 2:27.

[22] Gerhard von Rad, *Genesis: A Commentary* (Philadelphia, 1961), p. 60.

[23] Jer. 27:5.

[24] Chap. 31:35-37.

[25] Isaiah 56:4, 6, associates the Sabbath rest with the holding fast of the covenant, and Ezekiel 20:12, 20 points it out as a "sign" between God and His people. In Exodus 31:12-17 the Sabbath rest is designated as the "sign" to Israel that the Lord is her Sanctifier. One who rejects this sign by violating the Sabbath has also rejected God (verses 14, 15).

[26] Ex. 16:29.

[27] Lev. 23:3; Ex. 16:23, 25; 35:2.

[28] Lev. 23:38.

[29] Ex. 31:15.

[30] White, *op. cit.*, p. 48.

[31] It is with regard to the Sabbath day that the Creation narrative uses the term *holy* for the first time. The earth and the heavens were declared "good" (Gen. 1:12, 18, 21, 24), man "very good" (verse 31), but the seventh-day Sabbath was called "hallowed," i.e. "holy" (chap. 2:3).

[32] Ex. 20:8-11.

[33] The prophets' words speaking out against business on the Sabbath contradict natural man's inclinations to make his life secure or to add to life's abundance by a nonstop, uninterrupted work. See Ex. 33:14; Isa. 58:13, 14; Jer. 17:19-27; Neh. 13:15-22.

[34] To Willy Rordorf, the original Sabbath was a social-ethical institution providing rest and refreshing. He

REFLECTIONS ON A THEOLOGY OF THE SABBATH

considers the religious dimension as a later addition. See his *Sunday* (Philadelphia, 1968), pp. 15-18, 45-54.

[35] "Had the Sabbath always been kept, man's thoughts and affections would have been led to his Maker as the object of reverence and worship, and there would never have been an idolater, an atheist, or an infidel," remarks Ellen G. White (*The Story of Redemption* [Washington, D.C., 1947], pp. 382, 383).

[36] Pointing out that in the case of the Sabbath rest the last rather than the first is consecrated to God, A. M. Dubarle remarks: "The offering of time, accomplished on the last day of the week, and not on the first as was the case in the offering of the material goods, had the effect of consecrating the whole time, in as much as it tended toward the day of meeting with God."—"La signification religieuse du sabbath dans la Bible," in *Le Dimanche*, Lex Orandi 39 (Paris, 1965), p. 52. See also Matitiahu Tsevat, "The Basic Meaning of the Biblical Sabbath," *Zeitschrift für die Alttestamentliche Wissenschaft* 84 (1972):454.

[37] Jean Daniélou, *The Bible and the Liturgy* (South Bend, Ind., 1956), p. 223.

[38] Ex. 20:11.

[39] See on this point H. K. LaRondelle, *Perfection and Perfectionism* (Berrien Springs, Mich., 1975), pp. 69-72.

[40] Deut. 5:12.

[41] Verse 15.

[42] In the Deuteronomy rendering of the Sabbath commandment, the rest of Israel's slaves and domestic animals (verse 14) seems to be the essential purpose of the Sabbath rest. There are, to be sure, other instances in Deuteronomy where slaves are invited to rejoice with the Israelites in their worship of the true God (cf. Deut. 12:12, 18; 16:11, 12, 14) in an attempt to underline man's intrinsic dignity. But in this instance God's concern is much more a salvation-history motif. The Israelite will grant his slave this day of rest because God delivered Israel from slavery in Egypt and led her to the rest of the Promised Land. See Jenni, *Die theologisch Begründung*, pp. 16-19.

[43] Notice the reminder, in this passage, of the already existing commandment, as indicated in verse 12: "'Observe the sabbath day, to keep it holy, *as the Lord your God commanded you.*'"

[44] "The Doctrine of the Sabbath in the Old and New Testaments," *Grace Journal* 6 (Spring, 1965):10.

[45] Titus 2:14; Eph. 1:7; Col. 1:14; Heb. 9:11-22.

[46] John 16:11; Heb. 2:14-18.

[47] 2 Cor. 5:17; Gal. 6:15.

[48] Eph. 4:24.

[49] See esp. verses 1-5, 8-10. It is true that Christian devotion and thought concern themselves most with God's redeeming activity as revealed in Jesus Christ. This is at the foundation of our knowledge of God as a loving father, of our hope for salvation. But who is that God who is supremely righteous and loving, who judges and redeems us, if not the Creator of heaven and earth? The gospel promises of salvation are rooted in the Biblical doctrine of Creation, for Creation is the activity of God by means of which we define what we mean by the word "God". Without this transcendent aspect of God that describes Him to our faith as the source of all existence, His judgment and love would ultimately be unimportant to us, and the redemption promise impossible to perform. His promise to redeem is "good" only if God is the Creator of the powers that rule our lives. The Christian faith requires that the God who saves be also the God who brought us into existence. It is only as we believe that God is Creator that we can believe that He has power to re-create us, that is, to redeem us, for redemption is essentially a creative act. This has been brought out admirably by Gilkey, *op. cit.*, pp. 79-82, 231, 234.

[50] "Given to the world as the sign of God as the Creator," the Sabbath "is also the sign of Him as the Sanctifier," remarks Ellen G. White in *Testimonies to the Church*, 9 vols. (Mountain View, Calif., 1948), 6:350. This unity between Creation and redemption decisively sets the Biblical message of salvation apart from all dualistic religions that regard salvation as release from the created world rather than the restoration of the world.

[51] John 1:1-18, Hebrews 1:1, 2, and Colossians 1:15-17 identify in their different ways creative wisdom and the word of the Creator with Jesus Christ. There is also an unmistakable reference to the role of Christ in Creation when the words "through" Jesus Christ are added to the "from God" of 1 Corinthians 8:6.

[52] The Sabbath rest reminds man that the world and human life are essentially good, that they are God's creation, endowed with many beautiful things. Thus the Sabbath is an invitation to rejoice in God's creation.

[53] The seventh-day Sabbath is the day of, to, or unto the Lord. Quite often, however, in the Scriptures the term "day of the Lord" carries a clear eschatological connotation. See Isa. 13:9; Eze. 13:5; Joel 2:31; Amos 5:18; 1 Cor. 1:8; 5:5; Phil. 1:6; 2:16; 1 Thess. 5:2, 4; 2 Tim. 1:12.

[54] Rom. 8:20-22. As in the past God did His mighty works and overcame His enemies through His initial creative act and the deliverance of His people from Egypt, so He also acts now in the final decisive struggle that is to usher in the eschatological age.

[55] Barth, *op. cit.*, III/1, p. 214.

[56] Heb. 4:1-13. With Oscar Cullmann, Seventh-day Adventists make a clear distinction between the New Testament concept of eternity as everlasting time and the familiar philosophical concept of eternity as the opposite of time, as timelessness. See Oscar Cullmann, *Christ and Time* (Philadelphia, 1950), pp. 61-80. In the New Testament the eschatological rest is described not as a rest of negation but, on the manward side, as a time of worship and praise. See Rev. 22:3-5.

[57] See particularly Barth, *op. cit.*, III/1, pp. 213-228; III/4, pp. 47-72.

[58] See, for instance, Barth, *op. cit.*, III/1, p. 218f.

[59] Barth, *op. cit.*, IV/1, p. 508: "The biblical saga tells us that world-history began with the pride and fall of man. ... There never was a golden age. There is no point in looking back to one. The first man was immediately the first sinner." By the same token Barth denies the historicity of Adam's fall as a transition from the *status integritatis* to the *status corruptionis*.

[60] For a more detailed Adventist critique of Barth's views, see LaRondelle, *op. cit.*, pp. 69-86.

[61] Rev. 1:17; 2:8; 22:13; 21:5, 6.

[62] As unequivocally indicated in Col. 1:15-20; Eph. 1:3-14.

[63] Hans Walter Wolff, "The Day of Rest in the Old Testament," *Lexington Theological Quarterly* 7 (July, 1972):65.

[64] Worship is a human act that, like all other human actions, can be diverted from its true object, thus losing its meaning. One can hardly forget the prophets' warnings to that effect or Amos' denunciation of Israel's assemblies (Amos 5:21-24).

[65] The true ground of worship—not just on the seventh day, but of all worship—is found in the distinction between the Creator and His creatures. As a memorial of Creation, the Sabbath, which keeps this distinction ever present to man's mind, lies at the very foundation of true worship. See J. N. Andrews and L. R. Conradi, *History of the*

Sabbath and First Day of the Week, 2d ed. (Battle Creek, Mich., 1873), pp. 509-512.

[66] "Nothing is as hard to suppress as the will to be a slave to one's own pettiness," observes Abraham Joshua Heschel. "Gallantly, ceaselessly, quietly, man must fight for inner liberty. Inner liberty depends upon being exempt from domination of things as well as from domination of people. There are many who have acquired a high degree of political and social liberty, but only very few are not enslaved to things. This is our constant problem—how to live with people and remain free, how to live with things and remain independent."—*The Sabbath: Its Meaning for Modern Man* (New York, 1951), p. 89.

[67] In spite of their dramatic efforts, the attempts of those who observe Sunday to give the first day of the week Sabbatic qualities have utterly failed. See Herbert E. Saunders, *The Sabbath* (Plainfield, N.J., 1970), pp. 12-17.

[68] Heschel, *op. cit.,* p. 21.

[69] Gen. 2:3. "God had previously blessed the fish of the sea [1:22] and man [verse 28]. This blessing provided them with the power to be fruitful and to multiply." Then the seventh day was blessed, "provided with life-restoring powers, so that from it man's time might be made new and fruitful."—Wolff, *op. cit.,* p. 70.

[70] The Sabbath commandment is the only one to take "a step in the direction of making all men equal before God."—*Ibid.,* p. 71.

[71] Eph. 2:6.

[72] By its very nature the Sabbath commandment underlines all the other commandments and provides for their keeping. It is the one commandment that grants time for worship, for the reception of the Word and the Spirit of God. It is a time set aside for the purpose of reflecting on and responding to life in relation to God, nature, self, and humanity.

[73] Efforts to relate the origin of the seventh-day Sabbath with phases of the moon, agricultural seasons, or any other natural phenomenon have utterly failed. See De Vaux, *op. cit.,* p. 480; Walter Harrelson, *From Fertility Cult to Worship* (Garden City, N.Y., 1969), pp. 30-32; Tsevat, *op. cit.,* pp. 456-458; Jenni, *Die theologische Begründung,* pp. 11, 12; Guillén, *op. cit.,* p. 78, 79; Felix Mathys, "Sabbatruhe und Sabbatfest," *Theologische Zeitschrift* 28 (1972):245, 246.

[74] While the greatest rewards are associated with the keeping of the Sabbath (Deut. 28:1-14; Isa. 56:2-7; 58:13, 14; Jer. 17:24-26; Eze. 20:12, 20), continued violation of the fourth commandment stood for years as a spiritual thermometer revealing Israel's plight of having broken God's covenant (Ex. 31:15; 35:3; Num. 15:32-36; Neh. 13:15-22; Jer. 17:27; Eze. 20:13, 16, 21, 24; 22:8, 26).

[75] For a pertinent analysis of the current forces in Western culture and their threat to the traditional Christian day of rest, see Christopher Kiesling, *The Future of the Christian Sunday* (New York, 1970), pp. 3-15.

[76] Arthur W. Spalding, *The Sabbath and the Sabbath Day* (Mountain View, Calif., 1937), p. 5. In the first chapter of his book Spalding discusses several categories of negative Sabbathkeepers: the "Sabbath-burdened," the "Sabbath-bound," and the "Sabbath addicts."

[77] See, for instance, the Mark 2:23-28 episode.

[78] Mark 2:27.

[79] Verse 28.

APPENDIXES

APPENDIX A

The Planetary Week in the Roman West

S. Douglas Waterhouse

AS a septenary time unit the seven-day week is peculiar, for it is entirely independent of the month and unrelated to an event in nature, such as the movements of the sun, moon, or stars. In the whole of the pre-Hellenistic, ancient Orient it can nowhere be clearly perceived, except among the Hebrews.[1] The ancient Etruscans of Northern Italy, and their cultural descendants, the Romans, are said to have possessed an "eight-day market week." Such an assertion is not technically correct. Neither the Romans nor their predecessors possessed a word to denote this space of time. The country people were accustomed to coming to an urban center, such as Rome, for their market days, called *nundinae*, or "ninth days." By our mode of reckoning, which is not inclusive like the Romans', the "nine days" actually count out to mean "eight days."[2] Since the classics never placed *nundinum* by itself to indicate a time unit, it cannot be claimed that this was an eight-day weekly cycle.[3]

The Jewish historian Flavius Josephus correctly noted toward the end of the first century A.D. that the week introduced into the Roman Empire was in imitation of the Jewish septenary time observance. As he put it: "There is not one city, Greek or barbarian, nor a single nation, to which our [Jewish] custom of abstaining from work on the seventh day has not spread."[4] Indeed, our modern week, observed worldwide, which employs the Jewish system of enumeration, counting the days up to the Sabbath, goes back to the authority of the Hebrew Scripture and Jewish practice.[5]

The Astrological Week and the Roman World

While it was the Hebrews who brought the weekly cycle to the attention of the world, it is the planetary week, arising in Hellenistic times, that popularized the weekly cycle, until it finally gained a widespread acceptance throughout the Roman Empire. That the nature of our present week has a secondary dependence upon the astrological week of the Roman Imperial Age, is made obvious when the distinguishing features of the planetary week are listed:

1. Instead of beginning the day in the evening (Lev. 23:32; Gen. 1:5), the astrological day began at midnight.[6]

2. Instead of starting the first day of the week as that which follows the seventh-day Sabbath (Matt. 28:1), the first day of the planetary week is Saturday.[7]

3. Instead of honoring the scriptural Sabbath (Ex. 20:8-11), Sunday is honored.[8]

4. Further, each day is given a name, not simply enumerated, as was the Hebrew custom.[9]

5. Finally, and most important, each hour, as well as each day, is given a planetary ruler, considered a god, whose qualities influence its ruling hour, or the day to which it is assigned.[10]

The Roman Empire thus came to promulgate a seven-day week whose sequence and names are: *Saturni dies,* ruled by Saturn; *Solis dies,* ruled by the Sun; *Lunae dies,* ruled by the Moon; *Martis dies,* governed by Mars; *Mercurii dies,* lorded by Mercury; *Jovis dies,* ruled by Jupiter; and *Veneris dies,* ruled by Venus. These astrological names for weekdays are still current in present-day European languages derived from Latin. Translated into Germanic names of the equivalent gods, these names survive in present-day English.[11]

The evidence for the arrival of the astrological week into the West, that is, to Rome and to European peoples under her control, dates from 27 B.C., the first regnal year of the first emperor, Augustus. For it was soon after the triumph of Messala in that year that Albius Tibullus published what he had mournfully written prior to Messala's departure: "Without me will ye go, Messala, across the Aegean wave. . . . I . . . sought . . . for reasons to linger and delay. Either birds or words of evil omen were my pretexts, or there was the holy-day of Saturn to detain me."[12] Since Saturn and Mars were considered malevolent planets, Saturday *(Saturni dies)* and Tuesday *(Martis dies)* were unlucky days, impropitious for the start of a new enterprise, especially that of an overseas journey.[13] The enrapturement of Tibullus with the concept of planetary control over time periods is made evident further on in the same passage, when he refers to the planets as guiding patrons of successive ages in Roman history.[14]

A complete listing of lucky and unlucky days is provided by a type of early Roman farm calendar (termed *menologia*),[15] a fragment of which dates to the first century A.D. Possessing an astrological character, each of the twelve months is introduced by its own zodiacal sign. Of interest here is the fact that along with the *nundinae,* the marking off of the Roman eighth-day market holidays, is the employment also of the seven-day planetary week, with each day having twenty-four hours and each hour containing sixty minutes.[16] Erasing all question of the widespread existence of the astrological week in Italy before A.D. 79 are the contents of wall inscriptions and graffiti uncovered from pre-Vesuvius Pompeii. A Greek inscription prefaced with the title "Days of the Gods" lists the gods of the seven planetary days in order, beginning with Saturn and ending with Venus.[17] A Latin graffito, explicitly dated to A.D. 60, states: "In the Consulship of Nero Caesar Augustus and Cossus Lentulus, 8 days before the Ides of March, on Sunday, on the 16th of the Moon, Marketday at Cumae, 5 days before the Marketday at Pompeii."[18]

The biography of Apollonius Tyanaeus, while not altogether trustworthy, may indicate that by the mid-first century A.D. the planetary week was observed as far east as India![19] Apollonius, born at Tyana in Cappadocia about four years before the Christian Era, built up a reputation as one knowledgeable in ancient lore and possessing supernatural powers. Between his fortieth and fiftieth year Apollonius set out from a Pythagorean "retreat" in Aegae, in Cilicia, on a five-year journey toward Eastern lands. At Nineveh he met Damis, the future chronicler of his actions. From there he proceeded to Babylon and on to India. At Taxila, in the Upper *Panjáb*, he met Iarchas, the chief of the Brahmans. As a gift, Iarchas presented his visitor with seven rings, each named after "the seven stars." It is stated that Apollonius wore each of these in turn on the day of the week that bore its name.[20]

While this account is supposedly based on the memoirs of Damis, it actually is preserved for posterity by Philostratus, who wrote between A.D. 210 and 220. Hence, the tale of a Brahman's gift commemorating the days of the planetary week is open to question, especially since Philostratus' account abounds with incongruities and fables. The fact that Apollonius was a Pythagorean philosopher and studied in Cilicia, however, is of great interest. Both factors are intimately connected with the spread of the planetary week. In the first century A.D. it was being said that Pythagoras (who flourished in the sixth century B.C.) had discovered the Greek planetary sequence,[21] an assertion that indicates (along with other evidence) that the Pythagorean philosophers of Cilicia and elsewhere were interested in planetary theology. The region of Cilicia, as will later be noted, was steeped in Eastern astrological lore. Here were to be found the adherents of the god Mithras and his rites—a cult that hailed Sunday as the preeminent day of the week.[22]

At this point it would be well to divert our attention to look at the historic rise of astrology, particularly its introduction into the West. For not only is the planetary week the product of Eastern astrology but it never could have become so popular were it not for astrology's captivating influence in Western lands, which by Augustus' reign (27 B.C.-A.D. 14) had permeated religious speculations throughout the Mediterranean world.

Astrology, containing the primary concept that the heavenly planets and zodiac signs are divine powers that exercise a manifold patronage on earth, originated in Babylonia.[23] Geographically it was Chaldea (the region from Babylon to the Persian Gulf) and historically it was the Persian reign (538-331 B.C.) that marked the rise of horoscopic astrology to paramount importance in the ancient world. While the zodiac belt of constellations had long been known in Babylonia, not until the fifth century B.C. did a blend of Persian and Chaldean/Babylonian beliefs result in horoscopic predictions concerning individuals, based on the configuration of the heavens at the hour of birth.[24]

Meanwhile, the lack of astrological knowledge in fifth-century Greece was illustrated by the usually knowledgeable Plato (428-347 B.C.), who in his *Republic* (Book X) knew of the planets but not their names. Plato, who perhaps had gained some of his heavenly knowledge from the Pythagoreans, was at least ahead of his contemporaries, for Greek literature of the fifth century knew nothing of the distinction between planet and fixed star. In the generation following Plato, the situation dramatically changed. The Greeks not only had a concept of the planets as deities but also had even learned to name them after their own Olympian gods

(Zeus, Aphrodite, et cetera).[25] What caused the dramatic change? The contact of Greek intellectuals of Asia Minor with the learned Chaldean astrologers. It was Eastern, Asian Greeks, men such as Eudoxos from Knidus (390-340 B.C.)[26] and Hipparchus from Nicaea (190-126 B.C.),[27] who lent their prestige and astronomical discoveries to the art of Chaldean astrology/astronomy. Through such intermediaries in Asia Minor, the Greeks of the mainland came to possess the Babylonian zodiac with its twelve signs.[28]

Since the Babylonians were interested mainly in characteristic phenomena, their planetary system began with the big, slow-moving planet Jupiter (identified with Marduk, the patron deity of Babylon). His size and brightness suggested kingly power. Second in sequence came the luminous queen star Venus (the Babylonian goddess Ishtar). First to appear in the night sky, while the lesser celestial lights still were eclipsed from view by the Sun's evening glow, Venus' light (when nearest the earth) was the most brilliant of all the stars. Her warm radiance, which seemed so near in the evening sky, suggested love and desire.[29] Third was Saturn (the god Ninurta). His dim light and slow movement suggested the old dethroned Sun—the retiring distant Sun of the night sky.[30] The subsequent fourth position was relegated to Mercury (the god Nabu), who was perceived as the scribe of the gods. His quick motion, because of his nearness to the Sun, gave him a nervous, mercurial quality, as though he always was transmitting learning.[31] Fifth in sequence was the fiery red planet Mars (the god Nergal), who was thought of as the source of plagues—the ruler of the realm of the dead. To this planetary sequence the Moon (Sin) and the Sun (Shamash) were appended.

The Babylonian hierarchy of celestial gods, Jupiter-Venus-Saturn-Mercury-Mars-Moon-Sun (the seven *bibbi* of Mesopotamian astrologers),[32] was rearranged by Greek mathematical calculations, a rearrangement that may have been made as early as 300 B.C. or as late as the time of Hipparchus (*c.* 150 B.C.). Greek spherical trigonometry and astronomical observations established an order of eight spheres, the criteria of order being based on their respective distance from the earth. First was the sphere of the fixed stars, marking the bounds of the cosmos. Within this outermost boundary were the seven inner spheres of the planets, which in order (from distant to near) are: Saturn, Jupiter, Mars, the Sun, Venus, Mercury, and the Moon. This new Greek "spacial" sequence significantly perceived that the Sun was set in the middle. The three planets above this preeminent ruler were thought of as male and less humid (except for Saturn); the three below were female (except Mercury, who was considered hermaphroditic) and humid.[33]

The Babylonian zodiacal year was then made to conform to this new sequence.[34] The annual rising of the Sun, from the winter to the summer solstice, began with the zodiac sign of Aquarius and ended with the sign of Leo. The ancient winter-solstitial month of Aquarius (now dated January 20-February 18)[35] was given to Saturn, the most distant of the visible planets. The next month, Pisces (February 19-March 20), was assigned to Jupiter, the secondmost remote planet; Aries (March 21-April 19), the third, to Mars. Since the yearly cycle of the Sun was conceived of as a "great day," the next in sequence, the Sun, was reserved for the year's "noon," the zenith position directly opposite its rising. Hence, the fourth month, Taurus (April 20-May 20), was given not to the Sun but to the following planet, the "dawn-star" of spring, Venus. Gemini (May 21-June 21), the fifth, was assigned to Mercury; and Cancer (June 22-July 22), the sixth, to the Moon.[36]

Marking the seventh month in this sequence was Leo (July 23-August 22), the month that begins the annual descent of light down to the short days of winter darkness. As just noted, this turning point was reserved for the Sun itself. The remaining months of the solar setting then were given to the five planets in reverse order, so that Virgo (August 23-September 22) fell to Mercury; Libra (September 23-October 22), to Venus; Scorpio (October 23-November 22), to Mars; Sagittarius (November 23-December 21), to Jupiter. Finally, with the twelfth month, Capricornus (December 22-January 19), Saturn once more is brought to view as ruler. In this manner Saturn emerged as the pivotal planet that both began and ended the cycle of the solar year (holding two consecutive months in a row). Consequently, he became the Hellenistic god of time, Kronos (Saturnos-Aion), who not only controlled the circle of time but also appears as the ancient father figure who presides over the birth of Light at the moment of winter solstice (the shortest day of the year).[37]

Of continued importance is the Sun's influential position. As just seen, it is the solar rising and setting that predetermined which two months each respective planet was to rule (only one month each being assigned to the Moon and Sun). Beginning at "midnight," that is, the winter solstice, the astrological year followed the course of the Sun as it rose, "dawning" at spring and reaching a high "noontime" during the height of the summer season. With this observation in mind, one could erroneously assume that the beginning (New Year's Day) of the astrological year would be assigned to deepest winter, starting with the Sun's nativity.[38] Actually, however, the twelve zodiacal months begin their enumerated succession with the "dawning" of spring, at the moment of the Sun's "exaltation" (at the vernal equinox).[39] This twofold beginning is of interest, because the same analogy holds true for the astronomical day of the Hellenistic age. Again, as with the yearly solar rising, it was midnight that marked the start of computing the hours of the day. But following the longstanding Persian custom, the Magi astrologers continued to reckon the natural day from sunrise.[40]

The connection between the intellectual mathematical advances being made by the Greeks in Asia Minor and what was taking place in Hellenistic Egypt is illustrated by the position of Hipparchus (190-126 B.C.), the greatest astronomer of his time. While he made his celestial observations and calculations in Asia Minor, and toward the end of his life on the island of Rhodes (just off the southwest coast of Asia Minor),[41] his discoveries, including his defense of astrology, made the greatest impact upon the Greek thinkers of Alexandria, Egypt (the most important center of Hellenistic learning of that age). The measure of this impact can be noted in the works of Ptolemy (Claudius Ptolemaeus) of Alexandria (died c. A.D. 150). It is Ptolemy who created the *Almagest,* which served as the astronomical bible until the seventeenth century. It was this same savant who authored the *Tetrabiblos,* the main astrological treatise to the present day. But what should be noted is that the basis of Ptolemy's works, which represent the culmination of Greek astrology, was largely derived from that of the Asian Greek, Hipparchus.[42]

Indeed, it was in Hipparchus' own lifetime, around 150 B.C., that one of the earliest manuals of astrological techniques was drawn up in Alexandria. The work was given the name of a sixth-century Pharaoh, Nechepso, and his scribe,

Petosiris. A product of Hellenistic scholarship, it became the most quoted handbook of astrology at Rome during the late second century B.C.[43] At about the same time a synthesis of Babylonian, Greek, and Egyptian methods of measuring time units took place. This was a most significant event for both the development of what presently is understood as astrology and the origin of the planetary week. For it was at Alexandria that astronomers first designated the equinoctial "hours" as the parts of the day. Babylonian priests long had divided day and night into twelve equal parts each, and the Greeks had adopted this system.[44] However, the Egyptian priests traditionally were inured to dividing the complete night-day cycle into twenty-four constant units. The aura of ancient Egyptian practice eventually made its mark on the Greek-speaking astronomers of Alexandria, causing them to adopt the Egyptian division of the calendar day. However, still being under the aegis of Chaldean astrological thought, the astronomers applied the Babylonian sexagesimal counting system to the Egyptian hour so that each hour fell into sixty equal parts, creating sixty minutes to the hour.[45]

Thus it came about that the ingredients for the planetary week were brought together; the concept of planetary gods being taken from the Babylonians, the mathematics having been supplied by the Greeks, and the *dekans*, or hours,[46] adopted from the the Egyptians. Alexandria, possessing a large, indigenous, and influential Jewish population,[47] was well suited for bringing in a final ingredient, that of the Hebrew weekly cycle. Apostate Hebrew thought had long associated the highest sphere of the heavens, ruled by Saturn, as the sphere of the Ancient of Days.[48] The antiquity of this association can be dated centuries back to the time of the Old Testament prophet Amos. Rebuking idolatry, the Hebrew prophet singled out for special condemnation Israel's chief star-god Kaiwan *(kywn)*, the Chaldean and Persian designation for Saturn (Amos 5:26).[49] The two basic components that form the foundation for the astrological week thus were present within the community of Alexandrian Jews. Not only did they possess a unique septenary time cycle, but even more interesting to the Hellenistic astrologers was the fact that they long had associated their "high" day (cf. John 19:41) as a day ruled over by the planet Saturn.

It is the scholarly Roman historian Dio Cassius, in a passage dating between A.D. 210 and 220, who tells posterity about the origin of the astrological week. According to Dio, the planetary week, "now found among all mankind," was instituted in Egypt. He further asserted that it was a comparatively recent innovation, an institution unknown to the ancient Greeks. As Dio tells it, the concept of days ruled by planets originated with the recognition that the planets ruled the twenty-four hours of the day. Beginning with the highest planet and the highest day of the Hebrew week, Saturn and Sabbath, it followed that the initial hour and initial day both were to be allotted to Saturn. As each of the seven planets (assigned in sequence according to their distance from the earth) took its respective turn as ruler over an hour, the first, the eighth, the fifteenth, and the twenty-second hour of Saturn's day fell to Saturn's special jurisdiction. As Saturday drew to a close, the twenty-third hour went to Jupiter, the twenty-fourth to Mars. The first hour of the next day went to the fourth in sequence, the Sun, which then was given Sunday to rule. In this manner, as the hourly rulers rotated their respective positions, every day of the week was named after the lord of its first hour.[50]

Interest in the advanced, Alexandrian mathematical-astrology reached Rome in the first century B.C. Its reception by the Roman upper classes is illustrated by the astrologic diagram that was found on the dead body of the consul Octavius in 87 B.C.[51] By the time the planetary week began to spread westward into Italy, the Emperor Augustus himself was placing the zodiacal sign of his birth, Capricorn, on his coins (by 24 B.C.).[52] Undoubtedly it was the Emperor Septimius Severus (A.D. 193-211) who set the stage for the final diffusion of the planetary week. Born in the North African town of Leptis Magna, he had been a fervent believer in astrology from his childhood.[53] Hence, it is not surprising that it was during his reign that the Romans officially began to mark the most important dates according to the weekdays as well as according to the year. The earliest extant evidence of this custom comes from May 23, A.D. 205.[54]

Sunday Observance in the Pagan World

In a relatively brief essay such as this, the full complexity of how *Solis dies,* the day of the Sun, rose to paramount importance in the pagan Roman world can only be touched upon.[55] The ancient sources, however, do pinpoint one religion as the vehicle that promulgated Sunday religious observance. While the prestigious Alexandrian center of learning fostered astrology and its offspring, the planetary week, it was the so-called "Persian" religion of the god Mithra that extolled Sunday as the most important day of the week.[56] Replying to the taunt that he honored the day of the Sun, Tertullian, the Christian Church Father from North Africa *(c.* A.D. 150-230), makes the illuminating admission that a day of festivity to the Sun was in his time popularly thought of as a "Persian" institution: "Others . . . believe that the sun is our god. We shall be counted Persians perhaps, though we do not worship the orb of day painted on a piece of linen cloth." [57]

In a book attacking Christianity, the Epicurean Celsus *(c.* A.D. 140-180) speaks of the "reasoning of the Persians and the initiation rite of Mithra" as postulating a figurative "road" that led through the planets. This path, for those who would escape earthly matter, was perceived as a ladder of seven gates, each associated with one of the seven planets. At the top was an eighth gateway, representing the final sphere of the fixed stars.[58] This otherworldly sequence of an ascent through planetary incarnations seems to have been in imitation of the growth and rise of Mithra, the deified Sun-Light, to his zenith position in the astrological solar year. For like the ascendant light of the Sun, which moves from its birth position (the shortest day of the year) through planetary "spheres" and zodiacal signs, so too the planetary ladder of Celsus begins with distant Saturn, ruler of the winter solstice, and ends with the dominating Sun, ruler of the summer solstice (the longest day of the year). But in addition, this growth of deified light now is made to conform to the planetary week. From Saturn the ladder moves through the sequence of the gods of the week in a reverse direction, enabling the Sun to attain a significant seventh position (Saturn-Venus-Jupiter-Mercury-Mars-Moon-Sun).[59]

The importance of the Sun for the followers of Mithra is illustrated also by archeological work done at Ostia, a coastal port city of Roman Italy. In the Mithraeum of the Seven Portals, seven gates are represented in mosaic, covering the floor of the sanctuary's entranceway. Attention is immediately drawn to the large center gate, which is flanked on either side by three smaller portals. Within the inner sanctuary itself, the seven planets are in attendance, depicted on the faces of the side benches. As with the seven gates mentioned by Celsus, seemingly these gates are to be associated with the planets. The pictorial presentation at the very threshold of the sanctuary, with its large middle gate, very likely reflects the Greek "spatial" sequence of the planets, with the Sun holding the expanded center portal. It presumably is the Sun's "door" that brings the initiate into the sanctuary.

A more startling similarity to the gateways of Celsus is found in the nearby Mithraeum of the Seven Spheres. Once again seven gates are depicted in mosaic. This time, however, the seven portals fill the whole central floor of the inner sanctuary. Here it becomes obvious that the gates are connected with initiation rites, that is, the seven spheres through which the mystes must pass. That each gateway was thought of as a transition point, marking death and rebirth, is suggested by the picture of a death-inducing dagger in the pavement at the entrance. Again in evidence are the celestial patrons, the seven planets presented on the front of the reclining benches that surround the central aisle. Above, on the surrounding walls, are placed the signs of the zodiac. Once more the idea is conveyed that here is a star-studded planetary ascent through seven "heavens."[60]

That the veneration paid to the day of the Sun was linked to what Tertullian and Celsus termed "Persian" theology needs clarification. While Mithra indeed was a very ancient Persian deity, the late, Hellenistic form of Mithraism that spread far and wide in the Roman Empire actually was unknown in Persia, The astral mystery religion of western Mithra had its roots in an unorthodox *daevic* cult of the god as practiced in Chaldea and Anatolia, and not in the cult of the Zoroastrianized Mithra of Iran.[61] The historic antecedents to this apostate "demon" offshoot of orthodox, Iranian religion trace back to events that were to find their denouement in Asia Minor, where western Mithraism was first formulated as the result of the intercourse between Magi and Chaldeans.

The first of these events came in 539 B.C., with the fall of Babylon to the Medo-Persian Empire. The rustic and nonliterate Persian Magi immediately were subjected to the sophisticated influence of Chaldean astrologers, whose impressive literature and urban temples abounded in mystic emblems of the elements, signs of the zodiac, and symbols of the planets. An even more momentous event unfolded in 521 B.C. when Darius I of Persia decreed a death penalty, the so-called *Magophonia,* or "killing of the Magi," which aimed at exterminating the whole caste of *daevic* (apostate) Magi in one day.[62]

The Magian priesthood against whom Darius bitterly fought were Iranian polytheists who had blended their worship with Chaldean astral beliefs.[63] In sharp contrast were the true Magi of the prophet Zoroaster (the Mazdayasnians), who insisted that there was only one good god, Ahura-Mazda. Adored as a supreme deity, transcendent and without equal, Ahura-Mazda was held by the orthodox to be too great and spiritual to have images made to contain him.[64]

The divergent polytheists received a further blow in 482 B.C. when Xerxes I, who had succeeded Darius on the Persian throne, prohibited the worship of *daevas,* or demons. By imperial decrees, all the temples of Chaldea were dismantled. The imposing temple of Babylon, Esagila, was leveled, and its eighteen-foot, eight-hundred-pound gold statue of the god Marduk was melted into bullion.[65]

These catastrophic blows directed against Babylonian religious influence abated somewhat with the rise to power of the Persian monarch Artaxerxes II

(404-359 B.C.). Because of his conflicts with his half brother, Cyrus the lesser, Artaxerxes felt a need to claim a legitimate place in the Persian (Achaemenid) royal line. The traditions of the past therefore became important. Ancient pre-Zoroastrian idolatry was everywhere elevated. Ahura-Mazda, who had ruled uninterrupted as supreme god since the reign of Darius I, now *(c.* 400 B.C.) was forced to share his once-supreme position with the goddess Anahita and the god Mithra. Polytheistic temples, complemented with the presence of idols, were erected throughout the empire.[66]

By this time, however, the adherents of Chaldean astral theology had been scattered to Anatolia and to the Mediterranean littoral. Illuminating the gulf of difference that remained to separate the *daevic* Magi, who had been driven from their homeland, from that of the orthodox Mazdayasnian Magi, who still were to be found in the East, is the new Testament witness. On the one hand are the Magi whose Mazdayasnian background shunned the worship of idols, who come from the remote East to adore the Christ child (Matt. 2:1). On the other hand are the Magi who live in the near West, the authors of demonic magic (Acts 8:9-24; 13:6-11), the "black magic" of medieval times.[67]

The emergence of the most spectacular Hellenistic city-state in Asia Minor, the kingdom of Pergamum (263-133 B.C.), provided the arena for the final amalgamation of Chaldean and *daevic* Persian beliefs that resulted in the birth of Hellenistic Mithraism. The glorious days of Pergamum began under Attalus I (241-197 B.C.). Rendering important services to the Romans, Attalus amassed such wealth that his name became proverbial for riches. Becoming a patron of arts and eastern Chaldean learning, he invited from Babylonia the famed astrologer Sudines (Babylonian *Šuiddina*). As court adviser, Sudines made predictions based on divinations, particularly during the king's war against the Galatians *(c.* 240 B.C.). The importance of this Chaldean as a learned instructor to Greek-speaking students is found in the fact that his lunar tablets were still quoted some four hundred years later (A.D. 154-174) by the "mathematician" Vettius Valens.[68] Under such cultural patronage, which remained a dynastic tradition at Pergamum, a great library was established during the reign of the next monarch, Eumenes II (197-159 B.C.). Its size was superseded only by the number of volumes found in Alexandria. During the same reign of Eumenes, Pergamum was able to expand from that of a mere enclave on the Aegean Sea to include the whole of Asia Minor west of the Taurus Mountains.[69]

While the details of how western Mithraism was first formulated remain unknown, the facts speak for themselves as to the time and place. The post-Hipparchian, Hellenistic astrology, which forms an integral part of the mysteries of this syncretistic religion, makes it certain that *daevic* Mithraism, which the Romans first encountered in 67 B.C.,[70] was formulated within the last two centuries B.C. Lactantius Placidus *(c.* A.D. 300) states that the cult passed from the Persians to the Phrygians (the natives of Asia Minor) and from the Phrygians to the Romans.[71] Everything known about Hellenistic Mithraism bears out this assertion. The Phrygian dress that continually garbs the god Mithra and his companions, wherever in the Roman Empire they are encountered, makes it obvious that the place of the god's origin is Asia Minor. Fortifying this conclusion is the type of artificial cave in which the arcane Mithra was worshiped, for artistically it is derived from western Asia Minor.[72] The place and time thus are

THE PLANETARY WEEK IN THE ROMAN WEST

narrowed; the finger of evidence unmistakenly points toward the Hellenistic kingdom that encompassed Asia Minor, that is, Pergamum, patron of the arts and Eastern learning.

The nature of the western Mithra is of interest. While the god Mithra is, of course, Persian, the liturgy of the emergent astral religion remained Chaldean (Aramaic). The teacher of the mysteries was called a *Magus,* that is, a Persian priest, but he taught from a scroll called "a Babylonian book."[73] While a number of the classics speak of this syncretism between Persian Magi and Chaldean astrologers, a late Latin inscription from Rome, which dates from A.D. 377, beautifully sums up the nature of the fusion by speaking of the mystery teacher as a "Babylonian priest of Mithra's Persian temple."[74]

Two factors have usually been pointed out as especially important in facilitating the rapid spread of Mithraism: first, the bankruptcy of indigenous authoritarian religions, and second, Rome's peculiar religious dependence upon Asia Minor. These are beyond the scope of our discussion here, but it is important to ask: When was Mithraism introduced into Rome, and what impact did it have after its arrival?

Plutarch reports that when the Roman general Pompey conquered the pirates on the coast of Cilicia (the southeastern shore of Asia Minor) in 67 B.C., he carried back with him to Rome some prisoners who were devotees of Mithra. It was these Cilician pirates, the report states, who introduced the mysteries into Italy.[75] Two archeological finds tend to substantiate the report. The first is a series of rock reliefs authored by Antiochus I Epiphanes in 62 B.C., giving evidence of the major importance of astrological, Hellenized Mithraism in the region lying immediately to the east of Cilicia in the very time of Pompey. Found on the summit of Nimrud Dagh, at Commagene, the rock inscriptions and reliefs not only contain a reference to what seems to be the Mithraic mystery-grade of the "Lion" but, more important, depict the god Mithra shaking hands with Antiochus.[76] The other archeological find comes from Italy, about a century later. A graffito from Pompeii, dating from before A.D. 62, sketches out the Mithraic magic emblem, the so-called ROTAS-SATOR square. Using the Latin alphabet, the mystery square significantly was found in the area of the *Iuvenes,* that is, the region set aside for young men to perform military exercises.[77] Here, then, is confirmative evidence that Mithraism had become rooted in mid-first-century Italy, its devotees being drawn especially from Roman soldiers. Because of its emphasis on fighting against evil and the forces of darkness (interpreted to include Rome's enemies), Mithraism was to gain an ascendant position as the religion of the Roman troops. Beginning with the reign of Trajan (A.D. 98-117), material evidence shows that wherever the Roman legions planted their standards, Mithra and his cult were in prominent attendance.[78]

The strength of Mithra's impact on first-century-A.D. Rome also can be gauged by Statius, who mentions *(c.* A.D. 90) seeing the *Tauroctonous Mithra* (the depiction of the god Mithra in the mystery rite of slaying the bull) in Italy.[79] Nero, the first Roman emperor to listen formally to the judicial merits of the Christian gospel (Acts 25:12 with 2 Tim. 4:16),[80] also is the first emperor to acknowledge the appeal of Mithra. When, in A.D. 66, Tiridates I, king of Armenia and a Mithraic priest, came with his attendant Magi to reverence the emperor, Nero was addressed by the Eastern potentate with these words: "I have come to thee, my god, to worship thee as I do Mithras."[81] Tiridates went so far as to initiate Nero into the Mithra cult.[82] In return, the grateful Nero confirmed Tiridates' position as ruler over Armenia.

Christian and Mithraic influences again were brought to bear on the person of another emperor, Constantine the Great (A.D. 306-337). By this time, Mithra, the deified light, had become popularly identified with the unconquerable Sun-god *(Hēlios, Sol Invictus)* of the Roman state religion.[83] Of import for the future of the planetary week was Mithra's position as the titulary divinity of the reigning emperor's family. This explains why Julian the Apostate, the nephew of Constantine, would later make much of the fact that he was under the guardianship of Mithra. In A.D. 312, Constantine proclaimed that he would henceforth be a follower of Christ. Nevertheless, the monarch continued to perceive the Christian faith through the externals of Mithra worship. An illustration of the emperor's failure to detach himself from pagan theology is obtained from the comment of his contemporary, the Church Father Eusebius, who of the supposedly Christianized Constantine said: "He taught all armies zealously to honor the Lord's Day [Sunday], which also is called the day of light and of the sun."[84] How significant the phrase "day of light and of the sun"! Was it not the armies of Rome who held Mithra to be Light deified, the offspring of *Sol*, the Sun? While each planet was held to be "lord" of a particular day, who but Mithra himself was lord of the "day of light and of the sun"?[85]

On the seventh of March, A.D. 321, Constantine issued his famed "Sunday law" edict, commanding that: "All judges, city people and craftsmen shall rest on the venerable day of the sun. But country-men may without hinderance attend to agriculture."[86] With the issuance of that decree, the day of the sun, in its paganized dimension as a civil day of the astrological week, officially was accepted by those who ruled Christendom. Henceforth, the week of the planetary deities was to be the "sanctified" septenary time unit that the Western world was to inherit.[87]

NOTES

[1] The seven-day-unit was well known in the ancient Near East, but it was not employed as a weekly cycle. The seventh day of seven-day-units within the lunar month (the seventh, fourteenth, twenty-first and twenty-eighth days of the month) appear now and then as unlucky days in Babylonian texts. In ancient Greek, Sumero-Akkadian, and Ugaritic epic literature, the seven-day-unit is utilized as a schematic device: an action continues for six days but is completed on the seventh day. It is the lunar month, however, that formed the basis for time reckoning in the ancient Orient. In Assyria and Babylonia the word *Sabbath (šapattu*, originally *šabāttûm)* may have designated, at an early period, a division of the month; later it was applied in cuneiform texts of Babylonian origin to the fifteenth day of the month, eventually coming to mean "full moon." It follows that there is no real basis for the popular hypothesis that Hebrew *šabbāt* meant "full moon" and not "week." See S. E. Loewenstamm, "The Seven-Day-Unit in Ugaritic Epic Literature," *Israel Exploration Journal* 15 (1965):121-133; Arvid S. Kapelrud, "The Number Seven in Ugaritic Texts," *VT* 18 (1968):494-499; Roland de Vaux, *Ancient Israel* (London, 1961), pp. 476-479; Niels-Erik A. Andreasen, *The Old Testament Sabbath*, SBL Diss. Ser. 7 (Missoula, Mont., 1972), pp. 1-7, p. 97, n. 5. William Foxwell Albright, review of Julius Lewy and Hildegard Lewy, "The Origin of the Week and the Oldest West Asiatic Calendar," *Hebrew Union College Annual* 17 (1942/1943):1-152, in *JBL* 64 (1945):288-291.

[2] Inclusive reckoning was used by ancient peoples generally, including Bible writers. According to this system of reckoning, any parts of the first and last units of time are reckoned as whole units. Van L. Johnson, "The Primitive Basis of Our Calendar," *Archaeology* 21 (1968):15.

[3] Following the comments of Alexander Adam, *Roman Antiquities* (Philadelphia, 1872), p. 218. The fact that a market day of one city fell on a different day than the market day of a nearby, neighboring city also militates against the assumption that the *nundinum* was generally held as an eight-day week. Like the later seven-day week, however, the *nundinum* days frequently were identifiable in writing and conversation. Market day was called "the *Nundinae*"; there was "the day before the *Nundinae*," "two days before the *Nundinae*," and so on. See J. P. V. D. Balsdon, *Life and Leisure in Ancient Rome* (New York, 1969), pp. 60, 61.

[4] Josephus *Contra Apionem* (LCL) 2. 39. The statement of Josephus is well borne out by the evidence. Two examples from the first century A.D. may suffice. Emperor Augustus wrote to Tiberius that he had kept his fast on the Sabbath more strictly than a Jew (Suetonius *Divus Augustus* 76. 2). Tiberius himself, before he became emperor, attempted to hear the public disquisition of the Greek grammarian Diogenes of Rhodes, but was refused admission as

THE PLANETARY WEEK IN THE ROMAN WEST

the disquisitions were held on every seventh day only, on the Sabbath (Suetonius *Tiberius* 32). As a rule, the Romans jeered at the Jewish use of the Sabbath as a rest day. See Jack Lindsay, *Origins of Astrology* (London, 1971), p. 234.
    [5] E. J. Bickerman, *Chronology of the Ancient World* (Ithaca, N.Y., 1968), p. 59; Eduard Lohse, "σαββατον," *TDNT*, 7:32.
    [6] Because the chronographer of A.D. 354 *(Chronica Minora* I: *Monumenta Germaniae Hist., auctores antiquissimi,* ed. by C. Frick [Leipzig, 1892], 9. 120) shows that night hours were reckoned to be under the control of the same planet as that of the succeeding day, some have assumed that the planetary week was reckoned from evening to evening. See Willy Rordorf, *Sunday* (Philadelphia, 1968), p. 34. The data supplied by the chronographer, however, does not conflict with the fact that Chaldean astrologers began their computations from the hour of midnight, the planetary ruler of the first hour being considered the lord of the succeeding day. Significantly, the astrological year also was computed from what was considered the winter "midnight" of the annual rising and setting of the sun. On the astronomical cuneiform texts from the seleucid period showing that advanced astronomical reasons were used in computing the day from midnight, see O. Neugebauer, "The Survival of Babylonian Methods in the Exact Sciences of Antiquity and Middle Ages," *Proceedings of the American Philosophical Society* 107 (1963):529; Bickerman, *op. cit.,* p. 14. Coincidentally, the ancient Romans began their civil day at midnight. Leonhard Schmitz, "Dies," *Dictionary of Greek and Roman Antiquities,* ed. by William Smith (Boston, 1870); Plutarch *Quaestiones Romans* 84.
    [7] Dio Cassius *Roman History* 37. 18 (LCL). See Bickerman, *op. cit.,* p. 61; Lindsay, *op. cit.,* p. 233; Johnson, *op. cit.,* p. 20.
    [8] Gaston H. Halsberghe, *The Cult of Sol Invictus* (Leiden, 1972), p. 120; Rordorf, *op. cit.,* p. 36; C. C. Richardson, "Lord's Day," *IDB,* 3:152.
    [9] Johnson, *op. cit.,* p. 20; Lohse, *loc. cit.*
    [10] Bickerman, *op. cit.,* p. 61; O. Neugebauer, *The Exact Sciences in Antiquity,* 2d ed. (New York, 1957), p. 169.
    [11] The first day of the week presents an exceptional case. While Northern Europe perpetuates the pagan name "Sunday," the Romance languages term that day: *dimanche, domenica, domingo,* the "Lord's Day." See F. H. Colson, *The Week* (Cambridge, 1926), pp. 117-120.
    [12] Tibullus *Elegiac* 1. 3. 1, 15-19 (LCL).
    [13] While both Mars and Saturn were reputed to be unlucky, Saturn was considered the more dangerous of the two. In the Zodiac, Saturn had as houses the two winter months of Capricorn and Aquarius, cold, wet signs. Traversing his houses, he supposedly begot not only winter rains but also within the body cold humors, intestinal fluxes, and so on. See Lindsay, *op. cit.,* p. 127. In the Greek world Hesiod is the first to mention lucky and unlucky days *(Works and Days* 765-825). Possibly the medieval ban on the "seventh" tone in church music as the "interval of the devil" was because of the association with the unlucky planet Saturn, to which the seventh day was consecrated; for anciently it was held that as the planets followed their orbits they produced sounds whose pitch depended on the speed of the planets and that together formed the "music of the spheres." For a discussion, see Martin A. Beek, *Atlas of Mesopotamia* (New York, 1962), p. 150; Charles Peter Mason, "Pythagoras," *Dictionary of Greek and Roman Biography and Mythology,* 3 vols., ed. by William Smith (Boston, 1849), 3:624.
    [14] *Elegiac* 1, 3. 35-50.
    [15] The *menologia* were cut in stone or laid out in mosaic, and were more for public display than use (see Balsdon, *op. cit.,* p. 59; Theodor Mommsen, *Corpus Inscriptionum Latinarum,* 2d ed. [Berlin, 1893], 1:280-282; and more recently: Attilio Degrassi, *Inscriptiones Italiae* [Rome, 1963], 13, fascicle II: 284-298). Also displaying the seven-day week in Roman Italy is a Sabine calendar that dates between 19 B.C. and A.D. 14. Consisting of three columns, the first column marks the days of the seven-day week, the second the eight days of the *nundinum,* and the third records whether the day is *fastus* (the praetor was allowed to administer justice in the public courts), *nefastus* (neither courts of justice nor comitia were allowed to be held) or *comitialis* (the comitia could be held). Modern scholars take differing opinions as to the type of week found in the Sabine calendar. Rordorf is of the opinion that the *"fasti Sabini"* is "probably the Jewish week" *(op. cit.,* p. 10, n. 1); Johnson would see the calendar as evidence for the spread of the planetary week in the first century after Christ *(op. cit.,* p. 19). "There are two other very fragmentary calendars, one of the time of Augustus, the other from the early Empire, on which also the seven-day week is marked."—Balsdon, *op. cit.,* pp. 62, 63.
    [16] See Samuele Bacchiocchi, *From Sabbath to Sunday* (Rome, 1977), p. 245, n. 35; Balsdon, *op. cit.,* p. 59.
    [17] Colson, *op. cit.,* p. 32.
    [18] Lindsay, *op. cit.,* p. 234.
    [19] It is known that Hellenistic astronomy penetrated into India at least as early as 150 B.C. See Neugebauer, "Babylonian Methods," p. 532, and the literature cited there. On Apollonius of Tyana, compare Colson, *op. cit.,* pp. 22-24; Benjamin Jowett, "Apollonius Tyanaeus," in Smith, *Biography and Mythology,* 1:242-3.
    [20] Philostratus *The Life of Apollonius of Tyana* 3. 41.
    [21] Pliny *Natural History* 2. 22.
    [22] While the Neo-Pythagoreans of the first century B.C. had a predilection for astral theology, modern scholarship has demonstrated that the founder, Pythagoras of Samos (whose career in southern Italy flourished between 540 and 510 B.C.), had nothing whatever to do with the invention or establishment of the Greek "spatial" sequence of the planets; Neugebauer, "Babylonian Methods," p. 530. It was Mithraic ("Persian") theology that "contributed largely to the adoption of the week throughout the Roman Empire." Franz Cumont, *Astrology and Religion Among the Greeks and Romans* (New York, 1960), p. 90; compare Bickerman, *op. cit.,* p. 61.
    [23] Astrology, which operates with the use of mathematical astronomy, is an extremely ancient art, dating back to Old Babylonian and Sumerian times. See Willy Hartner, "The Earliest History of the Constellations in the Near East and the Motif of the Lion-Bull Combat," *Journal of Near Eastern Studies* 24 (1965):1-16.
    [24] B. L. van der Waerden, "History of the Zodiac," *Archiv für Orientforschung* 16 (1952/1953):224. While equinoctial hours of constant length were unknown until Hellenistic times, the ancient Babylonians did possess twelve day-hours and twelve night-hours (Lindsay, *op. cit.,* pp. 35, 69, 153). The earliest horoscope, written in cuneiform by a Chaldean scribe, dates to April 30, 409 B.C. *(ibid.,* p. 49). A systematic list of the twelve zodiacal constellations (their names extremely old, going back to Sumerian times) appears for the first time in a Babylonian text from year 6 of Darius II (419 B.C.). See Lindsay, *op. cit.,* pp. 57, 58; Neugebauer, *The Exact Sciences,* p. 140; Van der Waerden, *op. cit.,* pp. 217, 220.
    [25] The earliest Greek horoscope is that of Antiochus I of Commagene, dating from July 6 or 7, 62 B.C. The earliest known horoscopes in which Olympian Greek names are given to the planets are from Egyptian papyri dating from A.D. 4 and 14 (Lindsay, *op. cit.,* pp. 126, 137). In a dialogue called *Epinomis,* probably by one of Plato's pupils, the

planets are named after Greek gods, showing the increase in planetary knowledge in the generation following Plato. See the discussion by Jean Rhys Bram, trans., *Ancient Astrology: Theory and Practice (Matheseos Libri VIII* by Firmicus Maternus) (Park Ridge, N.J., 1975), p. 306, n. 24.

[26] Van der Waerden, *op. cit.*, p. 225.

[27] Bram, *op. cit.*, p. 324, and the literature cited there.

[28] The reason Greek science (including astronomical knowledge) was born in Asia Minor is to be found in the traumatic events that transpired in the Persian Empire, events that drove out the Chaldean scholars from their temple schools in Uruk and Babylon. The problem of how the transmission of astronomical knowledge from Babylonia to Greece took place remains unsolved. "Even if we completely disregard the very serious practical difficulty of utilizing cuneiform material, we must assume a careful and extended training by competent Babylonian scribes and computers in order to account for the profitable use of any of the Babylonian ephemerides."—Neugebauer, "Babylonian Methods," p. 534. Pliny claims that the Greek zodiac with its twelve signs was introduced all at once by Cleostratus, 548-545 B.C. (*Natural History* 2. 31). In 432 B.C. Meton publicly displayed in Greece a "stellar calendar which, using the zodiacal division, indicated the daily progress of the sun" (Bickerman, *op. cit.*, p. 57). "The light of history begins to shine only about 400 B.C. Zodiacal schemes were then used by Euctemon and Eudoxus in their calendars" (Van der Waerden, *op. cit.*, p. 225).

[29] Even though the ancient Semites realized that the evening and morning star were different manifestations of the same entity, they looked upon the planet as male in the morning and female in the evening. See W. F. Albright, *Yahweh and the Gods of Canaan* (London, 1968), p. 117. Hence the Romans spoke of the morning star as *Lucifer*, "the light bearer," who became the feminine Venus of the evening sky (cf. W. Robertson Smith, *The Religion of the Semites* (New York, 1956), p. 57, n. 3). The glow of dawn's early light was personified, in antiquity, as a goddess (the manifestation of Ishtar-Venus in the morning) who victoriously gave birth to the wonderous male child, the morning star, who in turn became transformed into the ruling Sun. Cf. Isa. 14:12-15; J. W. McKay, "Helel and the Dawn-Goddess," *VT* 20 (1970):451-464.

[30] Luis I. J. Stadelmann, *The Hebrew Conception of the World (Analecta Biblica* 39; Rome, 1970), p. 70. The slow, steady movement of Saturn's revolution around the sun took 29½ years; Jupiter's period of rotation was 12 years; while the fluctuating period of Venus lasted only 225 days. See George Sarton, "Chaldaean Astronomy of the Last Three Centuries B.C.," *JAOS* 75 (1955):168, n. 4. Saturn (in the Hellenistic period) came to be called "the winter or hidden sun." See Ptolemy *Tetrabiblos* 2. 3. 64; Leroy A. Campbell, *Mithraic Iconography and Ideology* (Leiden, 1968), p. 70.

[31] Cf. W. F. Albright, "Some Notes on the Nabataean Goddess 'Al-Kutba' and Related Matters," *Bulletin of the American Schools of Oriental Research* No. 156 (December, 1959):37.

[32] The sky, in the eyes of the first observers, was a great revolving vault, set nightly, attached with tiny flecks of fire (the fixed stars). Inside this celestial vault were the erratic planets, or "wanderers" (which is the meaning of the Greek word *planetai*). The Chaldean astrologers figuratively spoke of the fixed stars as a flock of sheep. Among the ordered ranks of these ordinary sheep were the "wild sheep" (Akkadian *bibbi*), that is, the seven "travelers." The sequential order of the five planets in Babylonian thought begins with the two beneficent deities Jupiter and Venus, moves on to malign Saturn and the doubtful influence of Mercury, and ends with the underworld ruler Mars. See the discussion by Stadelmann, *op. cit.*, pp. 91, 92. (It should be noted that the later Seleucid texts provide a different sequence of planets.) While the reason for the standard order of the seven *bibbi* is not known possibly the order's structure was of an "envelope" type. Jupiter (A) was paired with the Sun (A'), Venus (B) was coupled with the Moon (B'), and Saturn (C) with Mars (C'). In the very middle was the ambivalent Mercury (D), the intermediary scribe. Such a structural arrangement was well known in Akkadian literature; cf., for instance, William L. Moran in the *Bulletin of the American Schools of Oriental Research* No. 200 (1970):48.

[33] Lindsay, *op. cit.*, pp. 127, 128; Cumont, *op. cit.*, pp. 66, 67.

[34] Prior to Hellenistic times and the establishment of the Greek "spatial" order of the planets, the Babylonians had only one house (that is, one stationary division of the zodiac) per planet. This one-house system was referred to by Firmicus Maternus: "The Babylonians called the signs in which the planets are exalted their 'houses.'"—*Matheseus libri VIII*, 2. 3. 4; see Bram, *op. cit.*, pp. 34, 305, n. 23. The mathematical astronomy that Hellenistic astrologers employed was not fully developed until about 300 B.C. (Neugebauer, *The Exact Sciences*, p. 102).

[35] In the fully developed zodiac of the Greco-Roman world, Aquarius ("Water Carrier") and Leo (the "Lion," a solar emblem) marked the months that immediately followed the winter and summer solstices. But between 3000 and 1000 B.C. these two zodiacal constellations marked the positions of the Sun at those two periods of the year. See Bickermann, *op. cit.*, p. 58; Campbell, *op. cit.*, p. 46. Aquarius, which stands in the confines of the zodiac that is diametrically opposite to Leo, was in Sumero-Babylonian times also conceived of as an ibex or mouflon, comprising the main stars of both Capricorn ("Water-Goat") and Aquarius. The heliacal rising (the ascent above the horizon at the moment of dawn) of the ibex's horns (formed by Aquarius) served as the signal that marked the winter solstice for the early Babylonians (Hartner, *op. cit.*, pp. 9, 11).

[36] Campbell, *op. cit.*, p. 76.

[37] The pater ("father") who held the highest grade in the Mithraeum was considered under the protection of Saturn. In his office, he presided over the death and rebirth of the initiate, just as Saturn, in the celestial sphere, was thought to preside over the death and rebirth of the Sun (Campbell, *op. cit.*, p. 76). On the role of Saturn (represented with a lion's head and wings) as the god who rules the cycles of time, see Walter O. Moeller, *The Mithraic Origin and Meanings of the Rotas-Sator Square* (Leiden, 1973), pp. 5, 6, and the literature cited there.

[38] The moment of winter solstice (anciently held to be the 25th of December) was honored by the Chaldeans as the emergence of light—the offspring of the Sun. It is from this Babylonian concept that there later originated the Mithrakana, a festival dedicated to Mithra (*lux mundi*, "the light of the world"), an event that marked Mithra's ascent from the nether regions (December 25). The Syro-Phoenicians, on the other hand, held a different doctrine. For them the winter solstice was when the old, decrepit Sun became transformed into a youthful, vigorous, invincible other self. Elagabalus, the emperor (A.D. 218-222), introduced the Syrian sun cult to Rome, and Aurelian (A.D. 270-275) established December 25 as the outstanding Roman festival of the year (A.D. 274). In imperial Rome, few distinguished between the two doctrines; the *dies natalis Solis Invicti* was celebrated by a profusion of lights and torches. The day honoring the birth of Light and the Sun was chosen by Pope Julius I (A.D. 337-352) as the day to remember Christ's nativity. Cf. the remarks of Theodor H. Gaster, *Myth, Legend, and Custom in the Old Testament* (New York, 1969), pp. 569, 570; Halsberghe, *op. cit.*, pp. 55, 56, 120, 158, 174; Julian Morgenstern, "The 'Son of Man' of Daniel 7:13f: A New Interpretation," *JBL* 80 (1961):68, 69.

[39] The progression of the light of the Sun through the ecliptic (the apparent annual path of the Sun in the heavens) served as a great celestial archetype for earthly horoscopes. While the Sun was born at winter solstice, the counting of his "houses" began with his "ascendant" sign at the vernal equinox. Hence, in earthly horoscopes, the start of enumerating an individual's "houses" is the sign of the zodiac that was ascending in the East at the exact time and place of birth. On the exaltation of nativity, see Lindsay, *op. cit.*, p. 426.

[40] *Natural History* 2. 188. When Pliny states that the Babylonians reckoned their day from sunrise, presumably he was referring to the "Chaldean" Magi of the Hellenistic Age, for the ancient Babylonians, like the Hebrews, reckoned the start of the day from sunset. Cf. Bickerman, *op. cit.*, pp. 13, 14; Neugebauer, "Babylonian Methods," p. 531. On the Magi custom of reckoning the complete day from dawn, see Lindsay, *op. cit.*, p. 96. Traditional folk societies, in their personification of the phenomena of nature, would anthropomorphize celestial events. Possibly Hellenistic astrologers thought of the vernal equinox (fertility season) as the moment of conception; nine months later came the birth of deified Light at the winter solstice.

[41] Augustus de Morgan, "Hipparchus," in William Smith, *Biography and Mythology*, 2:476, 477. Cf. above, n. 27.

[42] George Sarton, *Ancient Science and Modern Civilization* (New York, 1954), pp. 47-49; and *idem*, "Chaldaean Astronomy of the Last Three Centuries B.C.," *Journal of the American Oriental Society* 75 (1955):172.

[43] Bram, *op. cit.*, pp. 5, 303, n. 7.

[44] Herodotus *Persian Wars* 2. 109.

[45] Bickerman, *op. cit.*, p. 16; Lindsay, *op. cit.*, pp. 35, 153, 156, 157. About 135 B.C., Ctesibius, a celebrated mathematician of Alexandria, made an ingenious invention in which water was made to drop upon wheels in such a way as to turn them. The regular movement of these wheels was communicated to a small statue, which, gradually rising, pointed with a little stick to the hours marked on a pillar that was attached to the mechanism (Leonhard Schmitz, "Horologium," in William Smith, *Greek and Roman Antiquities*, pp. 615, 616). In 1901 divers working off the isle of Antikythera found the remains of a clocklike mechanism dating from 80 B.C. The mechanism indicated the annual motion of the Sun in the zodiac, an amazingly complex astronomical clock that happened also to indicate the time. For details, see Derek J. de Solla Price, "An Ancient Greek Computer," *Scientific American*, June, 1959, pp. 60-67.

[46] The *dekans*, "or Calendar Stars, which were supposed to rise and set at intervals of 10 days throughout the year, and to culminate at intervals of 1 hour throughout the night" represent the only Egyptian contribution to the Greek planetary theory. But even the Egyptian doctrine of the *dekans* was molded into Hellenistic astrology in such a way as to conform to Babylonian theology; it was the Babylonian elements that prevailed (Van der Waerden, *op. cit.*, p. 229, 230).

[47] In Jeremiah 24, the Jews who did not go into Babylonian exile, who remained in the homeland or who fled to Egypt to dwell, were labeled "bad figs," unfit to eat. E. Badian speaks of the Jews in Alexandria as "the largest of the foreign communities," who were strongly organized and "formed a city within the city" (*Studies in Greek and Roman History* [Oxford, 1964], p. 186).

[48] Tacitus *Historiae* 5. 4.

[49] Stadelmann, *op. cit.*, p. 88.

[50] *Roman History* 37. 18, 19. The custom of naming the days after the planets also may have arisen, Dio says, by regarding the gods as originally presiding over separate days assigned by the "principle of the tetrachord" (which was believed to constitute the basis of music).

[51] Lindsay, *op. cit.*, p. 217; see also the remarks of Bram, *op. cit.*, p. 5.

[52] Johnson, *op. cit.*, p. 21.

[53] Halsberghe, *op. cit.*, pp. 49, 50.

[54] Bickerman, *op. cit.*, p. 61. "Juvenal suggests that by the early second century schools were following a seven-day timetable" (Juv. 7. 160, 161, in Lindsay, *op. cit.*, p. 234). "Further we may note that an inscription belonging to A.D. 205 has been found in Karlsburg in Transylvania, where the date is given not only by the year and the month, but also by the weekday, in this case Monday."—Colson, *op. cit.*, p. 25.

[55] Cf. Halsberghe, *op. cit.*

[56] Cf. note 8.

[57] Tertullian *Apology* 16 (*ANF* 3. 31). This statement should be read in conjunction with Tertullian's defensive assertion: "Do not many among you [pagans] . . . likewise, move your lips in the direction of the sunrise? It is you, at all events, who have even admitted the sun into the calendar of the week; and you have selected its day [Sunday], in preference to the preceding day, as the most suitable in the week. . . . You deliberately deviate from your own religious rites to those of strangers" (*Ad Nationes* 13 [*ANF* 3. 123]); see *SDABSSB*, Nos. 1567, 1582. In antiquity there was no one commonly accepted name for the followers of Mithra, but they were loosely referred to as "Persians"; indeed, Perses ("Persian") was an alternate name for Mithra; Campbell, *op. cit.*, p. 4; Moeller, *op. cit.*, p. 15.

[58] Origen *Contra Celsum* 6. 21, 22; Campbell, *op. cit.*, p. 342, n. 3.

[59] True, Celsus, in describing his planetary ladder, makes no connection with the days of the week. However, in Mithraic iconography it is common to vary the arrangement of the gods of the weekdays, while at the same time not disrupting the sequential order of the planetary deities. Examples: on the Bononia relief, the planetary gods are placed on the face of the tauroctone arch so that the week opens in the East (running counterclockwise) with Monday (*Luna*), followed by Tuesday (Mars), and so on, closing with Sunday (*Sol*) as the seventh day. Here, too, the sequence may have been thought of as a ladder, from the Moon (*Apogenesis*) souls ascending) to Saturn and the Sun (a new *Genesis*; to an ethereal world of pure light). In the Brigetio relief the order begins with Saturn (running clockwise) and ends with Venus, which is the normal sequence of the planetary week. See Campbell, *op. cit.*, p. 392, n. 3, and Plates XVII, XXXIII. When the planets act as the protectors of the seven grades in the Mithraic cult, the weekly order is not kept; then the sequence is (starting with the top grade): Saturn, Sun, Moon, Jupiter, Mars, Venus, and Mercury. "There was probably as little agreement among Mithraists about the details of eschatology as among the early Christians."—Campbell, *op. cit.*, p. 392.

[60] Campbell, *op. cit.*, pp. 300-302, figs. 19, 20; M. J. Vermaseren, *Mithras, the Secret God* (New York, 1963), p. 157. The concept of an otherworldly ladder, each step marking a transition point, is very ancient. The Sumerians and Babylonians held that the goddess Ishtar traversed downward through seven gates before reaching the Netherworld, home of the dead. As she descended through each gate, Ishtar was made to surrender those parts of her clothing that symbolized her office and rank (*ANET*, pp. 106-109). In the earlier Sumerian version, the goddess had to abandon seven cities on her journey of descent (*ibid.*, p. 53). In order to ascend upward to the place of eternal life, Gilgamesh, the legendary king of Uruk, acquired fame, raising up a "name" for himself, as he climbed up seven mountain peaks

(ibid., p. 47-50). The *ziqqurat* temple towers of ancient Mesopotamia each possessed a stairway ramp that supposedly served as a link between heaven and earth. In going up the steps to the topmost shrine, the priest figuratively was climbing to the home of the gods in the uppermost heavens. See Mircea Eliade, *Images and Symbols* (New York, 1969), pp. 42, 43. The step-pyramid of the Egyptian Third Dynasty possibly was designed as a gigantic stairway. The deceased Pharaoh's ascent would transform him into a star or a companion to the Sungod. Cf. the remarks of Kurt Mendelssohn, *The Riddle of the Pyramids* (New York, 1974), pp. 28, 47. Jacob, too, saw in a dream a ladder that was "set up on the earth, and the top of it reached to heaven: and behold the angels of God ascending and descending on it" (Gen. 28:12). Here again, the ladder communicates a transformation process. This is emphasized by Jesus, who claimed that He was the ladder that linked heaven and earth (John 1:51). On Jacob's ladder, see the observations by Harry A. Hoffner, Jr., "Second Millennium Antecedents to the Hebrew 'ŌḆ," *JBL* 86 (1967):397 and n. 30.

61 Richard N. Frye, *The Heritage of Persia* (New York, 1963), p. 185; I. Gershevitch, *The Avestan Hymn to Mithra* (London, 1959), pp. 66 *et passim;* Richard T. Hallock's review of Frye's book in *Journal of Near Eastern Studies* 25 (1966): 62, 63.

62 Herodotus *Histories* 3. 79; Josephus *Antiquities of the Jews* 11. 3. 1.

63 See the brief comment by W. F. Albright, *From the Stone Age to Christianity,* 2d ed. (Garden City, N.Y., 1957), p. 360; Vermaseren, *op. cit.,* pp. 20, 21. The slaying of the Magi by Darius I also is celebrated on the rocks of Behistun. See George G. Cameron, "The Monument of King Darius at Bihistun," *Archaeology* 13 (1960):162-171.

64 Herodotus *Persian Wars* 1. 131, 132. See Albright, *From Stone Age,* pp. 360, 361; John B. Noss, *Man's Religions,* 5th ed. (New York, 1974), p. 346.

65 A. T. Olmstead, *History of the Persian Empire* (Chicago, 1959), pp. 232, 237.

66 "About 400 B.C. the inscriptions of Artaxerxes II abandon Mazdayasnian phraseology and frankly list the chief gods of the pantheon as Ahura Mazda, Mithra, and Anahita. About the same time, according to Berossus, as cited by Clement of Alexandria, supported by a passage in the Avesta, the Iranian gods were first represented in the form of images" (Albright, *From Stone Age,* pp. 360, 361). On the historical events that influenced Artaxerxes II, see George G. Cameron, "Ancient Persia," in *The Idea of History in the Ancient Near East,* ed. by Robert C. Dentan (New Haven, 1955), p. 96; also Roland G. Kent, "The Oldest Old Persian Inscriptions," *Journal of the American Oriental Society* 66 (1946):206-212.

67 Franz Cumont, *Oriental Religions in Roman Paganism* (New York, 1956), pp. 188-190; Vermaseren, *op. cit.,* pp. 20-23. The discovery of the Precession of the Equinoxes, attributed to Hipparchus in 129 B.C., along with other discoveries, may have been knowledge the Chaldeans already knew. There is some evidence to believe that arcane Chaldean astronomy continued to exist in what was considered black magic; see the interesting observations made by Moeller, *op. cit.,* p. 28 and n. 1.

68 Cumont, *Astrology,* pp. 33-36; Lindsay, *op. cit.,* p. 61; Neugebauer, *The Exact Sciences,* pp. 137, 175, 176.

69 M. J. Mellink, "Pergamum," *IDB,* 3:733-735; Leonard Schmitz, "Pergamum," *A Dictionary of Greek and Roman Geography,* ed. by William Smith, 2 vols. (London, 1857), 2:575, 576.

70 Plutarch *Vita Pompei* 24.

71 L. Placidus *Ad Statius Thebaidos* 4. 717; Cumont, *Oriental Religions,* p. 143.

72 Campbell, *op. cit.,* pp. 8, 34, 39; Vermaseren, *op. cit.,* pp. 22, 23, 184, 185.

73 Vermaseren, *op. cit.,* p. 23.

74 *Ibid.,* pp. 155, 156.

75 *Vita Pompei* 24.

76 Lindsay, *op. cit.,* pp. 137-140; Albright, *From Stone Age,* p. 361.

77 Moeller, *op. cit.,* p. 2, n. 1.

78 Vermaseren, *op. cit.,* pp. 30, 31. In the study of the spread of Mithraism throughout the western Roman Empire, it too often is overlooked that the increase in carved Mithraic representations (especially along the *limes,* that is, the fringes of the empire) during the second and third centuries A.D. cannot be used as a final criterion in dating the popularity of this mystery cult, for it is to be noted that in the evolutionary development of Roman art, the increase in the use of figures and florid architectural decoration did not really come into its own as an art form until late in the first century A.D. See, for example, the comments of Morton Smith, "Goodenough's *Jewish Symbols* in Retrospect," *JBL* 86 (1967):60. There is no doubt, however, that the Roman army was the principal agent in the diffusion of the Mithraic religion. Franc Cumont, *The Mysteries of Mithra* (New York, 1956), p. 40.

79 *Ad Statius Thebaidos* 4. 717-719 (LCL).

80 The confrontation between Paul and Nero is interestingly reconstructed by Emil G. Kraeling, *I Have Kept the Faith* (Chicago, 1965), pp. 257-267. Like Mithraism, an import from Cilicia to Rome, Paul too hailed from Tarsus in Cilicia. Cf. the comments by Albright, *From Stone Age,* p. 396 and n. 80; Campbell, *op. cit.,* p. 4.

81 *Roman History* 63. 5 (LCL).

82 *Natural History* 30. 6 (LCL).

83 While Mithraism itself was never accepted as a state religion, it was merged and identified with the cult of the Sun *(Deus Sol Invictus)* established by L. Domitius Aurelianus in A.D. 274. See Halsberge, *op. cit.,* pp. 118-122; F. W. Beare, "Zeus in the Hellenistic Age," in *The Seed of Wisdom: Essays in Honour of T. J. Meek,* ed. by W. S. McCullough (Toronto, 1964), pp. 99, 112; see also note 38.

84 Eusebius *Vita Constantini* 4. 18. See Richardson, *loc. cit.,* Sarton, *Ancient Science,* p. 99, n. 30. The *labarum,* the war standard of the Emperor Constantine, comprising a monogram of the letters X *(chi)* and P *(rho),* apparently was not originally a Christian symbol, but a longstanding pagan symbol of the victorious Sun (or Dawn personified), which defeats night's darkness. See in particular the valuable discussion by Marvin H. Pope, "The Saltier of Atargatis Reconsidered," in *Near Eastern Archaeology in the Twentieth Century: Essays in Honor of Nelson Glueck,* ed. by James A. Sanders (Garden City, N.Y., 1970), pp. 178-196. Moeller sees the *Chi Rho* cross not only as a sun symbol but also as an abbreviation of *Chronos* (Saturn). The solar cross as a + *(crux quadrata)* seemingly is the major symbol of the Mithraic Rotas-Sator square, possessing the numerical value of 666 (cf. the number and mark of the beast in Rev. 13:18); see Moeller, *op. cit.,* pp. 8 (n. 2), 18-20, 24, 30.

85 Interestingly, the book of Revelation presents Christ as "Lord" over His own special day (chap. 1:10) in the context of possessing ruling authority over the celestial bodies of heaven (verse 20). Mithra, too, in his guise as Kronus/Saturn, the ruler of time, is pictured as lord over the starry heavens. Cf. Campbell, *op. cit.,* Plate XVII.

86 *Codex Justinianus* 3. 12. 3. See Bickerman, *op. cit.,* p. 61; *SDABSSB,* No. 1642.

87 Our modern week, however, still retains the scriptural system of enumeration, counting the days up to the Sabbath.

APPENDIX B

The Sabbath and Sunday From the Second Through Fifth Centuries*

Kenneth A. Strand

THE authors of chapters 5 through 7 (pp. 92-150) provide evidence that Sunday was not substituted for Saturday as the Christian weekly day of worship or rest during New Testament times. In addition, persuasive evidence is set forth in chapter 7 that Jerusalem was not the place of origin for Christian Sunday observance. Indeed, the earliest direct evidence for Christian weekly worship on Sunday comes from second-century Alexandria and Rome. About A.D. 130 Barnabas of Alexandria, in a highly allegorical discourse, declares, "Wherefore, also, we keep the eighth day [Sunday] with joyfulness."[1] Some two decades later Justin Martyr in Rome actually describes in some detail the type of Christian meeting held on Sundays there, possibly as a very early morning service.[2] (Part of Justin's statement is quoted by Samuele Bacchiocchi on p. 137; it appears in full at the end of this appendix.)

Rome and Alexandria *Not* Typical

The situation in Rome and Alexandria, however, was not typical of the rest of early Christianity. In these two cities there was an evident early attempt by Christians to terminate observance of the seventh-day Sabbath, but elsewhere throughout the Christian world Sunday observance simply arose *alongside* observance of Saturday. Two fifth-century church historians, Socrates Scholasticus and Sozomen, describe the situation in the following way:

"For although almost all churches throughout the world celebrate the sacred mysteries [the Lord's Supper] on the sabbath [Saturday] of every week, yet the Christians of Alexandria and at Rome, on account of some ancient tradition, have ceased to do this. The Egyptians in the neighborhood of Alexandria, and the inhabitants of Thebaïs, hold their religious assemblies on the sabbath, but do not

---

*Even though various details treated here receive random attention in chapters 8 to 10, it seems useful to provide this more comprehensive and cohesive survey concerning the Sabbath and Sunday from the second to the fifth centuries.

participate of the mysteries in the manner usual among Christians in general: for after having eaten and satisfied themselves with food of all kinds, in the evening making their offerings they partake of the mysteries."[3]

"The people of Constantinople, and almost everywhere, assemble together on the Sabbath, as well as on the first day of the week, which custom is never observed at Rome or at Alexandria. There are several cities and villages in Egypt where, contrary to the usage established elsewhere, the people meet together on Sabbath evenings, and, although they have dined previously, partake of the mysteries."[4]

Thus, even *as late as the fifth century* almost the entire Christian world observed *both Saturday and Sunday* for special religious services. Obviously, therefore, Sunday was not considered a substitute for the Sabbath.

Observance of Both Saturday and Sunday

Let us notice a further sampling of the ancient sources that give evidence for the early Christian observance of both Saturday and Sunday.

We may begin by querying whether even in Rome and Alexandria the Sabbath was immediately displaced completely by Sunday, or whether the process was gradual. This question is raised, for example, by the fact that early in the third century Hippolytus of Rome rebuked those who were giving heed to "doctrines of devils" and "often appoint fasting on the Sabbath [Saturday] and the Lord's Day [Sunday], which Christ did not appoint, and thus dishonor the Gospel of Christ."[5] Fasting was considered negative to a proper joyful observance of a weekly Christian day of worship, and it is of interest that Hippolytus opposed fasting on *both the Sabbath and Sunday!*[6]

Moreover, Origen, an Alexandrian contemporary of Hippolytus, makes reference to proper "Sabbath observance" in these words: "Forsaking therefore the Judaic Sabbath observance, let us see what kind of Sabbath observance is expected of the Christian. On the Sabbath day, nothing of worldly activity should be done. If therefore desisting from all worldly works and doing nothing mundane but being free for spiritual works, you come to the church, listen to divine readings and discussions and think of heavenly things, give heed to the future life, keep before your eyes the coming judgment, disregard present and visible things in favor of the invisible and future, this is the observance of the Christian Sabbath."[7]

This evidence from Rome and Alexandria is admittedly scant, but at the very least it does seem to suggest that not all Christians in those two cities abandoned the Sabbath immediately and totally during the second century. By the time of Socrates Scholasticus and Sozomen in the fifth century, however, it is clear that the omission of special Saturday worship services in Rome and Alexandria was an established fact having some degree of antiquity.

But what was the situation elsewhere? As we look at the rest of the early Christian world, the evidence for honor to *both* Sabbath and Sunday multiplies. For example, the *Apostolic Constitutions,* a fourth-century compilation with probable Syrian or other Eastern provenance, gives a number of prescriptions relating to the Sabbath as well as Sunday. Among them are the following:

"Have before thine eyes the fear of God, and always remember the ten commandments of God. . . . Thou shalt observe the Sabbath, on account of Him who ceased from His work of creation, but ceased not from His work of providence: it is a rest for meditation of the law, not for idleness of the hands."[8]

"But keep the Sabbath, and the Lord's day festival; because the former is the memorial of the creation, and the latter of the resurrection."[9]

"Oh Lord Almighty, Thou hast created the world by Christ, and hast appointed the Sabbath in memory thereof, because that on that day Thou hast made us rest from our works, for the meditation upon Thy laws. . . . We solemnly assemble to celebrate the feast of the resurrection on the Lord's day, and rejoice on account of Him who has conquered death, and has brought life and immortality to light."[10]

"Let your judicatures be held on the second day of the week [Monday], that if any controversy arise about your sentence, having an interval till the Sabbath, you may be able to set the controversy right, and to reduce those to peace who have the contests one with another against the Lord's day."[11]

"Let the slaves work five days; but on the Sabbath-day and the Lord's day let them have leisure to go to church for instruction in piety. We have said that the Sabbath is on account of the creation, and the Lord's day of the resurrection."[12]

The interpolater of Ignatius of Antioch, who enlarged the writings of this second-century Church Father during the fourth century, states: "Let us therefore no longer keep the Sabbath after the Jewish manner, and rejoice in days of idleness; for 'he that does not work, let him not eat.' For say the [holy] oracles, 'In the sweat of thy face shalt thou eat thy bread.' But let every one of you keep the Sabbath after a spiritual manner, rejoicing in meditation on the law, not in relaxation of the body, admiring the workmanship of God, and not eating things prepared the day before, nor using lukewarm drinks, and walking within a prescribed space, nor finding delight in dancing and plaudits which have no sense in them. And after the observance of the Sabbath, let every friend of Christ keep the Lord's Day as a festival, the resurrection-day, the queen and chief of all the days [of the week]."[13]

Gregory of Nyssa in the late fourth century referred to the Sabbath and Sunday as "sisters," and about the same time Asterius of Amasea declared that it was beautiful for Christians that the "team of these two days come together"—"the Sabbath and the Lord's Day."[14] According to Asterius, each week brought the people together on these days with priests to instruct them.

In the fifth century John Cassian makes several references to church attendance on both Saturday and Sunday. In speaking of Egyptian monks, he states that "except Vespers and Nocturns, there are no public services among them in the day except on Saturday and Sunday, when they meet together at the third hour [9:00 A.M.] for the purpose of Holy Communion."[15]

Cassian also refers to a monk "who lived alone, who declared that he had never enjoyed food by himself alone, but that even if for five days running none of the brethren came to his cell he constantly put off taking food until on Saturday or Sunday he went to church for service and found some stranger whom he brought home at once to his cell."[16]

An aged presbyter named Paphnutius, so Cassian further tells us, lived in the desert of Scete, five miles from the nearest church. This man, even "when worn out with years" was not "hindered by the distance from going to church on Saturday or Sunday."[17]

Cassian has brought us once again to the fifth century, to the time when Socrates Scholasticus and Sozomen reported that in general, except in the cities of Rome and Alexandria, Christians were holding services on both Saturday and Sunday. In subsequent centuries, the Sabbath was eventually displaced by Sunday quite generally throughout Europe—as Sunday finally began to take on the character of a rest day (a story told in chapter 10). However, in Ethiopia the practice adopted was that of making "Sabbaths" of both Saturday and Sunday (see chapter 9).[18]

Whence Sunday?

The preceding discussion has alluded to the fact that Sunday's achievement of predominance as the weekly Christian day for worship and for rest occurred in two major stages: (1) it originally arose as a day for *worship* services only, and (2) it later took on the character of a day of *rest*. In the former role, there would be no reason for conflict with the Saturday rest day—and indeed, for centuries both days were honored, as we have seen. In the latter role, however, the potential for conflict of Sunday with the Sabbath is obvious. That such conflict was appearing even as early as the fourth century is revealed in the literature, a point to which we shall return later. But first we must query, How did Sunday originate as a weekly day for Christian *worship* services?

Obviously, the situation of a concurrent rise of the Christian Sunday and demise of the Saturday Sabbath, as described by Bacchiocchi for Rome in chapter 7, was not characteristic of most of the Christian world. As we have seen, for centuries Saturday continued to be observed alongside the emerging Sunday throughout Christendom generally. Moreover, a fact of considerable importance regarding the rise of the weekly Christian Sunday is that when it did emerge it was regularly looked upon by the Christians as a day to honor Christ's resurrection. This resurrection connection is important to investigate, particularly in view of recent discoveries.[19]

In the New Testament, Christ's resurrection is symbolically related to the first fruits of the barley harvest, just as His death is related to the slaying of the Paschal lamb (see 1 Cor. 15:20 and 5:7). The offering of the *omer* or wave sheaf of the barley harvest first fruits was an *annual* event among the Jews. What has generally gone unrecognized about this annual festival is that at the time of the rise of the Christian church the Jews had two different methods of reckoning the day for its celebration.

The time of observance is based on Leviticus 23:11, which states that the wave sheaf of the barley harvest was to be offered in the season of unleavened bread on "the morrow after the Sabbath." The Pharisees interpreted this as the day after the Passover Sabbath. Their procedure was to celebrate the Passover Sabbath on Nisan 15 (the Paschal lamb had been slain on Nisan 14) and to offer the first fruits wave sheaf on Nisan 16. In different years, these dates would fall on different days of the week (similar to our Christmas and New Year's days).

On the other hand, the Essenes and Saducean Boethusians interpreted "the morrow after the Sabbath" as the day after a weekly Sabbath—therefore always a Sunday. The day of Pentecost also always fell on a Sunday—"the morrow after the seventh Sabbath" from the day of the offering of the barley-harvest first fruits (see Lev. 23:15, 16).[20]

SABBATH AND SUNDAY FROM 2D THROUGH 5TH CENTURIES

It would be natural for Christians to continue a first-fruits celebration. However, they would not keep it as a Jewish festival. Instead, they would keep it in honor of Christ's resurrection. After all, was not Christ the *true First Fruits* (1 Cor. 15:20), and was not His resurrection of the utmost importance (see verses 14, 17-19)?

But when would Christians keep such a resurrection festival? Would they do it every week? No. Rather, they would do it *annually*, as had been their custom in the Jewish celebration of the first fruits.

And which of the two types of reckoning would they choose—that of the Pharisees, or that of the Essenes and Boethusians? Undoubtedly, *both*. Those who had been influenced by the Pharisees would hold their Easter festival on a different day of the week year by year, and those who had been influenced by the Boethusians or by the Essenes would hold their Easter festival on a Sunday every year.

This harmonizes precisely with the situation existing in the Easter controversy toward the end of the second century.[21] At that time Asian Christians (Christians in the Roman province of Asia in western Asia Minor) placed emphasis on Nisan 14, regardless of the day of the week. But Christians throughout most of the rest of the Christian world—including Gaul, Rome, Corinth, Pontus (in northern Asia Minor), Alexandria, Mesopotamia, and Palestine (even Jerusalem itself)—held to a Sunday-Easter observance. Early sources indicate that both practices stemmed from apostolic tradition.[22]

A reconstruction of church history that sees the earliest Christian Sunday as an *annual* Easter rather than as a weekly observance makes historical sense. The habit of keeping the annual Jewish first-fruits festival day could easily have been transferred into an *annual* Christian resurrection celebration in honor of Christ, the First Fruits. There was, by contrast, no such habit nor even psychological background for keeping a weekly resurrection celebration.

The later-emerging *weekly* Christian Sunday would then have arisen as an extension of the annual Easter Sunday. This sort of rise of the weekly Christian Sunday indicates, moreover, how and why it took on the character of a resurrection festival: It was simply an extension of the annual celebration of Christ's resurrection.

Precisely what factors were operative in the rise of the weekly Christian Sunday from the annual one in this way is not clear; but one interesting suggestion has arisen because of the fact that almost all early Christians not only observed both Easter and Pentecost on Sundays but also considered the whole seven-week season between the two holidays to have special significance.[23] J. van Goudoever feels that perhaps the Sundays in that entire season from Easter to Pentecost had special importance too.[24] If so, other concerns already present could have aided in extending Sunday observance from an annual to a weekly basis, spreading first to the Sundays during the Easter-to-Pentecost season itself and then eventually to Sundays throughout the entire year.[25]

Such an annual Sunday celebration could have furnished a source from which Christians in Alexandria and Rome inaugurated the weekly Sunday as a substitute for the Sabbath. But their early rejection of the Sabbath was on grounds other than that of simply introducing worship services on Sundays, for there was nothing inherent in this Sunday weekly resurrection festival to cause it to replace the Sabbath. In fact, as we have seen, generally throughout early Christendom, with the exception of Rome and Alexandria, it was simply a special day observed *side by side with the Sabbath*.

Sunday Becomes a Rest Day

The story of Sunday's becoming a rest day, and as such displacing the Sabbath, is told at some length in chapter 10; hence only highlights will be noted here.

Undoubtedly, one of the most important factors that influenced Sunday's taking on the character of a Christian day of rest is to be found in the activities of Emperor Constantine the Great in the early fourth century, followed by later "Christian emperors." Not only did Constantine give Christianity a new status within the Roman Empire (from being persecuted to being honored) but he also gave Sunday the status of becoming a civil rest day. His famous Sunday law of March 7, 321, reads:

"On the venerable Day of the Sun let the magistrates and people residing in cities rest, and let all workshops be closed. In the country, however, persons engaged in agriculture may freely and lawfully continue their pursuits; because it often happens that another day is not so suitable for grain-sowing or for vine-planting; lest by neglecting the proper moment for such operations the bounty of heaven should be lost." [26]

This was the first in a series of steps taken by Constantine and by later Roman emperors in regulating Sunday observance. It is obvious that this first Sunday law was not particularly Christian in orientation. We may note, for instance, the pagan designation "venerable Day of the Sun." Also, it is evident that Constantine did not base his Sunday regulations on the Decalogue, for he exempted agricultural work—a type of work strictly prohibited in the Sabbath commandment in Exodus 20:8-11.

In A.D. 386, Theodosius I and Gratian Valentinian extended Sunday restrictions so that litigations should entirely cease on that day and there would be no public or private payment of debt. Laws forbidding Sunday circus, theater, and horse racing also followed.[27]

The question arises, How did the Christian church react to such *civil legislation* making Sunday a rest day? As desirable as such legislation may have seemed to Christians from one standpoint (for example, there had been earlier reference to leisure *for church attendance* on Sundays[28]), it also created a dilemma. Except for church attendance, Sunday had heretofore been a workday; therefore, what kinds of change would have to be made to accommodate it as a rest day? What, for instance, would happen to nuns such as those described by Jerome in Bethlehem, who, after following their mother superior to church and then back to their communions, devoted the rest of their time on Sunday "to their allotted tasks, and made garments either for themselves or else for others"?[29]

Moreover, there already was one Sabbath rest day each week. Could Christians afford to have *two* rest days—both Saturday and Sunday? As already mentioned, this latter concern was generally answered in the negative, though in Ethiopia two "Sabbaths" each week were observed.

Perhaps a first hint of the new trend regarding the weekly Christian Sunday comes as early as the time of Constantine himself—in a work commonly attributed to the church historian Eusebius: a commentary on Psalm 92, "the Sabbath Psalm." The author of this commentary writes that Christians would fulfill on the Lord's day all that in this psalm was prescribed for the Sabbath, including worship of God early in the morning. He then adds that through the new covenant the Sabbath celebration was transferred to "the Lord's Day."[30]

Later in the same century Ephraem Syrus suggested that honor was due "to the Lord's Day, the firstborn of all days," which had "taken away the right of the firstborn from the Sabbath."[31] Then he goes on to point out that the law prescribes that rest should be given to servants and animals. Here the reflection of the Old Testament Sabbath commandment is obvious.

The earliest church council to deal with Sunday as a day of rest was a regional one, meeting in Laodicea about A.D. 364. Although this council still manifested respect for the Sabbath as well as Sunday in the special Scripture readings, it nonetheless stipulated the following in its Canon 29: "Christians shall not Judaize and be idle on Saturday but shall work on that day; but the Lord's day they shall especially honour, and, as being Christians, shall, if possible, do no work on that day. If, however, they are found Judaizing, they shall be shut out from Christ."[32]

The regulation with regard to working on Sunday was rather moderate in that Christians should not work on that day *if possible!* However, more significant was the fact that this council reversed the original practice regarding the seventh-day Sabbath, which was now to be considered a workday.

Further conciliar enactments, as well as decrees by rulers, including Charlemagne, belong primarily to the sixth century and onward, a story told in some detail in chapter 10.

Evidence of Controversy

In the references from early Christian literature noted above, we have found that especially during the fourth and fifth centuries there was an increase in mention of *both* Sabbath and Sunday. This influx of references, particularly those of a polemical nature, bears added testimony to the conflict that was arising between the two days subsequent to Constantine's Sunday law.

On the one hand, the *Apostolic Constitutions,* for instance, stressed observance of *both* Saturday and Sunday, requiring that slaves work only five days and on Saturday and Sunday have leisure to go to church. On the other hand, we have found the Council of Laodicea requiring work on Saturday.

Another pointed reference with polemical tone comes from John Chrysostom (died A.D. 407), who declared, "We are become a laughing-stock to Jews and Greeks, seeing that the Church is divided into a thousand parties. . . . You will now understand why Paul calls circumcision a subversion of the Gospel. There are many among us now, who fast on the same day as the Jews, and keep the sabbaths in the same manner; and we endure it nobly or rather ignobly and basely"![33]

The controversy regarding fasting on the Sabbath, a controversy particularly prominent in the literature from the mid-fourth century into the fifth century, may add its weight of evidence to the changing situation for the Sabbath in relationship to Sunday. Although in Rome and in some other places in the West such a fast was adopted as a regular weekly practice, thus making the Sabbath a gloomy and rejected day, other places in the West (including Milan in northern Italy) and the entire Eastern Church resisted the innovation. Important witness to this general situation is afforded, for instance, in various statements by Augustine of Hippo (died A.D. 430) and by his later contemporary John Cassian.[34] Also, a half century to a century earlier, two particularly poignant statements with strong polemical overtones come from the interpolater of Ignatius and from the *Apostolic Constitutions:*

"If any one fasts on the Lord's Day or on the Sabbath, except on the paschal Sabbath only, he is a murderer of Christ."[35] (All Christians considered it appropriate to fast on the Paschal Sabbath, the anniversary of the Sabbath during which Christ was in the tomb.)

"If any one of the clergy be found to fast on the Lord's day, or on the Sabbath-day, excepting one only, let him be deprived; but if he be one of the laity, let him be suspended."[36]

At the time when Alexandria and Rome rejected Sabbath observance in the second century, polemical overtones negative to the Sabbath were evidenced in the writings of Barnabas of Alexandria and Justin Martyr.[37] Now, some two centuries later, after the time of Constantine the Great, the polemics begin to appear on a widespread basis as the new Sunday *rest* day began to conflict with the original Saturday *rest* day.[38]

Summary

It has become obvious that the displacement of Saturday by Sunday as a day of weekly Christian worship and rest was a long and slow process. Until the second century there is no concrete evidence of a Christian *weekly* Sunday celebration anywhere. The first specific references during that century come from Alexandria and Rome, places that also early rejected observance of the seventh-day Sabbath.

In this early substitution of Sunday for Saturday, however, the Christian churches in Alexandria and Rome were unique. Evidence from the fifth century indicates that also at that time *both Sabbath and Sunday* were observed generally throughout the Christian world—except in Rome and Alexandria.

Moreover, when the Christian weekly Sunday first emerged, it continued to be a day of work, although it included a worship service in honor of Christ's resurrection. This weekly celebration of Christ's resurrection appears to have been an extension of an *annual* Sunday-Easter resurrection festival. The latter, in turn, found its antecedent in the Jewish first-fruits celebration mentioned in Leviticus 23:11—also an *annual* event.

Finally, from the time of Constantine onward, a trend developed toward making Sunday a Christian Sabbath. This process brought about a widespread conflict of Sunday with the seventh-day Sabbath, and eventually in medieval times this Sunday "Sabbath" came to displace the original Saturday Sabbath generally throughout Europe. In Ethiopia, on the other hand, both Saturday and Sunday were considered to be "Sabbaths."

Addendum

Inasmuch as the significant early reference to Sunday by Justin Martyr of Rome *(1 Apology* 67) is not stated in full in the main text of this volume, it is appended here as it appears in *ANF* 1:186:

"And on the day called Sunday, all who live in cities or in the country gather together to one place, and the memoirs of the apostles or the writings of the prophets are read, as long as time permits; then, when the reader has ceased, the president verbally instructs, and exhorts to the imitation of these good things. Then we all rise together and pray, and, as we before said, when our prayer is ended, bread and wine and water are brought, and the president in like manner offers prayers and thanksgivings, according to his ability, and the people assent, saying Amen; and there is a distribution to each, and a participation of that over which thanks have been given, and to those who are absent a portion is sent by the deacons. And they who are well to do, and willing, give what each thinks fit; and what is collected is deposited with the president, who succours the orphans and widows, and those who, through sickness or any other cause, are in want, and those who are in bonds, and the strangers sojourning among us, and in a word takes care of all who are in need. But Sunday is the day on which we all hold our common assembly, because it is the first day on which God, having wrought a change in the darkness and matter, made the world; and Jesus Christ our Saviour on the same day rose from the dead."

NOTES

[1] Epistle of Barnabas, chap. 15 *(ANF* 1:147).
[2] Justin Martyr, *1 Apology* 67 *(ANF* 1:186). Willy Rordorf believes this Sunday-morning worship service as described by Justin took place *"before daybreak"* (see his *Sunday* [Philadelphia, 1968], pp. 264, 265).
[3] Socrates Scholasticus *Ecclesiastical History* 5. 22 *(NPNF/2* 2:132).
[4] Sozomen *Ecclesiastical History* 7. 19 *(NPNF/2* 2:390).
[5] Hippolytus *Commentary on Daniel* 4. 20. 3. For Greek text and French translation, see Maurice Lefèvre, *Hippolyte, Commentaire sur Daniel* (Paris, 1947), pp. 300-303.
[6] For details on the Sabbath fast, see K. A. Strand, "Some Notes on the Sabbath Fast in Early Christianity," *AUSS* 3 (1965):167-174, as well as the material on this topic given in the present volume by Samuele Bacchiocchi in chapter 7.
[7] Origen, Homily 23, on Numbers, par. 4 *(PG* 12:749, 750). It is clear that in the context Origen is definitely speaking of Saturday. What may not be equally certain, however, is how the reference to church attendance on Saturday may apply to Alexandria.
[8] *Apostolic Constitutions* 2. 36 *(ANF* 7:413).
[9] *Ibid.*, 7. 23 *(ANF* 7:469).
[10] *Ibid.*, 7. 36 *(ANF* 7:474).
[11] *Ibid.*, 2. 47 *(ANF* 7:417).
[12] *Ibid.*, 8. 33 *(ANF* 7:495).
[13] Pseudo-Ignatius, *Magnesians*, long version, chap. 9 *(ANF* 1:62, 63).
[14] Gregory of Nyssa, *On Reproof (PG* 46:309, 310); Asterius of Amasea, Homily 5, on Matthew 19:3 *(PG* 40:225, 226).
[15] Cassian *Institutes* 3. 2 *(NPNF/2* 11:213).
[16] *Ibid.*, 5. 26 *(NPNF/2* 11:243).
[17] Idem, *Conferences* 3. 1 *(NPNF/2* 11:319).
[18] Apparently the first documentary evidence we have for Sunday's being referred to as a "Sabbath" is found in an interpolated passage in the Ethiopic version of the *Egyptian Church Order*. After a heightened version of a statement from the *Apostolic Constitutions* ("Ye and your slaves and your servants, do your work five days. And on the sabbath and first day ye shall not do any work in them"), an explanation is given regarding the institution of the Sabbath at Creation, followed by this unique commentary: "Then the First day is the day of the resurrection of our Lord Jesus Christ. And the first (day) was named sabbath, and both were named sabbaths. And in the prophets also he plainly declares that both are sabbaths, and says: Honor my sabbaths. . . . And all of those who honor my sabbaths, and profane them not, and continue in my ordinances, I will bring to my holy mountain. . . . Attend and understand when he said, My sabbaths, he said (it) of both days."—Eng. trans. in G. Horner, *The Statutes of the Apostles* [London, 1904], pp. 210, 211. See my further discussion in "A Note on the Sabbath in Coptic Sources," *AUSS* 6 (1968):150-157.
[19] For a more detailed discussion of the matters treated in the next few paragraphs, see my following publications: *The Early Christian Sabbath* (Worthington, Ohio, 1979), pp. 43-52; "John as Quartodeciman: A Reappraisal," *JBL* 84 (1965):251-258; and "Another Look at the 'Lord's Day' in the Early Church and in Rev. I.10," *New Testament Studies* 13 (1966-1967):174-181. The Dead Sea scrolls, including the recently published "Temple Scroll," have been important in illuminating the situation in Judaism just prior to and at the time of the rise of the Christian church.
[20] The Essenes and Boethusians actually chose Sundays a week apart because of a difference in their understanding of whether the Sabbath of Lev. 23:11 was the Sabbath *during* or the Sabbath *after* the Feast of Unleavened Bread. They appear also to have reckoned on the basis of a solar calendar in contrast to the lunar calendar used by the Pharisees.
[21] Eusebius *Ecclesiastical History* 5. 23-25, provides the details *(NPNF/2* 1:241-244). See my further discussion in the publications mentioned in note 19.

²²*Ibid.*, 5. 23. 1 (*NPNF*/2 1:241); also Sozomen *Eccl. Hist.* 7. 19 (*NPNF*/2 2:390). It may be added that this view regarding the origin of the Sunday Easter, at a time when Christian influences were still moving largely from East to West rather than *vice versa*, is certainly more realistic than to suppose that a Sunday Easter of Western origin had so early in church history replaced the Nisan 14-15-16 commemoration virtually everywhere throughout the Christian world—both East and West.

²³ The special importance of this season is indicated, e.g., by Tertullian, *The Chaplet*, chap. 3; *On Baptism*, chap. 19; and *On Fasting*, chap. 14 (*ANF* 3:94, 678, and 4:112).

²⁴ J. van Goudoever, *Biblical Calendars*, 2d ed. (Leiden, 1961), p. 167.

²⁵ Philip Carrington, *The Primitive Christian Calendar* (Cambridge, England, 1952), p. 38, offers another suggestion: Since crops could hardly have been ripe everywhere on the two Sundays especially set aside (day of barley first fruits and Pentecost day), may it not have been implied that *any* Sunday within the fifty days was a proper day for the offering of the first fruits? For an excellent discussion of the whole question of Easter in relation to the weekly Sunday, see Lawrence T. Geraty, "The Pascha and the Origin of Sunday Observance," *AUSS* 3 (1965):85-96.

²⁶ *Codex Justinianus* 3. 12. 3, trans. in Philip Schaff, *History of the Christian Church*, 5th ed. (New York, 1902), 3:380, note 1.

²⁷ See, e.g., *Theodosian Code* 11. 7. 13 and 15. 5. 5, trans. by Clyde Pharr (Princeton, N.J., 1952), pp. 300, 433.

²⁸ E.g., Tertullian *On Prayer* 23 (*ANF* 3:689), refers to "deferring even our businesses" on Sundays. The context of this statement suggests that what is meant is not total rest on Sundays, but leisure for church attendance (see the discussion by Rordorf, *op. cit.*, pp. 158-160).

²⁹ See Jerome, Epistle 108. 20 (*NPNF*/2 6:206).

³⁰ See Eusebius, *Commentary on the Psalms*, on Ps. 91 (92):2, 3 (*PG* 23:1172). The attribution to Eusebius is not certain.

³¹ *S. Ephraem Syri hymni et sermones*, ed. by T. J. Lamy (1882), 1:542-544.

³² Charles J. Hefele, *A History of the Councils of the Church*, 2 (Edinburgh, 1876):316. Canon 16 (*ibid.*, p. 310) refers to lections; and Canons 49 and 51 (*ibid.*, p. 320) reveal that Saturday as well as Sunday had special consideration during Lent.

³³ Comment on Galatians 1:7 in *Commentary on Galatians* (*NPNF*/1 13:8).

³⁴ See especially Augustine, Epistle 36 (to Casulanus); Epistle 54 (to Januarius), par. 3; Epistle 82 (to Jerome), par. 14 (*NPNF*/1 1:265-270, 300, 301, 353, 354); and John Cassian, *Institutes* 3. 9, 10 (*NPNF*/2 11:217, 218). Augustine's epistles may be numbered somewhat differently in editions other than *NPNF*.

³⁵ Pseudo-Ignatius, *Philippians* 13 (*ANF* 1:119).

³⁶ Canon 64 in *Apost. Const.* (*ANF* 7:504). The canon is numbered "66 (65)" in Charles J. Hefele, *A History of the Christian Councils*, 2d ed. 1 (Edinburgh, 1883):484.

³⁷ Epistle of Barnabas, chap. 15 (*ANF* 1:146, 147); and in Justin Martyr, e.g., *Dialogue with Trypho* 12, 18, 19, 23, 43 (*ANF* 1:200, 203, 204, 206, 216). In chapter 7, Samuele Bacchiocchi deals briefly with Justin Martyr's attitude toward the Sabbath (see p. 137).

³⁸ It may be mentioned that a forerunner of the *Apostolic Constitutions* entitled the *Didascalia Apostolorum*, usually dated third century, contains some anti-Sabbath polemic. However, it should also be noted that the *Didascalia Apostolorum* had an evolution (especially in its Syriac and Latin forms) that undoubtedly involved addition or interpolation of materials during the fourth century or even later. In any event, the context of the anti-Sabbath remarks shows a proclivity for "the Romans"—a group that as we have seen, already substituted Sunday for the Sabbath in the second century. For the main anti-Sabbath polemic in the *Didascalia* and its context, see R. Hugh Connolly, trans., *Didascalia Apostolorum* (Oxford, 1929), p. 238.

APPENDIX C

On Esteeming One Day as Better Than Another—Romans 14:5, 6*

Raoul Dederen

ONE man esteems one day as better than another, while another man esteems all days alike. Let every one be fully convinced in his own mind. He who observes the day, observes it in honor of the Lord. He also who eats, eats in honor of the Lord, since he gives thanks to God; while he who abstains, abstains in honor of the Lord and gives thanks to God" (Rom. 14:5, 6, R.S.V.).

What was in Paul's mind when he indicated in the above text the Christian's perfect liberty either to esteem one day above another or to fail to make any distinction at all among them? Was he objecting to Sabbathkeeping and attempting to prove that the "Jewish Sabbath" was "nailed to the cross" as some would hold? What was he saying to the Christian community in Rome?

Little is known regarding the beginning of this Christian community. It seems certain, though, that there was a large church at Rome around A.D. 58 when Paul wrote this Epistle, a church composed, like most churches, of mixed Jewish and Gentile membership (see chaps. 1:13-16; 2:9, 10, 17; 11:13, 31). "When the Neronian persecution broke out (c. 64)," writes C. H. Dodd, "the Christians of Rome were 'a large body' (I Clem. VI, I), 'an immense multitude' (Tacitus *Annals* XV, 44).[1]

The passage under study is part of the ethical or practical section of the Epistle (chapters 12-16). Far from being a new development in Paul's outline, this section is in fact rooted in the first main part of the letter (chapters 1-11). The recurring theme in the first part is that of justification by faith, the universal sinfulness of man, and the universal grace of God. The statement we are considering (chap. 14:5, 6) falls within the large section of the Epistle devoted explicitly to the application of Christian truths to the daily Christian life.

---

*Abbreviated from "On Esteeming One Day as Better Than Another," *AUSS* 9 (January, 1971):16-35.

The Immediate Context

It will be helpful to take a closer look at the immediate context:

"As for the man who is weak in faith, welcome him, but not for disputes over opinions. One believes he may eat anything, while the weak man eats only vegetables. Let not him who eats despise him who abstains, and let not him who abstains pass judgment on him who eats; for God has welcomed him. Who are you to pass judgment on the servant of another? It is before his own master that he stands or falls. And he will be upheld, for the Master is able to make him stand.

"One man esteems one day as better than another, while another man esteems all days alike. Let every one be fully convinced in his own mind. He who observes the day, observes it in honor of the Lord. He also who eats, eats in honor of the Lord, since he gives thanks to God; while he who abstains, abstains in honor of the Lord and gives thanks to God" (verses 1-6, R.S.V.).

A cursory reading of Romans 14 indicates that there existed in the Christian community of Rome a controversy in connection with both diet and the observance of certain days. In fact, the matter of "esteeming one day as better than another" is merely interjected in a passage that has to do entirely with a controversy that existed in the Roman church on the matter of meat eating *versus* vegetarianism and abstinence from wine (see verses 1, 21).

Exactly what the problem was remains uncertain. But after having dealt with the more general aspects of Christian behavior, Paul turns to a problem that was perplexing that particular community.[2] As in most Christian communities, tension arose between the "old-fashioned" and the "emancipated," or "enlightened," in T. W. Manson's words.[3] In this particular case the "weak" were vegetarians, the "strong" were prepared to eat all kinds of food.

Who Were These Ascetics?

The tendency has been to point immediately to Jewish Christians who still adhered to the shadows of the Old Testament laws and whose minds were not yet sufficiently established as the "weak" believers mentioned in this passage. Ascetic trends, however, existed in paganism as well as in Judaism.[4] Those who followed the Orphic Mystery cult and the Pythagoreans appear to have been vegetarians. Gnostic tendencies toward asceticism, too, may have obtained some following in Rome.[5] But those do not satisfy all the circumstances. Roman Christians were in the habit, says Paul, of observing scrupulously certain days; and this custom did not, as far as we know, prevail among any heathen sect.

It seems difficult also to retain the possibility that Paul was speaking of Jewish Christians who rejected wine (verse 21) and who would have serious scruples about eating unclean meats of which others among the congregation partook. Judaism did not reject wine except for the duration of a vow; and in Rome, the "weak" brethren objected to eating flesh at all, an objection that was not founded on the law of Moses but on ascetic motives foreign to the eleventh chapter of Leviticus.[6]

Since all meat was refused, some have postulated that the reason could very well be the same as that given in 1 Corinthians, namely, the difficulty of obtaining meat that had not previously been offered in sacrifice to deities.[7] There is, in fact, a rather close affinity between Romans 14 on the one hand and 1 Corinthians 8 and 10 on the other.[8] But Paul's silence concerning idols and demons in Romans

ON ESTEEMING ONE DAY AS BETTER THAN ANOTHER

14, as well as the mention of the observance of certain days, inclines many to conclude that there is no real parallel between the two situations.[9]

It is equally possible that those refraining from meat and wine might have been Christians of Jewish origin influenced by Essenism. We know that at that time there was a large Jewish colony in Rome, and that the Essenes sought to attain a higher sanctity by depriving the flesh of the satisfaction of its desires. As a possible outgrowth of Pharisaism, Essenism had much in common with it, although it also found itself at great variance with it. Not only was ceremonial purity an absorbing passion with the Essene, but in his desire to observe carefully the distinction laid down by Moses regarding meats as lawful and unlawful, he went far beyond the Pharisee. Many believe that he even drank no wine nor touched any animal food, at least at times.[10]

Less objection applies to this proposed solution if it is presented, not with the idea that Essenism existed in Rome as a strict organization (which is highly improbable), but that there was an Essene influence in the Jewish community there. Such is probable, and the view fulfills the three conditions of the case. The Essenes were Jewish and ascetic, and they observed certain days. "There is some evidence," writes F. F. Bruce, "that such 'baptist' communities were found in the Dispersion as well as in Judaea. The Jewish community of Rome, in particular, appears to have preserved some characteristic features of this 'non-conformist' Judaism—features which, as we may gather from the Hippolytan *Apostolic Tradition*, were carried over into Roman Christianity."[11]

On Esteeming Certain Days Above Others

At this point, in a discussion that has to do with a controversy on the matter of meat eating versus vegetarianism, Paul interjects another issue, that of esteeming "one day as better than another" (verse 5, R.S.V.). The statement presents no particular difficulty as far as its translation is concerned. It has been very faithfully rendered by the translators. But is it possible to determine what days Paul had in mind when he wrote that a Christian is at perfect liberty either to esteem one day above another or to fail to make any distinction at all among them?

Some commentators have argued that the distinction here touched upon refers to the seventh-day Sabbath. "What other day would any Roman Christian judge to be above other days?" asks R. C. H. Lenski.[12] In this interpretation, Paul considers that all distinction of the Sabbath day from other days has been abolished by Christianity.

It is to be noted, however, that the attempt to connect the Sabbath of the Decalogue with the "days" mentioned in this passage is not convincing for everyone.[13] Who could have a divine commandment before him and say to others: "You can treat that commandment as you please; it really makes no difference whether you keep it or not"? No apostle could conduct such an argument. And probably no man would be more surprised at that interpretation than Paul himself, who had utmost respect for the Decalogue, God's law, which is "holy, and just, and good" (chap. 7:12). Christ, the norm of all Pauline teaching, was indisputably a Sabbathkeeper. And Paul himself, who evidently cannot be reckoned among the "weak," worshiped on the Sabbath "as was his custom" (Acts 17:2, R.S.V.; cf. Luke 4:16).

There is no conclusive evidence to the contrary. Paul was in no doubt as to the validity of the weekly Sabbath. Thus, to assume that when they were converted to Christianity by Paul, Gentiles or Jews would be anxious to give up the "Jewish" Sabbath for their "own day" is hardly likely. This could be expected only at some later time in the history of the Christian church, and for other reasons.

The Jewish Ceremonial Sabbaths

It has been argued with a great deal of plausibility that Paul was simply referring to the sacred days of the Jewish economy, the seven annual ceremonial Sabbaths instituted by God after Israel's deliverance from Egypt.[14] Some regarded them as having abiding sanctity, while others considered them as abrogated with the passing away of the ceremonial institutions.

Paul may have had in mind the case of Jewish converts endeavoring to make a case for the observance of these yearly feasts and sabbaths. But the special days of the week referred to in our passage were probably fast days. This suggestion is based on the context itself, in which abstinence is the predominant feature. It may even be that among the faithful who strictly abstained from flesh and wine—or in addition to them—there were others who did so only on certain days. Paul's statement in Romans 14:2, "One believes he may eat anything, while the weak man eats only vegetables" (R.S.V.), is curiously analogous to his thought in verse 5, "One man esteems one day as better than another, while another man esteems all days alike" (R.S.V.). He mentions the two cases together, and later in the chapter he declares that a man should not be judged by his eating (verses 10-13), which may imply that Paul is referring to fast days. It appears quite probable from the context that Paul here is correlating the eating with the observance of days. Most likely—although it is impossible to ascertain this—the apostle is dealing with fast days in a context of either partial or total abstinence.[15]

Here again the Essenes may have caused the problem. It is certainly significant that besides abstaining from meat and wine—at least at times—they were also very specific in the matter of observing days. They sanctified certain days that were not observed by the general stream of Jews. Although the Essenes' principal feasts were the same, "as in the rest of Israel, others have been added which seem to have been unique to the sect."[16] Their liturgical calendar, set up according to the calendar of Jubilees, was different from the official priestly calendar in Jerusalem. Some have suggested that the calendar of Jubilees represented the ancient liturgical computation of the Temple itself, later abandoned at Jerusalem in favor of the lunar-solar calendar in use in the Hellenistic world. "It is not impossible that this substitution gave rise to the Essene secession," remarks Marcel Simon.[17] As might be expected, there was a predilection for these particular days.

Some pertinent observations emerge now that could well tie in the matter of diet with that of esteeming certain days above others. The Essenes scrupulously abstained from meat and wine—at least at times. They added certain feast days to the regular Jewish calendar. The discussion over the point existed in Jewry prior to the advent of Christianity. Could it be that the controversy was carried over into the Christian church and finds itself reflected in Romans 14? In this case, the practice of the weak may be compared with the early Christian custom indicated in the *Didache* of fasting twice every week.[18] Is it not significant, and relevant as well, that we have in this document too a matter of diet *and* days connected in a controversial issue?

Although the aforegoing interpretation cannot be considered as an established fact, it cannot be ignored, and indeed seems to be the most likely possibility in a context in which abstinence is a predominant feature. Therefore I suggest that Paul in Romans 14:5, 6 is referring to practices of abstinence and fasting on regular, fixed days.[19]

NOTES

[1] C. H. Dodd, *The Epistle of Paul to the Romans* (London, 1954), pp. xvii-xx.

[2] Although some have suggested that Paul might simply have been giving general counsel arising from past experience (see, for instance, William Sanday and Arthur C. Headlam, *A Critical and Exegetical Commentary on the Epistle to the Romans*, 5th ed. [Edinburgh, 1958], pp. 399-403), I believe with Emil Brunner that "a certain split had occurred in the church at Rome" *(The Letter to the Romans* [Philadelphia, 1949], p. 114).

[3] T. W. Manson, *Romans*, in *Peake's Commentary on the Bible*, Matthew Black, ed. (London, 1964), p. 951.

[4] For a list of the major groups, see Otto Michel, *Der Brief an die Romer*, 10th ed. (Göttingen, 1955), p. 297.

[5] Hans Jonas, *The Gnostic Religion* (Boston, 1958), p. 33.

[6] Most vegetarians in those days abstained from meat on the basis of their metaphysical concept of the world. Most Christian vegetarians today do so mainly in striving for good health. For the significance of Κοίνος used in Romans 14:14, see my article "On Esteeming One Day as Better Than Another," *AUSS 9* (January, 1971):20, note 12.

[7] Anders Nygren, *Commentary on the Romans* (Philadelphia, 1949), p. 442. Cf. A. M. Hunter, *The Epistle to the Romans* (London, 1957), p. 117.

[8] For a closer look at this affinity, see my article (in note 6), p. 21.

[9] Cf. Adolf von Schlatter, *Gottes Gerechtigkeit*, 4th ed. (Stuttgart, 1965), pp. 364, 368; Michel, *op. cit.*, p. 256; Ernst Gaugler, *Der Römerbrief* (Zürich, 1952), 2:326.

[10] Whereas some, on the basis of the Dead Sea scrolls, consider that the Essenes used wine, others regard it as improbable in view of the use of the word *tirosh*: see J. van der Ploeg, *The Excavations at Qumran* (London, 1958), p. 212, and E. F. Sutcliffe, *The Monks of Qumran* (Westminster, Md., 1960), p. 110. Archeologists have uncovered numerous deposits of bones in jars and pieces of jars, bones of animals (mainly sheep and goats) that had been cooked or roasted. Whether these are the remains of animals the flesh of which was eaten or are evidence of the sacrifices that the Essenes felt necessary to offer within the purity of their own community is a matter of debate; see Kurt Schubert, *The Dead Sea Community* (New York, 1959), p. 23; J. van der Ploeg, "The Meals of the Essenes," *Journal of Semetic Studies* 2 (1957):172; R. de Vaux, *Revue biblique* 63 (1956):73, 74, 549, 550; W. R. Farmer, *IDB* (New York, 1962), 2:148.

[11] F. F. Bruce, "'To the Hebrews' or 'to the Essenes'?" *New Testament Studies* 9 (1962-1963):227.

[12] R. C. Lenski, *The Interpretation of St. Paul's Epistle to the Romans* (Columbus, Ohio, 1945), p. 821.

[13] See, for instance, Joseph Parker, *Romans and Galatians, The People's Bible* (New York, 1901), 26:123-125; A. Barnes, "Romans," *Notes on the New Testament* (London, 1832), 4:299, 300; Wilber T. Dayton, *Romans and Galatians,* Wesleyan Bible Commentary (Grand Rapids, Mich., 1965), 5:85, 86.

[14] See Leviticus 23 and Numbers 28, 29.

[15] James Denney, "Romans," *The Expositor's Greek Testament*, W. R. Nicoll, ed. (Grand Rapids, Mich., 1961), p. 702; Joseph Huby, *Saint Paul, Epître aux Romains* (Paris, 1957), pp. 455, 456; Gaugler, *op. cit.*, p. 333.

[16] Marcel Simon, *Les sectes juives au temps de Jésus* (Paris, 1960), p. 62.

[17] *Ibid.*, pp. 62, 63. Cf. A. Jaubert, *La date de la Cenè, calendrier biblique et liturgie chrétienne* (Paris, 1957), pp. 51-56.

[18] The *Didache* (8:1) warns Christians not to fast with the hypocrites on the second and fifth days of the week, but rather on the fourth and sixth days.

[19] See F. J. Leenhardt, *The Epistle to the Romans* (London, 1961), pp. 348, 349. M. J. Lagrange declares, "Il est assez clair, d'après le contexte, qu'il s'agit d'abstinence."—*Saint Paul, Epître aux Romains* (Paris, 1950), p. 325.

APPENDIX D

The "Sabbath Days" of Colossians 2:16, 17

Kenneth H. Wood

THE historic position of the Seventh-day Adventist Church on Colossians 2:16 is that the "sabbath days" mentioned in this verse are festival sabbaths prescribed by the laws of Moses (Lev. 23:32, 37-39), not the seventh-day Sabbath of the fourth commandment of the Decalogue. Individuals here and there have recognized that the arguments used to support this position are not coercive, but the position has seldom been challenged. A review of church publications reveals that writers have set forth and defended the historic view using one or more of the following four arguments.

1. The Colossian believers, being confused by a heresy that sought to impose on them various requirements of the Jewish ceremonial law, needed to distinguish between the moral and ceremonial aspects of the Torah, or law. The heresy very likely included some pagan and Gnostic elements, but the heart of it, as at Galatia, seems to have been legalistic, Jewish ceremonialism. Logically, then, Paul would have set forth the truth that to perform ceremonial rites as a means of salvation was not only futile but an implicit denial of the fact that Jesus was the Messiah, the One who, by fulfilling the types, made them meaningless. And, to help the Colossians identify the parts of the Torah that no longer were binding, he mentioned several rituals and festivals prescribed in the ceremonial law.

2. The religious activities listed in verse 16 are similar in order and content to those mentioned elsewhere in the Scriptures where the sacrifices and festivals of the ceremonial law are set forth. For example, in Ezekiel 45:17 God says: "It shall be the prince's part to give burnt offerings, and meat offerings, and drink offerings, in the feasts, and in the new moons, and in the sabbaths, in all solemnities of the house of Israel." (See also 2 Chron. 2:4; 8:13; Hosea 2:11.) Though some believe that the sabbaths mentioned in Ezekiel and other passages refer primarily to the seventh-day Sabbath, doubtless the ceremonial sabbaths also are included.

3. Both the larger context and the immediate context strongly suggest that

THE "SABBATH DAYS" OF COLOSSIANS 2:16, 17

Paul was referring primarily to the festivals and ordinances of the ceremonial law. Throughout Colossians 1 and in the early part of chapter 2 Paul extols Christ as the Son of God, the Creator, the One who deserves worship and honor, the One who provides forgiveness and redemption, the One whom all should accept as Lord. He emphasizes one of his favorite themes—that to be "in Christ" is the *summum bonum* of religious experience. He sets forth Christ as the One who on the cross reconciled the world to God, the One who is Head of the church. Paul is determined to make clear that only that faith which focuses on Christ is of value. Neither thrones, dominions, principalities, nor powers (chaps. 1:16 and 2:15) are to be feared or venerated, for they are under the authority of Christ, having been created by Him. Thus, while the immediate context of verse 16 speaks of the complete forgiveness offered by Christ to believers (verses 13, 14), the larger context, the main theme of Paul's message, is the greatness of Christ and the importance of being "in Him," adhering to His teachings and recognizing that circumcision and ceremonial meats, drinks, holy days, new moons, and sabbaths have no value for salvation.

The key word in the passage, the word that argues strongly that the "sabbath days" of verse 16 are ceremonial sabbaths, is "shadow" (*skia*, as opposed to *sōma*, body), a word used in a similar way in Hebrews 8:5 and 10:1. Paul says that the meat, drink, holy days, new moons, and sabbath days "are a shadow of things to come" (Col. 2:17). A shadow has neither substance nor ultimate value. It is dependent for its existence on something substantial (the *sōma* casts the *skia*). It ends when it reaches the reality. Thus "shadow" describes well the various elements of the ceremonial law, including the annual sabbaths, for they pointed forward to Christ's life, ministry, and kingdom as the reality. Paul can hardly be referring to the seventh-day Sabbath of the Decalogue, for the seventh-day Sabbath is not a shadow of anything, it is the reality. Further, although to some extent the Sabbath points forward to the promised rest in Christ (see Hebrews 4), it does not obtain its primary significance from "things to come" but from an event in the past—the creation of the world in six days (Gen. 2:2, 3; Ex. 20:8-11).[1]

Adventists acknowledge that of the approximately sixty times the word *sabbath* is used in the New Testament, fifty-nine are references to the weekly Sabbath. But they hold that in Colossians 2 it means "ceremonial sabbath." They defend this view not on the basis of linguistics but on the basis of context. They argue that the number of times a word is used in a certain way does not determine its meaning in all situations. Context is decisive.

The word *frog*, for example, has a wide variety of meanings. It may mean a small, leaping, tailless amphibian; it may mean a swollen, sore throat; it may mean the triangular horny pad in the middle of the sole of a horse's hoof; it may mean an ornamental loop used as a fastening for a button on a coat or dress; it may mean a device on one rail of a train track that can be switched to permit wheels to cross an intersecting rail. Clearly, to argue that because fifty-nine times the word means a four-legged creature it must mean the same in the statement "I have a frog in my throat" is nonsense. Meaning must always be decided by context.

This principle is so obvious that it hardly needs elaboration; yet because some seek to show from Colossians 2 that the seventh-day Sabbath was abolished at the cross, we wish to add two further illustrations. The Hebrew word *torah*, for example, has many meanings, all of which must be determined by context.

THE SABBATH IN SCRIPTURE AND HISTORY

Sometimes *torah* refers to the Pentateuch, sometimes to the Ten Commandments, sometimes to the entire expressed will of God, sometimes to the instruction given by a king, a teacher, a mother, a father, wise people, a wise wife, or a poet.[2]

Likewise, the word *day* may mean a twenty-four-hour period; or it may mean only the light part of the twenty-four-hour period; or it may mean an extended but indefinite period of time (e.g., "The day in which we live is one of international tensions" or "The antitypical day of atonement began in 1844"). Clearly, even if the word *day* is used fifty-nine times to mean a twenty-four-hour period, this does not require that it mean twenty-four hours the sixtieth time it is used.

While many commentators hold otherwise, several of the most respected Bible commentators have declared that Paul was referring to ceremonial sabbaths, not the seventh-day Sabbath, in Colossians 2:16. Adam Clarke, a Methodist, said: "There is no intimation here that the *Sabbath* was done away, or that its moral use was superseded, by the introduction of Christianity.... *Remember the Sabbath day, to keep it holy,* is a command of *perpetual obligation,* and can never be superseded but by the final termination of time."[3]

Jamieson, Fausset, and Brown noted that the annual sabbaths "of the day of atonement and feast of tabernacles have come to an end with the Jewish services to which they belonged (Leviticus 23:32, 37-39)," but "the weekly sabbath rests on a more permanent foundation, having been instituted in Paradise to commemorate the completion of creation in six days."[4]

Albert Barnes, a Presbyterian, observed: "There is no evidence from this passage that he [Paul] would teach that there was no obligation to observe *any* holy time, for there is not the slightest reason to believe that he meant to teach that one of the ten commandments had ceased to be binding on mankind....He had his eye on the great number of days which were observed by the Hebrews as festivals, as a part of their ceremonial and typical law, and not to the *moral* law, or the ten commandments. No part of the moral law—no one of the ten commandments—could be spoken of as 'a shadow of good things to come.' These commandments are, from the nature of moral law, of perpetual and universal application."[5]

4. If the apostle Paul had intended to announce to the Colossian believers that the seventh-day Sabbath was no longer of consequence, surely this news would have created quite a stir, not merely in Colossae but in other cities. Adventists recognize that the argument from silence is not a strong argument, but they feel certain that as copies of Paul's letter were made, and these copies were taken to other churches and read, the shock of the believers in learning that Christ's death on the cross abolished the Sabbath would have been so great that the ensuing discussions would have been recorded, as were those regarding circumcision, idol worship, fornication, and other matters (see Acts 15).

But Paul's letter sent no shock waves through the community of believers. The people apparently understood that he was speaking of the rites and ceremonies connected with the Jewish faith. They understood him to mean that the cross abolished the ritual sacrifices, festivals, regulations involving meats and drinks, ceremonial sabbaths, special days governed by the new moon, and even the ceremonies that had been performed on the seventh-day Sabbath.

In using the four arguments reviewed above to support their position that Paul is speaking primarily of ceremonial sabbaths in Colossians 2, Adventists are aware that the word *sabbath* in verse 16, though apparently plural in form,

THE "SABBATH DAYS" OF COLOSSIANS 2:16, 17

probably should be translated as a singular. But they feel that this fact does not undermine their view and can be harmonized with it. Careful students have noted that in most passages where the Greek word for *sabbath* is used with a singular meaning, the form is *sabbaton*, a neuter noun in the singular, and that in some places the neuter nominative in the plural—*sabbata*—is used to express a singular meaning. In Colossians 2:16 the genitive of this form is used.

In the Septuagint the plural form with a singular meaning is found in numerous places. For example, in Exodus 16:23, 25; 20:8; Deuteronomy 5:12; Jeremiah 17:21, 22; and Ezekiel 46:1. The New Testament contains similar instances, for example in Matthew 12:1; 28:1; and Luke 4:16.

Adventists feel that A. T. Robertson, the well-respected New Testament scholar, has offered the best explanation as to why *sabbata* and *sabbatōn*, though plural in form, often stand for the singular. The Aramaic word for Sabbath is *shabbetha*, transliterated into Greek as *sabbata*. But *sabbata*, although representing the singular *shabbetha*, happens to be spelled as a plural in Greek and has been misunderstood to represent the plural of the Greek *sabbaton*, "Sabbath." Therefore in any occurrence of *sabbata* (or its other case forms such as *sabbatōn*) one must inquire if it represents the Aramaic *shabbetha*, in which case it is singular, or whether it is genuinely the plural of *sabbaton*, in which case it is a plural.[6]

The most defensible position seems to be to regard the genitive plural *sabbatōn* in Colossians 2:16 as a singular. Not only from a linguistic point of view is this logical, but from the context. Apparently the apostle Paul used *sabbath* generically in the singular, to correspond with the four other words in the series—meat, drink, holy day, and new moon, each of which is singular. Inasmuch as some ritual observances commanded by the laws of Moses were held on the weekly Sabbath—for example, the daily burnt offering was doubled on that day—perhaps Paul used *sabbath* generically, intending to include these ceremonies along with those that specifically involved annual sabbaths, as part of the "shadow" that was done away in Christ. These ritual ceremonies, of course, did not make the seventh day a Sabbath; it was a Sabbath already, established at Creation and commanded by the moral law, and abolition of the ceremonial observances that fell on that day would abolish neither the Sabbath nor God's command to keep it holy.

Among the references in Seventh-day Adventist literature that discuss Colossians 2:16 the following are typical:

Bible Readings for the Home (Washington, D.C., 1958).

William Henry Branson, *Drama of the Ages* (Nashville, Tenn., 1950).

Earle Hilgert, "'Sabbath Days' in Colossians 2:16," *Ministry*, February, 1952, pp. 42, 43.

W. E. Howell, "'Sabbath' in Colossians 2:16," *Ministry*, September, 1934, p. 10; idem, "Anent Colossians 2:16," *Ministry*, April, 1936, p. 18.

Arthur E. Lickey, *God Speaks to Modern Man* (Washington, D.C., 1952).

Francis David Nichol, *Answers to Objections* (Washington, D.C., 1932); idem, *Problems in Bible Translation* (Washington, D.C., 1954); idem, *The Seventh-day Adventist Bible Commentary* (Washington, D.C., 1957), 7:205, 206.

Ellen G. White, *Patriarchs and Prophets* (Mountain View, Calif., 1913); idem, *Selected Messages* (Washington, D.C., 1958), book 1.

Milton Charles Wilcox, *Questions and Answers* (Mountain View, Calif., 1911); idem, *Questions Answered* (Mountain View, Calif., 1938).

NOTES

[1] See also Ellen G. White, *Patriarchs and Prophets* (Mountain View, Calif., 1913), p. 48.
[2] See *SDABC*, 1:372, 887, 888, 1063.
[3] Adam Clarke, *The New Testament of Our Lord and Saviour Jesus Christ* (New York, n.d.), 2:524.
[4] Robert Jamieson, A. R. Fausset, and David Brown, *Commentary Critical and Explanatory on the Whole Bible* (Grand Rapids, Mich., n.d.), p. 378.
[5] Albert Barnes, *A Popular Commentary on the New Testament, Being Notes Practical and Explanatory* (London, n.d.), 7:267.
[6] A. T. Robertson, *A Grammar of the Greek New Testament in the Light of Historical Research* (London, n.d.), pp. 95, 105.

APPENDIX E

A Note on Hebrews 4:4-9

Roy E. Graham

NO STUDY on the topic of the Sabbath in Biblical teaching would be complete without reference to Hebrews 4:4-9, especially verse 9 with its use of the term *sabbatismos*. One Seventh-day Adventist publication included the statement that this text, i.e., Hebrews 4:9, "is perhaps the strongest argument in the New Testament for keeping the seventh-day Sabbath." [1]

More generally it is understood by Seventh-day Adventists to refer to the symbolic aspect contained in the Sabbath concept whereby the memorial of Creation becomes, through extension, the memorial and symbol of man's redemption.[2] This position is carefully worked out in the *Seventh-day Adventist Bible Commentary* in such sentences as: "The Sabbath thus bears witness both to the creative and to the sanctifying power of God, and its observance is an acknowledgement of faith in His power to create and to re-create, or sanctify, individual lives."[3] Again it is stated: "The 'rest' that remains (verse 9) is obviously the 'rest' into which the believing Christian of verse 10 enters."[4] It is significant that Ellen G. White, whose writing is considered to be authoritative in Seventh-day Adventism, refers to the "rest" of Hebrews 4:9 as being the "rest of grace."[5] More recently, Samuele Bacchiocchi, while emphasizing the "redemptive meaning of the Sabbath," has argued cogently for seeing the relationship of the literal observance of the seventh-day Sabbath within the context of its "true meaning in the light of the coming of Christ."[6]

The discussion, of which Hebrews 4:9-11 is the conclusion, begins earlier in the Epistle. After extolling the superiority of Jesus Christ, "the apostle and high priest of our confession,"[7] the writer explores the wilderness wanderings of the national forebears of those whom he was addressing. He concludes that the reason for the failure of those who left Egypt in the Exodus experience to enter into Canaan, which had been promised to them, was their unbelief. In chapter 4 the apostolic writer seeks to relate this experience to the Christians of his time. They also have received a promise of rest; they, too, may fail to enjoy its fulfillment through a lack of faith. William G. Johnsson has raised the questions evoked by this passage. He states them as follows: "(1) What is the 'rest' that remains for God's people? (2) When is it to be entered into—now or in the future? and (3) How does the Sabbath figure in the argument?"[8]

The noun used for "rest" in this passage is *katapausis* (chaps. 3:11, 18; 4:1, 3 [twice], 5, 10, 11); the related verb *katapauō* is also used three times (chap. 4:4, 8, 10). Only in Hebrews 4:9 is the word *"sabbatismos"* used for "rest."[9] There appear to be four ways in which the term "rest" is used here. In chapters 3:11, 18, and 4:3, 5, it is evidently an expression to describe what would have been the experience of those who left Egypt and who were planning to enter the literal land of Canaan—"Canaan rest," it might be called. This literal occupation of Canaan appears, however, as only a part of what God envisaged for His people. In Canaan they were to be a nation of priests, a means of proclaiming salvation to the world (cf. Ex. 19:4-6). This is a deeper meaning of the term "rest," with which the writer of Hebrews chooses to invest it. Thus he is able to speak of the time of Joshua and David—periods when the conquest of the land was taking place or had been realized—as still not meeting the requirements of God's rest (see Heb. 4:6-8). "Rest" is also applied to the Seventh-day Sabbath, although in an almost casual way in chapter 4:5. Here the seventh-day Sabbath appears as an illustration of what God's "rest" is. Then in verses 1, 3, 10, and 11, the term "rest" is used to describe the Christian's rest from the works of sin and from any attempt to earn salvation. The emphasis, therefore, seems to be on that "rest" that comes when the life is submitted to God. The whole discussion is reminiscent of the words of Jesus as recorded in Matthew 11:28, R.S.V.: "'Come to me, . . . and I will give you rest.'"

It may be noted, further, that in this chapter 4 of Hebrews the words *katapausis* and *sabbatismos* are used synonymously. This is seen especially in the context of verses 9 and 10. Both are taken to refer to that experience that characterizes the Christian's assurance, of which the seventh-day Sabbath is both symbol and part.[10] It is considered, as the rabbis described it, a type of the world to come (cf. 2 Macc. 15:1).

It would seem appropriate to follow the argument of the writer of the Epistle in this manner: "For if Joshua had given them rest (evidently the entrance to Canaan did not accomplish this), then would he (i.e., the Holy Spirit, cf. chap. 3:7) not afterward (through David or in the days of David) have spoken of another day." The glorious state of Israel was yet future, and, while other "rests" that had existed prior to the times of David might be symbolic of what was to come, it was the ultimate fulfillment of God's plan for His people that was being emphasized. Since this was not achieved through their unbelief, the "rest" was still future. Yet through the experience of personal salvation the individual might enjoy that "rest" here and now through grace while preparing for the full experience ultimately in the kingdom of glory.

NOTES

[1] *Senior Sabbath School Lesson Quarterly*, May 15, 1948.
[2] See, e.g., M. L. Andreasen, *The Sabbath*, pp. 86-89; W. G. Johnsson, *In Absolute Confidence* (Nashville, Tenn., 1979); Sakae Kubo, *God Meets Man* (Nashville, Tenn., 1978), pp. 65-69. (Cf. Karl Barth, *Church Dogmatics* [Edinburgh, 1956], III 4, pp. 47-72, 470-564, especially pp. 550-564.)
[3] *SDABC*, 7:420.
[4] *Ibid.*, p. 423. This may be seen as a midway point between those advocates of the traditional view as mentioned above and those who would wish to use Hebrews 4:9 to prove that the seventh-day Sabbath is still to be observed in the Christian dispensation. Cf. David Louis Lin, "An Investigation Into the Meaning of the Sabbatismos of Heb. 4:9" (M.A. thesis, Andrews University, May, 1946). Lin concedes that it may mean Sabbathkeeping now and have a future application but denies that the author of Hebrews would have the two separate ideas in mind.
[5] *SDABC*, 7:928. Cf. Ellen G. White, *Thoughts From the Mount of Blessing* (Mountain View, Calif., 1956), p. 1.
[6] Samuele Bacchiocchi, *From Sabbath to Sunday* (Rome, 1977), pp. 63-69.

A NOTE ON HEBREWS 4:4-9

[7] Heb. 3:1, R.S.V.
[8] Johnsson, *op. cit.*, p. 130.
[9] In the Septuagint, *katapauō* is used with reference to the Sabbath in Genesis 2:2, 3; Exodus 34:21; 31:17.
[10] Cf. a more recent writer's approach: "God's seventh-day has no closing refrain as do other days. 'Evening came and morning came.' His rest is everlasting and it is holy, and in the world of man the Sabbath is the way provided to 'enter into his rest.'"—George T. Montague, *The Holy Spirit: Growth of a Biblical Tradition* (New York, 1976), p. 64.

APPENDIX F

The "Lord's Day" in the Second Century

Kenneth A. Strand

BY the third Christian century "Lord's day" had become a common designation among Christians for the weekly Sunday, on which a special religious service was held.[1] Although certain early-second-century references (to be discussed below) have often been set forth as Sunday "Lord's day" statements, the first clear patristic evidence in this matter appears toward the end of the second century. We will first notice this evidence and then move back through the second century until we come to three so-called "Lord's day" statements that are thought to have been penned before A.D. 120 (two definitely before 120 and the third probably so).

Clement of Alexandria and Irenaeus

The first Church Father whose extant writings use the term "Lord's day" to apply to the weekly Christian Sunday was Clement of Alexandria near the close of the second century, probably about A.D. 190. Clement, who allegorized extensively in his theological discussions, thought that the Greek philosopher Plato some five and one-half centuries earlier had made a prophetic reference to Sunday: "The Lord's day Plato prophetically speaks of in the tenth book of the *Republic,* in these words: 'And when seven days have passed to each of them in the meadow, on the eighth they are to set out and arrive in four days.'"[2]

Obviously, a future Christian Sunday (or even a future Christianity) was totally foreign to Plato's mind, but the point of interest here is that Clement designates the Christian weekly Sunday as the "Lord's day."

A slightly earlier "Lord's day" reference (about A.D. 180 or 185) was made by Bishop Irenaeus of Gaul, but Irenaeus appears to have been speaking of Easter Sunday rather than a weekly Sunday: "This [custom], of not bending the knee upon Sunday, is a symbol of the resurrection, through which we have been set free, by the grace of Christ, from sins, and from death, which has been put to death under Him. Now this custom took its rise from apostolic times, as the blessed Irenaeus, the martyr and bishop of Lyons, declares in his treatise *On Easter,* in

THE "LORD'S DAY" IN THE SECOND CENTURY

which he makes mention of Pentecost also; upon which [feast] we do not bend the knee, because it is of equal significance with the Lord's day, for the reason already alleged concerning it."[3]

As the editors of the *Ante-Nicene Fathers* have observed, this reference must be to Easter.[4] It seems clear that two *annual* events are intended; for Pentecost, an *annual event,* is placed in comparison with "Lord's day."

Some Apocryphal Sources

Certain apocryphal sources that were perhaps written about the middle of the second century also use the designation "Lord's day," but not in clear reference to a *weekly* Sunday. The *Gospel of Peter,* for example, twice applies the term to the very day on which Christ's resurrection took place.[5] And the *Epistle of the Apostles* makes a curious reference to the "Lord's day" as the "Ogdoad."[6]

In the *Acts of John* there is a reference to "Lord's day" that seems to have *Saturday* in view.[7] But on the other hand, the very fanciful *Acts of Peter* would appear to mean the weekly Christian Sunday in its use of the term.[8] The dating of the *Acts of Peter,* as well as of the section of the *Acts of John* that mentions "Lord's day," is especially difficult, however, and it is possible that both of these references may be later than from the second century.[9]

Barnabas of Alexandria and Justin Martyr in Rome

Whether Barnabas of Alexandria (*c.* A.D. 130) and Justin Martyr in Rome (*c.* A.D. 150), whose main Sunday references have been called to attention above in chapter 7 and appendix B, were acquainted with the term "Lord's day" for the weekly Sunday has been raised in recent discussions.[10] The fact is that neither of these Church Fathers in their extant writings uses the term, but they use instead the designations "eighth day" and "Sunday" for the first day of the week.[11]

Obviously, this silence precludes calling upon these two Church Fathers for evidence that Sunday was termed "Lord's day" in their time and locale. On the other hand, the same silence should not be utilized as proof that Barnabas and Justin were totally unfamiliar with the term "Lord's day" as a name for Sunday, inasmuch as their specific Sunday statements are in contexts that would preclude their use of this term even if they were acquainted with it. Barnabas made his "eighth day" statement in the context of a highly allegorical and eschatological discussion, and Justin used the term "Sunday" in his apology addressed to the Roman emperor and Senate ("Lord's day" would surely have been misunderstood in this setting) and the term "eighth day" when disputing with a Jewish rabbi (again, the reason for his choice of terminology is clear).[12]

In short, we may say, therefore, that any debate regarding whether or not Barnabas and Justin knew of Sunday as the "Lord's day" is meaningless. There simply is no evidence one way or the other.

We now turn to three earlier sources that have often been set forth as evidence of a Sunday "Lord's day": The *Didache,* Ignatius' letter to the Magnesians, and Pliny's letter to Trajan.

Didache, Chapter 14

The *Didache,* a sort of baptismal, organizational, or instructional manual, has been dated anywhere from the late first century to the late second century, but scholarly opinion now favors a fairly early date, at least for a good deal of the material compiled in the *Didache*. The document seems to have originated in Syria.[13]

The statement in chapter 14 of interest here reads as follows: *Kata kuriakēn de kuriou sunaxthentes klasate arton kai euxaristēsate*—"On the Lord's of the Lord [or, "According to the Lord's of the Lord"] assemble, break bread, and hold Eucharist."[14] The word "day" (Greek *hēmeran*, in the accusative case) does not actually appear in the text, but most translators have added it in their English translation, making the text read as follows: "On the Lord's day. . . ." Some students of the text would, however, suggest the rendition "According to the Lord's commandment . . ."—also a possible translation of the original Greek.[15] Samuele Bacchiocchi, following a rendition of John Baptiste Thibaut and supporting it with a rather impressive line of evidence, gives a similar translation: "'"According to the sovereign doctrine of the Lord."'"[16]

Some years ago a noted British scholar, C. W. Dugmore, set forth arguments that the *Didache* terminology, which he refers to as "Lord's day," really meant an *annual* Easter Sunday. In fact, Dugmore also noted the paucity of reference to a weekly Christian Sunday in New Testament and subapostolic literature and felt it strange that if this day were indeed the most important day of the week for Christians there would not have been more mention of it until Justin Martyr at the middle of the second century![17]

Lawrence T. Geraty has followed up on this possible meaning for the *Didache* statement, commenting as follows: "Undoubtedly one of the earliest [hints that the Pascha was celebrated as an annual Lord's day festival] is the phrase 'Lord's Day' in the *Didache*, an ancient baptismal or organizational manual. Although this rendition from καρὰ κυριακὴν δε κυρίου συναχθέντες has been disputed, it is nevertheless the preferred translation. If so, the context would indicate that this could be an annual day for baptism and the celebration of the Eucharist."[18]

Geraty has further called attention to the fact that "a recognition of this possibility existed in the nineteenth century when J. Rendel Harris tried to show from the tenor of the *Didache* and its context, that it must have had reference to some great annual festival, perhaps similar to the day of atonement." Geraty goes on to point out with reference to Dugmore's work that this scholar, "after an analysis of similar passages in the *Didache* and *Apostolic Constitutions,* has argued convincingly that 'the use of κυριακή as a technical term for Easter Day thus seems to be reasonably attested. Its use as a normal description of the first day of every week would only have been possible after Sunday had become a regular day of worship among Christians and had to be thought of as a weekly commemoration of the Resurrection.'"[19]

Ignatius to the Magnesians, Chapter 9

About A.D. 115 Ignatius, Bishop of Antioch, traveled through the Roman province of Asia on his way to martyrdom in Rome. On this journey he penned letters to various of the Asian churches, giving them counsel in view of Judaizing and Gnostic tendencies that appeared to be creeping in.[20]

Ignatius' so-called "Lord's day" statement occurs in chapter 9 of his letter to the Magnesians, and reads as follows from a commonly accepted edition of the Greek text: *mēketi sabbatizontes alla kata kuriakēn zōntes*—"No longer sabbatizing, but living according to the Lord's."²¹ It should be noted that the Greek word for "day" (*hēmeran,* in the accusative case) is *not* in the text.

The manuscript evidence favors, however, a longer version of the Greek—a version that contains the word *zōēn,* "life." This word has been omitted by modern editors in the commonly accepted Greek wording given above. The actual text as found in the earliest extant manuscript reads as follows: *mēketi sabbatizontes alla kata kuriakēn zōēn zōntes.*²² The normal rendering of this expression (unless a cognate accusative was intended²³) would be: "no longer sabbatizing, but living according to the Lord's life."

Probably the strongest evidence that not *days* but *ways of life* are in view in this passage comes from a consideration of the entire context. The persons to whom Ignatius refers as "no longer sabbatizing, but living according to the Lord's" are the *Old Testament prophets.* In chapter 8:1, 2 he had declared that "if we are still living according to Judaism we admit that we have not received grace; for the most divine prophets lived in accord with Jesus Christ." In chapter 9:1, 2 he goes on to declare, "If, therefore, those who lived in ancient ways came to new hope, no longer sabbatizing, but living according to the Lord's [life], in which also our life arose through him and his death, . . . how shall we be able to live without him of whom even the prophets were disciples in the Spirit—looking forward to him as their teacher?"

It is also worth noting that the fourth-century interpolater of Ignatius did not see in this passage a conflict between two different days, for he approved the observance of *both* days. In his version of this passage in Magnesians 9 (quoted at length in appendix B) he prescribes that the Sabbath should be kept in a "spiritual manner," after which the "Lord's day" should also be observed.²⁴

A distinguished patristic scholar, Robert A. Kraft, has provided the following translation of the original Ignatius of the early second century: "If, then, those who walked in the ancient customs [i.e., the aforementioned prophets] came to have a new hope, no longer 'sabbatizing' but living in accord with the Lord's life—in which life there sprang up also our life through him and through his death."²⁵

Pliny's Letter to Trajan

About A.D. 112 Pliny the Younger, governor of the province of Bithynia in northern Asia Minor, wrote a letter to Roman Emperor Trajan regarding the situation he met in dealing with Christians in his province. He indicates that he interrogated some former Christians who, under this questioning, indicated "the whole of their guilt or their error" when they were Christians to have been that "they were in the habit of meeting on a certain fixed day [*stato die*] before it was light, when they sang in alternate verses a hymn to Christ, as to a god, and bound themselves by a solemn oath, not to any wicked deeds, but never to commit any fraud, theft or adultery, never to falsify their word," et cetera.²⁶

The statement, it is clear, is *not really a "Lord's day" reference,* for it does not use this terminology (indeed, the term "Lord's day" would have had quite another meaning for a Roman governor than what we know it later came to have for Christians). The reason for noting Pliny's statement here is that various modern writers have dealt with it as if it were a Sunday "Lord's day" proof text.

In discussing this passage, Geraty points out that until the Jewish-Roman war of A.D. 132-135 the observance of a weekly day of worship would not, in Roman eyes, "necessarily have involved guilt, but an annual vigil service in honor of the Lord's resurrection" might have done so. "The Romans were used to, and permitted, the weekly religious rites of the Jews on their Sabbath, and possibly of pagan sun worshippers on their Sunday. However, now they had on their hands a new sect, the Christians, meeting on a *stato die ante lucem* and attributing divine honors to some person other than the Roman emperor; and this could certainly be looked upon as a danger to the Roman peace. Thus the reaction of the Romans, the time of meeting, and to a lesser degree the content of the service, would seem to indicate an Easter vigil celebration—if indeed earlier examples of this celebration were anything like what they later came to be."[27]

Summary of the Second-Century Evidence

In sum total, the evidence from the second century for application of the term "Lord's day" to a weekly Christian Sunday is nonexistent in patristic literature until near the end of that century, the first such reference by a Church Father coming from Clement of Alexandria. Possibly "Lord's day" was used earlier in some quarters to designate an *annual* Easter Sunday. This could not have been true in the Roman province of Asia, however, for that province remained Quartodeciman until the end of the second century.[28] One curious reference in an apocryphal work from there, the *Acts of John*, seems to apply the terminology to Saturday.

Barnabas of Alexandria and Justin Martyr of Rome in their respective writings of about A.D. 130 and A.D. 150 should not be adduced as evidence of whether or not in their day the weekly Sunday had come to be known as the "Lord's day." In their extant works, neither of these fathers used the term, nor could they be expected to have used it.

Finally, none of the three earliest so-called "Lord's day" references from the second century—in the *Didache,* Ignatius, and Pliny—actually uses the term. In fact, the weight of evidence in each case favors a meaning other than a weekly Christian Sunday.

NOTES

[1] The earliest evidence for the usage comes from late-second-century Alexandria, as will be noted below; but beginning as early as Tertullian of Carthage, whose writings spanned the period from about A.D. 197 to 222, various patristic sources from elsewhere than Alexandria also use the term "Lord's day" as a designation for the weekly Christian Sunday. Especially noteworthy are the fourth- and fifth-century sources called to attention in appendix B, above, as mentioning both the Sabbath and "Lord's day" *(Apostolic Constitutions,* John Cassian and other sources).
[2] Clement of Alexandria *Miscellanies* v. 14 *(ANF* 2:469).
[3] "Fragments from the Lost Writings of Irenaeus," 7 *(ANF* 1:569, 570).
[4] *ANF* 1:569, note 9.
[5] *Gospel of Peter,* 9, 12 *(ANF* 8:8).
[6] *Epistle of the Apostles* (English trans. in M. R. James, *The Apocryphal New Testament,* cor. ed [Oxford, 1953], p. 491). Precisely what "Ogdoad" means in this context is not clear.
[7] *Acts of John (ANF* 8:560, 561). The passage reads as follows: "And the soldiers, having taken the public conveyances, travelled fast, having seated him [John] in the midst of them. And when they came to the first change, it being the hour of breakfast, they entreated him to be of good courage, and to take bread, and eat with them. And John said: I rejoice in soul indeed, but in the meantime I do not wish to take any food. . . . And on the seventh day, it being the Lord's day, he said to them: Now it is time for me also to partake of food." The "seventh day" here may refer specifically to the seventh-day Sabbath, or it may refer to the seventh day of the journey. If the latter, the day would evidently still be Saturday. This is so because fasting on Saturday was not allowed in the region to which the document pertains—the Roman province of Asia, in the Eastern Christian world, which did not adopt the Sabbath fast. On the problem of date, see note 9.
[8] The *Acts of Peter* contains a strange mixture of possible fact and obvious fiction (in the latter category, for example, a talking dog carries messages between Simon Peter and Simon Magus!). The "Lord's day" references of

THE "LORD'S DAY" IN THE SECOND CENTURY

primary interest are from paragraphs 29, 30 (James, *op. cit.*, pp. 329, 330).

[9] In addition to introductory materials in *ANF* and James (*op. cit.*) cited in the foregoing notes, see Edgar Hennecke's *New Testament Apocrypha* (Philadelphia, 1963) (i.e., Eng. trans. of Wilhelm Schneemelcher's edition of Hennecke's *New Testament Apocrypha*); esp. 2:195, 196 for discussion regarding the introductory seventeen chapters of the *Acts of John*, where the material on "Lord's day" occurs (see note 7). The "Lord's day" reference itself receives no mention, however. Also giving brief attention to some apocrypha we have mentioned above is Jacques Hervieux, *The New Testament Apocrypha* (New York, 1960).

[10] See, e.g., Walter E. Straw, *Origin of Sunday Observance in the Christian Church* (Washington, D.C., 1939), p. 35. Also, Robert L. Odom, *Sabbath and Sunday in Early Christianity* (Washington, D.C., 1977), p. 130, mentions Justin as "not once" speaking "of the first day of the week either as 'the Sabbath' or as 'the Lord's day.'"

[11] "Eighth day" in Barnabas, chap. 15, and in Justin's *Dialogue with Trypho*, chap. 41 *(ANF* 1:147, 215); "Sunday" in Justin's *1 Apology* 67 *(ANF* 1:186).

[12] See note 11.

[13] See, e.g., Jean-Paul Audet, *La didachè: instructions des apôtres* (Paris, 1958); and Robert M. Grant, *The Apostolic Fathers*, vol. 1, *An Introduction* (New York, 1964), p. 75. However, cf. also Robert A. Kraft, *The Apostolic Fathers*, vol. 3, *Barnabas and the Didache* (New York, 1965), p. 76: "The Didache contains a great deal of material which derives from very early (i.e., first-century and early second-century) forms of (Jewish-) Christianity; but it would be difficult to argue convincingly that the *present form* of the *Didache* is earlier than mid-second century."

[14] LCL, *Apostolic Fathers*, 1:330 (Greek), 331 (English), LCL; other English renditions available in various editions of *Apostolic Fathers*, such as Kraft, *op. cit.*, p. 173 (see note 13); Cyril C. Richardson, trans. & ed., *Early Christian Fathers*, LCC (Philadelphia, 1953), p. 178; Edgar J. Goodspeed, *The Apostolic Fathers* (New York, 1950), p. 17.

[15] See, e.g., Frank H. Yost, *The Early Christian Sabbath* (Mountain View, Calif., 1947), p. 32: "A number of words, appropriate both grammatically and in meaning, could be supplied . . . and make as good or better sense than 'day'; for instance, the word 'commandment.'"

[16] Samuele Bacchiocchi, *From Sabbath to Sunday* (Rome, 1977), p. 114, note 73. He adds to Thibaut's linguistic argument some six further arguments, mostly relating to contextual concerns.

[17] C. W. Dugmore, "Lord's Day and Easter," in *Neotestamentica et Patristica* (festschrift for Oscar Cullmann), supplements to *Novum Testamentum* 6 (Leiden, 1962):272-281.

[18] Lawrence T. Geraty, "The Pascha and the Origin of Sunday Observance," *AUSS* 3 (1965):87, 88.

[19] *Ibid.*, p. 88, note 15. The reference to Harris is *The Teaching of the Apostles* (London, 1887), pages 105, 106. The reference to Dugmore is to pages 276-279 in Dugmore's work ci.ed in note 17.

[20] See, e.g., the brief treatment in Richardson, *op. cit.*, pages 74-86, 94, and Goodspeed, *op. cit.*, pages 203-205 (see note 14). An excellent general account of Ignatius' trip to Rome and of his letters is given in Philip Carrington, *The First Christian Century*, vol. 1 of *The Early Christian Church*, (Cambridge, Eng., 1957), pages 445-459. English translation of the letters is found, e.g., in *ANF* 1:49-126 (including a number of spurious epistles as well); *Apostolic Fathers*, 1:173-277, LCL; Goodspeed, *op. cit.*, pages 207-235; Richardson, *op. cit.*, pages 87-137; Robert M. Grant, trans., *Ignatius of Antioch*, vol. 4 of *The Apostolic Fathers*, (New York, 1966), pages 29-137.

[21] The transliteration given here is from Greek text as given in *Apostolic Fathers*, 1:204, LCL.

[22] See the facsimile reproduction in Fritz Guy, "'The Lord's Day' in the Letter of Ignatius to the Magnesians," *AUSS* 2 (1964), plate facing p. 8. The text clearly reads, ". . . κατὰ κυριακὴν ζωὴν ζῶντες."

[23] For discussion of the possibility of a cognate accusative, see Guy, *op. cit.*, pages 10, 11, 16. In this case the translation *could* be: "No longer sabbatizing, but living a life according to the Lord's [day]." The specific Greek word for "day" is still lacking from the text, of course.

[24] *ANF* 1:62, 63.

[25] Robert A. Kraft, "Some Notes on Sabbath Observance in Early Christianity," *AUSS* 3 (1965):27.

[26] Pliny, *Letters* x. 96, LCL.

[27] Geraty, *op. cit.*, pages 88, 89.

[28] For a brief discussion of this matter, see Kenneth A. Strand, *The Early Christian Sabbath* (Worthington, Ohio, 1979), pages 47-50, 52, 53. The Quartodeciman Controversy of the late second century is treated in some detail in Eusebius *Ecclesiastical History* v. 23-25 *(NPNF/2* 1:241-244).

APPENDIX G

Joseph Bates and Seventh-day Adventist Sabbath Theology*

C. Mervyn Maxwell

SEVENTH-DAY ADVENTISTS constitute by far the most numerous group of Christians observing Friday night and Saturday as the Sabbath. General aspects of the background and development of their Sabbath theology have been surveyed in chapter 13. The pioneer contributions of Joseph Bates to this development deserve closer analysis.

Although, as has been noted in chapter 13, the Sabbath theology of Seventh-day Adventists owes much to the views held by Seventh Day Baptists in the early nineteenth century, Seventh-day Adventists have constructed a unique Sabbath theology by taking what they learned from the Seventh Day Baptists and uniting it to a complex Biblical eschatology. Joseph Bates, along with other Seventh-day Adventist[1] pioneers, was guided into this eschatological Sabbath theology partly as a consequence of his experience as a leading proponent of Millerite Adventism. His step-by-step contributions to Seventh-day Adventism will be better understood after a brief look at some of the beliefs of the Millerite Adventists.[2]

Millerite Adventism

The Millerite Advent movement, under the leadership of William Miller, of Low Hampton, New York, was the North American aspect of a more-or-less worldwide phenomenon of the early nineteenth century that is sometimes referred to as the Great Second Advent Awakening. Three themes that especially identified Millerism were (1) that the "2300 days" of Daniel 8:14 would terminate with the second coming of Christ around 1843 or 1844; (2) that the cleansing of the sanctuary mentioned in the same verse was to be equated with the Second

---

* This appendix enlarges on one significant aspect of the treatment given in chapter 13. Though duplication of material has been avoided as much as possible, there may be some repetition here for the sake of clarity. For the broad historical backgrounds, see chapter 13.

Coming *and* with the judgment scene of Daniel 7:9-14; and (3) that therefore the time had arrived for the proclamation of the first angel's message of Revelation 14:6, 7: "The hour of his [God's] judgment is come."

When Miller reluctantly began to preach in 1831, he discovered to his surprise a warm and enthusiastic reception among Protestant pastors. Besides some 50,000 to 150,000 lay persons, several hundred ministers in various denominations appear to have accepted his views. But during the summer of 1843 and especially in 1844, while the Millerites were concentrating on their final spiritual preparation for the judgment and the Second Coming, a change of feeling came about, and large numbers of Millerites were disfellowshiped from their Presbyterian, Methodist, Congregationalist, Baptist, and other Protestant churches.

Reexamination of Revelation 14 led the Millerites to the understanding that before the second coming of Christ could take place, the first angel must be followed by a second one (verse 8), who declares that "Babylon is fallen, is fallen." Millerites concluded that Babylon was a symbol of the churches that had rejected the judgment-hour message of the first angel and that the time had come to preach the second angel's message and to call the true people of God (chap. 18:4) out of their fallen churches.

This, briefly, was the core of the characteristic doctrines held by the Millerites—Joseph Bates among them—when Bates received his first exposure to the seventh-day Sabbath.

Joseph Bates's Initial Sabbath Theology

The story of Joseph Bates's acceptance of the Sabbath through reading T. M. Preble's publications in March, 1845, has been told in chapter 13. As was also noted in that chapter, in August, 1846, Bates came out with the first edition of his influential pamphlet *The Seventh Day Sabbath, a Perpetual Sign, From the Beginning, to the Entering Into the Gates of the Holy City, According to the Commandment.*[3]

This initial publication on the Sabbath question by a pioneer of the Seventh-day Adventist movement contained many elements likely to have been familiar to its Millerite readers; but as we shall see in a moment, it also contained a germ of the future, unique, Seventh-day Adventist position.

T. M. Preble had reflected Seventh Day Baptist theology in his publications; it is not surprising, therefore, that Bates's tract also was essentially Seventh Day Baptist in content. But it should be remembered that the Seventh Day Baptist position was itself a modification of Puritan Sabbatarian theology (see chapter 12). Congregationalists, Presbyterians, and Baptists (who in America stemmed directly fom Puritanism), and Methodists (who in America were much influenced by it), could agree with many of Bates's arguments. They could acknowledge, for example, that the Sabbath commandment is moral and binding, that the Sabbath is holy and is to be kept strictly, and that the "handwriting of ordinances" spoken of in Colossians 2:14-17 as having been nailed to the cross was the ceremonial law, not the Decalogue.

Even the reference to a "perpetual" Sabbath in Bates's title was as Puritan as Nicholas Bownde himself, for he, in 1595, had contrasted the annual Jewish Sabbaths "of weekes and yeares" with the "perpetuall Sabbath of daies"—intending Sunday, of course.[4] Jonathan Edwards in the early eighteenth century also had defended the "perpetuity" of the Sabbath commandment in a sermon titled "The Perpetuity and Change of the Sabbath."[5] Even more to the point, William Miller had gone on record as defending the Sabbath as a "perpetual sign," once again with application to Sunday.[6]

As a matter of fact, early Seventh-day Adventist Sabbatarianism owed a twofold debt to Puritanism. As noted in chapter 12, early English Puritanism, with its emphasis on the fourth commandment, led the founders of the Seventh Day Baptists to discover the "seventh-day" orientation of the Sabbath, a discovery which they later passed on to Seventh-day Adventists. In addition, the emigration of early Puritan ideals provided a culture in mid-nineteenth-century America that was familiar with the concept of a weekly holy day and which thus facilitated propagation of Seventh-day Adventism. For that matter, it appears that the seventh-day Sabbath itself was fairly widely agitated among the Millerites during the summer of 1844, to the consternation of their chief leaders.[7]

Thus when people read Bates's first edition of *The Seventh Day Sabbath, a Perpetual Sign*—and most of its readers were Millerite Adventists—a good many found themselves in harmony with much of what it said, most being startled mainly by its insistence that the Sabbath should be kept holy on Saturday rather than on Sunday.

But in addition to its familiar emphases and its presentation of the Seventh Day Baptist Sabbath, Bates's pamphlet also contained a totally new idea. After Bates had begun to keep the Sabbath in March, 1845, he noticed something that most Millerites had overlooked, namely, that before the second coming of Christ, the first and second angels of Revelation 14 were to be followed by a third angel with a warning against the mark of the beast. Bates also noticed that Revelation 14:12 describes the last-day saints as a people who "keep the commandments of God, and [have] the faith of Jesus."

This reference to commandment keeping helped confirm Bates in his new conviction about the Sabbath. It seemed to him that in a special sense the time had come for the people who had proclaimed the first and second messages to recognize the third angel's message and to keep the Sabbath of the Ten Commandments—and he mentioned this briefly in his book.[8]

Bates's Correlation of the Sabbath and the Heavenly Sanctuary

By the time Bates was ready to prepare the second edition of *The Seventh Day Sabbath, a Perpetual Sign,* he had added to his thinking two additional concepts which also were to become uniquely characteristic of the developing Seventh-day Adventist position. In order to understand them, it will be helpful to take yet another look at Millerite Adventism.

We have indicated that the Millerites assumed that a parallel exists between the cleansing of the sanctuary of Daniel 8:14 (King James Version), the judgment scene of Daniel 7:9-14, and the second coming of Christ. Indeed, Miller took Christ's coming on clouds to the judgment (Dan. 7:13) to be the same event as His coming on clouds to the earth at the end of the present age.[9] Thus, he seems to have given inadequate attention to the fact that in Daniel 7 the Son of man comes for judgment "to the Ancient of days" rather than to the earth.

But on the day following the disappointment of October 22, 1844, the seminal difference here was caught by Hiram Edson, a Methodist Millerite layman and later a Seventh-day Adventist minister. According to his personal account, Edson came suddenly to understand "distinctly, and clearly, that instead of our High Priest coming out of the Most Holy of the heavenly sanctuary to come to this earth on [October 22, 1844] . . . that he for the first time entered on that day the second apartment of that sanctuary. . . . That he came to the marriage at that time; in other words, to the Ancient of days to receive a kingdom, a dominion, and glory." [10]

Thus Edson observed that the Son of man goes to the Ancient of days, not to the earth, at the time of the judgment in Daniel 7, and that His marriage to His kingdom takes place in heaven, not on the earth.

Edson says that he also found himself taking a new interest in Revelation 11:15-19: "The seventh angel sounded . . . and, the temple of God was opened in heaven, and there was seen in his temple the ark of his testament." [11] When one of T. M. Preble's publications about the Sabbath reached Edson's home in Port Gibson, New York, sometime later, Edson associated the Sabbath of the fourth commandment with the ark of the testament [that is, the ark containing the Ten Commandments] in the heavenly temple or sanctuary. He began to wonder whether Christ's entry into heaven's Most Holy Place in 1844 would result in a new emphasis on Sabbathkeeping.[12]

Over the ensuing months Edson studied the Bible with O. R. L. Crosier, a teacher, and F. B. Hahn, a physician. Their conclusions were published by Crosier on February 7, 1846, in the form of an "Extra" edition of the *Day-Star,* a Millerite periodical edited by Enoch Jacobs, of Cincinnati, Ohio.[13] In this extra, Crosier argued from Scripture that the sanctuary of Daniel 8:14 is indeed the one in heaven, and that in October, 1844, Jesus entered its Most Holy Place to commence a work of atonement analogous to the cleansing of Israel on the ancient Day of Atonement (see Leviticus 16). Without any mention of a judgment concept, Crosier portrayed Christ's contemporary ministry as the blotting out of sins (Acts 3:19) in preparation for the Second Coming (verses 20, 21).

As already mentioned, Joseph Bates accepted the Seventh Day Baptist teaching on the seventh-day Sabbath from reading T. M. Preble in March, 1845. In February or March, 1846—that is, about as soon as it appeared—he also read Crosier's article in the *Day-Star* extra. Convinced by Crosier's argument that the sanctuary of Daniel 8:14 is the one in heaven, Bates soon composed a thirty-nine-page tract, *The Opening Heavens,*[14] in which he endorsed the concept with observations from the Bible and from astronomy. (This was still some five months before he published his first full tract on the Sabbath referred to above.)

Near the end of *The Opening Heavens* Bates inserted a short section on the Sabbath question, relating the seventh-day Sabbath to the ark of the testament in the sanctuary described in the Old Testament. But even though this little work as a whole dealt with the heavenly sanctuary and contained a reference to the Sabbath, Bates apparently did not at this time see any connection between the Sabbath and the ark of the testament in the sanctuary *in heaven.* It appears that on the Sabbath issue Bates was still an adherent of the Seventh Day Baptist position, not advancing beyond that theology until several months later, when, in his *Seventh Day Sabbath, a Perpetual Sign* (August, 1846), he linked the Sabbath to the third angel's message.

History and theology cannot meaningfully be separated in the development of Seventh-day Adventist theology. The marriage of James White and Ellen Harmon in the same month (August, 1846) that this tract appeared, and their soon-after adoption of the seventh-day Sabbath, provided a congenial foundation for further interaction between the Whites and Bates in the ongoing development of Seventh-day Adventism.

A second historically significant event was the visit Bates made about November, 1846, to Edson, Hahn, and Crosier in Canandaigua and Port Gibson, New York.[15] It was evidently while in conversation with these creators of the *Day-Star* extra, the paper which had influenced Bates so effectively earlier in the year, that Bates first began to sense a connection between the Sabbath and the entry of Christ in 1844 into the Most Holy Place of the heavenly sanctuary.

In January, 1847, after his return home to Fairhaven, Massachusetts, Bates issued a second, enlarged edition[16] of his *Seventh Day Sabbath, a Perpetual Sign*, the first edition having been exhausted. He made use of the opportunity to expand his exposition of the third angel's message by offering an identification for the mark of the beast referred to in that message and in Revelation 13:16, 17. "Is it not clear," he asked, "that [keeping] the first day of the week for the Sabbath or holy day is a mark of the beast?"[17]

In this second edition Bates also developed, for the first time in print, Edson's suggestion, mentioned above, about the fulfillment of Revelation 11:15-19. Specifically, Bates noted that many persons (Preble? J. B. Cook? himself? others?) had recently published material in favor of the seventh-day Sabbath.[18] As a possible reason for this upsurge of interest in the Sabbath, he proposed that when the seventh angel (Rev. 11:15) sounded his trumpet and the temple of God was opened in heaven and the ark of the testament was spiritually revealed, God's spirit "made an indelible impression" on people's minds to "search the scriptures for the Testimony of God."

He added cautiously, "I do not say that this view of the Ark in Revelation is positive, but I think the inference is strong. I cannot see what else it refers to."[19]

This was in January, 1847. Bates's hesitancy was quickly removed. On March 6, in Fairhaven, Massachusetts (probably in Bates's home),[20] and on April 3, in Topsham, Maine (in the home of another Sabbatarian Adventist),[21] Ellen White, in a visionary state, saw Jesus in the Most Holy Place of the heavenly sanctuary calling attention to the tables of the law in the ark and to a halo of glory around the fourth commandment. These were Ellen White's first visions concerning the Sabbath, both of them seen some months after she became a Sabbathkeeper.[22] They convinced Bates that his Bible study had been divinely led. Soon he published an account of the April 3 vision in volume 1, Number 1, of *A Vision*, dated April 7, 1847.

Bates, the Whites, and perhaps a few dozen or so other persons were now convinced that the seventh-day Sabbath was the message of the hour. But they found it difficult to persuade the other disappointed Adventists to adopt their view. To their dismay, they realized that almost all of them had abandoned the idea that October, 1844, had any significance at all.

To restore confidence in the Advent experience and, by doing so, to establish a basis for his Sabbatarian emphasis, Bates produced in May, 1847, an eighty-page booklet entitled *Second Advent Way Marks and High Heaps, or a Connected View, of the Fulfillment of Prophecy, by God's Peculiar People, From the Year 1840 to 1847*.[23] From

Scripture, the apparent fulfillment of prophecy, the Millerite experience in general, and the publications of Millerite leaders, Bates argued that God had most certainly led the Adventists to focus on the 2300 days of Daniel 8:14, and that the real significance of the Advent Awakening lay in its witness to Christ's entry in October, 1844, into the Most Holy Place in heaven. (This publication was a review of the Millerite Advent experience; thus, to anticipate a later Seventh-day Adventist term, it constituted an "Advent review.") On this basis Bates proceeded to argue for the timeliness of the Sabbath in relation to the three angels' messages and to the opened temple in heaven. He stated that "the first message [of the three angels in Rev. 14:6-11] that issued on the commandments came from the presentation of the ark.... This was the point of time that this message was urged on God's people, to test their sincerity and honesty in the whole word of God."[24]

Bates's various publications stimulated a vigorous debate on the Sabbath question within the Adventist community, articles on the subject appearing in the *Advent Harbinger* of Rochester, New York, and in the *Bible Advocate,* of Hartford, Connecticut. C. Stowe, J. Croffut, J. B. Cook, and A. Carpenter were among those who defended the seventh-day Sabbath. Timothy Cole, editor of the *Bible Advocate,* Joseph Marsh, editor of the *Advent Harbinger,* Joseph Turner, G. Needham, and "Barnabas" (possibly Jacob Weston) opposed it.[25]

In the context of this debate Joseph Bates sat down late in the autumn of 1847 to compose *A Vindication of the Seventh-day Sabbath, and the Commandments of God: With a Further History of God's Peculiar People, from 1847 to 1848.*[26] His own commitment to the propagation of Sabbatarianism is attested by the reduction of his cash resources at this time to a York shilling.[27]

Bates's most significant theological innovation in *A Vindication of the Seventh-day Sabbath* was the identification of the sealing process of Revelation 7 with the development of character. In this document he also associated the Sabbath more intimately than ever with Christ's new ministry in heaven's Most Holy Place.

The sealing process, Bates said, had been going on over the previous eight years, ever since Miller's movement first attracted wide attention in 1840, and it would be completed in the upcoming "time of trouble" of Daniel 12:1, 2. Specifically, he believed that the seal of God applied to the experience of the 144,000 saints—people who would show such a clear development "of Christian character in their lives and shining foreheads (or faces), that it will be clearly understood that Jesus has redeemed them from all iniquity, by purifying 'unto himself a *peculiar people, zealous of good works.*'"[28]

Bates further taught that as Jesus completes the work of atonement in heaven—that is, "in *this day* of atonement, while our Great High Priest is cleansing the sanctuary, (blotting out his people's sins,) preparing his jewels (Mal. iii:17) "[29]—Christ's people "enter into ... rest by keeping for the first time the right Sabbath of the Lord our God in their *patient waiting, or trying time;* resting from their labors, in these messages, from the world: ... waiting for their great high priest to finish the cleansing of the sanctuary, which blots out their sins, and purifies them to enter into the holy city."[30]

For Joseph Bates the concept that Christ entered the Most Holy Place in 1844 was not an exercise in metaphysics. Bates believed that Christ's new ministry imparted a vital new awareness of the privileges and responsibilities of Sabbath observance. For him, Christ's cleansing of the sanctuary connoted more than removing sins from records in a heavenly temple; it involved purification of the characters of the 144,000 saints on earth as the Sabbath message, voluntarily accepted, served to sanctify them and render them zealous of good works in essential preparation for the second coming of Christ.

Ellen White later made several references to this same concept of spiritual development in connection with the Sabbath and with Christ's ministry in the heavenly sanctuary. For example, in *The Great Controversy,* published in 1888, she wrote that "the people [that is, the Millerite Adventists of 1844] were not yet ready to meet their Lord. There was still a work of preparation to be accomplished for them. Light was to be given, directing their minds to the temple of God in Heaven; and as they should by faith follow their High Priest in his ministration there, new duties [including Sabbathkeeping] would be revealed. Another message of warning and instruction [the third angel's message] was to be given to the church. . . . Those who are living upon the earth when the intercession of Christ shall cease in the sanctuary above, are to stand in the sight of a holy God without a mediator. Their robes must be spotless, their characters must be purified from sin by the blood of sprinkling. Through the grace of God and their own diligent effort, they must be conquerors in the battle with evil. . . . When this work shall have been accomplished, the followers of Christ will be ready for his appearing."[31]

Group Study and Confirmation

We have seen enough to know that Bates did not develop his Sabbath theology in isolation. He served, rather, as the exponent of views developed by a band of Sabbatarian Adventists that included besides himself James and Ellen White, Hiram Edson, Stephen Pierce, and some others. This small group, in the words of one of them written much later, "searched for the truth"—sometimes all night—"as for hidden treasure."[32]

Historical developments in 1848, following the January appearance of *A Vindication of the Seventh-day Sabbath,* acted to encourage Bates and his associates in their Sabbatarian convictions. They also led Bates by the end of the year to a further significant interpretation.

Along with the Whites, Bates attended a series of seven "conferences" in 1848 that were organized for the benefit of those Adventists who were interested in the Sabbath. These occasions were attended by anywhere from a handful to around fifty persons. They convened in private homes or in farm buildings in Rocky Hill, Connecticut, in April and September; in Bristol, Connecticut, in June; in Volney and in Port Gibson, New York, in August; in Topsham, Maine, in October; and in Dorchester, Massachusetts, in November.[33]

The primary function of the conference series was to unify and confirm the laity in the sanctuary-Sabbath concept. James White reviewed the evidence of God's leadership in the Advent Movement. Bates traced the relation between the sanctuary and the Sabbath. And Ellen White exhorted to a quality of life harmonious with such ideas. (The impressive agenda sometimes conceived of for the series is speculative.)[34] Varying amounts of opposition were voiced at the first three gatherings. At the third and largest meeting (in Volney), Bates and the Whites stated firmly that they had not come to listen but to teach. They urged the people to concentrate on the "great truths" before them.[35]

JOSEPH BATES AND SDA SABBATH THEOLOGY

Unity and confirmation having been achieved well before the series ended, the company that gathered in Topsham in October looked to Bates to produce yet another publication on the Sabbath theology. While Bates hesitated, he and the Whites met in Dorchester in November. There, as the discussion focused on the seal of God in Revelation 7, Ellen White in vision saw that the seal was the Sabbath and that Revelation 7:1-3 implied that the Sabbath message would increase in prominence until, like the sun, it shone around the world.[36]

After the vision, Ellen White indicated that she believed God wanted her husband to launch a periodical and Bates to prepare a further publication (as some had suggested at the Topsham gathering). After the group satisfied itself that the Bible supports the view that the seal of Revelation 7 is the Sabbath, Bates, in January, 1849, came out with a booklet entitled *A Seal of the Living God. A Hundred Forty-four Thousand, of the Servants of God Being Sealed, in 1849*.[37] In this work he explicitly linked the seventh-day Sabbath to the eschatological seal of Revelation 7. He also associated this new understanding of the seal with his earlier view that it represented character development. He said that as Jesus cleanses the heavenly sanctuary, He seals and blots out the sins of only those persons who demonstrate strength of conviction by stalwart Sabbath observance.[38] He also taught that the 144,000 who will be sealed by the Sabbath are the saints, and the only saints, who will be alive at the Second Coming.[39] The prospect that the Sabbath message would be spread from a few American towns to the entire Christianized world and that the number of its adherents would increase from a few dozen to 144,000 did nothing to lessen Bates's confidence in the significance of his theology!

James White, in July, 1849, inaugurated *The Present Truth*, and in August, 1850, *The Advent Review*. In November, 1850, White merged the thrust of both papers into the enduring *Second Advent Review, and Sabbath Herald*. The title of the magazine had nothing to do with the future second coming of Christ. Instead, it promised the reader that the paper intended to keep reviewing the evidence that God had been in the Advent Awakening that had climaxed in October, 1844, and that therefore Christ's new function in the heavenly sanctuary since that date provided salient significance to the theology and practice of the Sabbath.

The Second Advent Review, and Sabbath Herald was the direct successor to Bates's own series of publications. Its masthead carried the names of James White and J. N. Andrews. With communication now entrusted to his younger colleagues, Joseph Bates closed his service as the principal publisher of Sabbatarian Adventist theology.

Other Important Concepts in Joseph Bates's Sabbath Theology

Before moving to a short survey of the relationship of Bates's Sabbath theology to later Seventh-day Adventism, we should pause to summarize what we have done so far and to note a few additional concepts and developments that deserve at least passing reference.

We have seen how Bates, after adopting the Seventh Day Baptist theology of the Sabbath, added to it one eschatological concept after another. This eschatological growth was rooted in his Millerite Adventist background. Successively Bates related the Sabbath to (a) the third angel of Revelation 14, (b) Christ's new ministry beside the ark in the heavenly sanctuary, conceived to have begun in 1844 in fulfillment of Revelation 11, (c) the "mark of the beast" of Revelation 14:9-11, (d) the "seal of God" of Revelation 7, and (e) the 144,000.

In addition to these concepts, it can be said that Bates was also interested in a theme of T. M. Preble's to the effect that Sabbathkeepers are the "true Israel" of the last days. In the first edition of *The Seventh Day Sabbath, a Perpetual Sign*, Bates concluded that, as the true Israel, Sabbathkeepers are heirs of the promises and obligations of Isaiah 58:13, 14: "If thou turn away thy foot from the sabbath, . . . then shalt thou . . . ride upon the high places of the earth," et cetera.[40] Bates also related the Sabbath to the "restitution of all things" promised in Acts 3:21, commenting, "I understand that the *seventh* day Sabbath is not the *least* one, among the *all* things that are to be restored before the second advent of Jesus Christ."[41]

In the second edition of *The Seventh Day Sabbath, a Perpetual Sign*, Bates developed logically from the concept of restitution in Acts 3 and the Sabbath promises in Isaiah 58 to the restitution prophecy of Isaiah 58:12. In doing this he presaged an emphasis that was to become characteristic of Seventh-day Adventism for many decades: "'They that shall be of THEE shall *build the old waste places—thou shalt raise up the foundation of many generations, and thou shalt be called the* REPAIRER *of the breach, the* RESTORER *of paths to dwell in.*'"[42] Bates observed that in view of verses 13 and 14, which immediately follow this prophecy, "repairing the breach" refers to the restoration of the Sabbath.

In *A Seal of the Living God*, in January, 1849, and in an 1850 tract called *An Explanation of the Typical and Anti-Typical Sanctuary, by the Scriptures. With a Chart*, Bates revived from earlier Adventist literature the concept of a pre-Advent judgment based on Daniel 7 and 8 and commencing in 1844.[43]

Not to be overlooked is the use Bates made of church history in support of his Sabbatarian theology. In both editions of *The Seventh Day Sabbath, a Perpetual Sign* he devoted several pages to the history of the so-called change of the Sabbath from the seventh to the first day of the week. In doing this, he followed the Seventh Day Baptists, who, in turn, had evidently taken their cue from the early Sabbatarian Puritans. Nicholas Bownde had shored up his theology of Sunday Sabbatarianism by attempting to deduce from history that the change from Saturday to Sunday occurred within the apostolic era and hence was Biblically approved. The Seventh Day Baptists—and Bates—used history to prove that the change occurred much later than the apostolic era and hence was *not* Biblically sanctioned. It was, in fact, on the basis that the change was made by the church in the age of apostasy that Bates demonstrated that Sunday was the characteristic, or "mark," of the beast. In mid-nineteenth-century America, the first beast of Revelation 13 was widely regarded, as it had been in Reformation Europe, as a symbol of historic apostate Christianity.

As for Bates's understanding of the third angel of Revelation 14, it underwent a significant shift during the years under observation here. When Bates commented on the third angel's message in the first edition of *The Seventh Day Sabbath, a Perpetual Sign*, he limited it to Revelation 14:9-11 (omitting verse 12), and he assumed that, like the messages of the first two angels, it had met its fulfillment within the Millerite movement. On this point James White disagreed with him. The matter not yet having been resolved, the identity of the third angel's message appears not to have been discussed at the 1848 conferences. Hiram

Edson leaned at first to Bates's view, but he changed to White's while writing on the subject in 1849. By 1850 Bates, too, had accepted White's position, and all three agreed that whereas the first two angels' messages were fulfilled in the Millerite movement, the third (including verse 12) did not commence its fulfillment until after 1844.[44]

The Course of Bates's Legacy

Bates's contribution to subsequent Seventh-day Adventist Sabbath theology was immense and has remained largely effective. Inevitably, of course, there have been developments and departures.

The three angels were very soon regarded, for practical purposes, as all flying currently with their messages, the first two no longer confined to the Millerite period. As new people adopted the Sabbath who had not participated in Millerism, they had to be taught the first two messages in order to understand the third.[45] In 1857 James White gave to the pre-Advent judgment the name "investigative judgment," by which it is still popularly designated.[46]

Bates's identification of the mark of the beast with Sunday observance underwent significant modification. Theoretical theology notwithstanding, it made little sense to say that all Sundaykeepers have the mark when so many are obviously devout. Ellen White effectively urged that no Sundaykeepers should be thought of as having the mark of the beast until they have chosen to reject clear evidence that Sunday stems from apostate Christendom.[47]

The quest for ever clearer evidence that, in fact, the Christian observance of Sunday does have a non-Biblical origin continued to stimulate interest in Sabbath-Sunday history. J. N. Andrews far surpassed Bates's treatment of the subject with his scholarly *History of the Sabbath and First Day of the Week,* which appeared in three editions during his lifetime. L. R. Conradi did not improve on Andrews' work in his fourth edition (1912), when, unwisely, he followed Adolf Harnack and cited Gnosticism as a major factor in the change of the day.[48] Nor did C. M. Sorenson help much when, following Franz Cumont, he cited Mithraism as a major cause.[49] Ellen White simply—and defensibly—attributed the change to incipient worldliness, misunderstanding of the gospel, distaste for Jewish legalism, and the attractiveness of Sunday in view of Christ's resurrection.[50]

The relationship that Bates stressed between the Sabbath and Christ's High Priestly ministry in developing character and blotting out sins has not been lost sight of but has been somewhat obscured. Contemporary North American Adventist writers seem somewhat more interested in Abraham Heschel's "cathedral in time" concept than in Bates's sanctuary in heaven.[51] As early as 1853 James White eagerly accepted a Seventh Day Baptist tract, *Elihu on the Sabbath,* and turned it into a sort of instant Seventh-day Adventist classic. It was still being distributed at least as late as 1903, by which time half a million copies must have been in print, *even though it omits* all of the Christ-centered sanctuary eschatology that characterized Bates's Sabbath works.[52]

Obfuscation of the sanctuary Christ, represented by the popularity of *Elihu and the Sabbath,* was paralleled between 1850 and 1890 by a partial but serious eclipse of the crucified Christ in the presentation of the Sabbath. Ellen White pleaded with the Adventist ministry to make the "burden" of its message "the mission and life of Jesus Christ."[53] A change was at last inaugurated by the

THE SABBATH IN SCRIPTURE AND HISTORY

Christ-centered presentations of Ellen White and Ellet J. Waggoner at the General Conference session held in Minneapolis in 1888. By October, 1893, 166,000 copies were in print of W. W. Prescott's *Christ and the Sabbath*,[54] a work that employs the name of Christ meaningfully some 260 times in its thirty-nine pages. Its central burden is that no one can keep the Sabbath holy without a personal involvement with Jesus Christ, the Lord of the Sabbath.

Summary

In 1845 Joseph Bates adopted the Sabbath theology of the Seventh Day Baptists and, in a series of publications over the succeeding five years, wedded it to a systematic Biblical eschatology that was influenced by his former experience in Millerite Adventism. In doing this he was associated with Hiram Edson, Stephen Pierce, and others, and especially with James and Ellen White. His spiritual successors, the Seventh-day Adventists of today, still seriously, but not slavishly, advocate and propagate his views.

NOTES

[1] The name "Seventh-day Adventist" was not adopted officially until October, 1860. For convenience, however, it is used in this appendix for appropriate persons, events, and ideas prior to that date.
[2] The best study of William Miller and the Millerites is Francis D. Nichol's *The Midnight Cry* (Washington, D.C., 1944). See also C. Mervyn Maxwell, *Tell It to the World* (Mountain View, Calif., 1976), chaps. 1-16.
[3] New Bedford [Mass.].
[4] *The Doctrine of the Sabbath, plainely layde forth, and soundly proved by testimonies both of Holy Scripture, and also of olde and new ecclesiastical writers*, 2 vols. (London, 1595), 1:21. See the discussion of this work in chapter 12, p. 493.
[5] Jonathan Edwards, *Twenty Sermons on Various Subjects* (Edinburgh, 1789), p. 208.
[6] William Miller, "Lecture on the Great Sabbath," *Life and Views*, p. 157, in T. M. Preble, *A Tract, Showing That the Seventh Day Should Be Observed as the Sabbath, Instead of the First Day; "According to the Commandment'* (Nashua/[N. H.?] 1845), pp. 3, 5.
[7] See editorials in *The Midnight Cry*, Aug. 22, Sept. 5, and Sept. 15, 1844.
[8] *The Seventh Day Sabbath, a Perpetual Sign*, p. 24.
[9] See, e.g., William Miller, *Evidence From Scripture and History of the Second Coming of Christ, About the Year 1843*, Second Advent Library, No. 2 (Boston, 1840), esp. pp. 45-47, 55-57, in his third sermon, "The Two Thousand Three Hundred Days."
[10] Hiram Edson, manuscript fragment, deposited in the Heritage Room, James White Library, Andrews University, Berrien Springs, Michigan.
[11] *Ibid.*
[12] *Ibid.*
[13] His article was entitled "The Law of Moses."
[14] *The Opening Heavens, or A Connected View of the Testimony of the Prophets and Apostles, Concerning the Opening Heavens, Compared With Astronomical Observations, and of the Present and Future Location of the New Jerusalem, the Paradise of God* (New Bedford [Mass.], 1846), esp. p. 25.
[15] This visit is referred to in Edson, *op. cit.*
[16] New Bedford (Mass.).
[17] 2d ed. pp. 58, 59.
[18] *Ibid.*, pp. iii, iv.
[19] *Ibid.*
[20] In 1860, Ellen White located this first sanctuary-Sabbath vision in New Bedford, the city across the river from Fairhaven. See Ellen G. White, *Spiritual Gifts*, 4 vols. (Battle Creek, Mich., 1858-1864), 2:82. However, in the "Remarks" Joseph Bates attached to his publication of the similar April 3 vision, he said that "at a meeting in Fairhaven, 6th of last month, I saw her a similar vision." The contemporaneousness of Bates s statement, not to mention that he lived in the area, justifies assigning preference to his data. The first vision appears to be the one described in *Spiritual Gifts*, 2:82, and in Ellen G. White, *Life Sketches of Ellen G. White* (Mountain View, Calif., 1915), pp. 95, 96.
[21] See *A Vision*, April 7, 1847; reprinted, with editorial changes, in Ellen White, *Life Sketches*, pp. 100-103.
[22] Cf. Ellen G. White letter 2, 1874: "It was months after I had commenced keeping the Sabbath before I was shown [in vision] its importance and its place in the third angel's message."
[23] New Bedford (Mass.). The publication date of May is inferred, in part, from page 73, which refers to a copy of the *Voice of Truth* for April 28, 1847, as having just come to hand. James White, in a letter dated May 21, 1847, reported that "Brother Bates is out with a book on our past experience."
[24] Bates, *Way Marks*, pp. 72, 73.
[25] Articles on the Sabbath question appeared in the *Advent Harbinger*, June 29, 1847, and the *Bible Advocate*, Aug. 26, Sept. 2, 16, 28, Oct. 21, Nov. 4, 11, and Dec. 2, 9, 16, 23, 30, 1847, and Jan. 13, 1848.
[26] New Bedford (Mass.). Godfrey T. Anderson discovered a copy in 1976, in the Boston City Library.
[27] James White, *Life Incidents in Connection With the Great Advent Movement, as Illustrated by the Three Angels of*

JOSEPH BATES AND SDA SABBATH THEOLOGY

Revelation XIV (Battle Creek, Mich., 1868), p. 269.

[28] Bates, *Vindication*, p. 96.
[29] *Ibid.*, pp. 73, 74.
[30] *Ibid.*, p. 108.
[31] *Ibid.*, pp. 424, 425.
[32] Ellen G. White, *Selected Messages From the Writings of Ellen G. White*, 2 vols. (Washington, D.C.: 1958), 1:206.
[33] Contemporary and reminiscent data on the 1848 conferences by persons who attended them can be found in James White letters, July 2, Aug. 26, and Oct. 2, 1848, and in Ellen G. White letter, May 29, 1848. Also in James White, *Life Incidents*, pp. 270, 271, 274, 275, and in Ellen White, *Spiritual Gifts*, 2:91-108; *Life Sketches*, pp. 107-115, and Joseph Bates, *A Seal of the Living God. A Hundred Forty-Four Thousand, of the Servants of God Being Sealed, in 1849* (New Bedford [Mass.], 1849), pp. 24-27, 32. Gordon O. Martinborough, "The Beginnings of a Theology of the Sabbath Among American Sabbatarian Adventists, 1842-1850" (M.A. thesis, Loma Linda University, 1976), offers helpful insights.
[34] See, for example, LeRoy Edwin Froom, *The Prophetic Faith of Our Fathers*, 4 vols. (Washington, D.C., 1946-1954), 4:1030-1048.
[35] Both James White ("The Work of the Lord," *Review and Herald*, May 6, 1852, p. 5) and Ellen White (*Spiritual Gifts*, 2:99) say that Ellen White urged the people to unite on the "third angel's message." This is certainly an interpretation, looking back from the time when unity had been reached, that the "third angel's message" did in fact encompass what Bates and the Whites were presenting. See note 44.
[36] Bates, *A Seal of the Living God*, pp. 24-26.
[37] See notes 33, 36.
[38] *Ibid.*, pp. 20, 37.
[39] *Ibid.*, p. 54.
[40] *Idem.*, *Perpetual Sign*, 1st ed., p. 44.
[41] *Ibid.*, p. 2.
[42] *Ibid.*, 2d ed., p. 60.
[43] *Idem, Seal*, p. 39; *idem, An explanation of the Typical and Anti-Typical Sanctuary, by the Scriptures. With a Chart* (New Bedford [Mass.], 1850), p. 10. Compare James White, "The Day of Judgment," *The Advent Review*, September, 1850, p. 49.
[44] See Bates, *Way Marks* (1847), pp. 19, 27, 61, 62, 68, 72; James White, "Thoughts on Revelation 14," in James White, Ellen G. White, and Joseph Bates, *A Word to the "Little Flock"* (Brunswick [Me.], 1847), pp. 10, 11; Bates, *Seal* (1849), pp. 33-37, 61; Hiram Edson, *The Time of the End; Its Beginning, Progressive Events, and Final Termination. A Discourse* (Auburn [N.Y.], 1849), p. 20.
[45] See, for example, Ellen G. White manuscript 11, 1850, and James White, "Babylon," *Review and Herald*, June 10, 1852, p. 20.
[46] James White, "The Judgment," *Review and Herald*, Jan. 29, 1857, pp. 100-102.
[47] Ellen White, *The Great Controversy* (Mountain View, Calif.: 1888), p. 449.
[48] J. N. Andrews and L. R. Conradi, *History of the Sabbath and First Day of the Week*, 4th ed., rev. and enl. (Washington, D.C., 1912), pp. 232-237.
[49] Unpublished proceedings of the Seventh-day Adventist Bible Conference, Takoma Park, Washington, D.C., 1919.
[50] See esp. Ellen White, *The Great Controversy*, pp. 52, 53. Cf. *ibid.*, pp. 43, 62, 384, 444, 577, and *idem, The Acts of the Apostles* (Mountain View, Calif.: 1911), pp. 553, 587.
[51] Abraham Joshua Heschel, *The Sabbath*, expanded ed. (Cleveland, Ohio, 1951, 1952). Cf. references in a sophisticated Adventist publication, Jack W. Provonsha, *God Is With Us* (Washington, D.C., 1974), p. 34, and in a trendy youth radio production, "The Sabbath," *His Way*, cassette 13 (Charlotte, N.C., 1975).
[52] See R. F. Cottrell, "A Visit to Brother 'Elihu,'" *Review and Herald*, April 1, 1880, p. 210; *idem, Elihu on the Sabbath*, Bible Students Library, No. 42 (Mountain View, Calif., Oct. 15, 1889), introduction; and a copy of the tract printed by the Review and Herald Publishing Association sometime after its 1903 move to Takoma Park, Washington, D.C., on file in the Heritage Room, Andrews University.
[53] Ellen G. White, "The Work of the Minister," *Review and Herald*, Sept. 11, 1888, p. 578.
[54] Rev. ed., The Religious Liberty Library, No. 14 (Battle Creek, Mich., 1893).

APPENDIX H

The Sabbath on a Round World

Raymond F. Cottrell and Lawrence T. Geraty*

A SUNSET-TO-SUNSET Sabbath on a round world is determined by the natural phenomenon of a spherical planet rotating on its axis in relation to the sun. This process of nature results in the night-day sequence, which is marked off by alternating sunset and sunrise.

Reckoning Time on a Round World

As the earth turns on its axis from west to east, the sun appears to rise in the east and set in the west, making one complete revolution around the earth in approximately twenty-four hours (more precisely, about twenty-three hours, fifty-six minutes, and four seconds of mean solar or clock time). Whereas clock time is calculated according to time zones that have been established and that are based on longitude, the *precise moments of sunrise and sunset* vary not only with longitude but also with latitude north or south of the equator, with altitude, and with the season of the year. These moments of sunrise and sunset are constantly moving along the "day-night line" that divides light from darkness. This "day-night line" encircles the earth at right angles to the sun and is known as the "terminator."

In order to reckon time on our spherical rotating planet, it is obviously necessary to think of each twenty-four-hour day as moving continuously westward as the earth turns eastward on its axis. In terms of clock time, with days reckoned midnight to midnight, the place where any day (Sunday, Monday, Tuesday, et cetera) first begins (at midnight) and terminates twenty-four hours later (at midnight) is known as the "international date line."

The International Prime Meridian Conference of 1884 in Washington, D.C., designated the meridian of Greenwich as the world's prime meridian, or 0° longitude. Halfway around the world, the 180th meridian is the "date line." When it is noon along the prime meridian, it is midnight along the date line.

Useful as the date line is for determining days on a midnight-to-midnight basis, the inclination of the earth's axis 23° 27' perpendicular to the ecliptic, or

---

* Cottrell is the primary author; Geraty authored most of the last section ("In the Land of the Midnight Sun").

plane of the earth's orbit about the sun, makes it impossible to use the 180th, or any other, meridian as a basis for determining the beginning and ending of days measured *sunset to sunset*. At the summer solstice (June 21), for instance, when the sun sets at the intersection of a given meridian with the equator at 6:00 P.M., it will set approximately five and a half hours later at the same meridian just south of the Arctic Circle and five and a half hours earlier on the same meridian just north of the Antarctic Circle, a difference of about eleven hours. Only at the spring and autumn equinoxes are day and night of equal length everywhere.[1]

Thus, to determine the arrival of a day on the basis of midnight, it is necessary simply to note the moment of midnight in the particular time zone within which a person lives. But to determine the anticipated arrival of the sundown-to-sundown Sabbath, it is necessary to ascertain in advance the moment of sunset at each particular location. For this information Seventh-day Adventists and various other observers of the seventh-day Sabbath refer to sunset time given in meterological tables for any given location, or the time is computed specifically for this purpose and published in church periodicals.

To attempt to synchronize observance of either the Sabbath or Sunday the world around would be, for all practical purposes, impossible. Nor is there any Biblical basis for doing so. When the apostle Paul was in Jerusalem, for instance, he obviously observed the Sabbath from sunset to sunset Jerusalem time, and when he was in Corinth he evidently did so when the sun set at Corinth—a difference of about twenty-five minutes.[2] For early Christians, wherever they were, sunset *local time* determined the commencement of the Sabbath.

Function of the International Date Line

The facts of geography, the migrations of peoples east and west, trans-Pacific voyages of discovery and commerce, acceptance in 1884 of the meridian of Greenwich as the prime meridian, and international usage were all involved in the eventual acceptance by all nations of the international date line, generally coinciding with the 180th meridian, as the place where each calendar day first begins.

Geographically, the 180th meridian is the logical location for the date line because it passes through fewer habitable land areas (the far eastern tip of Sibera and the northern island of New Zealand) than any other direct line that might be drawn between the North and South Poles. In order to avoid inconveniencing the people of Siberia, the Aleutian Islands, and New Zealand, the date line deviates locally at those places a short distance east or west from the meridian.

Every degree of longitude east or west (a distance of about fifty miles in midtemperate latitudes) translates into a difference of four minutes of clock time. When one travels eastward, the sun rises and sets four minutes *earlier* with every degree of longitude. On the other hand, when one travels westward, the sun rises and sets four minutes *later* for each degree of longitude. People traveling from a point in Europe or Asia eastward to the Pacific Ocean and people traveling westward from the *same point* of origin until they reach the longitude of San Francisco, California, in the U.S.A. would, by resetting their watches, have accumulated a difference of some sixteen clock hours (two thirds of a calendar day).

Expressed in another way, the sun looks directly down on San Francisco sixteen hours after it has done so above Shanghai, China, on the opposite side of the Pacific, and eight hours before it will do so again. Thus, when it is high noon in San Francisco, it is already 4:00 A.M. *the following calendar day* in Shanghai. Accordingly, a person in San Francisco is two thirds of a calendar day *behind* a person in Shanghai, figured around the world from east to west as the sun travels. If the person in San Francisco were to cross the Pacific without omitting a calendar day from his reckoning, to compensate for the calendar time lost, he would be a full calendar day behind Shanghai when he arrived there.

For this reason a person moving across the date line in a westerly direction must omit one calendar day from his reckoning, while a person going in the opposite direction must insert an additional calendar day by repeating one day. It became customary for ships traversing the Pacific Ocean to make this adjustment in their calendar reckoning in midocean, originally at noon but eventually at midnight, immediately after crossing the 180th meridian.[3]

The first travelers to become aware of the loss of a calendar day in circumnavigating the globe from east to west were those who sailed with Magellan on his famous voyage, 1519 to 1522. Having kept an accurate record of the days en route, they arrived at the Cape Verde Islands on what was, to them, Wednesday, July 9, 1522. Imagine their consternation upon discovering that it was Thursday, July 10, local time, in the islands! When they made port at Seville, Spain, on what they thought was Saturday, September 6, it was actually already Sunday, September 7, in Seville.[4] They had lost an entire calendar day from their reckoning without knowing it, though the actual elapsed time was the same for them as for those who had remained in Spain.[5]

Similarly, when Sir Francis Drake returned to Plymouth, England, after sailing around the world in 1580, again east to west, it was Sunday, September 26, aboard his ship but Monday, September 27, in Plymouth.[6]

If these pioneer globetrotters had journeyed in the opposite direction—from west to east—they would have *gained* a day of calendar time.

During the nineteenth century most missionaries and colonists from Europe to the islands of the Pacific sailed eastward around the Cape of Good Hope. Many of them located on islands east of the 180th meridian without realizing the need to add a day into their reckoning by repeating one day. This was true of those who located on Pitcairn Island and of missionaries to the Society, Samoan, Cook, and Friendly islands, for instance.[7] It was also true of the Russian colonists who settled Alaska.[8] As a result, Christians on these islands and in Alaska were actually observing Saturday, thinking the day to be Sunday (as it actually was, just across the date line and in Europe).[9] Decades later, Alaska and all of these islands except Tonga made the official change in order to coordinate their calendar days with their geographical location east of the 180th meridian.[10]

In contrast, the Philippine Islands were colonized by Spaniards who sailed westward across the Atlantic and the Pacific. Thus their Sunday actually fell on Monday, until the proper adjustment was made.[11]

In the United States the general public became aware of the reality of a "date line" with the purchase of Alaska from Russia in 1867. As mentioned earlier, the location of this date line was stabilized as the 180th meridian by the International Prime Meridian Conference of 1884.

In the closing decades of the nineteenth entury, burgeoning travel and commerce between the west coast of North America and the Orient intensified an awareness of the existence of a date line, and ill-informed critics of the seventh-day Sabbath latched onto the date-line enigma, then in the public eye, as a convenient ruse for confusing the Sabbath issue, though at least some of them were evidently honestly confused in their own minds as well.[12]

It is interesting to note that whereas prior to 1867 there had been only four articles about the Sabbath on a round world in *The Advent Review and Sabbath Herald*,[13] in that one year there were three.[14] The climax came four years later, in 1871, with twenty-one articles on the subject![15]

The purpose of this spate of articles was to clarify the fact that dropping or inserting a *calendar* day in crossing the Pacific has no effect on *real* time, despite the fact that those making the journey have one week with only six calendar days if their direction of travel is east to west, or a week with eight calendar days if they are going in the opposite direction. The solution to the problem, according to the articles, was that the Bible requirement of a seventh-day Sabbath can be kept on a round world when it is observed from sunset to sunset, local time, *wherever a person may chance to be*.

Especially noteworthy is the protracted series of eight lengthy front-page articles on the subject by J. N. Andrews, from May 30 to August 22, 1871.[16] He, as well as other writers, repeatedly pointed out that critics of the Saturday Sabbath who substituted the more general seventh-part-of-time concept for the more specific, God-appointed seventh day of each week faced the very same dilemma of having one week with only six days if going west, or a week with eight days going east.

In the Land of the Midnight Sun

Above the Arctic Circle (66° 33' north latitude) or below the Antarctic Circle (66° 33' south latitude), observance of the Sabbath is complicated by the fact that for a period of time each summer the sun remains above the horizon continuously without setting, while for a comparable period of time each winter it remains below the horizon without rising, for several days, weeks, or months (depending upon latitude).

Most Seventh-day Adventists residing in the Arctic begin the Sabbath during these periods of perpetual light or darkness at the time the sun reaches its lowest point (i.e., its nadir)—always above the horizon in the summer and below the horizon in the winter.[17] Since the sun is never seen during the winter, these times are calculated and printed in "sunset tables" for their respective locales. Others begin their Sabbath at the same hour as the last visible sunset (which is identical with the first visible sunset at the close of these periods).[18] In so doing they apply the Biblical evening-to-evening requirement to the actual earth-sun relationship. Depending on latitude, the last visible winter sunset occurs about Friday noon, and the last visible summer sunset about Friday midnight.[19] Still others, during the winter when the sun is not visible, employ the "twilight theory." According to this practice, the Sabbath is bordered by the time between twilight (the diminishing of light) and the arrival of full darkness.[20]

In recent years a 6:00 P.M.-to-6:00 P.M. view for the observance of Sabbath has been suggested.[21] In order to bring about greater unity of practice, the Northern European Division of Seventh-day Adventists appointed a study committee to review the history of practice, to research the Biblical and theological data that have a bearing on the borderlines of the Sabbath, and to make recommendations with regard to its findings. After a February 28 to March 1, 1980, meeting at Skodsborg, Denmark, the committee concluded that from a study of the Biblical material the following points become evident: "Evening" (Hebrew *'ereb*) marks the beginning and the ending of the twenty-four-hour day. "Evening" is the transitional *period* (not *point*) between light and darkness. Within "evening," sunset is the most specific point marking this transition. Thus the cycle of the twenty-four-hour day (including the seventh-day Sabbath) is governed by *natural* phenomena. Since Ellen G. White, by both statements and practice, demonstrated her support after 1855 for sunset as the point of time that marks the beginning and ending of the Sabbath, and since this has been the traditional teaching and practice of Seventh-day Adventists, even in Arctic regions, the committee reaffirmed sunset to be the time for the beginning and ending of Sabbath.

However, it was recognized that the Biblical data do offer some flexibility in defining "evening," making it cover the period of diminishing light prior to actual darkness. Consequently, for areas where this diminishing of light, rather than a visible setting of the sun, provides the observable natural phenomenon that indicates the end of the twenty-four-hour day, it was recognized that use of this sort of Sabbath-evening "border line" meets the spirit of the Biblical injunction given in Leviticus 23:32. The committee therefore recommended that in those regions this period of diminishing light be used as a guideline for beginning and ending the Sabbath, rather than fixing upon an arbitrary, rigid rule. Furthermore, it urged ministerial workers and lay members to respect one another's conscience, looking with genuine Christian love upon those who conscientiously differ in regard to the time for beginning and ending the Sabbath, particularly during the winter period of darkness.[22]

This arrangement may seem strange to people unaccustomed to life in the Arctic, but it is an entirely logical application of the Bible requirement "even to even" to reality in the land of the midnight sun. Furthermore, it provides for continuity in Sabbath observance based on *natural* phenomena, without resort to either artificial astronomical tables or clocks. This arrangement occasions no more difficulty for persons accustomed to it than the more conventional procedure does in the rest of the world.[23]

The principle has been aptly stated by a Seventh-day Adventist authority: "God made His Sabbath for a round world; and when the seventh day comes to us in that round world, controlled by the sun that rules the day, it is the time, in all countries and lands, to observe the Sabbath."[24]

NOTES

[1] What is known as the equation of time—the fact that the sun may actually be, at times, as much as about seventeen minutes faster than mean sun time, and at other times that much slower, because of the acceleration of Planet Earth as it approaches perihelion and corresponding deceleration as it approaches aphelion—introduces still further minor variations in sunrise and sunset time.

[2] A favorite ploy once used by critics of the seventh-day Sabbath held that it had to be observed synchronously around the world, with sunset in Palestine. Early articles in *The Advent Review and Sabbath Herald* (hereafter, *Review*) often pointed out the fallacy of this ploy. See, for example, Uriah Smith, "How Can the Sabbath Be Kept at the North Pole?" Feb. 28, 1856, p. 172; F. J. Bideler, "'Turning the World Upside Down,'" March 21, 1871, p. 111; Uriah Smith, "Uncalled-for Solicitude," Aug. 9, 1887, p. 505.

[3] Discussed by Uriah Smith, "Time on a Round World," *Review*, Oct. 15, 1889, p. 648.

[4] Robert Leo Odom, *The Lord's Day on a Round World* (Nashville, Tenn., 1970), p. 70.

[5] *Ibid.*

[6] *Ibid.*, p. 73.
[7] *Ibid.*, pp. 105, 118, 139, 145, 164.
[8] *Ibid.*, p. 128. Following the purchase of Alaska by the United States in 1867, the numerous articles in the *Review* dealing with the Sabbath-Sunday problem included, e.g., J. M. Aldrich, "Witty," July 2, 1867, p. 44; Uriah Smith, "A Very Poor Joke," Jan. 17, 1871, p. 36; *idem*, "The Facts in the Case," Feb. 21, 1871, p. 76; J. N. Andrews, "The Advantages of the Sunday-Sabbath in Being Easily Kept All Over the Globe," Aug. 22, 1871, pp. 73, 74.
[9] See note 8.
[10] Odom, *op. cit.*, pp. 105, 128, 164; K. H. Wood, "From the Editor's Mailbag," *Review*, May 16, 1968, p. 13; L. A. Smith, "It Makes a Difference," *Review*, Nov. 18, 1902, p. 6.
[11] See "Date Boundary Line," *Review*, Feb. 10, 1891, p. 87, from *Scientific American*. For a map showing the date line curving west of the Philippine Islands, see Uriah Smith, "Time on a Round World," *Review*, Oct. 1, 1889, p. 616.
[12] Numerous articles in the *Review* sought to abate the confused and confusing arguments advanced by critics of the seventh-day Sabbath. For example: Uriah Smith, "The Sabbath in the Arctic Regions," Sept. 9, 1862, pp. 117, 118; "Defense of the Truth in Saginaw Co., Mich.," July 16, 1867, p. 74; J. H. Waggoner, "A Day All Around the World," Feb. 28, 1871, p. 85; F. J. Bideler, "'Turning the World Upside Down,'" March 21, 1871, p. 111; J. N. Andrews, "Solution of Problems Relating to the Day Line," July 4, 1871, pp. 17, 18; C. W. Stone, "'A Curious Fact,'" May 10, 1877. p. 148; Uriah Smith, "Impotent Opposition," April 4, 1878, p. 108; *idem*, "Uncalled-for-Solicitude," Aug. 9, 1887, p. 505; G. B. Thompson, "The 144,000 of Revelation 14," Oct. 8, 1889, pp. 627, 628; L. A. Smith, "The Sabbath and the Calendar," April 26, 1906, p. 5.
[13] A. H. Hutchins, "The Sabbath," *Review*, Jan. 6, 1853, p. 134; Uriah Smith, "The Sabbath in the Arctic Regions," *Review*, Sept. 9, 1862, pp. 117, 118; J. N. Loughborough, "The Sabbath on a Round World," *Review*, Oct. 11, 1864, pp. 157, 158; Uriah Smith, "How Can the Sabbath Be Kept at the North Pole?" *Review*, Feb. 28, 1856, p. 172.
[14] J. M. Aldrich, "Witty," *Review*, July 2, 1867, p. 44; "Defense of the Truth in Saginaw Co., Mich.," *Review*, July 16, 1867, p. 74; Uriah Smith, "Where Does the Day Begin?" *Review*, April 2, 1867, p. 201.
[15] Twelve by J. N. Andrews, including a special series of eight articles, and nine by other authors.
[16] Each article in this series bore a separate title. No explanation accompanies the series, but the length of the articles and the position of prominence accorded them reflects considerable agitation over the subject.
[17] Oral communication from Finn H. Opsahl, secretary-treasurer, West Nordic Union Conference of Seventh-day Adventists, Feb. 28, 1980. This time can be as early as 10:30 A.M. on Friday because of the attempt in Norway to keep the entire country on one time zone even though it stretches through three from Bergen in the west (longitude 5°) to Kirkenes in the east (longitude 30°).
[18] Odom, *op. cit.*, p. 201.
[19] *Ibid.*
[20] This view, everywhere applicable, was advocated by the Northern European Division committee on May 18, 1955, after having been proposed as early as 1951 by local conference and union committees in Norway.
[21] Especially an article by H. Nordnes in *Advent-inform*, November, 1979.
[22] This paragraph follows closely the wording of the committee minutes that were subsequently accepted by the General Conference Committee.
[23] This point with regard to the "last visible sunset" method of reckoning the time to begin Sabbath was emphasized in numerous *Review* articles: Uriah Smith, "The Sabbath in the Arctic Regions," Sept. 9, 1862, pp. 117, 118; S. N. Haskell, "The Midnight Sun," Aug. 27, 1889, pp. 537, 538; Uriah Smith, "Sunset in Norway," May 28, 1901, p. 344. Haskell and Smith both reported conversations with permanent residents north of the Arctic Circle who told how they kept account of "sunrise" and "sunset" and the beginning and ending of the day, and who expressed surprise that anyone should believe it difficult to do so.
[24] Ellen G. White letter 167, 1900.

GLOSSARY

Glossary

Note: Definitions given below are not intended to include the full range of dictionary definitions of the terms listed, but rather reflect the specific or special meanings of those terms as used in the chapters and appendixes of the present volume.

Aggadah An Aramaic form of *Haggadah* (see *Haggadah*).

Akkadian An extinct Semitic language of the Mesopotamian region, used by the Assyrians and Babylonians.

Anagogical Having a spiritual meaning or a sense referring to the heavenly life. Medieval interpretation also saw in Scripture three other meanings: literal, allegorical, and tropological (the last pertains to morality or moral life).

Anthropomorphism Attribution of human shape or characteristics to God.

Antinomians Opponents of (God's) law, usually in the sense that faith alone brings salvation and that obedience to the Decalogue is unnecessary.

Apocryphal Uncanonical; of doubtful authenticity or authority. Often reference is made to a corpus of material known as "Old Testament Apocrypha" or "New Testament Apocrypha," depending on time when written and frame of reference. The "Old Testament Apocrypha" (often simply called "Apocrypha" and including 1 and 2 Esdras, Tobit, 1 and 2 Maccabees, and other works) normally no longer appear in Protestant Bible translations, though the King James Version originally included them.

Apodictic The form of legal statement that expresses general truth or obligation but does not detail specific causes or indicate (usually) sanctions (see also Casuistic).

Astral Pertaining to the planets and stars or "starry heavens." In ancient times the sun and moon were also treated as part of the astral family.

Bruchae Monstrous legendary animals.

Casuistic The form of legal statement (i.e., statement of laws) that deals with specific cases and their special or individual sanctions.

Casuists Persons expert in, or inclined to resort to, casuistry. In both Judaism and Christianity, casuists were experts in law who refined and redefined legal requirements to meet the situations current in their time and place.

Catechumens Persons, especially adults, receiving instruction in the fundamentals of Christianity before baptism.

Codices Plural of *codex*, a manuscript in book form (as contrasted with a scroll). The term is used especially of those copies of Scripture or of classical texts that appeared in this form.

Coptic Pertaining to the Copts (natives of Egypt, descended from the ancient inhabitants of that country), their language, culture, et cetera.

Coracle A short, wide boat made of a waterproof material stretched over a wicker or wooden frame.

Crypto Jews Jews who practiced their religion secretly and not by public avowal.

Cubits (2,000) An ancient measure of length, about 18 to 22 inches; originally, the length of the arm from the end of the middle finger to the elbow. The "Sabbath-day's journey" of 2,000 cubits would therefore be about three-fifths of a mile.

Cushitic Designating or pertaining to a group of languages spoken in Ethiopia and East Africa, constituting a subfamily of the Afro-Asiatic family of languages.

Decretalists Decretal—relating to or containing a decree; hence, specialists in the study of decretals, particularly papal decrees.

Diaspora Jews A term to indicate the widespread settlement of Jews outside Palestine.

GLOSSARY

Enthusiasts Religious fanatics or zealots, often believing themselves to be inspired or possessed by a divine power or spirit. In Christianity these have appeared throughout the history of the church. Mainstream Reformers of the sixteenth century (e.g., Luther) considered various radical reformers, including Anabaptists, as "enthusiasts."

Equinoctial Relating to either of the equinoxes (spring or autumn), when night and day are equal in length.

Erastian Advocating the supreme authority of the state in church matters.

Esoteric Intended for or understood by only a chosen few, as an inner group of disciples or initiates; said of ideas, doctrines, literature, et cetera.

"Etiological myth" The concept that a story is created and told to assign or seek to assign a cause for some monument, landmark, structure, boundary, et cetera.

Familists Members of a mystical and somewhat antinomian sect of sixteenth- and seventeenth-century Europe who believed that law was somehow restricting to one's personal relationship with God.

Form criticism A method of Biblical criticism that seeks to classify units of Scripture into literary patterns (as love poems, parables, sayings, elegies, legends) and that attempts to trace each type to its period of oral transmission in an effort to determine the original form and the relationship of the life and thought of the period to the development of the literary tradition.

Haggadah Nonlegal lore of Judaism, including anecdotes, historical accounts, and other illustrations of legal principles.

Halakah (Halachah) The authorized and normative law of Jewish religious life, based principally upon the Mosaic law together with the post-Biblical Rabbinic codes and interpretations.

Hasidism A belief that emphasizes joyful worship of an immanent God by members of a sect of Jewish mystics that originated in Poland in the eighteenth century.

Imago Dei The image of God (Gen. 1:26, 27).

Imitatio Dei Imitation of God.

Interdiction An official prohibition or restraint.

Intertestamental Of, relating to, or being the period of several centuries between the composition of the last canonical book of the Old Testament and the writing of the books of the New Testament.

Kenites A nomadic or seminomadic tribe of smiths, who in the latter half of the second millennium B.C. appear to have made their livelihood as metal craftsmen and lived in the northern part of the Sinai Peninsula.

Kiddush cup In Judaism, used during a benediction recited over wine or bread on the eve of the Sabbath or a festival.

Levirate A custom of the Jews in Biblical times by which a dead man's brother was obligated to marry the widow if there were no sons.

Libertines Freethinkers, especially in religious matters.

Logia Maxims attributed to a religious leader; especially sayings attributed to Jesus.

Menology A calendar of the months, with their events.

Monotheism Belief that there is only one God.

Mystes One initiated into the mysteries.

Nimbus A bright cloud supposedly surrounding gods or goddesses appearing on earth; or, an aura of splendor about any person or thing.

Ogdoad The number eight; or any group or series of eight. In the early Christian centuries, certain Gnostic heretics referred to the "Ogdoad" in their antimatter mythology (the Valentinians, e.g., had an Ogdoad, a Decad, and a Dodecad in their system of aeons).

Ostraca Pottery fragments containing writing.

Paraenesis An exhortatory composition.

Pentecontad Based on fifty; specifically, an ancient system of calendation supposed to have been structured upon fifty-day periods.

Philo Hellenistic Jewish philosopher of Alexandria, who lived *c.* 20 B.C.-A.D. 50.

Phylactery Either of two small leather cases holding slips inscripted with Scripture passages; one is fastened with leather thongs to the forehead and one to the left arm by Orthodox or Conservative Jewish men during morning prayer on weekdays (see Deut. 6:4-9).

Piel (pi'el) A Hebrew verbal form that intensifies the meaning of the word.

Proleptic Of, relating to, or exemplifying prolepsis, i.e., anticipation of an event. Especially, prolepsis can be the describing of an event as taking place before it could have done so, or the treating of a future event as if it had already happened.

Pseudepigrapha A group of early writings not included in the Biblical canon or the Apocrypha, some of which were falsely ascribed to Biblical characters. (See also Apocryphal.)

Punic The Northwest Semitic language of ancient Carthage, a dialect of Phoenician. It survived until *c.* A.D. 500.

Quadriga In ancient Rome, a two-wheeled chariot drawn by four horses abreast.

Quartodeciman Pertaining to observance of the Passover celebration on the basis of the fourteenth of Nisan as the day when the Paschal lamb was killed. In early Christian history, the Christians who celebrated their annual commemoration of Christ's death and resurrection on the basis of this sort of reckoning were called Quartodecimans ("Fourteenthers").

Quotidian Daily; recurring every day; usual or ordinary.

Rebbes In Judaism, Hasidic rabbis (singular, *Rebbe*).

Redactors Editors—those who arrange in proper form for publication.

Sarcophagus Among the ancient Greeks and Romans, a limestone coffin or tomb, often inscribed and elaborately ornamented.

Satrap The governor of a province in ancient Persia.

Septuagint The first venacular translation of the Old Testament. The translation was made in the Greek language in the third and second centuries B.C.

Sola Scriptura The famous Protestant principle enunciated by Luther of "The Bible and the Bible alone."

Soteriology Pertaining to, or the study of, salvation—especially the salvation believed in Christian theology to have been accomplished through Jesus Christ.

Spinoza Dutch Jewish philosopher (1632-1677) who taught that there is but one infinite substance, God (or Nature), having infinite attributes of which only thought and extension are knowable.

Syncretistic Combining or reconciling differing beliefs or practices in religion, philosophy, et cetera, or an attempt to effect such compromise.

Teleological Having the nature of or relating to, design, purpose, final intention, or cause.

Tzaddik In Judaism, a Hasidic saint or holy man.

Ugaritic Pertaining to Ugarit, an ancient city-state near the Mediterranean coast in northern Syria (near the modern Ras Shamra), where vastly important Canaanite materials were found. Frequently the term "Ugaritic" is used for the ancient Semitic language known from Ugarit.

Uncial Designating or pertaining to a form of large, rounded letter used in the script of Greek and Latin manuscripts between A.D. 300 and 900 ("capital letters").

Vernal equinox Occurs about March 21. One of the two times when the sun crosses the equator, making night and day of equal length in all parts of the earth.

SCRIPTURE INDEX

Scripture Index

GENESIS
1:1	23
1:26-28	24
1:31	23
2:1	23
2:1-3	24, 35
2:2	23
2:2-4	24
2:2, 3	23, 24
2:3	24, 25, 49, 235, 282
2:4	23
9:13	36
9:13, 17	36
9:15	35
17:11	36

EXODUS
16:5	26
16:5, 22, 29	27
16:13, 14, 26, 27	102
16:22	26
16:22, 23	27
16:23	25, 26, 27, 34
16:23, 25	29, 33
16:23, 25, 26, 29	27
16:23, 29, 30	27
16:25	26, 27
16:25, 26	26
16:26	27
16:26, 27, 29, 30	27
16:28	26, 27, 30
16:29	26, 102
16:30	26
20:2	234
20:8	25, 29, 30, 32, 33, 49, 72, 85
20:8-10	282
20:8, 10, 11	49
20:8, 11	29
20:9	29
20:9, 10	24, 49
20:10	24, 29, 32, 33, 127, 235
20:11	22, 23, 24, 29, 32, 35, 282
20:16	35
23:12	33
31:13	34, 35, 36, 51
31:13-17	30
31:13, 14, 16	34, 36
31:14	24, 25
31:14, 15	24, 25
31:15	29, 33, 34
31:16	34, 36, 283
31:17	22, 23, 24, 32, 35, 36, 87
34:7	33
34:21	33, 95
34:28	33
35:2	24, 25, 29, 33

LEVITICUS
18:4	77
23:1-3	46
23:2	33
23:2-4	102
23:3	29
23:4-15	46
23:11	326
23:15, 16	326
23:15-22	46
23:23-25	46
23:26-32	46
23:33-43	46
26:42, 45	47

NUMBERS
15:32-36	83
28:26	46

DEUTERONOMY
5:12	25, 30, 31, 32, 33, 34, 49
5:12, 14, 15	49
5:12, 15	34
5:13	13
5:13, 14	32
5:14	24, 31, 32, 33, 49
5:14, 15	31
5:15	31, 32, 298
5:15, 16	73
7:8, 9, 12	33
9:9, 11, 15	33
16:10	46
20:20	76
23:25	95
29:1, 9	33

1 SAMUEL
21:1-6	95

2 KINGS
4:23	51

2 CHRONICLES
36:21	52

NEHEMIAH
9:14	52
13:17, 18	52

ECCLESIASTES
11:2	143

ISAIAH
1:10-20	47
1:13	46
6:3	74
30:15	72
43:12	72
56:2	47
56:4	47
56:6	47
58:12	360
58:13	48, 127
58:13, 14	47, 48, 360
66:23	45, 49, 216

JEREMIAH
7:1-8, 30	49
17:22, 24	49
17:27	49
23:24	74
27:21, 22, 24	49
31:31	156

LAMENTATIONS
1:7	50
2:1, 21, 22	50
2:6	50

SCRIPTURE INDEX

EZEKIEL
20:12-24	50
20:12, 20	51
20:20	36, 50
22:8-26	50
23:38	50
44:24	50
45:17	50, 51, 338
46:1-4, 12	50
46:3	45

HOSEA
2:11	45, 46
2:11, 13	45, 46
2:13	46

AMOS
8:5	45

MATTHEW
5:17	94
11:28	344
12:2	95
12:5	95, 96
12:6	96
12:7	96
12:8	96, 127
12:10	97
12:11	98
12:12	98
16:21	121
20:19	121
23:23	96
24:4-8	118
24:4-36	102
24:20	102, 280
27:55	116
27:61	116
27:62-66	116
28:5, 6	105
28:8	118
28:9	118

MARK
1:27	97
2:24	95
2:25	95
2:27	32, 96, 279
2:28	96, 127, 288
3:4	98
3:14	116
8:31	121
9:31	121
10:34	121
13:5-37	102
13:18	102
15:42	103, 115
15:43	116
15:47	115
16:2	115
16:6	115
16:9	116
16:10	116
16:11	116
16:14	116

LUKE
2:39	93
4:16	93, 108, 335
4:33	97
4:35	97
6:1	95
6:2	95
6:5	96, 127
9:22	121
13:10-17	98
13:14	99
13:17	99
18:12	92
18:33	121
21:8-36	102
21:20, 21	102
23:54	117, 118
23:55-24:1	104
23:56	118
24:21	119
24:27	119
24:39, 40	119
24:46, 47	119

JOHN
5:1-9	99
5:16	100
5:17	74, 100, 288
7:23	101
9:6, 7	101
9:16	101, 102
19:14	103
19:31	103
19:42	103
20:1	120
20:2	120
20:8	120
20:10	121
20:15	121
20:17	121
20:19	121
20:20	121
20:21, 22	121
20:25	121
20:28	121
21:1-8	122
21:2	120
21:20	120
21:24	120
21:35	120

ACTS
1:12	74, 106
3:21	360
5:16	106
5:26	106
5:42	107
5:43	107
5:44	107
5:49	107
6:7	134
8:1	134
13:5	106
13:5, 14, 42, 44	134
14:1	107, 134
15:1	109, 110
15:20	110
15:20, 21	134
15:20, 29	110
15:21	111
15:22	110
16:9	107
16:10	107
16:12	108
16:13	108
17:1	108
17:1, 10, 17	134
17:2	108, 335
17:2, 3	108
17:4	108
17:12	109
18:1-3	109
18:4	109
18:4, 19	134
18:8	109
18:19	109
19:8	109
19:9, 10	109
19:10	109
20:6	134
20:7-12	122
20:16	134
21:20	111, 134
21:24	134
25:8	124
26:22	124

ROMANS
7:12	335
11:13	136
14:1-6	334
14:2	336
14:5	336
14:5, 6	333

1 CORINTHIANS
5:7, 8	127
11:26	133
15:20	127
16:2	124

GALATIANS
1:19	134

COLOSSIANS
2:14-17	353
2:17	339

1 PETER
4:19	282

REVELATION
1:5	127
1:9, 10	125, 126, 238
1:10	126, 127, 288
11:15-19	355
14:6, 7	353
14:9-11	360

GENERAL INDEX

General Index

A

Abelard, Peter, 203
Acra, 62
Address to the Christian Nobility of the German Nation (Luther), 216
Adomnan (biographer of Columba), 194
Advent Awakening (19th cent.): in America. *See* Millerites
Advent Harbinger: Bate's Sabbath articles in, 357
Advent Review, The: its beginning, 359
  its role, 251
Advent Review and Sabbath Herald, The, 367
Adventist Review, 251
Against the Jews (Dionysius), 156
Against the Jews, Concerning the Sabbath (John of Damascus), 156
Agricultural work: forbidden on Sabbath, 95
  permitted on Sabbath, 328
Agrippa II, 65
Ahaz, 52
Ahimelech gave Temple bread to David, 95
Ahura-Mazda, 315, 316
Akiba: his rule, 75, 76, 83
  martyred, 73
  on circumcision, 75
Aksum: Christianity in, 174
  forerunner of Ethiopia, 174
  Sabbath and Sunday observance in, 185
Alan of Lille: verbal attack against Waldenses, 208
Alcuin, 191
Alexander of Hales, 205
Alexander III, 204
Allen, W. C., 102
Almagest (Ptolemy): as early astronomical bible, 312
Alopen: arrival in China, 159
Alt, A., 28
Alvarez, Francisco: mission to Ethiopia, 180
Amabili ecclesiae concordia, De (Erasmus), 209
Ambrose, 138, 238
American Hebrew (Jewish journal), 267
Amos: Sabbath in, 44-45
Anabaptists: and the Sabbath, 220-222

Anahita, 316
Anastasius: anti-Sabbath position, 156
Andrews, John Nevins: articles in *Review,* 255
  in Transylvania, 224
  investigation of beginning of Sabbath, 252
  on Sabbath conferences, 250
  publisher, 359
  representative to Seventh Day Baptist General Conference, 253
  Sabbath history classic, 251, 361
  writings on Sabbath, 367
Anglicans: position on Sabbath, 229
Anilaeus, 65
Annals (Tacitus), 333
Anselm of Alessandria: on sandal wearing of Waldenses, 208
Ante-Nicene Fathers, 347
Anthology (Valens): sequence of stars in relation to days of week, 140
Antinomians, 239
Antiochus Epiphanes: and Samaritans, 67
  Jews oppressed by, 62, 64
Antiochus I Epiphanes: author of Mithraic rock reliefs, 317
Antiochus VII Sidetes, 63
Antoninus, 86
Aphrahat, 154-155
Apion: explanation for Sabbath, 67
Apocalypse: "the Lord's day" in, 125, 126
Apocryphal books (NT): Acts of John, 347, 350
  Acts of Peter, 347
  Epistle of the Apostles, 347
  Gospel of Peter, 347
Apollo: in synagogue for worship, 134
Apollonios, 62
Apostolic Canons, 153, 176, 179
Apostolic Constitutions (prescriptions for Sabbath and Sunday), 153, 155, 179, 194, 324-325, 329, 330, 348
Apostolic Tradition (Hippolytus), 173, 179, 335
Aquinas, Thomas, 205-206
  developed Sunday observance for Catholic Church, 284
Aramaic papyri, 57
Armenia: Christianity in, 162-163
Armenian Uniates: establishment of, 162
Armstrong, Garner Ted, 254

Armstrong, Herbert W., 254
Arndt, W. F., 99
Artaxerxes II, 315-316
Asinaeus, 65
Aslak Bolt, Bishop, 209
Asochia (Galilee): attacked on Sabbath, 63
Asterius of Amasea, Bishop, 152, 325
Astrological week: in Roman Empire, 308-309
Astrology: in Hellenistic age, 312
 influence in Western lands, 310-314
Athanasius, Bishop, 142, 174
Athanasius Anaphora (Ethiopia text), 180
Atonement, Day of: offerings on, 75
 on Sabbath, 84
Attalus I, 316
Augsburger, Daniel, 218, 219, 220
Augustine, 137, 138
 and Sundaykeeping, 190, 191, 192
 flexibility of worship requirements, 194
 resurrection reason for Sundaykeeping, 142
Augustine of Hippo, 330
Augustus, Emperor of Rome, 309, 310, 314

B

Baal Shem Tov, 273
Babylon: fall of to Medo-Persia, 315
 symbolizing churches rejecting judgment-hour message, 353
Babylonian: planetary system, 311
 sexagesimal counting system (hour), 313
 zodiacal year, 311, 312
Bacchides: Sabbath-day attack on Jonathan, 63
Bacchiocchi, Samuele, 343, 348
Baeck, Leo, 270, 271, 274
Ball, Bryan W., 239
Bampfield, Thomas, 238
Bang, Bishop: on Sabbathkeeping revival in Norway, 209-210
Barabas, Steven, 124
Barkokeba war: Jewish persecutions, 136
Barley harvest, 326
Barnabas, 68, 133, 142, 143
Barnabas: and Paul at Jerusalem Conference, 110
Barnabas of Alexandria, 330, 350
 joy of keeping the eighth day, 323
 Sunday references, 347
Barnes, Albert, 340
Barth, Karl: neo-orthodox theology on Sabbath, 280-284, 292, 300
Bartholomew, Bishop, 177
Bates, Joseph, 250, 252
 conversion to Adventism, 248
 correlation of Sabbath and heavenly sanctuary, 354-355
 identifies "mark of the beast," 356
 offers additional concepts, 352, 354, 357-360, 362
 Sabbath theology, 352-355
 speaker at Sabbath conferences, 249
Baumgarten, 67
Bavarian Laws: on Sundaykeeping, 199
Bavinck, 287

Baxter, Richard, 236
Bede, 191
Berea: Sabbath in, 109
Berechiah, 82, 87
Berenice (sister of Herod the Younger), 137
Bermudez, Joao, 180, 181, 185
Bernard, Jacques, 218, 219
Bernard, Richard: advocates Sunday Sabbatarianism, 236-237
Beth ha-Midrash, 86
Bethel, 58
Bezae, Codex, 97, 103
Bible Advocate: Bate's Sabbath articles in, 357
Bietenhardt: gave cosmic and metaphysical meaning to Sabbath, 59
 differences between Zadokite Document and Book of Jubilees, 61
Blumenkranz, B.: on Judaizing currents, 196
Bobiensis, Codex, 115
Boethusians, 326
Bond, Ahva J. C., 259, 290
Book of Sports (James I): condemnation of Sabbatarianism, 232-233
Borowitz, Eugene B., 276
Bownd, Nicholas, 230, 231, 237, 353, 360
 propagation of transfer theory, 235-236
Brabourne, Theophilus, 234
 defense of seventh-day Sabbath, 237
 asked to recant, 238
Breaking of bread: at Troas, 123-124
Brown, David, 340
Bruce, F. F., 98, 122, 123, 335
Buber, Martin: writings on Sabbath, 270-271, 272-273, 274
Bucer, Martin: on strict Sunday observance, 217-218, 220, 226
Budge, E. A. Wallis, 176
Bultmann, Rudolf, 279
Burnt offering(s): on Sabbath, 53, 341

C

Cadbury, 123
Calendar(s): of Jubilees, 336
 Roman farm, 309
 liturgical of the Essenes, 336
 determination of dates, 76
 pentecontad, 22
 Qumrân, 67
Callistus, Bishop, 137
 decree for Sabbath fast, 138
Calvin, John: and Barth in agreement on Sabbath, 280-282
 and Jewett in disagreement on Sabbath, 288-289
 Sabbath-Sunday theology, 215, 218, 220
Cam Domnaig (Law of Sunday), 200
Cannon, W. W., 30
Canones Poenitentiales (Archbishop Peter of Alexandria), 169
Canons, Collection of. See Fetha Nagast
Capitula (Rudolf of Bourges), 202
Capitula (Theodulf of Orleans), 202
Carlstadt, Andreas: treatise on Sabbath com-

mandment, 217
Caroli, Pierre: Catholic-Protestant debate (1535), 219
Cassian, John, 137, 330
  customs of monks, 170-171, 194, 195
Catechismus Romanus: theological position of Sunday worship in Catholic Church, 284
Celsus: his planetary ladder, 314
  his seven gates, 315
Celtic Church: Sabbath in, 194-195
Ceremonial law, 339
  nailed to cross, 353
Ceremonial Sabbaths, Jewish. *See* Sabbaths, Ceremonial
Cerularius, Michael, 197
Chafer, L. S., 289
Chappius, Jean, 219
Charlemagne: attempt to enforce Sunday rest, 201-202, 203
Charles, 59
Charles I, 237
Charles II, 238
  ejection of Puritans from Anglican Church, 233
Charles V, 222
Chelini, 197, 198
Childebert II: law prohibiting Sunday work, 198
Christ. *See* Jesus Christ
Christ and the Sabbath (Prescott), 362
Christian Pascha. *See* Easter (Sunday)
Christianity Today (magazine), 286
Christology of the New Testament, The (Cullman), 288
Chronicles, I and II: Sabbath in, 52
Chrysostom, John, 144, 154, 238, 329
  homilies, 196
Church Councils: Chalcedon, 162
  Clermont, 207
  Däbrä Mitmaq, 177
  Frioul, 196
  Laodicea, 175, 196, 329
  Les Estinnes, 201
  Macon, Second, 198
  Manazkert, 162
  Narbonne, 198
  Nicea, 175
  Orleans, 192, 193
  Quinisext, 154, 162
Church Dogmatics, Barth, 280
Church History of Britain (Fuller), 237
Church of Jesus Christ of Latter-day Saints, 291
Circumcision, 110, 157, 170, 173, 221, 329
  custom condemned, 137
  exemption of Gentiles become Christian, 134
  no value for salvation, 339
  observed by Waldenses, 209
  on Sabbath, 75, 101
City of God (Augustine), 191
Clarke, Adam: on Sabbath, 340
Claudius, 181
  "Confession of Faith," 181
  death of, 182
Clement VIII, 182
Clement of Alexandria, 346, 350
Clementine Recognitions, 155
Clifford, Sir Lewis, 209

Coccejus, Johannes, 287
Cohen, Gary, 299
Cohen, Hermann: set foundation for Reform Judaism thinking, 269, 271, 274
Cole, Timothy, 357
Colossians 2:16; bibliography on, 341-342
Columba, 194-195
Conferences (Cassian): on monks and sacraments, 171
"Conferences" of 1848: sanctuary-Sabbath concepts, 358, 360
Congregationalists, 353
Conradi, L. R., 224, 251, 361
Constantine: constitutions of, 140
Constantine I, 153
Constantine the Great, 330
  his "Sunday law" edict, 152, 318, 328
Constitution of the Holy Apostles (Syria), 151
Contans II, Emperor, 162
Contra Judaeos (Isidore), 191
Conybeare, F. C., 123, 162
Coombs, K. F., 291
Coptic Christians, Egyptian, 173
Coptic Church, 185
  in Alexandria, 176
Corinth, Sabbath in, 109
Cosmic week, 73, 143
  See also Creation week
Cottrell, Roswell F., 247
  and Seventh Day Baptist General Conference meeting, 252
  articles in *Review,* 255
Councils. *See* Church Councils
Craig, 125
Cranfield, C. E. B., 98, 114, 115
Cranmer, Thomas, Archbishop:
  influence on change of Sabbath, 234-235
Crautwald, Valentine: response to Fischer doctrine, 221-222
Creation, 283, 341
  and Sabbath, 279, 289, 295, 296
  covenant between God and man, 297, 299, 300, 343
  early theology of, 142-143
  relationship to Sabbath, 271-272
Creation week: in Jewish and Jewish Christian circles, 143
  of Genesis, 280
Crosier, O. R. L., 257, 355, 356
Cross, Frank, 58
Crypto-Jews: first Jewish settlers in Western Hemisphere, 244
Cullmann, Oscar: theology of, 287-288, 292
Cult of Sol Invictus, The (Halsbergher), 139
Cumont, Franz, 361
Cyril, Archbishop of Alexandria, 172, 185
Cyril II, 175
Cyrill III, 175-176

D

Damis, 310
Darius I, King: his *Megophonia,* 315, 316
Dawit, King, 177

Day of Atonement. *See* Atonement, Day of
Day of Saturn. *See* Saturn, Day of
Day of the Lord. *See* Lord's day
Day of the Sun. *See* Sun, Day of
Day-Star (Millerite periodical), 355, 356
Dead Sea scrolls, 74
Decalogue: Sabbath day of, 278, 282, 296, 301, 335, 338, 339
and Augustine, 328
not nailed to cross, 353
Defence of that most Ancient and Sacred Ordinance of Gods, the Sabbath Day, A (Brabourne), 237
DeHaan, Richard W., 290
Deissmann, 125, 127
Dellon, C.: on Inquisition imprisonment, 161
Demetrius, 63
Dengel, Sartsa, 182
Deuteronomic Decalogue, 279, 282, 283
Deuteronomic law, 103
Dewin (Tevin), Synod of, 162
Dialogue with Trypho (Justin), 141, 143
Diamper, Synod of, 160, 161
Diaspora, 335
Jews in Egypt, 61
Didache (manual), 103
fasting, 336
Lord's day, 347-348, 350
Didascalia, 175, 179, 182
Didascalia Apostolorum (manuscripts), 162-163
Dilthey, Wilhelm, 272
Dimi, 76
Dionysius Bar Salibi, 156
Disputation of Sergius the Stylite against a Jew, The, 156
Disappointment of Oct. 22, 1844:
theological divergence on sanctuary following, 257, 354-355, 356
Dispensationalism, 292
Dispersion. *See* Diaspora
Dissertation against the Jews (Anastasius), 156
Divine rest: its implications, 296-297
Doctrine and Covenants, The (Mormon), 291
Doctrine of the Sabbath, The (Bownd): its influence, 230-232
Dodd, C. H., 100, 106, 333
Dolabella: military exemption of Jews, 62, 63
Dominique de Monbouson, 219
Domitian, 137
Dugger, A. N., 254
Dugmore, C. W., 127, 348
Dumah (angel), 73
Durand of Huesca, 208

E

Earle, Ralph, 94
Easter (Sunday,), 126-127, 348, 350
Ebionites, 135, 152
Ebrard of Bethune, 208
Ecclesiastical History (Lucius), 238
(Socrates Scholasticus), 194
(Sozomen), 171
Edesius, 174

Edson, Hiram, 248, 358, 360-361, 362
on mark of the beast, 356
on true concept of sanctuary cleansing, 257, 354-355
Education of the Clergy (Maurus): on Sunday sacredness, 202
Edwards, Jonathan, 353
Egyptian Church Order, 173, 179
Eight-day market week, 308
Eighth day: as endless time, 68, 191
as first day of week, 203, 323, 347
Augustine and, 191
circumcision on, 170
early theology of, 143
Jerome and, 143
market holidays, 309
Eleazar ben Azariah, 76
Elephantine: Jewish garrison, 62
Ostraca discovery, 57
Elephantine-Syene: Aramaic papyri of, 37
Elihu on the Sabbath: Seventh Day Baptist tract, 361
Eliot, John, 240
Elizabethan settlement, 230, 232
Eössi, Andreas: inauguration of Sabbath movement, 223
Sabbath writings of, 224
Epiphanius, 135
Epistle of Barnabas (anti-Judaic), 143, 172
Erasmus, 209
Erastians, 232
Erub, 74, 81, 82
Erubin, 74
Essenes, 74, 75, 326, 335
abstinances of, 336-337
Essenism, 335
Etruscans, 308
Etymologies (Isidore), 191, 192
Eucharist, 123, 127
celebration forbidden by Church of Rome, 138
in *Didache*, 348
in Egypt, 171, 173
Sunday celebration, 159
Waldenses' unbelief in, 208
Eudoxos, 311
Eugene II, 199
Eumenes II, 316
Eusebius, 135, 141, 172, 318, 329
Euthathius, 162, 176, 177, 185
house of, 176-177
Evangelicalism, 292
Evangelists, 94
Exile, the, 52
Explanation of the Typical and Anti-Typical Sanctuary, . . . An (Bates), 360
Ezana, King, 174
Ezekiel: Sabbath in, 50-51

F

Fackenheim, Emil L., 275
Falashas, 74, 75, 174
Familists, 239
Farel, Guillaume, 218-219

Fasiladas, King, 184, 185
Fasting: abstention from as Sabbath observance, 152
  controversy of Sabbath, 329-330
Fausset, A. R., 340
Feast day(s), 58, 278
  of Baal, 46
Feast(s), 46, 52
  celebration of, 51
  termination of appointed, 50
Festival(s), 63
  days be abolished, 216
  of barley harvest, 326
Fetha Nagast ("Legislation of the Kings"), Ethiopic, 175
Filipos, Abba, 177
Fine et Adomonitione, De (Pseudo-Ephraim), 154
Finland: Sabbath observance in, 225
1 Apology 67 (Justin Martyr), 330-331
First day of the week, 347
  in John, 120-122
  in Luke, 118-119
  in Mark, 114-116
  in Matthew, 116-118
  meeting at Troas, 122-124
  offering collection on, 124-125
  resurrection of Christ, 115, 290
  worship on, 289
Fischer, Andreas, 221-222
Foakes-Jackson, 123
Fohrer, G., 28
Frankel, Zechariah: founding of Conservative Judaism, 267
Freer Gospels, 115
Frioul, Synod of, 203
Frontius, 139
Frumentius of Tyre, 174
Fuente, Constantino Ponce de la, 222, 223, 226
Fulbert of Chartres, 196
Fuller, Thomas, 231, 237
Furbity, Guy, 218-219

G

Gabriel, Abba, 177
Gaius: death of, 65
Gamble, Samuel Walter, 291
Gates of Prayer—The New Union Prayerbook, 275
Geesink, W., 285, 287
Gemara, 71
General Conference: Minneapolis session (1888), 362
"General meetings." See Sabbath conferences
Geraty, Lawrence T., 348, 349
Gese, H., 28
Gilfillan, James, 237
Giovanni da Imola, 180
Gischala, 65
Glait, Oswald, 221, 222
Gnosticism, 361
God Meets Man: A Theology of the Sabbath and Second Advent (Kubo), 260

Goppelt, Leonard, 136
Gorgias, 63
Gospels: nature of, 105
Great Controversy, The (White), 358
Great Schism of 1054, 196
Great Second Advent Awakening (19th cent.):
  in America. See Millerites
Great War, 63
Greenhorn, Richard: advocate of Sunday Sabbath, 236
Gregory IX: decree for Sundaykeeping, 204
Gregory of Nyssa, 194, 325
Gregory of Tours, 198, 199
Gregory the Great, 191, 192, 193, 194
Grosheide, 125
Grunfeld, Isidor, 268
Guillaume de Rennes, 206
Gunthram, King: his edict for Sunday observance, 198
Gustavus II Adolphus, King, 225
Tustavus I Vasa, King, 225
Gutbrod, W., 110

H

Habdalah, 86
Hadrian, 137
  his edict, 135-136
  outlaws Sabbathkeeping, 136
  siege of, 135
Haggadah, 72-74
Haggai, 87
Hahn, F. B., 355
Halakah: Sabbath rules in, 74-75
Hall, D. P., 253
Halsberghe, Gaston H., 139
Hampton Court Conference, 232
Hanina, Jose ben, 72, 81, 85
Harmon, Ellen, 248
Harnack, Adolf, 361
Harris, J. Rendel, 348
Hasel, Gerhard F., 221
Hasidism, 270, 272-273
Healings on Sabbath. See Sabbath, Healings on
Helena, 180
Hellenistic Mithraism, 315-318
Hellenistic period: Sabbath observance, 57-58
Hellenists, 134
Hennequin of Langle: death of, 209
Henry of Auxerre: ecclesiastical origin of Sunday statement, 203
Heraclius, 155, 162
Herculaneum, 139
Hering, J., 125
Heschel, Abraham Joshua, 275, 302, 361
  on concept of holiness in time, 260
  on universality of Sabbath, 273-275
Heylyn, 233, 235
Hipparchus, 311, 312
Hippolytus, 137, 138, 324
Hirsch, Samson Raphael, 267, 268
Historia Lausiaca (Palladius), 170
History of the Sabbath and First Day of the Week (Andrews), 251, 361

Hiyya bar Abba, 79, 87
Holdheim, Samuel, 266-267
Homilia de Semente (Pseudo-Athanasius), 169
Homilies (Aphrahat), 154
Homilies against the Jews (Chrysostom), 154 (Jacob of Serug), 154
Homily Two against the Jews (Isaac of Antioch), 154
Honorius: law of, 153, 154
Hope of Israel, as A Tract Showing that the Seventh Day Should Be Observed as the Sabbath, The (Preble), 248
Horace, 139
Hosea: Sabbath in, 45-46
Hours: equinoctial, 313
Howson, 123
Huitfeldt, Christopher: his edict imposing fine for Sabbathkeeping, 225
Huna, 80
Huss, John, 207
Hymn for Saturday Vespers (Abelard), 203
Hyrcanus, John, 63

I

I and Thou (Buber): its impact on Jewish theology, 272
Ibn al-Assal, 175
Ibrahim, Ahman ibn: incursions of, 181
Iconium, 107
Ignatian Epistles: on Sabbath observance, 151
Ignatius, Bishop, 325, 348-350
Ignatius II, 176
India, Christianity in, 160
Innocent I, 137
Innocent III, 208
Inquisition, 161, 209, 244
Inquisition at Goa, The (Dellon), 161
Insabbati. See Waldenses
Institutes of the Christian Religion (Calvin), 220
Institutes of the Coenobia (Cassian), 170
International Bible Students Association (Jehovah's Witnesses), 291-292
International date line, 364
function of, 365-367
International Prime Meridian Conference of 1884: date line established, 365-366
Invincible Sun: feast of, 141
Ioane de Calabria, 180
Ireland: Sabbatarianism limit reached, 200
Irenaeus, 116, 346-347
Isaac, 84
Isaac, Ephraim, 177
Isaiah: Sabbath in, 46-49
Ischius, 238
Ishmael, 76, 77
Ishu'-Yab, 158
Isidore of Seville, 191-192, 196, 202
Iskindir, King, 180
Islah, 57, 58

J

Jacob of Serug, 154
Jacobite, 163, 176

James I, 232, 233
Jamieson, Robert, 340
Jannai, 72
Jehoiada: his arrangement of *coup d'état*, 51
Jenni, Ernst, 287, 288, 292
on Sabbath commandment, 282-283
Jeremiah: Sabbath in, 49-50
Jerome of Jerusalem, 97, 141, 152, 154, 192, 196, 328
Jerusalem: battles on Sabbath in, 62
Conference and Sabbath, 109-111
destruction of, 135
not original place of Sunday worship, 323
Jesus Christ: Sabbath observer, 93-94, 288, 335
Jesus-Messiah Sutra (document), 159
Jewett, Paul K., 94, 288-289, 292
Jewish rebellion, 65
Jewish revolt, 64
Jews: denominations of, 70
massacre of, 64-65
observance of Sabbath in conflict situations, 61-65
Sabbath religious activities, 66-67
welcoming of Sabbath, 85-86
Johanan, 72, 76
John of Damascus, 65, 156, 190
Johns, Alger F., 61
Johnsson, William G., 343
Jonathan, 63
Jones, A., 182
Jose, 75, 86, 101
Joseph, 61
Josephus, Flavius, 60, 62, 63, 64, 66, 67, 103, 116, 308
Jubilees, Book of, 61, 62, 74, 75
Judah, 71
Judah ben Bathyra, 76
Judah the Prince, 85-86
Judaism, American: Conservative, 244-245, 267
Orthodox, 244-245
practice outlawed, 111
Reform, 244-245
"Judaizing Craze," 195-196
Judas, 63
Judith, 58
Julius III, 181
Justification by faith, 333
Justin Martyr, 347, 348, 350
condemnation of Sabbath, 137
day of the Sun, 140
resurrection as basis for Sunday worship, 133, 142
Sunday meetings, 141, 323, 330
Justinian I, 153
Juvenal, 137

K

Karaites, 74, 75
Karo, Joseph, 71
Käsemann, Ernst, 279
Kehathites, 52
Kenite origin: theory, 22
Kenites, 278

Kerygma, 106
Kidan, 179
Kiddush (ceremony), 85, 86
Kierkegaard, 272
Kimbrough, 60
Kings, I and II: Sabbath in, 51-52
Kline, M. G., 35
Knud, 202
Koelman, Jacobus, 284-285
Koole, J. L., 287
Kraft, Robert A., 349
Kubo, Sakae, 260-261
Kuriake (Greek for Sunday), 126
Kuyper, Abraham, 285, 287
Kyriake (Sunday), 173

L

Lake, 123
Lamentations: Sabbath in, 50
Lamm, Norman, 268, 269
Laodicea, Council of: anti-Sabbath canon, 196
Laodicea, Synod of, 151, 153
Laud, William, 233, 237, 238, 240
Laws of the Alemani (on Sundaykeeping), 199
Lebna Dengel, 180, 185
  his defeat, 181
LeCoq, A. von, 159
Lenski, R. C. H., 335
Lentulus, Cossus, 309
Leo the Isaurian 153-154
Les Estinnes, Council of, 201
Let God Be True (Jehovah's Witnesses), 291-292
Letter from Christ (on Sundaykeeping punishments), 200
Letter from Heaven (on Sundaykeeping), 192, 193-194, 199, 201
Letter from Jesus (woes to Sundaybreakers), 200
Letter to the Disciples of the Lord, A., 255
Levi, 72
Levi Isaac, 275
Levi, Testament of, 58
Lewis, A. H., 230, 290
Liber Antiheresis (Ebrard of Bethune), 208
Liber ex Lege Moyse (Mosaic commands), 200
Licinianus, Bishop, 192, 193
Life of Columba (Adomnan), 195
Life of Patrick (Muirchu), 195
Life of Severus (Zacharias Scholasticus), 172
Lindsell, Harold: on State legislation for "Lord's Day" observance, 286
Literature, Anti-Jewish, 154-157
Lohse, Eduard, 96, 102, 104, 107, 117, 278, 279
Lollards, 209
Lord's day, 195
  applied to Sabbath, 172, 238
  applied to Sunday, 152, 190, 194, 198, 200, 236, 240, 285, 324, 325, 329, 346, 349, 350
  Barth's theology of, 281
  in apocryphal sources, 347
  in *Apostolic Constitutions*, 330
  in *Didache*, 348
  in Revelation 1:10, 125-127, 289
  resurrection theology motivation, 142, 144

Lord's Day, The: A Theological Guide to the Christian Day of Worship (Jewett), 288
Lord's Day Alliance of the United States, 286
Lord's Supper: at Troas, 123
  cessation of in Rome and Alexandria, 323
  forbidden in Rome, 142
  on Sunday, 142, 280
Lucius, 238
Luminous Religion (China), 159
Luther, Martin, 215, 216-217, 220, 281, 288, 289
Lydia, 108

M

Maccabean period, 63
  defensive warfare permitted on Sabbath, 76
MacGregor, 123
McKay, D. O. 291
Maggid, 275
Maimonides (Moses ben Maimon), 71, 96
Manna and the Sabbath, 26
Manson, T. W., 99, 334
Marcionites, 138
Marduk, 311, 315
Mark of the beast, 361
Market day(s), 22, 278, 283, 309
Maronites, 152
Marqos, Bishop, 180
Marsh, Joseph, 357
Martial, 137
Martin of Braga, 197
Martin, Ralph, 124
Martrydom of Polycarp, 103
Maruthas, Bishop, 157
Marvelous Work and a Wonder, A (Richards), 291
Mashafa Berhān (Book of Light) (Zara Yaqob), 177, 179
Mashafa Tomar (Book of the Letter), 182
Mattathias, 62
Maurus, Rabanus, 191, 196, 202-203
Mayence, synod of, 204
Mazdayasnian, 315, 316
Meat eating: versus vegetarianism in Roman church, 334-335
Medieval Institutions and the Old Testament (Chydenius), 197
Meesters, J. H., 278
Megaphonia ("killing of the Magi"), 315
Meir, 70
Melakah: meaning, 78, 82
Melakhah: Talmudic concept, 268
Melanchthon, Philip, 217
Mendenhall, G., 28
Mendez, Alphonso, 184, 185
Menezes, Aleixo de: his decree, 160
Messala: triumph of, 309
Methodists, 353
Metzger, Bruce, 97
Midnight Cry, The (Millerite paper), 247
Mikael, Abba, 177
Millenary Petition (reform measures of Puritans), 232
Miller, William, 352, 353, 354

Millerism, 361
Millerite Advent movement: identifying themes, 352-353
Millerites, 354, 358
  Adventism, 352-353, 362
  groups now exant, 256
  imminent Advent proclamation, 247
  sanctuary concept divergence, 258-259, 359
Milligan, A., 104
Minas, 182, 185
Mingana, A., 157
Minha, 86
Mishnah, 71, 74, 78, 95, 97, 106
Mithra (Persian deity), 315, 316-317
  important to sun followers, 314
  origin, 316
Mithraea (day of the Sun), 140
Mithraeum (sanctuary): of the Seven Portals, 314
  of the Seven Spheres, 315
Mithraism, 361
  birth of Hellenistic, 316
  spread of, 317
  western, 315
Mithras (Invincible Sun), 141
  cult, 310, 314, 317-318
Mithridates (Parthian leader), 65
Monophyseism, 162
Monroe, E., 182
Moody Bible Institute, 290
Moore, G. F., 60
Morris, Leon, 101, 124
Mosaic Law: Barbarians' reliance on, 197-198
  for ceremonial act, 76
  on criminal death, 116
Motzaey Shabbath (rabbinic), 117
Moulton, W. F., 104
Muktzeh: Sabbath laws prohibiting things to be handled, 79
Mumford, Stephen: first Christian Sabbatarian in New World, 245
  Saturday Sabbatarian propagation, 240-241
Murray, John, 285

N

Naphtali, Testament of, 58
Narrative of the Portuguese Embassy to Abyssinia (Alvarez), 180
Nathan, 76, 85
Nazarenes, 135
Nazareth: Sabbath service in, 93-94
Neander, 125
Nehemiah: Sabbath in, 52
Neill, Stephen, 160
Nero, 317
  death of, 136
Nestorian: Church, 163
  documents in India, 160
  Monument discovery, 159
Nestorianism: adoption of by Persian Church, 157
New moon(s), 59, 339
  and Sabbath relationship, 45, 47, 49, 51, 52, 66, 76
  in Isaiah, 216
Nicanor, 63
  Sabbath attack on Judas, 62
Nicholas I, 196
Nietzsche, 272
Nimrud Dagh: Mithraic archaeological discoveries at, 317
Nisan, 76, 104
Noble, Abel, 241, 245
Novatianism, 157

O

Octavius, 314
On Easter (Irenaeus), 347
On the Lord's Day (Eusebius), 172
On the Sabbath and Circumcision (Athanasius), 142
180th meridian: day first begins, 365, 366
127 Apostolic Canons, The (Arabic), 173
Opening Heavens, The (Bates), 355
Opse de sabbaton: interpretation, 117
Oral law, 70
  of rabbis for Sabbathkeeping, 94
Origen, 324
Orphic Mystery, 334
Orthodox Church, 163
  persecutions, 210
Orthodox Jew: Sabbath is epitome of existence, 268-269
Ostraca, 57, 58
Oviedo, André de, 181, 182, 185

P

Pachomius, 170
Paez, Pero F., 182, 185
Pagan mythologies, 24
Palladius, 170
Paraskeuē (day of preparation), 103
Paris, Synod of, 202, 203
Parthians, 63
Passagini, 208, 209
Passover, 104
Paul: and Barnabas travels, 106-107
  and Silas travels, 108
  in Ephesus, 109
  vision of Macedonian pleading, 107-108
Paul V, 184
Paul of Burgos, 206
Pechi, Simon (son of Eossi), 223, 224
Penrose, C. W., 291
Pentecontad calendar. See Calendar(s)
Pentecost, 63
Pepin the Short, 201
Persius, 137
Peter (Archbishop of Alexandria), 169
Petosiris (handbook of astrology), 312, 313
Petronius, 137, 139
Petuchowski, Jacob J., 275
Pharisaism, 70
Pharisee(s), 75, 303
Philip (Abba), 180
Philip III, 182

GENERAL INDEX

Philo, 61, 64
  discusses synagogue services, 66
  on manna and Sabbath, 67
  theology of Sabbath, 67
Philostratus, 139, 310
Picards, 209
Pierce, Stephen, 358, 362
Pirke de Rabbi Eliezer, 73
Pirmin, 199-200
Pisidian Antioch: Sabbath services in, 106-107
Pittsburgh Platform of 1885, 267
Placidus, Lactantius, 316
Planetary week, 310, 313-314
  distinguishing features, 308-309
  in ancient Rome, 140
Plato, 310, 346
Plaut, W. Gunther, 275
Pliny, 350
Pliny the Younger, 349
Plummer, Alfred, 94
Plutarch, 137, 139, 317
Pompeii, 139
Pompey, 63, 65, 317
Popes. *See* Alexander III; Clement VIII; Eugene II; Gregory IX; Gregory of Nyssa; Gregory of Tours; Innocent I; Innocent III; Julius III; Sylvester
Porten, 57, 58
Pratt, Orson, 291
Preble, Thomas M., 353, 355, 360
  importance of his Sabbath articles, 248
Prescott, W. W., 362
***Present Truth, The*:** beginnings, 249-250, 359
  harbinger of Sabbath, 251
Preston, Rachel Oakes: first Sabbathkeeper to become Adventist, 247
Prosabbaton, meaning, 93
  day before Sabbath, 103
Protestant Sentinel (Seventh Day Baptist), 246
Pseudo-Athanasius, 170
Pseudo-Ephraim, 154
Pseudo-Gregory of Nyssa, 155
Ptolemaic period, 61
  Jews as soldiers, 62
Ptolemy (Claudius Ptolemaeus), 312-313
Ptolemy Lathyrus, 63
Ptolemy Soter, 62
Punishable Sabbathbreaking, 82-83
Purchas, Samuel, 152, 157
Puritan(s), 229, 232, 284, 292
  change of Sabbath, 234
  concept of the Covenant, 233-234
  kept Sabbath to honor God, 241-242
  Sabbatarian theology, 353
Puritanism, 354
Purkiser, W. T., 290
***Putnam's Hand Book of Useful Arts*,** 252
Pythagoras, 310
Pythagoreans, 334

Q

Quintilian, 137
Qumrân, 58, 60
Qumrân calendar. *See* Calendar(s)

R

Rabast, H., 28
Rabbinic Judaism, 70
  death penalty of, 61
Rabbinic period, 58
Rabbinic Sabbath: positive observance, 83-87
Rabin, 59
Rackman, Emanuel, 268
Rad, Gerhard von: on divine rest, 297
Radical Reformation, 220
Ramsay, William W., 118
Reform Jews, 274, 275
Reform Judaism, 266, 267
Reform rabbinical conferences (1844-1845), 267
Reformation Era: Sabbathkeepers, 223
Reformation in Spain, 222
Republic (Plato), 346
Resurrection of Jesus, 282
  argument for Sunday worship, 326, 330, 361
  His appearances after, 116, 118-119, 120-121
***Review*,** 252
Richards, Le Grand, 291
Richardson, Herbert W., 286
Richter, Julius, 160
Righetti, Mario, 141
Roberts, B. H., 291
Robertson, A. T., 341
Rodinson, Maxime, 174
Rodriguez, Gonçales, 181
Roman Catholics, 232
Roman Council of 826, 199
Rordorf, Willy, 279-280, 288, 292
Rosenzweig, Franz, 271-272, 273, 274
Ross, Alexander, 173
Rouen, Synod of, 203.
Rowley, H. H., 28
Roz, Francisco, 160
Rudolf of Bourges, 202, 203
Rules (Columba's for monks), 195

S

Sabbata, meanings, 92, 93, 108, 341
Sabbatarian: Adventism emergence, 248
  Adventists, 256, 257
  Anabaptists, 221
  Puritan(s), 230, 239, 360
  Sunday civil enforcement, 201-202
Sabbatarians (Moravia), 217
Sabbath, The (Heschel), 274-275
Sabbath: and Advent, importance to each other, 256-259
  and Covenant, 36, 297
  and sign, 33-35, 47, 51, 283
  arbitrariness of, 302-303
  as Creation ordinance, 280, 284, 287, 292, 296
  as relativization of man's work, 301-302
  cosmic and metaphysical meaning in the Jubilees, 59
  determination of beginning of, 251-252

etymology of, 67-68
evangelical theologies of transferred, 284
illumination of man's attitudes, 300-301
importance of to Jews, 71-72
interpretations of by small denominations and sects, 290-292
positive relevance of, 259-260
real nature of, 96
Sabbath—in history: catalyst for uniting Adventist believers, 250-251
controversies between Jesus and Jews, 94
conflict of plucking grain on, 94-95
cooking on, 79, 97
cubits, limits on, 81-82
death penalty for desecration of, 59, 61, 83
fasting introduced by Church of Rome, 138
in Carolingian period, 202
in Philippi, 107-108
in Thessalonica, 108-109
profanation of, 47, 51, 52, 60
profanation permitted, 76
Sabbath conferences, The, 249
Sabbath days: historic view of, arguments, 338-339
Sabbath day's journey, 74, 106
Sabbath, Healings on: demoniac, 97
Jesus' defense of, 100-101
man at pool, 99-101
man born blind, 101
man with dropsy, 99
man with withered hand, 97
Peter's mother-in-law, 97
woman with "spirit of infirmity," 98-99
Sabbath, How to keep, 25, 27, 48, 49
Sabbath Institution, The (Murray), 285
Sabbath, The: Its Meaning for Modern Man (Heschel), 260, 276
Sabbath prohibitions: by Jerusalem Conference, 110
in Book of Jubilees, 58-59
in *Mashafa Berhan*, 178
in Zadokite document, 59-60
rabbinic, 77-82
Sabbath observance: anti-Judaism influence on, 153
early anti-Jewish literature on, 154-157
in the Arctic, 367-368
in Reformation Era:
in Norway, 224-225
in Sweden, 225
motivations for:
day of hope, 299-300
day of rejoicing, 298-299
day of rest, 297-298
Sabbath Recorder, The, 246
Sabbath rest: meaning of, 295-296
Sabbath, The: Symbol of Creation and Recreation (Saunders), 260, 290
Sabbathai, 61
Sabbathkeeping: Amos on, 45
Sabbathkeeping sects: Adventist
Church of Promise, 255
Church of God, 254
Church of God and Saints in Christ, 254
Church of God, International, 254
German Seventh Day Baptists, 254

Seventh Day Church of God, 254
Strangite Church of Jesus Christ of Latter-day Saints, 254-255
World Headquarters of Church of God, 254
Worldwide Church of God, 254
Sabbaths, Ceremonial: after Israel's deliverance from Egypt, 336
in Colossians 2:16, 338-339, 340
numbering of, 67
weekly rest days, 46, 51, 52
Sabbatius, 157
Sabbato, De (Aphrahat), 155
Sabbaton, 341
Sabbaton: meanings, 92, 93, 105, 173
Saeki, P. Y., 159
Saga za-Ab (Zaga Zabo), 180-181
Saint Patrick, 195
Sambathion, 58, 61
Samaritans, 74, 75
and Sabbath, 67
Sampey, 94
Samuel bar Nachman, 87
Sanctuary, heavenly: cleansing of equated with Second Coming, 352, 353
Sanhedrin, 73, 116-117
abolished, 136
beginning of, 70
declaration of first day of month, 76
Saturday-Sunday observance, 324
in Armenia, 162
in Asia, 151
in Egypt, 169-173
in Ethiopia, 180-181
in *Mashafa Berhan*, 177-178
Saturn, Day of, 140
Saunders, Herbert E., 260, 290
Sawana Nafs (Refuge of the Soul), 183
Sawiros, 175
Sawma, Rabban, 159
School of Menasseh, 80
Schwenkfeld, Casper: his response to Glait's theology, 221
Scrutinium Scripturarum (Paul of Burgos), 206
Seal of God, 258
Seal of the Living God, A, . . . (Bates), 359, 360
Sealing: process of Revelation 7, 357
Second Advent Movement of 1844, 254
Second Advent Review and Sabbath Herald, The, 247, 251, 255, 257
beginning of, 359
Second Advent Way Marks and High Heaps, . . . (Bates), 356
Segal, M. H., 30
Selected Testimonies from the Old Testament against the Jews (Pseudo-Gregory of Nyssa), 155
Senchus Mor (ancient law), 195
Seneca, 137
Septuagint, 126, 341
Sergius, 156
Sermo Synodalis, 203
Seventh-day Adventism, 343, 354
Seventh-day Adventist Bible Commentary, 343
Seventh-day Adventist(s), 252, 253, 254, 256, 257, 259, 352, 354, 357, 361, 362, 368
Church, 249

name adopted, 250
publications, 251
Seventh-day Baptist Missionary Magazine, The, 246
Seventh Day Baptist(s), 247, 252-254, 246, 257, 258, 259, 352, 353, 354, 355, 359, 360, 361, 362
  Adventist indebtedness to, 255
  churches established, 245
  establishment in America, 241
  Sabbath as unification of world peoples, 291
  Sabbath observance, 251, 252
  Sabbath theology, 290
  Sabbath Tract Series, 255
  Saturday-Sunday position, 240-241
Seventh Day Sabbath, A Perpetual Sign, The (Bates), 48, 353, 354, 355, 356, 360
Severus, Septimius: diffusion of planetary week, 314
Shabbath (Mishnah tractate), 94
Shabbetha (Aramaic), 341
Shabbethai (Aramaic), 57
Shebuth (laws of Sabbath rest), 79
Shepard, Thomas, 240
Sherith Israel: first U.S. Jewish congregation, 244
Shim'on ben Menasya, 96
Shulchan Aruch (Karo): digest of Jewish law, 71
Shunammite woman, 51
Siculus, Nicholas, 207
Silas and Timothy: travels of, 109
Simeon, 82
Simeon ben Lakish, 72
Simeon ben Yohai, 72, 83
Simeon: rebellion of, 183
Simlai, 85
Simmel, Georg, 272
Simon, Marcel, 336
Sinaiticus (uncial codex), 115
Sinodos, 179
Smith, Joseph, 291
Smith, Uriah, 253, 255
  sanctuary and Sabbath correlation, 258
Socrates Scholasticus, 151-152, 157, 171, 172, 194
  on Saturday-Sunday observance, 323, 324, 326
Sol Invictus (cult), 139
Sola Scriptura, 219, 222, 288
Solis dies (day of the sun), 314
Soloveitchik, Joseph B., 268, 276
Sorenson, C. M., 361
Sozomen, 152, 171, 172, 323, 324, 326
Spalding, Arthur, 249
Spicer, W. A., 247
Stählin, Gustav, 98
Stephan (king of Hungary): his Sunday edicts, 202
Stewart, John, 160
Strang, James J., 255
Strong, A. H., 285
Sudines, 316
Summa contra Haereticos (Passagini beliefs), 209
Sun, Day of, 328
  importance in pagan Rome, 314-318
Sun: veneration of, 140-141

cults' influence on Christian worship, 140-141
worship and planetary week, 139
Sunday (magazine), 286
Sunday: becomes rest day, 328, 329
  change from Sabbath claim by Catholic monk, 218-219
  earliest worship evidence at Alexandria and Rome, 323
  early theology of, 142-144
  ecclesiastical institution, 204
  emergence of its predominance, 326-328
  first work curse, 172
  legislation in New World, 240
  Lord's day, evidences used for
    Didache (document), 347, 348
    Ignatius' letter to Magnesians, 347-349
    Pliny's letter to Trajan, 347, 349, 350
  substitution for Sabbath, 202-203
  sunset-to-sunset celebration, 203
Sunday observance: as rest day in medieval period, 192
  Constantine's law (321), 152
  date of beginning, 135
  Easter festival, 327, 330
  in pagan world, 314
  Roman Catholic basis for, 215
"Sunday Sabbath," 281
Sunday: The History of the Day of Rest and Worship in the Earliest Centuries of the Christian Church (Rordorf), 279
Sunday, The True Sabbath of God (Gamble), 291
Susenyos, 185
  edict against Sabbath worship, 183
  proclaims religious freedom, 184
Swete, H. B., 115
Sylvester, 137
Synagogue preaching: and Sabbath, 106
Syrus, Ephraem, 329

T

Tacitus, 136, 137
Talmage, James E., 291
Talmud, 71
T'ang dynasty: date of first Christianity in, 159
Tannaitic period, 76
Taor, 170
Tcherikover, 57-58
Teaching of Jacob, The (treatise), 156
Terian, Abraham, 163
Tertullian, 138, 140, 315
Testament of our Lord, The (Ethiopic), 179
Tetrabiblos (Ptolemy), 312
Textus Receptus, 107
Theodoret of Cyrrhus, 152
Theodosius I, 157
  extends Sunday restrictions, 328
Theodulf of Orleans, 202, 203
Theophilus, 119
Therapeutae, 66-67
Theses Sabbatica (Shepard), 240
Thibaut, John Baptiste, 348
Thomas (Abba), 176
Thomas Christians, 160-161

GENERAL INDEX

Three angels' messages, 258, 354, 357, 360, 361
  first angel's message, 353
  second angel's message, 353
  third angel's message, 249, 356
  third angel's message linked to Sabbath, 355
Thurin, Bertoul: execution of, 209
Tiberias (synagogue), 67
Tiberius, 140
Tibullus, Albius, 139, 309
Time reckoning: on a round world, 364-365
Timotheus I, 170
Tinneus Rufus, 73
Tiridates I, 317
Tishri, 76
Tithing: on Sabbath, 81
Titus, 65
Torah, 71, 76, 79, 87, 157, 244, 338, 339, 272
Trajan, 317, 349
Transfer theory, 234, 235, 237, 292
Transylvanian Sabbatarians, 223-224
Trask, John, 237
Travel: on Sabbath, 102-103
Trent, Counter-Reformation Council of, 215
True Sabbath—Saturday or Sunday, The (Coombs), 291
2300 days, 352, 257
Tyanaeus, Apollonius, 309-310

U

Ullendorff, Edward, 173-174
United Armenians. *See* Armenian Uniates
Unleavened Bread, days of, 134

V

Vagharshabad, Synod of, 162
Valens, Vettius, 140, 316
Valentinian, Gratian: extends Sunday restrictions, 328
Van Der Veen, R. J., 287
Van Goudoever, J., 327
Varthema, Ludovico di, 160
Vasco da Gama, 160
Vaticanus (uncial codex), 115
Veloso, Mario, 222
  on Reformation in Seville, 223
Vespasian, 64, 136
  introduced Jewish tax, 137
Victorinus, 138
Vincentius, 192
Vindication of the Seventh-day Sabbath, The (Bates), 357, 358
Viret, Pierre, 218, 219
Vision, A (tract), 356
Visser, P., 287
Voetius, G., 285
Vos, G., 285
Vuilleumier, Jean, 159
Vulgate, 126

W

Waggoner, Ellet J., 362
Waggoner, J. H., 253
Waldenses, 207-209
Wallis, John, 237
War: between Romans and Jews, 64-65
Washington, New Hampshire, Christian Church: first Sabbatarian Adventist congregation, 247
Waterman, G. H., 23
Welch, Charles H., 126
Wesbery, James P., 286
Wheeler, Frederick: first Adventist to observe Sabbath, 247, 248
White, Ellen G., 343, 358, 361-362, 368
  on divine rest, 297
  relationship of Sabbath and three angels' messages, 258-259
  visions
    confirming Sabbath observance, 248
    of God's seal as Sabbath, 359
    of heavenly sanctuary and Jesus in Most Holy Place, 356, 258
White, Francis, 238
White, James, 248, 252, 253, 255, 358, 360-361
  founder of Seventh-day Adventist Church, 247
White, James and Ellen, 250, 358, 362
  marriage date, 356
  speakers at Sabbath conferences, 249
Why Christians Worship on Sunday (DeHaan), 290
Williams, A. Lukyn, 154
Winter, G. B., 104
Wolff, Hans W., 301
Women: in Jewish culture, 114
  preaching by Waldensian, 208
Wycliffe, John, 209

X

Xerxes I, 315

Y

Ya'iqob, 176, 177
Yohannes I, 184, 185

Z

Za Dengel, 185
  edict of, 182
  excommunicated, 182
Zacharias Scholasticus, 172
Zadokite Document, 59-61, 74-75
Zahn, T., 104
Zara Yaqob, 175, 176, 177, 179, 180, 182, 185
Zenon, 62
Zerikah, 84
Zoroaster, 315
Zwingli, Huldreich, 215, 217, 288